PRIMARY AND EARLY YEARS COURSE READER

UG and PG Initial Teacher Training

PRIMARY AND EARLY YEARS COURSE READER

UG and PG Initial Teacher Training

**CHRISTINE SCREECH,
KARAN VICKERS-HULSE AND FAY LEWIS**

Los Angeles | London | New Delhi
Singapore | Washington DC

Los Angeles | London | New Delhi
Singapore | Washington DC

SAGE Publications Ltd
1 Oliver's Yard
55 City Road
London EC1Y 1SP

SAGE Publications Inc.
2455 Teller Road
Thousand Oaks, California 91320

SAGE Publications India Pvt Ltd
B 1/I 1 Mohan Cooperative Industrial Area
Mathura Road
New Delhi 110 044

SAGE Publications Asia-Pacific Pte Ltd
3 Church Street
#10-04 Samsung Hub
Singapore 049483

Typeset by: C&M Digitals (P) Ltd, Chennai, India
Printed and bound by CPI Group (UK) Ltd,
Croydon, CR0 4YY (for Antony Rowe)
Printed on paper from sustainable resources

British Library Cataloguing in Publication data

A catalogue record for this book is available from
the British Library

ISBN 978-1-4462-8564-0
E-ISBN 978-1-4462-8597-8

MIX
Paper from
responsible sources
FSC
www.fsc.org   FSC® C013604

Contents

Theory and Practice

EYFS

Primary

Cross–Curricular Approaches

Reflective Learning and Teaching

The Classroom Environment and Ethos

Communication and Language in the Classroom

Creativity and Play

Planning

Managing Behaviour

Special Educational Needs

Inclusion

Cultural and Linguistic Diversity

Preface

This course reader is designed to support trainee teachers embarking on the first and second years of the Primary and Early Years undergraduate teaching programmes (ITE) as well as those on the PGCE Primary and Early Years routes.

Both the undergraduate and post-graduate routes into teaching at the University of the West of England have seen significant change and development over the last year and we continue to be pro-active in responding to the on-going shifts in educational contexts, policy and curriculum that will impact on you as trainee teachers.

Introduction

The Transformational Professional

Training to be a teacher at the University of the West of England is about making a commitment to, and having an understanding of, the principles of the UWE transformational professional. There are three sites of learning within your training: centre based, school based and independent. All three come together within the undergraduate and post-graduate programmes to help you towards becoming an outstanding teacher. The concept of the transformational professional underpins all of your teaching and learning and is exemplified by the following characteristics:

- An outstanding educator – consistently striving for continuous improvement.
- Motivated by a sense of moral purpose – based on an understanding that educational experiences can transform lives.
- Dedicated to transforming the life chances of all learners – setting high expectations, overcoming barriers to learning and helping everyone to achieve their maximum potential.
- Committed to transforming their own practice through critical reflective practice
- Willing to open their practice up to scrutiny, support and challenge.
- Able to transform the practices of others through participation in professional learning communities.
- Passionate about co-construction of innovative solutions to enduring challenges and resilient and resourceful in pursuit of those ends.
- Ethically aware at all times, demonstrating honesty and integrity.
- Emotionally intelligent, able to create transformational relationships build on reciprocity and respect.

As well as the above characteristics there are three other key features which we also consider underpin the principles for your work in becoming a teacher: language and communication; innovation and participation. On the following pages you will be able to read more about the significance of these areas in your work towards becoming an outstanding teaching professional:

Language and Communication

Good communication is an essential tool for teachers. Teachers need to be able to communicate effectively on a number of different levels, both verbally and non-verbally. Quite simply, communication is a process that involves an exchange of information, thoughts, ideas and emotions but effective communication is much more than this!

Communication is *a complex process and at* any stage of this process things may go wrong, making the communication less effective. For instance, teachers may not express what s/he wants to say clearly; or the room may be noisy; or the student may not understand the words the teacher is using. To be effective, teachers have to try to minimize these *barriers to communication*. This can be tackled in a number of ways: ensuring we use words that the students will understand; creating a calm working environment and speaking clearly, however, the most important way to overcome the barriers is *two-way communication – ensuring that students understand what we mean by engaging in dialogue and using effective questioning techniques to ensure that communication is effective. Effective* communication does not only take place through our use of words but through non-verbal communication too: body language and facial expressions can send out very clear messages. This kind of communication is usually subconscious and we use it without thinking about it but it can be the first sign of boredom or disengagement and equally the pupils will be able to gauge confidence and interest levels of their teachers too!

Your training programmes will allow you to develop a thorough understanding of language and communication, particularly the impact of these on learning. The nature of classroom talk and how teachers communicate with children in classrooms and settings will also be prioritized. How young children develop early language and communication skills will be explored not forgetting the importance of understanding body language and alternative forms of communication. You will experience a variety of ways of working such as group work, presentations and written assignments which will enable you to hone and develop your own language skills. You will develop an awareness of different ways to communicate using a variety of mediums which will ensure that every student achieves.

Innovation

Innovative teachers think beyond the traditional. They aspire to get children excited about learning, to motivate them to achieve, to develop a love of learning and to prepare them for life in a rapidly changing world. They aim to create an ethos for change which allows a freedom to experiment and supports risk taking.

Innovation can take many different forms; from simple changes to the curriculum, timetable or physical environment through to major projects; but at the core will be a drive to create authentic child-centred learning experiences that enthuse children and thereby ensure engagement and interest.

There are, of course, many ways to achieve this, but most will fall under three main categories, as outlined below. As you read this book, be aware of activities and practices which:

Extend learning beyond the classroom

Life does not happen within the four walls of a classroom and learning should not therefore be confined to such a space either (or indeed within a 60 minute time slot). Links should be made with the wider community to create a more diverse and dynamic learning experience. Working in collaboration with other schools, institutions (farms, museums, art galleries, scientific bodies, etc.) and a range of outside experts (parents, local artists, practitioners in their field).

Integrate technologies

Today's children have never known anything but an immersion in technology. They should be learning in an environment that builds on their experiences in this area such as games, apps and independent research and should continue to do so as new technologies are developed. For example, collaborative work and reflection could be enhanced through the use of blogs and wikis, creativity through digital media such as podcasts and digital videos or even the creation of virtual learning experiences.

The following web sites provide some interesting approaches to innovative learning:

5x5x5=creativity

http:///www.5x5x5creativity.org.uk

An independent, arts-based action research organisation which supports children in their exploration and expression of ideas, helping them develop creative skills for life.

The Innovation Unit

http://www.innovationunit.org/

The Innovation Unit for Public Services is a not-for-profit social enterprise which is committed to using the power of innovation to solve social challenges. In particular look at their work on 21st century learning – The Engaging School and Work that Matters.

The Cambridge Primary Review

http://www.primaryreview.org.uk/

The Cambridge Primary Review (CPR) was launched in October 2006 as a fully independent enquiry into the condition and future of primary education in England. It sets out plans for a new curriculum that includes 12 aims for each pupil: wellbeing, engagement, empowerment, autonomy respect and reciprocity, interdependence, citizenship, celebrating culture, exploring, fostering skills, exciting imagination and enacting dialogue.

We hope that some of the ideas above as well as other discussions in this book will help you to question and challenge some of the ideas you may already have such that you are prepared to try out new approaches and really think about stimulating and engaging ways of working with children.

Participation

A good way of starting this section is perhaps to ask *you* what you understand by the term 'participation'? Undoubtedly it will mean different things to different people. A general definition might substitute the word, 'involvement' for participation. We are all involved in some things to some extent. For example, many people participate in family life in that they are parents, brothers, sisters, sons, daughters, etc. and in their role take an active part in activities that keep the family functioning. Outside the home there are many levels of involvement or participation; some you may do on your own, others may involve you working as a member of a group or organization. However, when we talk about the term participation in education or more specifically in terms of our role as teachers working in settings and classrooms, then it has a more specific and focused connotation.

In 1989, the most complete statement of children's rights ever produced and the most ratified international human rights treaty in history was approved by all United Nations member states except the United States, South Sudan and Somalia. Under Article 12 of the United Nations Convention on the Rights of the Child (UNCRC,1989), children and young people have the right to express their views, and for these to be respected by adults when making decisions on matters that affect them. Our own Government pertains to be committed to the UN Convention stating that:

> *The Government is committed to children's rights and participation. The Governmentbelieves that children and young people should be given opportunities to express their opinion in matters that affect their lives. Effective participation gives children and young people the opportunity to make a positive contribution to their communities and to develop the skills, confidence and self-esteem they will need for the future.*
>
> *Involving children and young people in the planning, delivery and evaluation of services that affect their lives is not only likely to improve services, but also helps in developing confident, engaged and responsible citizens.* (Dept of Education, 2011)

So, if we are to ensure that children have a voice in their school and classroom and that their views have value, what sort of practice will we adopt? In some of the schools and settings that you visit you may find that they have gained a UNICEF *Rights Respecting Schools Award* (RRSA) which recognizes achievement in putting the United Nations Convention on the Rights of the Child (CRC) at the heart of the school's planning, policies, practice and ethos. A rights-respecting school not only teaches about children's rights but also models rights and respect in all its relationships: between teachers / adults and pupils, between adults and between pupils. However, while this is an aspiration for the wider school community, it is you as a practitioner who will be working with children for around six hours each day in your individual classroom so how can *you* ensure that you really do listen and children really are heard? These are areas that your experience in school and the course will draw your attention to in more depth. As a starting point however, Vygotsky suggests that adopting a social constructivist approach where teachers co-construct knowledge alongside children based on the recognition that:

- learning takes place in authentic and real-world situations
- learning involves initiation, negotiation and mediation
- content and skill development is understood within the framework of the child's prior knowledge
- learning is assessed formatively, with the child actively involved in the process
- educators facilitate and encourage multiple perspectives and representations of realities and futures.

is very useful and may help you to think about your approaches to learning and teaching beyond that of the 'traditional teacher' leading from the front.

Of course, as learners yourselves we hope that you, too, will feel that your opinions and voices matter to us and another example of participatory practice is the student representative system run by the Student Union within the university whereby you have the opportunity for regular meetings with key staff to discuss your course.

So within that word, participation, there seems to be another concept emerging, that knowledge is not just individual but is social and collective, shared most effectively in what Wenger calls 'communities of practice. He contends that:

> *Communities of practice are formed by people who engage in a process of collective learning in a shared domain of human endeavour: a tribe learning to survive, a band of artists seeking*

new forms of expression, a group of engineers working on similar problems, a clique of pupils defining their identity in the school, a network of surgeons exploring novel techniques, a gathering of first-time managers helping each other cope. In a nutshell:

Communities of practice are groups of people who share a concern or a passion for something they do and learn how to do it better as they interact regularly.

We hope that you will become a member of a community of learners who is involved in participatory practice both within wider university life, your teaching course and, of paramount importance, when working with children in school.

How the course reader is organized

The book is divided into eight sections reflecting some of the essential knowledge and understanding that a primary or early years' teacher requires to become an effective educator of children from birth to 11 and beyond within an ever changing educational landscape. It also recognizes that underpinning all that you do both as a trainee and as an in-service teacher is an over-arching set of criteria and principles; the Teachers' Standards (2012). These are included at the beginning of the text to help you make connections between your on-going professional development and the materials and resources you engage with. While the course reader is primarily designed to support you within your initial teacher education programmes, we also hope that much of the material will remain useful as you move towards being an NQT and in further professional development opportunities.

Each section of the book begins with an overview, signposting you towards the key themes or areas included. The summary at the end of each section suggests some student activities that tutors may choose to include in modules as directed tasks. Alternatively, these may be areas that you wish to follow up independently. The final section will include 'top tips' when appropriate (e.g., behaviour management). These may reflect what we, as tutors and experienced teachers, have found work effectively in practice and once again provide continuity been your reading and practice in settings and classrooms. Additional readings are also included and it is important to see the course reader as a starting point for developing your understanding and a basis on which to build according to your interest, context and phase of teaching,

We believe that engaging with the readings in this volume alongside your own, personal wider reading, taught sessions in university and your diverse and varied experiences in schools and settings will set you on the path to becoming an outstanding, transformational practitioner.

Reference

Wenger, E. (2006) *Communities of Practice, a brief introduction*. [Online] available at: http://www.ewenger.com/theory/ [Accessed 24 June 2013]

Teachers' Standards

Preamble
Teachers make the education of their pupils their first concern, and are accountable for achieving the highest possible standards in work and conduct. Teachers act with honesty and integrity; have strong subject knowledge, keep their knowledge and skills as teachers up-to-date and are self-critical; forge positive professional relationships; and work with parents in the best interests of their pupils.

PART ONE: TEACHING
A teacher must:

1. Set high expectations which inspire, motivate and challenge pupils

- establish a safe and stimulating environment for pupils, rooted in mutual respect
- set goals that stretch and challenge pupils of all backgrounds, abilities and dispositions
- demonstrate consistently the positive attitudes, values and behaviour which are expected of pupils.

2. Promote good progress and outcomes by pupils

- be accountable for pupils' attainment, progress and outcomes
- be aware of pupils' capabilities and their prior knowledge, and plan teaching to build on these
- guide pupils to reflect on the progress they have made and their emerging needs.
- demonstrate knowledge and understanding of how pupils learn and how this impacts on teaching
- encourage pupils to take a responsible and conscientious attitude to their own work and study.

3. Demonstrate good subject and curriculum knowledge

- have a secure knowledge of the relevant subject(s) and curriculum areas, foster and main-tain pupils' interest in the subject, and address misunderstandings
- demonstrate a critical understanding of developments in the subject and curriculum areas, and promote the value of scholarship
- demonstrate an understanding of and take responsibility for promoting high standards of literacy, articulacy and the correct use of standard English, whatever the teacher's spe-cialist subject
- if teaching early reading, demonstrate a clear understanding of systematic synthetic phonics
- if teaching early mathematics, demonstrate a clear understanding of appropriate teaching strategies.

4. Plan and teach well structured lessons

- impart knowledge and develop understanding through effective use of lesson time
- promote a love of learning and children's intellectual curiosity
- set homework and plan other out-of-class activities to consolidate and extend the knowledge and understanding pupils have acquired
- reflect systematically on the effectiveness of lessons and approaches to teaching
- contribute to the design and provision of an engaging curriculum within the relevant subject area(s).

5. Adapt teaching to respond to the strengths and needs of all pupils

- know when and how to differentiate appropriately, using approaches which enable pupils to be taught effectively
- have a secure understanding of how a range of factors can inhibit pupils' ability to learn, and how best to overcome these
- demonstrate an awareness of the physical, social and intellectual development of children, and know how to adapt teaching to support pupils' education at different stages of development
- have a clear understanding of the needs of all pupils, including those with special educational needs; those of high ability; those with English as an additional language; those with disabilities; and be able to use and evaluate distinctive teaching approaches to engage and support them.

6. Make accurate and productive use of assessment

- know and understand how to assess the relevant subject and curriculum areas, including statutory assessment requirements
- make use of formative and summative assessment to secure pupils' progress
- use relevant data to monitor progress, set targets, and plan subsequent lessons
- give pupils regular feedback, both orally and through accurate marking, and encourage pupils to respond to the feedback.

7. Manage behaviour effectively to ensure a good and safe learning environment

- have clear rules and routines for behaviour in classrooms, and take responsibility for promoting good and courteous behaviour both in classrooms and around the school, in accordance with the school's behaviour policy
- have high expectations of behaviour, and establish a framework for discipline with a range of strategies, using praise, sanctions and rewards consistently and fairly
- manage classes effectively, using approaches which are appropriate to pupils' needs in order to involve and motivate them
- maintain good relationships with pupils, exercise appropriate authority, and act decisively when necessary.

8. Fulfil wider professional responsibilities

- make a positive contribution to the wider life and ethos of the school
- develop effective professional relationships with colleagues, knowing how and when to draw on advice and specialist support
- deploy support staff effectively
- take responsibility for improving teaching through appropriate professional development, responding to advice and feedback from colleagues
- communicate effectively with parents with regard to pupils' achievements and well-being.

PART TWO: PERSONAL AND PROFESSIONAL CONDUCT

A teacher is expected to demonstrate consistently high standards of personal and professional conduct. The following statements define the behaviour and attitudes which set the required standard for conduct throughout a teacher's career.

- Teachers uphold public trust in the profession and maintain high standards of ethics and behaviour, within and outside school, by:

  o treating pupils with dignity, building relationships rooted in mutual respect, and at all times observing proper boundaries appropriate to a teacher's professional position
  o having regard for the need to safeguard pupils' well-being, in accordance with statutory provisions
  o showing tolerance of and respect for the rights of others
  o not undermining fundamental British values, including democracy, the rule of law, individual liberty and mutual respect, and tolerance of those with different faiths and beliefs
  o ensuring that personal beliefs are not expressed in ways which exploit pupils' vulnerability or might lead them to break the law.

- Teachers must have proper and professional regard for the ethos, policies and practices of the school in which they teach, and maintain high standards in their own attendance and punctuality.
- Teachers must have an understanding of, and always act within, the statutory frameworks which set out their professional duties and responsibilities.

DfE V5.0 05.06.13

© Crown copyright 2013

You may re-use this information (excluding logos) free of charge in any format or medium, under the terms of the Open Government Licence. To view this licence, visit **http://www.nationalarchives.gov.uk/doc/open-government-licence/** or e-mail: **psi@nationalarchives.gsi.gov.uk**.

Where we have identified any third party copyright information you will need to obtain permission from the copyright holders concerned.

This document is also available from our website at www.education.gov.uk

Reference: DFE-00066-2011

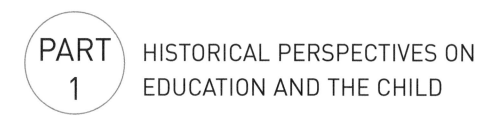

PART 1 HISTORICAL PERSPECTIVES ON EDUCATION AND THE CHILD

Overview

Part 1 introduces you to some historical perspectives on childhood and education which are significant in placing the current educational landscape into perspective. For those hoping to work with upper Key Stage 2 children, the ideas from Cleslik and Simpson are particularly interesting. For early years' trainees, Nutbrown and Clough is a useful sequential perspective on how ideas in early childhood have developed. However, in historical terms, just as in present day practice, it is helpful to see where children have come from as well as where they are moving towards. Therefore, reading each of these chapters would be helpful for all students, regardless of the chosen age phase for teaching.

REFERENCES

Cleslik, M. and Simpson, D. (2013) Chapter 1, 'Defining Youth' in *Key Concepts in Youth Studies* London: Sage.

James, A. and James, A. (2012) Chapter 1, 'Age and Maturity' in *Key Concepts in Childhood Studies*, 2nd edn. London: Sage.

Knowles, G. (2009) Chapter 2, 'The Child in Society' in *Ensuring Every Child Matters*. London: Sage.

Nutbrown, N. and Clough, P. (2008) Chapter 1, A short History of Early Childhood Education in *Early Childhood Education: History, Philosophy and Experience*. London: Sage.

Defining Youth

Cleslik, M. and Simpson, D.

We need a definition of young people so that we know exactly whom it is that we are researching, working with or developing policy for. Just as we note elsewhere in this book (see **theorising youth**) definitions of youth will reflect the biases of those doing the defining. Sociologists, youth workers and policy-makers will all have their own different notions of what constitutes young people and many of these understandings will be at variance with the ways that young people see themselves (Mannheim, 1952). Similarly writers document how conceptions of the youth phase are historically and culturally specific. In Western societies historical studies show that the category of youth as we understand it today is a relatively recent phenomenon dating from the eighteenth century (Gillis, 1974), though discussion of some notion of youth has been noted as far back as classical Greek society. The idea then of an intermediate stage between childhood and adulthood is commonly associated with the rise of Western modernity. Prior to the 1800s childhood was seen to merge into an early form of adult independence from the ages of eleven to twelve years of age as children took on waged employment and greater duties around the home (Gillis, 1974).

The past two centuries in Western societies have been the history of the gradual emergence and extension of the youth phase as the socio-cultural definitions of dependent childhood and independent adulthood have become more clearly demarcated producing a notion of the youth phase as an interstitial phenomenon – existing 'in between' the dependency of childhood and the autonomy of adulthood. During the late nineteenth century and throughout the twentieth century the development of adult citizenship rights (for example, around the franchise, education, housing and employment (see Marshall and Bottomore, 1997)) helped define the many facets of the transition to adulthood and with it the contours of the career routes and status passages that young people have to travel to achieve adult independence (Coles, 1995; Jones and Wallace, 1992).

In Western societies the late nineteenth century heralded the end of child labour and the separation of employment from the domestic sphere so commentators documented the emergence of common characteristics and experiences of young people. G.S. Hall (1904) and Erickson (1968), for example, discussed the developmental features of the youth phase and the inevitable 'storm and stress' that accompanied this period of identity formation and movement through status passages to adulthood. Key to these early ideas of adolescence was the notion that youth represented a time of flux where individuals had some time to experiment with ideas and identities as well as the actual routes they might take through life. Nevertheless one should be mindful of the fact that most young people during the twentieth century found their lives heavily conditioned by class, race and gender processes that defined much of their early lives and set limits to what they might possibly become through adulthood. Mannheim (1952) and Parsons (1942) were influential in the early twentieth century by noting how many young people came to recognise their common way of life (ideas, culture, life chances) and what they shared with other youth in contrast to adult society, thus setting up the possibility of generational conflict and tensions. As often the different generations had experienced very different forms of socialisation these authors pointed to a certain inevitability of culture wars springing up between the young and the old. Such ideas prefigured later concerns in wider society about the 'youth question' and how young people can be harbingers of disorder, change and conflict (see, for example, Cohen, 1997).

Through the latter part of the twentieth century in affluent societies we have witnessed the youth phase being extended from the teenage years of fourteen and fifteen to the early twenties and beyond as many young people spend longer periods of time in education and training and delay the entry into full-time work, family and household formation. For many, such delays are a result of unemployment, poor quality **work** and social exclusion. Recent commentators talk of a 'boomerang generation' of young people in their twenties and thirties who have tried to secure work and independent homes only to find themselves returning home through unemployment and the high cost of housing (Times Online, 2008). Hence the state has considerable power over the youth phase because of its influence on education and labour markets. Increasingly governments in affluent societies have called for the 'upskilling' of its citizens to help create 'knowledge economies' where all workers acquire higher level educational credentials (Lauder et al., 2007). In fifty years then we have witnessed the significant extension of compulsory **education** from a school leaving age of thirteen to fourteen years of age to one where most young people are in full time education until eighteen years of age and a majority in higher education until twenty-one years of age.

Young people's extended dependence on either their families of origin or on state welfare provision has led commentators to talk of the disempowering or infantilising of young people when they should rightly be enjoying greater independence associated with adult lifestyles. At the same time in many Western societies the commercialisation of childhood, and some suggest the sexualisation of children, has led to the emergence of the 'tweenies' phenomenon – young children whose fashion interests and way of life resembles those of earlier generations of much older teenagers (Hartley-Brewer, 2004). These social changes have consequently led some commentators to express doubts about the usefulness of the concept of youth as the boundaries between childhood and young people and between adulthood and adolescence have become increasingly fuzzy (Cohen and Ainley, 2000). One way of adapting to these social changes in the lives of young people is to understand the youth phase in different ways – for example, some talk of 'emerging adulthood' as a new phase between adolescence and adulthood and which reflects the different characteristics of young people as teenagers and those in their twenties (Arnett, 2004; Tanner and Arnett, 2009; see also Cote and Bynner, 2008). Others simply talk of young adults as a way of depicting the fact that some youth are indeed biologically old yet have lifestyles that lack the usual markers of independence associated with adulthood such as long-term relationships and their own home.

In recent years youth studies professionals have operated with definitions of youth transitions and youth identities that offer us an analytic map of the youth phase. **Transitions** are usually understood as comprising multiple routes into adulthood in relation to key aspects of young people's lives such as education/training and employment; intimate relationships and friendships; housing; and leisure. Some commentators suggest some routes such as education and employment are fundamental and structure the other transitions pathways (Roberts, 2003). In recent years writers in affluent societies have discussed the breakdown of once heavily structured and predictable transitions along classed and gendered lines and hence have moved from using metaphors such as careers and routes (Banks et al., 1992; Roberts, 1968) that denote transitions, to metaphors that convey greater fluidity such as navigations and niches (Evans and Furlong, 1997). The images of youth transitions developed by researchers tend to be socially constructed so they reflect the strong influence of culturally and historically specific events such as deindustrialisation of many European countries in the 1980s and 1990s

(Webster et al., 2004) and the economic growth and cultural transformation of many cities in developing societies during the first decade of the twenty-first century (Farrar, 2002).

Researchers in youth studies have also developed models of young people's social identities that contribute to our ways of defining young people. Prior to the 1970s youth were often understood in relation to quite crude notions of their structural class, race and gender positioning in wider society (Mungham and Pearson, 1976). More recently, however, such constructs have been superseded by concepts of youth identities that define young people as existing through multi-facetted, processual notions of the self where individuals undertake identity work and identity performances creating hybridised identities (Bennett, 1999; 2005). These developments in identity theory have been framed by the growing influence of mediazed interactions (via the web and other digital media) and diasporic, migratory experiences of many young people today. Writers still acknowledge the powerful way that economics, social relationships and cultural formations frame youth identities but many commentators speak of the loosening of conditioning processes so that young people have more space and opportunity to create their identities across what were once rigid and impermeable boundaries (Pysnakova and Miles, 2010). Young people's hybrid selves are also understood in relation to a greater sensitivity to the reflexive processes, so-called internal conversations and self-monitoring, that we all participate in and which make up our daily lives. Young people today then are more conscious of their self-identity than previous generations (compelled because of globalisation and de-traditionalisation and the 'risks' associated with these) and are thus mindful of the ways that one can pursue life projects and seek out self-development (Beck, 1992; Giddens, 1992; Taylor, 1991). Any definition of youth today needs to be sensitive to the effect that these historical processes such as individualisation and de-traditionalisation have had on how young people conceive and live out their lives.

REFERENCES

Arnett, J.J. (2004) *Emerging Adulthood: The Winding Road from the Late Teens through the Twenties*. Oxford: Oxford University Press.

Banks, M., Bates, I., Breakwell, G., Bynner, J., Emler, N., Jamieson, L. and Roberts, K. (1992) *Careers and Identities*. Milton Keynes: Open University Press.

Beck, U. (1992) *Risk Society: Towards a New Modernity*. London: Sage.

Bennett, A. (1999) 'Subcultures or neo-tribes? Rethinking the relationship between youth, style and musical taste', *Sociology*, 33 (3): 599–617.

Bennett, A. (2005) 'In defence of neo-tribes: a response to Blackman and Hesmondhalgh', *Journal of Youth Studies*, 8 (2): 255–9.

Cohen, P. (1997) *Rethinking the Youth Question: Education, Labour and Cultural Studies*. London: Macmillan.

Cohen, P. and Ainley, P. (2000) 'In the country of the blind? Youth studies and cultural studies in Britain', *Journal of Youth Studies*, 3 (1): 79–96.

Coles, B. (1995) *Youth and Social Policy*. London: University College London.

Cote, J. and Bynner, J. (2008) 'Changes in the transition to adulthood in the UK and Canada: the role of structure and agency in emerging adulthood', *Journal of Youth Studies*, 11 (3): 251–68.

Erickson, E. (1968) *Identity: Youth and Crisis*. New York: Norton

Evans, K. and Furlong, A. (1997) 'Metaphors of youth transitions: niches, pathways, trajectories or navigations', in J. Bynner, L. Chisholm and A. Furlong (eds), *Youth, Citizenship and Social Change in a European Context*. Aldershot: Ashgate Press, pp. 17–41.

Farrar, J. (2002) *Opening Up: Youth Sex Culture and Market Reform in Shanghai*. Chicago: University of Chicago Press.

Giddens, A. (1991) *Modernity and Self-Identity: Self and Society in the Late Modern Age*. Cambridge: Polity Press.

Gillis, J. (1974) *Youth and History: Tradition and Change in European Age Relations 1770–Present*. New York: Academic Press.

Hall, G. Stanley (1904) *Adolescence: Its Psychology and Its Relation to Physiology, Anthropology, Sociology, Sex, Crime, Religion and Education*, 2 vols. New York: D. Appleton and Co.

Hartley-Brewer, E. (2004) 'The trouble with tweenies', *The Guardian*, 15 September. www.guardian.co.uk/lifeandstyle/2004/sep/15/familyandrelationships.children (accessed 7 July 2012).

Jones, G. and Wallace, C. (1992) *Youth, Family and Citizenship*. Buckingham: Open University Press.

Lauder, H., Brown, P., Dillabough, J. and Halsey, A.H. (eds) (2007) *Education, Globalisation and Social Change*. Oxford: Oxford University Press.

Mannheim, K. (1952) 'The problem of generations', in P. Kecskemeti (ed.), *Essays on the Sociology of Knowledge*. New York: Routledge and Kegan Paul (1st edn 1927).

Marshall, T.H. and Bottomore, T. (1997) *Citizenship and Social Class*. London: Pluto Press.

Mungham, G. and Pearson, G. (eds) (1976) *Working Class Youth Culture*. London: Routledge and Kegan Paul.

Parsons, T. (1942) 'Age and sex in the social structure of the United States', *American Sociological Review*, 7, October: 604–16.

Pysnakova, M. and Miles, S. (2010) 'The post-revolutionary consumer generation: mainstream youth and the paradox of choice in the Czech Republic', *Journal of Youth Studies*, 13 (5): 533–47.

Age and Maturity

James, A. and James, A.

The number of years a person has lived.

Although in contemporary western societies age is commonly regarded as a fundamental aspect of a person's identity and is calculated numerically in terms of the passage of years since birth, this reckoning of time passing is not universal. Neither has it always been regarded as significant. In this sense, age can be regarded as one of the ways in which the passage of time across an individual's life-course is **socially constructed**. The historian Gillis (1996) argues, for example, that in western Europe it was only in the late 19th century that age became an important marker of social identity within the life-course. Prior to that, a person's chronological age might bear little relationship to the kinds of expectations and experiences that people had. So, unlike today, the pattern of life-course transitions was not fixed according to numerical age. Thus, for example, starting **work**, and then later marriage, did not always follow on from finishing attendance at school. Rather, boys and young men (though this was not so often the case with girls and women) might go in and out of school over a long period of time, taking up work in-between times, as their personal circumstances dictated. Thus, as Aries (1962) notes, the term '**child**' was traditionally not an age-related term; instead, it was more often used to describe a person's social dependency upon another.

In the modern world, however, as Hockey and James (2003) observe, there has been an increased institutionalisation of chronological age within the life-course and age is now key to the definition of what a child is:

> [F]rom legal imperatives through to consumer practices, age consciousness has intensified, such that what it means to be a child, for example, has become highly contextualized in relation to the age of criminal responsibility, consensual sex, leaving school, consent to surgery, access to contraception, participation in work and the right to vote. (2003: 64)

Although age is regarded as a key definitional marker of the status of 'child', when used to try to describe the lived experiences of children, age is revealed to be a less useful concept for a number of reasons. The first reason lies in the ways in which biological age has been used to chart out children's physical, psychological and indeed social development. Clearly, children share a common trajectory of physical change and development over time that is largely age-based, so that children achieve different stages of motor skills at different ages. Toddlers usually crawl before they walk, and may do this from around nine months old. However, the mapping of an age- and stage-based categorisation schema on to children's social, intellectual and psychological development, irrespective of social context, is now regarded as problematic. Not all children achieve the same stages at the same age, albeit that new research focused on **developmentalism** is shedding further light on the broad developmental changes that occur in the brain during childhood and adolescence. Nonetheless, age-grading remains a fundamental aspect of the ways in which, in modern society, children's lives are structured, because what the calculation of numerical age permits is the establishment of uniformly applicable boundaries to separate children from adults in particular cultural contexts.

The **school** system in many countries provides a prime example of age becoming institutionalised in this way. Schools divide children into different age-based classes, usually structured in relation to the annual intakes of children into the school system, ranging from early childhood through to the school-leaving age. Different age classes study different curricula, with different standards set for children's achievement. The result of this process is, however, to establish a process of age-based standardisation (James, 2004) such that some children may come to be judged as failing, as being 'behind' or 'backward' for their age, while others may be regarded as 'gifted' or 'precocious' because they achieve more than would have been expected *for their age*.

The second problem associated with the concept of age arises when it is used to define 'the child' and, through doing so, to place restrictions or protections on, or to give permissions for, children's activities. Not only does this place children of the same age together in the same group, irrespective of the differences among them, it also means that when age is used in this way, in a legal context, different ages may be used as boundary definitions for 'the child' in different social contexts. In relation to children's **rights**, for example, the **United Nations Convention on the Rights of the Child (UNCRC) 1989** defines a child as a person under the age of 18. Given the rather different social and economic circumstances that children across the world experience, such a universalising, age-based definition is problematic since it implies a commonality of experience that is not there. For example, the ages for consensual sex, for getting married and for leaving school vary enormously among different countries, and some **working children** of the majority South may enter the adult workplace at a very young age. But even within a single society, there may be little consistency about age-based definitions of 'the child'. In England, for example, within the youth justice system, a child is now deemed to be competent and responsible for his or her actions from the age of 10. In terms of the **welfare** system, however, children up to the age of 18 may not have their wishes and feelings taken notice of if it is thought that to accede to these may not be in their **best interests**.

This use of age to define 'the child' also raises issues in relation to ideas of maturity. While maturity can be defined in relation to developmentalism – for example, the achievement of sexual maturity –it is also commonly used to make a qualitative assessment or judgement about a child's actions, thoughts or behaviour. Indeed, 'maturity' describes the extent to which a child appears to behave or think more as an adult does. Thus, for example, when a child is described as being 'mature' for her/his age, the suggestion is that they are behaving more competently than would normally be expected of a child of that age. Maturity, then, is in effect a social construction and, as a consequence, understandings of what counts as 'maturity' are culturally relative. Notwithstanding the considerable problems that this raises for global childhoods, Article 12 of the UNCRC assumes that 'maturity' is something that, like 'age', can somehow be objectively assessed: 'States Parties shall assure to the child who is capable of forming his or her own views the right to express those views freely in all matters affecting the child, the views of the child being given due weight in accordance with the age and maturity of the child.' This is just one of the many examples of the problems that arise when trying to implement the UNCRC at the local level since what counts as evidence of ' maturity' in one setting may not in another.

Finally, age can also be problematic when seen from a child's **standpoint** since it may, for the reasons noted above, restrict children's activities. Solberg's (1997) study of Norwegian children shows, for example, how 10-year-old children manage to negotiate their parents' perceptions of their 'age'. By carrying out household tasks with **competence**, some children, she argues, act 'older' than their age, leading their parents to trust them to be alone in the house. In this way, through their everyday actions and interactions, these Norwegian children transformed age into a relative concept and circumvented the restrictions that fixed, numerical age can place upon them.

Age as a classificatory marker of identity has become, therefore, particularly important for children, since it is used not only to separate them out as a special group in society, but it may also restrict the kinds of activities and social **spaces** to which they have access. Indeed, many contemporary concerns about children's access to the **internet** and the **sexualisation** of children are underscored by views about age appropriateness and ideas about children's relative maturity and immaturity.

FURTHER READING

Aries, P. (1962) *Centuries of Childhood*. London: Jonathan Cape.

Gillis, J.R. (1996) *A World of Their Own Making*. Oxford: Oxford University Press.

Hockey, J. and James, A. (2003) *Social Identities Across the Life-Course*. Basingstoke: Palgrave.

James, A. (2004) 'The standardized child: Issues of openness, objectivity and agency in promoting child health', *Anthropological Journal on European Cultures*, 13: 93–110.

Solberg, A. (1997) 'Changing constructions of age for Norwegian children', in A. James and A. Prout (eds), *Constructing and Reconstructing Childhood* (2nd edn). London: Falmer.

The Child in Society

Knowles, G.

This chapter explores:

- how society's understanding of what is meant by the term 'child' has changed over time;
- what we mean by the notion of 'childhood';
- how different agencies working to support children and their families use different models of the child;
- how the Every Child Matters agenda requires tensions between agencies to be resolved; and
- how the Every Child Matters agenda requires the voice of the child to be at the centre of the agenda.

While education is concerned with learning and academic achievement, it is also very concerned with enabling children to explore and develop social, performance and physical skills. Early Years settings and schools have in turn increasingly realized that developing these skills and helping children to learn needs to be done in partnership with the child's home and family. Since, when a child comes to the Early Years setting or into school, the family come too, the beliefs and values held by the family come with the child; they are not left at the door. However, under the ECM agenda, settings and schools are now required to be even more proactive in listening to and working with children and their families to develop provision and to work closely with other agencies also working to support children and their families. For both these aspects of the ECM agenda to be successful, it is helpful for settings and schools to reflect on what model of the child they consciously – or subconsciously – use, as they go about their day-to-day business, and how that model helps – or hinders – their relationship with the child's parents and with other agencies. This chapter seeks to explore how dominant discourses with regard to what society views children as being have changed over time, what current models of the child are prevalent in different sectors in society and how these impact on the child's experience of 'being a child' and childhood.

How society's understanding of what is meant by the term 'child' has changed over time

If we look at a brief history of childhood and attitudes to childhood in Western Europe, beginning in the *Middle Ages* (*c.*1000–1453 CE) it is possible to find evidence that children were treated as being 'miniature adults'. They wore the same clothes, ate and drank the same things as adults, were expected to work and were regarded as having the same cognitive abilities as adults. However, this is not to suggest that children at this time were not still as cherished, wanted and loved as at any time in history. What is being explored here is that as society has changed, so too has its concept of the child and childhood.

The notion that children inhabit a special time – that is, childhood, which is somehow different and distinct from adulthood – began to emerge in the fifteenth century, and with it the idea that children may have different needs to adults. It has also been the case that at different times throughout history as different religious notions dominated society's views, these too have impacted on how children and childhood have been viewed. At times children have been seen as naturally wicked and in need of redemption, but by the *nineteenth century* children had come to be seen as being more naughty than wicked (Foley et al., 2001; Luke, 1989; Mills, 1999).

In terms of contemporary views of childhood, in *twenty-first century* Britain there are a range of concepts relating to what we mean by children and childhood. To some extent we are still operating with a romanticized view of childhood, which began to emerge in the *eighteenth century*, which saw children and childhood as a charmed time of purity and innocence (Foley et al., 2001). We still tend to see children and childhood in this way, seeking to protect children from the loss of innocence that comes with being an adult. However, this model of the child brings with it its own tensions, since most children want to explore the world, experiment and 'find things out for themselves', while the adults around them can seem to manage and limit their experiences and development towards adolescence and young adulthood.

The child in contemporary British society

To a greater extent all the models of children and childhood briefly explored above are as seen from an adult point of view. We examined in the previous chapter the notion of how dominant groups can oppress and control those more subordinate to themselves, not necessarily to intentionally cause harm or suffering, but because they believe they know what is best in any given situation. In terms of the adult–child relationship, adults are undeniably in control. This is in part because children are in the process of developing physically, emotionally and cognitively and, obviously, while still very young need a lot of attention, care and support to enable them to simply survive. For these reasons children are also very vulnerable and dependent on those around them who do have the capacity to provide for their needs, and it is in trying to define what the features of this relationship, between the developing and mature human being should be that the different models of the child and childhood proliferate and who holds the power to make their writ run is decided. It is possible to consider the child as being different from adults in that as *biological* entities they are different from adults. However, adults have invented and reinvented the idea of child and childhood as a social construct, to suit our own purposes and depending on the dominant discourse of the time (Cannella, 2002; Robinson, 2005).

We can discuss children as being distinct from adults in biological terms, since children are developing to a physical, emotional and cognitive maturity and because of that are vulnerable in ways adults are not, but we have translated this initial dependence into the industry of childhood, where, in the most extreme cases, children are kept infantilized and not required to have a view, an opinion or a direct input into what might be happening around them and to them, since 'in an important sense the child is an adult in waiting and therefore not part of the social world that counts' (Wyness, 1999: 24).

The concept of childhood

It is when we begin to consider these beliefs about the charmed, pure and innocent nature of the child and how they impact on what we believe children should and should not be exposed to, or encouraged to engage with, that we begin to shape our ideas about childhood. Wyness (1999) in discussing the work of Aries states how 'Aries was concerned with the historical shift in sentiments which shaped a set of ideas and values that gradually crystallized into the idea of the modern child' (Wyness, 1999: 22) and childhood being the space that the child is allowed to be a child in. There can be a tendency to believe that childhood too is a given and that childhood is experienced in a similar way by all young human beings and happens for all children in a similar way. Different families and societies, depending on tradition and cultural practices and, to a very great extent, the economic situation of any given family, will treat childhood in very different ways and have very different expectations for that child.

As we have seen, because childhood is to a greater extent, particularly in industrialized Western nations, a social construct (Barber, 2007: 82; Cannella, 2002) it can be and is defined in different ways by different societies, and for this reason

Activity

What, for you, are the defining features of childhood – how is childhood different and 'special' as compared to adulthood? What happens in childhood that is special to that time and ceases to happen as we become adults?

Now separate your ideas into the following categories:

- what children, as young human beings, actually need to thrive and grow into healthy adults;
- what society also encourages us to provide for children, believing that these are also necessary to enable children to thrive; and
- what society suggests children should not be exposed to as this will harm their development in some way.

Reflecting on this activity, what does this tell you about your model of the child and childhood?

Where did you get these concepts from?

Is there anything you would change in your thinking?

childhood is not experienced in a universal way, across the world. Any one child's experience of childhood will be determined by the society it grows up in and, in the same way, the society will determine how it views the child and what it will seek to provide for the child and expect from it. We have already seen how the notion of what a child is and what childhood might be is determined by prevailing cultural notions. However, one of the problems that this social construction of the notion of children and of childhood leads to is that we lose any sense of benchmarks that might guide us in knowing what it is best to do for children and what children themselves need from their childhoods.

In British society it is generally the norm that children are dealt with differently as compared to adults and often in a more marginal way. It is the adults who have a voice – they make decisions, they control the real power, in terms of money, the media and politics. This is not to say that children are not central to the economic and cultural identity of the adults around them; we can see this in the industry of childcare, education, toy-making and media provision that has developed, dependent entirely on children. Whether it meets the needs of the child we can debate, but what theses industries do achieve is the generation of adult employment and considerable economic wealth. For these reasons, there is a very strong economic argument for the version of childhood currently predominant in society to be perpetuated. However, the downside of this situation is that, again, it is the adults making decisions about what they believe children want from these industries. Even where there are claims that children are consulted with regard to developing toys and media products, these industries are still financed and run by adults (Cannella, 2002). This is not to marginalize caring for and wanting to provide for a loved one in all sorts of ways, because we want to be part of these people's lives and we are concerned for their well-being. Rather, what we are considering is what the actual needs of young human beings are against what we have come to believe they are, and the tensions between these two notions.

The voice of the child

In exploring the concept of child and childhood we have been doing so very much from the stance of being adults, deciding what ought to be the case for children. What we have been denying is that children are beings of themselves and for this reason have what Wyness (1999) describes as an 'ontology'. That is, because something 'is', it commands an authority to be considered and listened to, for its concerns to be canvassed and for its interests and needs – as it considers them to be – to be met. This notion of the ontology of children is what we might now call their 'rights'. Namely the very fact that human beings, and in this instance children, 'are' affords them the expectation of certain responses from those around them.

It is important to consider here the ontology of the child as it impacts on our model of the child and childhood, since a child is not a possession or an object; it is a human being of itself and therefore needs to be accepted on these terms and its wants, needs and desires considered – as are those of adults. This is an important concept to think through. Very often parents will use phrases such as 'this is my child and I decide what is best for it', which seems in the way it is expressed to be to do with ownership of a sort of material good. It often follows from this that parents will then go on to say that because the child is 'theirs' they can, therefore, 'bring it up' and treat them as they see fit. While parents, for many excellent reasons, are often the most-well placed people to bring up their own children, not least because most parents will do so selflessly, providing the best care, love and consideration for the child that they can, the child, from even before it is born, is a member of the wider community and the wider community has a role in bringing up the child. Children are present as beings in society, yet because they lack power (they do not have voting rights, for example) and they have no direct economic earning power (although through their parents they do have buying power) they are generally ignored in the wider social context. To a greater extent children are treated as being invisible – and they remain so, as beings, until the family has undertaken its role to socialize the child into adulthood. Only then will the person have an ontology and become a person with a voice that will be listened too.

The demonization of the child

Adults' attitudes to children are further complicated by the tension between conflicting views held about children, depending on the age of the child. While it is simply easier to romanticize the view of the young child being innocent and charming, even when they might also be actively rejecting this view of themselves by 'being naughty', it is much harder to continue to view children in this way as they become older, more independent and start to want to be young adults. Society has invested hugely in the charming, pure and innocent model of the child. We know that children do grow up and, indeed, must because we need them to take on the role of adult and eventually take over the adult world from us, but we are very unsure of how to actually support the child through the process of becoming an adult. Many of us further exacerbate this tension by giving children mixed messages about what we expect from them. We want children to be charming, pure and innocent, but there is a dominant discourse that also encourages us to think it is amusing to dress children as mini-adults and see them ape the behaviour of adults, although only when we allow it. Children who take licence to 'ape' adult behaviour and actually begin to behave like adults, in earnest, we are very uncertain about dealing with; indeed such children are reported by the media as being 'demon' children.

The dominant discourse of the demon child is one that began to gain its current momentum in the media in the early 1990s, although the notion that children, particularly those on the verge of adulthood, are particularly susceptible to behaving in demonic ways is an idea that has been prevalent since the 1840s, when the term 'juvenile delinquent' was first coined. There is also evidence of concern about adolescents, particularly young men, behaving delinquently, or demonically in reports about wild behaviour of gangs of apprentices, dating from the 1500s (Muncie, 2004). However, it was the terrible and highly atypical murder of the toddler James Bulger in 1993 by two ten-year-old boys that set the scene for the current concern with the demon child (Muncie, 2004: 3). Muncie states: 'The death of James Bulger triggered widespread moral outrage' (ibid.) the ongoing consequences of which Muncie suggests are threefold:

> First, it initiated a reconsideration of the social construction of 10 year olds as 'demons' rather than as 'innocents'. Second, it coalesced with, and helped to mobilize, adult fear and moral panic about youth in general. Third, it legitimized a series of tough law and order responses to young offenders which came to characterize the following decade. (Muncie, 2004: 3)

Barber (2007) suggests this tension arises because, while we encourage children to pretend to the clothes, behaviours and attitudes of adults, we are aware that they have less 'worldly' experience and, to adult eyes, children seem not always to understand the consequences of certain behaviours in particular contexts. We can provide them with the 'tools' of being an adult and encourage them to try them out at home, but we find it hard to accept the consequences of the children and young people then trying out these ideas in the 'real' world. 'Since young adults are knowledgeable and informed without necessarily being wise' (Barber, 2007: 85). Sometimes we 'have propelled children into places and positions before they are ready' (Wyness, 1999: 24). Rogers suggests that these tensions are compounded by adults' attitude to childhood having distilled into two distinct ideologies, or discourses, these being: 'the discourse of welfare and the discourse of control' (Foley et al., 2001: 30).

Further to this, the relativist nature of local practices in bringing up children can cause concern, particularly where not all families keep their children invisible. The media often seems to delight in presenting young people as being 'out of control'. However, in reality, crimes committed by children fell between 2002 and 2006, but the 'numbers of children criminalised had gone up by just over a quarter' (BBC, 2008). In Britain a child can be charged with some crimes at the age of 10, which is also in sharp contrast to other European countries that have a higher age of criminal responsibility and lock up far fewer of their children. Indeed, children in Britain are far more likely to be the victims of crime than to perpetrate them (Narey, 2007). What we do know from research is that where children live in poverty – with its attendant risk factors, of 'poor housing, poor health, educational underachievement, truancy and exclusion' – children and young people in these situations are also at more risk of becoming involved in crime (Narey, 2007). And as Martin Narey, Barnado's chief executive says:

> We can either support [these children] to grow into responsible citizens and valued members of the community or we can reinforce their disadvantage by ridiculing them in the media, expelling them from school and locking them up – pushing them further to the margins, when they most need our help. (Narey, 2007)

Activity

We have discussed how the media is very powerful in supporting and possibly even in establishing dominant discourses. Over the course of a day, note how different media report on the behaviours and actions of older children or adolescents.

Compare the reports in national newspapers and on national news channels with those on local news programmes and in local papers. Often local reporting conveys a better balance between the problems caused by a minority of adolescents and the celebration of the achievements and successes of local young people.

The child's experience

While the 'demon' child is a current dominant discourse, and one that does not stand up to rigorous scrutiny, what we do know about children is that, particularly in educational terms, they 'are achieving better than ever before – gaining good exam results, continuing to university, driving growth in higher skills sectors of the economy' (Narey, 2007).

Let us explore further behind the media spin and examine what children's actual experiences of childhood are. A further dominant discourse with regard to childhood is that children are 'better off' in material terms than they were a few generations ago (Foley et al., 2001: 18). While for many families levels of economic wealth have improved over the past 20 years, there is also evidence that there has been an increase in child poverty. This is further explored in Chapter 8. Although there has been material change, it has been different for different social groups (ibid.). However, all children come under the same pressure to have the same, possibly higher than previously, material expectations and 'change of this nature has led to a stereotyped picture of modern children as spoilt and over-materialistic' (Canella, 2002; Foley et al., 2001: 19). But, again, in this area of their lives, children can be seen to be modelling adult behaviour, since adults too use material goods to 'define their sense of identity', therefore 'we can hardly blame children for doing the same' (Foley et al., 2001: 19). We have allowed the advertising and media industry to pressure us as adults to 'buy' not only for ourselves, but also for children too.

Another common assumption about the change in childhood experience is that children today are healthier than children in the past, and although infant mortality rates fell by 65 per cent between 1963 and 1993, these improvements have only been for certain sectors of society. There is also evidence that suggests the rates of childhood asthma have increased, and that there has been a general deterioration in health and diet (Foley et al., 2001: 20). 'Children in the UK spend most of their waking hours in formal education ... compulsory education is the defining characteristic of modern childhood' (ibid.) and while there is evidence to show that children are attaining higher standards in the subjects they study at school, there is also evidence to show that the improvement in standards have reduced the opportunity for children's personal, social and creative abilities, plus their access to 'free-time' and the chance for unsupervised play. Although there is evidence that children are attaining higher levels in English, mathematics and science at school, this rise in achievement is not true for all groups of children; boys may be becoming increasingly alienated from formal education and 'there is evidence of persistent underachievement by children from some minority ethnic groups, gypsy and traveller children and children who are in care' (DfES 2003a; Foley et al., 2001: 21).

Research has also shown that parents are anxious about allowing children to freely roam without adult supervision and that there is concern about a rise in violent crimes against children, although it is less clear if these incidents have risen or it is the fear of them that has led to a change in parenting behaviour (Foley et al., 2001: 22). Compounding the concerns about children being able to play without adult supervision is the rise in the home as a place of leisure and entertainment, where most households have at least one television, video player and DVD player. Many households also have computers and access to the Internet. Not only do children have access to these forms of entertainment, but much of it is aimed directly at them, and while there is also concern that too much access to television and games consoles exacerbates anti-social behaviour, research shows that children are also quite able to reject media messages they do not like and are not 'at the mercy' of the media, passively soaking up everything they watch, as is sometimes suggested (ibid.).

Children's lives and experiences need to be placed in the wider social context in which we all live. Children and adults face, and deal with, a wide diversity of experiences. What must be considered is the control children have over their own lives and experiences.

Case study

James, known as Jimmy, was a 12-year-old boy in a Year 6 class in a North-West London primary school. He was an Irish, gypsy traveller whose family had recently moved from their trailer on the local authority travellers' site into settled accommodation.

Jimmy was the eldest of seven children, having five brothers and a very recent baby sister. Four of the boys were at school and the entire family was delighted the new baby was a girl, which was evident from the stories the boys told about their baby sister and how they would also write about her and want to take things home from school to show her.

Jimmy's dad, also called James, had recently, through the death of his own father, become the 'head' of the entire extended family in the local area. By default Jimmy then became 'head' of the family at school, being responsible not only for his brothers, but a number of cousins too.

This was Jimmy's second year at school, and the decision had been made to place him in a school year lower than his chronological age. He was physically bigger than the other children in his class and emotionally more mature; he was well liked by the other children but received a mixed response from teachers. He was very good at attending, rarely wore uniform to school, hardly ever badly behaved, was very funny and quick witted and, it also transpired, could drive.

Jimmy had a number of cousins at the school, two of whom caused the staff a lot of problems, their behaviour was very disruptive, sometimes violent, and the eldest boy's attendance was erratic since he often went to work with his father. This frustrated and pleased his teacher, since she was pleased he was absent and she did not have to deal with his behaviour, but it also interrupted the progress he was making. It further frustrated some staff that the cousin would do what Jimmy said, but would not obey them. Sometimes, they felt their authority and values particularly challenged when they were forced to seek Jimmy's help to manage his cousin. From Jimmy's point of view, this was a normal way to do things and he was often very embarrassed and apologetic that he could not control his cousin better and that the cousin was letting the family down so badly.

Jimmy's Year 6 teacher was very committed to working with traveller families in a supportive and proactive way, and in working with the Traveller Support Service from the local authority. To the teacher it was clear that in many ways Jimmy had 'out-grown' primary school, the very real responsibilities he was used to dealing with and the authority he was used to commanding with adults outside school caused tensions in the school. However, it was usually Jimmy who realized that power was organized differently in the school and generally he was

continued

continued

prepared to defer to the teachers. He was also bright enough to see the irony in that at one moment he was being treated like a child and in the next his help was wanted to deal with his cousin, and even to manage his aunt and uncle when they were aggressive towards the school.

Over the course of Year 6 Jimmy learnt to read and write. His parents were very pleased – for a number of reasons. His mother had come from a settled background and felt school to be important; for his father it was both expedient (particularly when having to deal with the settled community) and added to the respect he and Jimmy had in their own community. That Jimmy took his reading book home was an opportunity not lost on the teachers' of his brothers and cousins. If Jimmy took his book home – didn't they think they should too? However, Jimmy's mum often said having to listen to four boys reading was a mixed blessing.

Jimmy himself had put a lot of effort into this task, partly because being able to master these skills added to his authority and standing in the family, but also because he knew that it meant he would probably be allowed, by his parents, not to have to go to secondary school. Again Jimmy was quite astute enough to know the uneasy alliance he had struck with the authorities in his primary school he was unlikely to achieve at secondary. He also knew, from older members of his own family, that he would get a far rougher ride from the older children at secondary school. By the end of Year 6 Jimmy felt school had done as much for him as it could and that he too had done his bit for the school. However he had also come to the considered opinion that it was time to go and take up his place as a man in his community and help his dad in the more important tasks of managing and looking after his community.

Listening to children

Two of the most influential changes in terms of consulting with children and listening to their voice are:

- the United Kingdom's ratification of the United Nations Convention on the Rights of the Child (UNCRC) in 1991; and
- the Children's Act 2004.

In ratifying the UNCRC the British government has agreed to honour the rights set out in the convention, 'except in those areas where the government has entered a specific reservation' (Directgov, 2008). Since the treaty came into force in 1992, children in Britain have been entitled to over 40 specific rights, including having the 'right to have their views respected, and to have their best interests considered at all times' (Directgov, 2008). However, a convention is not the same as *law*, and the British government is not legally bound to adhere to the convention. In the same way, children can 'not bring a case to court if they believe that one or more of their Convention rights are being infringed'

(NSPCC, 2008a). Indeed the British government has been criticized by the UN Committee on the Rights of the Child, to whom it reports every year, for its failure to make progress in securing aspects of the articles it ratified. However, through the Children's Act 2004 the government has responded to some of the criticisms of the Committee and has also enshrined in British law the requirement that in separation or divorce proceedings that come before a court, the wishes of any children affected must be 'the court's paramount consideration in any decision relating to his or her upbringing' (DCSF, 2007c: 42). It is also from the Children's Act 2004 that we have the five outcomes of the ECM agenda, and the requirement for all agencies who work to support children and their families to work together and to work with children and families, listening to their voices in determining how provision should be 'rolled-out'.

One of the most important messages that the ratification of the UNCRC and the subsequent legislation that has been briefly outlined above signals, is that, by acknowledging children have rights, it gives them an ontology – it acknowledges, partly in law, that they are beings 'of themselves' and therefore can speak directly for themselves and are not at risk of having their wishes reinterpreted or misinterpreted through the channel of the adults around them. The notion of the child's voice is further discussed in Chapter 7.

Different agencies – different models of the child

Since the seventeenth- and eighteenth-century, philosophers and those interested in exploring what it is to be a child and that childhood might be different from adulthood, and how childhood might determine the adult the child will become, have tended to pursue the argument through two approaches. The first of these theoretical approaches stresses the role of a child's innate nature in determining the person they will be, including the part developmental psychology has to play in the nature of the child. The second approach stresses the role of the environment in which the child grows up in as the determining factor – that is, how they are nurtured.

Nature

In terms of the 'nature' side of the debate, some of the most influential work has been that of Jean Piaget, who formulated his theory of cognitive, or 'thinking abilities' development in the 1950s. Piaget is known as a cognitive developmental theorist and viewed biology – the genetic make-up of the child – as being the most important distinguishing effect on how a child will develop. Through working with children and observing how they solved problems he set them, Piaget theorized that childrens' thinking and thought processes are very different to those of an adult. He proposed that the combination of the environment a child grows up in and the experiences that the environment provides a child, coupled with the natural stages of cognitive development a child passes through to adulthood, will impact on the cognitive development of the child. His theory develops the notion that children learn by exploring their environment and essentially 'testing how things work'. Through these experiences they build up schemas of understanding about the world which, as they learn new things, they adapt to assimilate the new information. His work has been very influential in establishing the notion that children are 'different' from adults, not just biologically, but that they think in different ways too and need an environment that allows them to play, test and explore the world around them.

Piaget's four main stages of cognitive development are summarized below.

Stage 1 Sensorimotor thought (birth to 2 years)
In this stage thinking is in terms of responding to and possibly interpreting inputs from the senses. In this stage children cannot think in an abstract way, that is, hypothesize, or think about things that do not have a direct bearing on their senses at that point. If their primary care provider is absent and they want contact with them, they will respond to that desire, rather than be able to reason that he or she is elsewhere and will come back soon. By about 15 months children begin to become more exploratory and to make causal links between events and their actions. For example, a random action that results in an event that interests and pleases the child will be made deliberately and intentionally in the future. Pressing a button on a washing machine or toy will cause something to happen.

Stage 2 Pre-operational thought (2–7 years)
Children begin to acquire language and develop the capacity to hold mental images and remember things, although they cannot think logically and deal with more than one idea at a time. For example, a child who is in the pre-operational stage will not be able to answer a question like: 'I have a handful of sweets, 2 sweets are red and 3 sweets are green. What do I have more of, the number of sweets altogether or green sweets?'

Stage 3 Concrete operational thought (7–11 years)
This is a significant stage of development for children as it is at this point that they begin to be able to see the world, ideas and actions from the point of view of others. This is know as being able to decentre.

Stage 4 Formal operational thought (age 11 to adulthood)
It is in this stage that children become able to think hypothetically and outside their direct experience, for example, to imagine worlds, as in fantasy stories which do not exist in real experience; similarly, they are able to engage in abstract thinking such as is needed in mathematics.

One of the most significant things about this notion of child development is that the child must pass through each stage, and in the order as described by Piaget. It is important – and a developmental necessity in terms of the overall cognitive maturation of the child – that they 'complete' each aspect of cognitive development and understanding before they can move on to the next stage (Bentham, 2004). While it is unarguably the case that children change physically in their development from babies to adulthood, Piaget's notion of cognitive stages raises as many issues as it seems to explain. Other child development theorists have significantly challenged the work of Piaget, for example, the child psychologist Margaret Donaldson (Donaldson, 1984). While Piaget's work is useful in that it provides a framework, an overview, of how children's cognitive abilities might develop, it is criticized as being too rigid in tying development stages to chronological age and adhering to the notion that each stage has to be passed through before the child is able to master the cognitive challenges of the next stage.

Other theories that have impacted on and influenced our knowledge, understanding and beliefs about child development, and therefore our models of the child, are theories with regard to learning development. One of the most influential theorists in this area is B.F. Skinner (1905–90). Skinner was a leading 'behaviourist', behaviourism being a theory that focuses on behaviour as the objective of all human functioning. Human beings are motivated to behave in certain ways depending on the sense of innate or extrinsic reward they feel as a result of that action. These ideas are the basis of many reward/sanction-based discipline systems used with children in formal education settings. Children are rewarded, through praise or in other ways, to encourage them to behave in ways that are wanted. Conversely, sanctions are applied when children exhibit unwanted behaviours, to discourage such behaviour. However, critics of this method of managing children see this approach as being akin to coercion, or brainwashing, or that children only learn to do things if there is a reward attached and they will not learn to manage their own behaviour in the absence of an incentive.

John Bowlby (1969–80), is acknowledged as one of the most prominent theorists to begin to research social effects on development, in particular he is famous for his 'attachment theory' (Flanagan, 1999). When Bowlby first began discussing this theory his work centred on the importance, in developmental terms, of the attachment a child forms with its mother. However, the notion that a child can form the necessary nurturing attachment, needed for healthy social and psychological development, only with its mother has been developed by other theorists working in this area. The current accepted theory is that children can form a number of attachments with adults other than the biological mother, what is important is that children need caring and nurturing relationships in order to thrive, and not simply that basic needs for food and shelter are met (Foley et al., 2001: 211). This theme is picked up in the next chapter, in examining what children need from families.

A further influential theorist in the area of child development is Erikson who in the 1960s, devised a model of human social development that focuses more on the impact of background and environment on development, rather than genetic determiners. This is known as a psychosocial model (Miller, 2003). The importance of this theory of development is that it seeks to explore how the beliefs, attitudes and values we grow up to hold are shaped by our genetic pre-disposition towards stimuli and how the environment we grow up in impacts on those innate characteristics. Therefore, Erikson maintains, we are distinctly shaped by our formative experiences. If this is so, then the experiences a child will have while in an Early Years setting or in school will have a considerable long-term effect on the adult that child becomes, including on the attitudes, beliefs and values they will hold.

The models we have briefly looked at here are very much associated with educational model of the child. Those who are primarily concerned with a child in terms of their health may be focused on different signifiers of development. For example, there is already a range of ante-natal screening that takes place while the child is still in the womb, to determine if the child has any 'health problems' prior to birth. Parents, too, are given plenty of health advice about how to ensure the child is born into an healthy environment, that it is provided with the right nourishment and that its physical health and growth are monitored against 'normal' trajectories of healthy development. In part this is because we know that health during childhood will impact on the health of the adult and that a child that is healthy is more likely to thrive in all aspects of their life. This concern for monitoring children's healthy development is expressed by the Institute of Medicine Staff in the following way: 'the nation must have an improved understanding of the factors that affect health and effective strategies for measuring and using information on children's health' (Institute of Medicine Staff, 2004: 14). In exploring the notion of the model of the healthy child, Warsh writes of the growth of the 'health movement' that filled homes with 'the technology of personal hygiene (washbasins, toilets, toothbrushes, soap, and tissues) and then made sure that these products were used. It was the job for a new kind of expert: a professional health educator' (Warsh, 2005: 24). Warsh (2005) goes on to describe the three principles on which this movement was based: that no matter how meagre a families resources everyone could maintain their own good health through 'preventive health care based on good habits of eating, sleeping, and keeping clean' (Warsh, 2005: 25).

There is no doubt that monitoring children's health over the past few decades has greatly improved the overall well-being of children, and this has included 'reduc-ing mortality and morbidity from many infectious diseases and accidental causes, increasing access to health care, and reducing environmental contaminants' (Institute of Medicine Staff, 2004: 14). However, just as there are criticisms of the various cognitive developmental models educationalists use of children, so too the health sector has critics of its models, the significant issue of working with a 'model' being that the model presupposes that anything that does not fit the model is 'deviant'. Again, the child, that is, the person – the ontology of the child – can get lost in trying to fix the child to meet the model or in discarding the child that cannot be fixed. We have seen this happening in the past where children with disabilities and learning difficulties that cannot be 'fixed' are placed out of the way of mainstream society and their families left unsupported and marginalized.

In a multi-agency approach to working with children, there is the potential to have a range of different agents' models of what constitutes a child – and therefore the best way of dealing with the child may cause tensions between professionals. So far we have only considered the models used by educationalist or health-care workers. There are also the social care model of the child and the youth criminal justice model to take into account – to a greater extent the social care model of the child is explored in the following chapter of this book. Those who have central to their working lives the concern for the welfare of the whole child, have a duty to resolve any differences in approaches in working with children through agencies by talking to each other but, most crucially, by talking to and listening to the child.

Activity

Your model of the child and childhood
Think through the experience you have in working with children. Which of the models briefly outlined above seem to agree most with your ideas and experience?

What evidence do you have to defend your ideas? Can you talk about instances of working with children when they have behaved in the way described by your preferred theorist?

How has the model presented by your chosen theorist helped you provide better for the needs of children?

Of the other theories, what is it that you do not agree with? What evidence do you have to support your position?

This chapter has explored the concept of the child, and what childhood might be, through notions, or dominant discourses, that currently have a strong influence on how these concepts are viewed in society. More significantly, it is not only how these discourses explain children and childhood that we need to consider, but the impact these ideas have on public policy. The prevailing concept of what it is a child might be influences all practice that relates to children, from the way children will be treated in their own homes, to what happens to them in the Early Years setting and at school. These notions affect how children will be treated by health-care workers, child protection workers and how they will be dealt with by the Youth Justice System and the media. It is a symbiotic relationship, the dominant discourses feed public opinion and policy and vice versa.

The individuals in any group in society are linked to one to another by the means through which they communicate. A universally predominant way of communicating is through spoken and, often, written language, that is, through discourse. The 'centrality of language in social life' (Matheson, 2005: 2) serves a range of purposes: not only can we pass on information to each other, but the very language – choice of words – we choose to use to pass on information will shape the attitudes beliefs and values of the group, that is we 'cannot separate out people's thoughts and actions from the communicative means that they use to perform them' (Matheson, 2005: 3), what we say and write is what we do (Mills, 1997: 5).

> Discourse must be understood in its widest sense: every utterance assuming a speaker and a hearer, and in the speaker, the intention of influencing the other in some way ... It is every variety of oral discourse of every nature from trivial conversation to the most elaborate oration ... .(Mills, 1997: 5)

As has been explored in Chapter 1, the language of those groups that have the power in any given situation can be used, overtly or inadvertently, to disadvantage subordinate groups. In some instances the discourse of certain groups becomes a dominant discourse and is treated as if it is the belief of a wide audience, sometimes of a society itself, that is, 'certain representations of the social world' come to be predominant or accepted view of how things should be (Matheson, 2005: 1). In Britain, a society that has a well-established, very complex, media industry (ibid.), many ideas can be circulated in the public arena, and where certain notions are 'picked-up' by media that command a large audience, then the way in which they express ideas can establish what can go on to become a dominant discourse.

Some of the dominant discourses as they relate to children and childhood have been explored in some detail above, both those perpetuated by the media and those used by different professionals concerned with children's education, health or social care. We have also already touched on two further discourses, that of a discourse of welfare set against a discourse of control. These are important ideas to consider, particularly for those who work with children and write policy for children. That is, is social policy and legislation there to protect the welfare of children, or to control them? Under ECM, there may be further tensions here, where those agencies from a child protection and health backgrounds may have different notions of what is in the best interests of the child – the welfare of the child – while schools, education and the criminal justice system can be seen to derive from a tradition of the discourse of control.

It is not by accident that a central tenet of the ECM agenda is that of well-being. We know that many children, through poverty and other impoverishing experiences, do not experience well-being or have the means to achieving it in the future for themselves. Therefore, we need to be concerned, not only for the material aspect of children's lives, but also the wider aspects of how they experience their lives socially and emotionally. Traditional attitudes to children have not stopped abuse of adult power over children, whether intentional or unwitting; however, changing practice to ensure children's ideas and wishes are routinely considered is a model of working with children that will be very challenging for some practitioners, teachers and others.

One way of beginning to resolve these tensions is to discuss issues with the children themselves, 'Since Children themselves might have something particular to say about their own world and to contribute to decision-making in relation to this environment' (Foley et al., 2001: 82). The notion of children's voice is explored further in Chapter 7. But if we consider where the power has traditionally been when it comes to judgements about children, whether from a welfare or control perspective, it has not been with the child. This has changed somewhat with the Children's Act and the notion of Children's Voice however, if we consider where we are at present: 'What do all these stories tell us? First, they regularly present children's vulnerability. Second, they confirm adults' assertion of fundamental rights over young bodies and minds. Third, they demonstrate the diversity of children and their varying susceptibility to the control of the powerful' (Warsh, 2005: 15).

Further reading

'Say it your own way': Children's participation in assessment (that is, in consulting children to help practitioners and others make assessment about children's needs): www.barnardos.org.uk/sayityourownway

The full list of articles that comprises the UN Convention of the Rights of the Child can be accessed at: www.everychildmatters.gov.uk/_files/589DD6D3A29C929ACB148DB3F13B01E7 .pdf

Useful websites

www.dcsf.gov.uk/

www.cyh.com

www.bbc.co.uk/children/

www.surestart.gov.uk/surestartservices/childcare/childrensinformationservice/

www.familyinformationservices.org.uk/

A Short History of Early Childhood Education

Nutbrown, N., Clough, P. and Selbie, P.

The legacy of history

> Without words, without writing and without books there would be no history, there could be no concept of humanity.
> Hermann Hesse (1877–1962), winner of the Nobel Prize for Literature in 1946

We begin this book with a short chronology of developments in thinking and practice which have taken place in the history of early childhood education in the UK. We have identified some key moments and key international figures in history who have, in different ways, influenced thinking, research, policy and practice in the development of education and care for the youngest children. In opening the book with an overview of early years developments from the 1600s to the present day we have created a foundation for the rest of the book, and we have shown our view of the impact of individual men and women who, in one way or another, made their distinctive mark on the development of early childhood education.

History is what humanity creates, and policy itself is *realised* by people; as Hesse (1939) reminds us, history helps to generate a concept of humanity. In the sense that people *are* the history-makers, early childhood educators *make* both history and policy, though in another sense the inheritance of history is something from which they stand apart and the impact of policy is something over which they may feel they have no control. But, as Merleau-Ponty (1962) has it, 'although we are born into a [pre-existing] world, we [yet] have the task of creating it ...' (p. ix).

One of the aims of this book is to help readers to consider current policies and practices in early childhood education through the lens of history; it seeks to use history as a means of understanding present states and challenges of early childhood education and as a tool for informing the shape of early childhood education in the future – that is, in our *own* lives and careers.

Of course, we could say that nothing is new, and ideas simply recur; perhaps most topical at the end of the twentieth century was the example of the planned re-introduction of 'Payment by Results' signalled in a Department for Education and Employment (DfEE) Green Paper (DfEE 1999) with echoes of 'Payment by Results' in the Revised Code of 1862, where the notion of raising standards through the use of testing was introduced and teachers' pay was linked to the achievement of their pupils. This is not so much a case of history repeating itself but perhaps more an example of how events, developments and ideas can rhyme, or chime, or echo over time.

This book is structured to encourage critical engagement with historical ideas and developments, influences on early childhood education, issues of policy development and implementation, and the impact of research on policy. The development of early childhood education provision, and the key figures in that development, form the starting points for considering where early childhood education has come from and where present policies 'fit', or do not fit, with the lessons of history. The ways in which childhood has been constructed throughout recent history is also a topic which helps to inform the critique of policy which has moved from the central aim of 'nurturing childhood' to a situation where 'raising educational achievement' is the main goal. Central to this argument about the shift in priorities of policy in early childhood education is the change in language and the new terminologies imposed year after year upon early childhood education.

Finally, we are aware that there is no single history; it needs always to be seen from multiple perspectives, viewed through different lenses. In understanding what has happened in the UK, it is important, too, to look at international developments in early childhood education and the many influences from figures throughout history working around the world.

Early childhood education in the UK: a brief history

During the mid 1700s there were moves in political and social spheres to provide some form of education for young children. 'Monitorial' schools were set up from the end of the 1700s by the Quaker, Joseph Lancaster, and the New Lanark worksite elementary school was established by Robert Owen in the early 1800s. The National Society was founded in 16 October 1811; its aim:

> ... that the National Religion should be made the foundation of National Education, and should be the first and chief thing taught to the poor, according to the excellent Liturgy and Catechism provided by our Church.[1]

The National Society established a national system of education, supplemented by the State from 1870. In 2007 there were some 5,000 Church of England and Church in Wales schools (originally known as National Schools), most of which are primary schools, educating almost a million children. However, it was the protestant 'Evangelicals' who, through the Home and Colonial School Society (founded in 1836), had the insight to consider the development of schools for the youngest children and open 'infant schools'.

Thus, throughout the eighteenth and nineteenth centuries schools were being developed and systems devised and expanded, not only by religious organisations and benefactors, but also of course by the socially and politically motivated who were driven, not by religious conviction but by a belief that the education of young children could contribute to the development of a better society. By 1862, the Revised Code was introduced whereby grants were awarded to elementary schools, depending upon the achievement of their pupils. Forster's Education Act of 1870 established school boards in areas where there was a lack of elementary school provision.

Simultaneously, there was pioneering work on the nature of curriculum for young children, with the Mundella Code of 1882 advocating 'enlightened' teaching of young children. Particular figures can be seen as distinctly influential in such 'curricular development' (though of course it would not have been known as such!); these include: Johann Pestalozzi, Friedrich Froebel, Rachel and Margaret McMillan, Maria Montessori, Charlotte Mason and Susan Isaacs. All advocated ways of working with children which centred around the children themselves and where play was a central component of what was offered.

It was the development of industry which first prompted schooling for young children, and discussion about the age at which compulsory schooling should begin. The view was put forward in parliament during the enactment of Forster's Education Act (1870) that sending children to school a year earlier than some other countries in Europe would give them some sort of advantage in educational achievement (Szretzer 1964). Indeed, it was Mundella who, in an address to the 'National Education League', said: 'I ask you Englishmen and Englishwomen, are Austrian children to be educated before English children?' (National Education League 1869: 133). A further reason, put forward in the Hadow Report of

---

[1] (http://www.natsoc.org.uk/society/history)

1911, for supporting an early start to schooling was the desire to prevent childhood ill-health by the introduction of medical inspections of young children while at school. An early start to compulsory schooling was paralleled by early leaving too, a view supported by the industrialists who needed young workers.

Later, during the First World War years and the need for mothers of younger children to work, the development of nursery education flourished. The following account of the setting up of nursery education in Sheffield is typical of many cities in the North of England.

The Development of Nursery Education in Sheffield has paralleled National trends. Nursery Education began in this country at the beginning of [the twentieth] century at the instigation of people who were concerned about the plight of children in industrial cities: Sheffield children were typical of these. The social climate was such that by the late 1920s Sheffield was beginning to suffer in the Depression: unemployment was rife and poverty was very real. The then centre of the city buildings consisted of many terraced houses and factories, with little opportunity for the children to grow and develop in a healthy environment. In Scotland, Robert Owen had seen the necessity for young children to have good food, fresh air and rest in uncrowded conditions and started a nursery for his workers' children at the turn of the century. Rachel and Margaret McMillan began their Nursery School in Deptford with the intention of providing an 'open-air' school for young children in 1913. This was the beginning of thinking that young children needed special provision.

Children from poorer areas were often under-nourished with poor skin and pale complexions: rickets were common. Colds, coughs and catarrh seemed to perpetuate. Clothing was inadequate and unattractive: there was very little colour in their lives. The children were often stitched into their clothes for winter. Flea bites, sore eyes and lack of sleep were common and infection was easily passed on. The local Women Councillors (in Sheffield) decided to fight for a nursery school and, although it was an uphill battle, Denby Street Nursery School was opened in 1928 based on the McMillan open-shelter type. It was open from 8.30 a.m. to 5.00 p.m. and holidays. There was practically no money, very little equipment and a skeleton staff.

The emphasis was on physical care. The children were fed, washed, rested and loved. The food was simple and plentiful – buttered rusks, dripping toast, hash stew, shepherd's pie, lentil roast, milk puddings, custard and fruit and steamed puddings. The nurse and doctor visited regularly. Cod liver oil was administered and children monitored for impetigo, rickets, poor eyesight, etc. School became a haven especially if children were from families living in only one room, although the schools were very careful not to usurp the home.

Outdoor play was robust and skilful as many of the children had played in the streets from a very young age. The imaginative play – particularly domestic play – was very real. The children were independent, practical, capable and resilient, many having to be so from a very young age, especially if they came from a large family.

Sheffield Nursery Education grew slowly from its beginnings: there were only 4 nursery schools by 1939 when most children were evacuated or spent quite a lot of time in the air raid shelters after the outbreak of war. Nurseries did close at the beginning of the war but opened again in 1940 on a short-time basis because of the bombing campaign. Gradually the day became extended again as it was felt that children could catch up on sleep at the nursery and there was a need for the regular routine and stability it provided.

The war years did give an impetus to nursery education: there was some expansion because of the demand for married women in the labour force. The expansion of nursery education became a high priority and resources were found. For example in 1941 a new joint circular was sent out to set up special war nurseries financed by the Ministry of Health and the Maternity and Child Welfare Department. The full-time nurseries were open in some cases for 12–15 hours and only for children of working mothers. Part-time nurseries also gave priority to evacuated children and those of working mothers. The emphasis moved to include children's social and emotional needs.

Although the extension in provision of nursery education because of the pressures of war was considerable, compared with earlier years, it could not be regarded as 'spectacular' as only a very small proportion of the total child population in the age group were receiving some kind of nursery education. However, the war nurseries did much to popularise the idea of a nursery stage in education. In the emergency situation of the war, where married women were needed to work, the care of the children had been met by the nursery school. The idea that only mothers can look after children, lost its force during the war.

The 1944 Education Act implied that nursery education would become universal but the 50s and 60s marked a decline in state provision for a variety of reasons – economic pressures, demand for space and teachers for the over fives during the 'bulge' years. (Government) Circular 8/60 effectively stopped expansion until Addendum No. 2 in 1965 when a controlled expansion was allowed where this would increase the return to service of married women teachers.

In 1960, however, the Pre-school Playgroup Movement was formed, the lack of nursery places having given mothers the impetus to make their own provision. The continuous expansion of the movement and the commitment and dedication of those working in it has contributed significantly to greater awareness of the needs of the under fives.

Interest in the state provision of nursery education came to the fore once again when stimulated by the Plowden Report in 1967. It was recommended that nursery classes should be extended, and that an immediate start on building of new nursery schools should be made in 'educational priority areas': the idea being that good nursery schools could begin to offset the consequences of social deprivation. (Sheffield LEA 1986: 2–3)

Meanwhile, during the same period, in Scotland, following Robert Owen's initiatives, Nursery Education began with voluntary contributions in the early 1900s through the commitment of those who saw the need to provide something particular for younger children:

At the beginning of the 20th century as people became more aware of social and physical conditions, public interest was directed to the welfare of children under five years old. The first nursery school in Scotland was opened in Edinburgh in 1903.

Edinburgh's Free Kindergarten was established in 1903. Miss Howden, infant headmistress at Milton House School in 1881, who was concerned at 'babies' accompanying siblings to school, left her savings to found the free kindergarten which started in Galloway's Entry, Canongate in 1903.

St Saviour's Child Garden was established in 1906 by Miss Lileen Hardy in co-operation with Canon Laurie, Rector of Old St Pauls Episcopal Church in the church's hall in Browns Close. (Hardy, 1919:7)

Thus, His Majesty's Inspector of Schools (HMI) reported in 1913:

This school is a bright spot in a rather dark neighbourhood ... with two groups of about 20 children under 5 years of age. To these school lessons are not given. They engage in a variety of interesting kindergarten occupations and they learn to draw and sing. The rest of the time they spend taking care of pets, in attempts at gardening and in playing at housework. They mostly live in the open air and are obviously happy. Regular lessons in elementary subjects are given to those children whose ages are from 5–7 years. (City of Edinburgh Council/Early Education 1999)

All such developments in early education had social and welfare issues at their heart, as fundamental concerns. These, combined with the effects of war years and a recognition of the needs of young children, fuelled the development of early education provision, where establishments set up to care for the physical needs of young children also began to develop ways of providing opportunities for young children to learn. The summary of the HMI report on St Saviour's school describes what many would recognise as elements of an appropriate curriculum for young children. Extended opening hours for working mothers was often normal practice and balancing children's needs was a central feature of many nursery establishments.

Foundation stones: some key figures whose work has influenced thinking and development of provision for young children

The following section outlines some of the politicians, social pioneers, academics, industrialists, and educationalists who in different ways contributed to the development of early education in the UK. Table 1.1 provides a brief summary (in chronological order of date of birth) of some of the figures who influenced these developments in the UK, up to the early 1960s. This summary helps to identify 'key moments' in particular periods of history, and the links between various pioneers and the development of policies. It is not a comprehensive summary, but serves to provide an indicative 'archaeology' behind current UK practices.

Table 1.1 Some influential figures and key events in the development of early education in the UK, up to the early 1960s

Born	Died	Name	Summary of achievements
1592	1670	Jan Amos Komenský (Comenius)	In 1631 published *The School of Infancy* focusing on the early years of a child's education and, in particular, education by mothers within the home. In 1658 his *Orbis Sensualium Pictus*, the first picture book for children, was published.
1712	1778	Jean-Jacques Rousseau	In 1762 published *Emile* which expounded his view for a universal system of education through the experience of the child Emile.
1746	1827	Johann Heinrich Pestalozzi	1780: Published *Leonard and Gertrude: A Book for the People* in which he set out a view of education as central to the regeneration of a community. He wrote: 'The school ought really to stand in closest connection with the life of the home'. He believed that mothers should be educated sufficiently to teach their children at home.
1771	1858	Robert Owen	Mill owner in New Lanark, Scotland. 1816: Established schools for children of his workers. Schools were for children under 12 years with particular emphasis on the infant school. James Buchanan was the first teacher in the New Lanark school, exemplifying Owens' ideals of kindness, activity and co-operation.
1771	1855	Joshua Watson	A retired wine merchant and government contractor during the Napoleonic Wars, he was once referred to by Bishop Lloyd of Oxford as 'the best layman in England', was an influential Church of England figure in the nineteenth century, and one of the founders of the National Society for the Education of the Poor in the Principles of the Established Church in 1811.
1778	1838	Joseph Lancaster	One of the founders of mass education for the poor in the industrial age, and pioneer of the Monitorial school system. 1798: Set up the Borough Road School using the system of monitors to teach them. Supported by other Quakers, the system spread and by 1851, 826 British schools were established. Borough Road also became the earliest teacher training institution.

(Continued)

Table 1.1   (Continued)

Born	Died	Name	Summary of achievements
1782	1852	Friedrich Froebel	In 1826 published *The Education of Man* in which he argues for the importance of play in education. Froebel's ideas became influential in Britain around the mid nineteenth century.
1784	1857	James Buchanan	1814: Worked with Robert Owen in New Lanark to run the infant school. Though reported not to have been a good manager, he enjoyed working with children using methods that reflected 'progressive' infant school work.
1791	1866	Samuel Wilderspin	1820: After meeting James Buchanan took charge of the new Quaker Street Infant School in Spitalfields.
1793	1865	Elizabeth Mayo	1829: Wrote *Lessons with Objects* which claimed that by arranging and classifying objects and discovering their qualities the child would be stimulated to learn. This influenced elementary education throughout the rest of the nineteenth century, including some rote learning.
1798	1869	William Ewart	1850: Successfully introduced a bill to establish free public libraries supported from local rates.
1804	1877	Sir James Phillips Kay-Shuttleworth	1839–40: Established a training college at Battersea which became the model for nineteenth-century training of elementary school teachers.
1811	1892	Robert Lowe	Introduced the Revised Code in 1862 which included the introduction of 'payment results' whereby grants to elementary schools were based principally upon pupils' performances in annual examinations in reading, writing and arithmetic. 'Payment by Results' continued for 35 years until 1899.
1812	1870	Charles Dickens	Through his novels he drew attention to the poor social conditions which affected children and the importance of education.
1814	1897	Emily Anne Eliza Shirreff	Campaigned for education of girls and women. In 1875 became president of the Froebel Society (founded in 1874). She emphasised the importance of the proper training of kindergarten teachers.

Table 1.1

Born	Died	Name	Summary of achievements
1818	1886	William Edward Forster	1870 Elementary Education Act established school boards in areas where there was a lack of elementary school provision.
1825	1897	Anthony John Mundella	Member of the Hadow Committee and responsible with Lord Spencer for the Mundella Act which became known as the Education Act of 1880 which introduced universal compulsory education in England. The 'Mundella' Code of 1882 encouraged 'enlightened' teaching methods in schools and allowed for a variety of subjects in the curriculum.
1837	1931	Sir William Hart Dyke	Played a leading part in promoting and distributing the 1890 Education Code which paved the way for the ending of the system of 'Payment by Results'. 1891: Introduced the Free Education Bill, which opened up the way to provide free elementary education to children.
1840	1938	Sir James Crichton-Brown	1884: As Vice President of the Committee of Council on Education, investigated cases of alleged 'overpressure' in London schools caused by the demands of the Mundella Code.
1842	1923	Charlotte Mason	Headmistress of one of England's first infant schools at 22 years of age. Pestalozzi trained, she started the first infant school in the country and championed home education and play as being as important as lessons, with the key phrase 'education is an atmosphere'.
1850	1936	Edmond Gore Alexander Holmes	1911: Published *What Is and What Might Be: A Study of Education in General and Elementary Education in Particular.* This book condemned the formal, systematized, examination-ridden education system and advocated co-operation, self-expression and activity methods. Holmes also importantly, criticised the system of 'Payment by Results'.

(Continued)

Table 1.1   (Continued)

Born	Died	Name	Summary of achievements
1851	1920	Mary Augusta Ward (Mrs Humphry)	In 1890 founded centre for social work, bible teaching and 'children's play hours' at Gordon Square, London. The Children's Play Hours scheme led to establishment of recreational centres for London children, transferred to centres for London children, transferred to Tavistock Square in 1897, and became the Passmore Edwards Settlement. In 1898 Mary Ward began a scheme for 'crippled' children which contributed to the general recognition of the need for special resources and provision for some children.
1855	1931	Edward Parnell Culverwell	1913: Published *The Montessorian Principles and Practice* advocating modern, Montessorian teaching methods. Thus introducing the method to the UK.
1856	1936	Sigmund Freud	Developed an approach to psychoanalysis which provided a way of interpreting the behaviour of young children.
1859	1952	John Dewey	Promoted progressive and child-centred education through teaching based on integrated learning through projects rather than discreet subjects.
1859	1917	Rachel McMillan	1913: Established the Rachel McMillan Open-Air Nursery School in London, based on her ideas about preschool education with a large garden with shelters and other outdoor facilities. She focused particularly on work with children from slum areas.
1860	1931	Margaret McMillan	In 1899 Margaret McMillan participated in one of the first medical inspections of children under government auspices, before campaigning successfully for school medical inspections in 1902. 1913: With her sister Rachel she established Camp schools and a nursery school. She established the Rachel McMillan Training College in memory of her sister in 1930.
1860	1932	Catherine Isabella Dodd	1902: Opening of experimental elementary school and kindergarten based on new teaching methods.

Table 1.1

Born	Died	Name	Summary of achievements
1861	1925	Rudolf Steiner	Founded the Waldorf-Steiner Education movement. The first school opened in 1919 based on Steiner's Anthroposophical principles and promoting co-education for children based on imitation and example and Steiner's beliefs about child/human development and the parallel development of moral life and teaching.
1864	1933	Dame Maude Agnes Lawrence	School inspector and administrator. Became Chief Woman Inspector in 1905 when the Woman Inspectorate was set up. The six women, at first, inspected education of very young children and girls in elementary schools, mainly in domestic subjects.
1870	1952	Maria Montessori	In 1907 opened, in Rome, the first House of Childhood, for children living in tenement housing aged between 3 and 7 years. Montessori's work emphasised the importance of children's environments. She developed successful methods of working with children described as 'mentally defective'.
1872	1937	Edith Mary Deverell	1900: Appointed to the Inspectorate. Joined five other women inspectors who were inspecting girls' and infants' departments in elementary schools. Campaigned to secure the interest and co-operation of parents in the work of the school.
1882	1960	Melanie Klein	Psychoanalyst who employed 'free [therapeutic] play' techniques with children. In 1932 published *The Psychoanalysis of Children*. A pioneer of knowledge of the 'mental life' of infant children and an important influence on general attitudes to young children.
1883	1973	Alexander Sutherland (A. S.) Neill	In 1924 A. S. Neill founded his own school in Lyme Regis, which on moving to Suffolk became known as the famous Summerhill School, based on radically liberal, humanist and child-centred principles.
1885	1948	Susan Sutherland Isaacs	1924–27: Established the Malting House School, Cambridge, with a curriculum and pedagogy designed to further the *individual* development of children. Author of several books which include observations and reflections of children at the Malting House School. (Thus an early *systematic* researcher.)

(Continued)

Table 1.1 (Continued)

Born	Died	Name	Summary of achievements
1886	1939	Henry Caldwell Cook	1917: Published *The Play Way: An Essay in Educational Method*. Believed that the existing school system hampered 'true' education, arguing (as Dewey was to) that: 'Proficiency and learning come not from reading and listening but from action, from doing and from experience'.
1892	1946	Marion Richardson	Mostly influential as Inspector for Art during the 1930s in London. Influenced the teaching of handwriting during the late 1930s, with the publication of *Writing and Writing Patterns* (1935) which influenced the teaching of handwriting in primary schools.
1895	1976	Louis Christian Schiller	HMI, promoted child-centred learning and education through the arts. Worked closely with Robin Tanner running courses for serving teachers.
1896	1934	Lev Semenovich Vygotsky	Psychologist and educational theorist best known for his emphasis on learning as an act of social interaction and his theory of the 'Zone of Proximal Development'.
1896	1971	Donald Woods Winnicott	A paediatrician and psychoanalyst who developed a framework of human emotional development which supports the development of environments and practices to enable children to develop as secure and emotionally 'whole' human beings.
1896	1980	Jean Piaget	Psychologist who put forward stages of cognitive development which informed practice in early years teaching. Corresponded with Susan Isaacs.
1900	1969	Sir Fred Joyce Schonell	Most renowned for influence on primary school method of teaching – in particular, approaches to teaching children with learning difficulties. In 1944 wrote the *Happy Venture* reading scheme and developed the reading test of his name.
1901	1985	Sir James Pitman	Inventor of the Initial Teaching Alphabet (ita) – a simplified format to aid learning of reading which was in vogue in some schools during the 1960s but which did not become universally established infant teaching practice.

Table 1.1

Born	Died	Name	Summary of achievements
1902	1994	Erik Erikson	Psychologist and psychoanalyst whose theory of human development prompted the development of early childhood programmes which supported healthy social and emotional development.
1902	1987	Carl Rogers	Psychologist and psychotherapist who put forward an approach to education which was based on reciprocal relationships between children and between children and their teachers.
1904	1990	Burrhus Frederic (B. F.) Skinner	Psychologist who developed theory of behaviourism which promoted a system of learning which involved a 'stimulus-response' approach in order to modify undesirable behaviour.
1904	1988	Robin Tanner	Promoted the arts in education and ran courses for teachers with Christian Schiller at the Institute of Education in London.
1907	1990	John Bowlby	Psychoanalyst who is renowned for his 'Attachment' theory.
1909	1986	Sir Alec Clegg	Chief Education Officer of West Riding, Yorkshire 1945–74. Emphasising the importance of creativity in all educational processes, made key contributions to teachers' INSET and to the organisation and curricula of schools and settings. Made an extensive collection of children's artwork from West Riding schools 1930s–1974 and expounded the importance of creativity.
1910	1971	Sir John Hubert Newsom	Like Clegg, a pioneer of systematic development of school needs and processes. 1963: Chair of the Central Advisory Council on education which produced the Newsom Report, *Half Our Future*, reporting on education of 'average and below average' children. Deputy Chair of the Central Advisory Council, which produced, The Plowden Report, *Children and their Primary Schools* (1967). Wrote several books including *Willingly to School* (1944), *The Education of Girls* (1948) and *The Child at School* (1950).

Into the twenty-first century: twenty years of policy change

> How comes change? We read of its coming in the books of history – 'change was in the air', 'that was the decisive year', 'then came the breakthrough', but when we live through history it is quite different: change takes place on the ground not in the air, each year seems only too much like the next, and as for the breakthrough – we wait for it in vain. Yet, looking back over a period, somehow change has come. (Schiller 1979: 17)

Understanding recent history: 1998–2008

When we look back over these last few years, it seems that the slow and fitful development of early childhood education in the UK is now central to educational and social change. There has been something of an explosion of activity, a burgeoning of initiatives, interest and resources. Thus, in the last 20 years alone, from 1988 to 2008, there have been at least 20 major new policies (an average of one per year) which apart from their individual effects have, as a whole, changed the shape and status of early childhood education almost beyond recognition. A teacher recently told us: 'It's odd, I started teaching in 1988 and I've been looking back at old files and things and clearing out planning sheets, class lists, those kinds of things. Looking back I found myself plotting these 20 years almost exactly in terms of a policy a year!'

A brief survey of this period reveals how policy changes have involved early childhood educators in the following:

- the National Curriculum and subsequent revisions;
- rigorous and (sometimes) stressful inspection processes;
- the Children Act 1989;
- interpretation of expected 'desirable outcomes' of nursery education;
- new Codes of Practice for the identification of children with Special Educational Needs;
- changes in relation to national assessment of children on entry to school, known as 'Baseline Assessment';
- the National Childcare Strategy in 1998;
- working, during the 1990s, with diminishing resources followed by high profile, funded activity and increasing expectations during the 2000s;
- working with diminishing support and limited opportunities for professional development, followed by expectations of further qualifications and funded professional development;
- grappling with issues affecting the teaching of four-year-olds in school;
- Early Years Development and Childcare Partnerships (EYDCPs);
- working within a developing network of diversity of provision and EYDCPs;

- the National Literacy Strategy;
- the National Numeracy Strategy;
- new Foundation Stage curriculum developed from government guidance;
- transforming the Foundation Stage from policy to practice;
- the Foundation Stage Profile;
- *Every Child Matters* (2003)
- *The Ten Year Childcare Strategy* (2004);
- *Birth to Three Matters* Framework;
- the revised Early Years Foundation Stage (2007);
- acquiring Early Years Professional Status.

It is important to remember that this list is by no means exhaustive and, of course, is supplemented by other social and educational policies which have – equally, if less directly – impacted on the culture, structure and status of early childhood education. As well as these demanding policy shifts, recent years have seen the establishment of what might be called a new status for the early childhood workforce, with:

- unprecedented government investment;
- professional development opportunities (and expectations);
- networks of support;
- expectation of further qualifications of all staff working with children from birth to five.

Into the future, learning from the past

Learning from the past is one way of trying to ensure that new policies and investment do not repeat the mistakes of previous generations. We shall come to this later in the book where we examine the ways in which influential figures or deeds in the history and development of early childhood education the UK has helped to shape present-day policy and practice and serves to locate current experience within a history of ideas, beliefs and values. However, throughout the book it will become apparent that policy-makers do not always learn from the past and, as we shall see, ideas sometimes seem to return, are sometimes re-invented and appear in 'new clothes' but nevertheless bear distinctly familiar shapes (even if bringing new intentions).

The point of this examination of the work and thinking of people who have contributed to the development of early childhood education, is to try to understand how some of the most useful ideas can be drawn upon and developed. There is no 'history for the sake of history' here, rather a reflection on some of the lessons which might be learned in order to understand the present state of early childhood education and how it has come to be what it is.

Summary

From reading these chapters you will have gained an insight into childhood and education across the centuries and how some historical ideas have impacted on educational theory and policy today.

Student activities

- Think about how much of what you have learnt still applies today:
  - o What has changed dramatically?
  - o What aspects of childhood or education are still similar?
- Can you see how any of the historical educational debates have influenced policy or curriculum today?
- Is there anything about historical accounts of childhood or education that either surprised or shocked you?
- Do you think it is important to have some historical knowledge of how childhood and education have changed over time? If so, why?

Additional reading

Gray, C. and MacBlain, S. (2012) Chapter 2, 'The Founding Fathers and Philosophies of Learning' in *Learning Theories in Childhood*. London: Sage.

McDowall-Clark, R. (2013) Chapter 2, 'The Historical Context: The Emergence of Childhood' in *Childhood in Society for the Early Years*, 2nd edn. London: Learning Matters.

PART 2 — EDUCATIONAL THEORY

Overview

A theory is an orderly set of ideas which should allow us to describe, predict and explain human behaviour. It should be stated in such a way that it can be shown to be false and it must be open to scientific investigation. The key message is that it is a basis for action to enable us to find ways to improve the lives and education of children. Below is an overview of the key learning theories and theorists that you may come across during your studies:

Theory	Key theorists	Overview
Psycho analytical	Sigmund Freud Erik Erikson	*Beliefs focus on the formation of personality. According to this approach, children move through various stages, confronting conflicts between biological drives and social expectations.*
Behavioural and social learning	Joseph Watson B.F. Skinner Albert Bandura	*Beliefs that describe the importance of the environment and nurturing in the growth of a child.*
Biological theories	G. Stanley Hall and Arnold Gesell Konrad Lorenz John Bowlby	*Belief that heredity and innate biological processes govern growth.*
Cognitive theorists	Jean Piaget Lev Vygotsky	*Beliefs that describe how children learn.*
Systems theory	Urie Bronfenbrenner	*The belief that development can't be explained by a single concept, but rather by a complex system.*

These will be covered briefly in the chapter by Gray and MacBlain and if you wish to explore these in more detail it is worth looking at the whole book, which is on the reading list. You will also be exploring current issues, views and perspectives on learning theories and child development. As you read these theories, note the patterns and similarities between the ideas they describe and principles and practices of modern education. These theories are explored in context and in a modern setting; in the writings of Watkins et al. and Whitebread. Child development is defined as a change in the child that occurs over time. These changes follow an orderly pattern that moves toward greater complexity and enhances survival. The ways in which children develop and the impact upon us as professionals will be explored in this part.

An Introduction to Learning Theories

5

Gray, C. and Macblain, S.

This chapter aims to:

- familiarize the reader with the organization and structure of the book
- provide a brief synopsis of each chapter.

We are convinced that learning begins at inception and continues throughout life. Although this approach is frequently termed cradle to grave, we believe that learning precedes birth as babies become familiar with sounds heard frequently during pregnancy, including the sound of their mother's voice. Hepper (1996) had a group of mothers relax after their evening meal and another group keep busy. He found the group who relaxed tended to watch a popular Australian television programme, Neighbours, which aired at around 6.30pm on most evenings. After birth, mothers in the relaxation group were able to settle their babies more easily when they played the Neighbours theme tune. Babies in the busy mothers' group showed no reaction to this tune. Hepper (1996) concluded that, prior to birth, babies in the relaxation group had learned an association between the Neighbours theme tune and relaxation. From birth onwards, babies are interactive processors of information. Some learning is incidental, effortless and undirected, whilst other learning is effortful, purposeful, directed, creative and reflective. For example, you might settle down to show a toddler how to put a jigsaw together (directed learning) but find their attention drawn to (incidental learning) an activity at the writing table. By the end of the session, the child might be able to tell you that 'S is a snake, a slithering snake' but have no clue how to put the jigsaw together. This situation reflects the sheer complexity of human learning. It suggests that learning can be affected by situational factors such as the presence of others, background noise, or internal factors such as tiredness or level of interest. Once learned, how-

acquired in early childhood include walking, talking, riding a bike and reading and writing. Simply stated, learning is the acquisition of knowledge and skills (David et al., 2011).

For more than 2000 years, philosophers, academics and educators have attempted to explain and define human learning. The Greek philosopher Aristotle (384–322 BC) believed that learning develops through repetitive exercises. According to Aristotle, the State must be charged with responsibility for instilling virtue, habits, nature and reason into children and for ensuring they became citizens of benefit to society. Almost a hundred years later, Socrates (470–399 BC) described learning as a process of remembering. He believed that all knowledge exists within the human soul before birth but, perhaps due to the trauma of birth, the soul forgets all it previously knew. Through a process of questioning and inquiry, termed Socratic dialogue, the soul recovers some aspects of knowledge.

Definition

Learning is the acquisition of knowledge or skill.

In contrast, Locke (1632–1704) argued against the existence of innate ideas (formed before birth), describing the child's mind as a *tabula rasa* or blank slate. Consistent with Aristotelian philosophy, Locke believed that knowledge is acquired through experience, repetition, training and virtue. He emphasized the importance of enjoyable learning and insisted that teaching should begin in early childhood. Locke's assertions were radical for their time but were shared by a number of influential thinkers including, amongst many others, Pestalozzi (1746–1827), Froebel (1782–1852), Dewey (1859–1952) and Montessori (1870–1952). Whilst each offers a unique insight into children's learning, importantly for our discussion these philosophers and educators have a shared belief in the importance of educating the young child.

Rousseau (1712–1778), for example, argued that education should follow the child's natural growth rather than the demands of society. His emphasis on the innate development of human nature became the primary philosophical basis for many alternative movements in education. In the early 1800s, the Swiss humanitarian Pestalozzi opened schools for orphans, based on Rousseau's principles. His work inspired educators in Europe and America. Froebel, a teacher at Pestalozzi's school, later became famous as the founder of the kindergarten concept. Montessori shared Froebel's belief that children should be taught social skills and empathy. While Froebel used creative and imaginative play to achieve his goals, Montessori employed real-world experiences such as cleaning a room, caring for animals, building a toy house or making a garden to develop these skills.

Dewey shared with Montessori and Froebel the notion that education should be child-centred, active and interactive; and that education must involve the child's social world and community. Influenced by the teaching philosophies of the early pioneers in the field of early childhood education, Dewey emphasized the importance of experiential learning and the process of teachers and children learning together. The teachings of the founding fathers and mothers of early childhood education are explored in greater detail in Chapter 2 where their unique contributions are highlighted. Similarly, the topic of experiential learning is given a more thorough analysis in Chapters 4 and 5 of this book as we explore the theories of Piaget (1896–1980) and Vygotsky (1896–1934).

It is, however, theories of learning which form the central foci of this book. The last century witnessed a significant shift away from philosophical propositions to the development of a range of empirical theories of learning; each claims to explain the origins of some aspect of learning. Before considering influential educational theories of learning, it seems appropriate at this juncture to define the word theory. In common usage, the term can be used to denote a set of statements or principles devised to explain a group of facts or phenomena, especially one that has been repeatedly tested or is widely accepted and can be used to make predictions about natural phenomena (Dorin et al., 1990).

Definition

A theory is a set of statements or principles devised to explain a group of facts or phenomena.

According to Woollard (2010, p. 472), a theory is 'an unproven conjecture or hypothesis that gives a tentative insight into a complex situation through to a well established explanation of that complex situation'. Darwin's Theory of Evolution, Maslow's (1943) Hierarchy of Needs and Gardner's (1983) Theory of Multiple Intelligence are examples of frequently referenced theories. Arranged in a five-stage hierarchical pyramidal format, Maslow, for example, posits that lower order physiological needs must be met before higher order needs can be satisfied. The first level in the hierarchy concerns basic physiological needs such as water, air, food and sleep; the second is about the need for safety and security; the third involves belongingness, love and affection; the fourth relates to the need for esteem, personal worth, social recognition and accomplishment; at the fifth level, the summit of the hierarchy, is self-actualization. According to Maslow, very few people reach this level but those who do enjoy moments of profound happiness and find deep fulfilment as they achieve their full potential. Maslow's theory provides a useful tool for understanding the factors that impede or progress learning. Nevertheless, it is unsurprising to find that even popularly known theories are the subject of criticism. Maslow's theory, for example, has been heavily critiqued for its lack of scientific rigour and for failing to acknowledge contradictory aspects of human nature. Moreover, it is unidirectional and fails to take account of individual priorities. By way of example, 18-month-old Kevin is a quiet child who rarely cries. Small for his age, Kevin is frequently hungry and sometimes searches for food in the bin. Kevin has learnt that it is better to go hungry (biological need) than to risk the slap that comes when he cries. Even at this young age, Kevin has learnt to prioritize his safety needs (level 2) over his biological need for food (level 1).

In essence, the theories included in this book will provide the reader with a general rule or principle about some aspect of learning. Each theory has strengths and weaknesses. We aim to highlight both and, where appropriate, to compare and contrast them. It is not our contention that one theory is superior to another, or that any single theory holds the key to learning, or even that any of the theories discussed are sufficiently developed to explain all aspects of human learning. On the contrary, we hope to engage the reader in a level of critical reflection that may cause them to accept or reject aspects of each theory. We believe that by studying the content of each chapter, examining the tables included and completing the tasks provided, the reader will develop a greater insight into the complexities of children's learning.

Chapter 3 introduces the theories of Pavlov (1849–1936), Thorndike (1874–1949), Watson (1878–1958) and Skinner (1904–1990). Each explored an aspect of learning underpinned by the principles of stimulus–response. For that reason, they are typically referred to as behaviourists. A branch of psychology, behaviourism remained a dominant force in education for more than fifty years. Although it lost prominence in the 1970s, behaviourism continues to have an influence on pedagogical practice in twenty-first century classrooms. Behaviourists believe that all behaviour, no matter how complex, can be reduced to a simple stimulus–response association. They focus on measurable outcomes rather than on introspective processes (imagery, feelings and thoughts, etc.).

In the course of his experimental research with dogs, the physiologist Ivan Pavlov noted that dogs salivated when laboratory technicians entered the room. Further research revealed the dogs had made an association between the technicians (neutral stimulus) and food (stimulus) and this caused their drooling response. Termed classical or Pavlovian conditioning, the theory was developed further by Watson who demonstrated classical conditioning in humans using young boys known as Little Albert and Little Peter.

Skinner extended Watson's stimulus–response theory to explain more complex forms of learning. He believed it was possible to use the principles underpinning animal experimentation with infants and children. He coined the term operant conditioning to explain the influence positive and negative reinforcers have on shaping and maintaining the child's behaviour. Skinner's theory continues to exert a direct and profound influence on education and is particularly evident in the reward and punishment systems teachers use to shape and maintain pupil behaviour. Star charts, praise, positive feedback and circle time are examples of popularly used positive reinforcers whilst time out is a negative reinforcer. The work of the social learning theorist Bandura (1925 to present) is included by some theorists in discussions on behaviourism (Woollard, 2010). Although he employed the experimental methods favoured by behaviourism, Bandura's inclusion of imagery, mental representations and reciprocal determinism (the child influences and is influenced by their environment) marked a radical departure from traditional behaviourist approaches. For that reason, his work is discussed in Chapter 6 alongside Bronfenbrenner's (1917–2005) social learning theory.

Chapter 4 considers the constructivist theory of learning. Though they continue to co-exist, this theory offers a considerable departure from that of behaviourism. Constructivism views learning as an active, constructive process with the child engaged at every stage. Rather than focus on measurement, cognitive theorists use observations and discourse analysis (interviews) to explain the development of internal cognitive processes. The term 'cognition' refers to internal mental processes and cognitive development to the acquisition of 'knowledge in childhood'. Cognitive constructivism is based on the work of the Swiss biologist and naturalist Jean Piaget. Whilst working with the French psychologist Alfred Binet (the inventor of the first intelligence test), Piaget became curious about the structure of the child's mind. From an analysis of interviews with children of differing ages as they solved problems and his observations of the process, Piaget concluded that older children think in a very different way from younger children. It wasn't simply that older children knew more but that their thought processes had undergone some form of maturational (age-related) change. Piaget continued to study child development for several decades before positing the theory that intellectual development occurs in four distinct stages. Each of these stages is described in detail in this chapter with their advantages and shortcomings discussed.

Chapter 5 extends the concepts introduced in Chapter 4. Vygotsky, a Russian developmental psychologist, developed many of the concepts outlined by Piaget to incorporate the child's social environment. He stressed the fundamental role of social interaction in the development of cognition. Vygotsky believed that each child is born with a basic set of unlearned cognitive functions such as memory and attention that facilitate high-level learning. Since from their earliest moments children are absorbing the rules and mores of their culture, Vygotsky believed that learning can precede understanding; whereas Piaget believed that development precedes learning. According to Vygotsky (1978, p. 57):

> Every function in the child's cultural development appears twice: first, on the social level, and later, on the individual level; first, between people (interpsychological) and then inside the child (intrapsychological).

Both Piaget and Vygotsky believed that young children are curious and actively involved in their own learning and in the discovery and development of new understandings/schema. Whereas Vygotsky placed more emphasis on social contributions to the process of development, Piaget emphasized self-initiated discovery. These points will be considered in greater detail in Chapter 6 where the zone of proximal development, role of culture, social factors, language, peers and educators are explored in detail.

Chapter 6 explores the social learning theories of Bandura and Bronfenbrenner. As previously discussed (see Chapter 3 above), Bandura's social learning theory has its roots in behaviourism. Whilst sharing the experimental approaches of his contemporaries, Bandura argued that to exclude thinking from any theory of learning would be like reducing 'Shakespeare's literary masterpieces to his prior instruction in the mechanics of writing' (Bandura, 1978, p. 350). Social learning theory advocates that individuals, especially children, imitate or copy modelled behaviour from personally observing others, the environment and the mass media. Reflecting the central tenets of traditional behaviourism, Bandura believed that behaviour can be shaped and maintained by reinforcement. He extended this theory to include two aspects of indirect reinforcement termed vicarious and self reinforcement. Vicarious reinforcement or observational learning occurs when a child witnesses the effects of an event and stores it in memory. By way of example, pre-school children refused to wear their seatbelts after watching the children's cartoon character Peppa Pig and her brother George sitting in the back seat of a car without seatbelts. Following complaints from parents, the producers rectified the problem (BBC News, 2010). This example serves to indicate that, consistent with Bandura's theory, the relationship between viewers and television is reciprocal, with each reacting and shaping the other.

Similar themes inform Bronfenbrenner's ecological model of child development. Bronfenbrenner acknowledged the role of media, technology, culture and society on childhood development. Like Bandura, Bronfenbrenner believed that technology has the potential to change and even damage society (Henderson, 1995), and that the child influences and is influenced by their environment. Bronfenbrenner was one of the first psychologists to adopt a holistic perspective on human development. His ecological model of development comprises five interrelated systems each containing the roles, norms and rules that powerfully shape development. Bronfenbrenner recognized that not only is it necessary to understand how the family or school influences human development, but broader influences as well.

Chapter 7 considers Bruner's (1915–present) discovery learning theory of constructivism. Bruner was influenced by Piaget's ideas about cognitive development in children. During the 1940s, his early work focused on the impact of needs, motivations, expectations (mental sets) and their influence on perception. Like Piaget, he emphasizes action and problem solving in children's learning, but like Vygotsky he underlines the role of social interaction, language and instruction in the development of thinking. To achieve this goal, he devised the concept of scaffolding. Whilst the term scaffolding is most closely associated with Bruner, it was coined by Wood, Bruner and Ross (1976) to describe the type of support children need to achieve the zone of development. Though a psychologist by training, Bruner became a prominent figure in education and wrote several influential and highly regarded texts for teachers including *The Process of Education (1960), Toward a Theory of Instruction (1966), The Relevance of Education (1971)* and *The Culture of Education (1996)*. The final section of this chapter includes a detailed review of constructivist and social constructivist theories drawing out similar and disparate threads.

Chapter 8 examines children's learning through the lens of a newly evolving paradigm variously referred to as the new social studies of childhood and the new sociology of childhood. The origins of this theory can be traced to the United Nations Convention on the Rights of the Child (UNCRC, 1989), which was ratified in the UK in 1999. The UNCRC established children's rights to provision, protection and participation and changed the way children were viewed by many social and developmental researchers (Corosa, 2004). In challenging the objectification of children, the UNCRC heralded a well-documented shift away from research being conducted 'on' to research being conducted 'with' children (Porter and Lacey, 2005). Critical of traditional approaches to research on children's learning, proponents of the social studies of childhood reject the empirical methods favoured by behaviourists and critique Piaget's explanation of universal age-related competencies. Advocates of this newly evolving paradigm share the natural methods of enquiry favoured by Piaget and embrace key concepts of the socio-constructivist and ecological theories. This chapter seeks to explore this contemporary theory with reference to more traditional approaches to children's development and learning.

The final chapter of this book offers a departure from theory (Chapter 9). It is written especially for people who work with or care for young children and who would like to enhance children's learning. Consideration is given to the challenges inherent in creating a learning–teaching environment where children play together in creative, investigative and problem-solving ways, where they take ownership of and responsibility for their own learning, and where emotional and imaginative needs are met (Broadbent, 2006, p. 192). In addition, the role of the adult as a facilitator of learning is explored with reference to the theories of Vygotsky, Bronfenbrenner and Bruner. Practical examples from practice pepper and inform this chapter which seeks to demonstrate the dynamic relationship between theory and practice.

Exercise

Before reading further, consider which theorist best explains how children's learning develops. As you read each of the following chapters, we would ask you to continually review your decision and to consider whether the information provided has changed or strengthened your initial view.

RECOMMENDED READING

Fabian, H. & Mould, C. (eds) (2009). *Development and Learning for Very Young Children*. London: Sage.

A useful resource, this book concentrates on children in the 0–3 age range. Fabian and Mould cover a breadth of material, including the stages of child development, development and learning, and policy and practice.

Robson, S. (2009). *Developing, Thinking and Understanding in Young Children*. London and New York: Routledge.

This interesting and challenging text offers an in-depth study of children's thinking and learning. The developing brain and language and communication are discussed through the lens of thinking and learning. Limited to cognitive theory, it offers students an insight into the developing child.

REFERENCES

Bandura, A. (1978). Perceived effectiveness: an explanatory mechanism of behavioral change. In G. Lindzey, C.S. Hall & R.F. Thompson (eds) *Psychology*. New York: Worth.

BBC News (2010). Peppa Pig in seatbelt safety row. Available at: http://news.bbc.co.uk/1/hi/8460753.stm

Broadbent, P. (2006). Developing an understanding of young children's learning through play: the place of observation, interaction and reflection. *British Journal of Educational Research, 32, 2,* 191–207.

Bruner, J.S. (1960). *The Process of Education*. Cambridge, MA: Harvard University Press.

Bruner, J.S. (1966). *Toward a Theory of Instruction*. Cambridge, MA: Belknapp Press.

Bruner, J.S. (1971). *The Relevance of Education*. New York: Norton.

Bruner, J.S. (1996). *The Culture of Education*. Cambridge, MA: Harvard University Press.

Corosa, W.A. (2004). *The Sociology of Childhood (Sociology for a New Century Series)*, 2nd edn. Thousand Oaks, CA: Pine Forge Press.

David, T., Goouch, K. & Powell, S. (2011). Play and prescription: the influence of national developments in England. In M. Kernan & E. Singer (eds) *Peer Relationships in Early Childhood Education and Care*. London: Routledge. pp. 49–60.

Dorin, H., Demmin, P.E. & Gabel, D. (1990). *Chemistry: The Study of Matter,* 3rd edn. Englewood Cliffs, NJ: Prentice Hall.

Gardner, H. (1983). *Frames of Mind: The Theory of Multiple Intelligences*. New York: Basic Books.

Henderson, Z.P. (1995). Renewing our social fabric. *Human Ecology, 23, 1,* 16–19.

Hepper, P.G. (1996). Fetal memory: does it exist? What does it do? *ACTA Paediatrica Supplement, 416,* 16–20.

Maslow, A.H. (1943). A theory of human motivation. *Psychological Review, 50, 4, 370–96.*

Porter, J. & Lacey, P. (2005). *Researching Learning Difficulties: A Guide for Practitioners*. London: Paul Chapman Publishing.

United Nations Convention on the Rights of the Child (UNCRC) (1989). Available at: www.unicef.org/crc/

Vygotsky, L.S. (1978). *Mind and Society: The Development of Higher Mental Processes*. Cambridge, MA: Harvard University Press.

Wood, D., Bruner, J.S. & Ross, G. (1976). The role of tutoring in problem solving. *Journal of Child Psychology and Psychiatry, 17, 2,* 81–100.

Woollard, J. (2010). *Psychology for the Classroom: Behaviourism*. Oxon: Routledge.

Thinking about Young Children Learning

Nutbrown, C.

A 3-year-old sits on the edge of a river bank, her toes just touching the gently flowing water. She watches the insects skimming the surface, stares intently at a tiny fish which swims near to her feet. For some 20 minutes, this little girl watches patiently. No one knows what she is thinking, but there is no doubt that her diligent study of the environment around her is something which takes up the whole of her being. No one tells her to study the water and the wildlife around her, no one asks her to sit still, to be quiet and to watch. Her interest is fuelled by a natural and instinctive curiosity about the world around her.

Adults who teach young children must remain constantly aware that young children are capable of being patient observers, especially when given space and time to do so. Young children cannot be taught effectively if planned learning is always artificially divided into falsely defined compartments called 'subjects'. Just as the child on the river bank studied intently the experiences around her, children will explore scientific ideas, learn about mathematics and develop their language while engaged in many different experiences in home and community situations as well as through experiences specifically planned for such learning in early education settings.

In the following examples, children are learning through real and immediate experiences. They are all playing or working with water, and these observations show the immediate and engaging experience of water in providing playful learning opportunities. Three observations follow: Zoe (aged 4), Ashaq (aged 6) and Karmen and John (aged 8 and 7).

Zoe aged 4

Zoe was playing in the water trough at the nursery. She was experimenting with a jug and water wheel, spending a considerable time filling the jug, pouring the water over the wheel and watching it turn. She poured water at different speeds and from different heights. Her teacher watched and eventually asked: 'Can you tell me what is happening?' Zoe looked at her and began her explanation: 'The wheel doesn't like to get wet, so it runs fast to get away from the water. When all the water is gone, it stays still again!' Zoe knew that the water made the wheel turn but ascribed attributes of thought and feeling to the wheel. Early experiences of the scientific principles of force, gravity and power are present in this example, as well as the beginnings of reasoned thought. Zoe was beginning to grapple with ideas of speed and of cause, function and effect.

Ashaq aged 6

Ashaq was watching his mother using a jet spray at the garage to wash her car. He observed intently for some time and then asked if he could have a turn. After concentrating the jet of water on one muddy wheel and watching the dirt wash away, he said: 'If I put it nearer the dirt goes away faster. That's because the water hits it harder if it doesn't spray so far. If I spray a long way away then not all the dirt goes.'

This 6-year-old told his teacher about the car washing. She used jets, sprays and the advantage of a hot summer day to work with him to develop further this understanding and to extend his interest. Water flowed from the hosepipe in the yard outside the classroom as did questions of 'How?', 'Why?' and 'What if?' Ashaq made reasoned answers to all the questions the teacher raised. He also asked questions of his own. The principles of siphoning were mastered and the appropriate terminology was introduced by the teacher. A small group of children worked purposefully to create and solve their own water-oriented problems.

Learning does not begin and end in school. The visit to the garage with his mother opened up the child's thinking which Ashaq, with the help of his teacher, was able to build on with his peers in school.

Karmen and John aged 8 and 7

Karmen and John were at home in their garden bathing dolls and washing all their clothes. The dolls and clothes were covered in an ever-increasing amount of soap suds. The children had rather overestimated the quantity of washing powder they needed, reasoning that the dolls were extremely dirty and so must need a lot of soap to get them clean. John decided to change the water and wash everything again, this time not putting in any more soap. The following conversation gives an interesting insight into the children's reasoning and understanding:

Karmen: Make the water cooler this time, it disperses the bubbles.

John: How?

Karmen: Not sure, but it does, mum does that with the jumpers in the sink. It sort of pops them.

John: Is it that cold water is too cold for them and it makes them pop?

Karmen: Maybe, it's thinner and gets through the membranes.

John: Brains! Do bubbles have brains?

Karmen: No! Membranes! It's like an invisible sort of film, like a sort of skin thing to keep the air trapped, they have them on a programme on telly sometimes.

John: How does the air get in there?

Karmen: Well, it's the soap. Get the cold water now.

John: How cold?

Karmen: Cold! Don't put any warm in, though you could put a bit, tepid water, 'hand-hot' my mum calls it I think.

John: Does that mean as hot as my hand?

Karmen: It means you can put your hand in and it doesn't make it red hot or freezing cold so it hurts your fingers.

John: I bet we could do it quicker than changing all this water.

Karmen: How?

John: Stick them all under the tap till all the bubbles run off then squeeze them!

Karmen: Or! We could use that thing in the bathroom and give them a shower. That would work.

John: I saw that on telly.

Karmen: What, doing the washing?

John: No, spraying the oil.

Karmen: What?

John: If you spray oil it breaks up, pollutes the environment and the sea, oil does.

Karmen: Like if you get soap on your hair and use the shower to rinse it off. We'll do the dolls first, their hair is all bubbles.

John: The particles bombard oil and hit it to break it up. Dad said.

Karmen: Does oil have membranes?

John: Don't know. Give me that jacket. Oil's not as heavy as water though. It floats on top. I saw that on telly too!

Karmen: We've got brains!

John: If it works we have. But I bet it does. My mum puts me in the shower on holiday!

Karmen and John were transferring elements of their knowledge gleaned from different sources, including their parents and the television, and using what they knew to try to solve their present difficulty. They were exploring, discovering, checking out each other's meanings, predicting results, forming hypotheses and drawing conclusions. They played cooperatively and with intensity of purpose. Susan Isaacs' (1930, 1933) meticulous observations of children during her three and a half years at the Malting House School show how a rich environment and freedom to explore can lead children to form numerous questions which they are then motivated to find answers to.

As children get older and more experienced, if adults have spent time with them, extending their interests and explaining things about the world, stimulating their actions and thoughts into new areas and talking with them, children come to use different language and terminology to explain their reasoning. It is their language which indicates to us their grasp of meaning and their understanding. If children articulate their thinking, their parents, teachers and other educators are in a better position to help them to refine and further develop their ideas. It is important to take time to listen to and talk with children, to give them opportunities to share their hypotheses, ask questions and refine their ideas.

If we reflect on the use of language in the three examples of children using water, we see different thoughts and understandings. Four-year-old Zoe explained: 'It runs away from the water.' Six-year-old Ashaq observed: 'If I put it nearer the dirt goes away faster.' Seven-year-old John said: 'The particles bombard the oil and hit it to break it up.' Eight-year-old Karmen said: 'Membranes, it's like an invisible sort of film; like a sort of skin thing, to keep the air trapped.' If children have played in their earlier years with the stuff of the world (water, sand, mud and clay), they are in a better position to develop further concepts through these media (Hutt et al., 1989). Children who have had few encounters with these natural materials will need time to explore their properties and attributes so that they can then tackle other challenges and questions when they work with such materials.

Worries about children's safety and urban living now inhibit the freedom of children to explore their world. Beck (1992) in *Risk Society* argues that risk comes with modernisation, and as such must be either 'eliminated or denied and reinterpreted' (p. 26). Bauman (1993) discusses the view that a postmodern view of risk brings us to a new view of risk and crisis with new sets of rules to govern behaviour and thus to reduce risk. Yet, he argues:

> Even if we abide by such rules scrupulously, even if everyone around observes them as well, we are far from certain that disastrous consequences will be avoided. Our ethical tools – the code of moral behaviour, the assembly of the rules of thumb we follow – have not been, simply, made to the measure of our present powers. (Bauman, 1993, p. 18)

Whatever we do, risk remains. We can seek to reduce risk in society, but we can never wholly eliminate it. In part, risk is generated by fear (as well as by fact). Füredi (2002) argues that risk has come to mean danger and the 'positive connotations traditionally associated with "risk-taking" have given way to condemnation; consequently, in many situations, "to take risks" is to court social disapproval' (p. 18). But young children need adults who help them to learn about assessing and taking risks. To learn about taking risks (just as the children who used Bunsen burners and lit bonfires in Isaacs' day had to do) is to become more aware of oneself in the world, and better able to live and play safely.

Concerns for children's well-being include fear of illness from polluted rivers, beaches and food, and of abduction or abuse. Other threats to children's health and well-being centre around poor diet (Oliver, 2005), and concerns that the over-use of technology by children could inhibit their outdoor and creative play (Miller and Almon, 2004; Palmer, 2006). Adults who wish to support children's learning now often bring the stuff of the world into safe, defined but falsely created boundaries. The vastness of the seashore and the expanse of the river-bank are reduced to small quantities of sand and water in specially designed plastic containers, and children often wear aprons to protect their clothing from wet and dirt. But an essential part of the learning experience is the process of getting sandy, dirty and wet! Instead of making mud pies in the outdoors, children use small quantities of clay in a confined space at an allotted time. The role of the adult in protecting the opportunities for learning and enabling children's own ways of thinking and exploring is crucial. Children need the freedom to play and learn, and educators need to create opportunities which provide this freedom to learn in safe environments which, as far as possible, removes the inhibiting restriction which arises from exaggerated fear for children's safety. The restrictions which are placed on children and the consequences of this in terms of their subsequent development were considered almost 40 years ago by Tinbergen (1976), who discussed the ways in which young children learn through play in their natural environments. Tinbergen suggested, even then, that society had inhibited children's freedom to play and, just as young animals find their own way of learning, young children could do the same if they were in an appropriate environment. The concerns expressed by Tinbergen nearly four decades ago have now multiplied to the point where children's freedom to learn is restricted and limited (often in the interests of keeping them safe) and their opportunities to play outdoors are, in many cases, being seriously threatened.

John Brierley's contribution to our understanding of children's brain growth and development provided insights for all who have responsibility and concerns for young children. Brierley asserted that the years from 0 to 5 are crucial for brain development and that the first 10 years are the years during which the brain reaches 95% of its adult weight. He wrote:

> During these years of swift brain growth a child's eyes, ears and touch sense in particular are absorbing experiences of all kinds through imitation and exploration. It is obvious that the quality of experience is vital for sound development. In addition to sensory experience, talk is as vital to human life as pure air. (Brierley, 1994, p. 28)

Recent scientific research suggests that babies and young children are born with the capacity to understand a lot more than was previously thought to be the case (Gopnik et al., 1999). Such studies have challenged long-held views of babies' 'ignorance' suggesting that babies, indeed, have an innate capacity from the moment they are born (Gopnik et al., 1999, p. 27) and confirms the importance of providing babies with novelty and stimulation in their environments (Brierley, 1994, p. 81). Bruner's 1960 theory of 'cognitive growth' suggested that environmental and experiential factors were influences on a child's development (Smith, 2002). Trevarthen's (1977) focus on the communication of babies during their first six months of life concluded that a pattern of development in social behaviour was forming in all five infants in the study. While interesting and affirming of practices based on belief and observation, the results of the studies of neuroscience may be of limited use to early childhood educators. Hannon (2003) argues that such studies are unlikely to change current practice and Wilson (2002) also suggests that brain science has little to offer parents who struggle in circumstances of poverty and other social difficulty.

Gopnik et al. (1999) suggest that despite extensive studies, it is at times difficult to grasp the amazing phenomenon of how young children think. They summarise this notion in terms of three elements: *Foundation* where babies are able to translate information and interpret their experiences in particular ways predicting new events; *Learning* when babies use their experiences to modify and reshape their initial representation thus achieving more complex and abstract representations; and *Other People* who care for the children actively yet unconsciously promote, encourage and influence children's representations.

In his work, Brierley identified 21 principles for teaching and learning based upon knowledge of brain development. He made it clear that the more children learn, the more their brains have the capacity to learn. The following two principles help to focus on implications for young children's learning:

> All forms of play appear to be essential for the intellectual, imaginative and emotional development of the child and may well be necessary steps to a further stage of development. The brain thrives on variety and stimulation. Monotony of surroundings, toys that only do one thing, a classroom display kept up for too long are soon disregarded by the brain. (Brierley, 1994, p. 111)

It was variety, stimulation and the important experiences of talking with adults which prompted the questioning and thinking from the children in the following three examples. Young thinkers construct some wonderful and apparently bizarre reasons for why things happen, drawing on their present knowledge to create explanations which are logical to them at that time (Paley, 1981). The following examples illustrate children's skills as thinkers as they struggle to explain and reason things which puzzle them about their world.

A 5-year-old boy asked his parents, 'Why are there trees?' A satisfactory answer took his parents into many reasons and a long discussion which justified the existence of trees: shady places to sit on a hot day; for making wooden furniture; equatorial rain forests; conservation; food and habitats for wildlife; and finally 'somewhere for Robin Hood to hide'. This last reason followed a visit to Sherwood Forest and the Major Oak. One part of the answer led to another question or a further reason and so dialogue between parents and child continued with an interested and lively 5-year-old applying his mind and pursuing this line of thought, continuing to think, assimilate and understand, acquiring more information along the way which extended and further stimulated his thinking. The questioning stopped when, for the moment, he was satisfied with the explanation which had been generated.

A 4-year-old girl asked her father, 'Why does the sea go in and out?' Her father gave the most reasonable explanation he could, mentioning the Moon and the spinning of the earth and the need for the sea to come into the harbours of other parts of the world. She thought that the sea came into the harbour of the small town where she lived to let the boats float so that the fisherman could go fishing, and that it went out to stop children swimming in the sea all day so that their skin did not get wrinkled! She thought that this going in and coming out of the sea was all 'a waste of time' and that the sea should stay in the harbour all the time so that the boats could always float, people could go fishing whenever they wished and the children could swim whenever they wanted to. Her search for reason and justification led her to create an explanation and some logical reasoning from what she presently knew and how she wanted things to be.

A 4-year-old girl was in the car with her mother when she asked 'Mumma? Why are we here?' Thinking that her daughter was asking why they were where they were on their journey, she said 'because we are on the way to the shops'. 'No', replied the little girl. 'Why are we here ... why are we people, here, in this world?' Her mother was quiet, thinking of how to respond. 'I know', said the 4-year-old. 'I think God put us here. The world was sad with no people to enjoy it so he made us and put us here because it's a nice place.' Her mother, being able to come up with no better reason at the time, agreed that yes, quite possibly, that was why they were there! Perhaps this question was just too big for either of them to find another answer at that point in time.

Piaget's insights into children's thought and language contribute to our understanding of young children's minds. Piaget (1953) gave some fascinating lists of 'why' questions which were asked by children, providing illustration of children's thinking and their search for reason. The children about whom Piaget wrote asked questions of causality and questions of justification. Those who spend time with young children will find a familiar tone in questions like 'Why does the sea go in and out?' and 'Why are there trees?' and 'Why are we here?' Young children ask questions which Piaget would categorise as the 'whys of logical justification' when they look for logical and sensible reasons for the things they see and are told, and sometimes, it seems, God is the only answer to these unfathomable questions! While Piaget thought young children 'egocentric', this term need not be considered in a selfish sense, nor should children's egocentricity be thought of as a deficit (Piaget, 1972). Nathan Isaacs, an ardent admirer and follower of Piaget, put forward his own thesis on children's 'why' questions in an appendix to Susan Isaacs' book (Isaacs, 1930). He wrote:

> The topic of children's 'why' questions is, I believe, worth special attention in connection with the general issue of the relation of child thought to adult thought. Contrary to such views as Piaget's, these questions seem to me to bear witness to the essential identity of structure and function of thought throughout our life history …
>
> The child's 'why's' – or rather, one important and common class of them – appear to me to show him actively interested in his knowledge as such and directly concerned with the question whether it is *(a)* correct, *(b)* sufficient, and *(c)* clear and unambiguous. (p. 293)

Young children work hard to make sense of the things they encounter and use all that they know to try to understand. To reply to a child's why question with an answer such as 'because it is' or even 'because I say so!' or even 'because God did it', will not suffice because such responses will not satisfy children at their stage of thinking and do not do justice to children's capacity to think through what they encounter as they try to make sense of what they find.

Children's questions, puzzles, problems, solutions and fascinations have formed the substance of this chapter, demonstrating the active and creative ways in which children learn, how they think about the world and make sense of their experiences of it. The view of children as capable and serious learners and thinkers is a recurring theme throughout this book.

 ## Questions and activities

Consider your provision for open-ended and exploratory play. Does it offer rich and uninterrupted opportunities – indoors and out – for children to play and discover with each other and with adults?

Consider Gopnick et al.'s (1999) three elements of thinking: foundation, learning and other people. Is this a useful framework for thinking about how the children in your setting go about their learning?

Make a point of noting down the 'why' questions that children ask. Consider if your ways of responding are always appropriate.

Further reading 📖

Athey, C. (2007) *Extending Thought in Young Children: A Parent–Teacher Partnership* (2nd edn). London: Sage.

Bruner, J. (1977) *The Process of Education*. Cambridge, MA: Harvard University Press.

Isaacs, N. (1930) 'Children's "why" questions', in S. Isaacs (ed.) *Intellectual Growth in Young Children*. London: Routledge & Kegan Paul.

Isaacs, S. (1930) *Intellectual Growth in Young Children*. London: Routledge & Kegan Paul.

Piaget, J. (1953) *The Origin of Intelligence in the Child*. London: Routledge & Kegan Paul.

Piaget, J. (1962) *Play, Dreams and Imitation in Childhood*. London: Routledge.

Vygotsky, L.S. (1978) *Mind in Society*. Cambridge, MA: Harvard University Press.

What is Effective Learning?

Watkins, C., Carnell, E. and Lodge, C.

In this chapter
Conceptions of learning
The effect of context
Inquiring into conceptions and contexts
Models of learning
Models and classrooms
Effective learning
The wider context
Concluding thoughts

We now set out what we mean by effective learning, and start by considering different conceptions of learning. Ideas about meta-cognition and meta-learning are then examined. This will be related to learning in classrooms. We will pay attention to different cultural constructions of learning, that is, what learning may mean in different countries, cultures and contexts. To do this we will draw on our experiences of working with teachers from all over the world.

In the last chapter you undertook an appreciative inquiry of effective learning in a classroom. We presented some provocative propositions that we have collected from teachers undertaking this task. Underpinning each statement, and indeed implicit in teachers' and learners' activities, are beliefs and theories about how people learn. This section will introduce some conceptions of learning to help illuminate beliefs about learning drawn from research and your own experiences.

Conceptions of Learning

Take a moment to make a note of the first three words or phrases that come into your head when you think about what learning is. A number of research projects have investigated people's understandings of learning, showing that the word 'learning' has different meanings for different people. Marton et al. (1993) report the following hierarchy of meanings gathered from some Open University students. They referred to them as 'everyday conceptions of learning':

- getting more knowledge
- memorising and reproducing
- applying facts or procedures
- understanding
- seeing something in a different way
- changing as a person.

How does your response relate to the ones on this list? Are the words and phrases you thought of similar to one of them, or do they differ, and why might this be?

Different conceptions may be held by different people or by the same person in different circumstances and for different purposes. We notice that all the conceptions in Marton et al.'s list tend to imply learning as an individual activity. We also notice that the list begins with a mechanical view of learning: taking in or consuming more information. This is enshrined in the idea that to possess knowledge is to be brainy, a view which is quite common in everyday life and beliefs. 'Brain of Britain' is a general knowledge quiz on the radio, and children reflect the idea that knowledge is central when they say their teachers ought to know everything about their subject. The popular view can be resistant to change even in the face of children being able to find out what they need for themselves when they want to, for example by searching the internet. The conception of 'learning as getting more knowledge' also suggests that this knowledge is separate from the individual and to be consumed or banked. One teacher talked in these terms about the enthusiasm for learning shown by a class of 8 year-olds:

> In my class the more you give them that they haven't had before, the more they grab it. They eat it up if it's something new. I mean, my classes, I've been very lucky, they seem to be like that, they just eat all knowledge. (Lodge, 2002: field notes)

Usha, an 8 year-old girl in another school, used the image of getting things into your head or your brain: this is a common view among young people when asked about good learning:

> As soon as someone teaches you then you feel like you've got something else you know and it's like it's going to be locked up in your brain. (Lodge, 2002: field notes)

In this conception of learning, people's ways of talking about a 'good learner' emphasise things like memorising, and the evaluation of learning is seen as outside the person – it's about performance and compliance: someone completes their work which can then be evaluated with ticks and marks:

> Yes, like you're doing the work, and get all the ticks, and they've memorised all the work, and they've known all the sums, their times tables. (8 year-old boy: Lodge, 2002: field notes)

Here we can see that the approach to assessment may generate this conception of learning. We return to the influence of assessment in Chapters 4 and 10.

Further down Marton et al.'s list is 'applying facts and procedures'. We hear this conception when teachers say they value learning that enables children to apply their knowledge in different circumstances. One 14 year-old boy gave another example when he contrasted the first aid course he had recently taken with an English lesson on *Othello*:

> And you feel happy with yourself because you know you have learned something that you can use. Personally, this stuff about Iago, once we've finished the subject I'm never going to use it again in my life but first aid is always going to be useful. (Lodge, 2002).

The list of conceptions moves on to include seeing learning as making meaning, interpreting events and constructing knowledge or understanding. For example, one young person expressed his conception of learning in this way:

> Learning is what I do as a human, to become a better human. How can exams test really important learning, like learning to love someone, or learning to cope when that person dies? I will try to stop beating myself up about not getting 'A' grades in exams because I think I have more to offer to the world than the sum total of my school exam results. (12 year-old student: Williams, 2002)

We were impressed by this exceptional view of learning: the student is in a high-performing school, but it is about more than performance, it is about core human experiences and making a contribution.

The last conception 'changing as a person' should not be taken to mean 'all at once'! It can refer to a change in cognitive, social or emotional states. Gill, a 14 year-old student said "I think when you have a good learning experience it makes you feel better for the rest of the day" (Lodge, 2002). And one teacher who had been investigating learning with her science class of 8 year-olds described how it felt to be a different person:

> I felt the joy and exhilaration of a new teacher who encounters many fresh experiences without ever feeling like a novice. I am now a committed learner. (Ann Pilmoor, teacher-researcher quoted in Carnell and Lodge, 2002a: 67)

The crucial point about conceptions of learning is that they are influential, not just 'in the head' ideas, or merely academic. Someone's conception of learning has a big influence on what they do, how they go about their learning. Doubtless every teacher has experienced this in their interactions with pupils: some pupils display their conception of learning by implying that the responsibility for their learning rests with you! But we should also remember that conceptions of learning may vary for the same individual, depending on their context. This stops us as teachers thinking that our pupils come with a view of learning that was formed elsewhere and that we have no influence over. Far from it: the influence of the immediate context, for example the classroom, can be very influential.

The Effect of Context

The list of conceptions which Marton et al. provide resulted from research with adults learning at a distance, in the formal setting of a university course, and maybe the balance of their results reflects that context. Learners in other contexts, perhaps including you, may have different conceptions of learning. For example, when we talk with young people about their learning outside school, we often hear more active, experimental and social views than we do when they talk about learning in school. You might have noticed that Marton et al.'s list does not include learning through collaboration and dialogue, building knowledge together with others. Yet schoolchildren will remark on this, when their classroom context has supported it and they have a chance to review. For example:

> Working in a small group in class is really helpful. You hear everyone's ideas and you can say 'no he doesn't agree with me' and why not, and she does and she is sort of half way and it's really good because you understand what you think compared with other people's views. (14 year-old girl: Carnell, 2000)

So our pupils' examples may reflect a richer conception of learning than those included in Marton et al.'s list, depending on what their classroom experiences are like.

We now have considered three key elements, all of which have an influence on each other: an individual's conception of learning, their way of going about learning, and the immediate context of their learning. These are summarised in Figure 2.1, where the wider context is also indicated (and will be discussed later in this chapter). Note that all the arrows indicating influence go in both directions: individuals can be influenced by the context, but they can also influence the context, through their beliefs and actions.

Inquiring into Conceptions and Contexts

There are many ways to inquire into a pupil's conception of learning: informal conversations, listening to conversations between pupil peers, questionnaires of

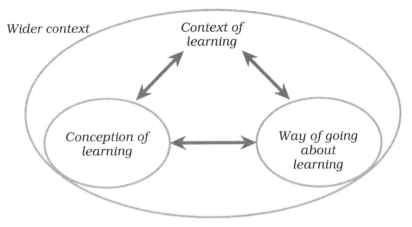

Figure 2.1 Conceptions, actions and context of learning

Note that this diagram could portray the elements and influences for a pupil, but it could equally portray them for a teacher.

various sorts, and open-ended writing. A rich form of enquiry, not depending too much on language, is to ask young people to draw. When asked to draw a good learner we have found that primary school pupils often draw a person with a big head and big ears! Thus they reflect the brainy, consuming, listening conception of learning which was discussed above. But learning is always influenced by context, so rather than invite them to draw a learner, we invite them to draw a learning context. When one of our teacher colleagues asked a young person in a class of 10 year-olds to draw a learning occasion she produced the drawing in Figure 2.2.

Figure 2.2 A 10 year-old's drawing of a learning occasion (Harris, 2002)

This picture is typical of the dominant response in Dean Harris's research. You will notice that the children are sitting in rows, facing the teacher and the blackboard on which is written some sums. Sums were the most frequently drawn element in many drawings. Many children see themselves as isolated, passive and dependent on the teacher for the acquisition of knowledge. Another teacher told us that when her class of 6 year-olds first began to talk about learning, the children said they only learned by listening to her.

Other students will have richer conceptions than those expressed in the dominant view. A drawing that captures some of this is portrayed in Figure 2.3.

Figure 2.3 Another 10 year-old's drawing of a learning occasion (Harris, 2002)

What we notice here is that the learner is not relying on the teacher; the learner is making connections, and learning with friends and family and other adults. There is an assumption that understanding is more significant than the acquisition of knowledge.

So if our inquiries into people's conceptions of learning demonstrate differences, are there some big differences between those views of learning which have been identified?

Models of Learning

A model is not the real thing, but it tries to say something important about the real thing by identifying key elements and describing how they relate to each other. So it is with models of learning. Amongst the very large body of literature on learning, and in surveys of how this literature developed over the last century (Mayer, 2001), it is possible to identify three major models of learning. These are summarised in Table 2.1.

Table 2.1 Three models of learning

Models of learning	
Reception	Concerned with quantity, facts and skills; assumes transmission of knowledge from an external source (e.g. teacher). Emotional and social aspects are not attended to. *Learning = being taught.*
Construction	Concerned with the learner's construction of meaning through discussion, discovery, open-ended learning, making connections. *Learning = individual sense-making.*
Co-construction	Concerned with the learner's construction of meaning through interaction and collaboration with others, especially through dialogue. *Learning = building knowledge with others.*

The important point is that these models are not just found in literature: they are found in everyday talk, in images of learning, in formal documents, and so on. And they are also found in pupils' communications. We suggest that in the drawings above, Figure 2.2 speaks of the reception model, and Figure 2.3 reflects more the construction model. It is not common for young people to draw the third model because they tend to have little experience of that approach and it may therefore seem difficult to represent. But Rosie (aged 6) has experienced a different form of classroom, as shown in her drawing (Figure 2.4). Here we see pupils voicing their own questions – including about learning – and stating that they learn by talking together. It is no coincidence that Rosie draws the pupils seated round a large table: her teacher, Zoe Bonnell, ran her classroom as a learning community, partly on the model by Vasconcelos and Walsh (2001) which emphasises the big table.

Models and Classrooms

Classrooms are very complex contexts, which vary in important ways. One of the ways that classrooms vary is that their practices and ways of working can

Figure 2.4 A 6 year-old's drawing of learning (Bonnell, 2005) "We learn by talking together", "Why are bees black and yellow?", "Why are snakes different?", "How do we learn?"

represent different models of learning. So for each of the three models introduced above, it is possible to imagine how that classroom operates.

On many occasions classrooms are operated on a simple view of learning ('Learning = being taught') with the idea that pupils receive in some simple way what teacher teaches. In England the reception model is the most common in classrooms. The teacher and teaching are dominant. The latter's purpose is often expressed as getting more knowledge 'in their heads'. Assessment is then used to work out whether they did get it in their heads, and focuses on the quantity of knowledge learned and the idea of 'basic' skills. This model is not dominant in all countries, though it probably is in most. Occasionally someone from another country can point this out, as with a visitor from New Zealand who noted that in the classrooms she visited there was plenty of time given to teaching. "When do the children get time for learning?" she asked.

In the second model, construction, the learner is more dominant, and as a result of the shift away from a focus on the teacher, the social context of the classroom is also brought into focus. The purpose is seen as the learner making meaning. In this model 'content' is not for delivery or coverage; it is for connecting with previous knowledge, extending understanding and helping learners to see things in new ways. Assessment in this model may rely partly on knowledge recall, but it also promotes individual interpretation and choice in order to assess understanding.

In the third model, co-construction, the classroom operates in a way where learners create knowledge together, and they may create a collaborative product from this. The teacher acts to encourage opportunities that promote dialogue and other collaborative activities to help the learners together to make sense of their learning experiences. In this model assessment is integrated into the process of learning and may take many forms, including feedback, self- or group-assessment and includes giving a collaborative account of the learning process.

It might be helpful at this stage for you to reflect on familiar classrooms.

- Which models of learning are dominant in your school and in your classrooms?
- To what extent do the teachers in these classrooms promote a particular model of learning?
- What are the factors that influence classroom interactions?

On that last question, we do not underestimate the numerous factors which operate on teachers in current times, many of which can lead to classrooms operating on the first model, reception. When teachers are under pressure (e.g. from exam performance, inspection and observations for judgemental purposes, concerns with behaviours – see for example Sullivan, 2000) teachers tend to become more controlling and promote the first model. Where the pressure includes making teachers 'accountable' for pupils' test results, we also notice what has been described as 'defensive teaching' (McNeil, 1988). We consider these themes further in Chapter 4. But these examples only emphasise some of the distortions in the purpose and context of classrooms, and they do not lead to effective learning.

Effective Learning

Having explored different understandings of learning, we now examine the concept of 'effective learning'. In many countries there has been an emphasis on 'effectiveness' in schools and in education systems, and the word itself has been contentious at times when interpreted in a narrow or mechanical fashion. The same applies when it is attached to learning. It is important to consider what effective learning means, and to ask "Effective for what?" "Effective for when?" This helps us remember that the term 'effective learning' only makes sense when the context of learning and the goals are specified. It helps us recognise that effective learning today is likely to be different from what it would have been a century ago, or in another era of the history of classrooms.

The contemporary context has some important features that mean that the goals of learning need to focus less on knowledge acquisition by individuals and more on knowledge generation with others. The reception model was dominant at a time when it was important for people to learn a finite body of information. While these features vary in their impact in different parts of the world we note the significant effects of the following everywhere:

- More information is available – learners, both adults and young people, need to know how to find and select relevant information, to process it, connect it, use it …
- The capacity to learn and to adapt needs to be lifelong because change is a permanent state.
- Employment requires being able to enhance and transfer knowledge and to operate collaboratively.
- Learning is increasingly taking place in different settings and with different relationships. Learning is a way of being. (Adapted from Watkins et al., 2002)

All over the world effective learning increasingly means more knowledge generation (construction) with others (co-construction), and less independent knowledge acquisition (coverage). This is recognised by an increasing number of governments. For example, in Hong Kong:

> Schools should also encourage students to inquire beyond the confines of 'curriculum prescriptions' and textbooks, and to process information and make their own judgements in order to enhance their knowledge-building capacity. (Hong Kong Education Department, 2002: 78)

And in Singapore, following their 'Thinking Schools, Learning Nation' initiative, the Minister for Education has said "Ironically, being prepared for the knowledge economy does not mean acquiring more knowledge. Instead, a change of paradigm is required." And new policies for secondary schools state:

> The changes will shift the emphasis of education from efficiency to diversity, from content mastery to learning skills, and from knowing to thinking. (Singapore Ministry of Education, 2002)

Another way of saying this is that in every context the nature and pace of change mean that learners need to focus more on *how they learn*, with others, and to be strategic about their learning. We focus in detail on what this means for classrooms in Chapter 9, but we find that teachers already have the core idea, especially when they look in detail at learners they know who seem to be effective.

Effective learners have gained understanding of the individual and social processes necessary to learn how to learn. They have acquired a range of strategies and can monitor and review their learning to gauge the effectiveness of these strategies. This point is especially important, since there are many examples where particular single strategies are sold to schools with claims for promoting learning. But the evidence shows that particular strategies are not effective: they often do not get used or transfered to other contexts. This only happens when a learner can notice, monitor and review how their learning is going. Effective learning includes this vital ingredient of learning about learning or 'meta-learning'.

In Table 2.2 we summarise the main features of effective learning and learners. We explore how the classroom may promote these features in turn in Chapters 6 to 9.

Table 2.2 Effective learning and learners

Effective learning is …	*An effective learner …*
an activity of construction	is active and strategic
handled with (or in the context of) others	is skilled in collaboration
driven by the learner	takes responsibility for their learning
the monitoring and review of the effectiveness of approaches and strategies for the goals and context.	understands her/his learning and plans, monitors and reflects on their learning

Learning is an activity of *making* meaning – construction – not simply of receiving. The social dimension is always present, and in social contexts collaboration supports learning. Effective learning has to be regulated by the learner, not the teacher. These aspects of effective learning are all connected by the fourth feature, meta-learning – being aware of the processes of their learning, how they are learning. Effective learners have learned to monitor their strategies, purposes, outcomes, effects and contexts (Ertmer and Newby, 1996; Sternberg, 2003). In Chapter 5 we will consider in more depth the implications of making changes in classrooms to promote more effective learning, and how these changes can contribute to changes in power, content, roles, responsibility and evaluation (Weimer, 2002).

The Wider Context

We have already briefly mentioned some examples of pressures on teachers from the wider context, and we will explore this in more detail in Chapter 4. But there is a wider influence which we might call the 'wider culture', which also needs to be considered. Here we want to note some themes that appear in a range of countries, and which influence how learning is viewed in classrooms.

In many parts of the world the teacher dominates the classroom. "In Jamaica the teacher is King!" one teacher told us. And pressures on teachers exist in many countries. In different parts of the world the examination system influences what happens in classrooms; for example, there is an emphasis on content and coverage in Greek secondary classrooms where they have annual examinations. In a Jordanian private school, one teacher observed that for younger students the social and extra-curricula activities of the school were regarded as important, but this changed when the girls were faced with examinations.

Classrooms around the world are recognisable on some basic features: there are a number of young people in the same space as one teacher. Some countries (for example, in the UK) organise same-age classes; others (for example, in Nigeria) organise classes according to attainment and not age. In every classroom there is often a physical boundary of some sort. The learners are usually engaged in the same or similar tasks as each other. The furniture is usually arranged so that the learners can write or draw at a table or desk. The desks are usually arranged so that the teacher can see what's happening.

A recent video study in seven countries highlighted other similarities: teachers talked more than students – at least 8:1 teacher to student words; at least 90 per cent of lessons used a textbook or worksheet (Hiebert et al., 2003; see also Stigler and Hiebert, 1998). No one country was distinct on all the features observed.

Alongside these consistent features the experience of young people in classrooms varies across the world in other ways. Variations we have noted in our conversations with teachers helped us to understand a range of influences which aided us in seeing how things can be different and what teachers need to take into account if they are planning changes.

Some of the themes we have noted were:

- Flexibility and routines: the degree to which classroom activities are seen to be in the control of teachers and young people, and the extent to which they are seen as routinised and regularised (usually by external influences).
- Beliefs about learning: for example, that there is a body of knowledge that young people have to absorb in order to progress through the school.
- Beliefs about learners: who has responsibility for the learning; that young people can be categorised and labelled as 'normal', 'gifted' or 'disabled' and then treated accordingly or that young people's intelligence is fixed.
- Assessment and accountability: many assessment systems focus on what is easy to assess. They have not caught up with some of the complexities of learning, such as skills in building knowledge with others. Assessment often triggers a response which reinforces learners' isolation, inactivity and skills in memory and reproduction.

Schools as organisations also affect classrooms in different ways, and the cultural context in different countries can influence how effective an organisation is in promoting learning. The culture of organisations or countries can be considered along similar dimensions. Table 2.3 is derived from Hofstede's (1980) work. He was a Dutch academic, who researched the relationship between 117,000 employees' core values and their practices in many different countries. He used this data to analyse cultures on several dimensions. The degree to which each of these dimensions affects ideas about learning, and about teaching, varies in different contexts, and it would be an oversimplification to assume that one culture pertains uniformly across a nation or a region, or indeed an organisation. The following table adapts Hofstede's dimensions and attempts to map some implications for effective learning in an organisation.

Table 2.3 Hofstede's cultural dimension considered in relation to effective learning

Dimension	Description related to possible impact on learning
Individualism – collectivism	The degree to which the organisation puts value on collaboration as significant in learning for organisations and individuals or for individual activity.
Power distance	How far an organisation encourages responsibility by learners for their learning or dependence on teachers. The degree to which deference to the teacher or engagement with the teacher is expected.
Uncertainty avoidance	The degree to which organisations encourage risk taking, openness and vulnerability, or encourage compliance in learning.
Status-relationships	How far organisations value performance in tests over effective learning practices.
Long-term – short-term orientation	The degree to which the institution values dispositions such as perseverance, persistence over protection of 'face' and respect for established authorities.

The implications of these dimensions can be seen in a number of aspects of classroom learning such as: the structure and length of lessons; the balance of oral and written work; pedagogical language; teachers' questions; learning tasks; the balance of emphasis on subject matter and affective or behavioural issues; the manner in which teaching messages are conveyed; the view of knowledge (Alexander, 1999).

Concluding Thoughts

In this chapter we have explored important 'big picture' ideas about effective learning: people's different conceptions of learning, the influence of context on these, major models of learning, and so on. These will stay with us throughout the book. We have also started to clarify effective learning and begun to examine how it may be promoted in classrooms – through activity, collaboration, responsibility and meta-learning (see Table 2.2).

But is that what we see in classrooms? And how are we looking at classrooms? We now turn in Chapter 3 to address these questions in detail. Then in Chapter 4 we examine influences that can work against the promotion of effective learning in schools and classrooms. And in Chapter 5 we consider teachers who have created conditions where effective learning flourishes, despite these constraints.

Learning and Language

Whitebread, D.

Key Questions

- What are the main theories of learning?
- In what ways is human learning different to that of other species, particularly other primates?
- Do adults think and learn differently from children?
- How do children develop as learners?
- Why are some children better learners than others?
- How does language help us to be better learners?
- How can we organise educational settings to support children's learning?

Early Behaviourist Theories of Learning

When I undertook my undergraduate degree in the late 1960s, I took a one-year course in learning theory. This represented an extremely thorough introduction to what psychologists at that point in time knew about learning and consisted almost entirely of experiments on rats, pigeons and the like learning to find their way through a maze or which lever to press to obtain a reward of food. This work was located within a school of psychology which is now referred to as behaviourism and was founded on the then very sensible proposition that, as we could not then directly observe and measure what was happening in people's brains or minds, if we wished to be scientific in our investigations of human psychology, we should confine ourselves to observing and measuring behaviour. This school of psychology was, to a degree, a reaction against earlier forays into understanding the workings of the human mind through the process of introspection, as practised by such early thinkers as William James (brother of the author Henry James).

In order to carry out truly scientific, rigorously controlled experiments, however, learning had to be reduced to very simple elements, removed from any kind of social context, and carried out on animals who could be confined, slightly underfed so that they were motivated by hunger, and treated in other ways which might not be considered as entirely acceptable or ethical with young children (even in the early part of the 20th century!). Perhaps the most well-known examples of this work are the Russian psychologist Ivan Pavlov's experiments with dogs, and the American B.F. Skinner's work with rats and pigeons. Pavlov showed that dogs could learn to associate a ringing bell with food, and eventzually would salivate at the sound of the bell alone. Skinner demonstrated that rats, pigeons, etc. could learn to press a lever to obtain food, and, given a choice of levers between which they could discriminate (such as by shape), they could learn to press the correct lever. He went on to show that what he termed a 'variable schedule of reinforcement' (when a correct lever press resulted in food randomly on some trials, but not all) was a far more powerful motivator to maintain a learnt behaviour than a fixed or regular schedule (when food was provided every time the lever was pressed, or every third time, for example). The parallel here with human gambling behaviour is quite striking. Imagine if fruit machines consistently just gave you back half of what you had put in every third go. The financial consequences would be the same, but not nearly so many people would travel to Las Vegas for the experience! Also, perhaps importantly for education, Skinner's work showed quite conclusively that providing a reward for correct behaviour was a far more efficient stimulus to learning than was punishing the animal when it made a mistake. Using his principles, he demonstrated that pigeons can count up to 7 and that they could be trained to roller-skate (two major scientific advances), but they are also the basis upon which dogs for the blind are trained, which underpin highly successful behaviour management techniques with children with severe conduct disorders, and sound principles used by many skilled early years teachers to help children learn how to behave in the social world of the school classroom. If we praise children when they are kind to one another, when they share their toys and so on, the classroom will become a far more harmonious place to be than if we concentrate on criticising and punishing behavioural lapses. According to one recent American study, involving 400 4–6-year-olds, who received stickers or verbal praise as rewards, it is even possible for young children to learn to like vegetables through these means (Cooke et al., 2011). I know – amazing, but true!

At the heart of behaviourism, then, there are a number of important insights that have been verified by later research. For example, as we shall see, the notion of learning as forming associations has been supported and extended in much more recent neuroscientific research (through which we can now directly observe the workings of the human brain). Nevertheless, despite these successes, it is clear that the behaviourists' model of human learning is quite inadequate. Indeed, this was gradually becoming clear in the 1960s when I was undertaking my own undergraduate education. In the introduction to his excellent book on children's learning, David Wood (1998) recounts this period when many young psychologists, trained in behaviourist methods, gradually became aware of the limitations of the approach. An important book (Hilgard, 1964), published at that time, represented a turning point in psychology's investigation of learning. In one chapter, for example, as Wood reports, a young psychologist called Pribram reported his experiences of experiments with monkeys which had caused him to doubt one of the major precepts of behaviourist theories of learning, that it relied upon external reinforcement (i.e. receiving food for a correct behaviour). One monkey, for example, quickly learnt to pull the correct lever, but then subverted the experiment by not eating peanuts it received on 'reinforced' trials, then feeding itself a peanut when the trial was not 'reinforced'. Eventually, when it had received more peanuts than it could eat, with its cheeks, hands and feet stuffed with them, it continued to pull the lever and, finally, to throw them out of the cage at the experimenter. Pribram concluded that the monkey's behaviour and learning could not be accounted for by the schedule of external reinforcement embodied in the experiment, but by the monkey's own 'intrinsic' interest in the task itself. He also, among a number of the contributors to the book, commented favourably on the new theories of children's learning being developed by the Swiss psychologist, Jean Piaget.

Piaget and the Constructivist Model of Learning

The fundamental problem with the behaviourist approach was that it characterised learning as an essentially passive process, consisting of forming simple associations between events, and being dependent upon external rewards or reinforcements. What was becoming increasingly clear in the 1960s, however, was that such a model could account quite well for the behaviour of relatively simple animals, such as rats or pigeons, but it could not account for learning in primates and was an entirely inadequate explanation of the richness, diversity and sheer creativity of human learning. As a consequence, when Piaget's work was translated and made available to the English-speaking scientific world, for example through the publication of John Flavell's (1963) book, *The Developmental Psychology of Jean Piaget*, it was greeted with enthusiastic acclaim. While much of the detail of Piaget's theory has now been discounted (as we discuss below), he is nevertheless rightly celebrated as the originator of a number of key insights into the nature of human learning.

Methodologically, he is celebrated for his demonstration that much can be learnt about children's learning and development by very careful naturalistic observation of children going about their everyday lives (much of his work was based on observations of his own children). As regards our understanding of the processes of learning, he is celebrated as the father of 'constructivism', which is the idea that children's learning is an active process through which they attempt to develop their skills and construct their own understandings of the world.

The kind of model of human learning which developed from this view is illustrated in Figure 6.1. Here, every aspect of the interaction between the learner and the environment is seen as active and dynamic. Rather than passively receiving information to be learnt, the learner actively perceives and selects the information they are seeking. The information is not simply stored, it is sifted, categorised and re-organised, patterns are detected and rules, 'schema' or concepts constructed. Similarly, the consequent actions or behaviour of the learner are not simply a 'response' to a 'stimulus' or a reward, as the behaviourists would have it, but are consequent upon hypotheses and predictions generated about the way the world works, and strategies and plans developed to act effectively upon it.

The example is often quoted of the way in which children learn language. According to a behaviourist view, this is a laborious process whereby every word and utterance the child learns is initially by imitating an adult and learnt as a consequence of reinforcement by external reward (such as adult smiling). However, it is clear that the rate at which children learn to understand and use language is far too rapid for this kind of explanation and, in any case, they typically produce a constant stream of completely novel utterances (in my family, we even have words and whole phrases which we now all use, but which were originally invented by the children). In English, many of these novel words and phrases that children produce, furthermore, are clearly the consequence of mis-applying patterns and rules which they have constructed for themselves. For example, you will hear young children say that yesterday they 'goed to the shops and buyed something'. They will not have heard an adult say this; nor has any adult taught them that you create the past tense by adding on 'ed'. This is a pattern or regularity that they have detected from the huge variety of their experience of spoken English.

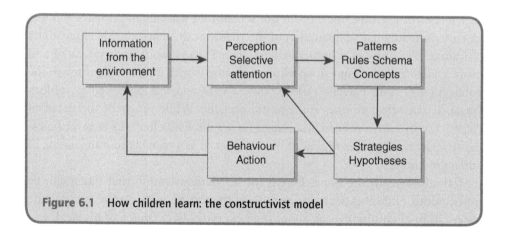

Figure 6.1 How children learn: the constructivist model

The Cognitive Revolution

Piaget was born in Neuchatel, Switzerland in 1896 and worked prodigiously until his death in 1980. His body of work was immense (around 50 books and 500 academic papers) and he is largely credited with having brought about what is termed the 'cognitive revolution' in psychological investigations of learning. The 'black box' psychology of the behaviourists (where the brain was seen as impenetrable and unobservable) was replaced by increasingly inventive and innovative methodologies and techniques which enabled psychologists in the latter part of the 20th century to explore much more directly the cognitive processes in the developing brain of the young child.

As it turned out, much of this work has directly contradicted Piaget's own theories about children's development, to the point where today the specifics of his theories are largely dismissed. As we shall see, the main criticisms of his work arise from his failure to take into account the social nature of learning, and the important role of social interaction and language in children's developing abilities as learners. As a consequence, in many of his studies, he set children tasks where they performed poorly because of the linguistic demands of the task, and misleading social clues, rather than because of an underlying failure of understanding. This led him, it is now believed, to significantly underestimate the capabilities of young children.

One of the earliest researchers to expose these limitations in Piaget's work was a Scottish psychologist, Margaret Donaldson. In her classic text, *Children's Minds* (Donaldson, 1978), she reports a number of studies where slight variations in the way in which Piaget's tasks were presented to children showed them to be much more capable than he had suggested. For example, Piaget's famous number conservation task consisted of showing the child two equal rows of buttons (as shown in Figure 6.2, Part 1) and asking the child whether there are more white buttons or black buttons, or whether they are the same. One of the rows was then transformed by the experimenter (as shown in Figure 6.2, Part 2) and the question was repeated. Piaget found that many young children could correctly recognise that the first two rows contained the same number, but said there were more white buttons in the second condition. He concluded that these young children were overwhelmed by their perceptions and that they lacked the logical understanding of the conservation of number.

When this task was repeated, however, by a colleague of Margaret Donaldson's, the transformation of one of the rows of buttons was effected by a 'naughty teddy' glove puppet. In these circumstances, many more young children were able to say that the two rows still contained the same number.

Donaldson concludes that the introduction of the naughty teddy changes the meaning for the child of the second question. This question is made sense of by the children in relation to the social situation and their own previous experience. When the adult transforms the pattern and repeats the question, this means to

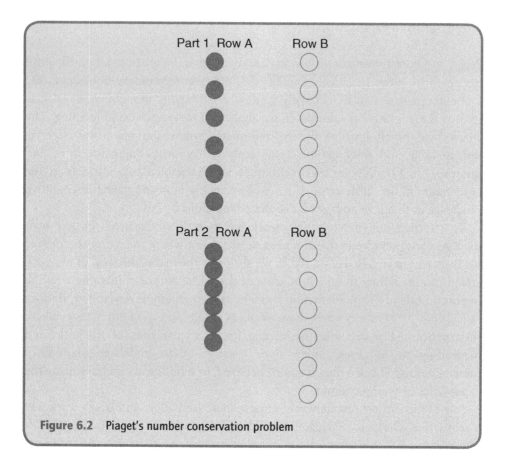

Figure 6.2 Piaget's number conservation problem

some children that their first answer was wrong and the adult is helping them to see the correct answer. In the amended version, the second question is a cue to check that the naughty teddy hasn't lost or added any buttons during his mischief.

What is more, lest we think that such reliance on the social context of a task is a sign of immaturity in children's thinking, it is now clearly established that human adults' thinking is equally reliant on these kinds of social cues, and that we all find abstract reasoning problems much more difficult than ones placed in a socially meaningful context or scenario. Wason and Johnson-Laird (1972), for example, posed the following 'four-card' problems (see Figure 6.3 for a slightly updated version). In the numbers and letters version (a), we are told that each card has a number on one side and a letter on the other. Your task is to name those cards, and only those cards, which need to be turned over in order to determine whether the rule (set out below the cards) is true or false. In the 'people with drinks' version (b) (my own cunning invention but with less skilful drawings), we are asked to pretend that we are working in a bar which serves beer and tea (stay with me) and where, to help preserve the law about under-age drinking, everyone is given a sticker on their back showing their age. Your job is to make sure that no one is breaking the law, i.e. you have to say which of the four people,

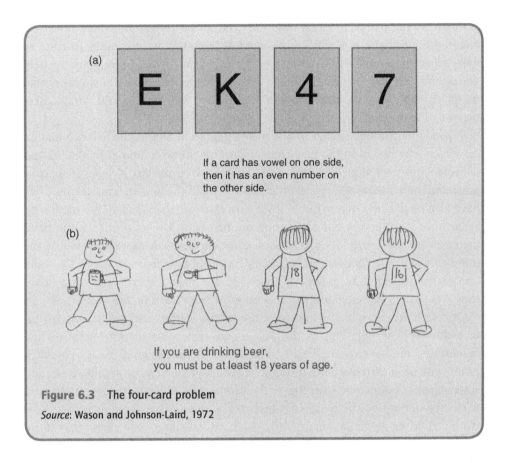

If a card has vowel on one side,
then it has an even number on
the other side.

If you are drinking beer,
you must be at least 18 years of age.

Figure 6.3 **The four-card problem**

Source: Wason and Johnson-Laird, 1972

and only which people, you would need to turn round to make sure that customers are obeying the law set out below the drawings. Write down your answers before you read on and find out if you have a typical human adult brain!

The correct answer to (a) is the vowel (E) and the odd number (7) – not the even number (4), which is a popular choice, but wrong since it would not contradict the rule if there were a vowel or consonant on the other side. Similarly, the correct answer to (b) is the person drinking beer and the person who is only 16. Most adults (even those brainy enough to be reading this book!) find the more abstract version (a) difficult and often make mistakes. The more socially contextualised version (b) is nearly always found to be much easier, although logically it is an identical problem. Ironically, this dependence upon the social contexts of tasks both makes sense in relation to the social origins of human evolution, as we have discussed in earlier chapters, but is also a logical consequence of Piaget's own theoretical position, that we construct our own understandings from experience.

This kind of work, by Donaldson, Wason and Johnson-Laird and many others, is important for developmental psychologists, as we try to unravel the complexities of the development of the human brain, but it also has some highly significant implications for those of us involved in the education of young children. Young children do not passively receive the information we provide for them. They are engaged continually in a process of active interpretation and transformation of new experiences and the information derived from them. If we want to help young children make sense of their educational experiences, we must ensure that we place new tasks in contexts with which they are familiar and which carry meaning for them.

Beyond this, through a range of newly emerging technologies, such as habituation (to which we referred in the Play chapter), eye-tracking, computer modelling and neuroscientific techniques, cognitive psychologists over the last 30 years or so, have uncovered an impressive range of processes by which the human brain learns. They have also established that many of these processes are there and fully functioning at birth, or mature very quickly during the first 4 to 5 years of life, as the brain increases in size fourfold (largely as a consequence of a rapid increase in the number of synaptic connections between neurons in the cerebral cortex). Goswami (2008) has provided an extensive review of the many experiments which have shown the very early emergence of this range of basic learning processes.

One such process which seems to be there from birth is referred to as statistical or inductive learning. This is the process by which we identify patterns and regularities in the stream of experience, and is fundamental to a very large proportion of human learning. It might be seen as a much more sophisticated and active form of association learning, of the kind explored by the behaviourists, and it clearly underpins the ways in which the human visual system learns, how young children learn language with such rapidity and ease, how they form concepts and detect categories from their experience, and how they seem so ready and able to understand causal relationships between events. Using habituation techniques, researchers have shown that, for example, babies as young as 2 months old can learn complex sequence patterns in a series of shapes they are shown, and will subsequently show a preference for 'novel' patterns which are made up of the same shapes but do not contain the same sequences (Kirkham et al., 2002). The patterns used, to a great extent, mirrored those found, for example, in language, involving 'transitional probabilities' of one shape following another, rather than just fixed sequences. Astonishingly, the 2-month-olds were just as proficient at this as babies 6 months older.

As we discussed in the previous chapter, neuroscientific work on memory has established that semantic information is stored in the cerebral cortex through a process whereby neurons establish increasingly stronger connections between themselves. So, the kinds of patterns (or rules, 'schema', or 'concepts' – see Figure 6.1) learnt through these processes of statistical or inductive learning appear to be physically held in networks of interconnected neurons. Quite a body of recent research, referred to as 'connectionist modelling', has attempted, with some success, to model neural networks that might be responsible for particular aspects of learning. So, for example, Plunkett (2000) has reviewed some of the key ideas and conclusions from this type of work and has reported, for example, very successful attempts to model young children's typical vocabulary growth, using a computer simulation.

Figure 6.4 shows a graph of a typical vocabulary learning trajectory, in which, after a period of relatively slow but steady growth over several months, there is a sudden spurt at around 22 months. As those of us who work with young children know, this kind of 'discontinuity' is very common in many areas of young children's learning. Plunkett and colleagues managed to construct a surprisingly simple neural network which learnt vocabulary (i.e. could reliably name a series of objects correctly) and produced a pattern of learning remarkably similar to that typically seen in vocabulary growth. What this seems to indicate is that the long plateaux and then sudden spurts so typical of young children's learning are a structural consequence of the ways in which the neuronal networks in the human brain learn.

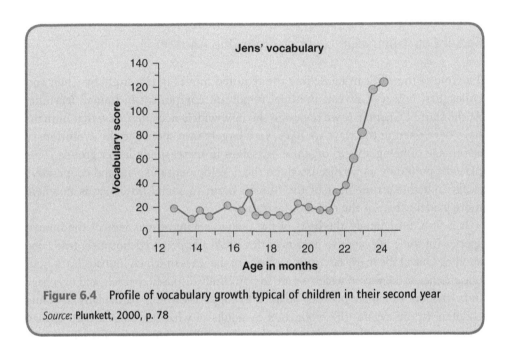

Figure 6.4 Profile of vocabulary growth typical of children in their second year

Source: Plunkett, 2000, p. 78

Closely related to these statistical or inductive processes, whereby patterns are actively constructed from experience, are processes of learning by analogy. This is an entirely active form of learning, perhaps not quite unique to humans, but infinitely more developed than in any other species, whereby a pattern identified and learnt in one context is used to make sense of a new experience or new information related to a separate context. This ability, sometimes referred to as the 'transfer' of learning, or 'generalisation', is of enormous significance in explaining human adaptability to new situations, and human capability in regard to novel problem solving. The vast changes in human civilisation and technology, since our ancestors lived as nomadic hunter-gatherers, would not have been possible without the ability to learn by analogy. Contrary to Piaget's conclusion that analogy is a complex form of reasoning which does not develop until later in development, Goswami (1992) was one of the first to demonstrate that it is, indeed, present in young children. She showed that children as young as 4 years old could reason analogically, provided that they understood the basic relationships involved. So, for example, a child of this age shown a pair of pictures of a bird and a nest could pick out a picture of a kennel to go with a dog. Chen et al. (1997), however, went further and managed to demonstrate basic analogical learning in children as young as 10 and 13 months. Their task involved learning a sequence of moves in order to retrieve an attractive doll (remove a barrier, pull a sheet with a string lying on it, then pull the string to move the doll). At these ages, the children required an adult to model the basic series of moves, but once learnt, they could then apply them (the 13-month-olds rather more flexibly than the 10-month-olds) to other similar tasks.

Social Constructivism: Learning from One Another

The role of the adult in modelling the required moves in the study by Chen and colleagues, however, reveals the final important component in human learning. At the start of Chapter 3, we reviewed the now widely accepted view that humans have developed in the ways we have, very largely in response to the evolutionary advantage of being able to organise ourselves in increasingly larger groups. This placed a premium, as we discussed, on the development of social and cooperative skills, and this attunement of the human brain to social influence is nowhere more evident than in the realm of learning.

It is also, intriguingly, the basis of the unique ability of members of the human species (of some relevance to readers of this book, I hope!) to deliberately teach one another. One of the many fascinating aspects of the ways in which humans learn from one another, is the way in which we are so powerfully disposed to teach, and to engage in behaviours which are perfectly adapted to support learning, particularly in young children. In this regard, the production by adults of what has usually been termed 'motherese' is an excellent example in relation to children's learning of language, and it points up very clearly the advantage of adults mediating children's experience for them (of which more later) in order to assist in the process of identifying patterns and regularities in their experience. When adults speak to babies and infants, they typically enunciate more clearly, use a more 'sing-song' voice exaggerating the intonations and stresses in speech, use a more limited vocabulary and shorter, simpler sentences, referring to the here-and-now, and respond to the child's productions in ways which would be odd, or even rude, if they appeared in adult-to-adult conversations (for example, repeating what the child says, or expanding a child's utterances into complete sentences). We all do this, without anyone teaching us, and it clearly helps young children to develop their receptive and expressive language.

Applying this approach to other areas of children's learning is often a characteristic of someone who is described as a 'natural' teacher, and, as we shall see, there are individual differences in adults' sensitivity and responsiveness to young children which have a clear impact upon children's learning. Within developmental psychology, the social interaction processes which relate to children's learning have been examined mainly in regard to learning by imitation (which relies, in the teaching context, on adult modelling) and learning through social interaction (which relies on the use of language).

Learning by imitation

We now know, chiefly through the work of American developmental psychologists Andrew Meltzoff (briefly mentioned in Chapter 3) and Keith Moore (Meltzoff and Moore, 1999), that young children are astonishingly adept at learning through imitation, from a very early age. In a paper published in the late 1970s, Meltzoff and Moore reported video data showing clear evidence of babies of 12 to 21 days old imitating both facial and manual gestures (see Figure 6.5). As is always the case with evolved behaviours, humans not only show the ability to imitate one another from a very early age, but brain mechanisms have also evolved to reward ourselves for doing it. We derive enormous pleasure, as children, and as adults, from imitating one another and being imitated. Imitative behaviour is often associated with playfulness and laughter; it is no accident, for example, that it is the basis of much adult comedy and satire, as well as many children's games.

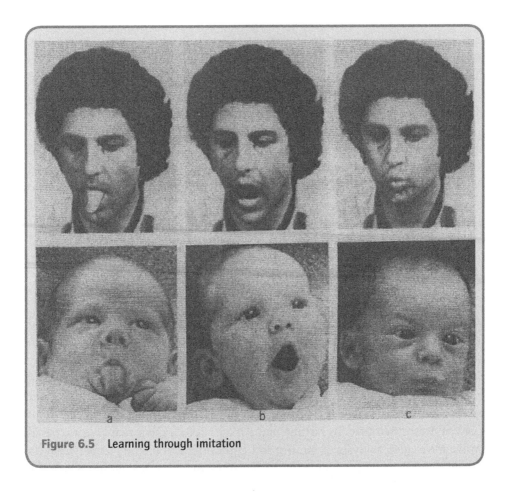

Figure 6.5 Learning through imitation

But it is worth considering what a phenomenal achievement even simple physical imitation represents. For a very young baby to be able to observe an adult performing an action, and then to be able to recognise which parts of its own body are equivalent, and, within its own immature motor cortex, to organise itself to perform the same action, shows a level of cortical organisation from birth which was not recognised until very recently indeed. Intriguingly, there is now some fairly strong evidence to suggest that this is achieved by what has been termed the 'mirror neuron' system (Rizzolatti and Craighero, 2004). What seems to be the case is that these same neurons fire, both when we observe another person performing a particular action, and when we perform it ourselves. This system seems to be fundamental to imitative behaviours, but also, in relation to issues discussed in Chapter 3, to understanding others' minds and intentions, and to empathetic responses to others' emotional states.

Within the context of learning, however, the ability to imitate the actions of another is clearly of enormous benefit in relation to learning a physical skill (for example, in learning a craft or in sports coaching – I am currently developing a golf swing of astonishing beauty by watching Tiger Woods!). In humans, furthermore, it is enormously enhanced as a tool for learning by the ability for imitation which is not only immediate (i.e. carried out while the to-be-copied behaviour is still perceptually available) but also deferred (i.e. performed on a subsequent occasion). Deferred imitation appears to be unique to humans as, of course, it crucially depends upon our ability to mentally represent objects and events in memory. This ability again appears to be present from a surprisingly early age, and to develop rapidly in very young children. Piaget observed deferred imitation in his own young children as long ago as the 1960s (Piaget, 1962), but only when they reached 16–24 months. In more recent work, Meltzoff (1988) identified deferred imitation in children as young as 9 months old. At this age, he demonstrated that they could reproduce novel actions they had observed up to 24 hours later (when presented with the same toy), but later work has shown that by 18 months this is up to two weeks, and by 24 months children are capable of showing deferred imitation after delays of 2 to 4 months. These are enormously valuable findings which inform our understanding of the development of young children's representational abilities, and their ability to hold mental representations in long-term memory.

Learning through social interaction

Modelling and imitation are, of course, a simple form of social interaction, and one can commonly observe adults and babies deriving enormous pleasure from pulling faces and blowing raspberries at one another. The astonishingly early predisposition and ability in babies to interact with others, and the powerful predisposition in adults to interact with babies and to read meaning into their actions and vocalisations, has been beautifully documented in the work of Colwyn Trevarthen (see Trevarthen and Aitken, 2001). Over many years, based on detailed video analysis of mother and child interactions, he has persuasively argued that they are best characterised as 'proto-conversations' within which the early establishment of children's abilities to derive meaning through interaction, or 'inter-subjectivity', is established. For example, he argues that:

> The interactions are calm, enjoyable and dependent upon sustained mutual attention and rhythmic synchrony of short 'utterances' which include, beside vocalisations, touching and showing the face and hands, all these expressions being performed with regulated reciprocity and turn-taking. Newborn and adult spontaneously display a mutually satisfying inter-subjectivity. (Trevarthen and Aitken, 2001, p. 6)

The establishment of 'mutual' attention is clearly a key element in these early communicative episodes. This develops within the first two years of life, it appears, as the growing child develops the ability for 'shared' attention, i.e. the ability to jointly attend, with an adult, to an external object or event. This most obviously emerges initially through the use and understanding of the pointing gesture. By 10–12 months, infants typically point to objects of interest which are out of reach and, shortly afterwards, they acquire the ability to locate objects pointed out to them by others (like most other primates, children under the age of 9 months respond to a pointing gesture by looking at your finger – try it!). During the second year of life, children then gradually acquire the ability to establish joint attention by following an adult's gaze. Once again, the predisposition of adults to support this development, by closely monitoring the infant's gaze, looking where they are looking, and using this focus of attention as the basis for further interaction (for example, by naming the object, commenting upon it, or fetching it for the child) has been clearly documented (Butterworth and Grover, 1988).

Extensive studies of these early adult–child interactions, however, have shown that, while there is a general disposition to support these early communicative developments, there are considerable variations in the sensitivity and style of communication between adults, and that these variations are clearly related to individual differences in children's learning, particularly in relation to language development. To begin with, a number of studies have shown that there are considerable differences in the amount of time 1-and 2-year-old children spend in joint attention episodes with their parents or caregivers (including joint play, conversation, book reading) and that this variation is related to the rate of language development of the child. Further, within joint attention episodes, significant differences exist in the sensitivity, or responsiveness, of parents or caregivers to their children, and this also impacts upon language development. Some adults appear to be much more aware of the child's pointing gestures or gaze as indicators of their focus of attention, and, having established the child's focus, some adults tend to use this as a basis for further interaction, including talk, while others tend to attempt to switch the child's attention to their own focus of interest. Not surprisingly, the former 'attention-following' strategy, building on the child's current interest and attention, has been found to support language development much more effectively than the 'attention-shifting' approach (for a review of this work, and research on language development generally, see Schaffer, 2004).

These findings are clearly of considerable interest to early childhood educators. Supporting early language development is clearly important in itself, if we wish to help children to become articulate adults, but it is even more important given its established relation to the ease with which children make the transition into literacy, and the now compelling evidence that, in the phrase popularised by Jerome Bruner, language is a 'tool of thought'. As regards the first issue, particularly given the current obsession in the UK with teaching young children 'phonics' divorced from meaning, I can do no better than recommend a recent excellent review by Catherine Snow, who has been foremost in research in this area for many years (Snow, 2006). As she notes, the two established predictors of literacy ability in early childhood are vocabulary size and phonological awareness. However, as she also notes, and as I would wish to argue, given what we know about children's learning more generally, direct instruction of vocabulary or phonology may not be the most productive approach. As we have seen, young children's learning is enormously enhanced by new information being placed in contexts which are of current interest to them and are, therefore, in a real sense, meaningful. Of course, it is perfectly possible to introduce the phonology of the written form of the language to young children in ways they find interesting. Given this, Snow cites rather strong evidence (from a meta-analysis of a considerable body of research) that about 20 hours of attention to phonological awareness is sufficient for almost all children (Ehri et al., 2001), and that supporting children to write, with their own attempts at spelling, supports phonological awareness as effectively as explicit curricula.

Language and learning: the contribution of Vygotsky

It is to the issue of the role of language in learning that I wish to turn in the final section of this chapter. The ideas of the Russian psychologist, Lev Vygotsky, to whom we have referred in Chapter 4 in relation to children learning through play, have been enormously influential in this area. While Piaget had argued that language development was a product of children's general ability to learn, and their increasing abilities for mental representation, Vygotsky argued the exact reverse. Happily, for those of us engaged in the education of young children, the evidence now overwhelmingly supports the Vygotskian view.

Piaget had emphasised the importance of the child interacting with the physical environment, and his followers in the educational sphere argued that the role of the teacher should be that of an observer and a facilitator. The general view of this approach was that attempting to directly teach or instruct young children was a mistake. It was claimed that whenever teachers attempted to teach children something, they simply deprived the children of the opportunity to discover it for themselves. This view was partly a reaction against the simplistic 'behaviourist' model that children only learnt what they were taught, and were rewarded for learning (as we have outlined in the first part of this chapter). This view, however, can be seen to have thrown the baby out with the bath water.

More recent research, inspired by the work of Vygotsky, has shown that there is a much more central role for the adult, and, indeed, for other children, in the processes of learning. This role is not as an instructor delivering knowledge, however, but rather as a 'scaffolder' (a metaphor suggested by Jerome Bruner and colleagues – Wood et al., 1976) supporting, encouraging and extending the child's own active construction of meaning and understanding. Based on observational studies of mothers and young children in experimental contexts, this group of researchers developed a characterisation of scaffolding which supports and develops many of the ideas emerging from other studies of early interactions, as we have reviewed above. So, they determined that a good scaffolder engages the interest of the child, simplifies the task if necessary, highlights critical features of the task, models key processes or procedures and, perhaps most importantly, sensitively monitors the child's success with the task and withdraws support when the child can proceed independently. The parallels with the work on adults supporting children's language learning are evident.

The central idea in Vygotsky's model of children's learning is that all learning begins in the social context, which supports children in the processes whereby they construct their own understandings. Thus, he argued that all learning exists first at the 'inter-mental' level (i.e. within the experience of joint attention and inter-subjectivity) in the form of spoken language, and then at the 'intra-mental' level (i.e. within the child's mind, in the form of internal language, or thought). This has been termed the 'social constructivist' approach to learning. Within this model, a further key insight is that of the 'zone of proximal development' (ZPD), as illustrated in Figure 6.6. Faced with any particular task or problem, Vygotsky argued, children (or any other learners for that matter) can operate at one level on their own, described as their 'level of actual

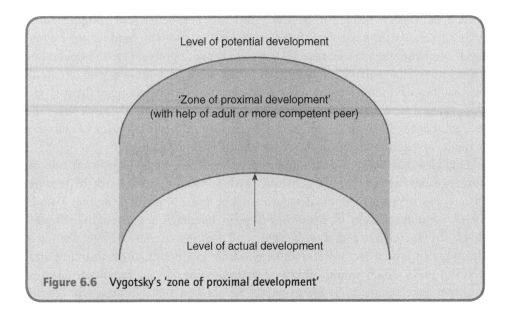

Figure 6.6 Vygotsky's 'zone of proximal development'

development', but at a higher level when supported or 'scaffolded' by an adult or more experienced peer, described as their 'level of potential development'. The ZPD is that area of learning between these two levels of performance or understanding, within which the child is really challenged, but which they can achieve with appropriate support.

Vygotsky and his followers have further argued that children learn most effectively through social interaction, when they are involved in jointly constructing new understandings, within their ZPD. Intriguingly, this view has been supported by a range of research, including that related to young children's production of what has been termed 'private speech', when they self-commentate on their own activities (to which we referred also in Chapter 4). Vygotsky's view was that this represents a crucial bridging mechanism between external 'social speech', produced in the context of social interaction with an adult or peer, and fully formed 'inner speech', which we all use as adults to help us to structure and keep track of our thoughts. It appears predominantly in young children up to the age of 7 or 8 years, and then gradually fades, as the capability for 'inner speech' is established, but is still commonly observed in older children and adults when they are dealing with a particularly challenging problem.

If Vygotsky's model is correct, it would be predicted that private speech would support young children's thinking and would be produced by young children at the highest rate when they are required to deal with a problem that is in their ZPD. It would also be predicted that the production of private speech would enhance children's problem-solving abilities. Extensive research into the phenomenon of private speech has fully supported both of these predictions (Fernyhough and Fradley, 2005, Winsler and Naglieri, 2003). The production of private speech by any individual child graphed against the level of difficulty of a task produces an inverted U shaped curve, or what might be termed a 'Goldilocks' pattern. That is, tasks which are too easy or too difficult lead to relatively low levels of private speech, but tasks which are at just the right level of challenge lead to significantly higher levels. At the same time, between children, those who produce the higher levels of private speech when faced with a challenging problem are those who are most successful in solving it. I have known early years practitioners who have told me that they have tended to discourage young children from talking to themselves; the evidence would suggest that we should be doing exactly the opposite and, indeed, that the incidence of 'private speech' is an excellent indicator of children being involved in tasks which they find appropriately challenging.

This view has been further supported by evidence of the significant role of language development more generally within learning. The work of Jerome Bruner has been influential in regard to this issue (see, for example, Wood, 1998, for a discussion of Bruner's ideas on language and thought). Bruner described language as a 'tool of thought', and demonstrated in a range of studies the ways in which language enables children to develop their thinking and perform tasks which would otherwise be impossible. In his famous '9 Glasses Problem' (see Figure 6.7), for example, he showed that children who could

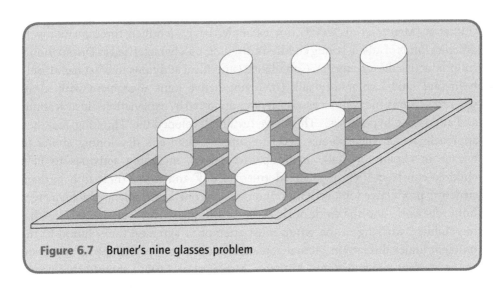

Figure 6.7   Bruner's nine glasses problem

describe the patterns in a 3 x 3 matrix of glasses (which were taller or shorter one way and thinner or fatter the other) were also able to transform the matrix (i.e. arrange the glasses in a mirror-image pattern). Children without the relevant language to call on, however, were only able to reproduce the pattern exactly as they had seen it.

It is now widely recognised that providing children with a relevant vocabulary and requiring them to formulate their ideas in discussion is a vital element in helping children to develop flexibility in thinking and construct their own understandings about the world. As long ago as the 1980s, Tizard and Hughes (1984), in a classic study of 4-year-old girls attending pre-school in the mornings, and spending time with their mothers at home in the afternoons, presented evidence of these young children engaging in intellectual search through conversations with their mothers. The kinds of meaningful dialogues they shared with their mothers, unfortunately, were sadly lacking in their pre-school experience. Sylva and colleagues (Sylva et al., 2004), more recently, in a large longitudinal study of factors leading to effective early years educational provision, have shown that high quality pre-school experience can significantly impact upon a range of intellectual and personal gains, even over-riding the effects of social disadvantage, for example, and that a key element in high quality provision appeared to be the occurrence of episodes of 'sustained shared thinking' between adults and children.

This kind of evidence has led to the recognition that a certain style of interaction between adults and children, along the lines emerging from the research we have reviewed in this chapter, and between pairs or small groups of children, can be enormously beneficial to learning. A range of recent and current classroom-based research has supported this view and has begun to identify in more detail the specific elements of a successful 'dialogic' pedagogy appropriate for children in the early years of education (Mercer and Littleton, 2007). Neil Mercer and colleagues

(Littleton, Mercer et al., 2005), for example, have identified three qualitatively different kinds of talk in young children's discussions, characterised as Disputational (unproductive disagreement), Cumulative (uncritical additions to what has already been said) and Exploratory talk (involving active joint engagment with ideas, where assertions and counter assertions are supported by explanations, justifications and alternative hypotheses). They have further developed the 'Thinking Together' approach, which incorporates tasks to support children's developing ability to engage in exploratory talk in group discussions, including activities to help children construct their own agreed 'rules for talk' and to use these to help them structure productive joint activities. Interestingly, one key element which emerges from this work, and the work of Howe and colleagues (Howe et al., 2007) is that the children working in the group must attempt to agree on the solution to the problem under discussion. Actual agreement does not appear to be as important as the attempt to achieve this. Littleton, Mercer et al. (2005) showed that young children could make significant strides in their ability to argue their case and provide explanations for their views, and that there were measurable gains in both the quality of their language and their non-verbal reasoning skills.

In a current piece of research which I have been conducting with Neil Mercer, with 5- and 6-year-old children in Year 1 classrooms, we have shown that this kind of approach can also encourage young children's self-regulation, measured both by their teachers' observational assessments (of which more in Chapter 7) and by their ability to reflect upon and talk about their performance on particular tasks. A recent American study (Vallotton and Ayoub, 2011) of 120 toddlers in New England has established a similarly exciting relationship between vocabulary size (which they distinguished from general 'talkativeness') at ages 14, 24 and 36 months and observed self-regulatory behaviour (such as the ability to maintain attention on tasks, and to adapt to changes in tasks and procedures). What emerges from this whole area of research is that a primary and fundamental goal of any early years educator must be to extend the language knowledge and skills of the young children in their care, as the evidence is now overwhelming concerning the significance of this area of development to learning in its broadest sense. Silence, in the modern early years classroom or setting, is anything but golden.

SUMMARY

We have seen that, as developmental psychologists have explored learning, we have become increasingly aware of the range and sheer power of the ways in which humans learn, right from the moment they are born. Piaget can be credited with having first established the dynamic, active model of young children's learning which is widely accepted today. But the particulars of his model of development, which characterised children as limited by logical deficiencies in their reasoning powers, have been largely dismissed. As Margaret Donaldson (1978) and others have demonstrated, adults make the same kinds of logical errors as children, and have difficulties with the same kinds of reasoning problems, particularly when they are divorced from meaningful contexts (as Philip Wason's four-card problem so brilliantly illustrates). In contemporary developmental psychology, children's learning is seen as being limited much more simply by their lack of experience and of accumulated knowledge. This makes it more difficult for them to see what is relevant in any new situation, and to see what is the best way to proceed. When this is made clear by the context in which a task is presented, however, children's potential for learning is phenomenal and often way beyond what was appreciated even quite recently. For those readers interested in what we know currently about the capabilities of very young children, I would enthusiastically recommend Tiffany Field's *The Amazing Infant* (2007), or either of Alison Gopnik's excellent books in this area (Gopnik, 2009; Gopnik et al., 1999). If you want to see what a 3-year-old can do, given the opportunity and the love and support, go to this YouTube clip (I promise you, it is amazing!): www2.choralnet.org/268945.html

The current view of the child as learner is one which recognises their considerable appetite and aptitude for learning, and the very active nature of learning processes, including statistical or inductive learning, learning by analogy, learning by imitation through social interaction with adults and more experienced peers, and learning through the formation of mental representations using language.

We have also seen how views about the role of the adult in supporting children's learning have veered from the early behaviourist view (beloved of our politicians) that children will only learn what they are taught, to the opposite Piagetian view that children must learn by themselves and adults getting involved will only interfere. The current view, supported, as we have seen, by a considerable and diverse body of evidence, is rather more measured and nuanced. The role of the adult (and peers) in supporting children's learning is established, but is seen not as that of an instructor, but rather as that of a facilitator and mediator, a more experienced tour guide taking children to all the important beauty spots in the world of learning, and pointing out the key cultural icons to which they should especially pay attention. As early years educators, in undertaking this role, the research evidence from developmental psychology we have reviewed in this chapter provides us with a number of clear principles to guide our practice, as follows:

- Children do respond to external rewards, such as stickers and verbal praise, but these represent a limited view of children's learning, and can encourage a passive, dependent style of learning in young children, so are perhaps best reserved as a means of dealing with anti-social and supporting prosocial behaviour in the early years; verbal praise for prosocial behaviours is far more effective than criticism of undesirable behaviour.
- Children are powerfully dynamic and active learners, who are highly motivated to learn about and make sense of their world; this is best supported by providing them with activities placed in contexts which are meaningful to them and relate to their current interests and enthusiasms.

(Continued)

(Continued)

- From a very early age, perhaps even a few weeks old, many of the processes through which the human brain learns are already in place; this includes learning by identifying patterns and regularities in the flow of experience and learning by imitating the actions of adults and older peers.
- During the first year or two of life, the learning of common patterns and regularities supports the ability to understand new experiences by analogy, and deferred imitation becomes an important part of the young child's learning repertoire.
- Much of this learning is supported by social interaction with adults and peers; from the first few weeks of life infants engage in 'proto-conversations' with adults, and their early endeavours to make meaning of their experiences are strongly supported during episodes of joint attention with adults during the first few years of life; these episodes are much more productive when the adult responds to and develops the child's focus of attention, rather than trying to re-direct the child's attention to a predetermined focus.
- In particular, these episodes of joint attention are instrumental in supporting children's language development; through a 'motherese' style of speech, adults help children to discern regularities in language, to develop their phonological awareness and their listening and speaking abilities, and to extend their vocabulary; in turn, these abilities support young children's early engagement with written language.
- Language is also a powerful 'tool of thought'; children's developing abilities to use language as a tool for learning is most powerfully supported by the experience of engaging in meaningful dialogues with adults and peers; in these contexts, adults can most purposefully 'scaffold' children's engagement with tasks or activities which would otherwise be slightly beyond their capabilities; the social speech used in these dialogic contexts is later used by young children, in the form of 'private speech', to enable them to undertake the same or similar tasks independently.
- Young children can learn to engage in productive 'exploratory' talk with peers, unsupported by an adult, provided they are given the opportunity to reflect upon and agree 'rules for talk', and are provided with collaborative problem-solving tasks which are appropriately structured to encourage genuine discussion and expression of views supported by arguments and explanations.

QUESTIONS FOR DISCUSSION

- Should we praise children when they have completed a task successfully, or should we ask them to explain how they did it?
- How can we help children to understand the important points or ideas in any new activity or area of knowledge we are introducing?

- How can we ensure that we spend time each day engaging productively in extended discussions with the young children in our care?
- Is teaching young children 'phonics' an important component in supporting their language and literacy development?

ACTIVITIES

A. Talking to children

Tape record some conversations with individual children, each lasting at least 2–3 minutes. In some of these conversations, decide beforehand on something you wish to 'teach' the child, and make a point of asking the child a number of questions to check their understanding. In other conversations, allow the child to determine the topic of discussion, listen to what they say and try to help them say more about their experiences and ideas, and share with the child some of your own experiences or thoughts.

These conversations could be stimulated by sharing a storybook, or by engaging in a joint activity (such as playing together with dough or a construction toy). Afterwards, listen to the conversations and answer the following questions:

- Who did most of the talking?
- Was it a genuine conversation, in which we both enjoyed sharing ideas and experiences, or was it just a question and answer session, with the child being fairly monosyllabic?
- Did I help develop the child's vocabulary?
- Did I help develop the child's ability to explain a narrative or justify an opinion?
- Do I feel I now know the child better, and appreciate his/her interests and concerns better than I did before?
- Do I see how I could do it better next time?

B. Private speech

Observe (or, ideally video-record) individual children engaged in construction or imaginative play. Note examples of their speech which do not seem to be directed at anyone else but are just 'private speech' to themselves. See if you can find examples of the following:

- *Planning*: talking about what they intend to do, or need to do next, or what they are trying to achieve
- *Monitoring*: talking about what is happening or what they are doing at that moment
- *Instructing*: talking to themselves to direct their current activity
- *Evaluating*: talking about how well they have carried out an activity, or how good they are at this kind of thing generally
- *Playing with sounds and words*: singing, humming, making sounds or exclamations to accompany the activity
- Inaudible mumbling.

Do you notice some children engaging in more of this private speech than others? Do you notice children producing more private speech when they are engaged in some kinds of activities than others?

C. Supporting 'exploratory talk'

In developing young children's abilities to organise productive discussions amongst themselves, it is best to start with some preparatory activities. Of course, children cannot usefully discuss activities of which they have no experience, so it is a good idea to set up a number of opportunities for them to try to have a discussion in small groups first. These generally work best if the activities are open-ended, require the children to make a decision, and cannot be solved in a straightforward manner. For example, try one of these:

- sorting out into groups a random collection of objects which do not fall into obvious categories; you could either decide on the number of groups to be formed or leave this open
- putting a set of five works of art in order from most to least favourite, as agreed by the group
- casting a puppet show: choosing from a selection of puppets which ones should play which characters in a well-known story.

After each of these sessions, discuss with the children how well it went and what problems they had in coming to an agreement. Ask them if they did all genuinely agree or if one member of the group made all the decisions. After a few trials, you can start to pick out with the children what you need to do to have a good discussion. Perhaps you could model good discussion and bad discussion with some puppets? Then set up further discussion activities for the children to decide their own 'rules for talk' for the class (see Dawes and Sams, 2004, for some proven ways of doing this, the associated issues and lots of excellent ideas for ways to extend this work further).

References

Butterworth, G.E. and Grover, L. (1988) 'The origins of referential communication in human infancy', in L. Weiskrantz (ed.) *Thought without Language*. Oxford: Oxford University Press.

Chen, Z., Sanchez, R.P. and Campbell, R.T. (1997) 'From beyond to within their grasp: the rudiments of analogical problem-solving in 10- and 13-month-olds', *Developmental Psychology*, 33, 790–801.

Cooke, L., Chambers, L., Anez, E., Croker, H., Boniface, D., Yeomans, M. and Wardle, J. (2011) 'Eating for pleasure or profit: the effect of incentives on children's enjoyment of vegetables', *Psychological Science*. Available at: http://dx.doi.org/10.1177/0956797610394662

Dawes, L. and Sams, C. (2004) *Talk Box: Speaking and Listening Activities for Learning at Key Stage 1*. London: David Fulton.

Donaldson, M. (1978) *Children's Minds*. London: Fontana.

Ehri, L.C., Nunes, S.R., Willows, D.M., Valeska Schuster, B., Yaghoub-Zadeh, Z. and Shanahan, T. (2001) 'Phonemic awareness instruction helps children learn to read: evidence from the National Reading Panel's meta-analysis', *Reading Research Quarterly*, 36, 250–87.

Fernyhough, C. and Fradley, E. (2005) 'Private speech on an executive task: relations with task difficulty and task performance', *Cognitive Development*, 20, 103–20.

Field, T. (2007) *The Amazing Infant*. Oxford: Blackwell.

Flavell, J.H. (1963) *The Developmental Psychology of Jean Piaget*. Princeton, NJ: Van Nostrand.

Gopnik, A. (2009) *The Philosophical Baby*. London: The Bodley Head.

Gopnik, A., Meltzoff, A.N. and Kuhl, P.K. (1999) *How Babies Think*. London: Weidenfeld & Nicolson.

Goswami, U. (1992) *Analogical Reasoning in Children*. London: Lawrence Erlbaum.

Goswami, U. (2008) *Cognitive Development: The Learning Brain*. Hove, East Sussex: Psychology Press.

Hilgard, E.R. (ed.) (1964) *Theories of Learning and Instruction*. Chicago, IL: University of Chicago Press.

Howe, C.J., and Tolmie, A., Thurston, A., Topping, K., Christie, D., Livingston, K., Jessiman, E. and Donaldson, C. (2007) 'Group work in elementary science: towards organizational principles for supporting pupil learning', *Learning and Instruction,*17, 549–63.

Kirkham, N.Z., Slemmer, J.A. and Johnson, S.P. (2002) 'Visual statistical learning in infancy: evidence for a domain general learning mechanism', *Cognition*, 83, B35–42.

Littleton, K., Mercer, N., Dawes, L. Wegerif, R., Rowe, D. and Sams, C. (2005) 'Talking and thinking together at Key Stage 1', *Early Years*, 25, 167–82.

Meltzoff, A.N. (1988) 'Infant imitation and memory: nine-month olds in immediate and deferred tests', *Child Development*, 59, 217–25.

Meltzoff, A.N. and Moore, M.K. (1999) 'Imitation of facial and manual gestures by human neonates' and 'Resolving the debate about early imitation', in A. Slater and D. Muir (eds) *The Blackwell Reader in Developmental Psychology*. Oxford: Blackwell.

Mercer, N. and Littleton, K. (2007) *Dialogue and the Development of Children's Thinking: A Sociocultural Approach.* London: Routledge.

Piaget, J. (1962) *Play, Dreams and Imitation in Childhood*. New York: W.W. Norton & Co.

Plunkett, K. (2000) 'Development in a connectionist framework: rethinking the nature–nurture debate', in K. Lee (ed.) *Childhood Cognitive Development: The Essential Readings*. Oxford: Blackwell.

Rizzolatti, G. and Craighero, L. (2004) 'The mirror neuron system', *Annual Review of Neuroscience*, 27, 169–92.

Schaffer, H.R. (2004) 'Using language', in *Introducing Child Psychology*. Oxford: Blackwell.

Snow, C.E. (2006) 'What counts as literacy in early childhood?', in K. McCartney and D. Phillips (eds) *Blackwell Handbook of Early Childhood Development*. Oxford: Blackwell.

Sylva, K., Melhuish, E. C., Sammons, P., Siraj-Blatchford, I. and Taggart, B. (2004) *The Effective Provision of Pre-School Education (EPPE) Project: Technical Paper 12 – The Final Report: Effective Pre-School Education*. London: DfES/Institute of Education, University of London.

Tizard, B. and Hughes, M. (1984) *Young Children Learning*, London: Fontana.

Trevarthen, C. and Aitken, K.J. (2001) 'Infant intersubjectivity: research, theory and clinical applications', *Journal of Child Psychology and Psychiatry*, 42, 3–48.

Vallotton, C. and Ayoub, C. (2011) 'Use your words: the role of language in the development of toddlers' self-regulation', *Early Childhood Research Quarterly*, 26, 169–81.

Wason, P.C. and Johnson-Laird, P.N. (1972) *Psychology of Reasoning: Structure and Content*. London: Batsford.

Winsler, A. and Naglieri, J.A. (2003) 'Overt and covert verbal problem-solving strategies: developmental trends in use, awareness, and relations with task performance in children aged 5 to 17', *Child Development*, 74, 659–78.

Wood, D.J. (1998) *How Children Think and Learn,* 2nd edn. Oxford: Blackwell.

Wood, D.J., Bruner, J.S. and Ross, G. (1976) 'The role of tutoring in problem-solving', *Journal of Child Psychology and Psychiatry*, 17, 89–100.

Summary

By now, you should have developed an understanding of learning theories and how these theories impact upon your teaching. Thinking again about the overarching themes of this book – Communication, Innovation and Participation – we can make links to the importance of communication in order to gauge how a child learns and whether what we think we have taught has actually been learnt. Communication is a vital tool for developing reasoning and the cyclical process of learning; where experiences are reflected upon and are assimilated into future learning. Innovative ways to approach learning is crucial – keep looking for interesting and engaging ways of learning and implementing a variety of strategies for learning in your classrooms. Learning is an active process which should be engaging and purposeful. Co-constructed learning is something that has been mentioned in the chapters and you should recognize the importance of involving children in their own learning. Knowing what strategies work best for individual students is imperative to ensuring good learning occurs in your classroom, every day!

Student activities
- Observe a child in your setting and begin to think about how their displayed behaviours link to what you know about the theories of learning.
- Look at the theories of learning that are practised in Montessori and Steiner schools. How do these compare to the learning that takes place in the settings that you have experienced?
- Watch this clip on operant conditioning from The Big Bang Theory and think about other examples of 'theories at work' that you may have seen in society or in schools. http://www.youtube.com/watch?v=Mt4N9GSBoMI

Top Tips
- Remember that whilst theories help us to understand learning there is no definitive answer: all children are individual and therefore respond to learning in different ways.
- These theories are a solid foundation for you to build upon; as you progress through the course remember to make links to how behaviour and assessment for learning strategies impact upon learning.
- Think about yourself as a learner – what works for you? How does this affect your teaching style?

Additional reading
Bolton, G. (2010) 'Reflective Practice: An Introduction', in *Reflective Practice: Writing and Professional Development*. London: Sage.

Year 3/PGCE
Kendall-Seatter, S (2005) 'Planning for all abilities: Differentiation', Chapter 2 in *Primary Professional Studies*. Exeter: Learning Matters.

PART 3   THE CHILD IN A SOCIAL CONTEXT

Overview

At UWE we believe that for all students to have an understanding of child development is a pre-requisite of becoming an outstanding/transformational teacher. How can you teach children if you know nothing about their development or significant areas: home, school, community, that impact on their lives? While in many early years' courses, this area is already well developed, it is often much less embedded within primary courses and we are determined to remedy this!

The Tina Bruce chapter provides a very useful introduction to what child development is and its significance. The two chapters on children developing as communicators look at a specific feature of child development, i.e., language acquisition and development and the Daniels chapter identifies the importance of developing strong relationships both in school and between all stakeholders in a child's education.

Further reading

Child development

Bruce, T. (2009) 'Introducing Child Development' Section 3, Chapter 8 in *Early Childhood: A Guide for Students*, 2nd edition. London: Sage.

Children developing as communicators

Levey, S. and Polirstok, S. (2011) 'An Introduction to Language and Learning' in *Language Development. Understanding Language Diversity in the Classroom*. London: Sage.

Whitehead, M. (2007) 'Talking With Parents and Carers about Communication and Language Development' Chapter 6 in *Developing Language and Literacy in Young Children*. London: Sage.

The child's social context – home, family, school and the wider community

Daniels, D.H. and Clarkson, P. K. (2010) 'The Primacy of Relationships in the Early School Years', Chapter 3 in *A Developmental Approach to Educating Young Children*. London: Sage.

Introduction to Child Development

Bertram, T. and Pascal, C.

Professor Tony Bertram is Co-Director of the Centre for Research in Early Childhood and its sister organisation, Amber Publications and Training based at the St Thomas Centre, Birmingham. He is Co-Founder of the European Early Childhood Education Research Association and Editor of its prestigious journal. His current research is a five-country, cross-national project looking at home/setting transition issues for children and families of the 'newly arrived'. He is a Ministerial Adviser to the Department for Children, Schools and Families.

Professor Christine Pascal OBE is Co-Director of the Centre for Research in Early Childhood based at the St Thomas Centre, Birmingham, which specialises in early childhood research and evaluation projects and its sister organisation, Amber Publications and Training, which offers con-

sultancy and advanced-level professional development. She is currently President of the European Early Childhood Education Research Association. She is Project Director of the Effective Early Learning (EEL) Project, Baby Effective Early Learning (BEEL) and of the Accounting Early for Life Long Learning (AcE) Project and is early years specialist adviser to the House of Commons Select Committee.

Aims

To develop understanding of:

- ☐ and gain an introduction to, child development in the western tradition
- ☐ and explore this knowledge in action
- ☐ and using the knowledge and ideas to improve your own professional practice.

Introduction

New research and theories about child development are appearing all the time and adding to our understanding about young children's lives. This chapter sets out some of the main ideas, predominantly from western traditions of research and theory, and shows how they help us to work more effectively with young children and their families.

Each section of the chapter sets out some key messages about what we know and understand about child development, and explores how this information can help practitioners and carers interact with children to support their learning. The chapter also provides ideas for putting the key messages into practice and offers some exercises and reflective questions for readers to try out these ideas within their workplace.

How children develop and learn

Key messages

1. *Pre- and post-natal experience is a major determinant in the long-term healthy progress of the child.* The mother's state of health, levels of stress and nutrition during pregnancy play a key part in the healthy development of the foetus and new-born baby. Smoking, alcohol and other substance abuse by the mother, are factors in the low birth weight of babies, and this is linked to long-term health problems in children. Breast-feeding can also offer the child significant health benefits. Research has shown the key part played by health visitors and other supportive practitioners or family members in helping parents and the wider family to prepare for the birth of their child and to support the new-born infant.

2. *The first 60 months of a child's life are critical in determining their future development, with the first four months being the most influential.* Research on brain development and emotional well-being has shown the critical nature of experiences in the first months of a child's life, and in particular, the first four months (Abbott and Moylett, 1997). During this period the architectural structure of the brain's connectivity is being formed. Small babies have an extraordinary range of capabilities, some of which they will lose before 3 years of age. The early thickets of synaptic connections begin to be pruned when not used and the connecting branches that are used and stimulated become the major pathways for thought. The quality of stimulation and interaction at this time will largely determine the child's capacity to learn in the long term and the associations they will make between learning and pleasure, or between stimulation and emotional well-being. The quality of stimulation, affection and care received by the child during the first five years of life has been shown to shape a child's life chances.

3. *There appear to be developmental phases that all children go through but a child's individual progress is shaped by their experience and culture.* Research has continued to show that developmental psychologists, like Piaget (Piaget and Inhelder, 1969), were

right in stating that all children go through a series of developmental sequences or stages as they mature and that the rate and timing of these stages are part of our biological and genetic programming. But to understand development we must go beyond biological explanations. Social constructivists like Vygotsky (1978a) and Bruner (1960; 1996) have also shown that a child's development and learning is significantly mediated by individual, social and cultural experiences. Social constructivists believe that the culture and society in which children are raised impacts on the pace and nature of development. So development is constructed, in part, by the social environment in which children live. Each child's developmental profile will be unique, and development may be non-linear and uneven.

4. *From birth children are competent and skilful learners, with a wide range of skills that are further shaped by their family and community.* Children are born full of capability, able to communicate, influence and make sense of the world and their experiences within it. Humans are characterised by a strong exploratory drive and curiosity. This capacity is further enhanced and extended in enriching environments and in particular ways by a child's family and community. Relationships, interactions and shared experiences feed this capacity. Children often indicate whether they are bored or involved in an activity, and children who are involved in stimulating, purposeful and meaningful activity will display confirming signals. Cultural diversity adds complexity and richness to our society and it is important that such diversity is acknowledged, valued and incorporated into practitioners' thinking and actions. Parents are valuable partners in ensuring a child's cultural identity is celebrated, reinforced and extended, in sharing information about a child's early experiences and in ensuring a child's capabilities are recognised and built upon.

5. *Children are born with a strong exploratory drive and seek active experiences and play.* From birth, children have a strong exploratory drive through which they experiment, explore, interact with and make sense of their world (Laevers, 1994; Pascal and Bertram, 1997). Young children are essentially active risk-takers and problem-solvers and they require an environment which is full of stimulation, opportunities to stretch themselves to their limits and take risks, to play for extended periods of time, both alone and with adult and child playmates. They also need encouragement to follow through their self-chosen activities and to be self-organised, persistent, resilient, creative and playful.

6. *Young children learn with and through other people, especially their parents/carers and other children.* As Vygotsky (1978a) has shown, development and learning is essentially a social activity. Children learn with and through significant others, who may be a parent or carer, an older child or sibling or other playmates. It is through interactions and collaborative play activity that seeks and solves problems, combined with plenty of supported opportunities to express their meaning-making, that a child develops and learns. Action and interaction are the twin keys to development and learning.

7. *Children's development is hugely affected by their social and emotional well-being.* Children's development and learning is fundamentally influenced by their emotional state (Pascal and Bertram, 1997). A child who has a confident sense of connection with, and attachment to, those around them will thrive. Laevers (1994) has demonstrated that children with strong well-being will be able to open themselves to deep levels of

involvement and immersion in their explorations of the world. Whereas a child who lacks social skills and is timid and insecure will miss the joy of experimentation, adventure and shared risk-taking.

EXERCISE 8.1

Exploring the first weeks of a baby's life

1. Make contact with the parent(s) of a child under the age of three months and arrange an interview.
2. Discuss and record how the pregnancy progressed and any facts about the child's pre- and post-natal history. Find out how the child developed during the first weeks after birth and any emerging issues that occurred relating to the child's progress. How did the parent(s) deal with these issues, where did they go to for help and advice, and what may have further supported them?
3. Share the information you have gained with a work colleague. Discuss how typical the issues raised are and how additional support may have been provided to the family and child.
4. Consider what your reading says about a child's development in the first few weeks of life and reflect in your journal how this pattern of development fits the baby you have been focusing on.
5. Write a plan of support for the parent(s) and baby for the next six months and state what difference this action might make to both the parent(s) and the child.
6. How will you evaluate the benefits of your planned action?

Reflective questions

- Do parents' concerns and priorities for their child match your own?
- What are the particular competencies that children are born with and how might you nurture these more effectively?
- How far do you feel children follow developmental patterns and how far are their learning journeys unique?
- What do you feel are the benefits of parents and professionals sharing knowledge about the child's development and learning?

Feelings, relationships and sociocultural development

Key messages

1   *Children's overall development is fundamentally affected by their relationships and feelings.* There has been a revolution in recent thinking about children's development and we now know that there is a close link between emotions and cognition (Bruner,1996).

Children who experience close, affectionate, loving relationships, and who are emotionally supported, develop better in all areas. Children who do not form strong attachments, have disrupted relationships and experience cold, distant care, especially during the first few months of life, are vulnerable to long-term developmental delay.

2. *Children's sense of self and their ability to form relationships with others is substantially shaped by their early interactions with others.* During the first few weeks of life children form strong bonds with those who care for them. Through the interactions with their carer(s) and other close family and community members, children start to develop a sense of themselves and their particular place in the world (Trevarthen, 2003). They are exploring where they 'fit' and who they are, seeking feedback continually from those around them on their actions and experiences and feelings. Their capacity to connect with others and make relationships is therefore critical if they are to receive the feedback and reinforcement they seek from these early interactions.

3. *The emotional life of the young child underpins the way they explore and make sense of the world.* Children's emotional state has a profound effect on the way they explore and attempt to make sense of their world (Pascal and Bertram, 1997). Children who have poor emotional well-being often respond with timidity, fear and rigidity to new experiences, lacking the open, exploratory state that learning about the world requires. Research has shown that such children can become withdrawn, hesitant and very clingy, in a way that inhibits their exploration. In contrast, children who are secure, attached and confident usually play, and become adventurous, enjoying risk-taking, and having the flexibility that new experiences need. These attitudes, dispositions and feelings will positively shape the way the child faces the unknown and ensure that their curiosity and exploratory drive thrives.

4. *The social and emotional life of the child is culturally embedded.* The way a child feels and expresses emotion, and the nature and shape of their social relationships, will be influenced a good deal by the particular family and community into which they are born. Each family and community has certain values and beliefs (or culture) that shape the way children are dealt with, related to and encouraged to behave. These experiences, in turn, will shape the child's emotional and social life, and the way the child will deal with feelings and relationships. It can sometimes be hard accurately to read the social and emotional signals that children from other cultures communicate.

5. *Children's identities are shaped by the nature of their interactions with different cultures.* In the early months of a child's life, children are forming a sense of themselves and their own identity(ies). In today's global and visual world, a child's sense of self and identity is shaped by a complex range of experiences and interactions with a culturally diverse range of sources. Young children become very adept at cultural brokering, and will draw on all these cultural sources when creating their own identity(ies) and sense of self. They are also capable early on of understanding when to display certain aspects of self, and when to suppress certain aspects. We should not underestimate the hybrid and multiple nature of identity and the choices young children make when constructing a sense of who they are and what constitutes their internal self.

E X E R C I S E   8 . 2

Who are the child's 'companions'?

1. Observe a child under the age of 4 over several days and record who are the child's favoured companions (both adults and other children).
2. Record the nature and content of the interactions between the child and her/his companions. What do you think the child is gaining from these companions?
3. Talk to the child's parents and or carers about the child's favoured companions and how these relationships have developed.
4. What does your reading say about 'companionship' or 'friendship' in the early months and years of life? Can you find evidence in your reading of cultural differences in 'companionship' patterns?
5. Reflect on how you might use both child and adult 'companions' to support children's development within an early years centre.

Reflective questions

- Why do you feel companions are important to young children's well-being?
- How might you support children's friendships more effectively?
- What do you think are the skills and competencies children need to be a good companion or friend?
- How would you help parents and siblings to become better companions?

Communication and language development

Key messages

1. *Children are born as gifted communicators*. From birth children are skilful communicators, using a whole range of verbal and non-verbal signals to reach out to, and manipulate, those around them. This capacity to direct others to tend to their needs is vital to a child's survival. The young child is also gifted at orchestrating the communication and effective partners, both adults and children, often follow the child's cues and leads, through imitation and improvisation. This is true of facial and bodily communication cues, as well as vocalisations (Doherty-Sneddon, 2003; Trevarthen, 2003).
2. *There are critical periods for the development of language*. Research on the development of the brain has confirmed the view that there are critical periods for the development of a child's linguistic ability (Chomsky, 1975). Experiences during the first weeks of a child's life appear to determine the child's capacity to vocalise in certain ways. Young children need lots of opportunity to both hear (listen) and vocalise (speak), and are very receptive to sound. The kinds of vocal patterns that they will be able to achieve are shaped by the vocal

patterns they hear and imitate. Rich and extended opportunities for interaction and communication are centrally important in these early months of development.

3. *The development of communication and language is intimately linked to the development of thought.* The capacity of the child to think, to internalise their growing sense of the world, and to extend their understanding through the development of higher order thinking skills, is to a large extent determined by their growing capacity to use and understand language or sign language (Vygotsky, 1978). Young children need to experience and participate in a language-rich environment, and to be encouraged to talk about and reflect on their experiences.

4. *Children have many languages that they use to communicate their thoughts, feelings and understandings about the world.* Children express themselves in many non-verbal ways before they use words (Doherty-Sneddon, 2003). They have many languages to draw on to communicate meaning and their non-verbal languages provide an important window on all aspects of their development and learning. Hand gestures, posture, eye gaze, facial expressions and touch are all key ways that children use to communicate. Understanding these important channels of communication can help parents and practitioners to support children's development and learning. Unfortunately, sometimes these other languages are ignored or misinterpreted with the emphasis largely on the significance of the spoken word.

5. *Children need adults and other children to respond to, and stimulate, their developing communication and language skills.* Children are inherently social beings and seek others to share their world and help in the co-construction of their growing understandings. The importance of interaction and talk within affectionate, caring relationships cannot be overestimated in the development of a child's communication and language skills. The sharing of stories, rhymes, singing and other play activities will provide further stimulus to the child's developing communication and language skills.

EXERCISE 8.3

Making sense of young children's communication

1. Observe a small group (two or three) of young children interacting together.
2. Make a list of the different ways the children use to communicate with each other and note what was the intention of the communication. Include non-verbal and verbal signed communication in your record.
3. Try and group the kinds of communication strategies you have recorded into various types, for example, hand gestures, body posture, eye gaze, facial expressions, touch, vocalisations.
4. Discuss with other practitioners how they interpret children's communications – in particular try to analyse how non-verbal communications are used by practitioners to make sense of children's experiences and feelings.

(Continued)

(Continued)

5. Read about how new-born babies communicate with the world and reflect on how far and in what ways these strategies are used by older children.
6. Plan a small-group session with young children that encourages them to use a range of communication strategies with each other and yourself.
7. Evaluate why there is a tendency to focus primarily on verbal communication in many early years centres and consider how this focus might be extended to better understand young children's experiences and feelings.

Reflective questions

- What do you feel are the key communication skills (verbal and non-verbal) a young child has?
- How might you more effectively support the development of these skills?
- How do you listen with all your senses to young children's communications?
- How far do you think children's communications are different at home and in the setting?
- What practices inhibit children's communication and what practices do you know enhance it?

Learning through the senses and direct experience

Key messages

1. *Children are born with a natural curiosity, and a strong exploratory drive.* All children are born with a strong inner exploratory drive that feeds their natural curiosity and inclination to investigate the world (Laevers, 1994; Pascal and Bertram, 1997). The inquisitive nature of young children feeds their development and learning, and is a disposition to be celebrated and encouraged. Challenge, risk-taking and adventure come naturally to the young child and adults need to ensure these dispositions can thrive within a secure and safe environment.

2. *All five senses are used in a child's exploration but sight and sound are critical.* Children draw on all their senses to explore and make sense of the world. Touch, sight, smell, sound and taste are the conduits of action and experience, and each of these senses needs stimulation from birth. Research has shown that the senses of sight and sound develop earliest and need vital stimulation if they are to develop normally. There appears to be a critical period in young children's development when the capacity for these senses to develop normally is set, and therefore stimulation of these senses from birth is essential.

3. *Children actively seek stimulation and need first-hand experiences with real objects and occurrences, and responsive adults or children who both support and model.* There can be no substitute for first-hand experience and active, self-directed experiences which flow from the child's own initiatives. Although children do learn through modelling, demonstration and imitation, offering active, problem-posing and play experiences with real objects within a rich environment will stimulate the child's development far more effectively (Bruce, 2001; Bruner, 1996).

4. *Children need lots of opportunities to be self-directed and should be encouraged to manage their own learning.* Research has shown that children should be given the chance from the earliest age to be self-directing and to take initiatives (Laevers, 1994). Adults can support a child's choices and progress towards self-identified goals. The capacity of children from the earliest age to self-manage and self-evaluate their own learning should be acknowledged and built upon, and where a child finds this difficult further support should be provided as a priority.

EXERCISE 8.4

Mapping involvement levels in young children

1. Read about Laever's (1994) 'Child involvement scale' and reflect on how this might help you 'tune into' a child's learning processes more effectively.
2. Using Laever's involvement scale, observe two children: (a) engaged in free play; (b) engaged in circle time; (c) engaged in a collaborative activity; and record their involvement levels.
3. Analyse where you found involvement levels were high and where they were low, and reflect on the reasons why these levels were observed.
4. Talk with practitioners and parents and ask them what conditions seem to favour high and low involvement levels in children.
6. Reflect on how the 'Child involvement scale' might be used to evaluate and improve the quality of practice within a centre.

Reflective questions

- Why is involvement a useful concept?
- How might you use this idea to develop your practice?
- What do you think stimulates 'high involvement' in your setting?
- Why do you think some children find getting highly 'involved' in your setting difficult?

Diversity and inclusion – gender, ethnicity and culture

Key messages

1. *Children are born into a diverse, intercultural society and seek to find their place and identity.* The world into which children are now born is diverse and made up of myriad different cultures and communities. Globalisation and increasing migration means that they are likely to travel and mix with children and families from different cultures and communities. Helping children to have a sense of both individual and collective identity, and also a feeling of connectedness to society as a whole, is an important task for those who care for and educate the young.

2. *All cultures are rich but not all cultures are given equal value in our society and this impacts on children's sense of self and self-worth.* It is important to acknowledge that while all cultures are rich, society tends to endow some cultures with more value than others. Often, there is an ignorance of other cultures, and this can lead to stereotypes and prejudices developing (Siraj-Blatchford, 1994). Young children are acutely aware of the responses of others towards them, their family and their community as they form their own sense of self worth and identity.

3. *Gender identity affects a child's progress.* There has been much written to document the differences between boys and girls in various areas of development. It appears that the developmental profiles of even very young children are affected by their gender. However, it is also evident that any biological determinism can be reinforced or challenged by the way boys and girls are treated, particularly in the early years. The feminisation of the early years workforce may be a factor in the superior progress of girls within the existing system. This raises important questions of equity and access for boys in early childhood settings.

4. *All children have the legal right to be treated equally and not suffer discrimination.* The United Nations Convention on Children's Rights, which has been ratified by the UK, gives children from birth important rights and entitlements. The appointment of the first Children's Commissioner for England and Wales in 2005 adds weight to the importance of children's rights. The UK also has strong laws to ensure that all children are treated equally and should not suffer discrimination on the grounds of race or gender. Early childhood practitioners are required by law to provide equal access to their services and to adopt inclusive, anti-discriminatory practice.

EXERCISE 8.5

Looking at diversity

1. Focus on a group of children who attend an early childhood centre and try and map the diversity of cultures that are present in the group.
2. Research the cultures represented in the group and in particular find out about the cultures with which you are less familiar.
3. Talk to a small group of parents from a range of a different cultures about their own childhood experiences and their aspirations for their children.
4. Find out from the practitioners within the centre how they support cultural diversity and difference within their practice.
5. Find out about the legal requirements on equality in public services. Look at an early years centre's policy on equality and diversity and talk with the centre manager about how this is put into practice.
6. Identify what you feel are the key challenges to achieving anti-discriminatory practice within all early childhood centres.

Reflective questions

- How far do you feel you acknowledge the diversity of cultures in your work with children?
- How might you encourage parents to share with you their stories of their childhood experiences and hopes for their own children's lives?
- Do you feel confident in challenging racism, stereotyping and prejudice?
- How do you balance acknowledgement of difference while encouraging a sense of social cohesion?

Children with special educational needs and disabilities

Key messages

1. *There is a wide range in the normal development of young children, and we should be cautious of pathologising variations in children's development.* Although it can be helpful to look at expected norms of development for children, recent work has shown that developmental expectations at different ages are also culturally embedded (Bruner, 1996). What can be expected of a 2-year-old in one culture may be very different to a 2-year-old child growing up in another culture. It should also be emphasised that there is a very wide range in the normal development of children and we should be careful about labelling children with developmental delay or precociousness (Bruce, 2001).

2. *Early diagnosis and intervention to support children's special needs can lead to more favourable long-term development.* The early identification of children with special needs and the provision of specialist support have been shown to make a remarkable difference to children's subsequent progress. All early childhood settings are required to have an identified member of staff with responsibility for co-ordinating specialist support for children with particular needs, but all practitioners have an important role to play in identifying a child's needs as early as possible and linking with specialist support where necessary.

3. *All practitioners need to work together with other professionals to ensure a network of support around children with special needs and their families.* Recent legislation requires all agencies and professionals working with young children to co-ordinate their efforts to ensure a 'joined-up' network of support for all children, and their families, based on individual needs. Each child and family should have a Lead Professional or Key Person who is the primary point of contact, and whose role is to identify and coordinate appropriate support. There is also a requirement to share information to ensure a seamless service, to avoid duplication of effort and ensure all children receive the support they need.

4. *Practitioners should ensure their practice is inclusive and anti-discriminatory towards children with special needs.* There is a legal requirement for practitioners to adopt anti-discriminatory practices towards all children and families. Services should be open and accessible for all children, and promote positive and inclusive practice that celebrates diversity and difference (Siraj-Blatchford, 1994). This means practitioners need to understand fully the nature of a child's needs and be aware of their obligations towards meeting these fully and respectfully. Parents too may need particular support in understanding and realising their child's rights.

5. *The pedagogy for children with special needs should mirror that for all children.* Children with special needs have an entitlement to a curriculum or programme that fully meets their needs and ensures access to experiences in all areas of learning. The pedagogy adopted for children with special needs should encourage independence, autonomy and choice, emphasising self-directed and self-managed learning, as recommended for all children. Practitioners need to provide additional support where necessary, but should not change the nature of learning experiences where this would discriminate against children with special needs (Bruce, 2005).

6. *Settings should ensure resources are accessible and appropriate to support the particular needs of all their children.* Anti-discriminatory practice requires that all resources, including materials, equipment, room layout and staffing, are reviewed regularly to ensure accessibility and appropriateness to the whole range of need within a setting (Siraj-Blatchford, 1994). This may require specialist resources and equipment that are geared to a child's particular needs. Accessing specialist advice is vital when reviewing access to, and equality of, programmes for all children within a setting.

EXERCISE 8.6

How inclusive are we?

1. What does your reading say about the legal requirements to support all children with special educational needs and disabilities?
2. Talk to a centre manager about their views on inclusive practice for children with special educational needs. What do they feel are the key challenges in ensuring inclusive practice works well?
3. Interview a parent of a child with special educational needs and discuss their experience of their child's inclusion in early childhood centres. Who do they deal with and where is their key point of support?

4. Observe a child with special educational needs or a disability within a centre and record how the practitioners involved ensure the child has equal access and entitlement to the experiences on offer.

5. How might you evaluate the inclusiveness of an early years centre for children with special educational needs? What evidence would you use?

Reflective questions

- What are the benefits of inclusive provision and how far do you feel these are recognised?
- How do you more effectively support children with special educational needs and disabilities?
- What additional professional development do you feel would help you provide better support?
- How do you encourage a climate of inclusion and equity in your setting?

The impact of economic poverty on a child's development

Key messages

1. *In England we continue to have unacceptably high levels of child poverty, which has a long-term impact on the life chances of many children.* In comparison with other developed countries, England continues to have high levels of child poverty and the gap between rich and poor persists despite government policies devised to address this. Growing up in poverty has a long-term impact on children's attainment and significantly shapes future life chances (OECD, 2000).

2. *The long-term development of the child is negatively affected by factors related to poverty.* Living in poverty is the single most damaging influence on a child's life and is associated with a range of negative factors connected with development in children. These factors include family stress, strained relationships, poor pre- and post-natal nutrition, poor physical and mental health, inadequate housing, low well-being and low aspirations. The impact of such factors on children's lives can be profound and hard to redress later.

3. *High-quality, integrated early childhood provision, with a strong educational component can make a difference to children's life chances.* There is robust evidence that providing high-quality, integrated early childhood services can be particularly beneficial to less advantaged families. Combining health and social care services with a strong and early educational focus for children and families can be particularly effective in improving life chances. The development of Children's Centres in all neighbourhoods, where multi-professional teams work collectively for children and families, reflects a more 'joined-up' approach to early childhood services, in an attempt to break cycles of poverty and disadvantage.

Issues of child development

Key messages

1. *Children's development is determined by both biological factors and sociocultural experiences*. Current evidence points to a dynamic and symbiotic relationship between biological or genetically determined patterns of development and socioculturally embedded development. Knowledge about genomes is revolutionising our understanding of genetic endowment and its impact on developmental progress. However, sociocultural studies reveal the significance of life experiences, especially in the very early years of life, in determining the realisation of capabilities and human potential.

2. *There is a rapidly increasing knowledge base about young children's development that is providing important insights for effective practice*. Rapid strides have been made in our knowledge and understanding of human development, and the factors that contribute positively and negatively to healthy progress. These factors provide valuable insights into what constitutes effective practice in the rearing of young children, both in home- and centre-based care. A key factor appears to be the nature of early relationships and interactions.

3. *The child's brain is at its most malleable in the first weeks of life and stimulation is critical at this time*. Brain research shows that during the first weeks of a child's life the brain has immense plasticity and that this is a critical time for shaping the architecture of the brain and the long-term capacity to learn. The brain is at its most impressionable during this early period of life. Stimulation, both sensory and socially through interaction with others, is hugely important and profoundly shapes a child's potential.

4. The impact of early experience on a child's developmental profile is profound and provides a critical challenge for practitioners to provide high-quality experiences. The long-term significance of experiences in the early weeks and months of a child's life provides practitioners with both a challenge and an opportunity. If high-quality, cognitive and affective experiences can be provided for children during these early years, life chances can be improved impressively. This is a huge incentive for practitioners to raise the quality of their services, to ensure maximum impact and outcomes for all children

5. Globalisation means that young children are increasingly likely to experience migration, transitions and cross-cultural experiences that will shape their development. It is important to acknowledge that modern life, and the impact of globalisation, means that migration, transitions and change are endemic in children's and families' lives. These experiences can be enormously beneficial for children when handled with sensitivity, empathy and support. They can certainly open doors to new worlds for children whose lives are marred by disadvantage and deprivation of various kinds. But, such experiences can also disrupt, dislocate and disturb children's progress, and practitioners need to respond actively and positively to the reality of children's lives.

6. *Every child's developmental profile is unique although there are universal patterns in human development*. Our ever-increasing knowledge of child development supports the view that although there are universal patterns which may be recognised and used

to guide practice, each child's growing journey is unique, shaped by a powerful cocktail of genetic endowment and life experiences which are culturally and socially embedded. This means that practitioners have to be able to respond to children as individuals with a unique and exclusive response to the world into which they are born and are living and growing. The skills required of adults who can respond to all children with insight, affection and expertise cannot be overestimated.

Further reading

Bruce, T. (2005a) *Early Childhood Education*. 3rd edn. London: Hodder Arnold.
This is a thoroughly practical and well-researched introductory text which shows how current understandings of child development build on from traditional approaches, and may be used to inform early childhood policy and practice during a time of radical reform in the delivery of early childhood services. The book provides a comprehensive overview of past and present understandings and looks ahead to explore how this knowledge of young children's development and learning might be incorporated into an agenda for change. It emphasises the sociocultural context in which children develop, and puts this alongside the biological aspects of child development and learning.

Bruner, J. (1960) *The Process of Education*. Cambridge, MA: Harvard University Press.

Bruner, J. (1996) *The Culture of Education*. Cambridge, MA: Harvard University Press.
Both these texts are rightly recognised as twentieth-century 'classics' and have had a direct impact on policy formation and the thinking and orientation of a wide group of teachers and scholars. In *The Process of Education* (1960) Bruner's view of children as active problem-solvers who are ready from birth to explore 'difficult' subjects challenged many of the accepted canons of educational practice. His later reflections in *The Culture of Education* (1996) show the changes in his thinking since the 1960s. He now places his work within a thorough appreciation of culture, which he sees as shaping the mind.

Piaget, J. and Inhelder, B. (1969) *The Psychology of the Child*. New York: Basic Books.
This is a seminal text that has profoundly shaped our understanding of child development. The concept of cognitive structure is central to his theory. Cognitive structures or schemas are patterns of physical or mental action that correspond to stages of child development. There are four primary development stages according to Piaget: sensorimotor, pre-operations, concrete operations and formal operations. In the sensorimotor stage (0–2 years), intelligence takes the form of motor actions. Intelligence in the pre-operation period (3–7 years) is intuitive in nature. The cognitive structure during the concrete operational stage (8–11 years) is logical but depends upon concrete referents. In the final stage, formal operations (12–15 years), thinking involves abstractions. Cognitive structures change through the processes of adaptation: assimilation and accommodation. Assimilation involves the interpretation of events in terms of existing cognitive structure whereas accommodation refers to changing the cognitive structure to make sense of the environment. Cognitive development consists of a constant effort to adapt to the environment in terms of assimilation and accommodation. In this sense, Piaget's theory is similar in nature to other constructivist perspectives of learning.

Sheridan, M.D., Sharma, A. and Cockerill, H. (2007) *From Birth to Five Years: Children's Developmental Progress*. London: Routledge.
This book is based on the pioneering work of Mary Sheridan, and has become a classic guide to the developmental progress of very young children. It is widely recognised as an invaluable reference for professionals training or working in health, education and social care. It provides charts describing key stages in the development of motor, perception, communication, play, independence and social

skills and detailed information on what we know about how children develop. Guidance is offered on ages at which children typically achieve key stages, while acknowledging individual variation in the rate of development and the influence of the child's environment. The evidence is based on an ethos of health promotion and the need for a common assessment framework.

Vygotsky, L.S. (1978) *Mind in Society*. Cambridge, MA: Harvard University Press.
Lev Vygotsky, born in the USSR in 1896, developed the social constructivist theory of learning and development. In this book he proposed that social interaction profoundly influences cognitive development. Central to Vygotsky's theory is his belief that biological and cultural development do not occur in isolation. He argued that the process of development is dependent on social interaction and that social learning actually leads to cognitive development.

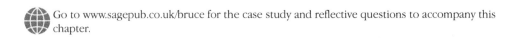 Go to www.sagepub.co.uk/bruce for the case study and reflective questions to accompany this chapter.

An Introduction to Language and Learning

Levy, S.

CASE STUDY: The role of language in the classroom

Kimberly, a first-grader in her first few weeks of school, was unable to answer questions about stories read aloud to the class. She appeared distracted during story time, and she fidgeted and played with her hands. Ms. Benjamin, the classroom teacher, decided that she had to make careful observations to informally assess the nature of Kimberly's inability to answer questions about a story read aloud to the class. The goal was to determine if Kimberly's behavior suggested developmental immaturity, inattention, impulsivity, or distractibility suggestive of an attention disorder or if she seemed to have problems understanding words, sentences, or stories read to the class, which would be suggestive of a language disorder. The teacher knew that Kimberly was a native English speaker and eliminated learning a new language as a factor in her inability to answer questions about stories. Consequently, the teacher planned to use her observations of Kimberly to create a more descriptive profile of how this child was performing. Such data can be very useful in making recommendations to the Child Study Team should a formal request for evaluation need to be made.

What might the classroom teacher do to help Kimberly respond to questions about stories read to the class? On what information and experience did you base your answer?

INTRODUCTION

Several factors play a role in children's academic success. Among them are good health, emotional well-being, and intact learning abilities (Hadley, Simmerman, Long, & Luna, 2000). In spite of the importance of all these factors, kindergarten teachers overwhelmingly report that language deficiencies are the most acute problems affecting children's school readiness (Boyer, 1991). Correspondingly, one of the major health problems reported for preschool-age children is language delay (Rescorla, 1989). The case described at the beginning of this chapter illustrates the importance of understanding how spoken language capability is vital for the development of literacy skills. For example, children must be able to attend to and understand spoken language in order to develop the skills needed in all academic areas.

New Language Rules

Within the classroom, children are exposed to new rules for using language. They must now understand the social rules for interacting with teachers and peers and must also learn to listen carefully to directions and information that relate to learning. Understanding the components of language and their impact on the academic and social functioning of students is key for classroom teachers.

Within the classroom, children are exposed to new vocabulary and rules for using language, along with learning to listen carefully to directions and information.

Observation and Intervention

Not only is spoken language the primary means of communication in the classroom, but teachers are in an optimal position to observe students' language development and level of function. In the modern classroom, a teacher must determine whether observed problems are a function of learning English as a second language; a function of a learning/behavioral challenge requiring other professionals trained to deal in these areas; or a symptom of a language disorder that requires referral, evaluation, and intervention by a speech-language pathologist. The first step for the classroom teacher is to make careful observations of the child's language or behavioral issues to understand the nature of the problem but not to affix a label to it. Once such an analysis takes place, the teacher can determine what she or he can do to address the performance or behavioral concerns and monitor how the child responds to these interventions. This process of observation and classroom-based intervention provides important data for the Child Study Team should a more formal evaluation need to be conducted relative to a child's communication development.

Chapter Concepts

To help the classroom teacher begin to understand what she or he should be monitoring regarding communication and language, the following concepts are discussed in this chapter:

- *Communication:* the exchange of information, ideas, and concepts
- *Speech:* a mechanical process involving a coordinated effort involving breathing and movement of the tongue, lips, and jaw to produce sounds
- *Language:* conveying meaning through words, signs, or written forms
- *Reading:* the process of understanding the meaning of characters/letters and words in written material
- *Writing:* the mechanical act of forming characters/letters to create meaning
- *Executive functions:* the cognitive functions that involve planning, organization, memory, and monitoring work for accuracy
- *Critical thinking:* the cognitive function that allows determining the meaning and significance of something that has been observed or read

THE COMPONENTS OF COMMUNICATION: SPEECH AND LANGUAGE

Communication is the process of exchanging information, ideas, needs, and desires (Owens, 2008). The speaker sends information (**encodes**), which the receiver of this information comprehends (**decodes**). We are able to communicate using various modalities: verbal, written, gesture, pantomime, drawing, or sign language. For verbal (spoken) communication, a speaker can convey intent (meaning) through words, sentences, or longer utterances, such as conversation or narrative (storytelling). Communication depends on speech and language.

Speech

Speech is the verbal production of meaningful sounds. The speech process involves movements of the articulators (e.g., lips, tongue, and jaw) and coordination of the muscles that move these articulators to produce sounds. (A complete description of speech skills is provided in Chapter 5.) The most important aspect of speech is that movement of the articulators results in the production of sounds that compose the language we hear—speech is the movement and language is the concepts or ideas that are expressed.

Language

Language consists of a socially shared code or conventions (set of rules) for representing **concepts** (beliefs, thoughts, and ideas) through the use of arbitrary symbols (words) as well as rule-governed combinations of those symbols in sentences (syntax). For every language in the world, there is a socially shared code that a speaker uses to represent meaning through beliefs (e.g., "I think she is coming soon"); thoughts (e.g., "I think that´s a great plan"); ideas (e.g., "Let's try to find a new way to get there"); space and time (e.g., *in front of* and *later*); and a description of things, people, and events in the environment (e.g., *objects, parties,* and *parades*). We would be unable to understand one another if this code were not shared.

As noted earlier, language involves the combination of words to form sentences (syntax). English syntax rules allow for the word order subject + verb + object (e.g., *Jane drank milk*). Other languages may use other orders, such as subject + object + verb (SOV), verb + subject + object (VSO), verb + object + subject (VOS), object + subject + verb (OSV), and object + verb + subject (OVS). This is one of the most interesting aspects of language: different rules for different language.

The importance of language in the classroom is described in the following section of this chapter and the chapters that follow in this book.

LANGUAGE AND THE CLASSROOM

The following language components are essential in children's academic development (Secord, 2002; Sotto & Prendeville, 2007): receptive language (understanding), spoken language (expression), literacy (reading and writing), social communication, and speech and phonological skills. Descriptions of these language components follow, along with examples of a child's performance in each of these components. Other essential factors for classroom success are the cognitive components, which include executive functioning and critical thinking. We begin with a discussion of receptive language, defined as the ability to understand spoken language.

Receptive Language

Receptive language consists of a child's listening skills. In the classroom, these skills involve understanding a classroom teacher's directions, instructions, and explanations. In addition, good receptive language skills allow a child to understand words, sentences, stories, and directions. Intact language requires that children understand directions that are short (e.g., "Open your books and read the first page") or long (e.g., "Get your coats, pack up your backpacks, line up at the door, and report to the gym teacher"). In the first case, children must remember two pieces of information and in the second, four. Children with receptive language difficulties frequently forget the earlier portion of directions, especially when lengthy or containing multiple steps.

Receptive language skills allow a child to understand words, sentences, stories, and directions.

Receptive language also allows a child to remember details from stories read in class by the teacher, especially in preschool and in earlier grades. These details may contain events or vocabulary items that contribute to language development and literacy. Children´s inability to respond to questions about these stories in the earlier grades allows early identification of potential language difficulties. The following vignette illustrates difficulty with lengthy directions.

Jonas was able to remember certain spoken directions (e.g., "Open your blue notebooks and find last week´s vocabulary words") but had difficulty with others (e.g., "Open your blue notebooks, find last week´s vocabulary words, and underline the words that were in the story we just read"). Note that the second example contains three pieces of information that must be remembered and understood in a particular sequence. His teacher noticed the problem and decided to express directions in shorter chunks of information. Each direction was given and followed by a pause (e.g., "Open your notebooks . . . pause . . .").

Sounds in words last only briefly after being spoken. It is in this brief time that the listener must make sense of the spoken message, analyze it, and figure out the speaker's meaning. Some children are unable to accomplish this rapid processing of the spoken signal and require additional support for their receptive language problems.

Receptive Language Problems and Solutions

Two behaviors may alert the classroom teacher to the presence of receptive language difficulties: missing longer directions and frequently asking for repetition. Children's receptive language abilities are supported when directions are shorter and repeated or when they are asked to repeat the directions to make sure they are understood. Good teaching practices should incorporate repetition of directions or asking students to recap directions to help teach listening skills. Both strategies are essential to academic success for all learners. For older children, tape recording and writing directions for homework assignments may be effective. Additional supports within the classroom are pictures on the wall to illustrate the topic at hand. These supports benefit all children within the class, not just those with receptive language difficulties.

There are also cases when children do not respond to questions because of expressive language difficulties. They understand the question but may not have the vocabulary or the knowledge to structure sentences to respond. To understand this component of language, we next examine expressive language.

Expressive Language

Expressive language consists of the ability to express ideas and needs in a meaningful manner that is understood by listeners. An essential factor in expression is the ability to convey meaning (semantics) in a manner that is understood by listeners. Another factor is the ability to sequence words in the correct order to produce sentences (syntax) and longer utterances (conversations and stories about events). Communicative interaction with others requires that a speaker express language according to certain rules (pragmatics) such as maintaining a topic or taking turns as a speaker or a listener.

Expressive Language Problems

Expressive language problems may be revealed when children cannot find the word they want to say (e.g., "It's that thing, you know") or genuinely have difficulty learning new vocabulary items. In essence, expressive language skills are illustrated by the fluent flow of ideas or concepts in a manner that is easily understood. The following vignette illustrates difficulty with this component of language. In this example, the child has difficulty expressing her ideas in a clear manner, often using fillers or empty words when responding to questions or retelling events.

It was difficult to understand what Erin wanted to say. Fillers interrupted her fluency (e.g., "and then," "uh...uh...uh..."), and empty words (e.g., "that thing") lacked meaningful reference. Her sentences were shorter and less complex than those of her classmates. Her classroom teacher noticed this problem and decided to provide props in the classroom to help her retrieve certain words. For example, pictures were placed around the room to illustrate the topic under discussion. She also asked children to draw a picture illustrating aspects of the topic at hand, thinking that this would provide rehearsal for vocabulary elements to be discussed in class. In this case, children were given the opportunity to talk about the picture they had drawn. The classroom teacher also sent home vocabulary word lists for all children to give them additional practice for words in current use in the class. The teacher made sure that vocabulary words were taught in context and not in isolation. Teaching words in context helps students remember these vocabulary items.

Expressive Language Solutions

Children with expressive language difficulties are helped when given the type of supports described above. Additional support can be supplied through intervention by a speech-language pathologist, working closely with the teacher to support academic activities in the classroom. A caution here is that teachers need to be aware of various cultural practices involving student interaction with adults. Expressive language skills are frequently a means of identifying children with language difficulties. However, some children who are learning English as a second language go through a period of silence because they are not comfortable or willing to take risks producing words or sentences in learning a new language. (This behavior is discussed in detail in Chapter 13, and additional information on second-language learning is provided in Chapter 14.)

One of the ways that expressive or oral language skills can be stimulated and taught in the classroom is through modeling. For example, the classroom teacher can talk about his or her actions when completing a task, and students can be asked to verbalize their actions. In this way, expressive language begins with a simple description of current activities. Another activity is to have students ask questions. These questions can be about an upcoming event or just something hidden in a box (e.g., "Is it round?" "Can you eat it?" "Is it alive?").

Another expressive language activity focuses on asking how things are different or what characteristics distinguish one thing from another when children are presented with two similar objects that differ in size, shape, or color. Other tasks consist of asking children to describe the scene of a story or object function (e.g., "How do we use a . . . ?"). More advanced tasks elicit expressive language by asking children questions like "What might happen next?" and "What would happen if . . . ?" It may be important to introduce the vocabulary needed to engage in the expressive language task before beginning. In summary, children talk more when they feel comfortable and when they are engaged and interested. Children who appear to have more significant difficulties may benefit from referral for additional help.

READING

Another component of language in the classroom is reading, an essential factor in academic success. The classroom teacher must keep in mind that reading depends on the earlier development of receptive and expressive language skills and that reading requires more than mere exposure to books. This exposure is essential but does not fulfill all the requirements for reading development, which begin well before children enter school.

The Foundations of Reading Skills

Emergent literacy skills are the early prereading abilities that support later literacy skills: holding a book and "pretending to read" at 2 to 3 years of age, understanding that words on the page have meaning, and understanding the connection between letters on the page and sounds that are heard. Later literacy skills consist of the ability to identify words and comprehend (understand) written materials appropriate to age and academic grade.

One of the skills essential to succeeding in reading is the ability to decode (to interpret print), especially when faced with new words. For example, in later grades, children may encounter a novel word. In this case, they use context or try to sound out the word, depending on their earlier acquisition of the correspondence of sounds with letters.

Reading Problems and Solutions

One of the signs of potential reading difficulties materializes when children avoid reading tasks.

> Rory didn't seem to enjoy reading time as much as his peers during independent reading time or when stories were read to the first-grade class. He preferred looking at books with pictures instead of books with words. He also chose the same books for reading each time, and even when a new book was added to his desk, he never opened it. The teacher noticed his lack of interest in reading materials. She decided to send books home and asked his family to engage in nightly story reading. Her goal was to familiarize Rory with the story that would be introduced to the class the following day. She thought that this might contribute to his engagement in reading tasks and his degree of comfort when asked questions about the reading materials.

In the classroom, before a book is read (to the class in younger grades or by the class in older grades), vocabulary items from the story can be placed on the board (pictures and words for younger children and words for older children). These words can be discussed even before the book is read. During the reading task, the teacher can ask questions that require responses (e.g., "Why do you think . . . ?"). After the story has been read, the teacher can ask students questions that target the children's ideas about the story (e.g., "What did you like/not like about . . . ?"). Children's interest in reading may also be developed when books are sent home to be read with family members and later read in class. Familiarity with the stories encourages children's participation when the teacher reads books or asks questions about the material. Asking children to "act out" stories is another way to encourage interest in reading. If a genuine reading problem is suspected, referral is essential to provide the early supports that will allow a child to develop good reading skills. In the case of genuine reading problems, it is appropriate to refer for specialized instruction.

WRITING

Another important language component in the classroom is writing, and reading and writing are two language skills that are closely connected. In fact, children need to learn that written text is simply someone's verbalization that was written down, and linking oral speech to written text is an important understanding. In addition, both reading and writing skills emerge from children's receptive and expressive language abilities. (See Chapters 7 and 8 for a deeper discussion of the precursors of reading skills.)

The Foundations of Writing Skills

Similar to the development of reading, emergent literacy skills later reinforce intact writing abilities. These emergent skills begin with toddlers' drawing and scribbling as they pretend to write. A broader discussion of these emergent skills can be found in Chapter 8. The language skills essential for good writing are semantics, the ability to express ideas and needs in written form; syntax, the ability to create well-formed sentences in written texts; and mechanics and organization, the ability to follow rules for letter formation, information organization, and structure. It is in grades one through three that literacy is introduced. Within the first-grade class, children will have varying levels of writing (and reading) skills. Some will need special guidance, while others can be helped with classroom strategies that enhance their skills. The following vignette describes good writing skills in the first grade.

Emily's writing was similar to that of other children in the first-grade class. Her sentences were short, and she sometimes used a combination of writing and drawing. She was able to write at least three sentences when asked to describe something that happened to her over the weekend. Her teacher noticed that other children had more difficulty expressing themselves through writing. She decided to initiate a strategy to engage children's interest in writing. She gave children an assignment to write/draw a story about a recent trip the class made to the science museum. She knew that, in the first grade, children should be given plentiful practice in using writing and drawing to express their ideas and concepts about the world. She also knew that some children would need additional tutoring to develop good writing skills.

SPEECH AND PHONOLOGICAL SKILLS

We next discuss speech and phonological skills: the vehicles for verbally expressing ideas and concepts derived from language. Both speech and phonological skills allow a child to be intelligible (understandable). Speech is the ability to produce sounds with accuracy, while phonology involves the ability to sequence sounds to produce words and longer utterances. Children with speech difficulties frequently have difficulty with certain sounds—generally *s*, *l*, or *r* sounds. Those with phonological difficulties have problems combining sounds or syllables in words. In this case, productions may consist of "wed" for *red* or "teep" for *keep*.

Sabrina has problems with speech, such as correctly producing some consonant sounds—for example, /s/ (see), /r/ (red), and /l/ (low). She also has some problems with phonology rules, producing "nana" for *banana* and "raef" for *giraffe*. At times, the kindergarten classroom teacher and Sabrina's peers cannot understand her speech.

Speech sound difficulties and phonological difficulties are typical for younger children but should be resolved by about 4 years of age. It is appropriate to refer children for speech-language pathology intervention if problems persist.

SOCIAL COMMUNICATION

The ability to follow social interaction rules for conversation and interaction allows children to interact with peers and with adults in conversation. These rules consist of eye contact, taking turns as speaker and listener, and maintaining the topic at hand. Children with social interaction difficulties often require support and training to improve the frequency and quality of their social interactions.

> Otis joined other children while they were engaged in a game. He enjoyed playing with the other children and had a number of friends in the classroom. On the other hand, Danny hung back, watching other children but seeming unsure how to enter an existing playgroup.

The Supports for Social Communication

Children with social communication difficulties can improve their interactions through observing appropriate models interacting with other children. The classroom teacher can ask children to role-play "wanting to play with another child" or "asking another child to play with you." The classroom can also be organized to encourage more interaction (a model for this goal is described in Chapter 3). Some of the strategies that target social communication include grouping children with more and less advanced social skills to provide models. Another method is to have children explain something to each other, again pairing children of unequal skill levels. Social communication difficulties can also be addressed through reading stories about children with these same difficulties and examining with the class how these difficulties are resolved in the story. Having students discuss these kinds of social problems can be a good way of increasing student awareness, especially for those students who do not experience these problems, and thereby sensitizing them to what they can do to help another student.

COGNITIVE COMPONENTS: EXECUTIVE FUNCTIONS AND CRITICAL THINKING

We follow the discussion of social communication with a discussion of the cognitive components that play a role in the classroom. These components involve the ability to understand, plan, organize, and process information. It is clear that these are essential factors in academic success. Executive functions and critical thinking are based on children's cognitive abilities. Cognitive abilities provide the ability to acquire knowledge and understand and process incoming and outgoing information.

Executive Functions

Executive functions consist of organization, initiation, planning, organization, problem solving, making changes when necessary, and/or implementing a task. Functions also consist of attention, the ability to attend to the task at hand; memory, the ability to remember spoken information; and self-regulation, the ability to stay focused on the task at hand and monitor output for accuracy. The following vignette presents an example of an executive function disorder.

> The teacher asked children in the class to complete three worksheets that involved cutting and pasting pictures and then matching them to words. The children promptly began working, first cutting out all the pictures. One of the children began a few minutes later, cutting only one picture out without pasting it or drawing a line to match it to a word. This child seemed to have no plan about how to proceed and was not able to self-monitor or know that he or she wasn't doing what the other children were doing. The teacher needed to intervene, focusing the child on the steps of the task and helping develop a plan for how to complete the assignment.

The question the teacher needs to consider is whether this behavior indicates planning problem or whether the student has difficulty recalling the directions. Determining which possibility is actually impacting the behavior can provide important insight into follow-up activities and supports. Frequently, children with executive function difficulties show poor organization, losing books and other classroom tools, and lack the ability to recognize or correct errors in work. (Additional examples of executive difficulties are presented in Chapter 6, along with classroom strategies.)

Critical Thinking

Critical thinking involves the ability to identify and gather important information, evaluate output to determine if the work is accurate, and problem-solve. The following vignette presents an example of a child who hasn't learned how to think critically about a problem.

> After reading a story to the class, the teacher asked each student to offer a solution to a problem faced by one of the characters in the story. One of the children could not come up with a solution and seemed surprised by some of the answers the other students in the class offered.

This child cannot identify the information necessary to solve a problem or propose a solution and evaluate the quality of that solution, even though he or she may have intact basic language abilities. It may be necessary to model various solutions to problems to develop critical thinking skills. In this case, all children can be involved in the process, but some time should be devoted to working with a child alone.

STRATEGIES FOR THE CLASSROOM

Language Development Across Grades

The role of the classroom teacher is to provide children with supports for their language development when needed and provide a nurturing environment for learning. Language supports for younger children are more readily available, given that early grades have pictures on the wall that portray classroom themes along with a number of other environmental supports that provide children with language cues (Bernstein & Levey, 2009). Pictures frequently act to remind children of words that they may not otherwise be able to produce from memory.

Later grades lack these environmental cues or supports, with children required to rely more on their internal language skills. In addition, classroom tasks become more complex as children encounter expository reading materials that require intact and age-appropriate language skills along with developed schemas, attention, and memory. Students also need to learn how to derive meaning from new words embedded in sentences, using context (the surrounding words) to provide the meaning of the unknown word. For students in later grades, "learning to read" is not the focus; the focus becomes "reading to learn," as concepts in science and history are presented in texts. Consequently, it is essential that classroom teachers become aware of the role that they can play in language development, in early as well as later grades.

Reading Skills

Frequently, young children are introduced to books for the first time in the classroom. Many classroom teachers are aware of the importance of print recognition as an early precursor to reading development. Children must also learn to associate the sounds they hear with the alphabet letters on the page to help them decode (interpret) words. Later reading skills require that children use their early knowledge of sound-letter association to identify unknown words in texts. Language also plays a role in mathematics, with children acquiring knowledge of the vocabulary associated with math problems (e.g., *more than, less than, dividend, multiplier*), along with the spatial terms associated with later mathematics tasks (e.g., *above, below, perpendicular, adjacent*). In addition, using words such as *because* helps them understand the connection between concepts (e.g., "He was mad because the dog stole his catcher's mitt").

Listening Skills

Teachers across all grades must continuously work to develop and maintain listening skills with respect to the teacher and peers. To ensure that listening skills are functioning optimally, students can be encouraged to repeat information. They can also be asked to elaborate on another child's productions, adding information of their own. The following strategies can help promote language learning in the classroom and support children's learning in the presence of potential language difficulties (Quale, Peters, & Matkins, 2010).

- Seat children so that all can see the classroom teacher's face.
- Monitor children's attention and pause until attention is focused on the task at hand.
- Pause to highlight important information and to capture children's attention.
- Allow children to express ideas versus lecturing or only asking them questions.
- Encourage children to ask questions and explain what is not clearly understood.
- Monitor background noise, such as noise from computers and other distractions, to enhance listening.
- Ask questions and ask children to repeat information to ensure that materials or information have been understood.

Connecting Language to Environment

Finally, the most important aspect of language and the classroom is that *language* needs to be related to the environment. Visual supports are necessary to relate spoken language to concrete examples for younger children. For both younger and older students, classroom language strategies can include reading, writing, drawing pictures, role play, and discussion to enhance learning concepts. Communication through language is the means by which the classroom teacher can identify children who may have language difficulties (Peets, 2009).

Visual supports help children associate spoken language with classroom tasks.

Additional classroom strategies in the following chapters provide teachers with methods for developing children´s language skills in the classroom.

We now return to the case study presented at the beginning of the chapter to determine the outcome of the classroom teacher's observations of Kimberly's difficulties in responding to questions about stories read in class.

CASE STUDY REVISITED

The vignette presented earlier in this chapter provided an example of a child experiencing difficulty answering questions when the teacher read books aloud to the class. The teacher planned to observe this child to determine why she could not answer such questions.

Observation of this child in different contexts was essential to determine if her language skills were better in certain situations than others. As you can see, this approach was successful in determining the basis of Kimberly's difficulties when books were read to the class.

Case Study Revisited: **The role of language in the classroom**

To determine if there was a problem with attention or focus, the teacher read a story to Kimberly in a one-to-one situation. The goal was to determine if being in a larger group setting with other children led to distraction. In the smaller group setting, she found that Kimberly was able to answer more questions about the story but still had problems providing details from the reading task. However, given leading questions (e.g., "But what happened after the little girl met the old woman on the path?"), she was able to retrieve this information. Consequently, her teacher determined that Kimberly understood the story but required help to retrieve certain details.

To improve her performance in the classroom, the teacher sent books to the child's parents each night, choosing books that she planned to read in class the next day. Kimberly's parents were encouraged to read the stories to her and discuss the events in the story. The goal was to provide Kimberly with familiarity with the story to enhance her success answering questions in the group-reading context, along with potentially improving her self-esteem. Over the next few weeks, Kimberly's performance became more consistent with that of her peers, even when the teacher introduced new books not read at home. Subsequently, she showed more engagement, less fidgeting, and provided more appropriate responses to questions. She also showed more interest in reading new books and less interest in picture books.

SUMMARY

This chapter introduced the basic components of language that are discussed in depth in the following chapters. Given that kindergarten teachers have reported that language difficulties are the main obstacle affecting children's school readiness, language is the focus of this chapter and this text. Language is the vehicle for communication within the classroom, and knowledge of its components allows the classroom teacher to identify children who may have language difficulties that may impact their learning. The basic components discussed in this chapter were:

- Communication as the means for exchanging information;
- Speech as the means for producing the sounds that comprise words;
- Language as the means for representing beliefs, thoughts, and ideas through spoken language;
- Social communication as the means for using language in interaction;
- Executive functions as the means for successful planning and monitoring work in the classroom;
- Critical thinking as the means for grasping important information.

To begin our journey into understanding language development and learning, Chapter 2 provides knowledge of the theories that underlie language development: the environmental theories of Vygotsky, Piaget, and Bates; the innateness theory of Chomsky; the emergentism theory of Bates and MacWhinney; and the Theory of Mind of Baron-Cohen and others. Chapter 2 also offers strategies to enhance language development related to these theories. As you prepare to move forward in this text, pay close attention to the role of the classroom teacher in facilitating language development.

KEY WORDS

Communication	Encode	Receptive language
Concepts	Expressive language	Speech
Decode	Language	

STUDY QUESTIONS

1. Explain the importance of decoding in the development of literacy.

2. Describe executive functions. Explain the importance of executive function difficulties in the classroom.

3. Explain the reason why the classroom teacher in the case study needed to observe Kimberly's responses to questions in other contexts.

4. Explain why empty words indicate a language disorder.

5. Describe the language disorders that would be associated with receptive language and with expressive language. How do these disorders differ?

PROJECTS

1. Observe a classroom. Make notes on how the classroom teacher interacts with the children in the class. Are there any children with speech or language difficulties? If so, make notes on how the classroom interacts with these children versus children with typical speech and language abilities.

2. Observe the interactions of children at play. Are there any children with speech difficulties? How do the other children interact with this child? Make notes on any differences between their interactions with this child and their interactions among themselves.

3. Choose five journal articles from this chapter's references. After reading your choices, write an article that compares these articles in the following manner: the main research project, the number and age of the participants, and results. In your article, describe how you would use the information you gained in your classroom.

STUDENT STUDY SITE

Visit the Student Study Site at **www.sagepub.com/levey** for these additional learning tools:

- Video Links
- Self Quizzes
- E-Flashcards

- Sample Forms and Assessment Tools
- Recommended Readings
- Web Resources

SUGGESTIONS FOR FURTHER READING

Fromkin, V., Rodman, R., & Hyams, N. (2006). *An introduction to language.* Florence, KY: Cengage.

Hall, B. J., Oyer, H. J., & Haas, W. H. (2000). *Speech, language, and hearing disorders: A guide for the teacher* (3rd ed.). Boston: Pearson.

Haynes, W. O., Moran, M. J., & Pindzola, R. H. (2005). *Communication disorders in the class.* Sudbury, MA: Jones & Bartlett.

McLaughlin, C. (2006). *Introduction to language development* (2nd ed.). Florence, KY: Cengage.

Power, B. M., & Hubbard, R. S. (2001). *Language development: A reader for teachers.* Boston: Prentice Hall.

Talking With Parents and Carers about Communication and Language Development

Whitehead, M.

All through this book there are references to children communicating, developing language and learning about literacy with parents, carers and families in a variety of local communities, home languages, cultures and traditions. This final chapter will pull together these central issues in child language development and make some suggestions for working together in children's best interests. However, this is not primarily a book about parental involvement in education and for a full background to the topic I would recommend an earlier volume in this series which is focused on Pen Green Centre for the under-fives and their families: *Learning to be Strong* (Whalley, 1994) and a study of further work with parents in the same centre, *Involving Parents in their Children's Learning* (Whalley, 2007). The role of parents and the extended family in the lives of babies and children under three is explored in detail in *Parents Matter: Supporting the Birth to Three Matters Framework* (Abbott and Langston, 2006). Practitioners who are concerned mainly with the early years of statutory schooling will still find powerful evidence and insights in *Parents and their Children's Schools* (Hughes, Wikeley and Nash, 1994). Research and legislation are now united in an awareness that children thrive in care and education settings where there is a close working relationship between home and setting (DfES, 2005a).

The focus in this chapter will be on the nature of the partnership with parents and carers; the role parents and carers play in early literacy; and ways of talking about language development for parents, carers and practitioners.

Partnership with parents and carers

Worthwhile talk about children's language development depends on a sound approach to practitioner and parent partnerships, so it is crucial that we examine our ideas about partnership.

Partners

Partners are equals, although they often have different roles and different kinds of expertise, and partners can be as unalike as any other individuals. When the partners are parents or carers and the practitioners who work with their children in a range of early years settings, there is lots of scope for misunderstanding these different roles and lots of scope for improving mutual respect and insight. We all need to understand the distinctive roles we play as parents and practitioners.

Parents and grandparents

Parents are as different as the rest of humanity and cannot be lumped together as 'the parents' – indeed, many of them are early years students, practitioners and other professionals! They bring many cultures, traditions, languages, temperaments, histories, strengths and weaknesses to their parenting roles, as we all do.

Parents are more knowledgeable about their own children than anyone else can ever be: they have a deeper emotional commitment to them and a wider background of experiences shared with them than can ever be achieved in settings which have the children for a comparatively few hours. Even when parent–child relationships are apparently poor and ineffective, they are still a potent factor, to be respected and handled with great sensitivity.

Grandparents are beginning to appear in the research literature on attachment in infancy, emotional development and early learning. It is some years since I published a lengthy case study of my grandson Dylan's very early experiences with picture books (Whitehead, 2002), but the UK Basic Skills Agency now has a Learning with Grandparents project and support materials (BSA, 2006). One small study in east London also highlights the emotional, cognitive and linguistic gains from learning to garden with grandparents (Ruby et al., 2007) and Tricia David (2006) has written sensitively about the role of grandparents as emotional buffers for young children and carriers of family intimacy and attachment styles across generations.

Parents and grandparents care about what happens to their children, now and in the future, and they are particularly concerned about what happens to them in early years care and education settings.

Practitioners

Practitioners who work with children are expert in relating to large numbers of children; they can observe them closely, manage and organise them in groups, and they develop warm professional relationships with them as individuals.

Practitioners have considerable knowledge, both practical and theoretical, about children's normal development and deviations from these norms. They understand how to engage children's interests, how to structure learning and how to provide worthwhile activities for them. The best practitioners know when to intervene and when to stand back in children's learning and investigations.

Practitioners are as individually different as parents – many of them are parents – and can be limited by their own histories, backgrounds and languages. Practitioners may have more access to, and understanding of, government legislation and the many official agencies that affect the care, education and lives of young children and their families. What are the implications for partnerships between such different and interesting people?

Clearly such diversity can only be handled successfully and in children's best interests if the partnership is open, democratic and based on consultation and respect. We have to know what our partners are doing and what their aims and aspirations are for the children who have brought us together. This means that creating effective channels of communication and sharing information will be crucial (Hurst, 1997). It is easy to give examples of the ways in which many early years settings do this, but the danger is that this can become very one-sided, with the flow of information and arrangements always coming from the professional side. Of course it is good to have family rooms on the premises, family noticeboards and newsletters, open sessions and workshops, talks and outings, and even a prominent description of the curriculum followed and the current focus for play and learning. But there must also be a more open kind of permanent invitation to parents and carers to say what they want, ask for particular activities, identify what puts them off coming to the setting, or what they find to be pointless, or even offensive. I have in mind here the occasional objection to finger-painting, or a deeply felt disapproval of children being allowed to play naked in very hot weather. Good partners respect such feelings, talk about them and explore possible compromises. This is particularly important for families who are new to a setting. Furthermore, they have a right to be fully consulted about their level of involvement in the gradual settling in of their children and about any home visits prior to their children's first attendance at the setting. Partnerships depend on mutual respect, trust, some shared goals and the acceptance of differences. These are not achieved instantly – we all have to work at being good partners.

Co-workers

In most early years settings and statutory schools, parents can be found working alongside professional practitioners. This makes for unique opportunities in partnership approaches to early years care and education, because there is nothing like hands-on involvement with groups of children alongside a colleague, to make sense of routines and curriculum activities. In these kinds of situations it is much easier for co-workers to ask each other questions, challenge assumptions, demonstrate how to do something, share their expertise and experience, or talk about ideas and anxieties. This approach deepens and broadens the idea of parental involvement so that it becomes 'a triangle of care' (Ball, 1994, p. 45) in which parents, professionals and the community work together for young children.

When we are working for children as a mixed group of parents, practitioners and multi-professionals, we learn an important lesson about education: it is social and collaborative. This is just as true for adult learning as it is for young children's learning. Every solitary scholar has a back-up team of tutors, librarians, family, friends and fellow scholars waiting to talk it all through, disagree and offer comfort. Similarly, every child in the sandpit wants someone to pretend to eat their 'pie', identify the ingredients and discuss the best method for cooking it. Parents and professional workers at the Pen Green Centre are successfully blurring many of the old 'them and us' dividing lines by taking seriously the claim that parents are their children's first educators and acting on it (Whalley, 2007). They *all* study together and share the latest child development research, keep child observation records at home and in the centre, and plan new curriculum initiatives together. Many other early years settings have begun to make similar moves towards full partnership by keeping 'open house' for families; supporting parents and very young infants in their homes with toys, books, advice and friendship; and de-mystifying early years practice by open and honest discussions about the 'whys' and the 'wherefores' of what goes on in early years settings. The rapid growth of integrated Children's Centres and extended schools is opening up many more opportunities and challenges for parental co-workers and multi-professionals to work and learn together (DfES, 2005b).

As co-workers we may also have the beginnings of an answer to the problem of finding enough practitioners of high quality to work with young children. We can create networks of learning and self-improvement. We can, for example, undertake shared action research into our own practice and seek to raise the quality of our work with young children. There are many historical precedents for this kind of self-help; perhaps we would not wish to re-create ragged schools and hedge schools, but we could take a pride in becoming paint-smeared and clay-daubed scholars and partners!

Parents, carers and early literacy

First educators

It is obvious that the great majority of parents are their children's first carers, but we now find a broad agreement that parents are also their children's first and most enduring educators. This consensus has been reached partly because of Piaget's pioneering studies of infant thinking in the earliest weeks and months of life, a period when it is parents, or other primary carers, who create the child's environment and the resulting stimulus for the rapid development of the brain. Modern brain studies (neuroscience) have strengthened these earlier theories by confirming that the brain literally changes as it is exposed to social and cultural experiences in the earliest months and years of childhood (Bruce, 2000; Blakemore and Frith, 2005). Linked to this evidence for the continuity of human learning from birth are the powerful modern studies of babies' sociability, and their ability to share feelings and states of mind in partnership with their parents and carers (Trevarthan, 1993; 2002). Another piece of evidence for learning with parents and carers is the everyday but stunning achievements of almost every baby: learning to communicate, talk, use narratives and become aware of marks and print. These achievements have been discussed in detail in this book and the point to be made here is that the role of parents in early learning, particularly language learning, is the foundation of all later educational success.

Many parents, across all social and economic classes, are very active in their role as first educators of their young children. Research in several cultures (David et al., 2000) has demonstrated that they talk in stimulating and challenging ways to their children; introduce them to second and third languages and written systems; share books, songs, stories and jokes with them; teach them to play card games, make cakes, count and identify letters; and keep them supplied with markers and scrap paper (Wells, 1981; Tizard and Hughes, 1984; Pen Green/SureStart, 2003). This evidence that parents teach their children has not always been welcomed and developed in early years settings. However, when professional practitioners have invited families to take an active part in monitoring and supporting their children's cognitive developments the outcomes for children, parents and practitioners have been very positive (Athey, 2007; Nutbrown, Hannon and Morgan, 2005). In no area has this been more fully developed than in early literacy and the claim that 'literacy goes to school' (Weinberger, 1996) is now widely acknowledged.

Babies and books

Perhaps there have always been 'bookish' families who share books with their babies (White, 1954; Butler, 1979), but in recent years there have been some determined efforts to help many more parents and grandparents do this (Figure 18). One of the most well-planned and carefully evaluated was the *Bookstart* pilot project in Birmingham which involved the city's library services and the South Birmingham Health Authority. *Bookstart* packs containing a book, a poetry card, a poster, an invitation to join the local library and information were given free to 300 parents/carers of nine-month-old babies in three areas of the city by the local health visitors. The project covered a wide ethnic and social-economic cross-section of the city and the families were asked to complete questionnaires at the start of the project and six months later. The evidence from the parents was that sharing books with baby spilled over into an enthusiastic sharing of books with all the family, including toddlers, older children and adults. In some families it also sparked off, or renewed, an interest in joining the public library and even buying books. The *Bookstart* scheme has now been extended to many parts of the UK and librarians and families report the same enthusiasm for sharing books, buying books and joining libraries. The evaluators of the Birmingham pilot study draw our attention to its significance by pointing out that it is about more than early reading and school achievement, or even combating adult illiteracy and crime:

> *Books are sources of shared and repeated pleasure, of insight and new knowledge and of new possibilities for living.*
>
> (Wade and Moore, 1993a)

The ongoing monitoring of *Bookstart* revealed that at eight years old the original *Bookstart* babies had increased their initial gains in literacy throughout the early years of schooling. They also demonstrated sustained high achievements in reading, mathematics and scientific thinking at the end of Key Stage 1 (age seven). The researchers conclude that their findings affirm the central role of parents and carers in educating children in the pre-school years and that *Book-*

start is a cost-effective way of ensuring a confident start at school and continuing higher standards through the primary years (Wade and Moore, 2000). This project has gained international recognition, for example, the Better Beginnings project (Rohl and Barratt-Pugh, 2006) in Western Australia supports parents from diverse communities in their role as a child's first teacher of communication and literacy.

Figure 18   Reading for pleasure, Dylan (17 months) with Grandad

Charting early literacy

Increased knowledge about the emergence of literacy (Hall, 1987; David et al., 2000) in the earliest years of childhood has aroused a great deal of interest in the part played in the process by families, communities and cultural beliefs and activities. One powerful example of involving families on a full partnership basis is the Sheffield Early Literacy Development Project, 'Raising Early Achievement in Literacy' (REAL) (Hannon, Nutbrown and Morgan, 2005). The approach of the researchers was based on asking families to share with them the ways in which they already helped their young children to get into literacy. Not surprisingly the parents talked about looking at labels on tins and in shops, writing notes together, looking at books and making words from alphabet spaghetti (Nutbrown, 2006, p. 88)! In return the researchers helped the parents to link their existing good practices to the broad patterns of language development and some major aspects of early literacy: environmental print, books, early writing and oral language. They also provided families with a literacy progress chart. This was designed as a sheet of interlocking jigsaw shapes, each of which named an achievement that could be coloured in by a parent or carer once it was noted. The chart covered looking at environmental print, beginning to write and sharing books; it provided a record of progress, from making marks to writing own name, or from telling stories about the pictures in a book to recognising the name on a food wrapper. The project also gives families separate jigsaw sheets for recording developments around environmental print, books and early writing (Nutbown and Hannon, 1997).

This research noted that parents supported early literacy in four ways: they provided *opportunities* for literacy for their children; they *recognised* their children's efforts as readers and writers; they shared enjoyable *interactions* around literacy with their children, and they were *models* of what it means to be literacy makers and users. Similar findings emerged when the parents of children from several different language communities brought examples of everyday literacy into the nursery and reception classes of a London school (Kenner, 2000; 2005) and created relevant multilingual learning materials and contexts for their children. Without this kind of literacy home–school partnership, young bilinguals often find the transition to early years settings and reception classes confusing and their powerful language and thinking resources remain unused as they struggle to make sense of these strange new worlds (Gregory, 2007; Brooker, 2002; Drury, 2006).

Reading at home

The previous examples have been focused on babies and children under five, but perhaps the largest number of projects about parents and literacy are concerned with reading in the early stages of primary school. There are many ways of doing this (Wolfendale and Topping, 1996), but some consistent attempts to ask parents to hear children read at home and share books with their children are made by most infant/primary schools. The sight of young children taking their 'book-bags' home each afternoon is now a part of the national scene, as is the classroom morning session of 'changing' books and handing teacher a parental comment card on home reading progress. These important partnerships in reading have a common ancestor in the research in Haringey in the 1970s which indicated that reading at home with parents was more effective in improving children's reading progress than any other kind of school support (Hewison and Tizard, 1980). Research continues to indicate that pre-school literacy experiences and long-term parental interest and involvement in children's reading at home, combined with genuine consultation between teachers and parents/carers about school-based help such as Reading Recovery (Wade and Moore, 1993b), make all the difference to progress in reading. However, common sense and sensitivity is required here as it would be disastrous if parents felt pressured into doing 'teachery' things like phonic drills and 'sound blending', instead of having fun with stories, rhymes, messages and books.

The storysacks approach has already been outlined in Chapter 4, but it should not be forgotten that the aim of the approach is to involve parents and local communities in the making of the sacks and their contents, the organisation of storysack lending libraries and, above all, in reading at home for pleasure with their children. There is a high level of play and pleasure potential in the storysacks approach and there is also considerable learning about language and literacy. Storysacks usually contain parent prompt cards, an example of which is shown in Figure 19. Cards like this enable parents to talk about books and language with their children in a relaxed and enjoyable way.

Talking about communication and language development

Finding the right form of language in which practitioners, parents and professionals can talk together about children's language development is a continuing challenge. It has been one of the main difficulties of writing this book and the problem it has set remains. How do we use straightforward language and yet do justice to the complexity of individual language development in the years before eight? There does not appear to be an easy answer, but we have to keep on talking.

Our children's language

About communicating, talking and listening

We are all conversational partners for our children. We are all models for our children of how to use language. The daily caring, talking, playing and routine

PARENT PROMPT CARD

Where The Wild Things Are, **by Maurice Sendak**

Understanding the story

1. Why was Max sent to bed without eating anything?

2. What happened in Max's room?

3. How did Max get to the place where the wild things are?

4. What did Max and the wild things do?

5. What did Max find when he got back to his very own room?

Illustrations

1. Which is your favourite picture? Can you tell me why?

2. Find a picture with a little white dog. What do you think is happening?

3. What colour is Max's boat? What colour are the sails? What is the name of the boat?

4. Find a picture of a tent. Where is Max? How do you think Max feels?

Figure 19a A parent prompt card from a storysack

Letter fun

1. How many names do you know that start with 'M' ?

2. Can you say this chant with me?

   'Wicked, wobbly, wild old things,
   Wearing wigs and woolly whiskers'

   Now say it as fast as you can!

Word fun

1. Think of any words that rhyme with 'still' .

2. Tell me what your favourite wild thing looks like.

3. What do you think 'terrible' means?

Other activities

1. Paint or draw a picture of your favourite wild thing.

2. Make up a wild rumpus dance.

3. Dress up as a king or queen.
   Do you know any rhymes about kings and queens?

Figure 19b

reading and writing we do with our children shapes their language development and their thinking.

Our babies communicate with us long before they talk – they do it from birth. They get in touch by gazing at us, making faces at us and by moving their hands, arms, legs and toes in response to our attention and our voices. We become skilled at listening to our babies and watching them closely. This helps us to get to know them and interpret their messages and their meanings; it helps us to share our lives and activities with them. Our babies become talkers by communicating without words and by constantly watching and listening to all that goes on around them.

We tend to share our conversations and little stories about the ups and downs of daily life with wakeful and attentive babies and toddlers. We even expect responses from them. So we look at them, pause in our talk and give them time to find the appropriate sounds or words. Later, we tell them the words they ask for or seem to need, and we repeat important words or phrases frequently. We really make it possible for them to give names to their world and talk about it.

Our children begin by talking about the people they know, the events of their days, their own feelings, the food they eat, their toys, animals and family pets, and their own feelings and ideas about things. These topics of conversation remain very important all our lives and our children learn to talk about them by telling stories. Their conversations with us are full of little tales about falling down, losing things, meeting people, seeing animals or cars, feeling frightened or finding something interesting. These are everyday stories of 'what happened and how I feel about it'; they are not very different from the stories in family reminiscences, television 'soaps', novels and myths.

There are many people who worry that television, digital versatile discs (DVDs) and video have changed all this talking between children and carers. On the positive side, we know that television is an important part of all our lives and our children grow up with it. They learn an enormous amount about the wider world beyond their homes and they hear a wide range of languages, voices, accents and plenty of standard English on it. However, it is still a one-way kind of communication in most homes and we should think about trying to watch as much as possible with our babies and young children. We can talk to them about what they have watched and even try to follow up some programmes by drawing and making things, dressing up, going on visits, finding books, singing songs, repeating rhymes and poems, doing some cooking or dancing round the room!

Television can be an excellent child 'minder' and entertainer, although too much sitting and watching is not healthy in terms of children's physical development and their need for frequent exercise. But any potential threat to very young children's language development is only likely to materialise if watching television totally takes the place of playing, helping and talking between young children and caring adults – and older children.

About writing and reading

It is not an exaggeration to say that learning to become a writer and a reader depends on already being a talker and listener (or a signer if deaf), and a gossip and storyteller. It also depends on finding out what is involved in writing and reading.

So, once again it is clear that children's first literacy teachers are their parents and families, followed by their surroundings and communities. We demonstrate writing for our children every time we scribble a shopping list, sign a document or fill in a form. We demonstrate reading for them every time we open a letter, read the instructions on a food package or flick through a newspaper. And these are only the most basic examples of daily literacy. Surroundings and communities swamp all of us with examples of what print looks like and how it works. Everywhere we take our children we can find exciting, free reading materials to point out, talk about and play with: from leaflets and carrier bags to road names and advertising posters. And we should not forget to talk about 'reading' the meanings of colour signs like traffic lights, the symbols on road signs, and familiar logos in supermarkets and fast-food restaurants.

But our babies and toddlers do not just wait to be taught, so let us think about them, in a sense, as their own best teachers. They show us what they have noticed and what they are interested in every day and they can teach us a thing or two about becoming literate in any language.

What are the signs that our very young children are starting to write and read the languages of our homes and communities?

They will show some interest in print and notice it everywhere, including: letters, numbers, the writing on clothes labels, in shops and on buses. They point to print and ask about it.

They will try to make print-like marks when they are drawing and painting, or using raw pastry or plasticine, or writing with their fingers on steamed-up windows and in spilt drinks or food! One little girl was filmed making elaborate patterns with a broom and a small brush as she swept a large pile of dry sand in the nursery garden (Figures 20 and 21).

Figures 20 and 21 Creating patterns in dry sand (four years)

They may ask us for help and advice, saying: 'Read that letter to me', 'What does that say?' 'Can I write something?' They will almost certainly want endless supplies of paper scraps, notepads, felt pens, biros, pencils, paints, chalks and crayons. And they will love plastic and magnetic letters, or rubber letter and date stamps and ink pads. With these materials they will be keen to write 'pretend' lists, letters, cards, labels, invitations and little books.

They will really enjoy owning and borrowing picture books, story books, information books and, even, mail-order catalogues. They will often show great affection for the books, or the pictures and characters in them, sometimes stroking the pages lovingly. These favourites are frequently hidden in special places or taken everywhere – to the potty or lavatory, to bed, or into the child's own preferred hidey-hole like a cupboard or under a table. Of course our children will ask us, or other special people, to read these precious books to them and we might have to struggle if it is a seed catalogue or a car handbook!

Our young children will be fascinated by listening to people and will tune in immediately to stories, jokes, gossip, poems, common sayings, songs and rhymes. They will also ask for some of these to be repeated again and again. They will insist on listening to favourite stories and books repeatedly and soon know them 'off by heart' and begin to join in with repetitive or amusing bits. They may also talk about favourite characters and their adventures, and some children will act out, dress up as, or draw and 'write' these stories.

They will certainly play and have fun with languages, especially with rhymes, nonsense, songs, tongue-twisters, brand names, advertising slogans and any rude words they come across. They will love dancing and twirling around at any time or place, as well as singing, stamping and clapping rhythmically, and taking part in traditional games, pastimes and rituals such as parties, carnivals, festivals and religious ceremonies. Mobile phones are now a significant part of many cultures and young children's play and talk also reflects this fact, as I observed when my 22-month-old grandson, Mattias, held a LEGO wheel base to his ear and had an intense conversation as he wandered in and out of the garden.

They will begin to recognise and name some letters, particularly the initial letters of their own name, or letters in the names of family, friends, favourite sweets, drinks and food, or popular television programmes. This will mean that they know quite a number of letter names and some of their usual 'sounds', so it is a good idea to start looking at really attractive alphabet books, as well as making home-made ones for fun. This can be started by cutting letters from magazines and leaflets and sticking them in scrap books, or on scrap paper.

They will begin to write their name, or special mark, on their books, drawings and other property and cover sheets of paper or the margins of newspapers and the covers of magazines with what almost looks like writing. There will probably be identifiable letters, or numbers, or even the child's name among these important scribbles. At this point, many children ask adults and older children to write down names and brief stories for them and clearly enjoy this chance to dictate to a helpful secretary.

What difference will compulsory school make?

In one sense it should not make much difference, because all that has gone on and just been described here is the very best kind of language and literacy development. Teachers should be planning to continue and build on all the good things that have gone on in homes, early childhood centres, playgroups and nursery settings. They will also be extending what we as parents, carers and early years professionals have begun with our children. The influence of the Early Years Foundation Stage in England should continue to ensure that many young children in the reception classes of schools experience an appropriate early years curriculum. The underlying principles of such a curriculum emphasise the need for sustained play opportunities, informal teaching styles and adequate outdoor space in which a rich hands-on curriculum can be experienced.

Teachers and teaching assistants should still be setting up classrooms with ample opportunities and materials for talking, drawing, reading and writing. They will aim to show children all the many uses of literacy and find enjoyable ways of presenting them with the need to read and write every day. One of their top priorities will be to inspire children with a love of stories, poetry and books: they may tell us that they want our children to be 'hooked on books'!

Teachers will be good listeners, tireless secretaries and enthusiastic publishers. They will always be willing to write for our children, listen to them read and tell stories, and make attractive books with them. This is where they may ask for our help as occasional classroom listeners, readers and secretaries to the children. One enthusiastic teacher with more than 30 children can almost work miracles, but parents and teaching assistants working alongside teachers can definitely transform children's lives.

Teachers will introduce our children to computers and word-processing programs, not just for speed and smart copy, but as one way of teaching them more about how the written forms of language work. Teachers will emphasise the spelling, grammar and punctuation of written standard English, but only as our children become more confident and enthusiastic as writers. However, children who do not use English in their homes and communities should be supported and helped in their first language in school, if at all possible, while they develop some level of bilingualism. Talking, reading and writing in their home languages are central to children's thinking and self-respect and should be encouraged in every way possible. Furthermore, this actually helps with the development of fluency and literacy in English.

Most experienced teachers are unlikely to believe that there is only one way to teach reading that will work for every child, despite the changes to the literacy strategy in England. This is because reading is a very complicated mix of thinking skills and experience. Consequently, teachers of reading prefer some carefully planned mixing and matching of methods. They do introduce children to the sounds of letters and groups of letters like 'th', 'ch' and 'ing' as children's confidence with reading and sharing books increases. Plenty of experience with everyday print and books is essential because children need to recognise instantly many English words that cannot be sounded out and blended. Just imagine trying to sound out 'said', 'thought' or 'night'! As a reader of words like this you are also helped enormously by the sentence or situation in which you meet the word. This is a warning to all of us to let children read interesting material and not just meaningless lists of words or phonically regular nonsense. The most important help for our children comes from having a good idea of what a whole book or story is about, what the pictures are suggesting, and what is likely to happen. So, do not restrict your children's reading at home to phonics 'books', worksheets and schemes.

It is now absolutely clear that if parents and carers share books with their children at home they make a huge contribution to their success at reading. When teachers hear children read at school they have a different responsibility. They must keep careful notes about how our children use clues such as the whole context of the book, the pictures, the meaning and sense of words, their knowledge of sounds and ability to sound out unknown words, and their ability to go back and correct themselves. This is how teachers have always assessed children's reading development and decided what help and what kind of reading our children need next. Reading from a 'reading scheme' or phonics book is only one way of assessing reading progress and these books do not actually 'teach' reading. Children have to learn about print and books for themselves and many will find the process slow and boring if they only meet school scheme books.

The best cure for some problems in the early years of reading is to return to all the approaches used before compulsory schooling in order to rebuild a child's confidence and enjoyment of books and print. Go on sharing books and writing together as much as possible; struggling, uninterested readers need more books, more stories and lots more being read to. Most of all they need to know that someone who loves them believes in them totally and knows that one day they will be a reader.

We cannot separate communication and language development from the rest of our lives and teach them separately to our children. What children do successfully with language, they do as part and parcel of doing really important things. Things like telling us about their quarrels; shrugging, gesturing and pulling faces; celebrating their good times; reading their names on labels; or writing a message of kisses on a letter to a far-away grandparent. Throughout our lives language development is bound up with just being ourselves.

The Primacy of Relationships in the Early School Years

Daniels, D.H. and Clarkson, P. K.

> ### *Window Into Practice*
>
> *Brandi had been a preschool teacher for over 10 years. She had been teaching in the PreK program for most of that time. The preschool's philosophy and mission statement reflected a desire to partner with parents in the education and development of their children. Parent conferences were held once a year and most parents participated. In addition, the preschool holiday programs and graduation ceremonies were well-attended by parents, grandparents, and neighbors. As a teacher, Brandi made sure that she wrote notes about potential issues and problems with children, many times speaking to parents in person at drop-off or pick-up times. Brandi felt good about her efforts to maintain a partnership with the parents of the children in her class, and she felt that parents were generally happy with her communication as well. Much to Brandi's surprise, a parent survey revealed otherwise. Several parents reported that although they felt their children*

were in a nurturing environment, there was something lacking in the communication and sense of "partnership" between the parents and the teachers. In the survey, parents noted that they missed some of their children's developmental milestones during school hours. The preschool staff had made efforts to communicate through all of the major events, but there was a lack of communication regarding daily activities in children's lives that were important to parents. One parent described her feelings as trying to watch your child in a championship game through a small hole in a wooden fence. Her view of her child was narrow and limited to the scope of the hole (i.e., holiday programs, conferences, infrequent small talks with the teacher).

Brandi, along with several of her colleagues, reflected on these comments and reevaluated their efforts for parent involvement. One of their conclusions was that the "involvement" had been only one way (teacher to parent) and that they had not really considered what channels of communication parents would prefer, what information parents would desire, and how they could foster a true partnership of two-way communication. Together with her colleagues, Brandi drafted another parent survey to ask more questions. After reading the responses, teachers made some changes in their practice of "partnership." Expanding the analogy of the "hole in the fence view," the teachers drafted activities that would create a "chain-linked fence view" for parents. This open fence would provide a view for parents which not only visually represented more of the whole game (children's daily experiences and milestones), but it would also allow parents to participate at their level of availability and comfort. The practical activities and practices Brandi and her colleagues collected included a wide variety of communication avenues. The teachers planned to provide digital pictures of individual children engaged in specific activities that could be used to tell parents a "story" about their child's day or skill development. Digital recordings of children's voices could also be used to narrate some of the thoughts about the event. This would help parents "feel like they were there" and experience school with their children. E-mail could also provide positive home interactions between parents and children about school and learning. Next, the teachers decided to personally call parents at home once a quarter to check in, offer support, and convey positive aspects of their child's growth and development. This would help alleviate the notion that phone calls home are "always about negative behavior." It would also help to get to know children better. The next plan was to use "Skype" with parents who had access to a computer webcam; parents could view and converse with their child in "real time" during the day, possibly taking part in a special party or activity as it was happening. For families with limited access to computers, teachers decided to produce photographs of children and brief descriptions of their daily activities. Brandi and her colleagues committed to following through with these ideas for the next 6 months and then reevaluate their effectiveness by taking another survey of parents' feelings about their involvement and communication.

Brandi employed traditional parental involvement methods that needed improvement. Parent surveys revealed gaps in communication and involvement that inspired teachers to develop specific action plans for improvement. Studies show that parental involvement encourages children's positive attitudes toward school, greater motivation to learn, and enhanced learning. Parental involvement activities are most effective when complemented by a true "partnership" relationship between teacher and parent, which also serve to improve teacher-child relationships.

This chapter focuses on the development of positive relationships or partnerships in the early years of school that are vital for children's adjustment, learning, and achievement. We begin with arguments made by major developmental psychologists and educators for this perspective and approach to school reform. We then point to research documenting the importance of relationships between (a) teachers and children, (b) children and their peers, and (c) teachers and parents. Furthermore, we note how children's relationships with teachers, parents, and peers influence one another (see Figure 3.1). Within each of these sections, we make recommendations for promoting positive relationships and partnerships based on research. These relationships provide the foundation for establishing positive classroom climates discussed further in the next chapter. Finally, we return to suggestions for fostering home-school connections and parental involvement in school.

SCHOOL REFORM MODELS

Fostering Positive Relationships Is Key

From contemporary developmental perspectives, relationships in school not only matter because they influence children's adjustment and learning, the quality of these relationships may be *the* best indicator of later school success

The simple idea here is that children cannot learn well unless they feel secure in their environment, and these feelings stem from their relationships with others.

Figure 3.1 Relationships in School

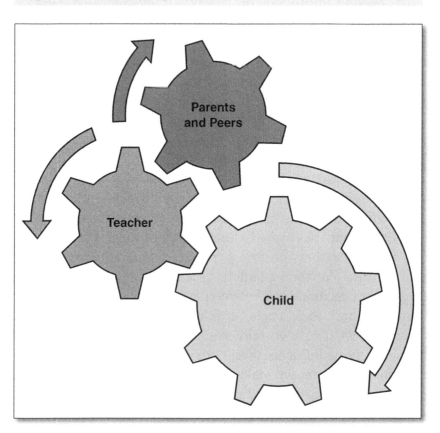

and well-being (Rimm-Kaufman & Pianta, 2000). Relationships between teachers and children, children and children, and teachers and parents may become patterned in the early years and affect later relationships, thus placing children on stable pathways through school. Thus, it is imperative to create quality relationships that direct children toward positive pathways. This focus on relationships is the motto of successful school reform efforts, such as the School Development Program, inspired by child psychiatrist, James Comer (2004). He argued that "good relationships make student, adult, and organizational development possible, which, in turn, makes a strong academic focus possible" (p. xiv). The development of relationship skills in schools is also central in other major organizational efforts to improve schools through research-to-practice connections, such as the Collaborative for Academic, Social, and Emotional Learning (CASEL), the National Association for the Education of Young Children (NAEYC), and the APA Center for Psychology in Schools and Education (CPSE) and promotion of learner-centered practices for school reform (e.g., Lambert & McCombs, 1998). Information about programs and organizations committed to creating caring relationships in schools is provided in Resources. These school reformers intentionally respond to children's basic needs for relatedness, as well as for autonomy and competence, based on psychological theories and research (e.g., Ryan & Deci, 2000). The simple idea here is that children cannot learn well unless they feel secure in their environment, and these feelings stem from their relationships with others.

TEACHER-CHILD RELATIONSHIPS

Teacher-child relationships play a formative role in children's self-regulation and academic skills in the early years of school (Pianta, 1999, 2004) and continue to forecast their later adjustment and achievement through eighth grade (Hamre & Pianta, 2001). Although children's earlier relationships with caregivers and regulatory skills (Valiente et al., 2008) may make forming positive relationships with them more or less challenging, studies suggest that sensitive, involved teachers can overcome difficulties and make a profound difference in redirecting children toward positive trajectories through school (NICHD ECCRN, 2005). Sensitive teachers are those that provide emotional support for children; they are adults to count on for understanding and guidance. Teacher-child relationships can be described in terms of their *affection* (i.e., how much the teacher likes and enjoys the child), *attunement* (i.e., the extent to which the teacher understands, sympathizes with, and knows the child), and *dependability* (i.e., the teacher's availability when needed; Skinner & Belmont, 1993). Research indicates that many teachers in the United States have positive relationships with children in their classrooms, and some do not.

The quality of teacher-child relationships can also be characterized in the following ways (sample items from the

Student-Teacher Relationship Scale are included in parentheses; Pianta, 1999):

- *Close.* Teacher and child share a warm relationship, openly communicate about personal items, appear comfortable with appropriate dependency, and display positive affect. (For example, "I share an affectionate, warm relationship with this child"; "If upset, this child will seek comfort from me"; "This child spontaneously shares information about himself/herself.")
- *Conflicted.* Teacher and child are often angry and at odds with each other, little warmth and personal communication is displayed, and they appear to be disconnected. Teachers often feel troubled by their inability to "reach" these children. (For example, "This child easily becomes angry at me"; "This child and I always seem to be struggling with each other.")
- *Dependent.* Child "clings" to teacher and asks for help when unnecessary; interactions with teacher are often emotionally negative. (For example, "This child reacts strongly to separation from me"; "This child is overly dependent on me.")

Of course, relationships can also be described in other ways, including "mixes" of the characteristics described earlier. As noted in Chapter 2, children with aggressive tendencies are prone to having **conflicted relationships,** and children with shyness tendencies are prone to having **dependent relationships** with teachers. It is no surprise that children with closer relationships with teachers fare better in school than children with negative relationships marked by conflict or overdependency. For example, Birch and Ladd (1997) found that children who shared a **close relationship** with their teacher demonstrated greater academic performance, school attitudes, and engagement in school activities (i.e., self-directed learning, cooperative participation) than children experiencing conflict or dependency. Researchers assume that close relationships provide children with felt security and positive feelings to boost their learning and confidence, allowing them to pursue further challenges.

Children's relationships with teachers may be patterned after their earlier relationships with caregivers (e.g., Pianta, 2004); thus, children with secure relationships may expect and elicit positive responses from other adults that serve to perpetuate close relationships, and children with prior insecure relationships may be more likely to expect and evoke negative responses which perpetuate dependent or conflicted relationships. Fortunately, teachers can circumvent negative cycles, but it may not be easy. Studies have shown that negative relationships with teachers in the earlier grades are sometimes perpetuated at the next grade level (Howes, Phillipsen, & Peisner-Feinberg, 2000). Consistent with **attachment theory** formulated by John Bowlby (1969), Howes and her colleagues proposed that children form mental or **working models** of relationships with earlier teachers that may lead them to expect future teachers to be positive (i.e., trustworthy, helpful) or negative; thus, they behave in ways that fulfill their expectations (Howes, Hamilton, & Phillipsen, 1998). The goal is to help children become appropriately dependent; this takes patience and perseverance. When children have not developed a sense of trust, they might test teachers' intentions many times. Because they also may not have developed age-appropriate social and emotional competencies in earlier relationships, they might display more emotional outbursts and harm others, making it even more difficult for teachers to like them.

Teachers can reflect on their relationships with individual children by asking themselves some of the questions researchers ask to characterize teacher-child relationships. For example, Table 3.1 includes sample questions from the Teacher Relationship Interview (TRI) developed by Pianta and his colleagues. Researchers consider themes as well as the affective tone of responses.

Pianta (1999) and other developmental psychologists provide several recommendations for enhancing relationships between teachers and children in the early grades. First, as we discussed in Chapter 2, it is important to encourage emotional

Table 3.1   Sample Questions From the Teacher Relationship
Interview

1. Choose three words that describe your relationship with _____ *child's name.*
For each word, tell me a specific experience or time that describes that word.
2. Tell me about a specific time you can think of when you and ___ "clicked."
How did you feel? How do you think _____ felt?
3. Tell me about a specific time you can think of when you and ____ really weren't "clicking."
4. What gives you the most satisfaction being _____'s teacher? Why?
5. Every teacher has at least occasional doubts about whether s/he is meeting a child's needs. What brings this up for you and ____? How do you handle these doubts?
6. What is your relationship like with _____'s family?

(Select items adapted from the Teacher Relationship Interview, Pianta, 1999.)

regulation. Second, it is important to organize the classroom schedule and activities to allow regular contact between the teacher and individual children, as well as design systems to prevent misbehavior (see Chapter 4). The value of having stable, predictable, and pleasant contacts between children and particular teachers cannot be overstated. Another recommendation is to implement a "Banking Time" intervention. This intervention is based on the notion that children must receive attention on an unconditional basis from the teacher. In other words, time needs to be built into the day so that the teacher can attend to each child. At the classroom level, teachers can arrange brief periods (e.g., 10 minutes) of Banking Time with small groups while engaged in child-chosen activities. Activities might include board games, arts and crafts, and interesting projects taken from the academic curriculum. Using this approach, a teacher can spend time with five or six children at a time, rotating groups so that during the course of a typical week, the teacher might be involved with each child two to three times. The following Banking Time principles apply: (a) Children are told that the time is theirs to do what they wish; teachers follow and participate as children direct; (b) the sessions occur on a predictable basis, and participation is *not* contingent on children's behavior; (c) the teacher is neutral and objective and does not focus on children's performance or skills; (d) the teacher draws attention to a few relationship messages (e.g., "I accept you," "You are important," "I am available," "I am consistent," "I am helpful when asked"). These messages convey the teacher as ". . . a helper, a person who is unconditionally available and predictable, a source of safety and comfort, and a resource for problem solving . . . common to most child-teacher relationships" (Pianta, 1999, p. 141). With consistent implementation over time, such messages will convey the experienced teacher-child relationship and override situational stressors.

Perhaps most important for reducing negative interactions with children, teachers need to reflect on their own beliefs and feelings. They should try to avoid a "within child" view of their relationships with children (Erikson & Pianta, 1989). This means that instead of thinking of children as "aloof," "clingy," or "mean," consider

Teachers also need to consider how they might inadvertently be perpetuating negative relationships with some children.

how children may have developed ways of interacting with others that need reworking in new relationships. Teachers also need to consider how they might inadvertently be perpetuating negative relationships with some children. Such awareness may involve reflecting on how their own earlier relationships impact their interactions with children. A few studies indicate that teachers with secure relationships (i.e., with their own parents) view their relationships with children more positively than those with less secure relationships (e.g., Pianta, 2004). Teachers also need to attend to their current emotional experiences as well, such as stress (see previous chapter) and depression (Hamre & Pianta, 2004), and look for means of support for themselves.

Creating a supportive context for teachers to support children's development is a cornerstone of Comer's School Development Program (SDP) implemented in schools across the country (Comer, 2004). In this program, social problems in the classroom are sometimes solved with the assistance of helping professionals in a school (e.g., social workers, special educator teachers, other health professionals) on the Student and Staff Support Team. One of the key operating principles of this team is "no-fault" problem solving: neither the child nor the teacher are blamed for problematic interactions; instead, adults in the school focus on how to solve the problem together. Teachers feel supported in this positive school climate and thus are better able to deal positively and effectively with children. Some SDP teams have decided to implement a looping system in their schools so that after teachers have worked hard to establish positive relationships with children, they can benefit for another year together. Sustaining positive teacher-child relationships for several years has also been a major reason for instituting multigrade classrooms where team-teachers stay with the same group of children for 2 or more years. Other model programs for meeting teacher as well as student needs are described in Resources.

Simple survey questions have been developed for primary-grade children to assess their perspectives of relationships in the classroom, including with their teacher, such as in the K–3 Assessment of Learner-Centered Practices (ALCP; McCombs et al., 2008). Children's views of the extent to which their teacher created positive interpersonal relationships in the classroom were related to their perceptions of competence and interests in school learning. Importantly, children's views were more powerful than teachers' reports of classroom practices in predicting their motivation. Sample items from the ALCP are shown in Table 3.2. In professional

Table 3.2   Interpersonal Relations in the Classroom: Sample
Items From the K–3 Student Assessment of
Learner-Centered Practices (ALCP)

My teacher likes me.	
My teacher makes me feel like I am part of the class.	
My teacher helps me feel good about myself.	
My teacher helps me get along with the other kids in my class.	

(Adapted from McCombs, Daniels, & Perry, 2008.)

development programs, children's views (as a group) can be shared with teachers in efforts to promote their awareness and understanding of how their practices influence children.

Note that the last item on the table involves how teachers help children get along with one another. This is a very important feature of teacher-child relationships, and it is the focus of the next section.

Before moving onward, we highlight suggestions made so far for promoting positive teacher-child relationships:

- Reflect on individual relationships with children. Attend to those that may not yet be close or positive.
- Help children develop emotional regulation skills so that they are better able to form positive interpersonal relations with others, including teachers.
- Create frequent opportunities in classroom routines for positive teacher-child interactions that children can anticipate and count on.
- Ensure that individual children have regular "unconditional" opportunities to develop positive relationships with a stable teacher (employ "Banking Time").
- Consider how previous relationships or stressors affect relationships with children. Obtain support from mentors or other school professionals when needed.

Stipek (2002) added the following suggestions to foster positive relationships:

- Respect and value children as human beings; take their ideas seriously and show interest in their personal lives outside school.
- Expect positive behavior and work from children; hold them to developmentally appropriate standards.
- Ensure that children are not humiliated; avoid embarrassing or making sarcastic remarks about them (young children are likely to take remarks literally).
- Let children know that there is no risk of disapproval or rejection when they do poorly on their work; praise children when they attempt challenging tasks, even when they fail.

Positive teacher-child relationships also appear to be fostered in classrooms with developmentally appropriate practices (DAP or child/learner-centered; see Chapter 4). Stipek and her colleagues (e.g., Stipek et al., 1998; Stipek et al., 1995) found that teachers were more warm, nurturing, and attentive to individual children's needs in child-centered classrooms than in teacher-centered, didactic classrooms. One of the reasons for this connection may be that children are happier, better behaved, and more engaged in these types of classrooms, making it easier for everyone to get along with one another. Another reason might be that there is more time in DAP classrooms for teachers to interact with children in small groups or individually (e.g., "Banking Time") than in classrooms where the teacher is directing whole class activities; thus, teachers and children have more opportunities to get to know one another and develop closer relationships. Yet another reason is that teachers in DAP classrooms use less adult-imposed responses to misbehavior, such as time-out. Howes and Ritchie (2002) found that classrooms were more caring in nature when teachers used alternatives to time-out. Thus, our final suggestion for promoting positive teacher-child relationships is to implement DAP, introduced in the next chapter.

Teachers' relationships with children impact their peer relations. Children with higher quality relationships with their teachers demonstrate fewer behavioral problems (Hamre & Pianta, 2001) and greater social skills with their peers (Howes, Matheson, & Hamilton, 1994). Researchers have also shown that the nature and extent of a teacher's interactions with a child influences classmates' views of and affiliations with that child (Hughes, Cavell, & Wilson, 2001). *The Child's Window* depicts a child who continues to struggle with teacher and peer relationships in school. The importance of promoting positive peer relationships in the classroom is the topic of the next section.

The Child's Window

Katie is 7 years old. She doesn't like her new second-grade teacher. She has already been in "time-out" twice today for yelling and bothering the girl sitting next to her in class. "She isn't my friend," Katie shouted before she stomped off to the time-out chair. Katie scooted the chair over to the pencil sharpener and started playing with it; after tiring of that activity, she started making chirping noises. Mrs. Snow wouldn't look at her. Finally, the bell rang, and Katie lined up at the door with the rest of the children and ran for the swings on the playground. She was there first—GOOD—she stayed on the swing for a long time despite seeing the other children waiting for their turns. She got off reluctantly when the yard duty lady told her to. When she returned to class, Katie went to her reading group. She didn't mind reading time because she was able to work with the student teacher, Miss Jill, who was nice and helped her with the hard words. She knew that most of the other children in the class were reading longer books. She wished that she could do this too. She didn't want to leave to go to lunch next, but Miss Jill had to go home. Katie walked to the lunch room alone. As she was walking, she thought about first grade. She was happier there because John played with her, but she didn't like her first-grade teacher either. She heard her teacher say a couple of times that she was a "problem child." Her mom called her that too sometimes, or more often, "strong-willed" when she screamed to do something she wanted to do. This usually worked with her mom but not with her stepdad, who usually ignored her when he was there and paid attention to "his" children—her older stepbrothers—instead.

When Katie returned to class after lunch, her teacher told her that she was calling her parents for a conference so that they could work together to make Katie's life at school better. Uh-Oh! Mrs. Snow smiled, but Katie still felt uncomfortable.

CHILD-CHILD RELATIONSHIPS IN SCHOOL

Children's acceptance by their peers in the classroom is essential for their school adjustment and learning. In a recent study, Ladd, Herald-Brown, and Reiser (2008) found that children rejected by their peers in grades K–3 exhibited significantly lower levels of participation in class activities. Indeed, rejection was associated with both lower independent *and* cooperative classroom participation. One can see how Katie (in *The Child's Window*) might miss out on learning opportunities in the classroom, not just because she is left behind in "time-out," but also because her classmates are probably reluctant to work with her; she's not very considerate of others. In addition, she is falling behind her peers academically and is beginning to realize this, making it more difficult for her to be inspired to do schoolwork. On the bright side, however, Ladd and his colleagues found that children who transitioned from rejection to acceptance increased engagement in class activities. There is hope. Obviously, engagement in class is central to learning and achievement in school, and fostering acceptance of children by their peers in the classroom must be taken seriously for this reason as well as to enhance their general wellbeing. Rejection hurts, even if children appear not to care. Ladd and his colleagues proposed a number of explanations for the connection between peer rejection and participation in classroom learning. One is that feelings of pain and discomfort associated with rejection impair executive functioning in the brain (see Chapter 1). Thus, children may be less able to focus, concentrate, and learn because of this interference. Another explanation might simply be that rejected children participate less because they are ignored or excluded from more activities. And negative emotions associated with rejection, such as anxiety or sadness or insecurity, may reduce children's motivation to become involved and cause them to

Engagement in class is central to learning and achievement in school, and fostering acceptance of children by their peers in the classroom must be taken seriously for this reason.

withdraw from challenging activities. In any case, it is clearly important for teachers to help children develop positive peer relations, feel accepted by their classmates, and learn to resolve social conflicts. These social competencies and relationships provide the foundation for a positive classroom climate (see Chapter 4).

However, Pellegrini and Blatchford (2000) warned that adults not become overly involved in children's peer relations. They argued on the basis of research and theory that children must work harder to engage their peers than adults and therefore develop better social competencies with moderate adult intervention. **Social competence** is defined as socially adaptive behavior. In early childhood, social adaptability with peers includes (a) the successful and positive seeking of peers' attention, (b) effectively using peers as resources, and (c) successfully leading peers. As we have seen, to accomplish these tasks, children also need to be able to manage their emotions and impulses. As children transition into middle childhood, they begin to develop more sophisticated perspective-taking and communication skills, allowing them to form and sustain close friendships and function in stable peer groups. Children are most likely to develop positive social competencies if they have been socialized in family and school contexts where adults are warm and nurturing, encourage independence, have clear expectations for mature behavior, but are not overly controlling—again, supporting a child- or learner-centered over an adult- centered approach.

Studies also show that high numbers of adults in early educational settings may inhibit social interaction with peers (e.g., Pellegrini & Blatchford, 2000). Interestingly, this particular perspective is embraced by teachers of young children in Japan where low teacher to child ratios are common (e.g., Lewis, 1995; Tobin, Hsueh, & Karasawa, 2009). Such findings are consistent with a Piagetian perspective that points to the importance of peer interactions for provoking children's cognitive and social development. With peers as equals, children must consider and accommodate different views (instead of merely accepting adult views). According to Pellegrini and Blatchford (2000), then,

preschool and primary-grade school teachers also need to provide opportunities for children to interact with their peers with
minimal adult direction. In particular, they suggest ensuring that
children have opportunities for free play in the classroom and on
the playground during recess and break times. The structure of
the classroom matters too; they point to earlier research showing
that children had more friends in relatively "open" multitask
classrooms than in traditional, ability-grouped classroom settings. Friendships in elementary school are also facilitated in
structured games on the playground (e.g., soccer).

Fostering friendships in school not only fosters children's
adjustment (they like school and cope in school better) but their
academic learning. Friends collaborate and solve academic
problems more effectively than nonfriends, and perhaps surprisingly, spend less time off-task (e.g., Zajac & Hartup, 1997).
A few studies even suggest that friends use more sophisticated
cognitive processes when working on academic tasks. For
example, researchers have found that 6-year-old friends were
more likely to reflect on language (e.g., "How do you
write ___?") and thought (e.g., "Try to put this one first.")
processes when writing and talking about books than acquain-
tances in the same classroom (e.g., Pellegrini & Blatchford, 2000).
These findings indicate that teachers should not always implement the common practice of separating friends in group activities. It is also important to note that not all friendships are
positive; as noted in the previous chapter, there are good reasons
for separating children with antisocial or aggressive tendencies.

Pellegrini and Blatchford (2000) concluded that there is
much work that can be done within schools to foster social skills
and friendships, but we also need to allow children opportunities to meet and sustain their interactions during recess and
other times relatively free from adult control. They are very concerned about policies that restrict these occasions in elementary
schools. Recess is a major part of school life for children
(Pellegrini & Bohn, 2005). In fact, when children are asked about
their day at school, their first responses often concern their activities at recess or lunchtime (see *Practice Exercises*). The arguments for reducing recess time tend to include cries for more

instruction and fewer problem behaviors (e.g., aggression). Counterarguments point to studies indicating advantages of recess for children's learning and performance in class as well as for their social relations and school liking. Also, proponents of recess note that aggression on elementary playgrounds is uncommon, accounting for 2 or 3 percent of total behavior (Pellegrini, 1988), and it is often instigated by very few children (i.e., bullies). (In some schools, however, bullying is more of a problem.) Further, with appropriate supervision in positive school climates, aggressive behavior drops dramatically (e.g., Olweus Bullying Prevention Program).

So when should teachers intervene in children's peer relations? Developmental psychologists and educators often agree that attending to children's regulatory and social skills in daily classroom activities is important for developing positive relations in school. And we have just reported arguments for disengaging at times from free-play activities so that children can develop other important social skills with their peers. Vivian Paley (1992), an acclaimed kindergarten teacher and author, reported her struggles with the accepted practice to leave children alone during free-play in *You Can't Say You Can't Play.* In particular, she struggled with concerns about children who are rejected year after year, as Ladd and his colleagues documented good reasons for concern, discussed earlier. She decided to bring the question about whether to intervene to children (as she often does), and she talked with older elementary students about the fairness and effectiveness of imposing the rule, "you can't say you can't play" before she implemented it in her kindergarten classroom. Some children thought that the rule was fair, but few thought it would work because it is an intrusion into friendship. The remainder of her book revealed children's responses to the rule and delightful (and sometimes heart wrenching) conversations and stories concerning its implementation in her classroom. Paley's abilities to respect, sympathize, and communicate with both the rejectors and rejected children, and her willingness to leave them to their own devices at times, encourages children to become more accepting and accepted over time.

Fortunately, integrating practices that foster other social skills is not nearly as challenging or controversial. There are well-established programs on social skill or social and emotional learning (SEL) available to guide school and classroom practices; some have been supported by research. For example, members of CASEL have created several guides for educators. One guide outlines the curriculum scope for different age groups (Elias et al., 1997); goals for promoting children's peer relations in preschool and primary grades include the following (p. 135):

- Being a member of a group (e.g., sharing, listening, taking turns, cooperating, being considerate, helping, handling disputes)
- Initiating interactions
- Resolving conflicts without fighting (e.g., learning to compromise)
- Understanding justifiable self-defense
- Demonstrating empathy toward peers (e.g., showing emotional distress when others suffer, becoming aware of others' experiences or perspective-taking, helping rather than hurting or neglecting, supporting rather than dominating, respecting rather than belittling others)

In a more recent guide, Elias and Butler (2006) provided specific suggestions for topics and activities that can be quickly and easily integrated into the regular curriculum. Topics include effective listening, self-monitoring, assertive communication, resisting provocations, working as part of a team, conversation skills, and joining a group, among many others. Table 3.3 includes suggestions for one second-grade activity: caring for friends. Recommendations for involving parents in activities—the subject of the next section—are also provided in this guide.

Thus, to foster positive peer relations, teachers must create a balance between directing children's activities and allowing them to direct their own. This theme is expanded in Chapter 4. To reiterate specific suggestions made for promoting healthy peer relations here, teachers can (a) attend to their own interactions with children as models for their students; (b) ensure that

Table 3.3   Promoting Social Competence in the Classroom: Sample Activity for One Topic

Selecting and Caring for Friends (Second Grade)	
1.	Introduce the new topic. Ask students to close their eyes and think of their best friend.
2.	Generate a list of what makes a friend a friend. (Prompts: What kinds of things does a good friend say? What does the person do that is nice or good for a friend to do?) Then generate a list of not-good friend behaviors. (Prompts: What are some behaviors that we do not like in a friend or that makes them not fun to be around?)
3.	Conduct a practice activity. Read vignettes or scenarios involving conflicts in friendship (provided in the guide). Ask the class to generate ideas for what to do when friends act in negative ways.
4.	Construct a reflective summary. Ask students to reflect on what they have learned about friendship.
5.	Conduct follow-up activities. Praise good friendship behaviors in student interactions both inside and outside the classroom. Have students pick "Secret Friend" names, and ask students to do one thing each day that shows good friendship behaviors. Discuss experiences at the end of the week (without revealing names).

(Adapted from Elias & Butler, 2006.)

Tips for Teachers and worksheets are provided for 29 topics for each grade level (see Elias & Butler's [2006] curriculum guide listed in Resources).

all children are included in small group activities, and prompt when needed; (c) take advantage of everyday social conflicts to discuss and resolve together in class meetings (can also relate to story discussions); (d) implement child-centered, developmentally appropriate practices; (e) allow some free time in class and at recess for children to interact with minimal adult control (adults observe and monitor from a distance); (f) encourage friendships in the classroom, and allow friends to work together on academic tasks at times; (g) initiate structured games on the playground (provide materials and guidance, then let children go); (h) watch out for bullying behavior; (i) implement a social skills curriculum shown to be effective (see Resources); (j) if problems with violent behavior persist, consider implementing a proven, schoolwide SEL or prevention program (e.g., SDP, Olweus Bullying Prevention, Second Step).

Teacher-Parent Relationships and Family Involvement in School

The opening window illustrated some admirable attempts by teachers to enhance their connections with parents and other family members. Teacher attitudes and efforts influence the extent to which parents and families become involved in their children's schools, and such involvement makes a big difference in children's success. Research shows that parental involvement is an indicator of children's school attendance and adjustment as well as their achievement. Parents may be involved in the education of their children at school or in the home. Attendance at school meetings, programs, and activities are the most recognizable forms of involvement. However, parents can also become involved in their children's education by providing places for educational activities, reading to them, having meaningful conversations about school, and helping children manage their time and homework. Research indicates that the extent to which parents assume these kinds of responsibilities for educating their children is important for fostering school adjustment and learning (e.g., Weiss, Caspe, & Lopez, 2006).

Joyce Epstein and her colleagues (2002) have identified six major types of family involvement and their expected impact on children, teachers, and parents (pp. 14–16):

1. *Parenting.* Help families establish home environments to support children as students. (Expected outcomes include strengthening children's attachment to school,

and their parents' confidence in parenting. Teachers also gain understanding and respect for families' strengths.)

2. *Communicating.* Design effective forms of school-to-home and home-to-school communications about school activities and children's experiences. (Expected outcomes include increasing children's understanding of their roles as students, and their parents' monitoring of their progress. Teachers also gain access to parent networks for communications.)

3. *Volunteering.* Recruit and organize parent help and support. (Expected outcomes include enhancing children's skill in communicating with adults, and parents' understanding of the teacher's job. Teachers also gain time to provide individual attention to children with volunteers in the classroom.)

4. *Learning at home.* Provide ideas about how families can help children with homework and other school-related activities. (Expected outcomes include enhancing children's attitudes toward schoolwork, and parents' awareness of their children as learners. Teachers also gain respect for family time.)

5. *Decision making.* Include parents in school decisions. (Expected outcomes include increasing children's positive experiences as a result of improved policies, and parents' feelings of ownership of school. Teachers become better aware of parent perspectives.)

6. *Collaborating with the community.* Identify and integrate community resources and services to strengthen school programs, family practices, and children's learning and development. (Expected outcomes include enhancing children's skills and talents through enriched experiences, and parents' use of needed services. Teachers become better aware of resources to enrich curriculum and services to refer families when needed.)

Sample practices are included in *School, Family, and Community Partnerships: Your Handbook for Action* (Epstein et al., 2002); see Resources.

Epstein and her colleagues (2002) noted that the type and quality of involvement matter, and they are affected by teacher-parent relations. For instance, if a teacher routinely contacts parents only when there is a behavioral or academic problem, then parents could become negative toward home-school inter-action and reduce their involvement. There are other reasons to consider why parents may be reluctant to become involved in their child's school. For example, some cultures view the teacher and the school as absolute authority and the parent's role is not to question those practices. There are often language barriers between school and home which inhibit conversation and clear understanding of expectations and goals. Also, research has indi-cated that parental educational level and socioeconomic status, as well as family size, influence the degree of parent involve-ment. Generally, those parents who are more educated and have middle incomes will be more involved than those who are poor and uneducated. Finally, research has documented the decrease of parental involvement across the grades, unless schools and teachers work to implement appropriate partnerships at each level (e.g., Rimm-Kaufman & Pianta, 2005). However, research continues to point to parental involvement being effective and needed throughout the child's entire school life. It is important to note that although we use the term "parent" here most often, we are referring to adult family members who are responsible for and provide primary care for children; these can be parents, grandparents, foster parents, older siblings, and others.

To enhance family involve-ment, we need to consider the motives of parents, teachers, and school personnel, and the resources or benefits they offer each other, as well as the costs of involvement (Halgunseth, 2009).

To enhance family involvement, we need to consider the motives of parents, teachers, and school personnel, and the resources or benefits they offer each other . . .

For example, teachers and schools can offer welcoming environments, opportunities for interactions with other parents and community service providers, two-way communication systems, parenting classes, and educational resources for parents. In exchange, parents can provide information about their children, enhance learning experiences at home, and volunteer at school. Such healthy exchanges contribute to stronger partnerships, enhanced family engagement, and more positive child and family outcomes. We also have to consider costs of involvement; for example, requiring extensive homework can undermine quality family time just as requiring extensive teacher-family-school activities can undermine quality teacher-student time. Inappropriate expectations and demands can also undermine trust. Developing mutual trust between teachers and parents is important for commitment and engagement in productive activities, as it is in teacher-child and peer relationships.

The establishment of a reciprocal relationship with children's parents is listed as one of the core values of an excellent teacher by the NAEYC (Copple & Bredekamp, 2009). Excellent teachers see the value of involving parents not only to better understand children's strengths and weaknesses but also to understand their cultural backgrounds and family environments that influence their learning and well-being in school (including their physical health, that is, sleep, nutrition, exercise habits). They see children as part of a larger interconnected social system, which influences their social and academic competencies (see Figure 1.1), and parents as vital in this system. Therefore, excellent teachers work hard to develop mutual partnerships that function with two-way communication channels and avenues for parents to become involved in their classrooms and schools. Table 3.4 provides recommendations for teachers to initiate such partnerships. Educators might also want to join the Family Involvement Network of Educators (FINE) to learn more about promoting partnerships with children's families (see Resources).

CHAPTER SUMMARY

The primacy of relationships in the early school years is becoming increasingly recognized. Relationships developed in school forecast later relationships and either support or challenge children's adjustment and learning; thus, fostering

Table 3.4 Creating Partnerships With Parents and Families

Partnership Values	Practical Suggestions
Create a warm, welcoming school and classroom atmosphere for parents to visit and participate.	• Welcome and communicate with parents using positive and relaxed body language, facial expressions, and tone of voice. • Provide a choice of activities for parents (e.g., a parent may feel more comfortable decorating bulletin boards than reading to students). • Create a parent resource room or space for parents to connect. • Address parents by name and find out some details about their lives and interests. • Spend time outside class getting to know parents (e.g., invite them to stay for lunch, come early for coffee, etc.).
Model positive communication behavior such as active listening and conflict resolution skills.	• Keep eye contact and maintain an open posture (e.g., don't cross your arms, sit behind your desk, etc.) when talking. • Listen with the intention of "checking in" to make sure parents' concerns are heard (e.g., "I can see that you are worried about your child's progress and stress level. Can you tell me more about why you are concerned?"). • Use language translators whenever there is a language barrier or when parents feel more comfortable communicating in their native language.
Commit to ongoing two-way communication channels that become part of the school and classroom culture.	• Distribute routine notes, memos, or photos about classroom news. • Provide a central place in the classroom where parents can go for more information. • Use the Internet, e-mail, and homework webpage to communicate ideas, events, quotes for the week, and so forth. • Incorporate home visits, especially for transitions to elementary school. • Use parent surveys to solicit input on various classroom practices, and identify their talents, skills, and availability.

Provide avenues of respect and sensitivity for parents to express their goals, choices, and concerns about their children.	• Value and model these beliefs. • Reflect (write about) your feelings about parents and potential conflicts. • Seek out a trusted mentor educator to discuss feelings and ideas.

positive relationships is central in successful school reform efforts. We began with a look at the quality of teacher-student relationships, how these relationships might be formed and perpetuated, and how to enhance positive relationships, even with children who challenge teacher efforts. We also discussed the importance of peer relationships in school and what teachers can do to promote (and refrain from inhibiting) these relationships in and out of the classroom. Finally, we looked at research demonstrating the value of creating partnerships with children's parents and families to further children's development and learning in school. A theme of this chapter is that children, parents, and teachers need regular opportunities for positive interactions to build relationships and the support of others to perform well in their roles.

Questions to Ponder

1. Think of individual children in preschool or the primary grades with whom you have enjoyed both positive and less positive relationships, and respond to the questions listed in Table 3.1. Considering the material in this chapter, attempt to explain the reasons for the quality of these relationships from the children's perspectives.

2. Think about Katie in *The Child's Window*. Considering the brief background provided, what do you think explains her current problems with the teacher and peers? What would you do at the parent conference

if you were in Mrs. Snow's shoes? How would you change things in the classroom? Refer to information from this chapter to form your responses.

3. As a prospective or practicing teacher, what are your attitudes toward "partnering" with parents? (See Table 3.4.)

Practice Exercises

1. **Relations in the Classroom.** Ask a preschooler or primary-grade child about his or her relationships in class using the items in Table 3.2. You can use a rating scale similar to the one described in the Practice Exercises in Chapter 2. Ask the child to explain his or her ratings. What other questions or items might you add to find out more about the child's relationships with classmates?

2. **How Was Your Day at School?** Ask a preschool or primary-grade child to "tell me about your day at school." What was the child's first response? You can probe a bit by asking, "What did you do in class, on the playground, at lunch," and so forth, to elicit more details. Note the mention of relationship themes.

3. **Parents as Partners.** Choose one or two of the partnership values and consider how you might express these as a teacher. What difficulties would you expect? What outcomes would you value?

Key Words

Attachment theory

Working models

Conflicted relationships

Dependent relationships

Close relationships

Social competence

Summary

While the material here has provided only a whistle-stop tour of the child develop-ment area, we hope it may have whetted your appetite for some further reading and exploration of what is such an important area for your work in school. Understanding children's language, for example, is about understanding their identity and their place within a given culture. Understanding what it is about a child's home background that means they are sometimes unable to focus on learning is also paramount. These chapters therefore have begun to give you an insight into the children in your class or settings as real children from a range of contexts and circumstances rather than purely learners to be taught.

Student activities
- A very significant figure in terms of child development is Urie Bronfenbrenner (his book is on the reading list below). His theory centres around an Ecological Systems Model that suggests that children are the product of wider society not solely a family. The following PowerPoint outlines this clearly and is well worth watching:

  http://www.slideshare.net/aislado/bronfenbrenner-ecological-theory
- In the year 2000, Professor Winstone in conjunction with the BBC and the Open University started to follow a group of 25 children born in the millennium year and has charted their progress in a series of documentaries since that point. The children are now 13. Access the Child of our Time website at:

  http://www.open.edu/openlearn/whats-on/tv/ou-on-the-bbc-child-our-time-2013
  - You might like to watch the latest programme and try and discover what issues have impacted on the lives of these 13 year old children to date.
  - The website also has a very useful range of materials and research relating to child development which you might like to investigate.

Additional readings
Bronfenbrenner, U. (2004) 'Bioecological perspectives on human development' in *Making Human Beings Human*. London: Sage.

Dowling, M. (2009) 'Living and learning with others', Chapter 2 in *Young Children's Personal, Social and Emotional Development*, 3rd edition. London: Sage.

Eaude, T. (2011) 'Making sense of young children's development', Chapter 3 in *Thinking Through Pedagogy for Primary and Early Years*. Exeter: Learning Matters.

Gerhardt, S. (2004) *Why Love Matters: How Affection shapes a Baby's Brain*. London: Routledge.

Gopnik, A. (2009) *The Philosophical Baby: What Children's Minds Tell Us about Truth, Love and the Meaning of Life*. London: Bromley Head.

Knowles, G. (2009) 'Families', Chapter 3 in *Ensuring Every Child Matters*. London: Sage.

Music, G. (2011) *Nuturing Natures Attachment and Children's Emotional, Sociocultural and Brain Development*. East Sussex: Psychology Press.

Palmer, S. (2007) *Toxic Childhood: How the Modern World is Damaging our Children and What we Can do About It*, 2nd edition. London: Orion.

Sylwester, R. (2010) 'Understanding childhood', Part 1 in *A Child's Brain: The Need for Nuture*. London: Sage.

Whitebread, D. (2011) 'Introduction' in *Developmental Psychology and Early Childhood Education: A Guide for Students and Practitioners*. London: Sage.

Whitehead, M. (2007) 'Talking with parents and carers about communication and language development', Chapter 6 in *Developing Language and Literacy in Young Children*. London: Sage.

PART 4 CURRICULUM

Overview

A school curriculum is intended to provide children and young people with the knowledge and skills to lead successful lives. It is made up of a challenging selection of subjects that help young children to understand the world. This includes skills necessary for learning throughout life, work, personal development and wellbeing.

The structure of curricula is a political issue and therefore is currently being reviewed; you will need to be familiar with these changes and the potential impact on practice. Your role throughout your time in university is to become a 'curriculum maker' not simply a curriculum provider; a practitioner who always keeps the learning of the children at the centre of their practice. This is discussed in more detail by A.V. Kelly.

With the primary curriculum being revised it is imperative that trainee teachers have a thorough and robust understanding of curriculum issues. This section begins with a reading by Copping which outlines the learning and pedagogy of curricula models and provides a solid frame of reference.

Following on from the Copping reading, Kelly provides an overview of the key aspects of curriculum studies focusing on the centrality of the teacher and the 'hidden' curriculum of values and ethos.

The next reading by Wood and Attfield explores recent developments which strongly endorse play at the centre of childhood education and links this to case studies of early childhood play based cross curricular activities.

The final reading by Barnes outlines the pedagogies of cross curricular learning and provides case studies to highlight what good cross curricular practice looks like in the primary classroom. While reading these, consider the overarching theme of innovation where Barnes discusses 'Wow' experiences, motivation and the creative curricula.

Curriculum Approaches

Copping, A.

Learning Outcomes

By the end of this chapter you will have explored:

- how beliefs about learning drive curriculum planning and teaching approaches;
- how children's learning and development is at the forefront of curriculum development;
- how a cross-curricular approach deepens learning through the joining of concepts and ideas;
- debates about integrated and single-subject learning opportunities.

TEACHERS' STANDARDS

A teacher must:

3. Demonstrate good subject and curriculum knowledge

- have a secure knowledge of the relevant subject(s) and curriculum areas, foster and maintain pupils' interest in the subject, and address misunderstandings
- demonstrate a critical understanding of developments in the subject and curriculum areas, and promote the value of scholarship
- demonstrate an understanding of and take responsibility for promoting high standards of literacy, articulacy and the correct use of standard English, whatever the teacher's specialist subject.

4. Plan and teach well structured lessons

- impart knowledge and develop understanding through effective use of lesson time
- promote a love of learning and children's intellectual curiosity
- contribute to the design and provision of an engaging curriculum within the relevant subject area(s).

8. Fulfil wider professional responsibilities

- make a positive contribution to the wider life and ethos of the school
- develop effective professional relationships with colleagues, knowing how and when to draw on advice and specialist support
- deploy support staff effectively
- take responsibility for improving teaching through appropriate professional development, responding to advice and feedback from colleagues.

Introduction

Chapter 1 outlined the statutory requirements and non-statutory components of the National Curriculum. For each subject in Key Stages 1 and 2, the National Curriculum programmes of study set out what children should be taught and it is for schools to choose how they organise their school curriculum to include the programmes of study (QCDA, 2010). Therefore, although teachers are statutorily obliged (that is, by law you are required) to teach the *content* of the National Curriculum (DfEE, 1999), schools and teachers are not bound in any way as to *how* they should teach. Indeed, the direction of travel for the 2014 National Curriculum remains the same. One of the key principles is that the new National Curriculum 'will set out only the essential knowledge that children require. This will free schools to design a school curriculum that meets the needs of the children in the school' (DfEE, 2011a, p.6). In light of that, this chapter explores how schools and teachers might design their curriculum to include effective learning experiences for their children.

Theoretical approaches to curriculum design and designing learning

In *The Framework for the National Curriculum*, the Expert Panel for the National Curriculum Review (DfE, 2011) outlined the structure of the new National Curriculum. This is illustrated in Figure 2.1.

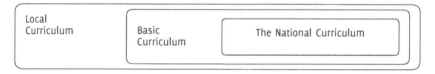

Figure 2.1: The proposed structure of the 2014 National Curriculum (from DfE, 2011: 18)

Table 2.1 outlines the proposed description of these components of the curriculum and the subjects.

A curriculum, be it a national one or a derivative made particular to a specific context, is created based on a series of beliefs about learning, and the perceived purpose of the curriculum. This section discusses the impact that your own beliefs have on how you plan for learning. The case study below exemplifies how the National Curriculum for England reflects a theoretical framework of learning.

The National Curriculum for England (DfEE, 1999) is based on the belief that in order for learning to occur, ideas and concepts should be re-examined and re-visited over time. This has been termed a 'spiral curriculum' where *'students return again to the basic concepts, building on them, making them more complex and understanding them more fully'* (Howard, 2007, p.1). Therefore, new learning builds on previous learning where the understanding of a concept is

	Description	Statutory basis	Responsibility	Proposed KS 1–2 subjects
National Curriculum	The essential knowledge to be taught in the core and foundation subjects. Core subjects will be specified for each key stage through Programmes of Study (PoS) and Attainment Targets Foundation subjects specified for each key stage through refined specifications.	Statutory.	Schools implement statutory programmes of study.	Core: English, mathematics, science Foundation: Geography, history, physical education, art and design, music, and from key stage 2 modern foreign languages.
Basic Curriculum	Schools should be able to determine for themselves the specific nature of this provision. (RE will follow locally-agreed syllabus)	Provision still statutory.	Schools implement requirements.	Design and technology, Information Communications Technology
Local Curriculum	Curriculum is determined at school or community level.	Should complement the mandatory National and Basic Curricula	Schools and communities innovate and determine additional educational provision for their pupils.	Schools determine specific content

Table 2.1 The proposed structure of the 2014 National Curriculum (from DfE, 2011: 18)

extended and enhanced through a process of *scaffolding*. This approach, outlined by Jerome Bruner, is rooted in the idea that learning is meaningful, has a purpose and that initial concepts have some validity and interest for the learner.

There are many other beliefs about how children learn and some of these are considered in Chapter 4, but it is important to remember as you read this chapter that a school's curriculum or scheme of work arises out of a belief in how children learn. The development of that curriculum, the activities contained therein, the progression of activities and teaching approaches indicated arise out of a particular belief about what learning is, how it happens and how children do it.

Additionally, it is shaped by how teachers perceive the wider curriculum itself. In light of this, the next section explores three ways of conceptualising a curriculum.

Conceptualising the curriculum

Activity

Read through the models below and consider to what extent they reflect how you see the curriculum. If necessary, have a go at developing your own model that uses a metaphor to reflect your own perceptions.

The curriculum as a blueprint for learning

This belief suggests that the curriculum is a blueprint on which knowledge is built. Instructions for the building suggest that the pre-ordained outcome must be reached and particular ways of working must be followed in order to get there. It is safe, secure and comfortable, provided the blueprint is accurate. It implies that there are no opportunities to explore alternative ways of constructing knowledge and is clearly focused on outcomes. This way of conceptualising the curriculum suggests a belief about knowledge which is propositional or declarative (knowing about facts, e.g. knowing the important events in Tudor England, how the water cycle works, or that Paris is the capital city of France) and that learning is procedural. Biggs (2003, p.41) explains that declarative knowledge *'is what is in libraries and text books, and is what teachers "declare" in lectures. Students' understanding of it can be tested by getting them to declare it back.'*

Whilst it could be argued that there is knowledge that should be known, it is limited in its use and application. Donald Schön, who developed the notion of reflective practice, explains how propositional knowledge or declarative knowledge is of limited value (Schön, cited in Brockbank and McGill, 2003). The implications of this belief are that learning could become rigid, concepts remain abstract and potentially irrelevant to the learner and that any learning that could take place through the process of an activity or created context is negated by the focus being on the arrival at the correct endpoint as provided by the instructions.

The curriculum as a set of outcomes to be able to quantify

This belief implies that a scheme of work (listing the statutory objectives, providing indicative activities that allow the learner to meet those and identifying suggested assessment designed to test the meeting of that outcome) can be tested, and the objective can be ticked off as having been taught and learnt.

This conceptualisation suggests something about how knowledge is gained. In this case, it is about knowledge being *procedural*. Biggs (2003) states that this procedural knowledge *is a matter of getting the sequences and actions right having the right... competencies* (2003, p.42). Just like the blueprint model, this is a very linear approach to the curriculum where the focus is on the outcome and passing the test which may indeed negate meaningful, constructed learning because in a sense this approach to curriculum is about the end result.

The curriculum as a map

This belief continues to use declarative knowledge as an end point. However, it may address the concerns of the models discussed above. The curriculum as a map model suggests that the curriculum is set within a particular environment and that participants within the environment are able to use a map to journey and explore within it. As long as a participant has the skills to be able to interpret the map, it is possible to reach a given destination using a number of possible routes. The route chosen will in turn offer new experiences and opportunities on the way to reaching the destination.

Boyle (2002, p.11) explains how a map metaphor can be used.

A map provides a systematic, integrated description of a particular geographical domain. This description, it should be noted, is both abstract and conventionalised. This knowledge base can be used to construct a route from any location on the map, through a series of 'valid steps', to any other location on the map. This is far more powerful than any set of procedural descriptions.

This belief builds on the notion that a curriculum should be designed to match the needs of the learners for whom it is intended because external guidance cannot be put into practice unless the context is considered. Boyle's map metaphor suggests a flexible and creative approach to learning knowledge and this places the learner (as the user of the map) and the teacher (as the expedition guide) in a position of being decision makers. Therefore, this takes into consideration the 'softer' skills a learner should possess, such as collaboration.

This approach reflects a belief that knowledge is useful and functioning. Biggs (2003) calls this *'functioning knowledge'* (2003, p.42). However, in order for a functioning knowledge to exist, Biggs suggests that the learner must have high levels of both declarative and procedural knowledge. These types provide the learner with the *what* and *how*. Additionally, Biggs (2003, p.42) suggests that the learner needs a further type of knowledge which he terms *'conditional'* that provides the learner with the *why* and *when*. As Biggs summarises *if the target is functioning knowledge, the declarative knowledge needs to be developed to relational levels in order to provide both the knowledge of the specific context, and the conditional knowledge that enable skills to be performed adequately* (2003, p.43).

Activity

Reflect on a recent school placement experience. Identify how the school's curriculum was designed. Which of the three beliefs about the curriculum, outlined above, were most prevalent in that design? Note down how the belief was exemplified in the learning and teaching. Also note what you consider to be the impact on children's learning.

Research Focus

In her work on trainee teachers' subject knowledge development in English, Twiselton (2006) identified three categories of trainee teacher: task managers, curriculum deliverers and concept/skill builders. She suggests that trainee teachers pass through these stages on a continuum.

The stages are important in thinking about curriculum design and the nature of knowledge. The belief about curriculum as a set of outcomes is very much about teaching through delivering the curriculum. Twiselton's findings suggest that

$\rightarrow$

> *Curriculum Deliverers appeared unable to link concepts and skills. Instead they appeared to treat knowledge as isolated and atomised pieces. In this view learning can be represented as a series of 'products' seen as ends in themselves (2006, p.91).* The implications for this approach to curriculum design are that the curriculum may lack cohesion and children may not be as able to make links between subject areas through the joining of concepts.

> Twiselton's (2006) notion suggests that trainee teachers move through categories on a continuum, rather than stay within discrete categories. Her research identified that ultimately trainee teachers should be aiming to develop into a 'concept/skill builder': a trainee teacher whose subject knowledge is not closed and who is able to link concepts and skills to situations outside of the classroom.

Earlier this section explored how Biggs suggests a joining up of knowledge types, and Twiselton (2006, p.93) supports this by stating that *'the bringing together of knowledge is the key to effective teaching'.* It is also evident that this is one key to effective learning.

The implications for this research and the 'curriculum as a map' model above are significant. It allows children to explore, problem solve and investigate. It also suggests that the learning that takes place during the process of meaningful activity is as, if not more, important than meeting a prescribed objective. However if this approach is the only one applied, a question must be asked about where does the solid foundation of declarative knowledge become built.

The case study below provides an example of how a trainee teacher on his final block placement planned and taught a lesson using Alfred Noyes' classic poem 'The Highwayman' as a stimulus.

Activity

As you read the case study, consider:

- Tom's beliefs about learning and teaching;
- how those beliefs may have directly impacted upon the children's learning and motivation to learn;
- where on Twiselton's continuum you would place Tom's subject knowledge.

Also consider your own response to the case study: would you be able to work in a similar way? As you read the case study, consider your own beliefs about learning and teaching and how they might impact upon how you would approach a similar unit of work.

Case Study: 'The Highwayman'

Tom, a trainee teacher working in a Year 6 class, planned an English unit for his placement class. The purpose of the unit was for the children to produce a news report about the two deaths that occur in the poem using processes such as enquiry, problem solving, reasoning and communication.

Prior to the children arriving, Tom had set the classroom up like a police murder scene using police cones and hazard tape to cordon off an area, taping outlines of two dead bodies on the floor and using anglepoise lamps to create subdued lighting. The chairs were arranged like a police investigation room, in pairs and in rows with police desk badges ready for the children to write their names on. A rolling slide presentation of images of highwaymen was playing on the interactive whiteboard and an action soundtrack supported this.

The effect was startling. The children came in for registration and were immediately asking questions about the classroom, investigating the artefacts, watching the slide show, discussing the images and there was an excited buzz of chatter and smiles and anticipation as to what would happen next.

Tom burst into the room in costume and introduced himself as the ghost of the highwayman lying dead on the floor and read/told the story from Noyes' narrative poem.

Tom then changed role to Detective Chief Inspector and charged the children with enquiring into the characters in the poem, what further information was needed to be found out, what might their motivation be for committing the murder and what questions might they like to ask the suspects. Tom used the dramatic technique of hot-seating and played the roles of the three main suspects. The children (in role as detectives) asked probing questions of the characters as to their motivation and 'where were you on the night of...' type questions whilst another child scribed useful information onto the board under a picture of each character. There was then an opportunity to share initial hypotheses and reflect on the views of others through small group discussion.

The children moved into role as journalists with the purpose of creating a news piece (a video presentation) in small groups. The teacher gave roles to each child (news anchor, camera operator, court reporter, crime scene reporter) and each group collated their ideas to form a news piece. A recording of a news programme was watched and the style analysed. A script was planned and prepared collaboratively in groups and then shared with the whole class. A 'good news report checklist' was used for evaluation purposes and each group had strengths and areas to improve to work on before final recording.

After recording, the class watched the news reports and assessed their performance in terms of news report criteria as well as understanding of the

$\rightarrow$

poem and story and a discussion about the key aspects of learning they had engaged in followed.

At the end of the unit some of the children made these comments:
- *I enjoyed being detectives, today we got be real police interviewing people;*
- *We were involved in everything;*
- *I learnt that English can be a bit like drama and acting;*
- *... that I'm more confident than I thought;*
- *... you got to do English physically as well as mentally.*

Interestingly, most of the comments came from the process of learning and were not particularly related with the end product of the video piece.

You are likely to have noticed that Tom was a very confident and creative trainee teacher. Crucially, he believed that children learn best from co-constructing their knowledge through experience and as a result he planned and taught in a way that reflected this. We see a social contructivist belief (Lambirth, 2005), where, in small groups, children bring their ideas and expertise together, share it and in so doing jointly construct new knowledge and skills with their peers.

Research Focus

Vygotsky (1978) and Bruner (1983) both emphasise the role of talk in learning. They claim that discourse can enhance thinking and support learning. Vygotsky even suggests that thinking and learning can come into existence through the act of talking, taking the idea that the verbal expression of a thought brings it into being. Both believed that learning was socially constructed. Firstly that new learning is built upon previous learning and experience and secondly that this construction process can occur through social discourse, a process that Bruner termed *scaffolding*.

Models of designing learning opportunities

This section focuses on the ways that you might design learning opportunities for the children you teach on placement. Regardless of the ways you conceptualise the curriculum, it is possible to approach planning the curriculum in several different ways.

Fogarty's models of curriculum design

Robin Fogarty has been writing about curriculum integration since the early 1990s. He has developed ten models for how school curricula may be conceived. This section considers four of these, but if you want to read more, see the further reading section at the end of this chapter.

Fogarty suggests that curriculum areas, knowledge, skills and understanding can be integrated in meaningful ways and that different models can be used by different teachers and in different times of the school year.

Shared

The shared approach is concerned with looking at two particular subjects and emphasising the common skills and concepts in them. Fogarty (1991, p.62) explains how the model *views the curriculum through binoculars, bringing two distinct disciplines together into a single focused image.* For example let's take English and history. Each circle in Figure 2.1 represents selected subject specific elements from the National Curriculum, and the area of overlap contains elements that appear in both. Therefore these can be shared when curriculum planning.

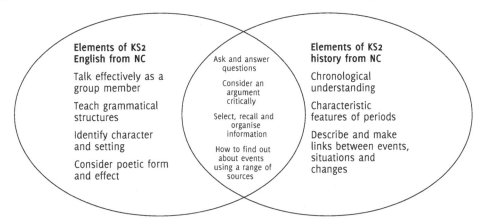

Figure 2.1 Example of shared integration: English and history

This approach has many advantages. It ensures that there is a strong link between two subjects and that any links made are meaningful and purposeful. It means that ideas and concepts can be applied easily and is relatively easy to organise. It does however mean that the rest of the curriculum might remain fragmented.

Threaded

The threaded approach is concerned with emphasising particular skills that can run through a subject and draws attention to the value of the process of learning, in particular thinking, social and study skills that can be threaded through a particular subject. Fogarty (1991, p.63) likens this model to viewing the curriculum *through a magnifying glass: the 'big ideas' are enlarged throughout all content with a metacurricular approach.* Let's take ICT as an example.

Figure 2.2 Example of threaded integration: Key Stage 2 ICT

This list is by no means exhaustive but it does demonstrate how skills in different areas can be considered through a subject, meaning that as a subject is taught or a curriculum area covered, key process skills can be threaded through to make learning more meaningful and coherent. With this approach there is the explicit teaching of thinking skills and the explicit consideration of multiple intelligences. It means that the transfer of skills is easier and provides opportunity for children to gain insights into their own skills, strengths and weaknesses. Brown and Campione (1998, cited in Watkins, Carnell and Lodge, 2007, p.72) suggest that these insights, known as *meta-cognition* are where 'effective learners operate best'. This approach does however mean that subjects remain separate and meaningful links may not be fully exploited and therefore arguably the full learning potential may not be fully realised.

Integrated

With the integrated approach there is a common theme and subjects are not explicitly emphasised. Fogarty (1991, p. 63) likens this to looking through a kaleidoscope where *interdisciplinary topics are rearranged around overlapping concepts and emerging patterns and designs.* The theme may be a curricular topic such as 'Britain and the world in Tudor times' but the emphasis is on the joining up of skills, concepts and attitudes rather than a focus on the subjects themselves. Let's use the theme of 'Britain and the wider world in Tudor times' as an example. The objectives stated within Fig. 2.3 are taken from the National Curriculum for History, Key Stage 2.

With this approach the interdependence of knowledge, skills and attitudes is clearly mapped out. This is the main advantage of this approach as learning is clearly identified as more than just knowledge being gained but to do with transferable skills and underpinning concepts as well as recognising that developing attitudes is a major part in learning. This approach emphasises whole child development and the role that these different elements play in learning.

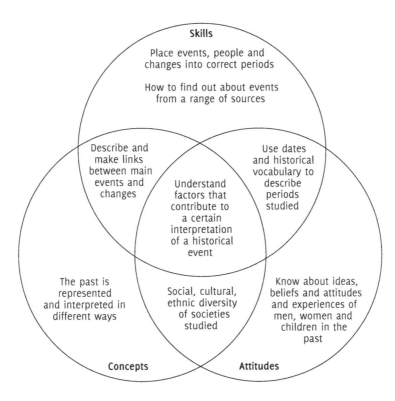

*Figure 2.3 Example of 'integration' approach using a KS2 British History unit
'Britain and the wider world in Tudor times'*

Webbed

Within the webbed approach a central theme or topic is identified, subjects treated separately but the consideration is what skills and concepts can each of those subjects contribute to the central theme. Fogarty (1991, p.63) suggests that this is like viewing the curriculum through a telescope, *capturing an entire constellation of disciplines at once.* As an example let's take a Key Stage 1 focused topic, 'the seaside' (Fig. 2.4).

The purpose of this approach is to consider the skills that can be taught through the theme. The advantages of this are that the central theme or hub pulls everything together and integrates the content. It also provides a holistic approach to learning and allows children to see links between concepts whilst also providing an opportunity for concepts, skills and content to overlap and be reinforced. However, its success is dependent on an appropriate theme and avoiding tenuous links. The content must also be relevant and meaningful.

Figure 2.4 Example of webbed approach using a topic heading and KS1 curriculum objectives

Activity

Consider a plan for a unit of work you have undertaken. Which of Fogarty's models of integration do you see and how did your planning in these ways impact on on the children's learning? Now that you have read about Fogarty's models of curriculum design, how might you amend the unit of work?

Integration versus single subject curriculum design

Case Study: The International Primary Curriculum

One published integrated curriculum growing in popularity is the International Primary Curriculum (IPC). The IPC is ostensibly a thematic approach to the curriculum. For schools that subscribe, it provides a menu of thematic units. These can be selected by schools so they best fit the interests of the children in the school. Each unit includes learning outcomes, a stimulus or entry point activity, tasks or activities, an explanation of the purpose of the theme and ideas for extending learning beyond what the unit suggests.

Fundamentally important to the thematic approach the IPC presents are the principles behind it. The IPC aims to ensure children:

- *Learn the essential knowledge, skills and understanding of a broad range of curriculum subjects.*

- *Engage with their learning so that they remain committed to learning throughout their school careers and their lives.*

- *Develop the personal qualities they need to be good citizens and to respond to the changing contexts of their future lives.*

- *Develop a sense of their own nationality and culture at the same time as developing a profound respect for the nationalities and cultures of others.*

www.internationalprimarycurriculum.com

This, like all other curriculum approaches, is built upon a strong set of beliefs about how children learn best and also about what knowledge is. For the IPC, knowledge is not just about the acquisition of sets of facts but about the desire to learn, to become life-long learners with a thirst for knowledge. Their approach is also more global, on two levels. The first level being about a more international perspective, children recognising and understanding the culture in which they live which will help them understand and develop a respect for the cultures of others. There is also a recognition that learning is about developing personal qualities such as flexibility, tolerance, interpersonal and intrapersonal skills essential in preparing them for jobs that may not yet exist. The IPC is also designed to take into account the idea that intelligence is multi-faceted.

There are other approaches and models to curriculum design. Although this chapter has focused on Fogarty's curriculum approaches that support ways of integrating subjects and consider the process of learning, Fogarty also identified as a curriculum approach a traditional, single subject design for organising the curriculum, which she called the *fragmented* model (Fogarty, 1991, p.61).

There is some debate to be had around many of the ideas suggested in this chapter. This debate primarily concerns two arguments: an integrated approach with the joining up of concepts from subjects and a single subject approach. The first argument is that an integrated approach to curriculum encourages the joining up of subjects, concepts, skills, knowledge and understanding and so, the proponents of this approach suggest, makes learning more coherent.

An integrated approach

A *fully* integrated approach to the curriculum by its very nature suggests that all subjects, including the daily mathematics lesson and the literacy hour will be absolutely amalgamated. It is interesting to note that the IPC does not include mathematics within its units and it also provides complex mapping guides for schools for them to identify where they need to address potential gaps in their bespoke unit choices in relation to statutory National Curriculum content. The question therefore must arise about what drove most schools to make the decision to have each morning dominated by these two subjects.

Alexander (2009) suggests that the government's drive to have schools demonstrate high standards in these subjects is likely to be the reason. This concerns government targets for schools at the end of Key Stage 2 to achieve certain percentages of levels four and five in Standard Assessment Tests (SATs).The publication of schools' results to parents, OFSTED and the world means that schools want to get the best results possible as these results can often be the first impression that a school gives. This in turn often gives rise to extensive preparation and a lot of SATs anxiety. Alexander (2009) goes on to say that this approach to curriculum and assessment compromises children's entitlement. The National Curriculum (2002, p.11) aims to *provide rich and varied contexts for pupils to acquire and develop a broad range of knowledge and skills.* There seems to be some conflict between this entitlement to a broad and balanced education and the emphasis on publically reported outcomes for English and mathematics. Alexander (2009) goes on to say that:

> The most conspicuous casualties are the arts, the humanities and the kinds of learning in all subjects which require time for talking, problem-solving and the extended exploration of ideas. A policy-led belief that curriculum breadth is incompatible with the pursuit of standards in 'the basics' has fuelled this loss of entitlement (2009, p.22).

This illustrates the two elements in the debate: curriculum breadth and pursuit of standards. Alexander reminds us that these do not have to be two opposing sides but that curriculum breadth can facilitate higher standards, but higher standards of what? This debate can only really have meaning once the question of the purpose of primary education is considered. If primary education is about enabling *pupils to think creatively and critically, to solve problems, to make a difference for the better...to become creative, innovative, enterprising and capable of leadership to equip them for their future lives as workers and citizens* (Alexander, 2002, p.11) then it seems that an integrated approach that supports the development of these in a joined up way may be more effective in achieving this first aim of the National Curriculum.

Medium Term Plan Checklist: Art and Design: Year 5

Learning objectives – linked to NC: skills, vocabulary, concepts and knowledge.	Learning experiences	Resources
To understand that landscape painting involves viewing from a single point and using perspective and scale according to distance. (4a, 5a,1b)	Children look at a range of landscape paintings: Constable, Monet, Cezanne, African landscapes in photographs and paintings, discuss similarities and differences. Look at colours: intense colours in foreground and paler colours further away. Look at scale and diminishing size.	Examples of landscapes by various artists and photographers
To have an appreciation of the use of colours to blend in paint and pastel. (2a,b,c)	Experiment mixing paler colours and intense colours and making patterns. Experiment with blending colours for African landscapes and creating vivid coloured skies and land with 'overpainting' areas, use pastels and watercolours in conjunction and blend together.	Paints, pastels, paper Mixing trays
To use colours, lines and 3D materials to create an impression of texture. (4b, 5b,c)	Experiment sketching a landscape with diminishing features in the distance, looking at landscapes by a range of artists.	Pencils, paper As above and examples of African landscapes
Outcomes • To make detailed observations of African landscape paintings.	Put painting and sketching together to produce an African landscape focusing on African prints and photographs. In small groups, use papier mache to make landscapes of Kenya based on pictures and photographs. Cover balloons with papier mache to produce hot air balloons to fly over African landscapes.	Papier mache, balloons, wire, card
• To imitate African landscapes taking into account colours used, blending and moods created.	Paint the papier mache when dry.	Paint, fabrics, thread, other media such as dried pasta and printing blocks. Canes to hang work
• To make 3D African landscapes, using papier mache, vivid colours and hot air balloons.	Use mixed media to create banners depicting people, flags, animals and symbols of Kenya, use different textures, threads, embroidery in small groups.	

Figure 2.5 Medium term plan for Art (single subject approach)
PoS taken from revised National Curriculum 2002

A single subject approach

One concern with an integrated approach to the curriculum is that individual subjects may lose some of their integrity. Indeed, OFSTED's summary of evidence related to improving primary teachers' subject knowledge across the curriculum begins with *The Independent Review of the Primary Curriculum accents the importance of subjects in primary education and the need for high quality teaching to ensure that pupils make all the progress that they are capable of* (2008, p.1). Additionally, it is not possible to ignore statistics about more students taking A-level mathematics in 2010 than ever before (STEM Advisory Forum, 2010) and how this is being linked to the implementation of the National Numeracy Strategy (NNS) which occurred when those students were in Year 2. This suggests that the NNS was a success in improving attitudes towards the subject. Furthermore, 80% of children in Year 6 achieved a level 4 or above in 2010. This is difficult to ignore when 54% achieved level 4 or above in 1997 (DfE, 2010).

Therefore, a single subject approach to curriculum design can also be highly effective. However, a clear progression of skills should be identified, planned for, and linked together in a structured way so that learners can gain initial skills and then learn how to use them effectively, particularly where an end product is identified. However this does not mean that links cannot be made to other curriculum subjects. Designing the curriculum in this way allows the teacher to use the skills, knowledge and understanding gained through one subject to transfer them to another.

Opposite is an example of a term's worth of work in Art. As you look at it, consider the build up of skills taught working towards the final product. You may notice opportunities for critical thinking, creative thinking, problem solving and also opportunities for developing meaningful cross curricular links.

Activity

Using the Art Medium Term Plan in Fig. 2.5, add any cross-curricular links you think are appropriate. Despite this being a plan for a single subject can you integrate any concepts and skills using any of Fogarty's models for integration? Use this to see how these different approaches to design are not incompatible.

During the activity you may have been able to pull in lots of ideas and thoughts and used the ideas in the plan as a central hub for other ideas around, perhaps a topic of Africa, continents or more specifically, 'Kenya'.

Now let's step back and consider what beliefs about learning drove this plan. First a belief in scaffolding: children need to have a purpose and then be taught the skills necessary to achieve that purpose. Each skill is then followed by an opportunity to try out, practise and explore. Just as in Tom's case study, we see a social contructivist belief (Lambirth, 2005) where, in small groups, children bring their ideas and expertise together, share it and in so doing jointly construct new knowledge and skills with their peers. Through this activity it is also possible to see how an integrated approach to curriculum design and a single subject approach do not have to be mutually exclusive. A skills-based art and design plan can certainly provide stimulus for an integrated approach to curriculum, similarly an integrated, perhaps webbed curriculum approach can facilitate a deep and exciting single subject plan. As stated before, subject knowledge is very important to success as a teacher, but it is what you do with that knowledge that is more important.

The case study below provides an example of how a group of trainee teachers in a year three class on a creative themed week placement. They planned and taught a series of lessons around the theme of enterprise.

Activity

As you read the case study, consider:

- the trainee teachers' beliefs about learning and teaching;
- how those beliefs may have directly impacted upon the children's learning and motivation to learn;
- what learning took place and how this was scaffolded for the children.

Also consider your own response to the case study: would you be able to work in a similar way?

Thematic approaches

Case Study: Enterprise week

A small group of PGCE trainees were planning a week on the theme of 'enterprise'. Their placement was undertaken as part of a module in their training and involved planning with members of staff in the school. The group began with a main end-product: creating a CD and/or podcast to help raise money for an appeal important to the children in the school. The idea was to post it on the school website and sell the CD at the school fair.

The week began with a role play and subsequent hot-seating and discussion about what it may have been like to be in the situation for which the appeal was raising money. It allowed children to respond physically, verbally and emotionally and begin to understand the world in someone else's shoes. This provided an excellent stimulus for the week as the children could mind map their thoughts and ideas and share them with others. The trainees brought in a range of subjects to their theme, providing subject knowledge in geography and science, marketing, persuasive writing and design. They were in role as rappers as well as business executives over the course of the week. The children had a large variety of learning opportunities not always measured in National Curriculum outcomes. The children learned how to make fruit smoothies, the technology behind making a music CD, the business of marketing and recording music using a mixing desk. They also had the opportunity to learn to express their thoughts, feelings and emotions and experience to a degree life in the shoes of people much less fortunate than themselves. Whilst some of the outcomes of this learning were demonstrated in more traditional acts of writing, drawing and mathematics, the main learning was taken from the processes the children went through and the shared experiences they had during the week of activities.

$\rightarrow$

One teacher commented that the children were more enthusiastic and engaged to work hard and the children's knowledge and understanding of issues outside their locality was definitely heightened. Interestingly the activities the children enjoyed most and articulated most learning from were those which they got practically involved in and made or created something. There was also a definite purpose to this week of work, raising money for people less fortunate than themselves and this purpose captured the enthusiasm and imagination of the children. This purpose was enabled by the theme of enterprise and all the learning opportunities derived from the activities shared that common goal. Fig 2.6 is a theme map such as the trainee teacher group used.

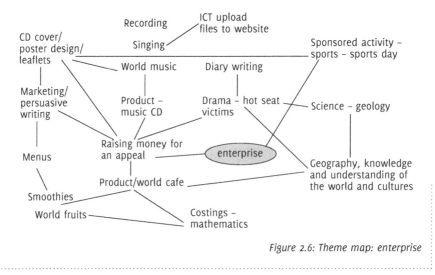

Figure 2.6: Theme map: enterprise

You are likely to have picked up on the children's comments about learning best and enjoying most the activities where they could get practically involved. When planning this themed week of work, the trainee teachers were keen to promote practical and purposeful activity, believing that the children would learn most if they could engage in a full experience that involved not just their minds but their bodies too. The children gained a lot from experiences not traditionally associated with school work such as making smoothies and making a CD. The trainee teachers believed that purposeful activity that was relevant and useful promoted learning and that the children would gain from it. They were able to define learning in broad terms.

This varied range of experiences and broad definition of learning encouraged more of the children to be successful and not 'turn off' those who found more traditional school work activities a challenge. Their planning demonstrates that they believed in the value of a range of different intelligences and that a child's intelligence is not defined by their ability in literacy and mathematics.

Research Focus

Howard Gardner (2006) terms this 'multiple intelligences'. This way of looking at intelligence recognises that intelligence should not just be measured in terms of being literate and numerate but in many other areas too. Alongside more 'traditional' intelligence, Gardner places spatial intelligence, interpersonal and intrapersonal intelligence, kinaesthetic intelligence and musical intelligence as part of a child's unique blend of intelligence and should not be ignored or allowed to stagnate at the expense of literacy and mathematics. This approach is clearly a way to provide children with the National Curriculum's aim of a broad, balanced and relevant curriculum through the profile raising of foundation subjects and mirroring the blending of intelligences with the blending of subjects through a themed approach. Perhaps this approach can offer an alternative to the government's standards agenda and assist in looking at education and approach to curriculum design and assessment in a more holistic way.

Activity

Examine the thematic web in Fig 2.6. Plot onto it opportunities for developing Gardner's intelligences: Visual/spatial, bodily-kinaesthetic, musical, interpersonal, intrapersonal, linguistic, logical/mathematical. More information on each of these is available at www.tecweb.org/styles/gardner.html. Consider whether you think the above approach is an effective approach to planning.

Now go to this website: www.infed.org/thinkers/gardner.htm. This article presents more information on Howard Gardner and on his multiple intelligences theory and identifies some additional intelligences for consideration. Towards the end there are some key questions or problems with his theory, surrounding his criteria for deciding on a particular intelligence, his conceptualisation of intelligence and a lack of empirical evidence. Read these carefully and add the information gained to your thinking about whether considering these intelligences is a good approach to planning.

Learning Outcomes Review

From your reading and from thinking about the school in which you are currently placed, or in which you most recently undertook a placement, respond to the questions which follow each of the intended learning outcomes, as a means of identifying your knowledge and understanding of the issues covered in the chapter.

- **How beliefs about learning drive curriculum planning and teaching approaches:**
  Give some reasons why some of the class teachers you have worked with have
  – organised their classroom in a certain way;
  – used particular teaching approaches;
  – used particular resources.
  Look at the planning that the class teacher uses for their teaching. Identify the main learning theory(ies) that underpin this planning. Find the evidence in the plan.

- **That children's learning and development is at the forefront of curriculum development:**
  – What can you do in your planning for teaching to ensure that children's learning is at the forefront of all that you do?
  – Think about a class you have recently taught, how did they learn best? How did you know? What will you do in the future?

- **How a cross-curricular approach deepens learning through the joining of concepts and ideas:**
  What different approaches could you use in your planning to join skills, concepts and ideas across subjects? Using the National Curriculum devise some examples.

- **Debates about integrated and single-subject learning opportunities:**
  Reflect on and evaluate your own planning on placement. Did you use integrated and/or single subject? Why? What was the impact on the children's learning and on your own subject knowledge understanding?

Further Reading

The texts below relate directly to the research foci outlined throughout this chapter. They will provide you with more knowledge and understanding of some of the key principles that have been outlined.

Brown, A. and Campione, J. (1998) Designing a community of young learners: theoretical and practical lessons. In Lambert, N. and McCombs, B. (eds) *How Students Learn: Reforming schools through learner-centred education.* Washington DC: American Psychological Association.

Cordon, R. (2000) Chapter 1 in *Literacy and Learning through talk: Strategies for the primary classroom*, pp.7–10. Buckingham: OUP in Lambirth, A. (2005) *Reflective Reader: Primary English.* Exeter: Learning Matters. pp.72–75.

Fogarty, R. and Stoehr, J. (2008) *Integrating Curricula With Multiple Intelligences: Teams, Themes, and Threads.* (2nd ed). Thousand Oaks, California: Corwin Press.

Gardner, H. (2006) *Multiple Intelligences: New Horizons.* New York: Basic Books.

References

Alexander, R. (2009) *An Introduction to the Cambridge Primary Review.* Available at: www.primaryreview.org.uk/Downloads/Finalreport/CPR-booklet_low-res.pdf accessed 22/7/10.

Alexander, R. (2004) Still no pedagogy? Principle, pragmatism and compliance in primary education. *Cambridge Journal of Education* 34 (1) pp.7–33.

Arthur, J. and Cremin, T. (eds) (2010) (2nd edn) *Learning to Teach in the Primary School.* London. Routledge.

Biggs, J. (2003) (2nd edn) *Teaching for Quality Learning at University.* Maidenhead: Open University Press.

Boyle, T. (2002) Towards a theoretical base for educational multimedia design. *Journal of Interactive Media in Education.* Vol. 2. From: http://www-jime.open.ac.uk/2002/2 accessed 14/5/08.

Brockbank, A. and McGill, I. (2003) *Facilitating Reflective Learning in Higher Education.* Buckingham: SRHE.

Brophy, J. and Good, T. (1986) Teacher behaviour and student achievement. In Wittrock, M.C. (ed.) *Handbook of Research in Teaching.* London: Macmillan.

Brown, A. and Campione, J. (1998) Designing a community of young learners: theoretical and practical lessons. In Lambert, N. and McCombs (eds) *How Students Learn: Reforming schools through learner-centred education.* Washington DC: American Psychological Association. p.540.

Bruner, J.S. (1983) *Child's Talk: Learning to use language.* Oxford: Oxford University Press.

DfE (2010) *Analysis of Year 6 Attainment in Maths by Level.* London: National Strategies.

DfE (2011a) *The Framework for the National Curriculum.* London: DfE.

DfE (2011b) *Teachers' Standards.* Available at www.education.gov.uk/publications

DfEE (1999) *The National Curriculum: Handbook for primary teachers in England Key Stages 1 and 2.* London: HMSO.

DfEE (2002) (2nd edn) *The National Curriculum: Handbook for Primary Teachers in England Key Stages 1 and 2.* London: QCA.

Fogarty, R. (1991) Ten ways to Integrate Curriculum. *Educational Leadership,* 49 (2): pp.61–65.

Gardner, H. (2006) *Multiple Intelligences: New Horizons.* New York: Basic Books.

Howard, J. (2007) *Curriculum Development.* Available at: http://org.elon.edu/catl/documents/curriculum%20development.pdf accessed 20/7/10.

Lambirth, A. (2005) *Reflective Reader: Primary English.* Exeter: Learning Matters.

QCDA (2010) *The Structure of the National Curriculum.* London: QCDA.

STEM Advisory Forum (2010) *Maths A-level Numbers Increase.* London: National Strategies.

Twiselton, S. (2006) The problem with English: the exploration and development of student teachers' English subject knowledge in primary classrooms. *Literacy: Teacher Education and Development.* 40 (2) pp.88–96.

Vygotsky, L. (1978) *Thought and Language.* Cambridge, MA: MIT Press.

Watkins, C., Carnell, E. and Lodge, C. (2007) *Effective Learning in Classrooms.* London: Paul Chapman.

14

The Curriculum and the Study of the Curriculum

Kelly, A.V.

It is stating the obvious to assert that education has changed drastically in the last twenty or thirty years. Both in the United Kingdom and elsewhere many important modifications have been made to all aspects of the education system. Nor is it surprising that the nature and structure of our education system should have been changing so extensively at a time when we have been experiencing social change of an equally dramatic kind, much of it prompted by rapid technological advance. The education system is a social institution which should be expected to change along with other such institutions. It would be more surprising, not to say disturbing, if the education system were to stand still while all else changed. And it is the need to ensure that it continues to develop, and that it responds appropriately not only to other changes in society but also to our increasing understanding of the educational process itself, which is, or should be, the central concern of Educational Studies and especially of Curriculum Studies.

One feature that characterized curriculum change in the latter part of the last century was the increased incidence of planning and preparation in curriculum development. Most of the curriculum change we saw before that was of a kind best described as unplanned 'drift' (Hoyle, 1969a). However, when in 1957 Russia launched its Sputnik 1 space rocket, the West, in particular the United States, fearing that it was falling behind in the race towards increased technological capability, began to look closely and deliberately at the curriculum, particularly its technological and creative dimensions. It was this which led soon after, in 1964, to the establishment of the Schools Council in Britain.

Thus educationists began to see the need for planned innovation, to recognize that if educational change is to keep pace with and match changes in society, if it is at the same time to maintain those standards and values which may be seen as transcending particular times and particular societies, it must be deliberately managed rather than merely left to happen. To recognize this is not, of course, to be committed to a totally revolutionary approach to curriculum development. The advantages of evolution over revolution are at least as evident in education as elsewhere. It is, however, to acknowledge that the process of evolution can be smoother, quicker and more effective, if it is not left to chance but implemented according to carefully thought-out strategies.

Recent experience has reinforced the case for curriculum evolution rather than revolution. For the shift we have seen towards central political control of the school curriculum has sometimes been revolutionary in its effect, so that it has often been far from smooth and thus less effective than it might have been.

One reason for this has been that there has been a failure to recognize that the changes which have occurred in society have been social, moral and political as well as, indeed as a consequence of, technological and economic developments. The natural evolution of the curriculum was reflecting this, especially in terms of attempts to overcome privilege and inequality and to move towards a more truly egalitarian system. Direct political intervention, by concentrating on the economic functions of the educational system, has largely ignored that dimension of educational provision along with its responsibility for promoting the personal development of the young, thus activating all of the consequences which that omission has for the quality of life in society.

It has also led to a technicist approach to the study of education by ignoring all or most of the insights which had been derived from explorations which had sought to go beyond concerns of mere methodology, to ask the 'why' questions concerning educational provision as well as those restricted to the 'how'. These insights have thus been placed at risk, and it is the central concern of this book, as has already been pointed out, to regain those insights and to reaffirm this kind of study of education and curriculum.

It is the aim of this chapter, then, to identify what is involved in this, to outline some of the essential ingredients both of the practice of curriculum planning and development and the study of curriculum. All or most of these points will be examined in greater detail in the chapters that follow, but an overall framework, a rationale, a cognitive map offered at the outset may help to establish and maintain the interrelationship of the many factors involved in curriculum planning.

What is the curriculum?

The first need is to achieve some clarity over what we are to understand by the term 'curriculum'. It is a term which is used with several meanings and a number of different definitions of it have been offered, so that it is important that we establish at the beginning what it should be taken to signify throughout this book, and, perhaps more importantly, what it should *not* be taken to mean.

The educational curriculum

From much of what follows in this book it will be clear that the term 'curriculum' can be, and is, used, for many different kinds of programme of teaching and instruction. Indeed, as we shall see, quite often this leads to a limited concept of the curriculum, defined in terms of what teaching and instruction is to be offered and sometimes also what its purposes, its objectives, are. Hence we see statements of the curriculum for the teaching of the most basic courses in many different contexts. We shall also see that much of the advice which has been offered for curriculum planning is effective only at the most simplistic levels, for teaching of a largely unsophisticated and usually unproblematic kind.

For this kind of definition fails to take account of the educational or moral dimensions of the school curriculum. To take an extreme view, this kind of model could be used to help us plan a curriculum which most people would regard as being quite immoral – to limit the pupil's scope for criticism, for example, to ensure political conformity and obedience or even to promote racist or religious intolerance.

Throughout this book, however, the concern will be with what we will be advocating as the *educational* curriculum. The focus will be not just on how one might plan any kind of curriculum, but on what it is that will ensure that our curriculum is justifiable in *educational* terms.

It is important, therefore, that at the outset we briefly define what we will mean by the term 'educational', because in all the many different dimensions of the curriculum which we will be exploring the concern will be to identify those which are acceptable educationally, that is, those which satisfy our educational criteria, and, perhaps more importantly, those which do not.

It is not the intention here, or at any stage, to debate these criteria in detail. It is important, however, that they be clearly stated. There is a sense in which the adjective 'educational' is as problematic as the adjective 'moral'; indeed, this is because the educational principles we are propounding are fundamentally moral principles, so that it must be accepted that they must be open to debate. There is also a sense, however, in which, if we accept that the curriculum we are discussing is a curriculum for education in a democratic society, its problematic nature, along with that of its moral base, begins to evaporate or at least to become less complex.

For few would wish to argue – at least openly – with the claim that, within a democratic society, an educational curriculum at all levels should be concerned to provide a liberating experience by focusing on such things as the promotion of freedom and independence of thought, of social and political empowerment, of respect for the freedom of others, of an acceptance of variety of opinion, and of the enrichment of the life of every individual in that society, regardless of class, race or creed.

Conversely, it is also the case that few would be prepared to argue – again at least openly – against the claim that the opposites of these principles have no place in an educational curriculum. Some of them, such as, for example, the promotion of intolerance, must be positively excluded from it. Others, however, such as that vocational focus which has become increasingly in evidence in recent years, while not meriting exclusion from the curriculum, must be recognized as not fitting appropriately with this definition of education, so that, to the extent that the emphasis of the school curriculum is on its vocational concerns and dimensions, to that extent it will fail to meet our criteria for an educational curriculum.

That the curriculum for schools in England and Wales has become increasingly vocational, almost to the exclusion of all considerations of education, is apparent from three related recent developments. First, the British government has decided that qualifications, claimed to be equivalent to A-level passes, are to be awarded by such commercial organizations as McDonald's. Secondly, schools have been warned that they must not attempt to direct their pupils away from the newly devised vocational diploma towards more academic A-level subjects. And, thirdly, parents are being addressed by television advertisements suggesting that they think again about encouraging their offspring towards academic study. These developments amount to a clear statement that the school curriculum is to be thought of in terms of its vocational rather than its educational content and purposes – at least for some pupils. It thus represents a return to the tripartite philosophy of the era prior to the 1944 Education Act with its promise of education for all, according to age, aptitude and ability. It also has implications for the role of state schooling in society and for the future of society's democratic base.

The rest of this book will be concerned to discuss and explore the many dimensions of curriculum from a genuinely educational perspective and to identify in all of these dimensions those aspects which satisfy these educational principles and those which do not.

With this in mind, there are several important aspects of the curriculum which we should immediately note.

The total curriculum

It will be helpful if, from the start, we distinguish the use of the word 'curriculum' to denote the content of a particular subject or area of study from the use of it to refer to the total programme of an educational institution. Many people still equate a curriculum with a syllabus and thus limit their planning to a consideration of the content or the body of knowledge they wish to transmit or a list of the subjects to be taught or both. The inadequacies of this view of curriculum as content will be explored more fully in Chapters 2 and 3. It will be immediately clear, however, that this kind of definition of curriculum is limiting in more than one way and that it is likely to hamper rather than to assist the planning of curriculum change and development. Indeed, some of the inadequacies of previous attempts at curriculum planning can be attributed to the fact that it has tended to proceed in a rather piecemeal way within subjects rather than according to any overall rationale.

This dimension of curriculum development is, of course, important, but it is the rationale of the total curriculum that must have priority. 'Schools should plan their curriculum as a whole. The curriculum offered by a school, and the curriculum received by individual pupils, should not be simply a collection of separate subjects' (DES/WO, 1981: 12). At the very least, the total curriculum must be accorded prior consideration, and a major task that currently faces teachers and curriculum planners is to work out a basis on which some total scheme can be built.

Any definition of curriculum, if it is to be practically effective and productive, must offer much more than a statement about the knowledge-content or merely the subjects which schooling is to 'teach' or 'transmit' or 'deliver'. It must go far beyond this to an explanation, and indeed a justification, of the purposes of such transmission and an exploration of the effects that exposure to such knowledge and such subjects is likely to have, or is intended to have, on its recipients – indeed it is from these deeper concerns, as we saw in the previous section, that any curriculum planning worthy of the name must start.

These wider concerns will be the focus of our discussions in this book, and we will understand by the term 'curriculum' the overall rationale for any educational programme. Much of what is said about curriculum development will, of course, be of relevance to the problems of developments within individual subject areas, but the prime concern must be with the totality.

The 'hidden' curriculum

A further question that needs to be resolved is whether we are to place any limit on the kinds of school activity that we will allow to count as part of the curriculum when it is defined in this way.

For example, some educationists speak of the 'hidden curriculum', by which they mean those things which pupils learn at school because of the way in which the work of the school is planned and organized, and through the materials provided, but which are not in themselves overtly included in the planning or sometimes even in the consciousness of those responsible for the school arrangements. Social roles, for example, are learnt in this way, it is claimed, as are sex roles and attitudes to many other aspects of living. Implicit in any set of arrangements are the attitudes and values of those who create them, and these will be communicated to pupils in this accidental and perhaps even sinister way. This factor is of course of particular significance when the curriculum is planned and imposed by government.

Some would argue of course that the values implicit in the arrangements made by schools for their pupils are quite clearly in the consciousness of teachers and planners, again especially when the planners are politicians, and are equally clearly accepted by them as part of what pupils should learn in school, even though they are not overtly recognized by the pupils themselves. In other words, those who design curricula deliberately plan the schools' 'expressive culture'. If this is the case, then, the curriculum is 'hidden' only to or from the pupils, and the values to be learnt clearly form a part of what is planned for pupils. They must, therefore, be accepted as fully a part of the curriculum, and most especially as an important focus for the kind of study of curriculum with which we are concerned here, not least because important questions must be asked concerning the legitimacy of such practices.

Others, however, take a less definite and perhaps less cynical line on this but wish nevertheless to insist that teachers do have a responsibility here. They accept that some of the values and attitudes learnt via the hidden curriculum are not directly intended by teachers, but believe that, since these things are being learnt as a by-product of what is planned and of the materials provided, teachers should be aware of and accept responsibility for what is going on, for what their pupils are learning in this unplanned way. It is this view which is at the heart of attempts to eliminate implicit racism and sexism from the experiences children receive at school.

It is because of the all-pervasive nature of such experiences and hidden forms of learning, however, and because of the assumed impossibility of eliminating such unplanned, and thus uncontrolled, learning, that some theorists, such as Ivan Illich (1971), have recommended a 'deschooling' of society and have claimed that all forms of organized schooling must involve the imposition of the values implicit in the selection of the content of such schooling on its recipients, and thus constitute an invidious form of social and political control through the distribution of knowledge. This is an important point and one to which we shall return in Chapter 2. What it suggests which is of importance here, however, is that, if we are not to go to the lengths of abolishing schooling altogether, we cannot merely ignore these hidden aspects of the school curriculum, and certainly must not adopt a definition of curriculum which excludes them from all critical consideration. Rather our definition must embrace all the learning that goes on in schools whether it is expressly planned and intended or is a by-product of our planning and/or practice. For it is difficult to exonerate teachers completely from responsibility for these implicit forms of learning. Rather they need to be sensitized to them and helped to recognize and identify the hidden implications of some of the materials and the experiences they offer their pupils.

The planned curriculum and the received curriculum

Much the same point emerges when we consider the distinction which has sometimes been made between the official curriculum and the actual curriculum, or between the planned curriculum and the received curriculum. By the official or planned curriculum is meant what is laid down in syllabuses, prospectuses and so on; the actual or received curriculum is the reality of the pupils' experience. The difference between them may be conscious or unconscious, the cause of any mismatch being either a deliberate attempt by the teachers or others to deceive, to make what they offer appear more attractive than it really is, or merely the fact that, since teachers and pupils are human, the realities of any course will never fully match up to the hopes and intentions of those who have planned it.

Both of these distinctions are important and we would be foolish to go very far in our examination of the curriculum without acknowledging both the gaps that must inevitably exist between theory and practice and the predilection of some teachers, and more especially national planners, for elaborate 'packaging' of their wares.

It becomes even more important, then, that we should not adopt a definition of curriculum which confines or restricts us to considerations only of that which is planned. What is actually received by pupils must be an equally important, or even more important concern, so that the actual or received curriculum must be seen as the teacher's or planner's responsibility every bit as much as the 'hidden' curriculum.

Furthermore, we must not lose sight of the fact that Curriculum Studies must ultimately be concerned with the relationship between these two views of the curriculum, between intention and reality, and, indeed, with closing the gap between them, if it is to succeed in linking the theory and the practice of the curriculum (Stenhouse, 1975).

The formal curriculum and the informal curriculum

Lastly, we must also recognize the distinction that is often drawn between the 'formal' curriculum and the 'informal' curriculum, between the formal activities for which the timetable of the school allocates specific periods of teaching time and those many informal activities that go on, usually on a voluntary basis, at lunch-times, after school hours, at weekends or during holidays. These latter activities – sports, clubs, societies, school journeys and the like – are often called 'extracurricular' activities and this suggests that they should be seen as separate from, as over and above the curriculum itself.

The reasons for this, however, are difficult to discern. For activities of this kind are usually regarded as having as much educational validity and point as any of the formal arrangements of the school. Indeed, some would even argue that in certain cases they have more point than many such arrangements. It was for this reason that the Newsom Report (CACE, 1963: para.135) recommended that they 'ought to be recognized as an integral part of the total educational programme' and that to this end they be included in the formal timetable of an extended day. And the inclusion of this kind of activity in the formal provision made by the school has also been a major feature of the philosophy of many of those concerned with the development of community schools (Cooksey, 1972, 1976a, 1976b).

Again, it would seem that, if we are concerned with curriculum planning, it would be foolish to omit by our definition of the curriculum a whole range of activities which teachers plan and execute with deliberate reasons and intentions. In looking at curriculum planning, therefore, there would appear to be nothing to be gained from leaving out of consideration any planned activity. It is for this reason that John Kerr (1968: 16) defined the curriculum as 'all the learning which is planned and guided by the school, whether it is carried on in groups or individually, inside or outside the school'. Such a definition provides us with a basis for planning all the organized activities of a school.

However, there are real difficulties in attempting to operate with a definition of curriculum which excludes from consideration the unplanned effects of teacher activity, as the notions of the 'hidden' and the 'actual' or 'received' curriculum indicate. There are more aspects to curriculum than are dreamed of in the philosophy of most teachers, and certainly of most politicians, and a definition of curriculum which confines its scope to what teachers, or politicians, actually plan will omit many of those important dimensions of Curriculum Studies we identified earlier. We need a definition which will embrace at least four major dimensions of educational planning and practice: the intentions of the planners, the procedures adopted for the implementation of those intentions, the actual experiences of the pupils resulting from the teachers' direct attempts to carry out their or the planners' intentions, and the 'hidden' learning that occurs as a by-product of the organization of the curriculum, and, indeed, of the school.

The problems of definition are thus serious and complex, and the chapters which follow will reveal that in planning for curriculum change and development we need to be aware of all aspects and dimensions of the educational experiences which pupils have during any period of formal education, and of their underlying principles and rationale. The definition adopted here, therefore, is that the curriculum is the totality of the experiences the pupil has as a result of the provision made.

If we take this broad definition of curriculum as our starting point, then, it becomes possible to identify the kinds of issue which the study of curriculum must address – the issues which subsequent chapters will explore in greater detail.

Before we do that, however, there is a further preliminary point which must be made. For a major premise of what follows is that in all successful curriculum development and implementation the teacher is the crucial element. And we must pause for an explanation of why this stance has been adopted.

The centrality of the teacher

It must first be stressed that all that is said about curriculum planning and development in this book applies as much to the individual teacher in the preparation of his or her individual 'lessons' or other programmes of work with children as it does to those who find themselves charged with curriculum development at school, local authority or even national level.

A major reason for stressing this is not merely to remind teachers of the degree of responsibility they must accept for their own professional work, nor only to emphasize their consequent need for the kinds of understanding of curriculum which this book is seeking to provide; it is, perhaps more importantly, because of the 'make or break' role that teachers have in all curricular activities, even in relation to those which originate outside their schools.

'Teacher-proofing' does not work

There have been many attempts over the last four or five decades to bring about curriculum change, most notably those sponsored by the Schools Council during its lifetime, some of the later work of the Assessment of Performance Unit (APU) and, most importantly, the decision to change the curricula of all schools to fit the demands of the National Curriculum. All these strategies for external manipulation of the curriculum we shall explore in greater detail in later chapters.

The most important point to be noted here, however, is what we have learned from the experience of these projects and activities about the role of the individual teacher in curriculum change and development. We must especially note the failure of all attempts by the Schools Council to produce 'teacher-proof' packages – schemes of work, versions of curriculum, supporting materials and so on of a kind which teachers would accept, use and apply in the precise form that the central planners had in mind. In every case, teachers adapted and used what they were offered in their own ways and for their own purposes. Some project directors were inclined to throw up their hands in despair at this phenomenon, at what they saw, and sometimes described, as 'cannibalism'. Others went along with it eventually and built into their schemes proper forms of allowance for this kind of personal and local adaptation by teachers. The Schools Council itself, just before its demise, adopted a policy of supporting school-based curriculum developments, assisting teachers and groups of teachers with the process of developing their own curricula rather than attempting to 'sell' them pre-packaged programmes which might not be geared appropriately to the specific needs of the individual school. And some of the later work of the Assessment of Performance Unit was concerned much more with offering its findings to teachers, while leaving it to them to decide whether and how they might use these in their own contexts, than with attempts at imposing the same solutions to teaching problems on all (Kelly, 1987). In short, there was developing a growing awareness that each school is unique and that its curricular needs are thus largely idiosyncratic.

The implications of this kind of experience for the implementation of forms of centralized control such as the National Curriculum are interesting and will be explored more fully later. We have here another example of the failure or the refusal of the architects of these policies to take any account or cognizance of the substantial experience and findings of earlier research.

The teacher's 'make or break' role

What we must note here, however, is that the teachers have a 'make or break' role in any curriculum innovation. Teachers have been known to sabotage attempts at change; certainly it is clear that such attempts can succeed only when the teachers concerned are committed to them and, especially, when they understand, as well as accept, their underlying principles. The practice of education cannot be a mechanical, largely mindless activity; it requires constant decisions and judgements by the teacher, and these he or she cannot make properly without fully appreciating and accepting the underlying rationale of any activity. Teaching, interpreted in a purely technicist sense, may be undertaken in a mechanistic manner. If, however, our concern is with *education*, in the full sense, as we have indicated that it is, much more than this is required, since education is essentially an interactive process. 'The building block is the moral purpose of the *individual* teacher. Scratch a good teacher and you will find a moral purpose' (Fullan, 1993: 10, original emphasis). Take away that moral and educational purpose, and you have a teaching machine.

Practically, every piece of serious and objective research into what happens in classrooms has focused on the teacher as the central figure and his/her competence as the crucial factor in the quality of the educational experiences provided for the pupils. And most pupils and ex-pupils will corroborate this – 'I like (liked) subject "x" or my second year in Junior school, because it was taught by Dr/Mr/Mrs/Ms "y"'.

The quality of any *educational* experience, then, will depend to a very large extent on the individual teacher responsible for it; and any attempt at controlling the curriculum from the outside which does not recognize that must be doomed to failure, or at best to triviality. An alternative strategy for ensuring compliance to external requirements is of course to introduce stringent measures for controlling the activities of teachers, through schemes of pupil assessment, regular inspections, teacher appraisal and accountability and control of the content of teacher training courses. Indeed, one can reasonably view the activities of the Office for Standards in Education (Ofsted) in England and Wales as those of a kind of 'thought-police' designed to prevent teachers from indulging in acts of 'sabotage' by acting on their own professional judgements. This aspect of current policies we must also consider later. Such a strategy, however, cannot ensure commitment or understanding; and obedience to authority on the part of teachers is not the best basis for the practice of education as we are viewing it here, although it may well be adequate if the concern goes no further than teaching or instruction. Hence it is for this reason that teaching in England and Wales has ceased to be education and has reverted to being merely a form of vocational training.

The corollary of this is that it becomes even more important for teachers to work at developing the kind of broader understanding of curricular provision which a study of the curriculum at the level we are advocating should bring.

Indeed, it might be argued that there is a major professional obligation on them to do so, since this is the only route to effective practice. Hence, we have seen the emergence of concepts such as that of 'the teacher as researcher' (Stenhouse, 1975) and of 'action research' as a key element in continuous professional development.

On the other hand, increased centralized control of teachers' work has had the effect of discouraging this kind of professional activity on the part of teachers. It has always been important, even when we acknowledge the central role of the teacher in education, not to lose sight of the fact that he or she is operating in a context hedged about with many constraints and pressures, social and political as well as physical and organizational. No curriculum planning of any kind can go on in a vacuum; it must take place in an environment which is prey to pressures and constraints of many kinds.

Recent developments, however, most notably the constraints imposed on teachers in England and Wales by the statutory requirements of the 1988 Education Act and subsequent policy decisions, have converted these indirect constraints into direct control. The more indirect influences of central government on the school curriculum have been slowly converted from influence to intervention and from intervention to direct control. The most important effect of this is that teachers now have little or no say in the official curriculum of the nation's schools, so that they are now expected to operate a curriculum which has been imposed upon them from without and to implement curricular policies over whose framing they have had little or no influence.

This latter point raises some interesting issues in the light of what we said earlier about the need for teachers to be committed to the curricular provision they are making if they are to make it properly and effectively. One of the strengths of the previous system was that most teachers did believe in what they were doing, or at least enjoyed a good deal of scope to make of it something they could believe in. No doubt there will be many who will believe in what they are now required to do. But for those who do not there are clearly important problems to be faced. At a more theoretical level, these are problems which highlight the distinction we referred to earlier in this chapter between the official and the actual curriculum, between the intention and the reality, between theory and practice. They also resurrect those difficulties we have also noted which arise from earlier attempts to manipulate teachers by remote control or to create teacher-proof curricula.

There is thus every discouragement in the present political climate for teachers who wish to view their professionalism in 'extended' terms and to pursue a study of curricular issues at levels beyond that of the mere 'delivery' of their subject knowledge. Indeed, the processes they are subject to have been described by many commentators as processes of deprofessionalization. If, however, their role is central, and if, further, the effective fulfilment of that role is dependent on a breadth of understanding of curriculum, the implications of the loss, or the suppression, of these insights are extremely serious for the long-term quality of educational provision.

Key aspects of Curriculum Studies

Now that we have established and explained the definition of 'curriculum' and the view of the role of the teacher within it which provide the major premises of the discussion which follows, we can identify briefly the broad issues which the rest of the book will seek to address in greater detail. All of these will be seen to reflect insights which have been gained from curriculum change, taken in its broadest sense, and reflection on that change. And all of them will be seen to be at risk in the current political climate.

Strategies for curriculum change and control

One family of issues we must concern ourselves with is that of the lessons which have been learned from the many attempts which have been made to change the curriculum.

We have just noted that one of those lessons has been that the teacher's role is central to the effectiveness of any attempt at curriculum change or development. The converse of this is what we have also learned concerning the role, effectiveness and, indeed, the value of national agencies for curriculum development and change. In particular, as we have seen, the work of the Schools Council and other national agencies of change in England and Wales taught us much about how such bodies, external to the schools themselves, might most effectively promote change and development within the schools – especially, as we have also seen, by supporting developments within rather than seeking to impose change from without. These are lessons which those responsible for the implementation of the National Curriculum are currently relearning, or, in their case, learning for the first time. The notion that all curriculum development is teacher development was first promulgated several decades ago (Stenhouse, 1975), and, indeed, had become almost a truism until it was rejected in favour of more coercive methods.

Those coercive methods, in addition to including the application of sanctions of various kinds, have also embraced more subtle strategies of change. We will see, for example, how effectively rhetoric, metaphor and the control of discourse generally have been used to bring about the changes which government has sought to impose on the school curriculum. And, at a more readily discernible level, we can recognize how testing and inspections have been employed as part of the same kind of coercive strategy.

This takes us to a second major family of issues the student of curriculum must address.

Assessment, evaluation, appraisal and accountability

Among the many insights into the workings of curriculum which emerged from the research and studies of the 1970s and 1980s were many in the related areas of pupil assessment, curriculum evaluation and, perhaps to a lesser extent, teacher appraisal. There was significant development both in techniques (for example, the introduction of some highly sophisticated forms of pupil assessment) and in our understanding of the effects and implications of the adoption of particular forms and approaches (for example, the ideas of self-evaluation and action research).

However, that move towards direct political control of the school curriculum which we have just noted has been accompanied by a major shift in the view taken of the purposes of these related elements of educational policy and practice and, as a consequence, in the procedures adopted to achieve those purposes.

For pupil assessment, curriculum evaluation, teacher appraisal and, indeed, school inspections have come to be regarded, and used, as key instruments in the establishment of direct political control, of combating that centrality of the teacher we have also just noted and of imposing a narrow and bureaucratic form of teacher accountability. We have experienced an era of 'assessment-led educational reform' (Hargreaves, 1989: 99).

Thus sophisticated forms of pupil assessment have given way to regular, and somewhat simplistic, tests, marking a shift from a formative and diagnostic function to a largely summative one, designed to provide figures for 'league tables' rather than to offer information about individual pupils which might guide the planning of their future provision, and using graded tests rather than pupil profiling (Hargreaves, 1989). The focus of evaluation has moved from a concern with the value of what is being offered to a concentration on the effectiveness of its 'delivery'. And teachers and schools are appraised also in terms of the effectiveness of their 'delivery' of whatever is dictated rather than in relation to the wider concerns of education.

This does not, however, mean that there is no longer a need for teachers to familiarize themselves with the issues and the techniques of assessment and evaluation. Teachers will continue to wish to assess their pupils in order to make adequate provision for them and to evaluate their own work with the same purposes in mind; and they will still need quite sophisticated techniques and understandings in order to do so. The insights gained in this area too, therefore, need to be maintained. One hopes also that, even with little direct power to bring about change themselves, they will wish to continue to evaluate the official policies and practices, if only to assert their professionalism and to maintain that curriculum debate we are suggesting is becoming more rather than less important in the new era.

This, then, is another major area we will need to explore in greater detail later in this book.

The politicization of curriculum

The uses and abuses of assessment and evaluation which we have just touched upon alert us to a further major area which the student of curriculum cannot afford to ignore, especially in the current social and political climate. For, as we have already noted, the flavour of the curriculum debate, as it has been conducted over the years which have passed since the publication of the first edition of this book, has become increasingly and strongly political.

The placing of the school curriculum in the hands of a series of politically motivated quangos, which reconstruct themselves – or, at least, rename themselves – almost annually, along with their use and abuse of devices such as assessment and inspections to achieve what are fundamentally political goals, has not only reinforced the need for continued and careful study of all of these aspects of curriculum; it has also called for a focusing of attention on this process of politicization itself.

We have long been familiar with the importance of education in the achievement of political goals. Indeed, it was the first exponent of education theory, Plato himself, who drew our attention to this and recognized educational provision as the key to achieving the kind of society he wished to see established. His advice has not gone unheeded by those engaged in social engineering of many forms since that time, most notably those seeking to establish and maintain social control in totalitarian societies – fascist Spain, for example, Nazi Germany and communist Russia.

The appropriateness of employing similar techniques in societies which purport to be democratic, however, demands to be explored. And so, it is no surprise to discover that the last decade or so has seen the appearance of a plethora of books and articles in the educational journals which have set about precisely this kind of exploration.

Hence, no attempt to fuel the curriculum debate at the beginning of the third millenium can ignore this crucial dimension of that debate. Indeed, we shall see, as perhaps we have seen already, that it is an area of concern which now permeates discussion of all other aspects of the study of curriculum.

Curriculum planning

Finally, we must note another crucial theme which underpins all of these issues – a series of fundamental questions about human knowledge and the implications of these for the ways in which we set about planning the school curriculum.

The content of what we expect children to learn during their schooling is clearly a crucial element in curriculum planning, whatever view we take of education, curriculum or, indeed, knowledge itself. There are important questions to be addressed, however, concerning how the knowledge content of a curriculum relates to its other dimensions. Indeed, an important first step in any study of curriculum is the recognition that other dimensions exist. For it has too often been assumed, again notably by the architects of the National Curriculum for England and Wales, that to plan a curriculum is merely to outline the knowledge content to be 'delivered' and imbibed.

Tyler's four questions

It has been suggested (Tyler, 1949) that the curriculum has to be seen as consisting of four elements, and curriculum planning, therefore, as having four dimensions: objectives, content or subject matter, methods or procedures and evaluation. In short, the claim is that we must distinguish in our curriculum planning what we are hoping to achieve, the ground we are planning to cover in order to achieve it, the kinds of activity and methods that we consider likely to be most effective in helping us towards our goals and the devices we will use to evaluate what we have done. Tyler's own way of putting this point is to suggest that there are 'four fundamental questions which must be answered in developing any curriculum and plan of instruction' (1949: i). These he lists as:

1 What educational purposes should the school seek to attain?
2 What educational experiences can be provided that are likely to attain these purposes?
3 How can these educational experiences be effectively organized?
4 How can we determine whether these purposes are being attained?

This analysis, then, if taken just as it stands, would give us a very simple model for curriculum planning, a linear model which requires us to specify our objectives, to plan the content and the methods which will lead us towards them and, finally, to endeavour to measure the extent of our success. It is, however, too simple a model for many reasons, as we shall see when we discuss the issue more fully later in this book.

What we must note here, however, is that rather than offering us a single, and simple, model for curriculum planning, Tyler's work can be seen as having alerted us to the possibility of adopting any of several planning models. For, if a curriculum can, or must, be viewed in terms of these four elements, different planning models will emerge according to the ways in which we might permutate those elements, the priorities we might give to them and the choice of focus we might adopt.

We have already noted that some planners see curriculum content as central, so that the acquisition of that content by pupils becomes the central purpose of the curriculum, the organization becomes a matter solely of effectiveness of 'delivery' and evaluation is focused on the degree of attainment achieved by the pupils. The most obvious example of this model is to be found in the predilection of politicians for planning by 'targets' and the generation of statistics.

Tyler's own concern, however, as we have just noted, was with the purposes of the curriculum, so that he is usually seen as one of the founding fathers of the 'aims-and-objectives' model of curriculum planning. Within that model, the purposes of the curriculum take pride of place, content is selected not for its own sake but for its presumed efficacy at enabling us to achieve those purposes, organization is similarly designed with these objectives in mind, and evaluation is framed so as to assess how far those objectives have been achieved.

Yet a third model has emerged more recently, as some have placed the emphasis on the organization of the educational experiences. This model has been described as a 'process' model (Stenhouse, 1975) or as a 'developmental' model (Blenkin and Kelly, 1987, 1996). With this model, the planner begins from a concept of education as a series of developmental processes which the curriculum should be designed to promote. The selection of both content and methods or procedures is made with the promotion of these developmental processes as the central concern. And evaluation is focused both on the suitability of the content and procedures selected and on an assessment of the development which may, or may not, have occurred.

Ideologies and curriculum planning
Thus we can immediately see that curriculum planning is not the simple matter some would have us believe. For it must begin with the crucial choice of

the most appropriate planning model for the work we have in mind. Furthermore, it must be accompanied by a justification of that choice. For it is not acceptable that we should plan something as important as a curriculum, at whatever level, by simply plucking a planning model out of the air without serious consideration of all possible alternatives.

This last point takes us into an additional complication. For it will already perhaps be clear that each of the three models which have been identified represents a quite distinctive concept of what education is about, what its purposes and functions are. In other words, each reflects a different educational ideology, which can in turn be related to a particular intellectual ideology and, perhaps most seriously, a particular political ideology.

It is this which makes curriculum planners, especially those working on behalf of political agencies, reluctant to advertise the fact that different models for planning the school curriculum exist. For to do so raises an obligation for them to justify their own choice and thus to make public the ideology they are seeking to impose. It is this also, therefore, that makes this an important area of exploration for the student of curriculum, and, indeed, for any teacher who wishes to lay claim to the title of professional educator.

It is this too that prompted the section at the beginning of this chapter which sought to stress the book's concern with the *educational* curriculum and the definition of this in terms of its location in a democratic moral and social context. For that is the ideology which underpins the definition of curriculum adopted here and which will determine the view adopted and proposed in relation to all of the dimensions of curriculum theory and practice which later chapters will explore.

Human knowledge

We must finally note that a major issue which lies behind this debate about models is the view taken of human knowledge. For, among the many insights which we are claiming are currently being lost from the educational debate are those which relate to questions about the nature of human knowledge and, in particular, the ways in which the distribution of knowledge can be, and is, manipulated in society for political ends. What has been called 'the politics of knowledge' has come to be seen as a major focus of consideration by the student of curriculum and its claims to importance have been much strengthened by official policies and practices in recent years.

For these appear especially sinister when one notes that nothing has characterized intellectual development in the twentieth century more than a growing appreciation of the problematic nature of human knowledge. That current movement known as postmodernism, while in itself problematic, has over the last three or four decades highlighted the dangers of dogmatism, raised important issues concerning the validity of knowledge claims and thus, above all, drawn our attention to the concept of ideology and the political dangers of ideological domination. Hence, there has arisen a recent emphasis on concepts of democracy and their implications for curriculum planning (Kelly, 1995).

It is with this fundamental debate concerning human knowledge that we will begin our explorations of curriculum in Chapter 2.

First, however, we must conclude this introductory chapter by asking, given the definition of curriculum which we have adopted and the consequent areas of concern we have identified, what are the key features of the kind of study we are about to embark upon.

What is involved in the study of the curriculum?

It is important from the outset to be clear about the kind of study we are involved in when we begin to explore issues related to curriculum planning and development. Curriculum Studies is an academic and intellectual exploration of all of the factors we need to take account of in order to devise an *educational* curriculum. In short, it is the kind of study which should be undertaken before planning the school curriculum for a democratic society and which, in most places, has been ignored for many years. It is an attempt to analyse every aspect of curriculum, which later chapters of this book will examine, with a view to assessing how far the different views and perspectives offered on them measure up to the *educational* principles and criteria we have identified as appropriate, indeed essential, to a democratic context.

There are several particular features of Curriculum Studies which it may be helpful to identify at this early stage.

A study in its own right

The first is that the area of study which has come to be known as Curriculum Studies has emerged from the attempts, over the last two decades, of researchers and some of those who have been concerned to teach Educational Studies to develop an approach to the study of education which would not be limited by being conducted within the confines of other disciplines, such as philosophy, psychology and sociology. The traditional approach to the study of education through these 'contributory disciplines', as they were once and in some places still are called, has led to serious inadequacies not least because of the approach's consequent inability to handle issues in an interdisciplinary way, in spite of the fact that it would be very difficult to identify any single educational issue which does not require a contribution from all these disciplines and often several others too.

Quite serious and extensive problems have arisen when the solutions to educational questions have been sought, and accepted, from psychologists or philosophers or sociologists, since inevitably such experts have a limited, uni-dimensional, and thus distorted view of the educational issues or practices to which they are applying the techniques and the methodologies of their own disciplines. Thus, for example, major problems were created by the establishment of a whole system of secondary schooling on the basis of the psychologists' view of intelligence and intelligence testing without the complementary and modifying contributions of a philosophical analysis of the concept of intelligence or of a sociological comment on the implications of such a system for the nature of society. Many other examples could readily be found in the history of the development of the schooling system in the United Kingdom or, indeed, in any other country.

Curriculum Studies, then, has emerged from an attempt to study education and to explore educational problems in their own right and not as philosophical problems or as psychological or sociological phenomena. The concern has been to end the practice of viewing the study of education as a sub-branch of any or all of these other disciplines.

Practice as well as theory

Allied to this has been a concern to study education as a practical activity and not merely as a body of theory, to get to grips with the realities of educational practice and to do so 'from the inside', in a manner that the philosopher, the psychologist or the sociologist can never do. Their studies have essentially and inevitably been conducted from the outside; their concern has been with the effects of educational practice rather than with its nature, with the realities of the classroom. If recently they have begun to turn their attention to these realities, they have in effect been developing as sub-branches of Curriculum Studies.

We must not, of course, lose sight of the value of such empirical research to the curriculum planner. For the evidence which emerges from such studies is of immense value to the student of curriculum, and especially to those engaged in curriculum planning at whatever level. We need to be made aware of the effects of our policies and practices in areas such as curriculum planning, approaches to teaching, the organization of schooling, the use of testing and other assessment techniques and so on. In particular, we need to be kept apprised of the side effects of what we plan and do, since these are the essence of that 'hidden' dimension of curriculum which we are suggesting should not be permitted to remain hidden. We will also discover as we explore these aspects of curriculum provision in detail in later chapters that it is research of this kind and the insights it offers which, along with the comparable insights which have arisen from reflection on practice, have been a major casualty of that centralized control of the curriculum which has been a feature of educational provision in recent years.

However, we must note a significant limitation on the value of empirical studies of this kind. For such studies must by definition be descriptive rather than prescriptive. It is not the part of any of those experts to tell us what we *ought* to be doing in education, any more than it is the part of the scientist or the technologist to tell us what we ought to do with his or her findings or inventions. Yet educational practice must essentially be concerned with questions of what *ought* to be done. Teachers in their practice must make such decisions – by the day and sometimes by the minute; they must be prescriptive. And so, if they, and curriculum planners generally, are to be assisted in this quite crucial aspect of their task, they need the support of studies which can and do take full account of the value dimension of education.

Not an applied science

In general, these difficulties illustrate the problems and the inadequacies of all attempts to adopt a 'scientific' approach to the study or the planning of education and/or curriculum. Curriculum Studies cannot be seen as a science, and especially not as an applied science. The history of attempts to theorize about education is littered with examples of this kind of scientist approach, and all of them have been theoretically misleading and practically harmful. Human beings seem to need the security of certainty in all areas of experience, and thus they are prey to all illusory forms of such certainty. This tendency is particularly odd, since it is the case that the more specifically human an activity is, the less susceptible it is to understanding through a search for objective 'truths'. Education is one such human activity, and thus does not lend itself to study of a narrowly scientific kind. It is what Maurice Holt (1981: 80) has described as 'a complex and ultimately impenetrable process'. And a major reason for this is that there are many areas, most notably those of values – moral and aesthetic (and thus educational) – in which knowledge with claims to some kind of scientific certainty cannot be attained. Indeed, when we come to look at the significance for the curriculum of that movement which has come to be called postmodernism, we will see that there are good grounds for questioning and challenging knowledge claims in all fields.

Unfortunately, attempts to make the curriculum the object of scientific exploration, and, more seriously, the practice of offering educational prescriptions as if they are indisputable deductions from, or conclusions of, such scientific study, continue to be made. Nor are these confined to those working in the 'contributory disciplines'. This kind of not-to-be-questioned assertion is all too prevalent, as we shall see later, in those many pronouncements we are now offered from official sources. S.J. Curtis (1948: 255) quotes a story about Robert Lowe: 'There is a story that when an HMI [Her Majesty's Inspector] went to consult him, Lowe said, "I know what you've come about, the science of education. There is none. Good morning"'. Whether or not Lowe himself was fully aware of the significance of that assertion – or, indeed, meant it in the sense in which we are taking it here – it is a pity that the said HMI did not pass this pearl of wisdom down to his descendants. For we are still beset by government officials, with little or no understanding of the realities of teaching, pressing on us the notion of teaching as an applied science and seeking to rubbish the 'quaint old-fashioned and ultimately highly damaging British view that teaching is an art' (Reynolds, quoted in the *Times Educational Supplement*, 22 May 1998: 2) – an assertion which could only be made by someone intellectually incapable, or, more likely, unwilling, to recognize the important conceptual distinction between education and teaching.

If, however, there is no science of education (as opposed to teaching), and thus no scientific and indisputable base for educational prescriptions, it must follow that all such prescriptions will reflect nothing more solid than the preferences, the values, the ideology of those who are offering them. And so, there is an obligation on such persons, first, not to behave as though this were not the case or as though their prescriptions enjoyed some kind of scientific objectivity that those of others do not, and, second, having recognized that, to see also the necessity of offering some justification of their views. To offer them as views without justification is to risk being totally ignored; to use a position of power to impose them without justification is to stand convicted of indoctrination and the abuse of authority.

Again we see, therefore, that the concept of ideology is an important one in Curriculum Studies, as is the concept of ideologies competing for dominance and of the curriculum as a battle ground for these competing ideologies. A study of curriculum, while not offering us spurious answers to questions of values, will, like Socrates of old, draw our attention to important questions which need to be asked about policies and practices and help us to achieve the kind of clarity which will enable us to see their underlying ideologies more clearly.

Beyond methodology

Curriculum Studies as it is being defined here, then, goes far beyond what is now often called by that name in many courses of teacher training. For the term is often now used to denote those courses which once were known as professional studies. The added ingredient of Curriculum Studies is the requirement it places on the student of curriculum to be critical and questioning in his or her approach, to face the value issues central to such studies and, in short, to recognize that the concern is not with mere methodology, with the *how* of educational practice, but much more with questions of the justification of such practice, with the *why* as well as the how. It is this critical dimension that is crucial to Curriculum Studies, at least as it is conceived throughout this book. Curriculum Studies must be seen as a form of professional studies which takes full account of the need for teachers to adopt what has been called an 'extended' professionalism, that attitude to their work which makes them professionals in the full sense rather than merely practitioners.

We can take this further. At one level, Curriculum Studies can be seen, and is seen by many, as concerned largely with the mechanics of curriculum planning, development and innovation. There is no doubt that this is an important area of study and that there are many curricula which could profit enormously from the application of the understanding of the mechanics of curriculum planning which has been acquired through recent studies. There is much more to Curriculum Studies than this, however, and this further, and crucial, dimension is lost when we settle, or allow ourselves to be forced into settling, for a purely technicist approach. We have already seen that, if it is to help teachers and other curriculum planners with the most difficult theoretical task they face – that of justifying their curricular practices or proposals – it must go far beyond this rather limited scientific and technological level. As Bill Reid (1978: 29) has suggested, curriculum problems 'are practical problems which are moral rather than technical in nature'. To deal with such problems, Curriculum Studies must embrace and tackle questions of what education is, or at least of what different approaches to schooling one might adopt. It must recognize that for some people the term 'education' means little more than instruction or the transmission of certain agreed bodies of knowledge; for others it carries connotations of the value of what is being transmitted; and yet again for some its central concern is the impact it makes, or is intended to make, on the development of the individual educands who are to be exposed to it.

To evaluate any curriculum plan or practice credibly, therefore, we need not only an understanding of the technicalities of curriculum planning and innovation but also the ability to discern the underlying values and assumptions of the curriculum specification. Indeed, it would not be difficult to argue that the latter may be far more important than the former. For to be subjected to some form of indoctrinatory process through lack of the ability to analyse critically and identify the value positions implicit in the forms of curriculum we are offered or exposed to is, in the long term, inimical to educational development in a way that some lack of understanding of the technicalities of curriculum innovation or planning or dissemination can never be. For, while the latter may diminish the quality of the educational experiences offered, the former must have the effect of rendering those experiences positively anti-educational.

The view of Curriculum Studies which underpins all that follows in this book will include, indeed emphasize, considerations of this deeper kind. For it is a major assumption that the narrower, mechanical, technicist version of Curriculum Studies, while important, does not in itself warrant a book of this scope or kind. In particular, it does not warrant a book whose prime concern is with the need for a critical approach to the study of the curriculum, since the mechanical view is by definition non-critical, value-neutral and raises no questions of whether the particular curriculum we might be planning is of educational value or not; its concern is merely with the mechanics of planning and 'delivery'.

Too much of what is called 'Curriculum Studies' these days is concerned with nothing more significant or more intellectually demanding than issues of methodology, usually within particular subject areas. Whatever one calls it, there is a need for a study of curricular theories and practices which goes far beyond this; and it is with that kind of study that we shall be concerned here. Perhaps we should call it 'pedagogialogy', or some such, a term which might have the advantage C.S. Peirce once claimed for one of his linguistic creations, namely of being 'ugly enough to be safe from kidnappers'.

Curriculum Studies, then, is seen throughout this book as a critical, analytical exploration of the curriculum as a totality, a theoretical/conceptual and practical/empirical examination of all the many dimensions of the curriculum debate and of curriculum planning, a critical evaluation of curriculum theories and practices, and a form of inquiry which goes far beyond considerations of mere methodology and transcends both particular subject specialisms and particular age ranges.

Conceptual analysis

It follows, therefore, and this must be stressed, that a major concern is conceptual analysis, since its prime purpose must be to achieve conceptual clarity in thinking about the curriculum as a basis for ensuring practical coherence in the implementation of that thinking – again a proper matching of theory and practice. Its concern is to conceptualize the practice of education – at both the general and the particular levels. It requires, therefore, as was suggested earlier, the development of an understanding of a wide range of theories, views and empirical insights of the kind generated by the work of psychologists, sociologists and many others, but, more than this, it demands the ability to sort through these ideas, theories and insights to identify and, if possible, resolve logical and conceptual mismatch and its resultant practical incoherence and confusion.

Many, perhaps most, of the concepts essential to any properly rigorous discussion of the curriculum or any attempt to implement curriculum proposals are highly problematic in nature, are complex in meaning and cannot, without detriment to the quality of both that discussion and its implementation, be treated as though they were simple, self-evident and non-controversial. This is another aspect of that attempt, which we commented on earlier, to treat educational planning and policy-making as forms of applied science. Concepts such as 'aims', 'objectives', 'processes', 'approaches', 'standards', 'ability', 'progression', 'continuity', 'coherence', 'evaluation', 'appraisal', 'accountability' and even 'subjects' or individually named subjects are far from being non-problematic in their meanings, just as they are equally far, as we saw above, from being value-free. Nor are they matters of empirical 'fact' or scientific 'truth'. One does not, or at least one should not, go out to 'discover' by empirical experiment aims, objectives, standards or any other of those things. This is another major intellectual flaw in many current policies and practices.

Further, the kind of deliberate obfuscation of these central educational concepts which characterizes recent official pronouncements on education and curriculum, such as that confusion of the concepts of education and teaching which we noted earlier, is intellectually dishonest as well as politically sinister. For one of its effects, and indeed intentions, is to sabotage and stifle the kind of open debate about the school curriculum which is essential to any genuinely democratic social context.

In any curriculum debate, therefore, a major concern must be with an analysis of what these concepts may mean, what, in the context of any particular debate or policy pronouncement, they are intended to mean, and, crucially, what, in that particular context, they actually do mean. In any curriculum planning conceptual clarity is a *sine qua non* of effective practice. In particular, it is crucial that the many concepts used in any statement of policy or practice be compatible with each other, and a major purpose in subjecting them to such conceptual analysis is to ensure that they are. A good example of this, and one we will find ourselves returning to constantly throughout this book, is the question of the compatibility of many of the concepts which are central to current policies with the notion of democracy.

Worthwhile and productive research into curricular matters, then, must embrace conceptual as well as, indeed perhaps more so than, empirical inquiry.

Engagement in Curriculum Studies of this kind, therefore, involves the development of the skills with which to make this kind of challenging critical analysis and evaluation of curricular schemes, proposals and theories – whether these are one's own or are offered by others – to explore rigorously their underlying conceptual structures and to make similarly critical evaluations of educational practices – again both one's own and those of others – in terms not only of their effectiveness but also of their educational worth and their conceptual coherence. In short, it necessitates a raising of levels of perception and awareness in relation to all aspects of curricular theory and practice.

Finally, we must again note that many of the insights which had begun to emerge from this kind of critical questioning of the school curriculum have been lost as that questioning has been largely pre-empted at the practical level by the imposition of centralized political control, such as that which has characterized schooling in England and Wales since the 1988 Education Act. Teachers have now been told what they are to teach, and their trainers are required to train them to 'deliver' the stipulated curriculum rather than to reflect on its major features, so that questions of the purpose or justification of this curriculum, or even of its logical or intellectual coherence, have effectively been removed from their sphere of influence. If, however, as a result of this, teachers and educationists generally cease to face these questions, even if at present they can approach them only in a largely theoretical way, then those questions will be faced by no one, and there are issues encapsulated in those questions which many would see as vital not only to the future of education but to the quality of the society in which future generations will live. The debate must go on, centralized control or not, and it must be conducted at a properly rigorous and critical level. It is that kind of debate Curriculum Studies endeavours to fuel. And it is that kind of debate whose importance this book is seeking to reaffirm and to which it is attempting to contribute.

All that follows, therefore, should be seen by the reader as an attempt to provide him or her with the understanding and, particularly, the critical apparatus needed to engage in this kind of rigorous study of curricular practices, both as a sound underpinning for his or her own practice and as a firm basis for evaluating official policy, especially when this is being imposed by force of law, and making appropriately professional contributions to what must be a continuing professional debate.

It is in this sense rather than in that of the purely mechanistic or technicist that the book seeks to improve the quality of educational provision at all levels.

Key issues raised by this chapter

1 What is the most appropriate form of intellectual study of education and the school curriculum?
2 Why is this kind of study important – for teachers?
                                        – for society at large?
3 How prevalent is this kind of study at the present time?

Suggested further reading

Carr, W. (1995) *For Education: Towards Critical Educational Enquiry*, Buckingham and Philadelphia, PA: Open University Press.

Play and the Curriculum

Wood, E.

The aims of this chapter are to:

- Understand the Model of Integrated Curriculum and Pedagogical Approaches (Wood, 2010b: 21) (Figure 4.2) as a socio-cultural framework for curriculum planning
- Understand the processes that link playing and learning, drawing on socio-cultural theories
- Critically explore your own values, beliefs and theories about planning for play
- Understand how to plan for progression and continuity into the Primary school

This chapter focuses on developing a continuum between playing, learning and teaching, based on a Model of Integrated Curriculum and Pedagogical Approaches developed by Wood (2010b). This model is underpinned by socio-cultural theories and research from different countries, and reflects the principle that adults cannot plan children's play, but can plan for children's play and other self-initiated activities. Practitioners can use the model to develop their practice in ways that extend beyond national policy frameworks. Play in early years settings is always structured to varying degrees, and practitioners are expected to justify play in relation to learning goals and outcomes. However, this is not the only (or even the most appropriate) way of understanding how play can contribute to 'high quality' and 'effective' provision. Practitioners can develop their own understanding of quality and effectiveness through adapting provision in ways that are responsive to social and cultural diversity, to children with additional and special educational needs and disabilities, and to families and communities. The model will enable practitioners to develop flexibility and responsiveness in their curriculum and pedagogical approaches.

Defining curriculum

As we have seen in Chapter 3, the early childhood curriculum is defined and constructed in different ways, based on images of children and practitioners, as well as principles and values such as community, citizenship and creativity in Reggio Emilia; children's rights, gender equity and education for sustainable development in Sweden.

All curriculum models reflect different beliefs and values about what forms of knowledge or areas of learning are educationally worthwhile for children's immediate and future needs and the wider needs of society. How that knowledge is organized and sequenced reflects ways of understanding progression in learning. However, knowledge is not value-free: the models described in Chapter 3 give status to different forms of knowledge, approaches to learning and to play. What links these different models is that practitioners have a professional and ethical responsibility to make informed decisions about how curricula will be created with young children through adult- and child-initiated activities, based on their interests, working theories and funds of knowledge (see Figure 4.1), and on the content defined in different frameworks. How the curriculum is experienced and interpreted will vary according to the children in the setting and will be influenced by dimensions of diversity: gender, home/family cultures, ethnicity, languages, religious affiliations, sexualities, social class, abilities/disabilities and special or additional needs. How progression is defined through curriculum content is not the same as progression in learning. Play itself does

The concept of funds of knowledge was developed from research by Moll et al. (1992) and González, Moll and Amanti (2005). In the context of play and early childhood education, these theories have been developed by Hedges (2010; 2011b). Funds of knowledge are conceptualized as the knowledges that are situated in everyday practices in children's homes and communities, including information, skills, strategies, ways of thinking and learning, approaches to learning and practical skills. These knowledges include 'subject knowledge' such as mathematics, literacy, technology, which are learned in everyday contexts, combining informal and formal approaches to learning through different cultural routines and practices. Children bring their everyday knowledge from their homes and communities and develop working theories about themselves and their social and cultural worlds. In the context of play, children may be taught important cultural rules and information through games, visual and creative arts, storytelling and traditional myths and legends. Children also participate playfully in activities such as shopping, gardening, cooking, caring for siblings, festivals and celebrations. The work of Hedges (2010; 2011a; 2011b), Brooker (2011) and Carruthers and Worthington (2011) indicates that children's funds of knowledge, and cultural approaches to playing and learning, may not always be recognized or valued within early years settings.

These concepts draw on Rogoff's argument (2003) that culture is not just 'out there' in our environments, but is profoundly situated within our minds, habits, beliefs, values, dispositions, behaviours, body language, interests and orientations to the world. Therefore, culturally responsive provision attends to children's deep cultural repertoires for learning and participation and not just to surface-level cultural representations.

Figure 4.1   Funds of knowledge

not constitute a curriculum, but should be integrated within the curriculum because it creates potential spaces for learning and development.

Activity

Identify a curriculum area and reflect on how your own funds of knowledge developed in home and education settings. What misconceptions did you have and how were these corrected or restructured? What funds of knowledge from home transferred or did not transfer into school?

The concept of potential spaces is quite challenging for practitioners who work with prescriptive curriculum models. However, curriculum cannot be defined only by performance goals in policy frameworks: in the Early Years Foundation Stage (DfE, 2012a) the learning goals and outcomes are expectations of what most children will achieve by the age of five, with an emphasis on 'school readiness' skills. Many children will exceed these goals and some will need further support in the transition to the Key Stage 1 curriculum. Curriculum frameworks do not define the deeper complexities of what is valuable for children to learn, particularly the ways in which they construct their unique identities, interests and dispositions. In addition, the curriculum that is experienced by children involves all the cultural practices within the setting: activities, rules and routines, how children are greeted, how the environment is organized, how they are expected to interact with peers and adults, and what behaviours and activities are encouraged, tolerated, ignored or banned. Into this mix are added children's cultural beliefs and practices from their homes and communities. So how can practitioners incorporate these complexities into curriculum planning? The following section describes a Model of Integrated Curriculum and Pedagogical Approaches which provides possible solutions to these challenges (Wood, 2010b).

Integrated Curriculum and Pedagogical Approaches

The Model of Integrated Curriculum and Pedagogical Approaches is pragmatic because it accepts that play in school is structured to varying degrees, but does not privilege the technocratic 'play as education' discourse. By incorporating flexibility and responsiveness, practitioners will be able to engage with children in planning some of their activities and to integrate ideas from different approaches (see Chapter 3).

The model is based on the concept of a continuum between work and play, as shown in the arrow that connects the two pedagogical zones (adult-directed

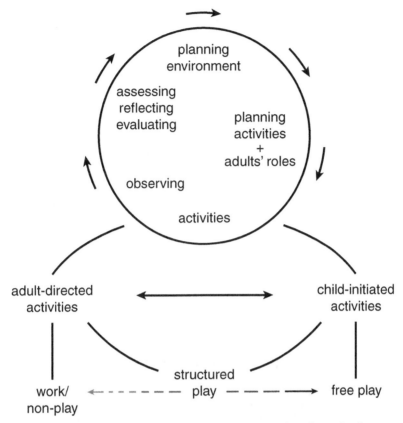

Figure 4.2   The Model of Integrated Curriculum and Pedagogical Approaches

and child-initiated). Looking at the centre of the continuum (structured play) the greater the degree of structure, the more the activity will be like work and less like play. Activities that are adult-directed may have playful and imaginative elements. The lesser the degree of structure that is imposed, the more the activity will be like play, with the recognition that 'free play' will never be truly free, but should be as free as possible within the setting. In the child-initiated zone, freely chosen activities are the closest to 'pure play' because they incorporate the qualities and characteristics of play outlined in Chapter 1. The players have choice and control; activities involve imagination and pretence, with little direction or intervention from adults; there is no pressure for 'outcomes' unless these are chosen by the children for their own purposes. Children are free to choose an adult as co-player, or refer to an adult for help; they set their own rules and possibly goals (but the goals will reflect the purposes of the play, such as building an airport or organizing props). Children may choose structured play activities, such as playing a game with rules or making a model from a plan, or activities that are more 'work-like', such as reading a story, carrying out a scientific investigation, making a sculpture or doing a mathematics game on a computer. In documenting activities in a Reggio-inspired school Parnell (2011) reports that workfulness and playfulness were indistinguishable in the children's activities and projects, but were linked by their creativity and multi-modal representational skills.

In the structured play zone, adult-directed activities can engage children in playful ways with curriculum content: there may be some elements of imagination and open-endedness, but the children's choices will be limited. For example, a practitioner may ask children to act a story with puppets or create imaginary mathematical problems to be solved. Adult-directed activities can be a precursor to play, for example taking children on community visits (vet, supermarket, fire station) and trips (Forest School, farm, zoo, local park). Adult-directed activities include introducing new equipment and resources or demonstrating technical skills, such as how to use tools and materials safely. Practitioners provide the bridge between adult-directed and child-initiated activities through interacting with and observing children, then planning with them for enrichment, challenge and extension in play, based on their emergent and working theories.

Emergent and working theories

Based on socio-cultural perspectives, the concept of emergence reflects the idea that children are always being/becoming: they are always 'ready to learn' and do not wait for readiness to develop. Emergent/responsive pedagogical approaches incorporate children's cultural practices, meanings and purposes (Wood, 2010a). They pick up snippets or fragments of knowledge and understanding in their everyday activities and interactions with people, places and things around them. From these they create working theories, which are combinations of dispositions, knowledge, skills and attitudes (Carr et al., 2009). Working theories may not be fully developed or understood conceptually, but over time they become connected and integrated as children learn to use and apply them in different contexts. Young children may not be able to 'read' in the sense of decoding symbols, but act as if they are competent readers in their play, because they understand that literacy as a social practice is purposeful, meaningful and empowering.

In the context of Te Whāriki, working theories can include making sense of the natural world, social relationships and social concepts, and social rules and understanding (Hedges, Cullen and Jordan, 2011). Working theories may constitute the gradual connections or bridges between everyday concepts and the conscious realization of scientific concepts (the concepts within the subject disciplines) that children use to transform their everyday lives (Fleer, 2010: 4). In the context of play, working theories may include understanding rules and rituals for entering play, the role of imagination and pretence, and acting with imagined competence and knowledge. Carruthers and Worthington (2011) provide many examples of the ways in which children use multi-modal mathematical graphics for communicating meaning and gradually making connections between their everyday working theories and curriculum knowledge.

Figure 4.3   Emergent and working theories

Adult-directed activities are defined as 'work' when they are tightly controlled, with focused instructional strategies, no choice or flexibility for the children, and defined outcomes. These pedagogical characteristics are associated with 'drill and skill' routines, where children may be sedentary and have to conform to regulatory practices such as sitting still, putting up their hands to answer, not calling out, taking turns or waiting to answer. There remain concerns about such formal practices, especially when children are kept in sedentary activities for long periods of time (often up to 40 minutes). This is not to underestimate adult-directed activities, because children often derive much pleasure from engaging with adults and peers in structured activities such as gardening, cooking, science investigations, mathematical challenges. However, long periods of sedentary activities often result in practitioners struggling to manage behaviour, rather than supporting learning.

This model combines two pedagogical zones which acknowledge the benefits of adult-directed and child-initiated activities, allowing for elements of playfulness and playful learning in different approaches, as recommended by Walsh et al. (2011) and Broadhead and Burt (2012). The model uses the recursive cycle of curriculum planning as described in Figure 4.4.

This model ensures flexibility and responsiveness in curriculum planning and pedagogical interactions, by allowing a flow of information and activity across the pedagogical zones. In each of the zones, there are contrasting and complementary modes of adult–child involvement and co-constructive engagement. Practitioners can move across zones to respond to children's interests, make connections between children's goals and curriculum goals, and build on their working theories and funds of knowledge. Planning can be informed by the children's play and practitioners can inspire further play by making or responding to suggestions. This model reflects contemporary interpretations of Vygotsky's socio-cultural theories about the zone of proximal development (ZPD) (Figure 4.5).

Play creates zones for potential development in which children perform 'a head taller than themselves' (Vygotsky, 1978). Play enables children to perform who they are and who they are becoming (Holzman, 2009). From these perspectives, learning leads development because learners actively seek new experiences which are within and beyond their current capabilities, to enhance their skills, knowledge and capabilities. They develop emergent or working theories, connect funds of knowledge and produce new learning through motivation, engagement and participation, and new ways of seeing themselves. Learning/teaching are co-constructive processes rather than a one-way transmission from the adult/more knowledgeable other to the child/learner. In peer play learning/teaching processes may focus on play skills – imagining, pretending, joining in, sustaining involvement, being seen as a good player.

Planning the play/learning environment

- Planning access to resources indoors and outdoors; space available for activities such as large and small construction; specific areas/learning centres for messy play, creative arts, technology, literacy, science, etc.; daily routines and activities
- Planning towards curriculum aims and objectives in adult- and child-initiated activities, including possible or potential outcomes in play. Planning for short-, medium- and long-term goals (but with an emphasis on the first two)
- Planning adult-directed activities and organizing adults' roles in one-to-one and group focus activities which may be adult-directed (teaching specific skills and knowledge in the curriculum areas; circle time)
- Planning for play and child-initiated activities

Implementing plans

- Organizing adults' roles to support play, carry out observations, monitor several areas, engage responsively with children 'on demand'
- Allowing time for play to develop in complexity and challenge
- Building on previous activities and interests, working and playing alongside children

Observing children's activities (see Chapter 5)

- Assessing, documenting, reflecting and evaluating: understanding patterns of learning, interests, working theories, dispositions
- Identifying learning outcomes from adult- and child-initiated activities
- Documenting learning to provide a feedback loop into planning and communicate with parents/caregivers
- Using evidence from all adults in the setting to evaluate the quality and effectiveness of the curriculum (see Chapter 7)

Figure 4.4   Planning for integrated curriculum and pedagogical processes

---

Activity

Chose two or three areas of provision (indoors and outdoors). What is the potential for learning in each area? In what ways do children extend the potential for learning through their own actions (such as combining resources?)

Within an integrated model, the concept of balance between adult- and child-initiated activities is fluid: it may change on a day-to-day basis and over time as children's play skills and friendships develop. 'Balance' may vary according to children's interests, choices and preferences. For example, because children who have autistic spectrum disorder (ASD) have difficulties with social communication, social interaction and imagination, dramatic and socio-dramatic play may be challenging. They may choose activities that are more structured and may prefer routines and repetition to challenge. However, research indicates variations in choices and activities. In an ethnographic study of five

> **Vygotsky's theory of the zone of proximal development (ZPD)**
>
> In the ZPD the novice moves from other regulation
>
> (interpsychological)
>
> *with*
>
> skilled assistance from more knowledgeable others
>
> (peers and adults)
>
> *in*
>
> an enabling environment
>
> *with*
>
> appropriate materials, experiences and activities
>
> *combining*
>
> social, cultural and historical influences
>
> *acquiring*
>
> tools for thinking and learning, knowledge, skills, dispositions,
>
> sense-making capacities
>
> *leading to*
>
> self-regulation (intrapsychological)

Figure 4.5   Play as zones for potential development

children, aged six to eight years, Kangas, Määttä and Uusiautti (2012) recorded different forms of lone play and group play, although in the latter, utterances tended to be short and interactions were directed towards action, for example in technological media-based play. Children with autism develop deep interests: in their home-based study of Rosie (aged 11), Goodley and Runswick-Cole (2012) document her interests and 'passion' for Greek myths and playful engagement with popular culture. The role of practitioners is to see the potential for playful learning in these interests. Drawing on post-structural theories about how 'disability' is framed in different contexts, Goodley and Runswick-Cole argue that 'disability' is constructed and intensified when there is a gap between the ways in which an individual child functions, the demands of society and of different environments. Macintyre (2001) provides skills-based observational checklists and a developmental record for children with additional or special educational needs. These are intended to enable practitioners to track children's learning and identify areas of difficulty, but as O'Brien (2010) notes, children may demonstrate skills and capabilities in their play which do not align neatly with developmental norms or checklists. For example, children who have physical disabilities will benefit from activities that build strength, stamina or flexibility to enable them to access large equipment or outdoor play. All children have the right to play; therefore the 'need' lies with the practitioners to provide opportunities for play as they consider the balance between adult-directed and child-initiated activities.

Processes that link playing, learning and teaching

There are three levels that can be used to understand the processes that link playing, learning and teaching. First, play contributes to learning in the cognitive, affective and psycho-motor domains of development (Figure 4.6).

At a second level, the cognitive processes and dispositions that link playing and learning are relevant across ages, phases and curriculum subjects, summarized in Figure 4.7. Positive dispositions lay the foundations for lifelong playing and learning, as we encounter new tools, technologies and new opportunities for work and leisure.

At a third level, children engage with the forms of knowledge that are defined as areas of learning, or the subject disciplines in pre-school and

---

Cognitive – all the skills and processes involved in learning, thinking and understanding:

- Self-concept and identity
- Language and communication skills
- Multi-modal representations
- Positive attitudes and dispositions towards learning
- Developing metacognitive skills and processes
- Mastery and control in learning
- Developing different forms of intelligence – visual/spatial, kinaesthetic, aesthetic and creative, musical/auditory, linguistic, logical/mathematical, interpersonal, intrapersonal, physical, scientific/technological, intuitive/spiritual, social/emotional
- Social and intellectual well-being

Affective – all the skills and processes involved in learning a repertoire of appropriate behaviours and interactions:

- Making relationships with peers and adults
- Reciprocal and responsive social interactions
- Expressing and controlling emotion
- Developing a sense of self
- Empathy and understanding the needs of others
- Emotional well-being

Psycho-motor – all aspects of physical development including:

- *Fine-motor skills* – use of hands, fingers, feet, hand/eye, hand/foot coordination
- *Gross-motor skills* – large body movements such as sitting, turning, twisting, balancing, controlled movement of head, trunk and limbs. Brain–body coordination, spatial awareness
- *Loco-motor skills* – large body movements involving travelling and an awareness of space such as crawling, running, climbing, walking, hopping, skipping, jumping
- Brain–body coordination, spatial and rhythmic awareness
- Learning about the body and gaining control of movement (body awareness); communicating and expressing ideas through movement
- Gaining confidence and competence in physical coordination
- Physical and emotional well-being

Figure 4.6   Domains of development

school curricula: literacy, mathematics, technology, science, the creative arts and humanities (knowledge and understanding of the world). The curriculum models outlined in Chapter 3 integrate the subject disciplines in different ways, but reflect the principle that children enjoy learning content knowledge, skills and concepts. Skilled practitioners understand the important pedagogical concept that young children can be introduced to the subject disciplines as long as these are presented in contextually appropriate and meaningful ways.

Cognitive processes and dispositions

- Attending, perceiving, observing, recognizing, discriminating, imitating, exploring, investigating, concentrating, memorizing, retaining, retrieving and recalling information, scanning for information, integrating knowledge and experience, categorization, classification, making connections and relationships
- Making intelligent use of past experience to formulate a plan of action, reflecting on action, noticing causes and effects, using metacognitive skills and strategies – awareness and conscious control of one's own learning
- Making and testing hypotheses, predicting, innovating, combining, recombining, reasoning, transferring knowledge and skills across contexts
- Making choices and decisions, constructing knowledge, creating sense and meaning from activities. Creating, recognizing and solving problems
- Communicating ideas, meaning, knowledge and understanding in multi-modal ways: written and spoken language, gestures, mime, signs, symbols, artefacts, drawings, plans, sculptures and so forth
- Creativity, imagination, flexibility, making novel connections across areas of learning and experience
- Convergent and divergent thinking, practice, repetition, rehearsal, consolidation, interpreting, retuning, accretion, mastery ('can-do' orientations to learning)
- Developing transferability, transferring knowledge and skills between similar and different contexts

Attitudes and dispositions

- Curiosity and interest; motivation – intrinsic and extrinsic; open-mindedness, flexibility, engagement, involvement, enthusiasm, originality, creativity, independence, interdependence; willingness to take risks; ability to struggle and cope with challenge and failure; perseverance, resilience, self-efficacy ('can-do' orientations)

Influences on learning

- Mood and feeling states; child and family health; home and community cultures and experiences; parental pressures and expectations; social skills; learning environments – home, school and community; quality of relationships between children, peers and adults; child's and family's orientations to education; socio-economic status

Dimensions of diversity

- Self-systems: self-concept, self-image, self-esteem, self-worth, self-efficacy

---

Figure 4.7   Processes that link play and learning

Play in and with zones of potential development

From a socio-cultural perspective, Bodrova (2008) questions whether play and academic skills are in tension or opposition. Many of the studies referred to in this book argue that play activities support and reveal children's learning in the subject disciplines, adding depth and detail to intended, possible and actual learning outcomes. Disciplined ways of knowing and understanding contribute to children's agency and growing mastery of their social and cultural worlds. Empowerment comes through being knowledgeable, skilful, confident and competent. By building on children's emergent and working theories practitioners can ensure that learning leads development. From this perspective, learning/teaching are co-constructive processes rather than a one-way transmission. However, these are not arguments for using play predominantly as a mode of curriculum delivery. The case study of Leanne's mathematical play illustrates these principles.

Case study

Outdoor play: hopscotch

Leanne (aged four) has chosen the chalks to draw a hopscotch grid. She measures out the grid with her feet, and counts out loud to 15. She draws the grid, writes the numerals in each square and counts backwards from 15. She runs off to look for a bike, but soon returns. 'I've no vehicle to go on.' She continues to draw the grid, counting backwards and completing the numerals in the squares: '15, 14, 13, 12, 11, 10, 9, 8, 7, 6, 5, 4 3, 2, oh no, I need another one'. She draws another square. 'There, that's one. That's all there now.'

   The grid is too small for her to play hopscotch, but the drawing and counting appear to be the main purposes of the activity. Leanne enjoys mathematics, and agency is evident in her confidence, self-regulation and competence in choosing and managing similar activities. In adult-directed activities she also enjoys the daily routines of counting and calculating how many children are staying for lunch/going home. She spontaneously copies numerals when recording her calculations and enjoys sticking her record on the notice board to 'remind the teachers'. Leanne has a good understanding of mathematics as a social practice and the contexts in which it can be used. In being a mathematician, she acts with competence and confidence and enjoys using and applying her knowledge for different purposes.

> **Activity**
>
> Consider this case study and reflect on how play enables Leanne to demonstrate her mathematical competence and funds of knowledge. Think about the different areas of provision and discuss what opportunities they afford for children to use and apply subject knowledge.

Play as an integrating process

Looking across these three levels, play acts as an integrating mechanism for internal and external motivations. Learning leads development because children are always in a state of readiness – trying out something that is just ahead of their existing competence. As children move along the play–work continuum, they combine their everyday knowledge, skills and understanding in different activities. As we have seen in Chapter 1, learning and development depend on internal cognitive structures that are complex in their origins and are intimately shaped by children's social and cultural experiences. The processes involved in playing and learning contribute to the architecture of the brain: rehearsal and practice may lead towards pruning and editing connections; exploration, repetition and revision help to create new connections and more complex neural networks. In play children develop exploratory as well as explanatory capabilities: they actively look for patterns, test hypotheses and seek explanations, leading to increased complexity in thinking, learning and understanding (Gopnik, Meltzoff and Kuhl, 1999). Play activities enable children to impose some structure or organization on a task, make sense of their experiences and engage in ongoing rehearsal of cognitive processes (Whitebread, 2010). As children develop playful minds, they make novel connections through combining materials, objects and ideas in creative ways, which indicates the importance of open-ended environments, materials and resources. Practitioners express concern that children's play is sometimes repetitive but closer examination often reveals subtle changes in play themes and patterns as children revise and extend what has previously been played at and played with. Where play is repetitive, practitioners can help to stimulate interests and ideas by offering new materials with creative potential.

Progression in learning is supported socially and collectively when children can connect their funds of knowledge across the play–work continuum. For example, exploration, enquiry and discovery are the building blocks of science; looking for patterns and relationships is fundamental to mathematics; history involves empathy and an informed imagination; technology and the creative arts involve planning skills as well as imagination, flexibility and spontaneity. Children's learning is enriched by the subject disciplines, including their distinctive methods of inquiry, skills, conceptual frameworks, and their powerful 'tools for use'. Playful orientations (playing with ideas, rules, relationships, materials) support learning within and beyond the subject disciplines.

The three levels of understanding playing, learning and teaching provide a framework for curriculum design, which takes into account breadth, balance, differentiation, inclusion, progression and continuity across phases. Planning the learning environment (indoors and outdoors) is integral to high quality provision.

The playing–learning environment

High quality environments support unity between playing, learning and teaching, and ensure access and inclusion for all children. Open access to materials and to indoor/outdoor spaces supports children's choices but some restrictions may be necessary (no sand and water near computers). Practitioners can either restrict or enable children's activities, as the following example shows.

Case study

Restricting or enabling children's choices?

In a private nursery, the practitioners had a rotating pattern of resources that were put out for the children on a daily basis. The children could not choose other resources or move them from one area to another. After attending an in-service course, the leader of the setting realized that they were constraining children's choices and learning opportunities. She acknowledged her own 'obsession' with tidiness, and was concerned about the mess that would be created and how long it would take for the adults to tidy up. Following some staff development work on the concept of affordance, the practitioners decided to allow the children more freedom to choose their own resources and use them in different areas. They were taught to take responsibility for tidying up and taking care of the resources. The practitioners noticed that the children extended the affordance of the resources and their play repertoires. Combining small-world resources with large construction equipment extended the children's imaginative play, by using hollow blocks to build towns, zoos, parks, space ships and developing role play with Lego™ and Playmobil™ figures. Small construction equipment was used in many different ways in role-play activities: Cuisenaire rods became chips in the cafe; small blocks became gold and jewels in the pirate ship; play people were used in the sand and water trays in dramatic scenarios of flooding, burying, drowning, getting lost and being rescued. The practitioners identified the increased complexity of children's creativity and symbolization, through new opportunities for playing and learning.

Activity

Consider the potential for children's choices in your own setting or in a setting that you have experienced. What factors enabled or restricted children's choices? Could some of the restrictions be overcome and with what potential benefits for the children?

The concept of affordance

Carr (2000) uses the concept of *affordance* to describe the relationship between learners and the setting (including people, spaces, places and materials). Affordance refers to the:

- perceived and actual properties of resources in the environment (people, objects, artefacts and tools)
- how these are used (this links with the idea of *tools for use*)
- how these might be used (this links with the idea of *tools and use*)
- how these may help or hinder learning.

In the Reggio Emilia approach, the underpinning philosophy is that children should have access to 'high affordance', intelligent resources to provoke learning (Thornton and Brunton, 2007). The specialist practitioner (*atelierista*) acts as the more/differently knowledgeable other, who helps children learn how to use authentic 'tools of the trade' in, for example, design, architecture, planning and a wide range of arts and crafts (Parnell, 2011). Following a visit to Reggio Emilia settings, Parker (2001) describes how she used familiar resources in different ways to support children's learning. These resources afforded opportunities to extend children's thinking and creativity with representation and mark-making, and particularly their language: talking, exchanging ideas, reflecting on home experiences, making connections between areas of learning, and playing with words and concepts.

The concept of affordance aligns with the socio-cultural theories that highlight the role of the 'more (or differently) knowledgeable other', and the concept of 'scaffolding' as a learning/teaching approach.

The concept of scaffolding

The concept of scaffolding is a popular metaphor for describing adult–child and peer interactions that support learning. Developed from the socio-cultural theories of Vygotsky, contemporary interpretations include a focus on joint problem-solving, reciprocal engagement and inter-subjectivity. The focus can be on teaching children how to use the tools and resources in their home and school communities, and providing optimum levels of challenge as they become more experienced and expert in their use.

Scaffolding has been interpreted in different ways and can imply a one-to-one relationship in which the teacher, expert or more knowledgeable other remains in control of what is to be learned and how the teaching will be carried out (Smidt, 2006). This underpins a transmission model and is not consistent with Vygotsky's ideas about learning leading development, the importance of mastering tools and the relationship between intra- and inter-psychological processes. Tools are psychological (ways of thinking, learning, memorizing, being and becoming) as well as material (games, computers, loose parts). The interpretation given by Bruner, Jolly and Sylva (1976: 24) is that the critical function of scaffolding the learning task relates to the ways in which the 'tutor' (a peer or adult) makes it possible for the child to internalize external knowledge and convert it into a tool for conscious control (tools for use/tools and use, as described in Chapter 2). The child's own activities and dispositions help to co-construct the interactions through reciprocal engagement. Scaffolding includes collective and culturally situated activity. There are cultural scaffolds that reflect the knowledges valued in different communities; collective scaffolds that reflect how peers teach each other about their play cultures and practices; and there are individual scaffolds that reflect personal interests, dispositions and identities.

Learning environments that have high-affordance tools, artefacts and materials can scaffold children's skills and abilities as they become real-world mathematicians, designers, artists, technologists and scientists.

Practitioners can support these processes by:

- teaching children how to use tools safely, correctly and with increasing competence
- providing tools and resources that are varied, of good quality and are maintained or replaced regularly (blunt scissors cause frustration and young children are remarkably safe with glue guns and drills)
- creating time to play with resources so that children learn to use them in creative ways and create their own problems and challenges.

Practitioners can extend the affordance of activities and resources for children with special educational needs in order to support access and inclusion. Dycem mats in the role-play area and tabletop activities provide a secure, non-slip base. Some musical instruments can be hung on the wall so that children with physical difficulties can use them. Visual props and puppets can be used to dramatize stories and encourage role play and multi-modal communication. The following sections demonstrate how practitioners can create unity between playing, learning and teaching through curriculum planning. The examples are related to the areas of learning in curriculum frameworks and illustrate the connectedness of children's experiences and activities.

Playing with literacy

The links between play and literacy have become clearly established in research, with strong justifications for planning literacy-rich play environments that include information and computer technologies and children's popular cultures (Marsh, 2012; Wolfe and Flewitt, 2010). Children use a wide variety of literacy skills, concepts and behaviours in their play and show interest in, and knowledge of, the many functions and purposes of print. When engaging in playful literacy, children are not just pretending to read and write; they are acting as readers and writers. This is a fundamental distinction which enables children to see the meaning and relevance of such activities. In Vygotskian terms, they are performing ahead of their actual level of development: their emerging capabilities and working theories anticipate future/potential progress, as shown in the four examples of children's writing (Figure 4.8)

Socio-dramatic play creates contexts for literacy practices because of the connections between story-making and telling, pretence, imagination and symbolic activity. In the case study on *Where the Wild Things Are* that follows Figure 4.7, a Year 1/2 teacher created a continuum between adult- and child-initiated activities, using a co-constructive approach which incorporated plan–do–review (described in Chapter 3).

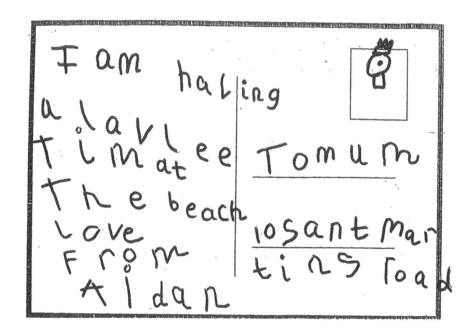

I am having
a lavlee
time at the beach
Love
From
Aidan

To mum
10 sant Mar
tins road

telephone messages

Hello mrs
Davja Son
I am at
the Park

rrg8/9

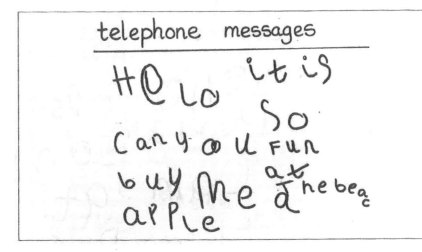

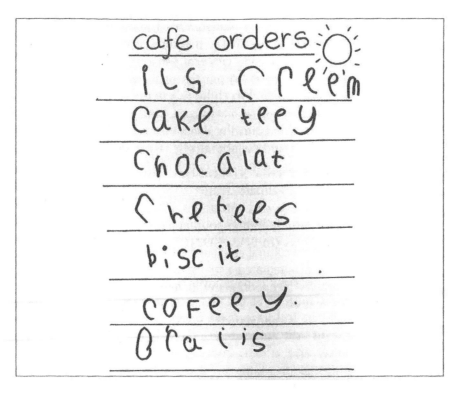

Figure 4.8   Four examples of children's writing

Where the Wild Things Are (Sendak, 1963)

Nicola decided to develop the children's role play through stories. The children chose *Where the Wild Things Are* by Maurice Sendak, which tells the story of how Max travelled to the island where the Wild Things lived, and enjoyed a wild rumpus party. The children planned to divide the role-play area into two sections – one for Max's house and one for the Wild Things' house. The children planned the area, making or bringing in props and resources. They made up names and characters for the Wild Things and represented their ideas through writing, drawing and painting. They extended the story by projecting themselves into different roles and scenarios and making up adventures. They talked and wrote about imagining the reaction of their parents to their absence, or what would happen if they brought home a Wild Thing to live with them. Salah described how he would teach him good manners and not to eat the cat. Jelika planned to make her own puppet, which she took home every day, and involved her family in writing stories and scripts that she shared with friends. One group made up a menu of Wild Things food and then planned a wild rumpus party, which involved many mathematical activities.

The children used geographical literacy: they drew maps of the land where the Wild Things live and the routes from their homes. They acted out their stories in the role-play area, which the teacher extended in dance and drama sessions (moving in the characters of the Wild Things, acting the wild rumpus). Materials and resources were always available in the writing corner and the children made books to record their stories, which became a shared resource for the class. As the children's interests developed, the teacher provided stories and poems about mythical creatures and lands, which reflected the multi-cultural community. Teacher-directed and child-initiated activities were integrated along a work–play continuum, with children having multi-modal opportunities for representing their ideas. The range of activities enabled all children to be included and to participate according to their abilities and interests.

This example demonstrates how role play can count as authorship because children co-construct play frames, scripts and texts, and understand the features of plot, characterization, sequencing, scripting and editing the dialogue and interactions to direct the course of the play. Such narratives interweave every-day funds of knowledge and imagination, drawing on their social and cultural knowledge. Play narratives can be inspired by stories (both fact and fiction) that adults tell to children, and stories that children invent.

As play progresses in complexity, children organize and structure their role play by sharing the creations of their imaginations through the following activities:

- Using story elements to structure their ideas
- Creating new worlds of meaning
- Communicating meanings explicitly to others
- Stimulating lateral thinking
- Playing out problems and possibilities
- Inventing, elaborating and extending themes
- Combining experience and creating knowledge
- Gaining new experiences
- Making connections between written and spoken language (Booth, 1994)

Linking play and literacy involves flexible planning, varied resources, engaging with children to value their activities, providing an appreciative audience, and supporting their developing skills and confidence. Marsh and Millard (2000) provide examples of how practitioners can use children's popular culture in the classroom, including comics, magazines, websites, computer games, television and films and popular music. They argue that comics can provide opportunities for supporting playful approaches to literacy, such as:

- analysing story structure
- understanding characters and how they change over time
- identifying playful uses of language such as puns, alliteration, assonance and onomatopoeia
- being critical of texts – identifying and challenging stereotypes
- making links between comics, websites, games and other 'spin-off' products.

Literacy is a social practice in which children can participate with increasing knowledge and competence. To ensure access and inclusion, books should incorporate different textures, noises that are activated by buttons, and communication systems such and Braille and Makaton. Information and computer technologies enable children to participate in structured games, as well as open-ended activities such as painting and drawing. Touch screens enable access to a wide variety of creative computer programs for children who have restricted mobility and movement.

Playing with numeracy

Children become mathematicians by participating in everyday practices in different contexts – home, community and school. Before they start school, many children demonstrate funds of mathematical knowledge and competences, but research shows that this richness and complexity is not always recognized in pre-school and school settings. Children invent their own strategies that enable them to solve a variety of addition and subtraction word problems, and develop their own systems for representing their calculations such as tallying and idiosyncratic notations (Carruthers and Worthington, 2011; Worthington, 2010). These strategies are evident in play contexts as children encounter problems and develop their own solutions.

Practitioners can build on children's invented strategies and create contexts in which they move through different stages of representation, learn the inter-relationships among ideas, and link their own informal strategies to the more formal symbol system of mathematics. From a socio-cultural perspective, Fleer (2010) argues that progression in learning happens when children make the links between everyday knowledge and scientific knowledge. But this is not the whole picture: as children become more experienced learners and players, they integrate cultural and social knowledge and, as the following example shows, demonstrate metacognitive awareness of the rules and conventions of play.

 Case study

Making a board game (Attfield, 1992: 85–87)

Linking everyday cultural and scientific knowledge, Jenny, Betty, Lee and Paul (aged between six and seven) decided to make a board game after discussion, initiated by the teacher, about the toyshop needing some more toys. The children went to a quiet area to discuss their ideas.

Betty:	Well we could have a race track.
Jenny:	Or we could have the first one to get home like a frog jumping on lily pads.
Lee:	In a jungle, in a jungle.
Jenny:	And you've got to go in your home in a jungle.
Betty:	Or you could have quite a big one and on one side have a race track. You've got to go round the race track the right way and then you get into the jungle.
Jenny:	Or what we could do is a little game for young children and put like sums on lily pads and they've got to add up the sums and they've got to jump on the next lily pad.
Lee:	I like Jenny's idea.

Paul:	It could be just like Jenny's but ... you could go along with a dice and a counter and you throw the dice and if you land on a square that's got writing on then you've got to do what it says.
Jenny:	That sounds good, like forfeits.
Betty:	I think Paul's is quite good cos it's fun.
Jenny:	What happens if it's really shy children, they might begin to cry with forfeits.
Paul:	We could have easy sums like 1 + 1.
Lee:	Easy peasy.
Jenny:	That's easy for you but not for little children.
Betty:	They put two fingers up and count with them.
Lee:	Why don't we have both ideas on it?
Betty and Paul:	Yes.
Jenny:	Why don't we have sums and forfeits? And what did you say about the jungle, Lee?

These children were skilled learners and communicators, using language for different purposes: explaining their ideas, reasoning, reflecting and sharing information. After presenting their ideas to the teacher, she extended their thinking by helping them to reflect on the design.

Teacher:	Before you start, so you've got it clear in your heads what the players can and what they can't do, there's something you need to do. How will the players know what to do?
Jenny:	Rules.
Teacher:	Right, you need some rules. How many people can play?

With further discussion and teacher participation the children clarified their ideas and decided to abbreviate the rules. In Jenny's list of rules (Figure 4.9) she is writing for a purpose: communicating the rules in order for the game to be successful. The children plan to have a pond at the end of the game as 'home' and hit another design problem.

(Continued)

(Continued)

Betty:	We'll stick the pond on the end here.
Lee:	Cut the pond about that big, turn it over and stick it here.
Jenny:	Yes, but what happens if the game breaks and that bit falls off and you can't find it and it isn't very nice in the game, you can't play it any more.
Lee:	Have it round here.
Betty:	Wait a minute. I think we should plan it before we draw.
Lee:	On this piece of paper. We don't have to put one enormous pond.
Jenny:	I know, we could have four ponds a different colour.
Paul:	Yes, red and blue.
Jenny:	The people with the green counters have to go to the green pond.
Betty:	Yes and red counters for the red pond, and yellow for the yellow pond and what's left?
Lee:	The blue one.

This case study illustrates several theoretical concepts that underpin an integrated approach to curriculum planning. The activity was initiated by the children and was scaffolded collectively: the teacher provided skilled assistance at the right moments, by responding to the problems identified by the children. Their metacognitive skills included joint recall of previous games (successful and unsuccessful), knowledge of social and cultural conventions in playing games, empathy and theories of mind (understanding the younger children's minds and feelings). The children's interests created spaces for enquiry which connected their individual and collective funds of knowledge from their home, community and educational experiences. Their working theories incorporated mathematical skills – they used mathematics as a psychological tool (knowing mathematical concepts, rules and conventions) and as a cultural tool (using and applying mathematics in a meaningful play context). Their play shows how older children develop structure, complexity and sophistication, with integration between processes and outcomes.

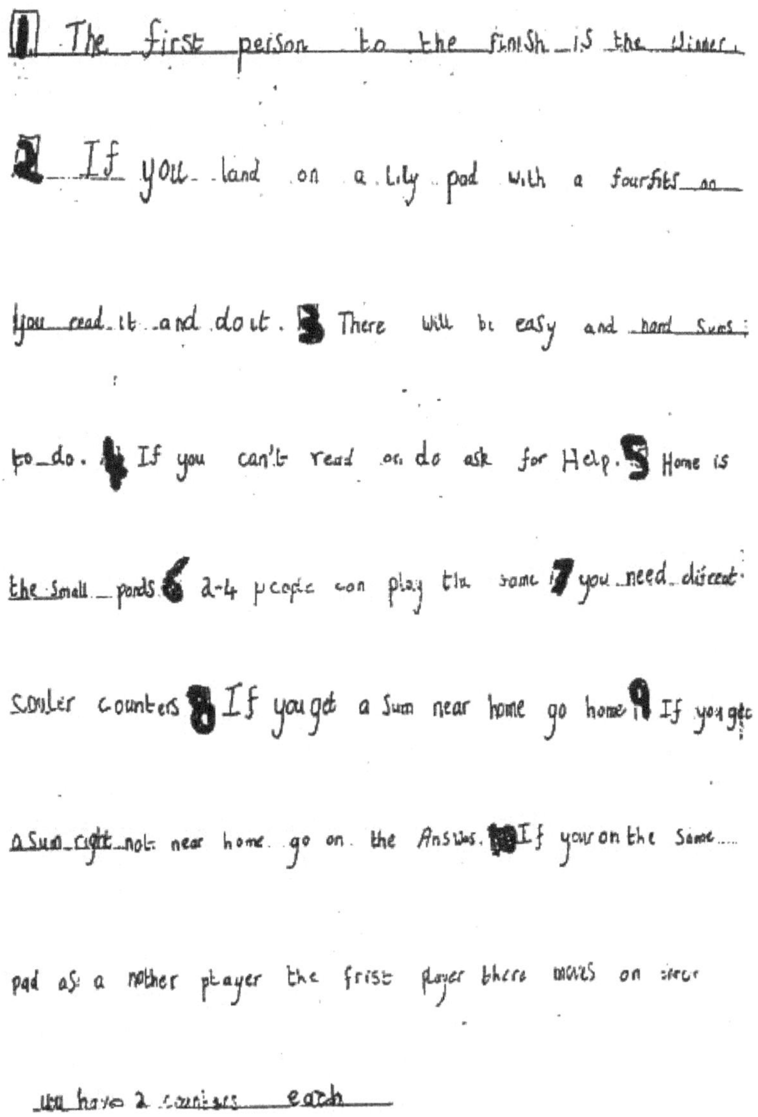

1. The first person to the finish is the winner.

2. If you land on a lily pad with a fourfits on

you read it and do it. 3 There will be easy and hard sums

to do. 4 If you can't read or do ask for Help. 5 Home is

the small ponds 6 2-4 people con play the same 7 you need diferent

souler counters 8 If you get a sum near home go home 9 If you get

a sum rigt not near home go on the Answer. 10 If yow on the same

pad as a nother player the frist player there moves on their

you have 2 counters each

Figure 4.9   Jenny's list of rules

Like all the subject disciplines, mathematics has its own discourse – ways of thinking, reasoning, problem-solving; methods, rules and procedures. Children's success in solving mathematical problems depends on their embeddedness in familiar, everyday practices and related discourses. Exploration and discovery are integral to children's mathematics (what does mathematics do?): the teaching of formal rules and routines enables children to think creatively within the discipline and solve problems independently and collaboratively (what can I do with mathematics?).

Play activities provide opportunities for integrating subject knowledge (scientific concepts) into everyday practices that children encounter in and out of school. The following examples show some creative pedagogical approaches that support continuity between work and play, and playful opportunities for learning.

Case studies

Playing with ICT

Hannah had a degree in media studies: she was keen to use her skills in her mixed-age class (Reception, Years 1 and 2), and wanted to improve her provision for ICT. The project was animals; after a visit to a local farm, the children wanted to bring in their pets. She videotaped these visits to record the discussions, which often involved family members. The children were interested in the camera and wanted to learn how to use it. Hannah was surprised at how competent and responsible they were and supported their idea for a 'Pet News' programme. This involved turning the role-play area into a TV studio, with children acting as reporters and presenters. They wrote news scripts and carried out interviews with children and family members. The older children provided expert models of literacy and language for the younger children: there was much peer interaction and co-construction, as well as extension from Hannah. The children used a wide repertoire of social skills, including allocating roles, sharing ideas, organizing presentations and learning from each other about caring for pets.

Playing with history

Julie, a newly qualified teacher, worked in a small rural school, which was planning centenary celebrations that involved the whole school in the theme of the Victorians. Julie did some research in the school's old log books and discovered a story about a strict teacher who was rather harsh with the children, but also very poor at spelling. The records showed that the teacher was subsequently sacked for her spelling (but not for her harsh punishments of the children). This story provided the impetus for some teacher-directed role play with a Year 1 and 2 class. Julie prepared her children for the role play by telling them the story of the teacher, and asked the children to come dressed in costume for a Victorian school day. She hired a Victorian costume from a theatrical shop and began the day in role. She carried out hand and nail inspections and planned her lessons based on rote learning and drill, with the children using old slates and chalk. She wrote some incorrect spellings on the board, which the children spotted. The head teacher, also in role, came into the classroom and sacked Julie for her poor spellings. At this point some of the children were a little unsure about the distinction between reality and fantasy and wondered whether they would get their teacher back.

Planning for progression and continuity

While there is clear validation for play in the Foundation Stage, there remain concerns about the transition to more formal approaches in Reception and Year 1, and continuing problems with continuity in curriculum and pedagogical approaches. As discussed in Chapter 3, just as children become more skilled in their play, opportunities for play are restricted. Policy-makers assume that young children need more challenging work, whereas a consistent argument throughout this book is that children need more challenging play, along with opportunities to develop and plan some of their own activities and projects.

The examples given throughout this book indicate that children's play preferences and approaches to learning change alongside their developing skills, knowledge and dispositions. Hughes (2010) identifies the major developments beyond the pre-school phase. The child's thinking becomes more orderly, more structured and more logical. Play becomes more realistic and rule-oriented and reveals a developing need for order, a need for belonging and a need for industry. Children's play involves more cognitive activity (what can I do with this?) as opposed to sensory exploration and physical manipulation (what does this do?). Children build knowledge about play and become increasingly skilled as players. As their play skills develop, they use abstract forms of thinking: from Vygotsky's perspective (1978), action arises from ideas and symbols rather than from concrete objects.

In their need for order, children show increasing levels of competence in how they organize, structure and perform in their play-based activities (as shown in the case studies). They become less dependent on an adult for support because they are more confident about sharing ideas, allocating roles, taking risks and defining rules within a group. In terms of the need to belong, older children orientate towards peer-group affiliations and away from the family unit. Increasingly they construct their identities in relation to their peers and enjoy demonstrating skills, expertise and talents, which define their status:

the peer group is a major socializing agent in middle childhood. It is from their peers, rather than from their parents or teachers, that children learn about the culture of childhood. Peers teach a child quite effectively – and sometimes harshly – about social rules and the importance of obeying them. Peers establish a certain moral order that may differ somewhat from that established by adults. (Hughes, 2010: 134)

Hughes (2010) argues that the developing need for industry is apparent in children's work and play: they need to be productive, to achieve a sense of mastery and a feeling of accomplishment. These attitudes and dispositions are related to their social status because play can bring positive or negative validation from peers. In the gradual shift from play with objects to play that is more abstract, structured and rule-bound, children create imaginative roles. When older children engage in socio-dramatic play, they are more likely to spend time negotiating the plot and story line, defining roles and directing the action. They understand the purposes of play, which influences its content and complexity. They gradually progress from spontaneous, unconscious actions towards more structured, conscious actions: their play becomes more like a performance that incorporates well-rehearsed themes, rituals and actions, often drawn from everyday experiences, stories, films and popular culture.

Children enjoy games with rules such as board games and computer games where they compete against a partner or a character, and where success contributes to their self-esteem and status in their peer group. Children's identities become defined by their play competence and how this is perceived by their peers. Hobbies, collections and interests often structure their play: for example football cards define social status and can be used in bargaining and exchanges with their peers.

Children (and adults) do not outgrow play but their preferred modes change as they develop their skills and competences. Therefore, planning for progression in play (not just for progression in the curriculum) needs to be considered within and beyond the Foundation Stage. Children from the age of six to seven enjoy the chance to compete with adults and peers in rule-bound activities (such as board games), but may need assistance to master the rules and conventions. In constructive play, there are many opportunities for progression. Much construction equipment can be linked to computer programs and enables children to integrate playfulness and industriousness as they use their skills and knowledge to solve complex problems and extend their creativity and imagination. Children draw increasingly on disciplined ways of knowing and reasoning so that play continues to provide contexts for extending and integrating subject knowledge.

Children's patterns of development vary significantly, as do their play preferences and approaches to learning. Planning for progression should take into account differentiation for children with special educational needs so that play/learning environments, both indoors and outdoors, promote capabilities and potential.

By continuing the unity between playing, learning and teaching, opportunities for play can be extended beyond the pre-school years. To summarize, children need:

- time, space and varied, good-quality resources (these need not be expensive, because quality is related to the affordances of the resources)
- opportunities for challenge, extension, practice, mastery, consolidation and transferability
- the support of more or differently knowledgeable others – peers and adults
- opportunities to make connections between cultural funds of knowledge from home and community contexts, and to perceive relationships between areas of knowledge and experience
- opportunities to develop confidence and self-esteem, to play considerately with others and take care of their playing/learning environments
- to have their play valued, with some freedom and flexibility to plan their environments and activities.

The following chapter examines how practitioners can integrate play with their pedagogical framing, techniques and strategies.

Activity

In what ways do you aim to achieve balance between children's and adults' choices? How does 'balance' vary for children in your setting? Think about dimensions of diversity – age, culture, language, ethnicity, gender, special/additional needs.

Are there any constraints on achieving balance? In what ways might you overcome these?

Further reading

Carruthers, E. and Worthington, M. (2011) *Understanding Children's Mathematics: Beginnings in Play*, Maidenhead: Open University Press.

Goodley, D. and Runswick-Cole (2012) 'Reading Rosie: the postmodern disabled child', *Journal of Educational and Child Psychology*, 29 (2): 53–66.

Hedges, H. (2011b) 'Connecting "snippets of knowledge": teachers' understandings of the concept of working theories', *Early Years: An International Journal of Research and Practice*, 31 (3): 271–284.

Hedges, H. and Cullen, J. (2011) 'Participatory learning theories: a framework for early childhood pedagogy', *Early Child Development and Care*, 82 (7): 921–940.

Hedges, H., Cullen, J. and Jordan, B. (2011) 'Early years curriculum: funds of knowledge as a conceptual framework for children's interests', *Journal of Curriculum Studies*, 43 (2): 185–205.

Kuschner, D. (ed.) (2009) *From Children to Red Hatters®: Diverse Images and Issues of Play. Play and Culture Studies, Volume 8*, Lanham, MD: University Press of America.

Lifter, K., Mason, E.J. and Barton, E.E. (2011) 'Children's play: where we have been and where we could go', *Journal of Early Intervention*, 33 (4): 281–297, http://jei.sagepub.com/cgi/reprint/33/4/281.

Marsh, J. (2004) 'The techno-literacy practices of young children', *Journal of Early Childhood Research*, 2 (1): 51–66.

Marsh, J. (ed.) (2005) *Popular Culture, New Media and Digital Literacy in Early Childhood*, London: RoutledgeFalmer.

Saracho, O. (2012) *An Integrated Play-based Curriculum for Young Children*, New York: Routledge.

 To gain free access to specially selected SAGE journal articles related to key topics discussed in this book please visit: **www.sagepub.co.uk/wood**

Pedagogy of Early Years

Papatheodorou, T. and Potts, D.

 Chapter roadmap

In this chapter the concept of pedagogy will be explored, by referring to different definitions, and consideration will be given to how different theories and policy requirements have informed and shaped pedagogical practice. A case study will illustrate the conscious and unconscious complex processes of reflection that take place during practice to reach a pedagogical approach that responds to children's individual needs and potential. It is concluded that early years practitioners need to espouse a pedagogy that is purposeful and intentional, appropriate and relevant to children's interest and potential, and is transformative and empowering.

This chapter aims to:

- develop a theoretical understanding of the concept of pedagogy
- understand key ideas that impact on pedagogy
- explore the impact of policy on pedagogy
- link current thinking and theory of pedagogy with practice in early years education and care.

Defining pedagogy

In the English context, pedagogy is often understood as being synonymous with teaching, defined as the act and performance of curricula delivery. Alexander (2000: 540), however, argues that 'Pedagogy encompasses the performance of teaching together with the theories, beliefs, policies and controversies that inform and shape it.' Within early years education and care Moyles and colleagues offer a similar definition, by stating that 'Pedagogy encompasses both what practitioners actually DO and THINK and the principles, theories, perceptions and challenges that inform and shape it' (Moyles et al., 2002: 5; original emphasis).

These definitions acknowledge *teaching* as being part of pedagogy, but it is the *thinking* behind teaching that is at the heart of pedagogy. Drawing upon Woodhead's (2006) work four major perspectives regarding child development and learning that have influenced pedagogical thinking and practice have been identified: developmental perspectives; socio-cultural perspectives; policy perspectives; and the rights perspective.

Developmental perspectives

The image of the developmental child has emerged mainly from biological and child development theories which understood development as a maturational process, taking place in different stages and ages. Notably, Piaget viewed children as progressing through a series of development stages with recognisable cognitive attributes. Through his studies Piaget demonstrated that young children are curious and intrinsically motivated to explore their environment and, through their doings, to work out the principles underpinning phenomena. Given suitable resources and an appropriate level of challenge, children are able to construct their own ideas and knowledge. Piaget's ideas have been particularly influential in creating learning environments that provide appropriate stimuli for investigation, experimentation and hands-on activities (Piaget, 1952).

In contrast to the Piagetian view, behaviourists saw learning as being the direct outcome of responses to environmental stimuli through a process of (positive or negative) reinforcement. According to this stimulus–response model, the child makes an association between a stimulus and the consequences which follow the triggered behaviour; a rewarding consequence is likely to increase the occurrence of the exhibited behaviour, while a punishing consequence would minimize it. The belief in the power and impact of behaviourism is better expressed in John Watson's (1930: 104) quotation below:

> Give me a dozen healthy infants, well-formed, and my own specified world to bring them up in and I'll guarantee to take any one at random and train him to become any type of specialist I might select – doctor, lawyer, artist, merchant-chief and, yes, even beggar-man and thief, regardless of his talents, penchants, tendencies, abilities, vocations, and race of his ancestors.

The unidirectional influence of the environment on individuals has been criticised from within behaviourism. Social learning behaviourists argued that environmental, biological, cognitive and other personal factors influence each other bidirectionally. Children are not passive in the learning process; instead their learning takes place within the social context and through observation, imitation, association and generalisation processes (Bandura, 1977).

Today the importance of the environment in which children live, and especially the early experiences they have there, cannot be disputed. Research in the field of neuroscience demonstrates that early stimulation and experiences shape the architecture of the brain and determine future development (SCDC, 2010). Lack of appropriate nutrition, health and care undermine children's survival, while adverse life experiences (such as care deprivation, chronic fear and anxiety, harsh punishment and mistreatment, and inadequate stimulation) affect negatively children's psycho-social and cognitive development. In contrast, early stimulation and positive experiences increase resilience and ameliorate negative effects (Shonkoff and Phillips, 2000; Fox and Shonkoff, 2011). The evidence from psychoanalytical theory, and mainly the work of Freud, as well as attachment theory (which will be discussed in Chapters 9 and 16), has been further supported by neuroscience which recognises the significance of early experiences with regard to children's attachment, emotional security and mental health in later life.

Child development theories raise awareness of early childhood as a discrete period of life that is characterised by certain needs and requires certain conditions for children to flourish. In many ways, these theories echo and further support the ideas of early pioneers, who had long before argued for age-appropriate resources to enable children's exploration through hands-on activities (e.g. Froebel's occupations and Montessori's learning resources) and the impact of environmental stimuli (e.g. John Locke, who claimed that children are *tabulae rasae*, blank slates, where environmental stimuli leave their imprint).

Some well-known ideas in the field of early childhood derive from developmental theories. For example:

- development takes place at certain stages and ages, determined by maturational processes
- children are viewed as being curious and intrinsically motivated and having enquiring minds
- children need access to resources that enable exploration, active experimentation, hands-on activities
- children thrive in stimulating, supportive and positively reinforcing environments
- early childhood is valued as a discrete period in life, where children's *being* itself is valued.

These ideas made significant contribution to pedagogical practice by:

- contesting traditional adult/teacher-centred pedagogical practice which focused on knowledge transmission
- introducing notions of child-centred, play-based, experiential and hands-on learning

- influencing the way learning environments are organised to offer rewarding and positive experiences
- contributing to the introduction of developmentally appropriate practice.

Socio-cultural perspectives

Socio-cultural theories have furthered our understanding of child development and learning as a social process. Vygotsky (2002) argued that development and learning take place within the social and cultural milieu: children are neither the lone scientists, isolated from their social environment (assumed in Piaget's theory), nor the product of direct stimuli of the environment and the process of positive or negative reinforcement (argued by behaviourists). Children are product of their socio-cultural milieu, its beliefs and values, and its customs and practices.

Socio-cultural theorists emphasise interdependence and relationships with others: how children learn to negotiate, problem solve and make meaning out of their experiences through the facilitation of knowledgeable others, be it parents, teachers or other children. Malaguzzi (1993: 10), the founder of Reggio Emilia pre-schools, saw children as being 'rich in potential, strong, powerful, competent and most of all, connected to adults and other children' and Bruner and Haste (1987) referred to them as *meaning makers*. Children reach their potential through adult *scaffolding* (Bruner, 2006), *guided participation* (Rogoff et al., 1993) and *sustained shared thinking* with knowledgeable others (Siraj-Blatchford et al., 2002), as they work within their *zone of proximal development* (Vygotsky, 1978).

Bronfenbrenner's (1979) ecological theory attempted to provide a broader framework for understanding children's development and learning. He highlighted the influence of dynamic interactions of many factors within and between different systems in which the children find themselves. It is not any single factor that is more important than others; instead it is the cumulative effect of the complex interactions of many factors, taking place over time, that influence and determine child development and learning.

Many contemporary theorists have also challenged the image of the *developmental* child in the light of the widespread diversity encountered in today's societies (e.g. of ethnicity, religion, social class, disability, linguistic) and the unspoken power of dominant ideologies and institutions. They have argued that notions such as stages and ages (the developmental child) assume distinct universal features that are applicable to all children, at all times and in all societies, and ignore social and cultural influences (Cannella, 2005; Dalhberg et al., 2007; Moss, 2008). Developmentally Appropriate Practice, in particular, was contested and became Developmentally and Culturally (or Contextually) Appropriate Practice (DCAP) to highlight that *what we learn* and *how we learn* are informed and influenced by the cultures of particular communities (NAEYC, 1996; Hyun, 1998).

These theories have furthered understanding of:

- the influences of the social and cultural milieu on child development and learning
- the significant role of cultural values and practices
- the role of knowledgeable adults/others in children's learning through processes of scaffolding, guided participation and sustained shared thinking
- the influence and power of dominant ideologies embraced by particular groups and institutions, and/or policies
- the importance of children's a sense of *belonging* in the context and place, where they find themselves.

These ideas have extended pedagogical thinking and practice to include:

- greater emphasis on social and contextual factors
- collaborative learning and group work, where children work together, support each other, encounter challenges, problem solve, cooperate, negotiate and arrive at shared meaning and action
- scaffolding, guided participation and sustained shared thinking to facilitate children's learning
- greater emphasis on the processes of learning (i.e. how and why we learn)
- acknowledgement of diversity and creation of cultures of inclusion and celebration of diversity
- forging relationships and a sense of belonging
- development of assessment and evaluation strategies that reflect diversity and capture contextual influences (e.g. introduction of documentation and learning journeys/stories; self-evaluation of early years settings).

Policy perspectives

Child-development theories have raised awareness of the importance of children's experiences and their being. These ideas became a double-edged sword, however. The notion of the *developmental* child, in particular, became the yardstick to measure children's development and progress according to universal standards, considered to be applicable to all children, ignoring contextual factors. Terms such as areas of development, desirable learning outcomes, stepping stones, benchmarking, standards, quality indicators and school readiness became the reference for defining indicators to measure/profile children's progress (Cannella, 2005; Dahlberg et al., 2007; Moss, 2008).

Developmental standards have been extensively used in the evaluation of early childhood programmes to demonstrate their immediate and lifelong impact (e.g. longitudinal studies such as EPPE in the UK – see Sylva et al., 2004; High/Scope and Head Start in the USA – see Schweinhart, 1994 and US Department of Health and Human Services,

2010). The accrued impact of early childhood on children, their families and societies, and the economic returns on investment for early years education and care became the cornerstone of international and national policies. As was demonstrated in Chapters 1 and 2, during the last two decades we saw a plethora of international policies that legally bind governments to make appropriate provisions for children to enjoy a certain level of living standards (for instance, the Millennium Developmental Goals – UNDP, 2000; Education for All – UNESCO, 1990, 2000; United Nations Convention on the Rights of the Child – UNCRC, 1989, 2006).

In the English context, since the mid-1990s there has been the introduction of curricula frameworks for the Foundation Stage and the Sure Start programme, plus the increase of external inspections and programme evolution (e.g. OFSTED inspections; National Evaluation of Sure Start). Both versions of the EYFS constitute a developmentally informed document. EYFS identifies language and communication, physical development, and personal, emotional and social development as its prime areas (DfE, 2012). Its specific areas focus on academic and cognitive development (e.g. literacy and mathematics) and offer opportunities for understanding communities and the world, and creativity and imagination.

Although it is located within a rights perspective (discussed in the next section), the EYFS highlights the importance of 'school readiness' and the need for acquiring a 'broad range of knowledge and skills that provide the right foundation for good future progress through school and life' (DfE, 2012: 2). It also requires that 'Each child's level of development must be assessed against the early learning goal' (DfE, 2012: 11), indicating that assessment remains child-centred and is the main factor for determining programme evaluation.

Policy has influenced thinking in:

- seeing the child *in the making*, *in becoming* tomorrow's productive citizen, by emphasising development and the acquisition of certain valued skills (e.g. the EYFS prime areas, literacy and numeracy)
- assessing and evaluating children's progress against identified learning outcomes
- viewing early years education and care as interventionist, especially for children and families experiencing disadvantage
- evaluating provision to measure its accrued impact.

The impact of policy on pedagogical practice is evident in:

- curricula frameworks that are learning outcomes-based/oriented (i.e. the EYFS)
- child assessment and profiling (e.g. Foundation Stage Profile)
- using developmental checklists for assessing children
- increased external evaluation of early childhood provision (e.g. Ofsted inspection)
- emphasising school readiness.

The rights perspective

The United Nations Convention on the Rights of the Child (UNCRC) has made an important contribution to understanding of young children as citizens of today rather than as individuals in the making (UNCRC, 1989). The UNCRC starts from the principle of acting in the best interest of the child and articulates specific rights that children are entitled to enjoy, including: adequate living standards (article 25), education (article 28), health (article 24), rest and recreational activities and enjoyment (article 31), social security (article 26), participation in decision making for matters that affect them (article 12).

The UNCRC discussed these rights in relation to young children (from birth to 8 years of age) in its fortieth session in 2005. It reiterated that these rights apply to young children too, and affirmed that children are 'rights holders' from birth. More importantly, it mandated that the quality of services for children should be evaluated to the extent that children's rights are observed (UNCRC, 2006). The UNCRC places the responsibility for ensuring that children enjoy their rights with parents and/or carers, but governments are held accountable in supporting parents for doing so.

The UNCRC has changed the landscape for early years education and care in many and different ways. At policy level, governments are expected to align aims, targets and priorities that meet children's rights. In the English context, for example, children's rights are reflected in the five outcomes of Every Child Matters, that is: being healthy; staying safe; enjoying and achieving; making a positive contribution; and achieving economic well-being (DfES, 2004). The revised EYFS is also positioned within a rights perspective by stating that children deserve 'the best possible start in life' and need support 'to fulfil their potential'. It acknowledges that: 'A secure, safe and happy childhood is important in its own right' (DfE, 2012: 2), ensured by adhering to four overarching principles: the unique child, positive relationships, enabling environments and that children develop and learn in different ways and at different rates (DfE, 2012: 3).

In terms of pedagogical practices, awareness of children's rights, and especially their participation in decisions that affect them, has raised awareness about listening to young children's voices. A growing body of research has enriched our understanding of the many ways that children can express their views and the attentive listening of adults that is required. This is reflected in Malaguzzi's (1993) idea of children's *hundred languages* and Rinaldi's (2001) concept of a *pedagogy of listening*. Children are natural communicators from birth, but adults need to invest in relational inter-subjectivity in order to capture and give meaning to children's many communicative signs (Trevarthen, 2011).

The UNCRC has:

- enriched our understanding of the child as a unique and potent individual, who is able to express her/his views and influence the care and education received
- recognised the importance of maturational factors (e.g. right to health and nutrition) and acknowledged the significance of the social and cultural context (e.g. right to education, leisure and enjoyment) for child development and learning

- explicitly articulated the obligations of families, communities and the state towards children.

As a result:

- policies are clearly aligned with the UNCRC
- pedagogical practices are gradually shifting to more participatory methods, enabling children's voices to be heard and listened to.

Pedagogy: a framework for practice

It is evident that the field of early years education and care draws upon a range of ideas from different theoretical perspectives and policy requirements to understand child development and learning and to inform pedagogical practice. In the next section this will be illustrated with reference to a case study.

CASE STUDY

Ben's story (through the voice of the teacher)

Ben spent two years in nursery and a full year in a Reception class. At the age of 6 years, he was admitted in Year 1. Due to his low Foundation Stage Profile score he was kept in a Year 1 class where he would continue the EYFS for the first two terms. There was concern for his low achievements in reading and writing and he was highlighted as a potential candidate for the Reading Recovery programme ... an expensive and intensive intervention programme for which Ben was assessed and qualified ...

Ben had very weak pencil control and was unable to form letters to write his name correctly. He was still undecided about his hand preference for writing. When he did attempt to put pen to paper he kept swapping hands, questioning the strength of his fine motor control. During initial assessments, Ben said, 'I can't read, I can't write.' 'I don't want to do it.' He had very low self-esteem and a poor concept of himself as a reader and writer and a negative disposition towards learning in general.

In the Reception year Ben would mostly 'choose' either the computer or to be outside on the bikes. At home, he spends his time playing on the computer.

I [the Reading Recovery teacher] called upon all of my known strategies trying to get Ben enthusiastic to articulate a sentence for writing. I tried to focus on his own experiences, but he just shrugged. I tried using playdough and paint to try to engage him in talking while developing his fine motor skills. Very, very slowly he began to gain trust in me and respond. I knew I needed to break through his attitude first and to get him to see what learning looked like. Finally, I found a picture of a boy sitting on the ground with a bleeding knee.

Me: What has happened to this boy?
Ben: *Shrug*
Me: Look at the picture and tell me what you see.
Ben: *Silent*
Me: I think he has fallen over and cut his knee. I bet you have fallen over and cut your knee before haven't you?
Ben: Yeah, but I ain't gonna write about it!

Reflection

I had a response and could see from it that he was sharp to be on to me so fast. It took 9 weeks – 22½ hours – of hard work and effort to build a relationship with Ben and get him to see that with my support he could begin to read and write and maybe even enjoy it. He suddenly started to see that he could do it for himself. I withdrew my support slowly as he gained in confidence. His attitude has turned around and he now sees himself more positively. When asked what he needs to do when he gets stuck he reels off the strategies he has learned (and has been taught!) in order to solve his problems more independently rather than wait and expect to be told.

Emerging issues

The case study above exemplifies what pedagogy looks like in practice and highlights the importance of reflection. It illustrates the importance of relationships, self-esteem and self-worth and the development of dispositions and skills. It raises awareness of the challenges and consequences of children's assessment and profiling against pre-identified learning outcomes and school readiness. It raises questions about interpretations and use of play for learning. The teacher's own response to Ben's needs and potential illustrates that pedagogy is not only a matter of skills and knowledge, but is an ethical stance.

Enacting pedagogy

The reported case study exemplifies the definition of pedagogy as the act of teaching and the thinking behind the teaching. Drawing upon 'known' strategies, the teacher started working with Ben in order to support his fine motor skills (concrete teaching strategy) required for pencil-control and writing (rationale). The teacher called upon ideas and notions from different theoretical and policy frameworks to inform her pedagogy. She employed, for example, a number of child-appropriate activities and materials, such as playing with playdough and painting, drawn from developmental perspectives. She drew upon Ben's possible experiences, such as falling from the bike and/or hurting his knee, adhering to principles of contextually appropriate practice. She tried to enthuse and enable Ben to enjoy learning, and to build up his confidence, self-esteem and self-worth, acknowledging developmental and rights perspectives, and she aimed at improving Ben's reading and writing skills (policy requirements). This, however, does not mean that the teacher's pedagogy was either arbitrary or selective. Instead, as is discussed in the following sections, this was a dynamic and ever-evolving process that was well reasoned against certain principles and substantiated with evidence and through reflection.

Reflecting on pedagogy

Confronted with Ben's refusal to engage with the tasks and his overall negative disposition to learning, the teacher embarked on a process of continuous reflection *in action* and *on action* (Schön, 1983). She became more aware of what she was doing when working with Ben (reflection in action) and stood back and looked at the whole experience to gain deeper insights (reflection on action) to inform her pedagogy. The teacher engaged in a process of what we might call *investigative* reflection, aiming at *seeing* the child behind the mask of observable behaviour and understanding the unspoken messages conveyed by such behaviour. This involved attentive listening and interpretation of Ben's overt messages (e.g. 'I can't read, I can't write', 'I don't want to do it.') and the effect of her strategies on him. Ben's refusal and avoidance techniques were interpreted in terms of his potential, not in the light of what he was lacking. She concluded that, while the concerns were about Ben's 'low achievement in reading and writing', the actual barrier was his 'low self-esteem and self-worth' and 'negative dispositions to learning in general'.

Building relationships

The teacher recognised that Ben's 'response' to and 'trust' in her and a 'relationship' with him were a prerequisite in order to engage him with reading and writing activities.

This required the teacher's attentive listening to Ben's explicit messages (e.g. I can't) and subtle cues (e.g. lack of confidence and self-esteem). The teacher took the time, watched Ben's responses and, in turn, modified her responses too. She waited and took the cues from Ben rather than applying her knowledge of what children need in general (Dahlberg and Moss, 2005).

It necessitated reflection on the impact of the teacher's planned learning activities on Ben and the subtle negotiation and renegotiation of activities that provided meaningful experience to both of them. Building a relationship with Ben meant that the teacher was in tune with him; she was able to think with him, not for him. Such a relationship made the teacher and the child co-travellers in the learning journey rather than the teacher trying to determine the learning journey and mould the child in dominant images.

Building self-esteem and self-worth

Building relationships is not an end itself; it is the building block for the child's self-awareness, self-worth and self-esteem, for these are attributes that derive from the ways others relate to the child and the acknowledgement of her/his efforts (Papatheodorou, 2006, 2009). The teacher noted, 'with my support he [Ben] could begin to read and write', 'started to see that he could do it for himself', 'I withdrew my support slowly as he gained confidence', 'his attitude has turned around and he now sees himself more positively'.

These strategies draw upon concepts of scaffolding, guided participation and sustained thinking, and the zone of proximal development. With the teacher's support Ben became aware of what he could do and this increased his self-worth and self-esteem. It gave him the confidence to engage with tasks that he might have thought of as being too challenging or beyond his skills.

Positive dispositions and skill development

Development of positive dispositions such as curiosity, creativity, independence, cooperativeness and persistence are at the heart of early years education and care. Katz (1993: n.p.) defines dispositions as patterns of behaviour 'exhibited frequently and in the absence of coercion … and that is intentional and oriented to broad goals'. Dispositions refers to all conscious and deliberate or habitual/automatic acts that seem to be intuitive and spontaneous. Carr (1995) suggests several ways of supporting the development of dispositions, namely valuing and modelling them, orchestrating interactions that support them, teaching them and providing support and affirmation to children.

Working with Ben the teacher herself demonstrated positive dispositions and modelled them (e.g. relating, trusting, showing perseverence and confidence). She created an environment where relationships and positive interactions were created; offered support and taught Ben skills and tools to use. The teacher noted that 'when he gets stuck he reels off the strategies he has learned (and has been taught!) in order to solve his problems'.

While skill training *per se* is questionable, provision of appropriate support and at the right time is necessary for the child to cross the threshold of challenge, gain confidence and persevere with the task at hand (Papatheodorou and Loader, 2009). Positive dispositions enable children to develop skills and competences, but supporting skills and competences can forge positive dispositions too. There is a dialectical and interactive relationship between the two, but it requires an insightful teacher with positive dispositions to learning to provide the right balance.

School readiness

School readiness figures highly in the revised EYFS, which also mandates children's assessment. The scores of the EYFS Profile are used to inform many decisions about individual children. Ben, for instance, 'was kept in a Year 1 class, where he would continue the EYFS for the first two terms' and was a 'candidate for the reading recovery programme ... an expensive and intensive intervention programme'.

School readiness is a contested notion, much debated and challenged in terms of its definition (e.g. certain level of cognitive skills) as to whether the child or the school should be ready (Pre-school Learning Alliance, 2011). Caution must be also exercised about decisions made on the basis of the EYFS Profile, for it may indicate the child's challenges, but it says nothing about why these challenges exist. In Ben's case, reading and writing were seen as his main difficulties, but as the teacher realised these were secondary to his lack of positive dispositions and skill, and low self-esteem and confidence.

To ignore the requirement for school readiness, however, may mean that a potent child, like Ben, will be left behind by his peers and his self-esteem and self-worth further lowered, or will be placed on expensive interventions (e.g. Reading Recovery). To act in the best interest of the child and serve her/him well entails careful considerations of the pedagogical options and choices to be made.

Playful learning

Working with Ben the teacher employed a playful learning pedagogy that, initially, was mostly adult-led, aiming at the particular objective of improving skills and competences necessary for reading and writing skills. The teacher appreciated that Ben's previous play was mainly static and around solitary activities (e.g. spending time on the bike or the computer), so she invested in joined and interactive playful activities (e.g. playing with playdough, sharing reading). She provided space and made time for both of them to find common ground of understanding in order to develop purposeful and playful learning that would be owned by Ben. This was a flexible playful approach that gave Ben (and the teacher) the opportunity to draw upon his experiences and interests and exercise his agency.

Play is enshrined in the consciousness and practices of early years practitioners for its impact on all areas of development (e.g. physical, cognitive, emotional and social), positive dispositions and skill development (for more on play see Chapter 5). Play and the pedagogy of play are not without challenges, however. In a culture and context of outcomes-based curricula and children's profiling, even the discourse of play has changed. This has shifted from play to playful learning; from child-initiated play to balanced child-led and adult-led play (for an extensive overview of play, see Moyles, 2010). Practices – as the case study illustrates – are also variable. In some cases play may become so open-ended as to allow children to engage with limited preferred choices and refuse to extend their play repertoire. In other instances play may be narrowed down to the extent that it is mostly, if not exclusively, adult-led.

Considering Ben's challenges, it is important to remember that whatever play or playful approach to learning is chosen, this should:

- contribute to children's positive dispositions to learning
- develop an appropriate level of skill and competences that enable children to engage with challenging tasks and enjoy them
- enable children to interact, collaborate and work with others and to problem solve
- instil a sense of self-esteem and self-worth and confidence
- lead to independence and self-reliance.

Relational pedagogy

The teacher's playful approach was also informed by her/his view of Ben as the 'sharp' individual, who was able to exercise his agency 'to solve his problems', to be 'independent' and 'reel off the strategies he had learned', to 'see what learning is like', 'not to expect to be told'. This was a pedagogical stance that acknowledged the child as a strong, powerful and meaning-making individual, but it placed the responsibility of enabling the child to do so on the teacher. The teacher's practice reflected the principles of relational pedagogy, articulated by Brownlee (2004), namely:

- showing respect to the child as a knower
- providing learning experiences that related to her/his own experience
- articulating and facilitating an approach that emphasised meaning making rather than transmission and accumulation of knowledge.

The case study illustrates that well-known and good practice needs to be framed against an appropriate pedagogy that leads to a meaningful experience for both the child and the teacher. This requires, to recall Dahlberg and Moss (2005: 1), investment in 'a relation, a network of obligation' and 'infinite attention to the other'. Reciprocal relationships inform and enable a pedagogy that is purposeful and intentional; are appropriate and relevant to the child's interest and potential; are transformative and empowering.

By investing in relational inter-subjectivity – to recall Trevarthen (2011) – relational pedagogy bridges dichotomies and polarised discourses such as child-centred/led/initiated versus adult-centred/led learning; learning processes versus outcomes/competences-based education; or children's *being* versus children's *becoming*. In doing so it necessitates continuous negotiation of different, and often conflicting, influences and ongoing reflection for developing meaningful and worthwhile practices.

Summary

In conclusion, pedagogy offers a broad framework that informs the ways early years practitioners engage with children and the planning of learning activities. It is the springboard for conscious and unconscious reflections and forms the basis for evaluating whether these actions are responsive to children's interests and/or brought about by intended outcomes. It offers the lenses and filters by which theoretical perspectives, policy requirements and established good practices are critiqued and questioned in order to act in the best interest of children and in safeguarding best outcomes for them.

It is neither the child's being here and now (developmental perspectives) nor her/his becoming in some distant future (policy perspectives) that is more important than the other. There is a moral and ethical obligation to observe children's being and becoming and instil a sense of belonging through an appropriate pedagogy (Papatheodorou, 2010). For this, engagement is needed in a dialectical manner with theoretical perspectives and policy requirements, as both inform and shape each other (Papatheodorou, 2012). The ability to critique and negotiate different and often conflicting and polarised discourses can only enable creativity and flexibility of thinking and thus advance practice.

Key points to remember

- The concept of pedagogy has been influenced by developmental theories, as the way we learn is influenced by development and children thrive in stimulating, supportive and positively reinforcing environments.
- The concept of pedagogy is influenced by policy in terms of curricular approaches, child assessment and external evaluation bodies such as Ofsted.
- The introduction of UNCRC in 1989 has enriched the understanding of the child as a social actor who is able to express her/his views, and has influenced the care and education received and consequently has impacted on our views on pedagogy.
- Pedagogy in the field of early years education and care draws upon a range of ideas from different theoretical perspectives and policy requirements and is influenced by ongoing dialogue and reflection among early years practitioners.

Points for discussion

- To what extent do the concepts of scaffolding, guided participation and sustained shared thinking reflect similar ideas, and how might they be different?
- What are the characteristics, similarities and differences between play, playful learning, child-initiated and adult-led learning?
- What does it mean 'acting in the best interest of children' and 'safeguarding children's rights'?

Reflective tasks

Consider your own practice and context to reflect on:
- whether any particular perspective, discussed in this chapter, is more evident than others, and why
- the ways and methods you use to capture children's voices and how these might be improved
- whether children's formative assessment and EYFS profiling do evaluate whether children's rights are observed, and how this might be improved.

Further reading 📖

Moyles, J. (2010) *The Excellence of Play*, 3rd edn. Maidenhead: Open University Press.
Papatheodorou, T. (2009) 'Exploring relational pedagogy', in T. Papatheodorou and J. Moyles (eds), *Learning Together in the Early Years: Exploring Relational Pedagogy*. London: Routledge.

Useful websites 🖱

United Nations *Convention on the Rights of the Child, General Comment No. 7: Implementing Child Rights in Early Childhood*: www2.ohchr.org/english/bodies/crc/docs/AdvanceVersions/ GeneralComment7Rev1.pdf

To gain **free access** to selected SAGE journal articles related to key topics in this chapter visit: www.sagepub.co.uk/Palaiologou2e

Curriculum as Content and Product

Kelly, A.V.

We have noted on several occasions the analysis by Ralph Tyler (1949) of the key elements of curriculum planning – purposes, content, procedures and evaluation. And we have suggested that a focus on any one of these, a selection of any as the prime consideration in curriculum planning will lead us to a quite distinctive form for such planning. Chapter 2, through its discussion of the problem of human knowledge also drew our attention to the fact that each of these forms will reflect and represent a different ideology not only of education but also of knowledge, of humanity and of society. This chapter and the next will seek to unpack the differing ideologies that each encapsulates. In particular, they will endeavour to elucidate what appear to be the three major ideologies which can be discerned – curriculum as content and education as transmission, curriculum as product and education as instrumental and curriculum as process and education as development.

Curriculum as content and education as transmission

We noted earlier that many people have not fully appreciated the force or the implications of Tyler's claim. For many, a curriculum is still a syllabus, and even among those who have discussed and even advocated a more sophisticated approach to planning there are those who continue, at least in the practical recommendations they make, to regard decisions of content as the starting point. Many of these people do operate with a concept of education framed in terms of the developing understanding of the child, the growth of critical awareness and other such elements which seem more closely related to the idea of education as development than to that of education as the mere transmission of knowledge. They still appear to assume, however, and sometimes endeavour to argue, that only certain kinds of knowledge will promote these forms of development or that exposure to certain kinds of knowledge will do so for all pupils.

And the politicians and those who produce the official documentation for them also continue to offer their curricular prescriptions in terms of the content to be transmitted, although they too wrap this up in a rhetoric of 'entitlement', 'progression', 'continuity', 'breadth', 'balance' and those other unanalysed and unexplained concepts which we noted in Chapters 1 and 2, again in a manner which suggests that they too assume that exposure to their chosen content will automatically, by some kind of magic or osmosis, ensure that these are the end results for all pupils.

The philosophical case

The philosophical case for planning the curriculum in terms of its content is based on the kind of absolutist epistemology whose difficulties we explored in Chapter 2. We saw there that to view knowledge as being in some sense God-given, independent of the knower, as *sui generis*, is to approach the problem of the status of human knowledge by studying knowledge itself rather than the social context and the social relations within which it is produced. It is thus a view which leads to a loss of status, and indeed of freedom, for the individual, since objective, absolute knowledge is not to be argued or disagreed with, even in the murky area of values. And we also noted that this is not merely an academic issue, since societies which have been based on particular and unquestioned views of knowledge and values have all of them in reality been characterized by an absence of individual freedom, not only of thought but also of speech and action.

When this form of absolutist epistemology is applied to the planning of the curriculum, it assumes a planning model whose first question is 'What kinds of knowledge enjoy this kind of absolute status?', and education is then defined, in the well-known words of Richard Peters (1965, 1966) as 'initiation into intrinsically worthwhile activities'.

There are two points to be identified here. First, as we saw in Chapter 1, if we are to see 'education' as a concept which is distinguishable from other kinds of teaching such as 'training', 'instruction', 'conditioning', 'indoctrination' and so on, one of the features which must distinguish it from these other teaching activities is that it must be focused on intrinsic value, it must be an activity we engage in for its own sake rather than as instrumental to some extrinsic purpose or purposes. This is an important distinction and one which has been largely lost in current policies and practices, as we shall see later.

The second point we must identify, however, is rather more controversial. For this approach to curriculum planning is asking us to accept, as its absolutist epistemology demands of it, that we see this intrinsic value as residing in some way in the knowledge itself rather than in the manner in which the learner approaches and views it. Like beauty also for the absolutist, it resides not in the eye of the beholder but in some sense in that which is beheld. Thus, on this view, in a very real sense, we must plan our curriculum with no reference to its potential impact on the recipients of it. The justification for that curriculum is to be found in its content rather than in its effects.

A further point arises from this. For, as will have been seen from our discussion of the problem of knowledge in Chapter 2, what is important is not merely *what* knowledge we present *via* our curricula but also, and more so, *how* we present it. In a context of serious doubts about the status of all human knowledge, what is crucial is that we invite critical reflection and challenge of all that is so presented. The knowledge component of a democratic curriculum must be what Habermas (1972) has called 'emancipatory knowledge'. This has been described by Wilf Carr (1995: 115) as deriving 'from a fundamental desire to be free from those constraints on human reason – constraints of authority, ignorance, custom, tradition and the like – which impede the freedom of individuals to determine their purposes and actions on the basis of their own rational reflections'. If knowledge is seen as emancipatory in this way (as it surely must in any genuinely democratic context), then some God-given status of its own cannot be the justification for its selection for inclusion in the curriculum. There must be some other basis or bases for selection.

This approach to curriculum planning, then, has the merit of being concerned to ensure that all pupils have access to what is regarded as intrinsically worthwhile; its concept of entitlement is genuine rather than rhetorical. However, noble as its intentions may be, it falls well short of offering a satisfactory basis for curriculum planning for a democratic society, since it produces a form of curriculum which leads to the stratification of society, to elitism, to the disaffection and alienation of those who find themselves in the lower strata of such a society, especially when this is due to social class, ethnic origin or gender. Hence there has been a rejection not only of this approach to curriculum but also of the theory of knowledge on which it is based.

Education as cultural transmission

A common example of this content-based approach to curriculum planning is that which derives from the view that the curriculum should be concerned to transmit the culture of society.

It must be recognized that schools exist in advanced or sophisticated societies as agencies for the handing on of the culture of the society, so that at least in part their purposes must be seen in terms of socialization or acculturation, attending to that induction of children into the ways of life of society which is achieved in more primitive societies by less formal methods. On this basis it has been argued that a good deal of what is to be taught in schools can be decided by reference to 'the common cultural heritage' (Lawton, 1973, 1975) of the society they are created to serve.

Even if one accepts the force of this claim in principle, in practice it creates more difficulties than it resolves. To begin with, difficulties arise because the term 'culture' has several different meanings (Kelly, 1986). In particular, confusions are created by the fact that the term is used, by anthropologists for example, to denote in a purely descriptive sense all aspects of the ways of life of a society, as when we speak of the cultural patterns of a primitive community. On the other hand, it is also used to denote what is regarded as being best in the art and literature of any particular society, what Matthew Arnold once described as 'the best that has been thought and said'. Thus a 'cultured individual', is not one who knows his or her way about the ways of life, the habits and beliefs of his or her society; he or she is an individual who has been brought to appreciate those works of his or her fellows that are regarded as being among the finer achievements of the culture.

When people talk, then, of basing the curriculum on the culture of the society, some of them are suggesting that we socialize the young, while others are encouraging us to frame the curriculum in terms of what is regarded as being best or most valuable, those things which are 'intrinsically worthwhile', among the intellectual and artistic achievements of the society.

Cultural pluralism

A further difficulty arises for those who wish to base decisions about the content of the curriculum on considerations of the culture of the society when we attempt to state in specific terms what that culture is. For it is clear that in a modern advanced industrial society no one pattern of life, and no single body of 'high culture', that can be called the culture of that society can be identified. Most modern societies are pluralist in nature; that is, it is possible to discern in them many different, and sometimes incompatible, cultures or subcultures.

The question whether schools should endeavour to promote a common culture or help diverse groups to develop their own different cultures is a vexed one, not least in relation to those minority ethnic groups that are to be found in most societies (Jeffcoate, 1984; Kelly, 1986). What concerns us more directly here, however, is the implication that, even if we believe that the content of the curriculum should be based on the culture of the society, it will be impossible to assert with any real expectation of general acceptance what that culture is and therefore what the content of the curriculum should be. As evidence of this we have only to note the problems which arise from proposals that schools in the United Kingdom should teach 'Britishness'. All that this line of argument will achieve is to remind us of the view of the curriculum as a battleground of competing ideologies and to bring us face to face with age-old issues concerning the appropriate educational provision for different social and ethnic groups. In fact, it is a line of argument which in the last analysis leads to a recognition of the need for diversity rather than uniformity of educational provision, and thus to an awareness of the inadequacies of any form of curriculum planning that lays too great a stress on the role of curriculum content.

This is one source of a further problem that arises if we attempt to establish as the content of our curriculum those things which we regard as being the essential valuable elements of the culture, a problem which we have seen is endemic to all forms of absolutist approaches. For recent practice has revealed very clearly that this can lead to the imposition on some pupils of a curriculum that is alien to them, which lacks relevance to their lives and to their experience outside the school and can ultimately bring about their alienation from and rejection of the education they are offered. This is probably the root cause of most of the problems that the educational system is facing today and it is certainly a real hazard if not an inevitable result of this kind of approach to curriculum planning. In a class-ridden society which is also multi-ethnic, it is not possible to break the cycle of poverty, unemployment, disaffection, alienation and social disorder by offering a middle-class, white, Anglo-Saxon curriculum to all pupils. In fact, to do so, as we shall see, is to aggravate and reinforce that cycle. So that the imposition of such a curriculum on all pupils is a clear indication that the breaking of that cycle is not high on the political agenda.

A selection from the culture

These last points lead us on to a much more general weakness of this line of argument. For it will be apparent that even if we see it as the task of our schools to initiate pupils into the culture of the society, it will not be possible to offer them the whole of that culture, however it is defined. A selection will have to be made and, since this is so, any notion of the culture of the society, no matter how acceptable in definition or content, will not in itself provide us with appropriate criteria of selection. We will need to look elsewhere for justification of the selection we do make, so that the arguments for a curriculum content based on the culture or cultures of society will not in themselves take us very far towards finding a solution to our problem. What they do offer, however, is a mechanism by which politicians can impose their own favoured versions of culture on a society, as is illustrated by those pronouncements we have heard from senior politicians about such things as history and literature syllabuses, echoed as always by their spokespersons in the curriculum quangos.

'Timeless' elements

This danger can be avoided only if it can be argued that what is valuable in the culture is valuable not merely because it is part of the culture but because it has some intrinsic merit which justifies its place not only on the curriculum but also in society itself. There are many people who would wish to argue that there are certain elements in the culture of any advanced society which go beyond the particularities of that society and reflect certain values which are 'timeless' and, indeed, transcendental in every sense. It is on grounds such as these that many would want to press the case for the introduction of pupils to literature, music, art and ideas that are felt to be 'great' and to constitute a cultural heritage which is the heritage of humanity in general rather than of one particular nation. And it is difficult to mount a contrary argument and claim that such things should have no place on the curriculum.

However, this does bring us back to the whole issue of the nature of knowledge and the question whether any body of knowledge has or can have an intrinsic, objective, absolute value or status. The focus of the matter, therefore, continues to be the nature of human knowledge, and, if we have doubts about absolutist versions of knowledge, we must ask important questions about the forms of curricula that these must lead us to.

Cultural change

The problem is further aggravated by the fact that most societies are far from static entities and this implies that one feature of their culture is that it is changing, evolving, developing. In particular, technological change must lead to changes in the norms, the values, the beliefs, the customs of a society; in other words, it must lead to a fluid culture. And moral change is more difficult in many ways to handle, since people shed or change their values more slowly and more reluctantly than they exchange their cars or their washing machines.

A recognition of the rapidity of social change and of the need for people to be equipped to cope with it and even to exercise some degree of control over it suggests that schools should in any case go beyond the notion of initiation of pupils into the culture of the society, beyond socialization and acculturation, to the idea of preparing pupils for the fact of social change itself, to adapt to and to initiate changes in the norms and values of the community. In short, it may be argued that the view of curriculum as cultural content is based on too narrow a concept of culture.

'Cultural amplifiers'

Thus more recent views have stressed that culture must be seen as the total environment within which the child develops and learns and which she/he must be helped to come to terms with, to operate effectively in and to gain some control over. Children learn, it is claimed, by making sense and constructing meaning through interaction with their environment, their culture. And so, the task of education is to help pupils towards this form of learning, 'to negotiate meaning in a manner congruent with the requirements of the culture' (Bruner and Haste, 1987: 1). In this sense, culture is viewed as supporting cognitive growth by providing 'cultural amplifiers' through which children develop those 'modes of representation' (Eisner, 1982) we noted in Chapter 2, access to public structures through which the meaning of experiences can be not only internalized and understood, but also shared. On this kind of analysis, learning is interactive and the relationship between culture and the curriculum is two-way. This discussion, however, is taking us into a quite different curriculum ideology and we must delay further pursuit of it until Chapter 4.

What we must note here is the support such a view of culture gives to the argument that pupils must be offered much more than a selection of the culture of the society as it exists at the time when they happen to be in schools, even if this could be identified and defined clearly enough for adequate educational practice. It also constitutes, as we have seen, a strong argument for planning the curriculum by reference to the capacities we are endeavouring to promote in pupils rather than the bodies of knowledge we are concerned to pass on to them.

Furthermore, if we are right to suggest that this is the only viable role the school can take in a rapidly changing society, if it can equip pupils to take their place in such a society only by developing in them the ability to think for themselves and make their own choices, the question whether the school is there to transmit or to transform the culture of society has already been answered. For the adoption of this kind of role takes the school well beyond the mere transmission of knowledge – a role which in a changing society would seem in any case to be untenable. If the school is not in itself to transform the culture, it is certainly there to produce people who can and will transform it. As Dennis Lawton (2003: 407) has said, 'schools must become better modes of cooperation and community as well as teaching and learning'.

The idea of education as transmission or of curriculum as content, then, is simplistic and unsophisticated because it leaves out of the reckoning major dimensions of the curriculum debate. In particular, it does not encourage or help us to take any account of the children who are the recipients of this content and the objects of the process of transmission, or of the impact of that content and that process on them, and especially their right to emancipation and empowerment. Their task is to learn as effectively as they can what is offered to them. If the effect of the process on them is of any significance, this model offers us no means of exploring or evaluating that effect, beyond assessing the extent of their assimilation of what has been fed to them, any other consequences of such learning being beyond its scope. So far as this model is concerned, these are an irrelevance, since to ask this kind of question is to go well beyond what the model permits or acknowledges. Yet many would wish to argue that it is precisely that effect or these consequences which are at the heart of what, as we saw in Chapter 1, we might mean by the term 'education', unless, as we have also seen, it is to be seen as synonymous with instruction or even training. And for that reason it is claimed by many that this model is inadequate for proper *educational* planning; it does not go far enough; it asks one kind of question only and takes into account only one kind of consideration; in particular, it pays little attention to the purposes of education; it thus offers a distorted view of education and of curriculum and a seriously flawed and limited model for educational planning.

The approach to curriculum planning through content, then, raises problems even when it is proposed within the context of an epistemology which seeks to proclaim the intrinsic value of this content. When no such epistemological basis is claimed, when the selection of the content of our curriculum is not justified by reference to knowledge itself or to the culture of society, then further difficulties arise, since that selection will now be a result of considerations of an instrumental or utilitarian kind. And it is this kind of consideration which underpins the forms of content-based curricula which are hatched by politicians and their aides.

The political selection of curriculum content

Planning by nothing more sophisticated than statements of content is becoming increasingly prevalent in current curricular policies. It is the view of curriculum which clearly underpins most official statements which have emerged from the Department of Education and Science (DES), which became the Department for Education and Employment (DfEE) and is now the Department for Education and Skills (DfES), and not only from the civil servants there, who might not be expected to show any depth of understanding of the complexities of educational planning, but also from Her Majesty's Inspectorate and that plethora of government quangos which recent years have spawned, whose ambitions to be regarded as the leading edge of professional planning and provision would seem to suggest that they should. Thus the series of publications under the general title *Curriculum Matters* (DES, 1984a, 1985a, 1985b, 1985c, 1985d, 1986a, 1986b, 1987b, 1987c) which presaged the establishment of the National Curriculum for England and Wales, was planned, like most earlier statements emanating from the same source, in terms of separate curriculum subjects, and each concentrated very largely on outlining what its authors felt should be the essential content of those subjects. When they were not outlining content they were listing 'aims and objectives' and thus demonstrating a different, although related, lack of understanding and sophistication, as we shall see later.

It was not surprising, therefore, that this same, simple model was adopted by the politicians and their aides for the planning of the National Curriculum, whose core is 'the overall content, knowledge, skills and processes' (DES, 1987a: 10) of every subject listed as an essential ingredient of the new national programme of instruction and testing. We will examine many aspects of this policy in later chapters, but we must note here that it is not only a good example but also a prominent and pressingly topical example of this view of education as transmission and of curriculum as content, but with the added dimension of a largely instrumental or utilitarian basis for the selection of the content to be transmitted. And the major weakness we should note is that at no stage does one find any justification, or even any attempt at justification, for either the subjects or their content, except in vague and unanalysed phrases such as 'which they need to learn' (*op. cit.*: 4), 'relevant to today's needs' (*op. cit.*: 10), or in overtly utilitarian considerations such as 'practical applications and continuing value to adult and working life' (*op. cit.*: 10) and 'the challenge of employment in tomorrow's world' (*op. cit.*: 2). We hear of 'bench-marks', of 'attainment targets', of 'programmes of study' and of 'standards', all defined in terms of subject-content and offered as though they are non-problematic, and we get an impression that attempts are being made to 'cash in' on the kinds of philosophical argument we considered earlier, but these arguments are nowhere adduced nor are the utilitarian arguments made explicit.

However, it is clear from the most superficial analysis that, behind the rhetoric, the fundamental thrust of these policies is instrumental (Kelly, 1990, 1994). And the survey of events leading up to the implementation of these policies which will be offered in Chapter 7 will lead us inexorably to the same conclusion. Indeed, the change of name from Department of Education and Science first to Department for Education and Employment and now to Department for Education and Skills indicates clearly a shift of ideology towards an instrumental view of schooling and the school curriculum. The education system is now geared to economic productivity and the curriculum planned to promote forms of learning which are regarded as useful, in terms both of future employment for individuals and the continued economic growth of society. Neither of these considerations, of course, can be responsibly ignored. In current policies, however, they are being bought at the expense of any notion that schools (or, even, universities) should also offer education in that full sense of learning for its own sake and for the development of the individual, which we outlined in Chapter 1. Indeed, as we have seen, any conceptual distinction between education and training, instruction or teaching is ignored, and even specifically rejected.

The implications of these policies

However, the merits of this approach are not the concern here. What we must identify are its implications and consequences. And those implications and consequences must be precisely the same as those we saw emerging inexorably from the content-based approaches we considered earlier, although this time there is not the saving grace of attempted objectivity in views of knowledge or culture, nor, as we have just noted, any associated concept of education for its own sake. For, if we have been right to claim that content-based approaches to curriculum must lead to elitism, inequalities, disaffection and alienation, then this must be, perhaps especially, the case when the choice of content is made not by reference to the knowledge itself nor by reference to the children who are the objects of the curriculum but in relation almost solely to the economic needs of society and the interests of social control.

Furthermore, it is clear that these consequences are accepted, if only tacitly, by the authors and the proponents of those policies. For, in spite of all the rhetoric of entitlement, it is clear from policies, practices and proposals, that there are strong and influential pressure groups whose weight is behind policies which would reduce entitlement for large sections of the child population and focus resources on those pupils deemed likely to make a useful contribution to the economy.

Indeed, this is the logic of this kind of instrumental ideology of curriculum. For, if it is not necessary for the economic health of society to educate every child, then there is no instrumental justification for universal provision. If the fundamental motivation behind the introduction of state-provided education for all was to produce a fully trained workforce, then, in an age when this is no longer necessary, a major part, perhaps *the* major part, of the rationale for mass education disappears.

Anti-educational ideologies

Hence we can see quite clearly the surfacing, or the resurfacing, of those ideologies (we might in this context call them sub-ideologies, since they are sub-variants of the general ideological position we are exploring) which Denis Lawton (1989, 1992, 1994) has drawn our attention to. For, in opposition to the faction he names 'the comprehensive planners', those who press for the provision by the state of 'a good general education for all' (Lawton, 1989: 52), he identifies three contrary ideologies which would deny such provision.

First, there are those he calls the 'privatisers'. These are those who, on the philosophical grounds of their objections to 'collectivism', interference by the state in individual privacy (what is now known as 'the nanny society'), and the much more practical grounds of costs, 'would advocate the dismantling of the whole state education service or gradually privatising the system' (1989: 49). A notable step in this direction was the introduction of vouchers for nursery education, a policy which has now been discontinued. This group would leave all to market forces, as, for example, by permitting, and indeed encouraging, the 'opting out' of schools from the state system.

The second group he calls the 'minimalists'. These hold to a tradition which derives from nineteenth-century 'Tory paternalism' (1989: 50) and which now reflects 'a set of values supporting the provision of a state education system provided that value for money can be demonstrated, and also that education can be shown to be "useful" particularly in the sense of servicing the labour market with well-trained and disciplined school-leavers who have been convinced of the value of such virtues as punctuality and hard work' (*ibid.*). Thus they 'support a state education service which concentrates on the basics' with parents having the right 'of buying additional extras or opting out altogether' (*ibid.*).

The third group are the 'pluralists'. This group favours the establishment of a good state system of education, but views such a system in meritocratic terms, 'favouring the metaphor of "ladder of opportunity" rather that of "the broad highway"' (*op. cit.*: 51). It may well be argued that in most countries, and especially in England and Wales, it is this group which is currently in the ascendant.

These then are all sub-variants of, and natural consequences of, the instrumentalist ideology we are describing. Their curricula will emphasize content, but they do not embrace an epistemology which requires them to select this content for its own sake. Rather, they lead to a viewing of all knowledge and all forms of learning as justified only on utilitarian grounds, so that the basis for the selection of curriculum content is a consideration of nothing more than its instrumental value.

It is perhaps worth noting here that this same trend can be seen in recent developments in higher education.

It is because of this fundamental instrumentalism that official policy statements and pronouncements, in addition to being framed in terms of subjects and knowledge-content, are also laden with references to the 'aims and objectives' of these subjects and this content. They can thus be seen as attempts to conflate the traditional model of curriculum as content with that model which emerged with the aims and objectives movement, with particular force in the second half of the twentieth century.

Before we consider the implications of such a conflation, however, we must turn to a detailed consideration of that movement and the ideology it represents.

Curriculum as product and education as instrumental

The aims and objectives movement

The growth of the movement
A concern with curriculum objectives was one of the most striking features of the move towards deliberate curriculum planning to which we referred in Chapter 1. Statements of objectives were, for example, the starting points for many curriculum projects developed under the aegis of the Schools Council, and we have witnessed a growing pressure on teachers to pay due regard to them in their planning. Indeed, current policies for the schooling system in England and Wales are framed almost entirely in terms of '*targets*', objectives to be achieved. And the same model can be seen in many other countries.

The impetus for this came initially early in the twentieth century from those who were impressed by the progress of science and technology and believed that the same kind of progress might become possible in the field of education if a properly scientific approach were to be adopted there also. From the beginning, therefore, the movement was clearly pushing educational provision in the direction of adopting a technicist form. As is so often the case, the origins of this movement can be traced to the United States; in the United Kingdom it appeared somewhat later.

The tone of the movement was set by one of its earliest proponents, Franklin

Bobbitt, who expressed great concern at the vague, imprecise purposes he felt characterized the work of most teachers, announced that 'an age of science is demanding exactness and particularity' (Bobbitt, 1918: ch.6; Davies, 1976: 47) and suggested that teachers be required to write out their objectives in clear, non-technical language that both pupils and their parents might understand. He also distinguished between what he called 'ultimate' objectives, those for the curriculum as a whole, and 'progress' objectives, those for each class or age group.

The cry was taken up by others. In 1924, for example, Werrett Charters attempted a 'job analysis' of teaching and offered a method of course construction based on this kind of approach. His suggestion was that we first determine what he called the 'ideals' of education, then identify the 'activities' that these involve and finally analyse both of these to the level of 'working units of the size of human ability' (Charters, 1924; Davies, 1976: 50), those small steps that need to be mastered one by one. In this way the curriculum could be reduced to a series of working units and its whole structure set out on a chart or graph.

Thus, early pioneers of the movement, like Bobbitt and Charters, gave it from the beginning a scientific, technicist, behavioural, job-analysis flavour, their general purpose being to introduce into educational practice the kind of precise, scientific methods that had begun to yield dividends in other spheres of human activity and especially in industry.

The spread of interest in testing that was a feature of educational development in the 1930s can be seen as another aspect of this same movement. For the link between the prespecification of objectives and the testing of performance has long been a close one, and that it continues to be so is apparent from the emphasis on attainment targets, allied to testing procedures, within the National Curriculum in England.

This link was made quite explicit in the work of the next major exponent of the objectives approach, Ralph Tyler. For Tyler's original aim was to design scientific tests of educational attainment and his solution to this problem was to suggest that this could be done most readily and easily if a clear statement had been made of the kind of attainment that was being aimed at. If course objectives had been formulated and those objectives defined in terms of intended student behaviour, that behaviour could then be assessed in the light of those intentions (Tyler, 1932; Davies, 1976).

This provided the foundation upon which Tyler was later to base what has come to be regarded as the classic statement of the objectives approach to curriculum design, based on the four questions which as we saw in Chapter 1, are concerned with the purposes, the content, the organization and the evaluation of the curriculum (Tyler, 1949).

The next milestone was reached in 1956 with the publication by Benjamin Bloom and his associates of their *Taxonomy of Educational Objectives Handbook 1: Cognitive Domain*. For this introduced a new dimension into this form of curriculum planning with its division of objectives into three categories or 'domains' – the cognitive, the affective and the psychomotor – and at the same time it offered the most detailed and ambitious classification of objectives in the cognitive domain that had yet been attempted. This was matched by the publication in 1964, under the editorship of D.R. Kratwohl, of a second handbook that offered a similar classification within the affective domain.

Recent and current developments

It was some time before the work of either Tyler or Bloom began to have any real impact but by the mid-1960s their influence was beginning to be felt not only in the United States but in the United Kingdom too. And, in an article published in 1969, Paul Hirst made the same kind of claim, that we should begin our curriculum planning with a statement of our objectives, arguing that not to do so is to transgress a basic principle of rationality, since, in his view, an essential feature of any rational activity is that it be goal directed.

At the level of educational practice, however, little interest was initially shown in this approach to planning, except perhaps in relation to relatively uncomplex vocational courses. Two main reasons were posited for this (Hirst, 1969). One is the fact that at secondary level that obsession with subject content which we examined earlier, reinforced by the demands of largely monolithic examination syllabuses, rendered it unnecessary for teachers ever to think about what their purposes or objectives might be. The second is the suggestion that at primary level the 'romantic' or 'progressive' movement, in particular because of its emphasis on 'child-centredness', also had the effect of deflecting attention from a clear formulation of objectives. Paul Hirst characterized this as an obsession with methods or procedures, but it has also been interpreted (Blenkin and Kelly, 1981, 1987) as a result of a concern to see education as a process of development, and this, as we shall see in Chapter 4, has very different implications and, in fact, reflects a totally different ideology of education and model of curriculum planning. In fact, it is clear that the unwillingness to embrace the 'aims and objectives' model can be seen as due to a continuing adherence to the two main models of curriculum planning and their associated educational ideologies which were already in place – curriculum as content and education as transmission and, the model we will consider in Chapter 4, curriculum as process and education as development.

The prespecification of clear course objectives, however, was a major feature of most of the curriculum projects that emerged during the period of innovation that followed the establishment of the Schools Council in the United Kingdom in 1964, and this was a key factor in the growth of interest in this approach to curriculum planning that came in the 1960s. The allocation of public money (although never a large sum) to curriculum development on this scale brought with it the requirement that a proper account be given of how that money was being spent. For this reason, as well as for considerations of a purely educational kind, evaluation was a central concern of most new projects from the outset, and in those early years a proper evaluation was interpreted as requiring a clear statement of goals, aims, purposes, objectives.

It was through the work of the Schools Council, therefore, after a long and interesting history, that the concept of curriculum planning by objectives finally entered the consciousness of the practising teacher. And so, when in the late 1970s, as a result of several factors of a largely political kind which we will explore more fully in Chapter 7, pressures began to be felt by teachers to plan their work more carefully and precisely, it was to this model that they were inclined and, indeed, encouraged to turn (Blenkin, 1980).

Planning by targets

The most obvious and, indeed, disturbing current manifestation of this approach to the planning of the curriculum is to be seen in the fad for planning policies for schools (and in fact all the social services) by setting targets for their achievement. Institutions can then be ranked and 'league tables' published. Targets, tables and testing have thus come to be described as the three central 't's of current policies (although some see them as their three central nonsenses). The ills of testing we will consider later in Chapter 6. What we must note here is that the implications and the difficulties we are about to identify of the objectives model of curriculum planning apply with equal, if not greater, force to the policy of planning by targets. To plan by targets is to place all of the emphasis on quantity rather than quality – on *how many* children reach the arbitrary norms of the testing procedures rather than on the nature and quality of the experiences they are having in the process of reaching these levels. Professional practices in every field (medicine, for example, as much as education) must be carried out and evaluated according to professional criteria and principles, that is, *qualitatively*, rather than *quantitatively* and by reference to statistical targets. The 'measuring' of target attainment may produce vote-winning statistics for the politicians; it provides nothing that can improve the quality of schooling or of any other form of social service.

It is one thing for teachers and even pupils themselves to set targets, since these can be educational and can be translated into educational principles rather than objectives, as we shall see in Chapter 4. It is quite a different matter for the government and its quangos to set targets, since, especially because the major concern is to 'measure' these and use them for the production of statistics, 'league tables' and the like, they must be translated into objectives with all the consequent threats to genuine education which we are about to note.

This approach to curriculum planning, therefore, requires more careful analysis than most teachers, and certainly most civil servants and politicians, have been able or willing to give it, and it is to that kind of examination that we must proceed.

Some problems presented by this model

The major characteristics of this approach to curriculum planning also reveal its major flaws. For, in contrast to that view of education which we elaborated in Chapter 1, it is fundamentally behavioural, linear, instrumental and leads to a loss, rather than an enhancement, of freedom for both teacher and pupil. It thus raises some fundamental ideological issues concerning the nature of education, the nature of human beings and, indeed, the nature of society.

A passive view of humanity

One fundamental criticism that has been levelled at this approach to curriculum planning is that its attempt to reduce education to a scientific activity, analogous to the processes of industry, commits it to a view of humans and of human nature that many people find unacceptable and even unpalatable. To adopt this kind of industrial model for education is to assume that it is legitimate to mould human beings, to modify their behaviour, according to certain clear-cut intentions without making any allowance for their own individual wishes, desires or interests. Like the materials upon which the industrial worker operates, children's minds are to be fashioned by teachers according to some preconceived blueprint. It thus represents a serious threat to individual freedom.

And, indeed, the major proponents of this view leave us in no doubt that they see objectives as behavioural and consequently regard schooling as a form of behaviour modification. Tyler, for example, tells us that 'the most useful form for stating objectives is to express them in terms which identify both the kind of behaviour to be developed in the students and the context or area of life in which this behaviour is to operate' (1949: 46–7). Bloom calls them 'intended learning outcomes' and says that they are to be defined in terms of the behaviour the pupil is intended to display through his or her thoughts, actions or feelings. Mager (1962: 13) says, 'A statement of an objective is useful to the extent that it specifies what the learner must be able to *do* or *perform* when he is demonstrating his mastery of the objective.' And Popham (1969: 35) tells us that 'a satisfactory instructional objective must describe an observable *behaviour* of the learner or a *product* which is a consequence of learner behaviour'. The observable behaviour might take the form of something like 'skill in making impromptu speeches or performing gymnastic feats' (*ibid.*). Products might be an essay or 'an omelet from the home economics class' (*ibid.*). This being so, 'a properly stated behavioural objective must describe *without ambiguity* the nature of learner behaviour or product to be measured' (*op. cit.*: 37). [All emphases original.]

The important thing to recognize, therefore, is that the notion of behaviour modification is essential to this model of curriculum planning. Again, we may note that there may well be areas, such as that of vocational training, where this is entirely appropriate. Whether it is appropriate to *educational* planning, however, is highly questionable. What we must note here is that to adopt this as the model for educational planning is to be committed to the idea of education as the modification of pupil behaviour, whether one defines what one means by 'objectives' in behavioural terms or not, or, indeed, even if one does not bother to offer a definition at all.

The focus of this approach to educational planning, then, is essentially on the modification of pupil behaviour, and the success of such a curriculum is to be gauged by an assessment of the behaviour changes the curriculum appears to have brought about in relation to those it was its stated intention to bring about. Fundamental to the view, therefore, is a psychological theory of a behaviourist kind and it is with behaviourist psychology that the movement has been associated from the start. In fact, most of its theoretical proponents have been psychologists rather than educationists or teachers.

This passive model of humans is endemic to the theory and it is thus not acceptable to those who take the view that the individual is to be regarded as a free and active agent, responsible for his or her own destiny and who, as a direct consequence of this, believe it to be morally wrong to deny him or her that responsibility and freedom by attempting to mould his or her behaviour to suit the ends of someone else. Such a process, they argue, is indoctrination rather than education and thus to be deplored. This, as we have seen before, is a problem which is endemic to all forms of instrumentalism in educational planning. This model, then, must be recognized as fundamentally at odds with the notion of education for emancipation or empowerment.

Controversial issues and areas of the curriculum

This becomes particularly evident when we consider the use of this approach in those areas of the curriculum which most obviously involve content of a kind which is highly controversial. For to approach these areas with a clear prespecification of intended learning outcomes in behavioural terms is to abandon education altogether for what must be seen as a much more sinister process. In the teaching and learning of music and the fine arts the prime concern is to elicit an individual response from the pupil; it is clearly not appropriate to decide in advance what that response should be (Eisner, 1969). In literature too, the whole purpose of introducing pupils to great literary works is lost if it is done from the perspective of intended learning outcomes (Stenhouse, 1970). Again that purpose is to invite the pupil to respond in his or her own way to what he or she is introduced to. To approach a reading of *Hamlet*, for example, in any other way is either to reduce it to an instrumental role, designed to promote an understanding of words, poetic forms, even philosophy, or to attempt to impose one's own moral and aesthetic values, one's own subjective interpretation of the play and response to it on one's pupils. If appreciation of literature or any of the arts means anything at all and has any place in education, it cannot be approached by way of clearly prespecified objectives.

It is this which is fundamentally wrong about the current approach to teaching literacy in schools in England and Wales (QCA 1999: DfES, 2004a, 2005a). It has been pointed out by Philip Pullman (2002) that in the whole of the official documentation devoted to advising teachers in this area and in the conduct of such developments as the 'literacy hour', the verb 'enjoy' does not appear once. And it is now becoming apparent even to those responsible for inventing these policies that, as any professional could have told them at the outset, they have missed the central point of a literary education.

This was one of the major reasons why the Schools Council's Humanities Curriculum Project (HCP), which may be identified as the first major rebellion against the use of this model, deliberately eschewed any kind of statement of objectives. Being concerned to introduce older pupils in secondary schools to some of the controversial issues that face modern society, such as relations between the sexes, living in cities, war and so on, and being of the opinion that these are issues upon which a number of different value stances can be taken with equal validity, it recognized that the involvement of pupils in these issues could not be undertaken justifiably with clear objectives as to what the outcome of their learning and discussions should be, but only according to certain procedural principles designed to allow them to reach their own informed opinions on them. To do anything else would be to indoctrinate rather than to educate, to deny them their right to think for themselves and to reach their own conclusions as emancipated human beings.

Children with special needs

This has also led some people to reject the behavioural objectives approach to the planning of the curriculum for children with special needs (Goddard, 1983). It is perhaps in this field that the model has been adopted most readily and extensively and in its starkest form. Indeed, in this kind of context the notion of 'behaviour modification' seems to have been adopted with few qualms, and there has been little objection to the view that in the case of children with special needs or learning difficulties it is not only acceptable but even necessary to concentrate all one's attention on modifying their behaviour and improving their performance of certain kinds of behavioural task. Thus Wilfrid Brennan (1979: 97) tells us that 'clarity of terminal and intermediate objectives in the curriculum is seen as essential if the teacher is to use the total learning situation in order to continuously "shape" [note the metaphor] the development of the pupil', and we are also told (Leeming *et al.*, 1979: 68) in relation to the education of children with special needs that 'the only way we can hope to change children and know we have succeeded, is to change their behaviour. This is the basis for the use of an objectives approach to the curriculum.'

However, if this approach leads to forms of indoctrination, if it treats human beings as passive recipients of experiences intended to bring about behavioural changes felt to be desirable by others, if it denies individual freedom, and if it negates the notion of learning for learning's sake, then it is at least as unsatisfactory as the sole approach to the teaching of children with special educational needs as it is in the case of other pupils. And it is right that Alan Goddard and others have insisted that there is, or should be more to the education of such children than that, that 'what we often want to teach is not behaviour, neither can it be reduced to behaviour' (Goddard, 1983: 272 – referring to Swann, 1981). Indeed, it is difficult to see the point of the Warnock Report's (DES, 1980c) recommendation for the integration of pupils with special needs wherever possible into ordinary schools and classrooms on any other grounds – unless, of course, behaviour modification is to be the aim for all pupils.

A view of learning as a linear process

A second feature of the aims and objectives model which has been seen as posing serious problems is its view of the learning process as linear. Aims are usually seen as very general statements of goals and purposes. Such aims by themselves, however, have often been regarded as too general and lacking in specificity to provide clear guidelines for planners or teachers, so that curriculum planning has been seen as a process of deriving more precise statements of goals from these general aims; these more precise statements of goals are normally termed objectives. Indeed, some writers have even suggested that we should recognize three or more levels of specificity (Kratwohl, 1965): general statements of goals that will guide the planning of the curriculum as a whole, behavioural objectives derived from these which will guide the planning of individual units or courses, and a third level of objectives appropriate in some cases to guide the planning of specific lessons; to use Wheeler's terms, 'ultimate', 'mediate' and 'proximate' goals, the last providing specific classroom objectives (Wheeler, 1967).

This, as we saw earlier, is the kind of structure that was envisaged by the early pioneers of the movement, and the important point to note is that this approach to curriculum planning assumes that education must be planned in a step-by-step linear manner. It is in fact an attempt to translate into classroom terms that linear step-by-step process which is not only claimed to be characteristic of industrial processes but which behavioural psychologists have discovered to be the most effective way of conditioning animals – dogs, cats, rats, pigeons and so on.

It is important to stress that it is only through this kind of linear and hierarchical scheme that one can make any real sense of the distinction between aims and objectives, in short, that it is an essential feature of the aims and objectives model of curriculum planning. The term 'objective' might of course be used to mean merely any 'goal' or 'purpose'. There is nothing fundamentally wrong or mistaken in such a usage. However, the attempt to distinguish 'aims' and 'objectives' implies that these terms denote different kinds or levels of educational goal or purpose, so that to make this distinction reflects either a clear acceptance of a hierarchy of goals, and thus of the objectives model and all it entails, or a disturbing failure to achieve conceptual clarity over what one's planning model really is. For, if there is a distinction between the two concepts, it can consist only in their hierarchical relationship with each other.

Thus, for example, the taxonomy which Bloom and his associates (1956) offer us requires us to prespecify our objectives at varying levels of specificity in order to outline in great detail the kinds of behaviour which are the objectives of our curriculum. We are offered a hierarchy of goals, of 'intended learning outcomes' defined in terms of the kind of behaviour the pupil is intended or expected to display through his or her thoughts, actions or feelings if we are to be able to claim that our objective has been achieved.

It is easy to see why this approach has proved, and continues to prove, so attractive to some curriculum planners. Indeed, as we will see shortly, the National Curriculum for England and Wales is firmly entrenched in this model, offering in fact a classic example of the combination of the content and aims-and-objectives bases, its statements of the essential content of each of its subjects having been set out in the form of attainment targets and levels of attainment in a step-by-step linear hierarchy. On a similar model, the curriculum for schools in Hong Kong was originally termed Targets and Target-Related Assessment (TTRA) and is now known as the Target Oriented Curriculum (TOC). In fact, in both curricula, the planning begins with, and is firmly based on the stating of its 'targets'.

The reasons for this are not difficult to identify. For this approach seems to inject a sense of purpose into our educational provision; it offers a flavour of scientific precision, accuracy and technological efficiency; and it provides a simple basis for assessment and evaluation, of a political kind, which might be seen to be vote-catching. The inadequacies of this will become apparent when we consider both assessment and evaluation in later chapters. What we must note here is that it is an essentially *technicist* rather than *educational* approach to planning.

However, the hierarchical form of the relationships between objectives that is characteristic of taxonomies such as that of Bloom and his associates (1956) does not reflect the realities of the learning process. The linear model that it assumes, which attempts to break down all learning into a step-by-step procedure, is not suitable for most of the learning that goes on in schools. We do not acquire knowledge and then, at some later stage, attain understanding; the two must go hand in hand. Real learning is developmental rather than linear. The acquisition of knowledge or the transmission of knowledge-content may be linear processes; the development of understanding certainly is not; it is a far more subtle process and much more likely to be brought about by some form of what Jerome Bruner has termed a 'spiral curriculum', where one returns to concepts at ever higher levels of complexity and understanding, than by a 'Thirty-Nine Steps', linear and hierarchical set of offerings. Any view of the learning process that does not recognize this must be regarded as too simplistic to serve as a basis for any but the most unsophisticated of teaching activities.

A good example of this is the suggestion often made by the advocates of this approach, and which is implied by all the assertions we hear about the need for the teaching of 'the basic skills', that we ought to set about teaching these skills before we attempt more sophisticated forms of teaching and learning; in short, that our approach to teaching and learning should be not only linear but also hierarchical. Again, we must note that this is the model which underpins current policies for the teaching of literacy and numeracy in schools in England and Wales (DfEE, 1999; QCA, 1999; DfES 2004a, 2004b, 2005a).

The teaching of basic skills, however, even those of a psychomotor kind, cannot be separated out from other kinds of goals without risking the loss of that essential ingredient of education that we must also be concerned with. It is possible to teach basic skills in an instructional manner – the basic skills of reading, for example, of using a saw or a wood-chisel, of drawing straight lines or circles and many others – and in this area the use of the behavioural model has appeared to be successful. Again, current policies in England and Wales for the teaching of literacy and numeracy (DfEE, 1999; QCA, 1999; DfES, 2004a, 2004b, 2005a) well illustrate this. However, if we do not at the same time have clearly in mind the educational dimensions of the activities we are engaged in, then, while our efforts might well result in highly skilled performance at the behavioural level (and thus in favourable statistics), they are likely to result in our achieving little beyond that and may even be counterproductive to any further attainment and, indeed, to education itself. For, as the Bullock Report (DES, 1975) pointed out, it is possible to help pupils to a high level of reading performance and at the same time to kill or to inhibit any love or appreciation they may have developed for the written word. Indeed, as the report also pointed out, even that high level of skilled performance itself will be short-lived. There are more 'non-readers' about than those who merely cannot decipher the symbols of the written word. Written language too is 'far too complex a system for any simple description in terms of a build up of sub-skills to account for it', so that 'if we try to offer a logically pre-programmed sequence of knowledge we simply interfere with the sense-making opportunities which real reading and writing offer to the learner' and 'any attempt to make learning literacy easy by offering only parts of the whole experience is almost certain to violate the meaningfulness of normal written language' (Money, 1988: 142). And, in mathematics too, it has been suggested (Metz, 1988: 187) that 'an emphasis ... on applying rules in a step-by-step manner ignores not only the need to make general sense of a situation first, but also the importance of reflecting on any solution obtained after the rules have been applied'. Education is far too complex a process to be broken down in this kind of way.

This is a major danger of attempts to measure standards of attainment in schools in terms simply of performance or behaviour. It is thus a danger not only of the objectives model of curriculum planning but also of those popular, public and political demands for improved standards in the 'basic skills' which have this kind of simplistic model of learning at their tap-root.

An inadequate concept of education

It is for this reason that this model has also been attacked as being based not only on inadequate and unacceptable models of humanity and of human learning but also on an equally unsatisfactory concept of education. The aims-and-objectives approach to curriculum planning, like all pseudo-scientific approaches to the study and planning of human activity, endeavours to be value-neutral. Those who have advocated it have been concerned only to present teachers and curriculum planners with a scheme or a blueprint for them to use as they think fit; it is not their concern to tell them how to use it. They regard education as a matter of changing behaviour but they do not accept responsibility for questions about what kinds of behaviour education should be concerned to promote or what kinds of behavioural change it should be attempting to bring about. They maintain their 'scientific' stance, therefore, and leave it to the persons using their scheme to make the decisions about how it should be used.

Thus this approach deliberately sidesteps the most difficult and intractable problem that faces curriculum planners – that of deciding what kinds of activity shall be deemed to be educational. And in itself it can offer no help or guidance with this aspect of educational decision-making. It sets out to provide a methodology for curriculum planning and nothing more. This must be regarded as a very serious disadvantage in this model as a basis for *educational* planning, and it may explain why most of those who have promoted the model (as opposed to those who have merely accepted and attempted to use it uncritically) have been inclined to use the word 'instruction' for what they are concerned to plan rather than the much more pregnant term 'education'. As a model for planning schemes of instruction, it may well have much to recommend it; as a model for educational planning, it is seriously flawed and inadequate.

However, although the proponents of this planning model have claimed that it is value-neutral, in fact there is implicit within it a very clear ideology of education. For its failure, or refusal, to distinguish education from teaching or learning itself constitutes an ideological position. As we have seen, those who have attempted to disentangle the concept of education from other related concepts such as training, instruction or indoctrination have done so by drawing attention to certain features of education that are not necessary parts of these other processes and, indeed, are sometimes explicitly excluded from them (Peters, 1965, 1966). One of these features is that of individual autonomy without a concern for which, it is argued, no process of teaching can be called education. Such a view of education clearly entails that we adopt an active model of humans and precludes an approach to educational planning that begins from a clear idea of the kinds of behaviour modification that teachers are to try to bring about in their pupils. In this context, it is interesting to note again how many of the books and articles written to promote an approach to educational planning through the prespecification of objectives contain the word 'instruction' in their titles or use that word to describe the kinds of teaching they have in mind. It is also interesting to consider the examples that they give, since most of them are of a relatively simple, instructional kind.

Instrumentalism

As we saw in Chapter 1, a second feature which it has been claimed is essential to education in the full sense is that the curriculum activities proposed should be undertaken for their own sakes. In a properly educational process the teacher must view the content of his or her teaching as being of value in itself and his or her intention must be to persuade his or her pupils so to view it. For if its justification lies in what it leads to, if, in short, the process is an instrumental one with ends or purposes outside itself, then, as we have seen, we would more naturally refer to it as 'training' or 'instruction'.

If one of the things that characterizes education as opposed to other activities that involve teaching and learning, such as training or instruction, is that education is essentially concerned with activities undertaken for their own sakes, such a notion of education is clearly at odds with the idea of activities planned according to extrinsic behavioural objectives, goals extrinsic to the activity itself. John Dewey first drew our attention to this feature of education when he asserted that education can have no ends beyond itself, since it is its own end. This view was subsequently developed more fully by Richard Peters (1965, 1966, 1973a) who claimed, for example, that 'to be educated is not to have arrived at a destination; it is to travel with a different view. What is required is not feverish preparation for something that lies ahead, but to work with precision, passion and taste at worthwhile things that lie at hand' (1965: 110).

On this kind of analysis not only does the notion of prespecified behavioural objectives run counter to the very concept of education but the broad aims of education must also be seen from a different perspective, not as what education *is for* but as what *it is*, so that to assert that education is concerned with the development of personal autonomy, understanding, a cognitive perspective, a recognition of the value of certain kinds of activity and so on is not to state extrinsic goals for education but to identify features that should characterize any process that is to be described as educational, a point we will pick up again in the next chapter.

Another way of expressing this is to say that education contains an essential value element, a commitment to the intrinsic worth of certain kinds of activity. Any approach to educational planning that ignores this element, that sets out deliberately to be value-neutral, as we have seen the behavioural objectives approach does, must be inadequate as a basis for the planning of activities which are educational in the full sense. Such an approach might be quite satisfactory for the planning of schemes of training or instruction. But for those activities that most teachers would wish to argue constitute the education they offer their pupils, the things they would claim were for their 'personal development' rather than for their vocational advancement, those things whose presence on the curriculum would be justified in educational or intrinsic terms, the model is quite inadequate. In fine, while the concept of an *instructional* objective is not difficult to grasp, that of an *educational* objective would appear to have no substance at all and to be, in fact, a contradiction in terms.

There is a further, important implication in this, and one that reveals an underlying ideology of society. For this form of schooling must lead to the emergence of a society which has never learned, except perhaps by accident, to value things for their own sake, a society in which utility is the sole concern, a society in which all are absorbed only by the means of existence and never by a consideration of its ends. This approach to educational planning, then, has wide-sweeping implications not only for education itself but for the nature, and indeed the future of society and for attitudes to human life and existence (MacIntyre, 1964). It represents what Enoch Powell (1985) once described as 'a modern barbarism'. Confucius once said, 'If you have twopence to spend, you should spend a penny on bread and a penny on a flower, the bread to make life possible, the flower to make it worthwhile'. The objectives model (and let us again note that included in this is the 'planning by targets' model) can offer no help or guidance with the second element of that advice. Its adoption as the planning base must therefore imply that its users have no interest in this aspect of human existence or, more likely, that they have not recognized the full implications of the model they have adopted. It must be emphasized, then, that the model must lead to an instrumental view of schooling and that it cannot accommodate, and thus offers no basis for, planning any other form of educational provision. It is for this reason that the current fad for planning by targets in the policies for schooling in England and Wales is leading to a lowering of *educational* standards, and even a failure to achieve its own standards and thus to produce the spurious statistics it is seeking.

An instrumental approach to the curriculum, then, precludes a number of characteristics deemed to be essential to education, and must therefore be seen as incapable of supporting, indeed as inimical to, educational provision in the full sense. Further, this ideology is one which implies a rejection of other concepts and dimensions of teaching and schooling which some would claim would make them more worthy of being described as 'education'; it requires us to settle for something considerably less than many would wish to see and/or get from an *education* system. One quite crucial effect of the adoption of this model, then, is that its use, as we have seen in relation to the current approach to the teaching of literacy and numeracy, places at risk all of those educational activities for which it cannot adequately cater. It thus leads to a loss of those essential dimensions of the educational process which, as we have seen, cannot be planned from the perspective of this linear, hierachical and behavioural approach.

Loss of freedom

The final criticism which has been levelled at this planning model and which we must note here is the charge which Charity James (1968) made that this approach restricts the freedom of teachers as well as pupils. For both will be inclined to see the objectives as fixed or given, just as secondary teachers have tended to see examination syllabuses as immutable, so that not only will they concentrate on what must be rather simple instructional goals, they will also lose the opportunity to play an active role in the educational process, a process which, it is claimed, is fully educational only if both teachers and pupils are active within it.

The curriculum on this view is seen as the dynamic interaction of teacher and pupil and this cannot be promoted by a scientific, 'industrial' model requiring careful pre-planning of outcomes. If education is seen as a continuous, ongoing, open-ended activity, and if the teacher's role is central to its effectiveness, as we claimed in Chapter 1, the idea of constant modification and reassessment must be endemic to it, so that any approach to planning an educational activity that starts with a clear specification of objectives will be based on a misunderstanding of what an educational activity really is. Every act of education takes place in its own individual context (Sockett, 1976a) and thus cannot be predetermined. Education is an art as well as a science and far too complex and sophisticated an activity to be elucidated in terms of this kind of simple model.

Again, therefore, we see the close connections between the model adopted for curriculum planning and the ideological stance of the planner. And again, we must note the significance of this in the context of current political realities. For the adoption of the aims-and-objectives model and target-based planning by politicians is a clear indication of an ideological position which cannot, or does not wish to, accommodate the notion of freedom for teachers or pupils. We can now see, however, that this means that they have also failed to recognize, or at least to acknowledge, what this implies for the quality of *educational* provision. As a consequence, their policies lack any clear concept of education; indeed, we have seen that this is deliberate and that they are choosing to regard state maintained schooling as merely a matter of teaching and instruction.

However, this view of education as an ongoing, open-ended process, subject to constant reassessment and modification as a result of pupil–teacher interaction is supported by the practical experiences of many teachers. Teachers and student teachers, even in the face of concerted pressures upon them to prespecify the objectives of their lessons, have in practice rejected this approach, and it is precisely those teachers who are concerned to offer something that goes beyond mere training or instruction who have found this model impossible to use. The realities of the teacher's task are too complex to be met by an approach like that of the industrial planner. This was reinforced by the experience of many of those curriculum projects that attempted to use this kind of model. For even when sets of objectives were presented to them in clear terms, many teachers found it impossible not to modify them continually in the light of the experiences that they and their pupils had from the moment the work began. As John Dewey once pointed out, objectives have a tendency to change as you approach them. It is thus not bloody-mindedness on the part of teachers that causes them to cannibalize what they are offered; it is a realization that, if they do not make this kind of constant adjustment, the goals of their teaching will remain at a simple level and that which is truly educational will be at risk. It is here that the most serious threats are posed to the quality of *educational* provision by the simplistic, objectives-based, 'target-oriented' prescriptions of the National Curriculum and its supporting policies and documentation.

One major reason, then, why some people have recently wished to argue against the prespecification of objectives is the conviction that education is a more sophisticated activity and curriculum planning as a result a more complex process than this simple theoretical model suggests. This is a point we have noted several times already. And, to foreshadow what we shall discuss in greater detail in the next chapter, what teachers need is a set of principles which will guide them in making the minute-by-minute decisions which this complex process requires.

Any model we adopt for curriculum planning must allow for a degree of personal and professional autonomy for the teacher. If we do not allow for this, we create constraints on the activity of teachers and their scope for exercising their professional judgement on the spot, and, far from ensuring that quality which the rhetoric proclaims, this will act to the detriment of the quality of their provision when that is defined in any but the most simplistic terms. This is clearly a very real danger with the aims-and-objectives model and with target-oriented planning.

All of these criticisms suggest that the aims-and-objectives model, along with the target-oriented approach to planning, is appropriate only for the planning of relatively low-level forms of teaching and aspects of the school curriculum. And attempts to develop it to a more sophisticated level, by, for example, suggesting we regard our objectives as 'provisional' (Blyth, 1974) or as 'mutable' (Kelly, 1973), or that we accept 'unintended learning outcomes' (Hogben, 1972), or that we seek to devise non-behavioural objectives (Eisner, 1969; Hirst, 1975), bring their own difficulties, not least in failing to provide adequate criteria and principles for practice.

What is needed is an approach which will guide us in the initial choice of aims, activities and, indeed, curriculum content and will then act as a constant source of assistance in the process of modifying these in the course of our continuing teaching and educating our pupils. And this would appear to suggest that, rather than seeking to modify the aims-and-objectives approach in some way in order to extend its use to the planning of the more complex and sophisticated aspects of educational provision, we might be better employed looking for a completely different and more appropriate model. It is to this that we shall turn in Chapter 4. First, however, we must note the attempts which have been made to marry the content and the objectives approaches to planning.

The combined model – 'mastery learning'

It is quite common to see the content-based approach to curriculum planning in practice – curriculum content selected without any real consideration of its aims and then 'delivered'. It is less common to see the aims-and-objectives model at work, at least in any genuine form, to see planners deciding on their aims and selecting the content felt most likely to achieve these. The tradition of viewing the curriculum primarily in terms of its content is too strong.

What is common, however, is to find a combination of the two, what the proponents of the aims-and-objectives model have called 'mastery learning' (Bloom, 1971). In many ways, it is this approach which is to be seen in the current policies of target-oriented planning. On this model, the content which is selected, on whatever grounds, for 'delivery' is viewed as the aim, and the objectives are the 'bite-sized pieces', attainment targets or whatever, into which the content is broken down for ease of 'delivery'. This approach has been characterized by Basil Bernstein (1996) as a 'performance' mode of pedagogic practice.

Thus we have a fundamental commitment to the content model and an adoption of the aims-and-objectives scheme as a methodology for achieving the most effective 'delivery' and assimilation of the selected content. This is the model employed, whether by design or accident, in the National Curriculum for England and Wales.

No doubt the advocates of this combined model feel that they are getting the best of both worlds. In fact, what they are getting is the worst of both, all of the inadequacies which we have identified as features of both models – in particular, the inequalities, potential disaffection and alienation of the content model, and the behaviourism, the instrumentalism and the loss of a genuine concept of education of the objectives model.

For the recommendation that content be broken down into 'bite-sized pieces' clearly indicates through its choice of metaphor that the 'education' process is seen as the force-feeding of content to pupils and its ingestion by them – whether this is also a process of digestion or not. And the use of the 'delivery' metaphor indicates that the process is seen as one of handing something over; it leads to a view of curriculum as an entity, a body of knowledge to be transmitted. 'Deliver' is a transitive verb; it must have an object; and, in this context, that object can only be a curriculum viewed as substantive rather than adjectival, as prescriptive rather than descriptive, as static rather than dynamic.

This is of course again an attempt to turn teaching into a scientific process. And it is perhaps worth noting here that, if completely successful, in an age of high technology, it will do away with the need for human teachers altogether; teaching machines will ultimately do the job far more efficiently – and more cheaply. Indeed, it has been pointed out (Kress, 2001) that knowledge-as-information is now available all the time through technological advances, so that schools must begin to conceive their role in terms other than this. It will also of course do away with *education* in the sense of 'what survives when what has been learnt has been forgotten' (Skinner, 1964: 484).

For such a curriculum is clearly based on a view of teaching as the transmission of knowledge in a form which does not and cannot adequately cater for those wider dimensions of education which we have identified – autonomy, personal and social development, aesthetic awareness, literary appreciation, the valuing of experiences and activities for their own sake and so on. All of these can only be promoted by the provision of appropriate experiences, since they all involve changes in the way that people view the world and not merely the acquisition of more and more of what A.N. Whitehead (1932) called inert knowledge. They involve the development of understanding rather than mere knowledge, and the development of understanding cannot be broken down into 'bite-sized pieces'; it is a far more complex matter than that. Education is much more than a form of mastery learning.

The underpinning curriculum model of current policies for England and Wales, then, is an amalgam of the content and the aims-and-objectives approaches. There is, however, no evidence of an awareness of the problematic aspects of either of these models. None of the documentation acknowledges that there are different models or approaches which might have been adopted; thus none attempts or offers any kind of justification for the model chosen. One can only assume that this is because their authors are not aware of, or are not permitted to acknowledge, either the fact that one might approach curriculum planning in any other way or the many inadequacies of the approach they have chosen or fallen into. As a result, they all reveal a disturbing confusion between a concern for the subject-content of their prescriptions, the wish to organize it in a linear and hierarchical fashion by the clear prespecification of objectives, levels or attainment targets and a lingering desire for the kind of educational justification which might come from viewing their subject as an 'area of experience' with something to offer to children's development above and beyond the transmission of the knowledge-content itself.

All this reveals a failure to appreciate the deep conceptual issues which underlie the differences between these approaches. This comes out perhaps most clearly in that failure to distinguish conceptually between aims and objectives, to which reference has already been made on more than one occasion.

It does seem too that the conceptual confusion arises from a desire to embrace the rhetoric of more attractive approaches to educational planning and the vocabulary of the increasingly fashionable process model, which we shall explore in Chapter 4, while at the same time advocating the more politically acceptable and 'hard-headed' view of education as instrumental and as primarily directed towards economic success. Or perhaps it reflects a conflict between the vestiges of a concern with education in the full sense and the realities of political expediency. Or again it may result from an unwillingness to acknowledge all the inevitable implications of the instrumental, economic, political view. Whatever the reason, it leads to a highly confused and unsatisfactory set of prescriptions for educational practice. Certainly, the policy of planning by targets has revealed more clearly what is the true intention of these policies – to win votes by convincing the electorate that 'standards' are rising through the production of statistics rather than any attempt to achieve genuine improvement.

The unsuitability of these models for planning which is to be genuinely educational

The simple fact which emerges from the whole of this discussion is that neither the content model nor the objectives model, nor even a combination of the two, can provide us with a template for the planning of a truly educational curriculum or one which is consonant with the underlying principles of a democratic society. In fact, and more seriously, the use of these models for the planning of the whole of the schooling system results in a curriculum which is quite inappropriate and which inhibits the attainment of education for all pupils.

These models are fine for planning programmes of *learning* or *instruction*, activities which are quite appropriately linear and instrumental, which do not have to be focused on pupil autonomy, empowerment or any of those other features we have identified as essential to education in the full sense, and which do not demand any necessary freedom for teacher or pupil. Hence they are models which work very well in contexts where education as such is not a central concern – in courses which are essentially vocational, for example. But the models are conceptually and logically incompatible with activities whose central point and purpose is educational.

More importantly, however, we must note that, as a result, the use of these models in contexts where education is the aim, or at least the stated aim, will lead to the erosion of all educational value. If courses or activities planned in this way do provide experiences or forms of learning which are educational, this will happen by accident and not by deliberate planning, since the planning model cannot of itself promote education. Hence, the advocacy of these models in England and Wales by HMI through their *Curriculum Matters* publications, along with the current fallacy of planning by targets which this has not surprisingly led to, has resulted in the emergence of a schooling system which is no longer planned with education in mind but merely as concerned with quantifiable and 'measurable' learning, and which provides genuine education only by accident or by those activities undertaken by teachers which attempt to transcend what they are officially required to do. Schools have been turned into those 'teaching shops' which the Plowden Report (CACE, 1967) tried to warn us away from, or what have more recently been called 'learning factories' (Watkins and Mortimore, 1999: 16). And so it is not inappropriate that the government department responsible for this has had the term 'Skills' added to its title, since these are now its main concern. The retention of the word 'Education' increasingly seems to be mere rhetoric.

Hence, as a consequence of the implementation of policies based on this kind of conceptual confusion, this is what the National Curriculum in England and Wales has resulted in. It is a *teaching/learning* rather than an *educational* curriculum, and its 'success' is measured in terms of quantifiable doses of knowledge to be acquired rather than in terms of educational goals achieved. Schools have been turned into teaching shops or learning factories and teachers are becoming instructors rather than educators.

Summary

What we have seen in this chapter, then, is that both the approach to curriculum planning through content and that through the prespecification of aims-and-objectives, and even, perhaps especially, the attempt to combine the two, have serious drawbacks in relation to the planning of *educational* provision. Whether we first select the content of our curriculum and use the aims-and-objectives schema as a methodology for planning the teaching of it, or establish our aims and objectives and select that content that we believe will achieve these most effectively, both models create more difficulties than they solve.

The objectives movement has rightly drawn our attention to the importance of being clear about the purposes of the curriculum, and that is a lesson we must not lose sight of, since there is nothing wrong with the advice of those such as Ralph Tyler who have told us we must begin our planning with a clear view of its aims and purposes. And the advocates of planning through content have raised important questions about the selection of the content of the curriculum, in particular by stressing the claims to inclusion of those aspects of culture which might be deemed to constitute that which is valuable in the heritage of human experience and understanding.

Neither, however, can help with the selection of what should be included in a truly educational and democratic curriculum, unless we are prepared to accept the absolutist epistemology of some of the proponents of the content model in its pure form. We need basic principles of a kind which will enable us to make these choices, and neither of these models can provide these.

Further, both of them can be seen to make tacit assumptions concerning not only education but also the nature of human beings and of the societies they form, assumptions which constitute ideological positions of a kind which must be challenged and questioned. In particular these are ideologies which in themselves are difficult to reconcile with any reasonable concept of democracy, so that, not surprisingly, they lead to practices which are clearly impossible so to reconcile.

What is needed for *educational* planning is a model which accepts the need for clear purposes and for the initiation of the young into that which is deemed to be worthwhile, but which at the same time seeks to do this while respecting the freedom of the individual and promoting social equality and empowerment. In short, we need a model which will provide us with fundamental principles to underpin our planning and one whose ideological base is genuinely democratic.

Those who have been exploring and advocating a curriculum planning model focused on education as development and curriculum as process have been doing so because they believe such an approach can meet these needs. It is to a detailed consideration of this model that we turn in Chapter 4.

Key issues raised by this chapter

1 Is the selection of content an adequate basis for an educational curriculum?

2 How might 'valuable' content be identified?

3 On what bases should content be selected?

4 How effective is the use of aims and objectives for the planning of classroom practice?

5 How might one reconcile the instrumental functions of the schooling system with its wider educational purposes?

6 Is the planning of schooling by the setting of 'targets' (and the allocation to schools of positions in a 'league table') an appropriate way to design and conduct an education system? Or is it essentially a political act?

Suggested further reading

Grundy, S. (1987) *Curriculum: Product or Praxis?* London: Falmer.

Kelly, A.V. (1994) *The National Curriculum: A Critical Review*, updated edn, London: Paul Chapman Publishing.

18 What does good cross-curricular practice look like?

Barnes, J.

The variability between us is surely humankind's greatest resource. Individual uniqueness does not apply simply to our DNA, irises or fingerprints, but to the almost infinite range of potential links making up each human's intelligence and personality. There is an immeasurable variety of possible connections between neurons controlling our senses, memory, physical and emotional responses, and those which process our conscious, rational and intellectual responses. Such a wealth of possibilities suggests that we each experience the world around us in subtly (and not so subtly) different ways. I believe that effective cross-curricular approaches mirror and maximize on this valuable diversity, but it would be foolish to give the impression that there could be a single or even a finite range of answers to the question, 'What does good cross-curricular practice look like?' Good practice in curriculum arrangement and approach is likely to be as diverse as any other aspect of human organization.

Aside from the consciousness of our mental diversity, a second wonder is that humans can communicate so effectively. Considering the potential for some of the billions of neural connections to misfire, it seems little short of miraculous that we ever establish shared perception. The teacher's job is to construct such understandings – mutually acceptable views of aspects of our world. Curricula are designed to support teachers in building minds by providing the intellectual and social settings for learning, but they vary in effectiveness and appropriateness.

Any curriculum that energizes, motivates, provokes and sustains high-quality, useful learning is doing a good job, regardless of whether or not it requires children to work across subjects. This book is *not* written to suggest that all teaching and learning should be cross-curricular. I claim rather that cross-curricular methods are a means of promoting learning that are highly motivating for some, even most, children.

The case studies

I have chosen seven case studies to illustrate a range of successful cross-curricular learning opportunities. Each case study has generated evidence of inclusive, creative thinking and deep learning on the part of the children and adults involved. Each sprung from strong and detailed planning, depended upon meaningful and shared experience and followed or resulted from focused subject application, real and relevant activity, and frequent formative assessment. The case studies include examples of multi-disciplinary, inter-disciplinary and opportunistic modes of learning and double-focus approaches to the school curriculum:

- two cross-curricular terms covering the entire curriculum for a 3–11 nursery/primary school (double focus)
- a cross-curricular module with a cross-phase group of Year 6/7 children (inter-disciplinary)
- a primary school following the Royal Society of Arts (RSA) competences curriculum (double focus)
- a two-day project for Year 4 pupils on 'our lane' (multi-disciplinary)
- a child-led term based on walks in the park with nursery children (opportunistic)
- a two-day session for Year 5 children working with an artist in school (inter-disciplinary)
- a combined arts project with adults and Year 7/8 children (opportunistic).

These seven studies are in no way an exhaustive set of examples. *Whenever* teachers and children apply learning in more than one subject to a problem, experience, issue or theme, cross-curricular practice is happening. When deep, transferrable, useful learning occurs as a result, good cross-curricular practice is happening.

In each example, the required cross-curricular and creative thinking did not just 'happen' – it was the result of thought, planning and usually of secure teacher knowledge. Objectives were met because teachers and other adults involved were constantly aware of them during planning and whilst children were working. Many case study schools brought in outside experts to take learning forward. Several teachers noted that their children were able cheerfully to accept pinpointed criticism and stretching targets from non-teacher experts in ways they would not have done from their regular teachers (see also Brice Heath and Wolf, 2005). The case study evidence confirms that partnership with members of the local community is not simply good for citizenship education but has wider learning benefits (Ofsted, 2010). Whether the expert was a carer, the mayor, an imam, nurse, artist, town planner or a great-grandmother, his or her knowledge helped raise standards of achievement, promoted the

Illustration 3.1 *Children studying full-sized reproductions of paintings in their school hall*

sense of belonging to a living, changing community and provided authoritative, rigorous alternatives to standardized assessments.

Creative curricula

Many schools are experimenting with what they call 'the creative curriculum'. There is no generally accepted definition or guide to such a curriculum, but very often cross-curricular approaches are associated with promoting creativity. Craft (2000) helpfully calls creativity, 'possibility' thinking, and a curriculum designed to help children make connections between different areas of learning in finding possible answers to real questions is likely to be creative. Indeed, in some schools, for example those using the International Primary Curriculum (IPC, 2006, website), they appear to have chosen a curriculum specifically intended to promote it. Arthur Koestler's (1964) insight that creativity is a result of 'bisociation' seems relevant here. Bisociation means the (usually unexpected) meeting of two distinctly different planes of thought. Sternberg (2003) picked up this idea as one of nine types of creativity and calling the bisociative type, 'integration', where creative input integrates two formerly diverse ways of thinking. We may, for example, be analysing in some detail the decorative markings on a Victorian teapot while carrying out an investigation in history, and something makes us think of the markings as reminiscent of music. This unpredicted link between applied pattern and music may result in an imaginative, original and valued musical composition. The chances of making unusual juxtapositions of ideas, approaches and knowledge are high but appropriately unpredictable, in a curriculum where different viewpoints exist side by side and unexpected links are expected (see Ofsted, 2002).

Case study 1: Two cross-curricular terms covering the entire curriculum for a 3–11 nursery/primary school – an example of double-focus cross-curricular activity

This school works with A New Direction (AND website), an organization dedicated to supporting the development of creativity in schools by promoting links between them, their community and local creative practitioners. Working specifically with schools in disadvantaged communities in London, AND hopes to bring positive, dynamic change to curricula, pedagogies and lives to its partner schools. The school has 300 pupils (3–11) and serves a deprived area of east London with a high percentage of first-and second-generation immigrants. More than 75 per cent of its children receive free school meals, whilst 90 per cent have English as a second language. The AND project in this school was based around a simple question: 'Where do we find the creative us?' This was a question which included both staff and children and its answer was to be found over two terms of curriculum work involving the whole school.

Planning with three creative practitioners, the school decided on a radical approach. Three major whole-school outings in the local area were to become the engine of curriculum and pedagogical change. The three trips and related activities would first be experienced by the teachers and assistants themselves and then a few days later the whole school would make the same trip. They chose three contrasting places to visit over the two terms:

- Canary Wharf
- a nature reserve developed from an abandoned Victorian cemetery
- (a tour of) the streets around the school (a visit to a local gallery of modern art had to be postponed).

The three visits shared a similar format and were built upon eight key principles:

- All should see themselves as learners (parents, lunchtime supervisors, governors were all represented as well as teachers, TAs and children).
- Children should be paired in differing age groups (a nursery child paired with a Year 6 child, reception with Year 5 and so on).
- Groups should be composed of three pairs of children and an adult.

(Continued)

> *(Continued)*
>
> - All focusing activities at the sites were to be sensory (using touch, smell, taste, sight, hearing).
> - Adults had to participate alongside children.
> - All activities were to be open-ended (having no particular end in mind).
> - Adults were to stress the 'present tense' experiential nature of the activities.
> - The visits would go ahead whatever the weather.

Illustration 3.2   *A wow moment at Canary Wharf*

'Wow' experiences and focusing exercises

Creative practitioners and staff agreed on the importance of meaningful experience in generating the desire to become involved in learning. So the whole-school trip was a crucial kick-start to each unit of work. A shared experience became a 'wow' experience, partly because of the locations, the large scale of the exercise and the unusual pairings. The places visited, though very near the school, were unfamiliar to well over half the pupils. The teachers and children had never experienced a whole-school outing before and it was very unusual for the Year 6 class to spend extended time with those in the nursery. The initial impact of each familiar yet unfamiliar environment was strong, children often expressed this in 'wow's and excited talk, but interest was sustained and deepened by a powerful series of focus exercises.

Focus exercises are sensory activities intended to be fully inclusive and help all learners experience aspects of a place, theme, object or person in fine detail. In each place, focused listening, careful looking, sensitive smelling and accurate seeing were encouraged through these open-ended exercises (see text box below for a sample of these exercises). They were open-ended because there was no initial objective other than to fully experience the sight, sound, smell or view of usually unnoticed features of the place visited. Children in their unfamiliar groupings entered into these exercises with gusto and real involvement. The social and sensory aspects of the learning process were fully exploited through them, but they also generated questions, thoughts and conversations which went well beyond the exercises themselves.

Following up experience

The big and little experiences of each day energized and motivated the children of all ages. Significantly, the experiences also excited the teachers. Back at school in the following weeks, class teachers picked up the excitement of the day and built a wide range of subject-based responses around them. Early years children talked enthusiastically about what they saw, smelt and heard with the aid of a video taken by a Teaching Assistant. They developed their newly extended vocabulary concerning where sounds came from, by doing more listening exercises around the school. Year 4 made a richly illustrated, three-week science project based upon the children's fascination with decay, re-growth and the minute creatures they found in the nature reserve. They also followed up the *spatialization* exercise with a series of group musical compositions based around four contrasting soundscapes found on the same visit. Year 1 also made a musical trail describing their journey from school to Canary Wharf in a series of sound pictures linked by a foot-tramping *Rondo* theme. The emotional maps of the nature trail led to a Year 6 group suggesting 'emotionally mapping' the school and then the neighbourhood. The children of all ages identified as particularly 'gifted and talented' made sculptures and environments based upon abstractions taken from either the made environments of Canary Wharf or the natural environment of the nature reserve. Children in Year 3 changed their smell trail into a 'taste trail', first of all being taught about the science of taste and then using blindfold sampling of stilton, mango, lime, coffee, 'raw' chocolate and other strong tasting foods to consolidate their learning. Later, they constructed a mapped treasure hunt based on taste identification and challenged another class to find their way to the treasure (chocolate of course!). Each of these provide further examples of multi-disciplinary

---

Outside School Focus Exercises

1. **'Key word' photo**
    Everyone is given a viewfinder with a different *key word* written on it (e.g. red, sad, lonely, awesome, dangerous, etc.). Using your viewfinder to frame it, look around for details (small ones are usually best) which visually illustrate or summarize that key word. Capture your decision in a photo and also include the key word on your viewfinder in the photo. This will remind you of the theme. (Thanks to Catherine Greig)

2. **Spatialization**
    Draw a circle to represent a bird's eye view of your head, put some ears at three o'clock and nine o'clock and a nose at 12.00. Listen carefully for sounds around you. Decide the location of the separate sounds and the direction of movement if the sound is moving (like an aeroplane or a car). Mark the location of each sound in the appropriate area around the diagram of your head. (Thanks to Robert Jarvis)

3. **Big picture**
    On a large sheet of paper (A1 or A2), each of four people draw a big impression of the skyline in front of them. One person should draw the skyline looking north, one east, one south and one west. You should use bold, colourful felt-tip pens. The four team members should then join their drawings to make a continuous collaborative image of 360° of the skyline.

4. **Texture rubbing and words**
    Find a place where two different materials and/or textures meet. Feel the join between them and then talk about the different textures which meet there. Make a rubbing of the join and a little of each material and annotate the rubbing with words describing the two textures. (Thanks to Stirling Clark)

5. **Colour match**
    Use coloured paint swatches to find natural and made matches in the environment. Peel off the double-sided sticky tape and attach as many examples of each colour to its corresponding paint colour as possible.

6. **Mapping**
    Make a map of a little journey you have taken showing significant landmarks (buildings, plants, shadows, furniture and unexpected things which strike you as important). Use your map in one of the following ways:

    (a) **emotional maps:** how do you feel in each place? Mark on your map with words or colours the emotions you feel in different places. For example, which place makes you feel small, lonely, excited, frightened, cold, happy, sad, etc.?

    (b) **sound maps:** what are the dominant sounds in different areas of your map? Draw symbols or write words which capture the locations of different sounds in the environment.

    (c) **smell maps:** what smells can you identify in this place? Mark on the boundaries between different dominating smells. For example, where is there a more natural woody, vegetation smell? How are the smells near the water different? (Thanks to Stephen Scoffham)

Figure 3.1   Some focus exercises to use in the locality of the school

cross-curricular responses – there was no intention to integrate learning in a number of subjects, classes simply responded in different subject ways to the same experience. Whilst subject-based activities related to the visits continued to occupy each class for three or four weeks, the remainder of the curriculum time was devoted to an unrelated programme of learning in the remaining subjects.

Illustration 3.3   *Using word frames*

Case study 2: A cross-curricular module with a cross-phase group of Year 6/7 children

The transition between Year 6 and Year 7 is a difficult one for children. Primary education practice and the pedagogies and curricula of secondary are often seen, even by teachers, as very different from each other. Two schools in the same locality wanted to work to break down these barriers and chose a cross-curricular language project to launch their new relationship. Both schools had identified their learning of modern foreign languages (mfl) as a target for improvement, in terms of motivation as well as outcome. Working with a team of music, English and mfl specialists, the schools developed a short inter-disciplinary module intended creatively to combine the three subjects and classes of Year 6 and Year 7 children. Their work was to be shared with and responded to by two parallel schools in France.

Motivation

Time, organization and money did not allow for a large-scale 'wow' experience to set the module going, but a series of focus exercises was chosen to engage

	Canary Wharf	Nature trail	Tour of streets around the school
Nursery			
Reception	Words: labelled photographs: 30 dark things, 20 red things, 45 cold things, 12 scary things, etc.	Collections – made and natural, colours	
Year 1	Musical journey – composition project		Shapes project – graphs of the most common mathematical shapes found in the locality
Year 2		Art gallery project – paintings of the woodland canopy and close-ups of natural detail collected in drawings and digital images	Designing and making 'Snow world' environments and learning about the history of the seventeenth-century winter markets on the Thames
Year 3	Taste trail – science of taste and geography plan-making project		
Year 4		Growth and decay – a science project on the life cycle of the minibeasts collected on the nature trail and the science of decay	
Year 5			Illustrated stories to be read to Reception children, based upon five personally collected items from the streets and gardens around the school
Year 6		Emotional mapping – geography mapping skills and knowledge, direction	
Gifted and talented cross-phase group	A geometric 'made' environment using forms, patterns and textures found in Canary Wharf – applying design/technology skills and mathematical knowledge		

Figure 3.2 A sample of class follow-up sessions for each year group after their three visits in the school locality

---

School and School Grounds Focus Exercises

7. **Key word viewfinders:** working in groups of four, use four coloured viewfinder frames to find five or six things around the school which express the meaning of each of the words printed on them. After discussing selection and composition, photograph the thing making sure that both the key word is readable and the subject is clear. (Thanks to Catherine Greig)

8. **Fridge magnet poems:** fold a piece of A4 paper into 16 rectangles by folding in half four times. Unfold the paper to reveal the 16 rectangles and then go on a private walk anywhere in the school or school grounds you are allowed. As you walk, write down single words (in English) to capture your feelings, observations, thoughts until you have 16 words. Return to class and gently tear the sheet into 16 separate word rectangles. Arrange your words into a meaningful poem – you can add extra ands, and buts or other short linking words if you like and leave out any words you don't really want to use. (Thanks to Rosanna Raymond)

9. **Spatialization:** as in Figure 3.1.

Figure 3.3 Some focus exercises to use in school grounds and buildings

the classes and give them a reason to want to express themselves in another language. The exercises were intended to help the children find English words to describe the detail and unique qualities of their school environment. These exercises can be done inside or outside school.

The chosen focus exercises are language-based and stimulated a great deal of agitated and enthusiastic talk. The teachers found that setting time limits – 10 minutes for the key words and the poems and 15 minutes for the spatialization helped focus minds more productively. Opportunities to work alone back in the classroom, as in the poem exercise, were particularly valued by some children. Many Year 7 children reported that they felt very motivated by these activities: 'It was great to get out and do real stuff', said one. 'I can't explain it, but when we were doing the exercises I felt really excited and wanted to do much more of it. I 'specially liked it when we were working in pairs on the key words, we kept sparking off new ideas from each other', said another.

Following up

The focus exercises provided motivation and a series of small-scale shared experiences for the children in both classes. When questioned, the vast majority of the class said they felt 'excited', 'energetic', 'happy', 'enthusiastic', 'interested' and 'questioning'. Teachers confirmed pupils' high levels of engagement by applying the Ferre Laevers Leuven Involvement Scale (see Chapter 6). Children's enthusiasm carried through the follow-up sessions which used music or geography skills hierarchically to take learning in French forward.

The pupils in Year 7 were given a degree of freedom in deciding on the relevance of the focus exercises for their learning in French. Several groups repeated the 'key words' idea in French, writing their own French 'emotional vocabulary' provided by the teacher, onto viewfinders. After taking 10 pictures, they used them to make a PowerPoint presentation on the meaning of French words like '*tranquille*'. Other groups used the poem idea and made up French poems from collections of 16 French words from a walk around the school. Motivation to complete and improve the follow-up activities was provided by the teacher introducing the class to a class in Boulogne via a Skype® link up. Some French children introduced themselves and then asked the English children to send them information about their school via email. Richly illustrated French poems and PowerPoints about their school were sent by email by the end of the second day of work.

The Year 6 class used similar focus exercises. Children constructed a series of 'I like .... ' poems about their school. The music specialist then taught the children how to use *Audiomulch*®, a computer programme which transforms recoded sounds digitally, and the children made electronic background music to their poems to illustrate their likes – creatively combining music skills and language skills in one 'product'.

Case study 3: A primary school following the Royal Society of Arts (RSA) competences curriculum

This school serves part of a garrison town and has a highly mobile population, with 60 per cent of its children likely to move into or away from the school in any year. The school describes its reasons for following curriculum guidance from the Royal Society of Arts rather than that of the Qualifications and Curriculum Development Agency as follows:

> Our views have been influenced by international, national, local and school based research and monitoring. We know that methods used in The Foundation Stage have been successful and believe that extending this approach and ethos will have a similarly positive effect on children as they progress through the school. We know that our school has unique characteristics, such as high mobility, and these were highlighted by OFSTED. We have responded to what we know about the school by preparing an appropriate model for teaching the curriculum. As part of this, we believe that building the RSA Competences for Learning into our curriculum will help our children to learn more effectively. (School prospectus, 2010)

The school launched one of the earliest primary versions of the RSA's competences-based curriculum called 'Opening Minds'. The RSA curriculum centres around developing five competences:

(Continued)

(Continued)

- learning
- citizenship
- relating to people
- managing situations
- managing information.

Each competence is chosen to cover an essential and generic aspect of modern life. Schools delivering the RSA curriculum decide upon curriculum themes which will generate development of the competences in a variety of experiential, learning and subject contexts. Working towards mastery of the RSA competences would result, they suggest, in internalizing essential and highly transferable life skills which will be meaningful to children whatever changes come about in twenty-first-century society. In the context of children's preoccupations and worries about the future, outlined in Chapter 1, such a curriculum appears potentially both relevant and timely.

The school has made its own detailed and levelled descriptors (levels 1–5) for each of these competences, but with no or little reference to subject content. Staff, parents and children have made many thoughtful and well-discussed decisions about curriculum. Their curriculum policy contains the following aims:

- For children to produce high-quality outcomes across all curriculum subjects – to bring out the best in everyone.
- To have a time-effective, relevant curriculum with real-life and cross-curricular links.
- To educate children and staff in the broadest sense of the word's meaning – 'to lead out'.
- To focus on children and how they learn best as a priority.
- To ensure children have appropriate access to learning activities that promote physical, moral, social, spiritual, cultural, academic and creative development.
- To encourage children's understanding and tolerance of the world in which they live and its peoples.

To achieve these aims, the school divided the curriculum subjects into what they term *'knowledge subjects'* (Geography, History, Science and Religious Education), each of which form the 'lead' subject for a term. The identification of knowledge subjects gives teachers a clear lead to be teaching knowledge and encouraging children to use it in different settings. What the school

---

What the competences mean

Learning

Children will understand how to learn and manage their own lifelong learning, they will learn systematically to think, to have explored and extended their own talents and have opportunities to develop a love of learning for its own sake. They will achieve high personal standards in literacy, numeracy and spatial understanding and be able to handle ICT with confidence and understanding.

Citizenship

Children will have developed an understanding of ethics and values and have experience of contributing to society. They will understand how the institutions of society work and their relationship to it. They will understand and value the importance of diversity, both nationally and globally, and will consider the global and social implications of technology. They will also learn to manage aspects of their own lives.

Relationships

Children will understand how to relate to people in a variety of contexts. They will have experience of operating in teams and understand how to help develop other people. They will develop a range of techniques for communicating in different ways and have an understanding of managing themselves and others emotionally. They will know techniques for managing stress and conflict.

Situations

Children will learn to manage time, change, success and disappointment. They will understand what it is to be entrepreneurial and how to take and use initiative. They will learn how to take and manage risks and uncertainties.

Information

Children will develop a range of techniques for assessing and differentiating information and will learn to be analytical. They will understand the importance of reflection and critical judgement and know how, when and where to apply it.

Figure 3.4 The RSA Opening Minds, competences-led curriculum

calls the *'process subjects'* (Maths, English, Design and Technology, Music, MFL, Art and PE) feature throughout the year. Here teachers concentrate more on the teaching of skills and opportunities for children to put those skills into practice in real projects. In consultation with the children, the curriculum designers decided that a literacy and numeracy 'hour' was too long and that the daily sessions should be cut to half an hour. Other English and mathematics and all science was to be subsumed in topic-based work and at other times throughout the week. Science is a term's focus three times a year, and English and mathematics have extra weighting to reflect their 'core' status. Look, for example, at Figure 3.5 to see the way the subjects are shared throughout the week during Key Stage 2.

Illustration 3.4   *Children planning their presentation*

This double-focus curriculum is divided into topics within which each year group chooses a strong and emotionally engaging shared 'event' as the focus for each of six terms. For every class, the event and 'lead' subject define teaching decisions for a six-week block. So a Year 1 or 2 group, for example, worked from (or towards) the following happenings:

- a trip to the seaside (with a history focus on how we used to live)
- a Christmas nativity play (with a science focus on light)
- an art exhibition (RE)
- an Easter fun day (with a science focus on new life)
- 'a day trip to India' (with a geography focus on a distant locality)
- the opening of a wildlife garden (with a science focus on biodiversity).

In this curriculum, 65–70 per cent of all subject-based work falls within the cross-curricular theme. Teachers are encouraged to use texts and examples in the remaining 30–35 per cent, which also relate to either a main or RE theme. Throughout the school, learning is interrelated and contextualized – the learning makes sense to the learners. Subject leaders support their colleagues by using the National Curriculum Attainment targets (DfEE/QCA, 1999) for their subject to construct progressions of skills, knowledge and attitudes. Teachers then use this levelled description to plan extra challenge or provide added skills.

Key Stage 2 total	23.75 hrs	
Literacy	**Hours per week**	**Percentage of time**
Discrete teaching of writing	1	4.2
Cross-curricular writing	1	4.2
Guided reading	1.25	5.3
Handwriting	0.25	1.1
Word and sentence work	2.5	10.5
Reading by/with teacher	1	4.2
Total	**7**	**29.5**
Numeracy		
Oral mental work	1	4.2
Number	2.5	10.5
Cross-curricular maths	1.5	6.3
Total	**5**	**21.0**
Other subjects		
Science	1.75	7.4
History and/or Geography	2	8.4
Art and/or Design and Technology	2	8.4
Music	1	4.2
Physical Education	2	8.4
Religious Education	1	4.2
Information Communication Technology	0.5	2.1
Personal Education	0.75	3.2
Modern Foreign Language	0.75	3.2
Total	**11.75**	**49.5**
Final Total	**23.75**	**100.0**

Figure 3.5   Key Stage 2 subject balance in a typical week

Case study 4: A two-day project for Year 4 pupils on 'What is a community?'

A Year 4 teacher wanted to contribute to a two-day unit of work as part of the Engaging Places (2010, website) project. The website, maintained by English Heritage and The Commission for Architecture and the Built Environment (CABE), aims to support schools in using aspects of the built environment as resources for learning. Providing a network of organizations able and willing to work with schools on built environment projects and a wide range of case

(Continued)

Whole School Topic Plan

Half/Term Curriculum Overview

National Curriculum Years 1/2

RE – Christianity/symbols and objects

Term 1	Term 2	Term 3	Term 4	Term 5	Term 6
HISTORY Special People (Changes in lifestyles) (SCIENCE – OURSELVES 1)	**SCIENCE** LIGHT	**RE** Islam (SCIENCE – SOUND)	**SCIENCE** MATERIALS (CHANGES)	**GEOGRAPHY** Contrasting locality [UK] (SCIENCE – INVESTIGATION UNIT)	**SCIENCE** LIVING THINGS IN THEIR ENVIRONMENT

RE – Christianity/symbols and objects

Term 1	Term 2	Term 3	Term 4	Term 5	Term 6
GEOGRAPHY Our School and Neighbourhood (SCIENCE – OURSELVES 2)	**SCIENCE** MATERIALS (GROUPING)	**HISTORY** Special Events (Changes in lifestyle) (SCIENCE – ELECTRICITY)	**SCIENCE** FORCES	**RE** Judaism (SCIENCE – INVESTIGATION UNIT)	**SCIENCE** GREEN PLANTS

National Curriculum Years 3/4

RE – Christianity/religious responses to current issues

Term 1	Term 2	Term 3	Term 4	Term 5	Term 6
GEOGRAPHY Locality in a Less Economically Developed Country (SCIENCE – HABITATS)	**SCIENCE** LIGHT	**SCIENCE** MATERIALS – THERMAL	**RE** Islam (SCIENCE – SOUND)	**HISTORY** Tudors (local study) (SCIENCE – INVESTIGATION UNIT)	**SCIENCE** TEETH & HEALTHY EATING

RE – Christianity/symbols and objects

Term 1	Term 2	Term 3	Term 4	Term 5	Term 6
SCIENCE MATERIALS – ROCKS & SOILS	**GEOGRAPHY** UK Locality (SCIENCE – MICRO ORGANISMS)	**SCIENCE** FORCES	**RE** Judaism (SCIENCE – FORCES CONT.)	**SCIENCE** GREEN PLANTS	**HISTORY** Victorians or Britain Since 1930 (local study) (SCIENCE – ELECTRICITY)

National Curriculum Years 5/6

RE – Christianity/religious responses to current issues

Term 1	Term 2	Term 3	Term 4	Term 5	Term 6
SCIENCE MATERIALS – CHANGES	**GEOGRAPHY**] UK Locality (SCIENCE – GREEN PLANTS)	**RE** Sikhism (SCIENCE – LIGHT)	**HISTORY** Romans, Anglo Saxons and Vikings (local study) (SCIENCE – SOUND)	**SCIENCE** EARTH, SUN AND MOON	**HISTORY** World Study – Egyptians (SCIENCE – INVESTIGATION UNIT)

RE Christianity/symbols and objects

Term 1	Term 2	Term 3	Term 4	Term 5	Term 6
SCIENCE MATERIALS – DISSOLVING	**GEOGRAPHY** Locality in a Less Economically Developed Country (SCIENCE – ELECTRICITY)	**HISTORY** European – Greece (SCIENCE – HEART RATE AND KEEPING HEALTHY)	**SCIENCE** FORCES	**RE** Hinduism (SCIENCE – INVESTIGATION UNIT)	**GEOGRAPHY** Changing Environment (SCIENCE – LIVING THINGS IN THEIR ENVIRONMENT)

Figure 3.6 Yearly topic grid for knowledge subjects

Illustration 3.5 *Intense faces and focussed body language often characterize collaborative projects. Photo: Ian Bottle*

(Continued)

studies, lesson plans and support materials, Engaging Places aims to be a 'one-stop shop' for all wishing to use real places as a focus for learning. The two-day unit of work is an example of multi-disciplinary cross-curricular teaching and learning in the context of a wider and values-based curriculum.

The wider aim of the school is to help all children feel they belong to the local community. This was in the teacher's mind when she decided that the question that would bind their cross-curricular work, would be: 'how is our street a community?' The class teacher set about helping the children answer this question in an oblique way: she asked a town planner, a geographer, a musician and a scientist to come in for the two days to work with her children. She asked these adults how their subject expertise would help them answer the class's question and then to lead the children towards finding answers along scientific, design, musical and geographical lines. The class was divided into four groups of seven and each worked with one of the adults:

- The music group took a 'sound walk' with the musician who wanted to show that musical compositions could construct a 'sonic sense of place'.
- The design/technology group talked with the town planner about the traffic dangers of their street at school opening and closing times. He wanted to help the children discover that they could do something as citizens to influence local government decisions.

(Continued)

(Continued)

- The scientists worked with the scientific advisor to a big company to find out if they could 'live lives any greener'.
- The geography option concerned discovering the uniqueness of their place, by taking a walk from top to bottom of the lane in which their school stood, and mapping together what was special about it.

Illustration 3.6 Six-year-olds showing thoughts about the possible changes in the view from a classroom window in 50 years time. (Left hand side, present; right hand side future)

The town planner (a friend of the teacher) showed the children how to use copies of a small-scale map to plan changes to a built environment. Children pooled and discussed the changes they felt would be needed to make the school lane safer. They arrived at four practical proposals: speed bumps, a one-way system, a safe crossing point and parking restrictions on a particularly dangerous stretch of the lane. A fifth suggestion, a school bus, was taken up by the scientist's group as they made detailed proposals for a 'green (electric) bus', supported by the scientist who told them about electric engines and their design implications. The scientist also had to help them with the practicalities of a calming fish tank the children wanted for the bus passengers.

The town planning group built a scale model of their proposals on to a base map of the school lane, carefully photographed each aspect and with the planner's help, composed a letter of proposals to the local district council. This decision supported the development of important PSHE targets for the class (for more details, see Engaging Places, 2010, website).

Case study 5: A child-led term based on walks in the park with nursery children

A speech therapist and a nursery leader in Liverpool decided to work together to address the communication barriers they had both observed through delayed development in many children. Emulating practice they had seen in Scandinavia, they planned a series of walks from the nursery to a Victorian park near the school with the aim of stimulating conversation and questions. Each walk took a path through a wood and out the other side to a meadow with a strange locked tower at one end and views across to a set of ornate mansions. With minimal adult leading, the children began to make up stories about the tower and the large decorated houses. The leaders eventually persuaded the local museum to open up the tower and on the fourth walk, the children were able to enter it and add to their stories about what it might have been used for. A museum curator brought a stuffed owl to show them one of the many creatures that currently occupied the tower.

The simple action of six walks in different directions through the park was enough to transform the atmosphere and the learning of the whole group. The walks, which happened rain or shine, took the whole morning and involved collections, woodland sculptures, den building, bird watching, tree, flower and butterfly identification, games and songs. The teachers, parents and helpers noted however that the chief benefit of these open-ended walks was the vast amount of talk they generated: real questions, imaginative solutions, genuine interactions and opportunities to help extend each child's language world at every turn.

The nursery school decided to timetable such walks weekly throughout the year and base much of the activity in the rest of the week on ideas, things and stories the children had brought back with them.

Case study 6: Two afternoon sessions for Year 5 children working with an artist

Case study 6 took place in a primary school in an economically deprived and ethnically mixed part of London; more than 60 per cent of its children had English as their second or third language and about 75 per cent were eligible for free school meals. External inspection and internal personal/professional development had identified two main aims for curriculum progress:

(Continued)

(Continued)

- to improve the standard of English literacy
- to improve the sense of community within the school.

Courageously, the school decided to take an unconventional route towards these two objectives – with a grant from Creative Partnerships, they employed an artist and a curriculum designer to work with children and staff on rethinking the curriculum. This case study records what happened in two sessions in a Year 5 class of 25 children representing 19 different languages. Many could not speak any English when they arrived at school. Analysis of these lessons formed the starting point for staff discussions and decisions about their curriculum for the coming year.

The observed class and their teacher worked with a Maori/Samoan artist for two afternoons. Coming from a culture outside all of theirs, the artist introduced herself by describing her *Tatau* (the Samoan word from which we get 'tattoo'). She described how personal and culturally important each image was to her and the meaning of some of the marks on her hands, arms and legs. After responding to many questions about her country, she suggested that the children might like to draw round their hands and design their own meaningful *tatau* which would symbolically show what was really, really important to them. Children were immediately keen to do this and the artist reminded children that the symbols should not be random but be attached to some kind of story to do with important things in their lives. After some 20 minutes of eager drawing, she said that if children wanted to they could write the story which linked their symbols, in poem form or as a story. After an hour, she called all 25 children into a circle, sat down with them and asked them to share what they had done. All children listened respectfully and attentively to the often moving and very heartfelt stories of the others. One boy who had drawn a flag and a heart and mountains and four dots said this when his turn came round:

> *You will not know this flag, it is the flag of my country Kurdistan, this is where I and my mother and father and sisters come from, they are the dots, there are lots of mountains there, I have drawn the heart because I have love for my enemies as well as my friends.*

Another, streetwise and mature nine-year-old Romanian, stood up and recited:

I love my mum and I love my dad
I love my grandma too

I like my cat when she's not scratching
I like coca cola but its not matching
I like my chicken but its not hatching

I love my mum and I love my dad
I love my mum and I love my dad.

(Continued)

(Continued)

All were deeply engaged by this simple exercise in celebrating both personal identity and the building of a respectful and diverse community.

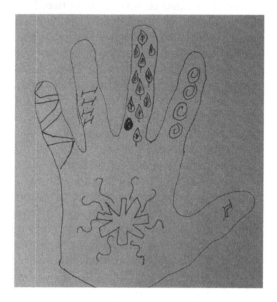

Illustration 3.7   *A tatau-ed hand*

Illustration 3.8   *Arranging found words in a poem*

(Continued)

(Continued)

The following day, the artist collected the symbols the children had designed and copied them onto the whiteboard. They discussed how these aspects of life that were so important to them might somehow be brought together and nurtured – under the influence of the previous day's session on Samoa, someone suggested an ideal Pacific Island where everyone lived peacefully together. One group thought the island could be turned into music and at that the whole class became energized. Under the artist's and class teacher's gentle guidance, groups began to compose a spiral-shaped score of Pacific Island music which used their symbols as graphic notation. Thus, the class creatively fused major progression in music learning (composing for the first time from a non-musical starting point, and using a spiral form as a musical structure), geography (detailed understanding of key features of a coral and volcanic island environment) and significantly developed their speaking and listening skills. This was inter-disciplinary in that creative fusion was both the aim and the outcome of these lessons, but also assessable subject progress was made in three subjects.

Case study 7: The Higher Education Arts and Schools (HEARTS) project (a Year 7/8 and ITE cross-arts project)

This project formed part of a teacher education programme, and exemplifies many of the personal and learning benefits for both teacher and pupil when they are involved in activities which seem to be mutually relevant.

The HEARTS project (Barnes, 2005b, 2006; Barnes and Shirley, 2007; NFER, 2007, website) was designed to investigate the power of the arts to enhance the learning of university tutors, trainee teachers and school children. It consisted of a series of practical encounters where cross-arts activities were used to answer profound questions and detailed investigations about environments. The project consisted of three discrete but linked experiences.

Experience 1: A mystery journey in a tiny steam train

Students and pupils were crammed into a half-gauge railway train with carriages just big enough to take four children and two students. Each group of six was given a sealed envelope to be opened as the train started its 50-minute journey. The letter in the sealed envelope simply gave an instruction:

> *Write a rap based upon the rhythms you can hear on the train and the sights you can see from it. Be ready to perform it on the station when you arrive.*

Neither the university students nor pupils were expecting this task and none were music specialists. In almost every one of the 15 groups of six, the school children took the lead. Students reported that the pupils '... just seemed more confident with open-ended challenges'. The pupils noticed the *tid-dly, tid-dly, tid-dly, taa, tid-dly, tid-dly, tid-dly, taa,* often interrupted by other rhythms as

(Continued)

(Continued)

Illustration 3.9 *Children and student teachers were placed together in the tiny carriages of a half-gauge railway to construct 'raps' about the journey*

wheels moved across points and crossings. They also noted the interruptions of whistles and frequent loud puffs of steam from the engine. As they looked from the carriage windows, the pupils recorded the things they saw: 'rubbishy gardens', 'miles of wires', 'traffic waiting', 'pylons, pylons, pylons', wrote one group. By half-way, the students had begun to catch up with the pupils and were making their own contributions. Students and pupils together started to make up their raps and write them down, some had repeated choruses which would hold them together, and some groups had discussed in detail how their raps were going to be presented to the audience of fellow travellers. One group punctuated their pithy take on what they saw as a spoiled landscape viewed from the train, with this repeated refrain:

This is my time
This is my place
This is my en-vir-on-ment
This is my rhyme

Experience 2: a beach on a drizzly November day

The 90 learners arrived at a forlorn and empty beach in light rain and strong winds. Aside from health and safety warnings, the student teachers had only

(Continued)

(Continued)

been given two instructions for their day: avoid using the words 'you' or 'I', and allow the children to take control of activities as soon as possible. Each group of six students and pupils were simply left with a set of focusing tasks and asked to 'capture the essence' of their place for a short presentation to their peers when they returned to school the next day.

Focusing exercises

9. **A sense of touch:** each member of the group is to go into their own space and sit or stand alone. Feel walls, pebbles, plants, fence, etc. nearest you. Jot down fragments of sentences which describe the fine detail of the physical sensations in the fingers as you feel the immediate environment.
10. **Haiku:** each person in the group is to write a three-line haiku (five syllables, then seven, then five syllables only) that captures the essence of a tiny detail of the place they are in. A haiku often starts with a sensitive description in the first two lines and in the last-five syllable line, the thoughts 'flip' to a 'higher' or more profound association.
11. **Snapshot view:** divide into pairs. In each pair, one of the partners closes their eyes and is led very carefully by their open-eyed partner. When the open-eyed partner sees an unusual or interesting image, they position their friend in the optimum viewing position and then squeeze the hand of their partner. The partner then opens their eyes for the length of the hand squeeze. Do this five times and then swap roles.
12. **One shot only:** each member of the group is allowed one still photograph only (so it has to be a good one). Discuss shots with the whole group but each individual must take a photograph.
13. **A dramatic happening:** plan a dramatic modern (or future) event which could only have happened in your place. Act it out. Summarize the story in three freeze-frame montages. Discuss and draw/plan/note what you would absolutely *have* to construct on your school stage if you wanted to act the scene out back at school. For example, would the light need to be coming from a certain side? Would there have to be a step here, an arch there? Would the arch have to be low/pointed/stone/crumbly? Etc.
14. **Say it in one:** each group has to produce five 'one-shot movies' lasting one minute. Each person will have the opportunity to make a movie. It should be a planned and continuous shot taken by one member but the shot should be discussed by the whole group.

(With thanks to Robert Jarvis for many of these ideas)

Figure 3.7 Excercises to widen and develop sensory and emotional engagement at the beginning of a project

Experience 3: adults and children working together

After a day together, students and children brought their collected data and impressions back to school. They worked on creative ways of bringing several aspects together and presenting them, and finally performed them to the rest of the year cohort. The 15 presentations could not have been more

(Continued)

(Continued)

Illustration 3.10   *Dungeness power station from the beach*

varied – they included two dramas, an art exhibition, a musical composition accompanying a silent film, a puppet show with characters made from pebbles, a dance where nature battled with humankind, a dramatically presented ghost story with music, a sculpture garden and a seven-minute documentary.

Students made detailed records of their impressions and observations, and wrote them up as part of an assignment. Several themes of general interest to those thinking of cross-arts work in schools emerged. Students noted many common outcomes from their three experiences. In each case, students remarked on the impact of placing control in the children's hands for significant periods. All remarked on the effective use of the arts to interpret and communicate the essence of a place. The following themes were commonly highlighted in student's assignments:

- Children's imagination was consistently recorded as being beyond that of the students themselves.
- The focus activities generated a great deal of genuine questioning.
- Children seemed so highly engaged that behaviour never became an issue.
- The atmosphere seemed very relaxed.
- The children displayed facial expressions of happiness and contentedness.
- The cooperation and friendliness of the children involved in the project were frequently remarked upon.
- The sense of pupil control significantly enhanced engagement.

(Continued)

- Children responded well to the open-ended nature of the project.
- The normal barriers between teacher and pupil were significantly broken down.
- Both children and students reported that they had learned significant arts and ICT skills and lots of unexpected place and science knowledge.
- A number of students commented that this activity had been the most enjoyable aspect of their whole course.

In a context where such positive outcomes are so evident, there remain serious pitfalls. University tutors assessing the students' work noted the following:

- Having stepped out of the role of teacher, many students forgot to step back in. Students were happy to see well-motivated, well-behaved, active and link-making children working on the project, but did not use the opportunity to help the children 'raise their game'. They did not step in to offer new challenges, teach new and relevant skills at a higher level or question pupils about ways they could improve their products.
- Having attended a crash course on creative teaching and learning, some students left with the idea that it was going to be easy to generate creativity in their classrooms. Some failed to understand that creativity does not 'just happen' when children are left to their own devices, but it needs serious preparation and discussion amongst teachers, and probably a clear framework to develop within.

Summary

- Each study illustrates different forms of local and child-centred relevance.
- There is no optimum timescale for good cross-curricular practice; a day, a week, a term, two terms and a whole-school curriculum are each represented.
- The fewer the curriculum subjects represented within a single theme, the more teachers are able to help raise subject standards and ensure curriculum progression and coverage.
- Each study relied upon and promoted maximum physical and emotional involvement in an authentic setting.
- Each study generated creative links across the curriculum.
- Each study integrated working adults as experts from the wider community.
- Activities and themes held equal fascination for both the adults and children involved.
- Each activity required and was founded upon detailed and lengthy planning in order to ensure progression and curriculum coverage.

- Every study was reported by teachers to have generated a high degree of focus, motivation and exemplary behaviour on the part of the children (and adults).

Key questions for discussion

- Can you identify the difference between interdisciplinary and multi-disciplinary cross-curricular activities?
- What kind of teacher do you think would be most at home with opportunistic methods of cross-curricular teaching?
- Are the kind of activities outlined in the case studies and focus exercises feasible for novice teachers? Give your reasons.

Further reading

Brice Heath, S. and Wolf, S. (2004) *Visual Learning in the Community School*. London: Arts Council.
Csikszentmihalyi, M. (2003) *Good Business*. New York: Hodder and Stoughton.
Wilson, A. (ed.) (2005) *Creativity in the Primary Classroom*. Exeter: Learning Matters.
Wyse, D. and Rowson, P. (2008) *The Really Useful Creativity Book*. London: Routledge.

Summary

These chapters should have given you a basis for developing an understanding of the purpose and process of a curriculum in a primary school. A curriculum is not a syllabus to be received and applied as seen but a document to aid planning and assessment which allows some scope for you, as a professional, to make judgements about how best to implement the necessary objectives and skills in each unique classroom.

Thinking again about our overarching themes of Communication, Innovation and Participation you should be able to see links to the curriculum. Communicating with children will not only allow you to assess their needs but will also allow you to ascertain their interests and skills which can be used as a starting point for a shared curriculum model. Creativity in curriculum design is essential when planning an innovative approach to any aspect of learning; such an approach, which encompasses the skills and abilities of pupils, colleagues and other groups such as parents, will allow all learners to participate and achieve!

Student activities
- Familiarise yourself with the new draft proposals for the primary national curriculum as well as the new Early years foundation stage curriculum and the exemplar materials that go with it. Compare this to the current curriculum – what will be the impact of these changes upon professional development, practice in the classroom and subject integrity?
- On your next school placement look for innovative ways of implementing the requirements of the national curriculum – make notes on good practice and share it with your peers.
- Put yourself at the centre of a learning experience. Note down two or three things that you are interested in – books, hobbies or skills; use one of these to build a programme of learning that begins with your interest! Look closely at the skills outlined in the national curriculum and try to think of innovative ways of implementing these within this framework.
- Investigate the findings of the Rose and Alexander reviews and consider the implications of these reports on curricula design. Begin to think about you as the professional and what your opinion is of the suggestions made within these documents.
- If you were tasked with implementing changes to the current curriculum what would you do? Consider the following questions: What would be the aims and values of your curriculum be? What objectives would you include and what sequence would these appear in? How should objectives be delivered? How would you assess students' learning?

Top tips

- Familiarise yourself with current documentation for curriculum as well as the draft documentation.
- Regardless of scheme or units of work that schools implement it is the objectives in the National Curriculum document that should be central to your planning; this is what is statutory.
- Impact on children's learning is the core of any curriculum! Thinking about how to implement the curriculum in innovative ways will engage not only the pupils but you!
- Planning is individual to every class and learner – what works one year will not always work the next. Ensure that you constantly reflect on your own practice and the learning of the pupils to ensure that your teaching remains fresh and up-to-date and enthuses all, including yourself!
- It is your responsibility as a professional to keep up to date with current developments in curriculum – be aware of what is around the corner and question how this will impact you as a practitioner.

Additional readings

Primary
Alexander, R. J. and Doddington, C. (eds) (2010) Children's Social Development, Peer Interaction and Classroom Learning Chapter 7 in *Cambridge Primary Review Research Survey*.
Peacock, Alison (2010) 'A voice for the future', *The Cambridge Primary Review*, 52 (3): 3373–80.
Rowley, C. and Cooper, H. (2009) 'Cross curricular learning and the development of values' Chapter 1 in *Cross Curricular Approaches to Teaching and Learning*. London: SAGE.
Hurford, D. (2009) 'Using dialogue to engage children with challenging ideas: Geography and global citizenship' Chapter 10 in Rowley, C. and Cooper, H. *Cross Curricular Approaches to Teaching and Learning*. London: SAGE.
Wyse, D. and Jones, R. (eds) (2005) *Creativity in the Primary Curriculum*. London: David Fulton.

Early Years
Athey.C. (1990) *Extending Thought in Young Children*. London: PCP. pp.113–57.
Brooker, L (2008) *Supporting Children's Transitions in the Early Years*. London: Open University Press.
Fabian, H. and Dunlop, A. W. (2002) *Transitions in the Early Years: Debating Continuity and Progression for Children in Early Education*. London: Open University Press.
Issacs, Barbara (2007) 'Bringing the Montessori Approach to Your Early Years Practice'. Read Part: Background to the Reggio Approach. Abingdon: Routledge.
Nicol Janni (2007) (available online – see library catalogue) 'Bringing the Steiner Waldorf Approach to Your Early Years Practice'Read Part 1: Background to the Steiner Approach. Abingdon: Routledge.
Nutbrown Review (2012) 'Foundations for Quality.The Independent Review of Early Education'. March.
Thornton, L. And Brunton P(2007) (available online – see library catalogue) 'Bringing the Reggio Approach to Your Early Years Practice' Read Part 1: Background to the Reggio Approach. Abingdon: Routledge.

NOTE: Ensure you are familiar with the new draft National Primary Curriculum and EYFS Link to web address for new EYFS and exemplification documents

PART 5

LEARNING AND TEACHING INTRODUCTION

Overview

This part is the 'nuts and bolts' of the teaching profession – planning and preparing for being in the classroom with a group of children is the foundation of your practice as a teacher.

This part looks at the role of the reflective practitioner and the importance of taking ownership of your own professional development. Smith will provide an overview of the terminology and practices of reflection and its purpose in the classroom as well as highlighting its usefulness as a tool for your own learning and development at university and beyond. Hansen will give an insight into the role of the reflective practitioner in the context of the classroom; outlining your role in developing as a teacher and concluding by looking at children as reflective learners.

Another focus is on the effect of classroom environments upon learners and how you can create an effective classroom environment and ethos. With our overarching theme of participation in mind, think about the role of yourself and the pupils in creating your classroom environment.

Creativity is an integral part of the primary and early years' classroom but is a word that is often used with little thought to what this would look like in practice. The aim of these chapters is to broaden your understanding of creativity and how to facilitate a creative learning environment.

'Failure to plan is planning to fail'. Planning is key to effective teaching and learning – it is the starting point for all activities within the classroom, with a clear focus on the learning objectives however, it should be a flexible, working tool which is adapted and refined as you teach in order to ensure the learning of the pupils is paramount.

In the theories of learning chapter you read about building upon prior and existing learning, knowledge and understanding; it would be impossible to ascertain these without due regard to assessment for learning practices. This section aims to provide an introduction along with some practical examples which will tie in with your centre-based seminars to give you a clear overview of the role of assessment.

Being a Reflective Early Years Practitioner

19

Hallet, E.

Chapter overview

Early years practitioners engaging in reflective learning within their work context has enabled them to become reflective practitioners working professionally with young children, families and other professionals. There is opportunity to reflect upon your work-based reflective learning throughout the chapter.

This chapter will:
- Explore the concepts of reflective learning and practice.
- Discuss theories of reflection.
- Examine qualities and attributes of being a reflective practitioner.
- Provide ways for practitioners to reflect upon their professional practice.

Reflective learning

The early years landscape is evolving and changing due to change in government-led policy and reform and international influences upon pedagogy and practice. These influences introduce new ideas, providing opportunities for reflection to inform professional practice. As practitioners work, they see new landscapes opening up ahead, while the landscapes of policy and professional practice they have just passed through appear different as they look back. Looking back through a reflective lens informs new ways of thinking of and developing professional practice to put policy into practice (Dahlberg et al., 2007).

There is an emerging importance for early years practitioners to be reflective in the continuously changing environment within the early years sector, particularly in regard to integrated working, which requires a reflective and sensitive approach to developing new ways for multi-professional working (Paige-Smith and Craft, 2011). Early years practitioners are particularly affected in developing their practice by shifts in policy. Practitioners use practical professional knowledge to interpret and respond to changes in policy and practice (Edwards, 2000). The purpose of reflective practice is to provide better quality experiences for children and their families. When practitioners engage in reflection, they can improve provision and practice by making informed decisions about whether their work with children is effective or not (Brookfield, 1995). The quality of children's lives does not depend upon government policy, but rather on the way in which practitioners interpret the policy (Foley and Rixson, 2008) using their professional knowledge and experience to reflectively learn from, subsequently modify and improve provision for children and families, as well as developing their own professional practice as early years practitioners.

The Every Child Matters policy (DfES, 2004) introduced a significant change in approach for practitioners from working in an educational service to working with health and social care agencies in a multi-professional way for the well-being of children, developing an integrated approach to service delivery for children and young people from birth to 19 years of age. The recommendations in the Allen Review (Allen, 2011) for intervening early with support for children's learning and development rather than later, build upon the integrated practice within the Every Child Matters approach to service delivery. The following case study describes how the Deputy Manager of a Children's Centre learnt about the recommendations for early intervention strategies in the Allen Review, enabling her to reflect upon her role as Deputy Manager in implementing the recommendations within her Children's Centre. It was the start of her reflective learning for implementing Government policy into practice.

 Case study: *Early intervention strategies*

Evie noticed 'The Allen Review: recommendations for early intervention' on the agenda of her local Children's Centre Network meeting. Before going she thought, what is this 'Allen Review' and the recommendations for early intervention? Is it something else we have to do? With these thoughts rumbling in her mind, she went to the local network meeting, hoping for some clarity.

(Continued)

(Continued)

The Head of the Local Authority's Children's Services was the speaker at the meeting; she gave some background information about the Allen Review, highlighting the importance of intervening early with support services for children rather than in children's later years, as the impact for children's educational outcomes and life chances was greater. She explained the underpinning philosophy of early intervention strategies, an integrated approach to working with children and families, recognizing the individual well-being needs of every child early and building a team of professionals around the child to meet his or her education, health and social needs.

On leaving the meeting, Evie thought, this makes it clearer. I now understand what the Allen Review is about and the importance of early intervention. We already have child-centred multi-agency review meetings, run parenting classes and have outreach family support provision in our children's centre. I'll talk with Deanne the Centre Manager and discuss how we can reflect upon what we already do and build upon it to further develop early intervention strategies and integrated practice within our provision.

The case study demonstrates how reflection can inform and develop practice. Reflection provides a process for practitioners to change the landscape in which they work, with the ability to reflect and challenge existing ways of working (Reed, 2008) through reading, discussing with others, thinking about theory, research and how these relate to, and inform, practice. Reflection concerns the further reprocessing and understanding of knowledge, part of meaningful learning where the practitioner seeks to make sense of new material, linking it to what she knows already, modifying existing knowledge and meaning to develop and accommodate new ideas (Moon, 1999). This is a reorganization of knowledge and meaning into new categories of knowledge and understanding for professional practice. The process is a bit like reorganizing a filing cabinet, adding file dividers for new knowledge, as learning about topics within the Early Childhood file grows. Evie, in the case study, has added a new file divider labelled 'Early Intervention' to her filing cabinet. Practitioners' engagement in knowledge informs reflective practice. Reflective practice within the framework of work-based reflective learning is now discussed.

Work-based reflective practice

Reflective learning and work-based learning are interrelated, both potentially powerful pedagogy for transformational change in practice

(Foundation Degree Forward, 2005), transforming learning at and from work, *through* the development of reflective learning abilities (Moon, 2006). Reflective practice, or practice that has been considered, has been likened to looking *in* a mirror and looking *through* a window (Jones and Pound, 2008). When looking in a mirror at practice, it is like looking at yourself in a mirror – the reflection is one way and only one image is seen. Considering practice, the reflection about practice is introspective and inward looking. When looking through a window upon practice, reflection has a wider view, with many different perspectives and ways of seeing provision and practice, providing more opportunities to reflect, review, modify, extend and develop professional practice. Biggs (1999: 6) further explains reflection using the mirror metaphor: 'reflection in professional practice, however, gives back not what it is, but what might be, an improvement on the original'. Practical experience is essential for developing expertise, but is not in itself sufficient (Maynard and Thomas, 2009); it is only when practitioners assimilate different ways of thinking and working that they can gain more progression in their own views and ways of working. It is through engaging in reading, research, professional development activity and reflective dialogue with colleagues and other professionals that practitioners acquire the characteristics of the 'reflective practitioner' (Schon, 2007).

Reflective practice should encourage practitioners to 'feel' their work, an approach that goes beyond observation but challenges knowledge and practice, moving to a place of understanding (Leeson, 2010: 181). Personal and professional self-knowledge gained through reflection can be unnerving, not everyone is prepared to take the risk and critically unpick their professional practice and their work as a practitioner. After reflection, modifying professional practice can be just as challenging and the process of reflective learning within reflective practice can be emotionally demanding. It is important to strike a balance between being reflective and professionally self-critical without being overly negative, which can be professionally destructive.

The reflective practitioner

The early years workforce is in a process of continuous change, as discussed in Chapter 1. What kind of workforce is required to work within the landscape of emerging policy and practice? What qualities and attributes should practitioners have to work effectively with young children, parents and other professionals?

How does reflection contribute to the development of an effective workforce?

Moss (2011) envisages a workforce with professional qualities of ethical and value-based reflective practice. Being reflective and being a reflective practitioner concern qualities and attributes in a person's behaviour, rather than a cognitive activity, a process of seeing and being that is part of the professional way an early years practitioner works, thinks and behaves (Paige-Smith and Craft, 2011). Moss (2008b: 125) further defines such a practitioner as 'a democratic reflective professional', an early childhood worker who is a critical thinker and researcher, a co-constructor of meaning, with identity and values, who values participation, diversity and dialogue. A practitioner with a self-reflecting pedagogy, able to engage in democratic discourse with others, through reflection develops a sense of self (Dalhberg et al., 2007). The emerging 'sense of self' as an early years professional workforce is discussed later in Chapter 7.

Reflective behaviour concerns attributes and qualities demonstrated in practitioners' interactions with children, parents and colleagues. These include the ability to reason, problem solve and find solutions; evaluate and discuss issues; give constructive feedback and be able to receive feedback from others; learn from others; explain values and pedagogical beliefs; consider others' views, theories, pedagogy and research and to think in a reflective way to improve provision and practice. The REFLECT (Reason, Evaluate, Feedback, Learn, Explain, Consider, Think) Framework in Figure 2.1 illustrates some of these reflective attributes and qualities.

- **R**eason
- **E**valuate
- **F**eedback
- **L**earn
- **E**xplain
- **C**onsider
- **T**hink

Figure 2.1 The REFLECT Framework

> ⟲ **Questions for reflection:** *The REFLECT Framework*
>
> There is opportunity for you to consider your own reflective behaviour using the REFLECT Framework.
>
> Consider your work over the last week and the reflective behaviour you used in your interactions with children, parents and professionals. How have you:
>
> - Reasoned or solved a problem?
> - Evaluated your work?
> - Given feedback to a colleague or received feedback from a colleague?
> - Learnt something new?
> - Explained to a child, parent or colleague?
> - Considered – a new idea? A colleague's point of view?
> - Thought – made time and space to think reflectively?

Theories of reflective practice

The concept of reflective practice and being a 'reflective practitioner' concerns how professionals think in their practice (Schon, 2007) through defining two processes of reflection:

- reflection *in* practice
- reflection *on* practice.

These terms highlight two levels of reflective practice. An early years practitioner may reflect *in* their practice by thinking about the activities they undertake with children as they carry them out. An early years practitioner who reflects *on* their practice, away from the physical activity of doing it, takes the reflective process to a higher level, by linking practice to theories, developing 'theories in use' and new ways of working (Schon, 2007). This reflective process and behaviour develops and expands professional knowledge and practice. Being a reflective practitioner is a characteristic of a person's behaviour rather than an intellectual activity (Moon, 2006).

Early years practitioners undertake routine tasks daily, without really thinking about why or how they are carried out. Reflective practice is a change agent for practitioners to modify, develop, improve or change provision for children. The following case study illustrates Schon's theory of reflective practice within an early years context; a Foundation Stage teacher in a primary school reflects upon the daily routine of children lining up.

Case study: *Children lining up*

Asking children to 'line up' is a frequent request made by teachers and practitioners, sometimes several times a day.

Reflecting in practice

Amera is a newly qualified Foundation Stage teacher; she 'herded' her class of 30 children several times during the day by asking them to 'line up'. The children lined up to go out to play, to go into assembly, to wash their hands before dinner, to go into the book corner for story time and to go home. Amera observed at these times, the children were herded like animals into small spaces. As a result, the children behaved in aggressive ways, pushing, pulling and poking each other. She ended up raising her voice above the children's noise, to manage the crowd of children and to keep them safe. This was a stressful time for the children and herself each day. What could she do to improve the situation, so it was calmer and more enjoyable for all?

Reflecting on practice

Amera remembered a comment made by a special needs adviser who attended her school. Teachers and practitioners tend to see a child's inappropriate behaviour and reprimand them for this, but it is not always the child's fault. We should look at the environment we create for children and consider the activity we ask them to do.

At break time as Amera drank her cup of coffee in the staffroom, she looked up at the shelf of books and she noticed a book about managing young children's behaviour. In reading this, Amera realized the importance of creating an environment in which successful behaviour can take place. A key strategy in behaviour management is to develop preventative approaches. Amera reflected that the daily routine of children lining up was developing into a behaviour management issue. She reflected upon her reading, what is my preventative strategy? She realized she did not have one, so devised a different approach to the routine of children lining up.

She decided to ask the children to line up in small groups, selecting the groups of four children in different ways. For example, she would invite: anyone who is wearing yellow, can line up; anyone whose name begins with an 's', can line up; anyone who is wearing stripes, can line up. Lining up in small groups would prevent the mass herding of children, and the inappropriate behaviours she had experienced, allowing the space in front of the door to slowly fill with children, rather than be filled all at once.

The next day Amera tried this approach out. The children listened expectantly to hear what she called out, would it belong to them? When it did, they jumped up and ran to the door to line up, standing quietly to see who would join them. On her way home Amera reflected upon her day . . . lining up in smaller groups had benefited children's behaviour, the children were calmer and she felt calmer too.

In the case study, Amera identified an aspect of her practice to review and modify by reflecting upon her practice, and then she modified a daily routine.

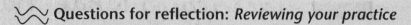

Questions for reflection: *Reviewing your practice*

Consider an aspect of your practice that you have reviewed and modified.

- How has reflection enabled you to modify, change or improve practice?
- How have children, parents, staff benefited?
- How have you as a practitioner benefited?

Theories of reflection

In the process of reflection, it is important to start from where the child is (Samuelson and Carlsson, 2008), to see the world through young children's eyes, the starting point for reflection. For reflection to be meaningful, it is important to identify the specific aspect of practice, which may be identifying a problem, to reflect upon and learn about it, with the aim of changing and improving provision and practice for the better. Schon (2007) and Dewey (1933) view reflection as a process of problem solving, the reflection begins when practitioners identify issues as problems within their provision and practice. An issue of practice may be seen as a problem by one practitioner and not by another, however an unidentified problem cannot be acted upon (Loughran, 2002).

Dewey (1933) identifies three attitudes as important for fostering reflective thinking: open-mindedness, responsibility and wholeheartedness. Practitioners who are 'open-minded' are willing to accept other perspectives, able to accept the possibility that their views and practices can be developed in light of other viewpoints. Other perspectives are gained through reading academic literature, journal articles about research, conversations with other professionals, visiting other settings, and attending network meetings and short and long courses.

Responsibility is part of reflective thinking. Practitioners with a responsible attitude are actively engaged in thinking about children in the broadest sense, not only thinking about what they are doing in their practice, but also considering factors beyond; for example, how will any change in practice resulting from their reflective thinking impact upon children's learning outcomes, or service delivery? The third of Dewey's attitudes, 'wholeheartedness' enables practitioners to be genuinely reflective, to have reflective agency for change, not only for the children and families they work with, but within the wider landscape of national, local and regional early years contexts for policy, provision and practice.

Hatton and Smith (1995) regard reflection as deliberate thinking about action with the view to improvement. Critical reflection is the ability to understand the wider social and political functions of experience and meaning-making and apply this understanding in wider social contexts (Fook, 2010). Dewey (1933) regards a reflective practitioner as a reflectively persistent one, engaging in continuous consideration of their underlying beliefs and knowledge, considering other beliefs and knowledge to illuminate their own values, beliefs and working practices. Dewey's notion of continuous reflection has relevance for the changing world of early years and child-care (Miller et al., 2005).

Pollard et al. (2002) describe aspects of the process of reflection within the framework of reflective practice. Reflection should include: a focus on goals, with consideration of how they are addressed and achieved; searching for evidence from practice as the main source of information for reflection; being open-minded with an inclusive attitude; modifying existing practice from insights from reading, research and prior reflections; having regular dialogue with colleagues; reflecting according to the situation; and realizing when to change practice or to keep existing practice. For reflection to be meaningful, it is important to consider what aspect of provision and practice to reflect upon and the level of reflection to engage in.

Van Manen (1977) broadens the meaning of reflection for practitioners, enabling them to reflect beyond their own professional practice. He suggests reflection has three levels: technical rationality, practical action of reflection and critical reflection. At the first level, reflection concerns techniques as a means to an end, to produce efficiency and effectiveness. Practitioners are mainly concerned with immediate effectiveness without considering how the goal or target was achieved. At the second level, 'practical reflection', practitioners think about the quality of the educational process. Practitioners using the third level of 'critical reflection' begin to think about wider social or educational implications beyond their own practice.

These theories of reflective practice are represented in a model of reflective learning in Figure 2.2. The model illustrates the essence of

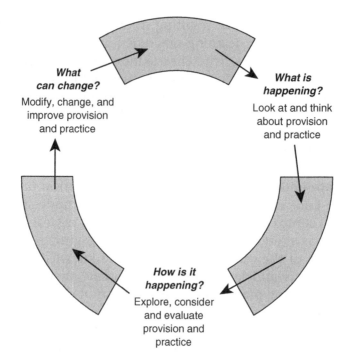

Figure 2.2 Reflective Learning: a reflective cycle for improvement and change

the theories of reflection within a reflective cycle for improvement and change, highlighting the role of the practitioner in reflectively evaluating provision and practice.

The three questions in the model provide layers of reflection.

- *What is happening?* A descriptive overview of provision and practice.
- *How is it happening?* A more in-depth analysis of provision and practice.
- *What can change?* Information from the two questions above informs the practitioner about what aspect of provision and practice they can modify, change or improve for better health, social and educational outcomes for children and families.

Reflective learning to improve provision and practice

Figure 2.2 provides a framework for reflective improvement and change. Practical ways of reflective learning used in early years contexts are now considered.

Reflective documentation, dialogue, questions and writing are ways for practitioners to individually and collectively engage in reflection, to learn about the children they work with, the provision and practice they provide, or about themselves as early years practitioners. Reflective learning provides a catalyst for personal and professional enhancement, and improvement in provision and practice.

Reflective documentation and dialogue

Documentation as pedagogy for reflective dialogue is used in pre-schools in the Reggio Emilia region in northern Italy. Pedagogues allocate time and space to meet together to reflect upon children's learning. By using a broad range of documentation such as video, tape recording and written notes, they discuss how their children are learning. Their reflective discussion around the documentation makes visible the learning processes and strategies used by each child (Rinaldi, 2005). There is a different emphasis in assessing young children's learning in these pre-schools than in some nursery schools in England. The Early Years Foundation Stage curriculum used in England is concerned with what children learn, recording children's learning as outcomes, rather than documenting the process of children's learning and using the documentation for discussion to understand how individual children learn, as in the pre-schools in Reggio Emilia.

Some pre-school settings in England have been influenced by reflective pedagogy and practices used in Reggio Emilia pre-schools. The introduction of accessible digital technology has enabled practitioners to use photographs for children to recall and reflect upon their learning, and for practitioners to have reflective conversations with the children and their parents, as the case study shows.

 Case study: *Reflective documentation*

Hannah is a Lead Practitioner working in a small nursery school attached to a primary school in a rural location. She explains how observation and photographs are used within her nursery to inform planning for children's learning.

We always say observation and reflection are part of our central strategy of how we teach and help children learn here. We observe the children through photographs, observing, writing things down and just generally being with them. At the end of the session, we always show the photos to the children in a slide show, displayed on the nursery wall. We have the photos printed off and stuck into their own diaries which they take home with them every day, so the parents can see them. The parents do the same, they put things in the diaries for us as well, so that forms a central hub of what we see.

Then as practitioners with the children we reflect on what the children have done. Quite often the children will say we did that today, we'd like to do that tomorrow, extending it in their own way. As practitioners, we also say, they were fantastic at that, for example like George who made his cake today, how can we extend this for him? Can we include some more children or where can it go next? The observation really feeds the reflection and the reflection feeds into our planning. It's a cycle, all the time encompassing everything we do.

The case study highlights the importance of professional conversations and reflective writing as key elements in reflective learning and practice and, importantly, the creation of time and space for reflective thinking and dialogue to take place. This has been created in the daily meetings for the nursery team to meet to reflect upon the learning that has taken place during the day.

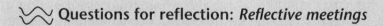 Questions for reflection: *Reflective meetings*

Consider your own work setting or work placement.

- When do you have time to meet together?
- What is the agenda for the meetings?
- Do you have time to reflect upon children's progress in the meetings?
- Do you have time to meet with children to share and reflect upon their learning?
- Do you have time when you can meet with parents to share and reflect upon their child's progress?
- How effective are the meetings?
- Are there any recommendations for improvement?

Nursery teams working together are reflective professional practitioners (Moss, 2008b) engaging in dialogue with others from a knowledgeable value base of early years principles and practice. Reflective practitioners have agency to change and improve provision and practice (Osgood, 2006). By personal and professional responsibility for the outcomes of children, practitioners use their personal and professional attributes and qualities to be part of a 'community of practice' (Wenger, 1998: 10) to make meaning, construct theories and testing them through listening and dialogue with others, then reconstructing those theories (Moss, 2008b). This process of reflective practice has similarities to Reggio Emilia's pedagogy of listening (Rinaldi, 2005) within a reflective culture of a learning community where pedagogues actively listen, engage in dialogue and make meaning with others about children's learning (Reed and Canning, 2010).

Reflective questions

The use of questioning in professional dialogue is central for reflective learning to take place. It is important for early years practitioners to work in a questioning culture in which provision and practice can be examined through a critical learning dialogue (Hallet, 2008b). The use of questioning guides reflection, further learning and finds solutions. The five words listed below, used as a Questions Guide, support and enable practitioners' reflection:

What?
- Is the focus for reflection?

How?
- Will the reflection be used?

Who?
- Will take part in the reflection?
- Will benefit from the reflection?

When?
- Time – when will reflection take place?

Where?
- Space – where is the best venue for reflection?

The use of questioning to solve emerging issues and problems, and within a cycle of review, evaluation and planning, provides a framework for reflective review and evaluation of provision and practice. The Review, Evaluate and Plan (REP) framework uses these five questions for reflection:

Review
- Ask the 'What' question – to identify the emerging issue or problem.

Evaluate
- Ask the 'How' question – to solve the emerging issue or problem, who or what resources could help me solve the problem?

Plan
- Ask the 'When' question – to provide a timescale to solve the emerging issue or problem.

〰 Questions for reflection: *The REP framework*

You are asked to identify an aspect of your practice that you are concerned about in your work as a practitioner, or that you have seen as a student in your work placement. Using the REP framework, reflect upon your practice and the process of reflective learning.

Review

- What aspect of practice are you considering?
- What emerging issue or problem do you wish to reflect upon?

Evaluate

- How can I find a solution?
- What knowledge or skills do I require?
- Who could help me?
- What resources could help me?

Plan

- What is the time scale for improving the issue or solving the problem?
- What is the time line?
- What are the short-term actions required?
- What are the long-term goals required?

Now consider the process of reflective learning. What have you learnt about:

- Addressing emerging issues and solving problems in provision and practice?
- Engaging in reflection?
- Planning for improving provision and practice?
- Yourself as a reflective learner?

Reflective writing

Throughout their work, early years practitioners write in different formats, such as school or setting evaluation reports, development and improvement plans, staff appraisal notes and children's records. All these have a specific genre of writing and are for a particular audience, an Office for Standards in Education (Ofsted) inspector, school governors, colleagues, parents and other agencies. The activity of writing provides a vehicle and space for reflective thinking, learning and practice.

Narrative writing in journals and diaries provides opportunity for personal and professional reflection. The use of narrative writing and storying is a powerful way for practitioners to make sense of their experiences (Bolton, 2010) in a reflective way. Reflective dialogue, documentation and writing are ways to enable practitioners to engage in reflective practice as reflective practitioners. The following case study demonstrates this.

 Case study: *Being a reflective practitioner*

Claire is a nursery teacher working in a primary school. She considers herself as a reflective practitioner and encourages reflective dialogue within her nursery team. She writes about this in an essay as part of her postgraduate study:

> Children need more than our enthusiasm. They need us as practitioners to think about what we are doing and why. Reflective practice has a deeply positive impact on setting provision. It ensures continuing professional development, deepens understanding of learning, supports planning, improves further pedagogical work and blurs the boundaries between research, theory and practice. A reflective practitioner is able to accept their subjectivity as strength and to embrace uncertainty as an opportunity to research and create new understandings and meaning through dialogue with others. In a landscape of shifting social and political contexts, reflective practice enables practitioners to maintain the continuous cycle of interpretation and response that is necessary when faced with complex and unique situations; this will ensure effective change and development in setting provision.
>
> There are numerous challenges to the nurturing of reflective practice; making time and space to reflect on our practice is of concern; how to document and share information about children's learning and our own reflections in and on practice. Perhaps the most significant of these challenges is to remain open. By remaining open to new perspectives, approaches and insights from others we enable a dialogue and facilitate the forging of new perspectives and understandings through collaborative meaning-making.

The case study shows how higher education studies have influenced Claire in being a reflective practitioner and leading reflective pedagogy within her nursery. Similarly this FD graduate from the case study considers her development as a reflective early years practitioner through her work-based studies.

Reflective practitioner's voice

It's made me think about things more. I now unpick what I do with children to understand more.

Summary

The chapter has explored the notion of reflection in its broadest sense, by examining theories of reflection, reflective learning and practice. These have been considered within frameworks for improvement and change. The concept of reflective practitioners behaving in a reflective way has been examined within the context of the early years. Through case studies and suggestions of how practitioners can be reflective within the work setting, reflective learning, abilities and behaviours within professional practice have been considered.

Further reading

This is comprehensive book about reflective practice:
Paige-Smith, A. and Craft, A. (2011) *Developing Reflective Practice in the Early Years.* 2nd edn. Maidenhead: Open University Press.

This is seminal book about the concept of a reflective practitioner:
Schon, D.A. (1983) *The Reflective Practitioner: How Professionals Think in Action.* New York: Basic Books.

Introduction to Reflective Teaching and Learning in Primary Schools

Hansen, A.

This book has been published to help you to develop the tools and strategies you need to improve your own teaching and learning and the learning and development of the children in your care. It is full of practical advice for how to use reflection during your initial teacher training course to its fullest effect.

This extended introduction sets the scene for the book and introduces the chapters that follow. It identifies the central place reflection has in learning and teaching for children and adults, and learning to be a teacher. First, before exploring the notion of reflective learning and teaching, it is prudent to clarify how learning and teaching is defined and used within this book.

'Teaching/learning'

As a trainee teacher, when do you see yourself as a teacher and as a learner? When you are in a seminar, are you passively learning from your tutor or are you expected to discuss and support peers to learn also? When you are in the classroom, what are your expectations about the children acting as teachers to each other, that is, learning from each other? I ask these questions to challenge your thinking about the artificial divide that the terms *teaching* and *learning* in the English language can create.

To my mind you will always sit somewhere along the teaching/learning continuum illustrated in Figure I.1. Sometimes you might find yourself at one end. For example where would you place yourself now, reading this book? I imagine towards the learning end (Point A). Often, however, your placement on the continuum will be dynamic, depending on what you are doing, who you are doing it with, and how you perceive it to be going. Can you think of situations where you may be at Points A, B or C on the continuum?

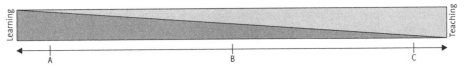

Figure I.1: The teaching/learning continuum

When you are a trainee teacher and teacher (and no doubt in many other roles in your life) you will be learning and teaching to some extent at any given time. Schön's notion of *professional artistry* (1983, pp.48–9), which will be revisited later in this introduction, reflects this. When you teach, you are consistently reflecting on your actions and those of the children in your care. Schön refers to this as *reflection in action* and this activity could be placed somewhere around Point B on the continuum. Schön also refers to *reflection on reflection in action*, where a teacher deliberately takes time to further develop his/her *repertoire of knowledge and experience* through a *conversation with the situation* (Schön, 1983, p.166). In these situations, placement is more likely to be around Point A on the continuum.

Therefore, it is rather difficult – and I suggest unnecessary – to artificially separate the two terms learning and teaching. Indeed, I hope that by the time you have read this introduction you will see that the act of 'teaching/learning' is symbiotic, that one does not exist without the other, and that reflection is a component within their relationship.

The idea of 'teaching/learning' is not a new one. For example, John-Steiner and Mahn (2003, p.133) use the term 'teaching/learning' to represent 'a joint endeavour that encompasses learners, teachers, peers, and the use of socially-constructed artefacts'. They cite Sutton (1980) as defining teaching/learning from the work of Vygotsky: 'The Russian word *obuchenie* does not admit to a direct English translation. It means both teaching and learning, both sides of the two-way process, and is therefore well suited to a dialectical view of a phenomenon made up of mutually interpenetrating opposites.'

Another term for teaching and learning is *pedagogy*. Through their ten principles for effective pedagogy, the Teaching and Learning Research Programme (TLRP) identifies evidence-informed pedagogic principles for all learner age groups and sectors in education. The principles are listed below, but you should visit the website (www.tlrp.org/themes/themes/tenprinciples.html) to read about each of them. As you work through this book, you will be able to see how you can use the principles in your own reflective practice as a learner and as a teacher to support children's development.

> *1. Effective pedagogy equips learners for life in its broadest sense.*
>
> *2. Effective pedagogy engages with valued forms of knowledge.*
>
> *3. Effective pedagogy recognises the importance of prior experience and learning.*
>
> *4. Effective pedagogy requires learning to be scaffolded.*
>
> *5. Effective pedagogy needs assessment to be congruent with learning.*
>
> *6. Effective pedagogy promotes the active engagement of the learner.*
>
> *7. Effective pedagogy fosters both individual and social processes and outcomes.*
>
> *8. Effective pedagogy recognises the significance of informal learning.*
>
> *9. Effective pedagogy depends on the learning of all those who support the learning of others.*
>
> *10. Effective pedagogy demands consistent policy frameworks with support for learning as their primary focus.*

(TLRP, online)

The chapters in this book often use learning and teaching interchangeably. When you are reading a discussion about what you can do as a learner, challenge yourself to think about how the ideas could be translated into the classroom and be used with children. Likewise, when you are reading about encouraging children to be reflective learners, step back and think about how you might use similar ideas in your own learning.

What is reflection?

Reflection is a broad concept used as a tool for learning in many different disciplines and it is a difficult notion to pin down. Biggs points out that 'a reflection in a mirror is an exact replica of what is in front of it. Reflection in professional practice, however, gives back not what it is, but what might be, an improvement on the original' (1999, p.6). Many identify reflection as a tool for 'deep' learning (Moon, 2001; Hinett, 2002; Race, 2004). Race (2004, p224) encapsulates many authors' definitions in how he talks about the impact of reflection.

> *Reflection deepens learning. The act of reflecting is one which causes us to make sense of what we've learned, why we learned it, and how that particular increment of learning took place. Moreover, reflection is about linking one increment of learning to the wider perspective of learning – heading towards seeing the bigger picture. Reflection is equally useful when our learning has been unsuccessful – in such cases indeed reflection can often give us insights into what may have gone wrong with our learning, and how on a future occasion we might avoid now-known pitfalls. Most of all, however, it is increasingly recognised that reflection is an important transferable skill, and is much valued by all around us, in employment, as well as in life in general.*
>
> *Race (2004)*

What is reflection in 'learning/teaching'?

John Dewey

Dewey (1933) is seen by many as the father of reflection in education. In his seminal book for teachers, *How We Think: A restatement of the relation of reflective thinking to the educative process*, he explained that reflective thinking is used by people when a solution to a problem cannot be found with certainty. This is particularly helpful to you as a trainee teacher because there is never anything certain in education, teaching and learning! Dewey defined reflective thinking as 'active, persistent, and careful consideration of any belief or supposed form of knowledge in the light of the grounds that support it and the further conclusions to which it tends' (Dewey 1933, p.118).

He went on to identify five thinking states, which are outlined below (1933, pp.199–209).

1. Dewey believed that individuals (and societies) are characterised by habitual patterns. It is only when a habit is disturbed that the process of *intellection* is employed.

2. When an individual directly experiences difficulty or perplexity then this turns into a problem that could be solved. This second stage involves an individual identifying the important aspects of the context in order to solve the problem.

3. The third stage involves identifying a hypothesis and coming up with a variety of possible solutions, perhaps through brainstorming ideas.

4. Considering and weighing up the possible solutions is the fourth stage.

5. Finally, testing the hypothesis (either in reality or by imagining) eliminates those ideas that do not work and identifies a favoured solution.

Perhaps you can see action research models you have followed reflecting these ideas more formally. This idea is discussed in more detail in Chapter 2.

Developments of Dewey's work

Many have taken Dewey's work forward and you will read a little of this in the chapters in this book. For more detail, the further reading section at the end of Chapter 2 provides suggestions for books that discuss these theorists and educationalists and their work.

King and Kitchener (2002) are researchers who used Dewey's notion of reflective thinking in their Reflective Judgement Model to define *reflective reasoning*. Their model describes how critical or reflective thinking skills are developed by adolescents moving into adulthood. The final stages of the model refer to reflective reasoning. They explain how people who use reflective reasoning accept

> *that knowledge claims cannot be made with certainty, but [they] are not immobilized by it; rather, [they] make judgments that are 'most reasonable' and about which they are 'relatively certain,' based on their evaluation of available data. They believe they must actively construct their decisions, and that knowledge claims must be evaluated in relationship to the context in which they were generated to determine their validity. They also readily admit their willingness to reevaluate the adequacy of their judgments as new data or new methodologies become available.*

> (King and Kitchener, 2002, p.40)

This is the type of reasoning that you will be expected to undertake on your initial teacher training course and beyond.

Criticisms of Dewey's work

There has been some criticism of Dewey's work. For example some feel that the five thinking states can be interpreted in a linear, process-oriented way (Smith, 1999). Approaching reflection as a systematic process is sometimes required in your professional work, as later chapters discuss in detail. For example, Chapter 2 talks further about reflection in action research.

Another criticism is that Dewey's work pays limited attention to emotions. Boud, Keogh and Walker (1985) address this. They define reflection as an activity in which people 'recapture their experience, think about it, mull it over and evaluate it' (p.19). They rework Dewey's five thinking states into three (pp.26–31).

- *Returning to experience* – retelling the salient events.
- *Attending to (or connecting with) feelings* – the purpose is twofold: identifying and building on helpful feelings and dealing with obstructive ones.
- *Evaluating experience* – analysing the experience while considering one's intent, knowledge and understanding of the event. This analysis supports the integration of new knowledge into one's existing understanding.

Later chapters address emotions in more detail. See in particular Mike Pezet's chapter on using coaching as a tool for reflection and Helen Davenport's chapter on reflective journals and portfolios.

A final criticism of Dewey's work is based on the notion that 'the individual student teacher learns to reflect on a particular experience individually' (Cinnamond and Zimpher, 1990, p.58), and that learning is not something that happens individually but is socially mediated. The social nature of reflection is revisited several times throughout this book and it is to this idea that we now turn.

Vygotsky and the social nature of learning and teaching

Social constructivism is a central theory that explains how we learn and how your role as a teacher is crucial in supporting children's cognitive development.

Vygotsky, one of the most well-known social constructivists, is perhaps most cited in relation to his work on the Zone of Proximal Development (ZPD). He defines it as 'the distance between the actual development level as determined by independent problem-solving and the level of potential to development as determined through problem-solving through adult guidance or in collaboration with more capable peers' (Vygotsky, 1978, p.86). Indeed, Eraut (1996, p.15) reminds us that interaction with a teacher and/or more capable peers is not merely desirable but is an essential requirement of development.

Think about your initial teacher training course. When do you feel you learn most effectively? What role do your peers, school colleagues and course tutors have during these times? Now think about your role as a teacher. How do you plan for children to experience the best possible learning opportunities?

The notion of the ZPD was developed by Wood, Bruner and Ross (1979), who considered how teachers and peers could build (*scaffold*) and withdraw (*fade*) support as necessary to help a child bridge the ZPD. Thinking about your course, identify where support is built and then fades appropriately. For further discussion about course design and the role of academic tutors, read Chapters 2 and 3.

Wells (1999, p.136) specifically comments on the importance of talk in Vygotsky's work:

> *Vygotsky's great contribution was to recognize that an even greater effect resulted from the development of semiotic tools based on signs, of which the most powerful and versatile is speech. For not only does speech function as a tool that mediates social action, it also provides one of the chief means – in what Vygotsky (1987) called 'inner speech' – of mediating the individual mental activities of remembering, thinking and reasoning.*

And Vygotsky explains (1978, p.280):

> *external speech is not inner speech plus sound any more than inner is external speech minus sound. The transition from inner to external speech is complex and dynamic. It is the transformation of a predicative, idiomatic speech into the syntax of differentiated speech which is comprehensible to others.*

Others have also identified talk as essential for learning. For example, Hoyles (1985) identified 'cognitive talk' that allows a child to 'step aside' and reflect on an aspect. In the first chapter, Emma McVittie continues the discussion about dialogue. Eraut (1996) also acknowledges that the wider social context is important for developing learners' understanding because their 'knowledge base' is developed through the social interaction (predominantly discussion) that occurs. He proposes, however, that even though a learner's knowledge base may share similar features with others', 'it still remains personalized and that it is important for a pupil's learning as well as their sense of identity that the personal nature of their knowledge is recognized' (p.15). John-Steiner and Mahn (2003, p.146) broaden this by explaining how our knowledge and understanding 'evolve from the sustained dynamic of individuals engaged in symbolic behaviour both with other humans, present and past, and with material and nonmaterial culture captured in books, artifacts and living memory'. Indeed, there are many aspects to consider such as how the classroom is laid out to allow particular directions of travel, groupings, access to resources, and so on (Arthur, Grainger and Wray, 2006).

So, while reflection is to some extent an internal, individual process, it does not need to be undertaken independently. Indeed, it is something that occurs most effectively when you are challenged by others through discussion of some sort. Therefore all the chapters in this book expect you to engage in dialogue – be it verbally or in another form – with children, peers and tutors throughout your course as part of your reflective practice.

Classroom norms and teacher expectations

As well as undertaking your own reflection as a trainee teacher, you also need to encourage children's reflective abilities. Emma McVittie provides many practical suggestions for doing this in Chapter 1. When analysing their own research about how children learned, Kafai and Harel (1991) referred to reflection as an 'incubation phase'. Additionally, Ackermann (1991) identified a 'cognitive dance' where children necessarily 'dive in' and 'step back' from a situation to create balance and understanding.

The discussion above about the social nature of learning and teaching, and Emma McVittie's discussion in Chapter 1 about creating a reflective classroom in practice, point to learning environments where there is a buzz in the air and where the learners and their teacher are working together to a shared outcome and developed understanding. Alongside this we also need to encourage learners to incubate their ideas to create balance and understanding. So we will turn our attention here to classroom norms and your expectations. How do you encourage this buzz and opportunity for the community of learners to reflect in your own classroom?

Yackel and Cobb (1996, p.460) offer one way forward. They discuss an evolving and increasingly sophisticated process that happens over a period of time as the teacher develops their understanding of the learners' conceptual development. This approach to classroom discussion (which Yackel and Cobb refer to as 'argumentation') is imperative because it creates the backdrop for the development of ideas. As argumentation evolves, the 'taken-as-shared communication' is subtly adjusted because it continues to form the backdrop for discussion, thus bringing about conceptual development. This validates the use of a reflective (and reflexive) approach to learning and teaching.

However, Goodchild (2001) provides a warning. He identifies a significant amount of literature that uses the phrase 'blind activity' (in contrast to reflective activity) when referring to children carrying out tasks set by their teacher. He cites Carr (1996, p.94) who states that 'students need to be made aware that [learning] is more than a set of procedural steps to be blindly followed', and Christiansen and Walther (1986, p.250) who explain that 'blind activity on a task does not ensure learning as intended'.

What activities are you encouraged to undertake as a trainee teacher, and what activities do you expect the learners in your care to participate in? When you are teaching, are you encouraging argumentation as a backdrop for children to develop their ideas? Or are you planning 'blind activity' for them instead? Which do you aspire to? How can you reach your goals?

Schön, reflection and the unique nature of every classroom situation

Teaching is complex. Its complexity is due to a huge number of variables which are in constant flux, leading to situations that are unique for every trainee teacher. Because of this, it is not possible, nor desirable, for any initial teacher training course to instruct, 'when X happens you should do Y' in a given situation. (The exception may be a child protection issue that requires a very specific, legally binding response.) In my experience many trainees can find this very challenging. They desire to become good teachers but just want to know what they should do. It is only after experiencing teaching, and as they learn more about learning and teaching, that they realise this is not an approach that will help them to become the best teacher they can be.

Schön's (1983) *reflection in action* helps to address this dilemma. He describes an iterative process, in which unresolved situations are developed into resolved situations through repeatedly defining the problem. Schön argues that while teaching, the teacher makes use of *professional artistry*. This *knowing in action* is where the teacher develops *theories in use*. These theories are created *from* the specific context *for* the specific context. They may involve scientific knowledge, but it is assumed that the teacher's experience steers the process of exploring, testing and refining/redefining theories in use. Schön explains that this can be seen as a *conversation with the situation* – a continuous communication between the teacher and others involved, as well as terminating specific avenues if they do not work, due to the *backtalk* of the situation.

How to use this book

In my work with trainee teachers and teachers the most common feedback about reflection I receive is that being reflective is a lot of additional work. However, you will already own an arsenal full of reflective tools that you have previously engaged to undertake a range of incidental or intuitive reflective activity in your professional and academic work. (You can read more about intuitive reflection in Chapter 2.) That activity has helped you to develop into the person and professional you are now. This book is designed to take your reflective practice beyond where it currently sits. It will extend the theory and ideas presented to you in this chapter and help you to make more use of those tools you have as well as introduce new ones. You will notice yourself moving around the learning/teaching continuum (see Figure I.1) more than you did previously, sometimes reflecting in action and at other times taking a careful step back to reflect on action. The skills, strategies and, most importantly, attitude you will develop will set you in the best possible direction to be the teacher you want to become.

Throughout this book the contributors have drawn upon their extensive experience of teaching and mentoring trainee teachers to present a wide range of case studies that you can adapt and use in your own classroom. The activities provided in each chapter will help you become actively engaged in strengthening your knowledge and understanding about the various skills and strategies that can be used for reflection. Each chapter concludes with a review of learning, and poses questions related to the content for you to reflect upon. Suggested responses to these self-assessment questions are included at the end of the book.

References

Ackermann, E. (1991) From decontextualized to situated knowledge: Revisiting Piaget's water-level experiment, In I. Harel and S. Papert (eds) *Constructionism*. Norwood, NJ: Ablex Publishing Corporation.

Arthur, J., Grainger, T. and Wray, D. (eds) (2006) *Learning to Teach in the Primary School.* London: Routledge.

Biggs, J. (1999) *Teaching for Quality Learning at University.* Buckingham: Open University Press.

Boud, D., Keogh, R. and Walker, D. (eds) (1985) *Reflection: Turning Experience into Learning*. London: Kogan Page.

Carr, M. (ed) (1996) *Motivation in Mathematics*. Cresskill, NJ: Hampton Press, cited in Goodchild, S. (2001) *Students' Goals: A Case Study of Activity in a Mathematics Classroom*. England: Hobbs the Printers.

Cinnamond, J.H. and Zimpher, N.L. (1990) Reflectivity as a function of community. In R.T. Clift, W.R. Houston and M.C. Pugach (eds) *Encouraging Reflective Practice in Education: An Analysis of Issues and Programs*. New York: Teachers College Press.

Christiansen, B. and Walther, G. (1986) Task and activity. In D. Christiansen, A.G. Howson and M. Otte (eds) *Perspectives on Mathematics Education*. Dordrecht: Reidel, cited in Goodchild, S. (2001) *Students' Goals: A Case Study of Activity in a Mathematics Classroom*. England: Hobbs the Printers.

Dewey, J. (1933) *How We Think: A Restatement of the Relation of Reflective Thinking to the Educative Process*. New York: D.C. Heath.

Eraut, M. (1996) Conceptual frameworks and historical development, In T. Plomp and D.P. Ely (eds.) *International Encyclopedia of Educational Technology*, 2nd ed. Oxford: Elsevier Science Ltd.

Goodchild, S. (2001) *Students' Goals: A Case Study of Activity in a Mathematics Classroom*. England: Hobbs the Printers.

Hinett, K. (2002) *Improving Reflective Practice in Legal Education*. UKLE.

Hoyles, C. (1985) What is the point of group discussion in mathematics? *Educational Studies in Mathematics*, 16: 205–14.

John-Steiner, V. and Mahn, H. (2003) Sociocultural contexts for teaching and learning. In W.M. Reynolds and G.E. Miller (eds) *Handbook of Psychology*. Hoboken, NJ: Wiley.

Kafai, Y.B. and Harel, I. (1991) Learning through consulting: When mathematical ideas, knowledge of programming and design, and playful discourse are intertwined. In I. Harel and S. Papert (eds) *Constructionism*. Norwood, NJ: Ablex Publishing Corporation.

King, P.M. and Kitchener, K.S. (2002) The reflective judgment model: Twenty years of research on epistemic cognition. In B.K. Hofer and P.R. Pintrich (eds) Personal Epistemology: The Psychology of Beliefs about Knowledge and Knowing. Mahwah, NJ: Lawrence Erlbaum.

Moon, J. (2001) *Reflection in Higher Education Learning*. PDP Working Paper 4. York: Higher Education Academy.

Race, P. (2004) *The Lecturer's Toolkit: A Practical Guide to Assessment, Learning and Teaching*. Abingdon: RoutledgeFalmer.

Schön, D. (1983) *The Reflective Practitioner: How Professionals Think in Action*, London: Temple Smith.

Smith, M.K. (1999) *Reflection*. Available at: www.infed.org/biblio/b-reflect.htm (accessed 4/1/12).

Sutton, A. (1980) Cited in John-Steiner, V. and Mahn, H. (2003) Sociolcultural contexts for teaching and learning. In Reynolds, W.M. and Miller, G.E. (eds) *Handbook of Psychology*. Hoboken, NJ: Wiley.

TLRP (online) *TLRP's Evidence-informed Pedagogic Principles*. Available at: http://www.tlrp.org/themes/themes/tenprinciples.html (accessed 9/1/12).

Wells, G. (1999) *Dialogic Inquiry: Toward a Sociocultural Practice and Theory of Education*. New York: Cambridge University Press.

Wood, D., Bruner, J.S. and Ross, G. (1979) The role of tutoring in problem solving. *Journal of Child Psychology and Psychiatry*, 17: 89–100.

Vygotsky, L.S. (1978) *Mind in Society: The Development of Higher Pyschological Processes*. Cambridge, MA: Harvard University Press.

Yackel, E. and Cobb, P. (1996) Sociomathematical norms, argumentation, and autonomy in mathematics. *Journal for Research in Mathematics Education*, 27(4): 458–77.

Classroom Organisation and the Learning Environment

Ashbridge, J. and Josephidou, J.

By the end of this chapter, you should be able to:

- discuss the key factors to consider when providing for an appropriate learning environment

- consider how theory and research impact on how the learning environment is designed

- reflect critically on learning environments you have observed on place-ment and question assumed practice

- examine how your own values and attitudes as a teacher can impact on the learning environment and the children's learning.

Introduction

In this chapter, we discuss a classroom scenario in order to explore the reasons why learning environments are complex, significant and shaped by a teacher's personal educational philosophy. Constructivist learning theories are drawn on to suggest starting points for creating effective learning environments which promote independence, social skills, self-esteem, positive attitudes to learning and give children a sense of ownership of their environment.

Different perceptions of the learning environment

The authors felt the best way to approach this was by giving you an insight into how the learning environment could be perceived by a child and by a teacher.

The child's voice

'It's in-time!'

Whistle goes and it's time to go into school but first I need to line up. If I'm really quick then I can get to the front. I make it in time but then Sally pushes ahead of me and stands on my toe. I dig her in the ribs with my elbow just as Mrs Jones is coming around the corner to collect us. Oh no, trouble again before I've even got into the classroom. I hate hanging my coat up because everyone pushes and the coat pegs are too near together. I get trampled on so I try to hang back until everyone one else comes back. Trouble again, I'm late.

'It's register time!'

I sit on the carpet quickly but then I realise that my name has been put on the amber traffic light and I'm really worried. Am I going to miss playtime? If I sit really still and listen Mrs Jones will put my name back on green but then I feel the cold, hard floor digging into my bottom and I realise that the Velcro on my left shoe has stuck to the carpet. I'm concentrating so hard on sitting still so the Velcro doesn't make a noise that I miss my name being called and I'm in trouble again.

'It's handwriting time'

Once register is finished it's handwriting time. I'm on the Yellow table. Books are ready in the middle of the table and the pencils are sharpened in the yellow pot. I try to get comfortable on my chair because I know I am not allowed to get up until the big hand is on the 6. Oh no, I should have gone for a wee when I was hanging my coat up. I know I have to look at the handwriting display and practise the letters on the yellow balloon. My teacher calls it being in-de-pen-dent. Red group have to practise the letters on the red balloon. Mrs Smith always comes to help Yellow table but she calls the letters differ-ent names to Mrs Jones and I get a bit confused. Rosemary gets a sticker because she is holding her pencil beautifully. Sometimes, near the holidays, we are allowed to play in the role-play area and with the sand and water. The holidays seem a long way off.

The teacher's voice

'Going into class'

The bell is about to go. Time to go and get the children in from the playground. You'd think by Year 2 they could make a straight line. Look at Sally, she's always at the front standing so smartly, having the maturity to ignore the little boy behind her who's trying to push in front. I'm so glad we line them up, it makes it so much easier. I have worked very hard on training the children to make them independent and most of them manage to sort themselves out quickly and come back to the classroom to sit quietly on the carpet. They know my expectations.

'Taking the register'

Simon is back 3 minutes after everyone else. I won't tell him off because I don't want to lower his self-esteem but I quietly get up and move his name from the green traffic light to the amber. The children sit beautifully for register and show really good listening. Everyone sitting still, all eyes towards me. I don't have to remind them, I just have to point to the good listening checklist on the wall.

'Handwriting practice'

It's good to start the morning off with handwriting because they can all get on with it quietly whilst I hear readers. To make sure they can be independent I have prepared all the resources and put them out ready on the table for the children. The activity is care-fully differentiated and all children know what level they are working at. My colour coding system works a treat. I have directed Mrs Smith to Yellow table today as they need an extra bit of input. Those who finish quickly will get 15 minutes to choose a free activity.

    Reflective task

Read the above scenarios and note down the key themes and issues where mis-matches in perceptions are apparent:

- What has the environment taught the child?
- What does the teacher believe the environment is teaching the child?
- How does the environment do this?

The importance of the learning environment

The learning environment is a complex and ever-changing place. It is a physical area with resources and furniture and has to fit in children and adults comfortably. It is an emotional environment too, where people form relationships, learn rules and develop attitudes, beliefs and values relating to themselves, each other and the world they live in. It is a place where children learn not only the curriculum but begin to understand their strengths, weaknesses and how they measure up to the others around them. Boundaries are set and particular behaviours are expected. It is not only where children learn but where children learn to learn. It is vital then to give much consideration to the way that it looks, feels and operates from a range of perspectives.

Organising the learning environment

The learning environment of the classroom is first and foremost a place where effective learning needs to take place. A key characteristic of this is where clear aims are agreed and teaching is purposeful. Theories of cognitive development tell us that for children to learn effectively they need to be actively involved in their learning: creating and constructing new knowledge in ways that are meaningful to them. It stands to reason, therefore, that the environment in which they are to do this must reflect their ways of learning and their individual needs. It must allow them to develop the skills they need to become independent learners and also to interact with the environment and resources as well as with each other in ways that make constructing knowledge purposeful and motivating. In order for this to happen, children need to be seen as central to the learning process not only in planning but also in the creation, organisation and management of the learning environment.

The scenario

Let us take the scenario above and consider what the teacher was trying to achieve. She is aiming to make the children in her class as independent as possible. She has done this through ensuring that the children know what is expected of them, ensuring that all necessary resources are easily accessible and that carefully differentiated work is provided along with additional adult support for those who may need it. The children are able to complete the activity with the minimum of fuss and noise. She aims to make them aware that their behaviour affects others and that they should respect the right of those others to be able to get on quietly. The clear ability grouping and the associated classroom display support this. She has set the environment up to enable the children to be able to learn by themselves.

Constructivist theories, classroom organisation and the learning environment

Exploration and stimulating experiences

What do theories of cognitive development have to tell us about the learning environment and how can they shed light on what happens in the scenario above? If we take the work of Piaget, we can see that his influential ideas about children needing developmentally appropriate activities are reflected in many classrooms, especially in Foundation Stage and Key Stage 1, although the same principles, differently interpreted, apply in any primary classroom. Piaget believed that the environment and children's interactions with it and within it are the key to children's learning and it is through engagement and exploration of real, concrete experiences that they are able to learn and develop. Piaget felt it was important for children to have stimulating activities, opportunities for symbolic play and an environment to actively explore (Daly et al. 2006). We can see that despite the teacher's good intentions, these opportunities are not offered and perhaps the learning needs of the children are not being met.

Social interaction and talk

Vygotsky focused more on the role of the adult in guiding children's learning. He also saw how important social interactions and language were to children's intellectual development. His work has influenced teachers and encouraged them to provide children with a challenging environment and activities. They also provide opportunities to work alongside adults and more knowledgeable others, including peers, to extend their understanding within the 'zone of proximal development'. More recent research has also stressed the importance of children developing effective communication skills with a broad cross-curricular vocabulary. This ability to articulate their thoughts helps them to make links in their learning and therefore their thinking (Daly et al. 2006).

Planning for exploration and talk

In the situation described above, although the children are grouped together, social interaction between the group or between groups is not encouraged; nor does the task given to the children encourage constructive talk. The way that teachers organise the physical environment (tables, chairs, etc.) sends out messages to the children about what kind of activities they are likely to be engaged in. Where children are all sitting looking at the front, they expect that the teacher will be talking to them and that they will be expected to focus their attention there and that any activity will probably be of an individual nature. When children are sitting around a table together, it appears that a more social and collaborative way of learning is expected and children will interact. It appears in the example above that there is a mismatch between the organisation of the classroom and the task given to the children. Social grouping is a valuable tool for teachers in supporting learning but it is very often used simply for convenience as a seating arrangement (Moyles 1992 p. 18). Conflicting messages such as this can be avoided by keeping the environment flexible and making the organisation match the task.

Effective adult interventions

In our scenario, the children on the Yellow table have access to a teaching assistant. She is available to scaffold the children's learning, helping them to achieve with support what they could not do unaided. This idea, first introduced by Wood, et al. (1976), requires the adult to match their interventions to the needs of the individual child and decide what sort of support is necessary (Doherty and Hughes 2009 p. 270).

Effective groupings

Vygotsky's model of social constructivism could perhaps best be played out where children were seated in mixed ability groups. This provides opportunities for 'less able' children to work within their zone of proximal development having input from a more knowledgeable other. 'More able' children who take on this role of more knowledgeable other can, therefore, both consolidate and articulate their learning. Gnadinger (2008) demonstrates in her research that peer collaboration is an effective learning strategy for children. In addition, other research has shown that higher achieving children who work in ability groups actually have their potential limited rather than enhanced, as they 'develop a crystallized view of their ability which may lead them to avoid challenges which are necessary for effective learning' (Dweck and Legget 1988 cited in MacIntyre and Ireson 2002 p. 250).

Moving around

All that we know about children's cognitive development tells us that active learning and problem-solving approaches can be beneficial. They enable children to engage with their learning in individual ways depending on their preferred way of learning and thinking. Active learning involves problem solving and this requires children to move around, talk, collaborate and gather resources. Any environment for learning needs to facilitate these approaches and teachers need to be sure they know the children well enough to be able to anticipate these needs and reflect them in the organisation of the classroom.

Reflective task

Consider the information above and your own experiences of classroom environments. What do you think a classroom for children of a given age needs to look like, in order to support children's learning as described? How might your use of the learning environment be reflected in your planning?

Encouraging independence and autonomy in the learning environment

Return to the scenario

Classroom layout and organisation

Let us return to the scenario. Consider for a moment what messages the classroom layout and organisation is giving to the child:

- How does he think that the class teacher wants him to use the environment?
- How does he think that the teacher views learning?
- How independently is he able to think and learn in this environment?
- What skills is he learning?
- What do you think the teacher's priority was for his learning?

Classroom organisation reflects your educational philosophy

Waterson (2003) claims that the classroom needs to reflect the way in which an individual teacher intends to organise and teach the children. It sends messages to the children about how they are going to learn and what their part in that learning is likely to be.

Much of what happens in primary classrooms is directed through print in the form of worksheets, over-reliance on schemes and lots of written recording. These are quite individual acts which do not necessarily develop children's critical thinking skills or their creativity – skills that are required if children are going to become independent and autonomous learners (Bowles and Gintis 1976). If we as teachers have abandoned the notion of the child as a 'tabula rasa' or 'empty vessel' (Kehily 2010 p. 5) onto which we transmit relevant knowledge, then surely as class teachers we should be encouraging those skills which enable the children to think for themselves and therefore to take some control over their own learning.

How much better it is not only to teach children, but also to ensure that our learning environment encourages the consolidation of skills such as 'information processing, reasoning, enquiry, creative thinking, [and] evaluation' (DfEE 2000 p. 22). We want to plan for and provide as many opportunities as possible for children to develop skills of metacognition, the ability to think about thinking (Goswami 2008 p. 295). If the children's learning is determined by how much we as teachers allow them to learn, then how limited will their learning be?

Encouraging independence

What do children actually need in order for them to become independent learners? The authors would argue that a good place for teachers to start is by overtly giving children the permission to learn in this way. Even so, the skills required for independent learning do not develop by themselves and need the teacher to provide structure and support.

Children need to be clear about what they are learning and how they are able to engage with this learning. If aims and objectives are shared clearly and reinforced through displays and resources, ambiguity is avoided and children are then able to focus on the task in hand. Teachers' own beliefs and attitudes about learning are thrown into stark relief at this point. As Alexander (1992) points out, 'notwithstanding the classroom layout and organisation, they are but the framework within which the acts and interactions central to teaching and learning take place' (Moyles 1992 p. 11). The objectives that teachers choose, the way they are shared and the ways that teachers expect that learning to be carried out, will influence the ability of the children to work in independent and autonomous ways just as much as the physical environment.

Teachers who believe that knowledge is a 'public discipline' (Kendall-Seatter 2005 p. 97) will create a classroom where the interactions and the environment focus on transmission of knowledge, whereas if knowledge is seen as being 'a fluid act of interpretation' (Kendall-Seatter 2005 p. 97) then a very different ethos pervades. Autonomous and independent learners have control and ownership over their learning. This needs to be supported by and negotiated with the teacher, who will use classroom interactions and the environment to encourage collaborative working and more meaningful contexts for learning.

Organisation of resources and classroom layout

If this is to succeed, the emotional and physical environment must be equally supportive. Resources must be easily identifiable, relevant and available, as well as flexible enough for the children to use them in the way that they need to. The physical layout of the room also needs to be flexible enough for children to work in ways that are appropriate for the task in hand. Planned opportunities for paired and group work, along with careful differentiation of tasks, are required in order to build up the skills to enable children to learn with and from each other and their environment.

The scenario again

In our scenario, the teacher believes that she is enabling independence, and within the context and purpose of this particular task, it could be argued that she is. The learning for the session is explicit to the children but it is tightly controlled by the teacher. If this is representative of other teaching and learning interactions within this classroom, then children become at risk of 'learned helplessness'. Children become accustomed to accepting extrinsic motivation and organisation and are not able to succeed without it. They do not have the necessary strategies. The teacher in our situation has created an environment where children have little need to be independent: they are lined up, sat down, moved to tables and given a specific task with specific resources. It is all organised and done for them. This teacher believes it is for the benefit of the children but in reality it could have more to do with convenience for herself. Children do not have to consider others or the effect of their behaviour as they are closely monitored. It is perhaps for this reason in the only part of the scenario where the children are not under the direct supervision of the teacher, in the cloakroom, that there is a breakdown of order. Children have not been helped to think independently and behave autonomously. These skills enable children to be resilient, to tolerate and adapt to new and different ideas and experiences and to stay engaged with things that are outside their comfort zone.

  Reflective task

Think about a classroom that you have spent time in. Make notes on:

- the routines
- the types of tasks
- the resources used and the ways they were organised
- the physical layout used in the classroom.

(Continued)

(Continued)

Put these into two columns – those that supported independence and autonomy and those that hindered it. How can you ensure that your learning environment encourages those skills that support independence and autonomy?

Supporting positive behaviour through the learning environment

Disruptive behaviour, whether low level or with greater impact, will of course always hinder effective learning so it is important to consider how our learning environment may help the children to choose appropriate behaviours which enable all to make good academic progress. Ecological psychologists note that the learning environment is important for children and that it can affect their behaviour (Bronfenbrenner 1979; Gump 1987; Pointon and Kersher 2000 cited in Pollard 2008). Learning dispositions can be influenced by the environment. An environment that is scruffy and untidy will not be respected by the children. If it is dull or cold, then they will not be happy about being there. If it is cluttered, it can make children feel stressed and overwhelmed, whereas a tidy, organised environment can help children to feel calm and positive, ready to learn in a place where there is a perception of order and structure (Cowley 2006). This can be achieved through carefully organised stations or areas of provision so children know how, and where, to access equipment. Signs, labels and displays will help to clarify these areas. Interactive displays are an effective learning tool which, alongside the use of music, sound and light, can encourage interest and focus engagement with the environment.

A sense of ownership

Learning environments are places where a complicated mix of factors come together – local community values, parental expectations, religious values, children and their attitudes, and so on. McNamara and Moreton (1997) cited in Kendall-Seatter (2005) showed that where children were actively engaged in their classroom a higher level of involvement was ensured and shared ownership, shared values and mutual respect were fostered.

Looking at the scenario, the child did not seem to feel any sense of ownership over the environment he was in. He was not involved in setting it up nor does it appear to consider the ways in which he needs to behave in order to learn effectively. Too many classrooms are sterile laboratories where the children are fenced in by table arrangements and not allowed to move from their places unless it is a key transition time. Everything is put in front of them – paper, pencil and books – so that they have to make few decisions or interactions with peers and adults.

The authors would argue that the classroom should be more like a workshop, a bustling busy place with children moving between different areas collecting resources independently, sometimes standing, sometimes sitting, sometimes even working on the floor. Sometimes it may look messy – workshops are full of very busy, productive people. This positive engagement appears to be the key to encouraging appropriate behaviours. It has been suggested that children should not only be involved in designing their classroom environment but also in working with teachers and architects in redesigning old buildings and in creating new ones (Alexander 2010 p. 355).

Evaluating engagement with the environment

As teachers, how can we tell if children are able to engage with an environment? Do the children sit still for too long? Are they uncomfortable? Do children know what is expected of them? Are instructions clear? Can they get the resources they need? What should they do if they finish the set task? What strategies can they use if they get stuck? Are they bored? Is the work too easy or too hard? Can they make decisions about their learning? Are they able to choose how to approach a task? Can they talk to their peers about their learning?

The scenario

Let us consider the scenario again. The child knows that he is expected to sit still for quite some time. He is also aware that he finds this difficult. Ouvry (2000 p. 23) asserts that 'the most advanced level of movement is the ability to stay totally still, which requires entire muscle groups to work in cooperation with balance and posture'. The struggle to do as he knows he should requires him to concentrate on the issue of staying still and as a result he misses other information. What is he engaged with? At all points, he is trying very hard to behave and this has a detrimental impact on his ability to engage with the learning he is being presented with. The teacher's perception of his behaviour is very different to his own desire to behave appropriately within the constraints of the environment she has created. How could the teacher have set the environment up differently to enable a more positive experience for this child?

Creating a work-centred atmosphere

Where the teacher creates a work-centred atmosphere, classes tend to behave better (Docking 2002). There is, however, a wide range of advice and research about how this is best achieved. Plowden (1967) advised teachers to put children in mixed-ability groups in order to promote active, problem-solving discussion. Later studies showed that although teachers grouped children, they were usually directed to work individually. The group situation but individualised nature of the task meant that children were often found to be off task and talking inappropriately (Whedall and Glynn 1989). In 1995, a study by Hastings and Schwieso found that primary children concentrated better in rows where disruptive children were less distracted. There was no eye contact to disturb them and the better they behaved, the more positive reinforcement came from the teacher. So are rows the answer? Probably as primary teachers, something inside us recoils at the idea! Why is this? Could it be that we really do believe that children learn better in a social environment and that our training tells us that it cannot be right that teachers' requirements for conformity and rules should override the child's need for 'understanding and engagement in high quality learning tasks' (Holt 1982 in Pollard 2008 p. 309). We need, therefore, to be challenged to provide a flexible environment where the needs of the children, the classroom, the tasks and experiences, groupings, levels of challenge, boundaries and routines, and expectations all come together to support children's positive behaviour. A challenge indeed!

Encouraging self-esteem and emotional development through the learning environment

Few would disagree that the learning environment may also have a powerful impact on the child's self-esteem and emotional development. Without a doubt, the class teacher in the above scenario will have spent many long hours planning and resourcing her delivery of the curriculum but one wonders how much time was spent planning the hidden curriculum and how to 'manipulate the environment' (Child 1997 p. 265) to offer opportunities to make the children feel valued, safe and that they have a contribution to make.

 Case study

Simon's low self-esteem was reinforced by the seating arrangements, the use of wall displays and his observation of rewarded behaviours. Teachers are fond of using and applying the label of low self-esteem and may take up a one-woman/man crusade to help re-educate parents or offer strategies to develop self-esteem in the home, but how do we know that Simon did not arrive at school aged 4 ready to conquer the world and it is actually school that has taught him he is failing?

Our understanding of brain development informs us that a child under stress is unable to learn effectively. If you re-read his perception of the scenario, you will note that there were many issues for Simon in his environment which were sources of stress for him and which could have prevented him from learning. Sometimes empathetic teachers or teaching assistants will recognise stress issues for children but may inadvertently impact on their achievement and therefore self-esteem even more by removing challenge from tasks they are required to do and encouraging the 'learned helplessness' we have already made reference to. Kendall-Seatter (2005) speaks of the necessity to provide environments which are 'low-stress-high-challenge' (p. 59) to ensure achievement for all children regardless of ability.

(Continued)

Simon's concerns will not just be with how his teacher perceives and values him but the opinions of his peers will also be of great importance to his positive self-esteem. The 'ripple' action (Jacques and Hyland 2003 p. 161) set into motion by the classroom teacher as she sets up the learning environment to reflect her own values and beliefs about learning and children will continue until all children included in that environment cannot help but be influenced by them. There will be a shared, if unspoken, understanding that some children are failing, therefore 'lesser', whilst others are successful and 'apart' and will always continue to be so. The failing children, the 'Simons' of this world, may feel they are powerless to move from the level in the hierarchy they have been assigned by the learning environment, the teacher and their peers and it is, thus, once they have decided there is no point any longer in trying, that disaffection may set in. If, on the other hand, the ripple that the teacher, through the environment, sets in motion is an inclusive one that demonstrates that all children are valued for the unique and individual talents and attributes they bring, all children will see themselves as learners regardless of their ability.

Children's perceptions of their place in society

The environment will dominate the children's understanding of their own role and place in society regardless of the teacher's discourse. This is why, as classroom teachers, it is so important to get it right and leave nothing to chance. We may feel we have a group of learners but in reality we have a group of individuals (Kendall-Seatter 2005 p. 62).

◻ **Summary**

To conclude, the authors believe that for effective learning to take place the environment needs to be flexible enough to be created around the needs of children. However loud the teacher's voice may be, the environment will always be able to shout louder, declaring to every child in that class the values and attitudes of that teacher. Children pick up these subliminal signals, adapting their behaviour accordingly where possible to fit into the requirements of their environment. Our challenge to you whatever your level of experience is to think hard about your underpinning values and attitudes towards teaching and learning and to create, within the limitations in which you find yourself working, an environment that will demonstrate to the children what you truly believe learning is.

Questions for discussion

- Children's voices: how might teachers find out how children feel about and respond to the learning environment they provide?
- How might children at each Key Stage be involved in creating their own learning environment?
- How might learning in the classroom be linked to learning outside the classroom at Key Stage 1? At Key Stage 2?
- What might your ideal learning environment at either Key Stage be like? What might be the constraints in creating this environment?

Further reading

Hewitt, D. (2008) *Understanding Effective Learning: Strategies for the Classroom.* Maidenhead: Open University Press.
This book explores these important concepts by examining learning in a range of classroom settings and drawing on evidence from teachers and pupils, through interviews and observations. The focus is two-fold: to understand learning in the classroom, and to develop practices which will support learning.

Roffey, S. (2010) *Changing Behaviour in Schools.* London: Sage.
Taking an holistic approach to working with students, the author provides examples of effective strategies for encouraging pro-social and collaborative behaviour in the classroom, the school and the wider community. Chapters look at the importance of the social and emotional aspects of learning, and ways to facilitate change.

Skinner, D. (2010) *Effective Teaching and Learning in Practice.* London: Continuum.
Based on excellent summaries of recent research on teaching and learning, this book presents a clear framework around which teachers can build their classroom practice. It provides an excellent starting point for new entrants to the profession as well as a source of reflection for their more experienced colleagues.

References

Alexander, R. (1992) *Policy and Practice in Primary Education.* London: Routledge.
Alexander, R. (ed.) (2010) *Children, Their World, Their Education: Final Report of the Cambridge Primary Review.* London: Routledge.

Bowles, S. and Gintis, H. (1976) *Schooling in Capitalist America*. London: Routledge and Kegan.

Bronfenbrenner, U. (1979) *The Ecology of Human Development*. Cambridge, MA: Harvard University Press.

Child, D. (ed.) (1997) *Psychology and the Teacher*, 6th edn. London: Continuum.

Cowley, S. (2006) *Getting the Buggers to Behave*, 3rd edn. London: Continuum.

Daly, M., Byers, E. and Taylor, W. (2006) *Understanding Early Years Theory in Practice*. Oxford: Heinemann.

DfEE (2000) *The National Curriculum Key Stages* 1 and 2 (revised edition). London: HMSO.

Docking, J. (2002) *Managing Behaviour in the Primary School*, 3rd edn. London: David Fulton.

Doherty, J. and Hughes, M. (2009) *Child Development: Theory and Practice 0–11*. Harlow: Pearson.

Gnadinger, C. (2008) 'Peer-mediated Instruction: Assisted Performance in the Primary Classroom', *Teachers and Teaching* 14(2): 129–42.

Goswami, U. (2008) *Cognitive Development: The Learning Brain*. Hove: Psychology Press.

Gump, P. (1987) 'School and Classroom Environments' in I. Altman and J.F. Wohlwill, *Handbook of Environmental Psychology*. New York: Plenum Press, pp. 131–74.

Hastings, N. and Schwieso, J. (1995) 'Tasks and Tables: The Effects of Seating Arrangements on Task Engagement in Primary Classrooms', *Educational Research* 37(3): 279–91.

Jacques, K. and Hyland, R. (2003) *Professional Studies: Primary Phase*. Exeter: Learning Matters.

Kehily, M. (ed.) (2010) *An Introduction to Childhood Studies*, 2nd edn. Maidenhead: McGraw Hill.

Kendall-Seatter, S. (2005) *Primary Professional Studies: Reflective Reader*. Exeter: Learning Matters.

MacIntyre, H. and Ireson, J. (2002) 'Within-class Ability Grouping: Placement of Pupils in Groups and Self-concept', *British Educational Research Journal*. 28(2): 249–63.

McNamara, S. and Moreton, G. (1997) *Understanding Differentiation*. London: Taylor and Francis.

Moyles, J. (1992) *Organising for Learning in the Primary Classroom*. Buckingham: Open University Press.

Ouvry, M. (2000) *Exercising Muscles and Minds*. London: The Early Years Network.

Plowden Report (1967) *Children and their Primary Schools: A Report of the Central Advisory Council for Education (England)*. London: HMSO.

Pollard, A. (2008) *Reflective Teaching: Evidence-informed Professional Practice*, 3rd edn. London: Continuum.

Waterson, A. (2003) 'Managing the Classroom for Learning' in K. Jacques and R. Hyland (eds) *Professional Studies: Primary Phase*. Exeter: Learning Matters, pp. 74–85.

Whedall, K. and Glynn, T. (1989) *Effective Classroom Learning: A Behavioural Interactionist Approach to Teaching*. Oxford: Basil Blackwell.

Wood, D., Bruner, J. and Ross, G. (1976) 'The Role of Tutoring in Problem Solving', *Journal of Child Psychology and Psychiatry* 17: 89–100.

22 Theoretical Perspectives on Learning outside the Classroom – Relationships between Learning and Place

Waite, S.

Chapter objectives

- A framework for developing a set of personal theories for teaching and learning outside the classroom
- An awareness of different learning theories that might help to understand learning outside the classroom
- An appreciation of the complexity of learning in relation to place: psychological, social, cultural, geographical and historical factors

A head teacher was recently asked to say why practical science, including the use of the outdoors – apparently under threat from health and safety concerns and science experiment videos – was so important to pupils. How would you have responded?

It might, or might not, come as a surprise to you that the head teacher with 30 years' experience was in certain respects unable to answer the question. She gave a fluent response that pointed to her conviction that 'pupils learn more' because it is 'hands-on', 'experiential' and 'enjoyable and engaging', but none of these go very deeply into *how* it makes a difference. Actually, such an explanation appears hard to provide; just how does 'the outside' and 'experience' make learning different? To begin to respond to the challenge of making sense of the relationship between place and learning – the central purpose of this chapter – let us return to the head teacher's comments above and think about what they represent. Pointing to practical science being 'hands-on' shows an implicit sense that *embodiment* is important; we use our bodies in practical activities, but why might this be beneficial? The conviction that pupils learn *more* might suggest that practical science is important to raise school outcomes. However, interestingly, it also points to an implicit model of learning that relates to the acquisition of knowledge in terms of cognition and which probably therefore values how much we know (quantity), rather than its form and its worth (qualities). Claiming that pupils learn more does not address the equally interesting question of more 'what'. The use of the term *experiential* might suggest that the *way* in which we come into contact with phenomena – rather than simply whether we do or not – might have a bearing on *what* is learnt. *Engagement* as the relationship between the learner and the focus of learning is important, and might again point to the need to consider *what* is being learnt and *how*; reinforced perhaps by *enjoyment*.

This analysis demonstrates that any conception of learning, particularly taking account of place and experience, is inevitably complex.

Developing a personal theory for understanding learning in different contexts

In this chapter we suggest that place plays an active part in learning and that developing a personal theory of learning outside the classroom that includes consideration of place can help planning for rich learning opportunities.

 Points for practice

- Consider the 'places' available to you for different learning purposes.
- Think about what meanings these 'places' have for staff, children, community.
- Consider what sorts of learning opportunities would be well supported by these places.

All the space beyond the four walls of the classroom is not a homogeneous 'other' to be regarded simply in contrast to what happens indoors and generally 'a good thing'. Although the UK government's Learning Outside the Classroom Manifesto appears to support this view, it does not go on to explain *why*:

> Learning outside the classroom is about raising achievement through an organised, powerful approach to learning in which direct experience is of prime importance. This is not only about *what* we learn but importantly *how* and *where* we learn. (DfES, 2006a: 3)

In fact, these questions form a useful shorthand evaluation of the appropriateness of place and pedagogy:

- *What* are we trying to teach/learn?
- *How* will this best be supported?
- *Where* is most likely to provide those conditions?
- *Why* is this so?

Different subjects bring particular cultural expectations, applicable regardless of where learning in that discipline takes place, but it might also be reasonable to assume that particular spaces are suitable for different kinds of learning because of the functions and activities that they support. For example, handling different materials can be beneficial in understanding their qualities. If materials are brought into the classroom, while the children may learn about some of their features through direct experience, they do not also learn where they occur in the world. Experiences outside the classroom may therefore seem more 'authentic' and grounded in 'reality' and certainly some of the children in our own research (Waite, 2011) have talked of knowing that something is 'real' in the sense of 'believable' through first-hand experience rather than just being told. Perhaps then, reference to 'reality' and 'authenticity' is understood in relation to *life beyond the educational setting.*

Nevertheless, this does not necessarily mean that the experiences are also 'relevant', another common claim for learning outside the classroom. Relevance comes from the meanings with which people imbue objects and spaces and from how activity fits with cultural expectations. Children in the Western world live their lives and learn both in and outside of formal education; perhaps their learning in both contexts is more easily linked and developed if the boundaries between the two are blurred by application of their learning in either context in the other, so that they see a purpose beyond the expectations of teachers as arbiters of their education. In some cultures such a distinction between places for formal and non-formal learning is less clear-cut and yet we see 'relevance' operating in their play (non-formal learning), where skills to be adopted later in their life are practised through play and participation (Smith, 2010). But the Learning Outside the Classroom Manifesto (DfES, 2006a) seems to yoke education outside the classroom to outcomes valued in schooling, saying it is about '*raising achievement* through an *organised*, powerful approach to learning in which direct experience is of prime importance' (p. 3, emphasis added).

So the opportunities inherent in places for 'relevance' and 'authenticity' to life beyond the educational setting are sometimes not taken up because of cultural transfers. Julian Sefton-Green (2006) notes that 'out-of-school learning' often actually takes place *within* schools in the form of clubs and after-school activities. Many are led by teachers. Although some of these activities are run in a less formal way, the cultural expectations of 'in-school' mean that many are simply 'extensions of the formal curriculum and function like study groups' (p. 4). They are only 'out-of school' in a temporal sense.

Other researchers in outdoor education (such as Brookes, 2002 and Stewart, 2006) argue strongly for awareness of cultural and historical meaning in place-based education. So in addition to emotionally mediated personal responses, students also learn how places have become as they are. However, relevance for the individual, or broader socio-cultural understandings of place, are often subservient to imposed demands, such as raising standards in learning. Yet, Greenwood (2008: 239) believes that the best place-based education 'emerges from the particularities of places, the people who know them best ... and the people who wonder about all the opportunities that might arise from action-oriented place study'. Such place-based learning refers to contexts that have long-term effects through long association with them. Ward Thompson et al. (2008: 132), in a study about how adults use green places, found that children who had not had access to outdoor environments in childhood were unlikely to spend time in the outdoors as adults, with consequent impacts on adult health and well-being.

Other ways of learning may be stimulated by novelty and adventure. Min and Lee (2006), indeed, suggest outdoor spaces for learning need a balance between challenge and security, private and public and meeting current and future, as yet unpredicted, needs. This suggests a high degree of flexibility in the resourcing and landscaping of such areas (Armitage, 1999). However, places may be better understood not simply as areas with geographical boundaries, but rather as places with particular social relations and understandings, which transcend time and space. Consideration of intersubjective experiences is vitally important when thinking about pedagogy and place (McKenzie, 2008), and there are several ways that we can consider learning to take account of subjectivity, culture and place.

Concepts of learning and different focal planes

Learning may be viewed using different focal planes, offering complementary ways to make sense of this complex process that defies any one single explanation. Zooming in tightly, one sees learning in terms of individuals. This is how the head teacher viewed the acquisition of knowledge by learners and echoes Cannatella's (2007) belief in the centrality of *self* in engaging with learning. Often this leads to a focus on the mind and claims that learning takes place through affective associations and (increasingly) reasoned thought, brought about through some conceptual challenge which requires the learner to rethink their conception of something. This is the basis of constructivism and represents a psychological plane of focus.

We cannot look inside the individual but we can take into account what that individual shows us through behaviour. The body is therefore one way we might gain insight into the learning process. How do we know how to adjust our teaching and planning to meet the needs of our children? It is not through X-ray vision of children's mental processes but what their behaviour tells us about how that teaching is being received. Are the children misbehaving, looking blank, fiddling with something? Beard and Wilson (2007: 5) put forward a psychologically based explanation of this conceptualisation in the form of a learning combination lock, where a series of tumblers represent the external environment, senses and internal environment as the person is seen as internalising the environment through their senses. Another way of looking at this positioning of self within the world is that through the mind *and* the social we come to 'know' and 'be' in relationship with our bodies and places and that culture is constructed from the interactions between these. In the model shown in Figure 1.1 this relationship is portrayed in a way that reflects an understanding of place as culturally constructed.

Using different ways of looking at learning in a context-sensitive way, this chapter aims to make more explicit some of the components of the 'holism' claimed for outdoor learning; how terms like *hands-on*, *experiential* and *practical* and the interplay between learning and place might be understood using these planes of focus.

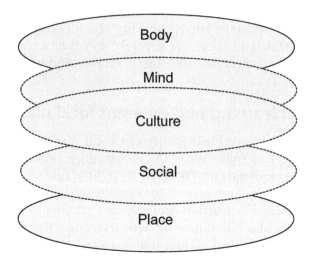

Figure 1.1 The embodiment of place: an individual's interaction in the construction of culture in place

A broader concept of learning

In considering concepts of learning, however, we need to be aware that we are also talking about concepts of education and schooling. Schooling implies a deliberate attempt to learn specific things that are valued within our society, so education can been understood as the manner in which this is organised and managed. Indeed, one of the prime motives for undertaking this book is a desire amongst the authors to unpick something new about how the wider education system has come to shape learning and what contribution 'place' might make to this. More specifically it stems from a shared concern with the way in which 'the classroom' tends to encourage a rather narrow view of what learning might involve and a desire to open up new ideas about this. An opportunity to revisit values for determining curriculum and pedagogy may be a possibility over the next few years. The UK coalition government claims that their invitation to all schools to become academies is 'offering them greater independence and freedom' (DFE, 2010), but since testing in the Primary National Curriculum is set to continue, it remains to be seen whether this 'freedom' and 'independence' is somewhat illusory. However, this is only one of the contributory factors that shape learning in and out of school.

Towards a relational model for learning outside the classroom

One way of reflecting upon the learning environment considers the interaction between the programme, facilitator, group, individual, culture, environment (place) and activity (Neill, 2008). Figure 1.2 illustrates the relationship between the national context of curriculum, standards and guidance, the cultural norms and expectations of the local context and the child, place and 'others' – adults and children – involved in their schooling. It is in the white space between these that pedagogic activity is enacted. Learning opportunities are created in this space through interactions between the three corners of the triangle (child, others and place); all in mutual interaction with the activity. Place will have new meanings and therefore new potentials as a learning context; the child and others will have learnt from the interactions and return to the place with developed expectations. Thus a micro-culture of that particular learning space may be co-constructed. Activity theory is one possible method for working with this conceptualisation. (For further details of activity theory, see Engeström, Miettinen and Punamäki, 1999.)

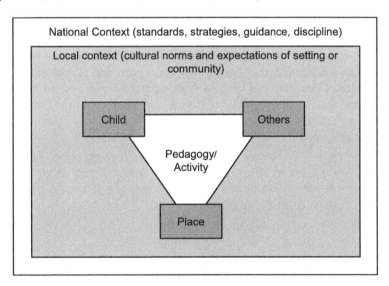

Figure 1.2 The possibility space in the relationship between place, pedagogy and learning (adapted from Waite et al., 2008)

Place in this relational model is an active partner in the learning activities in which the child engages and the pedagogies employed, but this model only captures a snapshot in a dynamic system of interactions. Spaces have particular possibilities, history and associations for children and adults that make them meaningful 'places' and these are constantly being revised by ongoing experiences in them. Repeated visits may result in the establishment of a different set of cultural expectations such as within Forest School programmes (see Chapter 12). On the other hand places that offer some novelty and unpredictability may be valuable in exciting a revision of our ideas (Jarvis, 2009). This might be why wild places lend themselves to transformative learning according to some researchers (Senge et al., 2005). If we accept that place contributes to cultural norms, an unusual context may reduce reliance on 'custom and practice' from the more usual site of learning and open another possibility space. Another explanation might be that power runs through teaching and learning, predominantly from teacher to taught, but if this usual distribution of power is disrupted in new places, different opportunities for learning may arise. Furthermore, if these places are not regularly revisited or stable, teaching and learning practices in them are likely to be more fluid. We therefore need to be alert to different sorts of places, what they make possible and how they are likely to interact with learning intentions.

 Points for practice

A framework for planning learning outside the classroom

Using the diagram in Figure 1.2, consider occasions where you have been teaching both in the classroom and elsewhere. Note down how these might be understood in terms of the model, as well as any implications for planning and practice. The questions below will prompt points to consider. Reflect how they cluster around certain aspects of this model.

- What are the powerful influences on your practice? How might you wish to change your practice to match your values? What theoretical perspectives are you using to interpret your pedagogy?
- What are your teaching intentions?
- Why are these important?
- What places are most suited to this sort of teaching and learning?
- How does the place particularly support the learning?
- What might the place mean to the children?
- What other valuable learning might therefore take place?
- How does this relate to priorities within the setting and nationally?

Review after activity

- What learning have you observed?
- How has the experience contributed on individual, local and national levels?
- Where to next – in learning and spaces?

We now turn to an example of learning outside the classroom taken from Economic and Social Research Council funded research (Waite, Evans and Rogers, 2008) to provide an illustration of how different focal planes allow us to take different perspectives on events and so can enhance our understanding.

Case Study 🗁

Pushes and pulls: forces at work in the play park

Laura feels some trepidation in taking this Year 1 class outside. As a supply teacher, she does not know the children very well, although certain ones have already been pointed out to her. The children gather around her on the carpet as she sets out the plans for the lesson on Forces, looking for examples of pushes and pulls in the play park. Nearly all the talking is done by the teacher. In fact, there are nearly twenty behavioural injunctions, principally about how they should *not* behave, and several of these remarks are targeted at the identified children directly; seven teacher comments are about practical arrangements such as who will hold the clipboard and pencil; a mere six relate to the substantive topic of the activity, why they are going out to the play park, and that they will need to put on their 'science hats'. The children are *very* excited about their trip.

In the play park the children are in their assigned groups with a leader (chosen by the teacher and indicated by possession of a clipboard) but they are pulled by the attractions of play in this context that they associate so much with freedom. They debate if play is allowed. One child says: 'We must be doing work, because I have a pencil.' Others are not so sure and lark about, making the most of their surroundings. The group leader adopts the teacher's role, while trying to get them to cooperate in compiling a group list of pushes and pulls in the environment. She herself has to be pushy to try to achieve this, but the interaction is very unidirectional, as it was in the classroom beforehand. 'If I see any silly behaviour!' she admonishes the boys throwing grass. Eventually, she calls on the teacher to reinforce behavioural control in this ambiguous area. 'Right,' says the teacher, 'we're coming away from this play area because you're all playing.' The child replies, 'I'm not playing. I'm just looking.' But the leader of the group rejoins, 'You *was* playing'.

How are we to make sense of what is happening here? The predominant way of thinking about learning is to consider how individuals make sense of the learning objects (forces in this case) and how interactions with others (usually teachers) can help them to develop this sense-making. In this situation though what is most noticeable is that pupils do not engage in the kind of conceptual thinking about forces that the teacher had hoped for. It is tempting to think that this is just misbehaviour, but it is also possible to make sense of it in other terms by looking at it on a wider plane.

First, we might consider why the supply teacher was perhaps more anxious about taking the children out of the classroom. Classrooms are associated with rules (explicit ones certainly, but also many more implicit ones) that allow teachers to control physical and intellectual behaviour, making everyone feel safe, but also strongly affecting what is deemed appropriate for learning. Leaving this haven affords the possibility that the children might 'misbehave' and show up both her and the school in public, perhaps accounting for her heavy emphasis on behaviour in the introduction. She may also have been given the lesson plan. Not only does this mean that she may not have thought through what specific learning points she wanted to support by the experience, but the practice of having 'plans' implies that there is specific learning to be achieved – and hence pressure to achieve it. This may then account for her organisation of pupils and resources. In setting up the groups, she chose children she thought would behave in ways that she deemed appropriate for schooling (mini-teachers), based on well-established social, cultural and historical patterns of 'school' behaviour. Ironically, this left the less motivated children with no symbols of work and perhaps confused therefore as to how this task was meant to operate, leaving them more likely to be seduced by the playful opportunities. Rather than becoming a 'new' experience that offered pupils the chance to appreciate forces in new ways, the group work didn't function as such but became a microcosm of the classroom. Children were not in fact free to engage in novel learning, but were implicitly required to learn in the same ways as a classroom would require. In effect, the class took 'the classroom' out there with them – and even increased the number of teachers! As a result, although the activity took place outside, it was not experiential or hands-on, and the relevance for the children (play) was seen as counterproductive because of the cultural norms that were exported with them from the classrooms.

This is just one of many possible readings of the situation. The learning itself does not differ but application of different focal planes, according to our own beliefs about learning and the questions we want to answer, can help make sense of how to set up and understand appropriate learning opportunities. We therefore turn now to a more detailed examination of these various planes.

A psychological plane

Cumulative learning refers to situations where there is no prior experience, so it is suggested this is how very young children may learn, like a sponge soaking up knowledge. However, anyone who has spent time with a baby is likely to agree that they are far from passive in their learning, encouraging repetition of actions and events that they find interesting. Although ideas of empty vessels to be filled may still linger in instrumental ticking off of 'things to be learnt', the most common form of learning found in schooling is probably *assimilation,* where the learner (and her teacher) incrementally build on existing knowledge. The knowledge that is taught or skills that are shown do not disrupt the expected progression from an existing and relatively circumscribed body of knowledge. However, *accommodative* learning also comes into play where a greater leap is needed to make sense of the new and is more likely to be present where challenge and complex problem-solving is required which calls on prior knowledge, understanding and skills *across* disciplines. It is this type of learning, where the learner makes more prolific and diffuse links with other experience, contexts and knowledge, which may be more easily transferred between situations. This is not to say that a 'piece of knowledge' is carted unchanged from one situation to another but that the many links made enable aspects of the original learning to be re-combined in and for new situations. (For more discussion of this, see Illeris, 2009.)

Jarvis (2009) argues that after initial experiences the cultural meaning rather than the experience is attended to by the learner, so that assimilation may be more likely. This has particular implications for outdoor and experiential learning which often offers opportunities to approach learning anew through novelty. However, we need to take care that such experience isn't understood as culture-free; even 'new' situations are only understood through reference to the past and anticipation of the future. Accommodative learning, though, is especially important for the rapid changing work/life contexts for which we prepare our children and ourselves, where many situations are 'new' to us. The apparent unpredictability of outdoor contexts therefore may afford a better preparation for real-life problem-solving than classrooms that conform to standard regular rituals, including perhaps 'taking the teacher's word for it'!

Reflective practice, which is drawn from one of the most common theories of learning used in outdoor education, Kolb's experiential learning cycle (1984), provides another theoretical vehicle for further engagement of the individual in making a learning opportunity their own. The simplest models of the cycle have been criticised for not taking the situated nature of learning into account and for portraying each 'stage' as discrete (Illeris, 2007: 55); in fact, we are constantly reflecting, planning and doing as we experience. (For further discussion and critique of Kolb's theory, see Jarvis and Parker, 2007: 6–7.) Another aspect of learning which is somewhat overlooked in this tidy model is that sometimes the experience is so out of the normal run of experience that it requires a drastic re-appraisal of what we think we know. A shake-up of our existing ways of thinking can lead to *transformative* learning (Jarvis, 2009). These are the occasions where experience or reflection leads to a re-adjustment not only to our previous ways of thinking but also to our understanding of ourselves, a sort of learning often claimed for wilderness experiences and adventure education.

Meanings may also be different for the individual and 'others' and it is therefore important that all children have an opportunity to be active in their learning, so that they can link these prior meanings to their present and to wider social and cultural meanings. If an adult takes control, the relevance to the child may be reduced, as the learning is mediated through the adult's cultural position (see Chapter 4 for an example of this). Sometimes the local context's cultural influences may be 'exported wholesale' to particular learning spaces, as we saw in the case study earlier. This is to be expected given teachers' investment in establishing norms for behaviour and relationships within schools. However, this practice may also jeopardise capitalising on the unique ways in which different places could shape learning. For example, imagine children being expected to ignore the 'distractions' of the outside world and listen to the teacher while they stand at the edge of the pond in order to learn about frogs, when supported direct observation would be a far more effective way of using that place.

We also know from our research that learning outside the classroom often allows the practitioner opportunities for close observation of children's natural behaviour. This is assessment that is not tied to a particular learning outcome but incorporates a rounded view of social and emotional aspects of learning for children, the holistic aspect mentioned earlier. In child-led activity, the teacher is able to observe and contingently develop the child's own interests enhancing the child's enjoyment. We see some particularly good examples of this in Chapter 3. This endeavour is worthwhile as *engagement* and *enjoyment* have both been found to be valuable in supporting motivation for learning from Early Years to Higher Education (e.g. Carver, 2003; Waite and Davis, 2006; Waite et al., 2009).

Another key question that must be asked in planning and observing learning outside the classroom is *what* is being learnt? Adopting a socio-cultural plane of focus can assist with this question.

A socio-cultural plane

A socio-cultural plane of analysis is not a common way for teachers to think about their work because of the deeply rooted emphasis in our education system on individual cognition (albeit with some social activity involved). There is no single social theory of learning (Jarvis and Parker, 2007), but the central ideas that we want to focus on here are twofold:

- the notion that people participate in activity that is socially orientated and organised;

- the idea that 'understanding' need not be viewed as an individual affair in which people (pupils) 'acquire' knowledge and carry it around with them, but can be seen as being linked more closely to context and experience.

Socially orientated activity

To illustrate further what we mean by activity that is socially orientated, we might ask you a question: have you been behaving normally today? Though we cannot access your answer, the fact that we can ask this and you can consider it points to the idea that there are 'normal' ways to behave within whatever social context you find yourself. We go about our life using well-established practices/ behaviours. These practices are embedded in the social context in which we live and work, and are cultural (what we do round here) and historical (we always do it this way).

Schooling is no different. Pupils and teachers operate in customary patterns; one need only watch young children 'playing' schools or consider the behaviour of the leader of the group in the case study above to know this. One way to make sense of classrooms therefore is to think about them in terms of:

- the common *practices* involved (people's actions);

- the *norms* involved (what is usual practice; what it is normal to do);

- the *discourses* involved (how people communicate meaning, both implicitly and explicitly, through language, action and symbolic means, such as clothing, status etc.).

As part of these ideas one can also consider 'rules' that operate within a situation (implicit as much as explicit), the notion of who does what (often referred to as the division of labour) and also the resources one has available to support activity. In thinking then about learning outside the classroom we can consider ways in which taking learning out of the normal environment encourages these practices, norms, discourses, rules and divisions of labour to change in ways that are desirable. If the value of working outside the classroom is in providing pupils with experiences that are different from those inside it, we need a framework and language that allow us to analyse and talk about such experience. So, returning to the class that goes outside to find frogs in the environmental area rather than simply reading books, this may be because we want them to learn to behave in ways that are different to classroom behaviour (as young environmentalists perhaps), as well as to learn 'about' frogs.

Understanding and experience

This example of youngsters learning to behave as environmentalists brings us to our second point about socio-cultural perspectives on learning; the idea that understanding need not always be thought of as an individual affair. This is more than simply saying context matters. The argument is that knowledge cannot be separated from the situation in which it is developed. Children learning about frogs through experiencing them around a pond don't learn 'more' or 'less' about frogs than children whose access is through books or a video; they learn a qualitatively different thing, a different way of 'knowing frogs'. This view of learning, which is often referred to as 'situated understanding', is not 'better' than an individualised, cognitive and affective view but it does offer ways to make sense of learning in terms of context, which is important in thinking about the role of place.

While culture itself is the product of social construction, the meaning of culture is continually being interpreted through our learning and enacted in our lives. So, in practice, it is not a question of nailing one's colours to the mast of socio-cultural or psychological/psychosocial theories of learning, but rather developing a personal theory about how these shed light and operate in the contexts in which one lives and works. Using different planes of focus helps us to approach different questions we may have about children's learning and our own teaching, but as Wenger (2009: 215) says: 'A perspective is not a recipe; it does not tell you what to do. Rather it acts as a guide about what to pay attention to, what difficulties to expect, and how to approach a problem.' In this book we hope that the stories we tell of practice and the theories we link with these in the following chapters will help readers each to make personal sense of what will help and guide them as practitioners.

Using different planes for different purposes

In terms of learning outside the classroom, our research leads us to think that cultural pressures associated with schooling (such as meeting standards, conforming to agreed targets, following plans) may be more intense where the social and institutional are more established, such as *within* schools. After all, where there are guidance documents, strategies and institutional policies, 'culture' is made more manifest. This is not to say that these outward signs are *the* 'culture' in any straightforward, unambiguous way; you probably hold your own views about what elements you agree with in these externally acknowledged policies and your personal beliefs (invisible culture) will inevitably colour the impacts of these policies (visible culture) on your practice. However, it is possible that novel situations, such as some of those outside the classroom, may represent a greater freedom for personal resistance to and inter-pretations of general norms. It is worth bearing in mind too that this freedom may not just be experienced by you as practitioner but also by learners. They too bring their own socio-cultural and historical values constructed from the histories of their family, community and peer group to the party!

Thus, our responses shape learning inside and outside the formal context of the classroom. Thinking of our own lives and of the children we have taught, we remember very different attitudes being shown to apparently identical sets of resources or places. This awareness of individual response may explain why the idea of 'personalisation' in learning is seductive. It is championed by government in a challenging and sometimes puzzling dynamic with recommendations for more objective-led teaching. Personalisation may be partly attributable to the uniqueness of experience through the distinct psychological understanding that each of us brings to our social and cultural worlds. Clearly it follows that places or learning opportunities are not always viewed in a standard fashion. On a psychological plane, our personality shaped by processes of socialisation throughout our lives means that we all experience events with potential for learning in different ways – what is offered is different to what is received because the learner brings her own past, present and aspirations for the future to bear on that. This personal response may be the 'engagement' that the head teacher spoke of, making links or 'engaging' with the learner's prior experience, and future hopes in the learning of the present and actual. Each child will ask (consciously or unconsciously): 'What does this (experience) **mean** *to* (in relation to my past and present) and *for* (in relation to my future) me?' Meaning and purpose are central for valuing what is learnt and, for that learning to be enduring, forging many links with other memories is helpful.

On the other hand, a wider lens suggests a problem with this tighter analysis. Although at the micro level each individual has experiences that are clearly different, at the macro level there is a strong sense of commonality between people, rooted in the social discourses within which they operate. The pupils in the play park mentioned earlier might, on the surface of things, have appeared to be free to 'see' anything they liked, but what is valued, and therefore what is valuable to see, is bounded by the social expectations of schooling, even when the children are not in the classroom. The trip was about forces and schooling dictates that objectives are met; issues of 'playing' therefore are only problematic because schooling is culturally and socially required to be about 'learning' and school learning means making focused, articulated observations about the issue under study. Interestingly, this plane of analysis is also always a political (small 'p') one in the sense that it asks questions about values. This is illustrated in considering notions of 'ability'. The main way we measure ability in schools is in the way pupils write and talk about ideas, but if outdoor learning offers pupils the chance to engage with the world in more tacit, experiential ways, then we need to reconsider this. An expert environmentalist is not expert because of his or her ability to talk about the environment. Rather, it is the ability to *do* the things that are central to expertise in the world of environmental science and indeed many other occupations. This mismatch between measures of achievement and desirable abilities brings into question how appropriate schooling in its current form might be for supporting vocational aspects of learning, but also implies that whilst working outdoors might seem like a good idea, it may conflict with other priorities within a teacher's professional life.

Returning to our head teacher's explanation for the value of practical learning, being 'hands on' makes learning potentially more direct and less mediated by another's meanings. An important skill as a teacher is in facilitating; after all, no one but the learner can learn *for* them. As learners, we implicitly call on our rich history of associations to forge links to make new knowledge, skills or understandings particularly meaningful, relevant and therefore more memorable for us. Involvement of the body in learning is another way in which more links are constructed. Children in our research have commented that 'hands-on' first-hand experience makes the learning more real and believable (Waite et al., 2006), but whether this leads to learning in a form that is useful for schooling remains an issue – and a challenge perhaps to develop new ways of understanding (and assessing) learning.

Furthermore, the head teacher's idea of 'enjoyment' is not simply a general hope that the learner will enjoy school but is underpinned by empirically evidenced associations, first from research into motivation (Hufton et al., 2002; Waite and Davis, 2006) and secondly from brain research which shows how important affect and emotional loading of memories are in their application in future situations (Carver, 2003; Waite, 2007). So the fact that children often mention wanting more outdoor and practical activities should indicate to us that it is worthwhile accommodating their preferences if we want them to remember. It may therefore be helpful to consider both emotional loading (psychological) and 'belonging' (psychosocial) in considering how to make learning experiences memorable. And so we come full circle to the value of personal theories employing various planes of focus in negotiating the relational complexity of learning and place.

 Thoughts on theory

- How do you conceptualise learning: as principally psychological, psychosocial, socio-cultural or a mixture of all three? [Your personal theory of learning.]
- Are some aspects more emphasised than others in your setting? [The local context.]
- What aspects of learning do you place the most/least value on? [Your personal values.]
- How could you better accommodate your personal concept of learning in your own practice? [Reconciliation of local context and personal values and theory.]
- What are the implications of this personal view for the way you choose to teach and use spaces beyond the classroom and for changes that might need to be made at the wider policy level of your teaching context? [Your plans.]

Summary

This chapter has outlined a number of ways in which learning and place can be viewed and has encouraged you to consider what your personal understandings are. Using different ways of looking may help to gain a better understanding of how learning in contexts within and outside the classroom occurs and this should support your thinking about how best to facilitate learning for different purposes. Clearly in a short chapter, we cannot hope to address this wide theme in great depth but we have provided pointers to further reading if aspects have caught your attention. The chapter should also be a useful resource to return to as you dip into the chapters that follow pursuing your own interests in supporting learning outside the classroom.

Further reading

Illeris, K. (ed.) (2007) *Contemporary Theories of Learning*. London: Routledge.

Jarvis, P. and Parker, S. (2007) *Human Learning: An Holistic Approach*. London: Routledge.

Nabhan, G.P. and Trimble, S. (1994) *The Geography of Childhood*. Boston: Beacon Press.

Offering Rich Experiences; Contexts for Play, Exploration and Talk

Warden, C.

This chapter explores:

- **The right that young children have to a rich outdoor environment full of irresistible natural stimuli, contexts for play, exploration and talk**
- **A consideration of how we offer real experiences and contact with the natural world within a 'community'**

Value: Young children must have a rich outdoor environment full of irresistible stimuli, contexts for play, exploration and talk, plenty of real experiences and contact with the natural world and with the community.

The rationale for rich experiences outdoors

Through outdoor play, young children can learn the skills of social interaction and friendship, care for living things and their environment, be curious and fascinated, feel awe, wonder and joy and become 'lost in the experience'. They can satisfy their deep urge to explore, experiment and understand and become aware of their community and locality, thus developing a sense of connection to the physical, natural and human world.

A particular strength of outdoor provision is that it offers children many opportunities to experience the real world, to have first-hand experiences, do real tasks and do what adults do, including being involved in the care of the outdoor space. An aesthetic awareness of and emotional link to the non-constructed or controlled, multi-sensory and multi-dimensional natural world is a crucial component of human well-being, and increasingly absent in young children's lives. The richness of cultural diversity is an important part of our everyday world; this can and should be explored by children through outdoor experiences. Giving children a sense of belonging to something bigger than the immediate family or setting lays foundations for living as a community.

The term rich environment has been used very frequently and so it is perhaps worthwhile to consider what we mean by 'richness' in terms of outdoor environments. Is it a space that has everything? Or one that has nothing? Is it the complexity of resources or complexity of thinking? Is it the people in our lives? Is it our place within a community that gives us the tools to interpret and understand richness? Can it be bought or is it a gift when we feel it? Can we be 'taught' to see it when we have it? Is it subjective in its interpretation?

In life, we create spaces around ourselves that mean something to us and have a connection to us as individuals. Children move into spaces that we have created in the hope they will meet the motivation and connection they seek. The closer the match between the child and their experience at a root level, then the more likely that the learning will be assimilated for later recall. Yet we do not place enough emphasis on the voices of children to direct and influence the spaces that they exist within. What about the lost voice of a generation who have not had the experience of playing outside in nature: are they able to reflect on their 'richness' of experience? Can their children, in turn, re-connect them through their motivation and engagement?

Joseph Clinton Pearce (1977) uses the term *magical thinking* to describe the child's way of knowing the world. These primary perceptions, Pearce notes, 'are developmental in that they tend to disappear'. Such primary perceptions are referred to as 'bondings to the earth' (1977: 136), and Pearce suggests that interaction with the physical substance of the living earth (e.g., rocks, trees, wind) is critical to the child's developing brain and intelligence. Even in naturalistic spaces, these magical thoughts may not appear if the space is devoid of creative stimulus. In areas that are over-structured and directive, the opportunity to let go, to create and develop are limited. Where activity driven 'programmes' create a given context, they will reduce the motivation to talk and explore if the child perceives their engagement as being secondary to the experience.

In his seminal work, Csikszentmihalyi (1975) outlines his theory that people are most happy when they are in a state of *flow* – a state of concentration or complete absorption with the activity. Many writers have spoken of their connection to nature being in line with this. Wilson (1997) talks of her experience:

> …picking cherries and plums from the trees in our yard, watching daffodils unfold in early spring, and rejoicing in the sweet scent of the lilacs that grew near our house. Such experiences filled my world with song, and I remember being swept away in a joyful childhood dance. Today, I miss the music, the dance, and the enchantment of childhood. 'Earth song' has been replaced by the noise of traffic, and daily life feels more like a race than a dance. The enchantment of knowing the world as a song is a treasured memory – a memory that still adds joy to my life. This memory, however, also brings a touch of sadness, because I feel that over the years to adulthood, I've truly lost something special along the way. This 'something special' is a way of knowing the natural world as a place of beauty and mystery. While I still maintain the belief that the world is full of mystery and wonder, my way of knowing it as such is not as direct and experiential.

The space created was enough to sweep her away in a joyful dance. The space, time and child came together to create a moment or a series of moments of connection. The context was one that was self-created as an interpretation and engagement with the natural environment around her. These memories have been retained by her into adulthood, and so tell us a great deal about the 'richness' of the moment.

Rachel Sebba (1991), a researcher from Israel, investigated children's relation to the environment from actual and retrospective points of view. In conducting her research, Sebba looked at the environmental preferences and the nature of the experiences of being outdoors as reflected in adults' recollections and in children's actual approaches to investigating the world. Her findings suggest that children experience the natural environment 'in a deep and direct manner, not as a background for events, but, rather, as a factor and stimulator' (1991: 395).

Sebba's findings are consistent with the work of Edith Cobb (1977), who concluded from her research that experience in childhood is never formal or abstract. 'Even the world of nature,' she says, 'is not a "scene," or even a landscape. Nature for the child is sheer sensory experience' (1977: 28–9). The context and its richness are supplied in a naturalistic outdoor space in a way that cannot be fully replicated by over-designed, closed materials for play.

Children seek contexts of excitement so that learning and discovery are at the very tip of the experience. When children decide to repeat an experience it is actually not static, it changes ever so slightly to assimilate new information, to make sure that each time the experience is different. Flemmen (2001) explores a concept of *systematic uncertainty* that children create in their play to make sure the outcome is unpredictable. It is this context of excitement that is a stimulus for play exploration. The talk wraps around the experience as a method of understanding, interpretation and sharing the moment with the community around the child.

The richness of a space can be linked to the level of *play affordance* proffered, or rather, what the loose materials within it offer. Many children seem to link more easily and directly with the open-ended materials that nature supplies. A stick must be the longest-standing toy of childhood. The concept of 'affordance' (Gibson, 1979) refers to what the environment offers; what it provides for the child. Affordances are opportunities that arise from the interaction between the physical properties of the environment and the interests, ideas and intent of the individual. Affordances arise through active detection: where the person is sensing and moving, observing and acting at the same time. This dynamic behaviour is the very aspect that attracts children to the outdoor environment. The richest contexts are linked to nature, so such things as mud and earth, winter holes, leaves, transparency, slope and gradients all repeatedly feature in our work in nature kindergartens. They reflect the motivation of children and the skill of the adults to create cross-references to the curriculum documents that seek to support work with children.

Any child will explore these open contexts. Schemas of repeatable divergent behaviours for the youngest children seem to be enabled to a greater degree than in convergent or structured spaces, but the concept of the schema, such as transporting, will be within the material interest of mud and earth. As the children mature, their schemas may move forward and combine, but the material context of the earth moves through an epistemic development to one of deeply understanding the material. This in turn leads to manipulation in order to sculpt and form. The context still has relevance to 5–7-year-olds as the creation of paint, ochre from the

Image 6.1   Deeply understanding the material

earth and application techniques all become about a more rigorous, detailed focus into the earth as a material.

In terms of children's play, the concept of affordance relates to what play possibilities are *afforded* by the physical environment. If the physical environment is over-designed and organised, it limits the very play it is trying to encourage.

Children play in response to both the objective and subjective qualities of an environment. Affordances are highly dynamic, with different features, elements and materials affording different play experiences for different individuals on different occasions. The number of affordances increases with the complexity of the environment. As highly complex environments, natural spaces provide limitless play affordances; the potential of the space matched by the inventiveness of the playing child. Through manipulating and changing more open-ended contexts and flexible environments through their play, children detect new affordances.

Principles into practice: what does this look like in practice?

Trees are a good example for us to explore across the age group of all the children in a setting. They have natural features that offer a large number of potential play affordances which in turn offer great provocations for talk.

Trees can be climbed and hidden behind; they can become forts or bases; with their surrounding vegetation and roots, they become dens and little houses; they provide

Image 6.2   Trees provide a backdrop for imagination

shelter, landmarks and privacy; fallen, they become part of an obstacle course or material for den-building; near them you find birds, little animals, conkers, fallen leaves, mud, fir cones and winged seeds; they provide a suitable backdrop for every conceivable game of the imagination (Ward, 1988).

Their place as a context is intertwined within their very play affordance. Let us take the experience of enclosure or den-building. A baby lying under the shade of the tree is in essence 'enclosed', stimulated by the light and movement. The tree as a place of context for experience offers many opportunities to be nurtured through nature. Den-building for a two-year-old is about thinking you are hidden when you cannot see the other person. For a four-year-old the den has become developed using the framing of the tree, the loose materials it offers to create features such as doorbells, window openings, bed areas and roof features such as chimneys. The complexity of thinking then moves into the use of tools and materials to develop and extend the concept of a den. Draft designs, a wider experience and knowledge of the types of dens and tree houses that could be built, use of tools and equipment such as saws, drills and measures, all deepen the learning and support children to create individual or small-group designs to keep the open-ended nature of the context.

The context of a tree also affords the learner an opportunity to talk about and consider the emotional aspects of their learning. Trees create shelter and privacy that are root experiences for all children, especially when the children are outside all year round. The seasonal variation offers more than printing with leaves. The youngest children feel the world through all their senses, so changing temperatures are good and should be experienced, through to the ground temperature and the

Image 6.3   Opportunity for being together

changing effects on leaves. Those settings running Forest School or who are moving towards a Nature Kindergarten will know that the context of a wood, a place of silence, has an emotive affect on the group; children and adults alike. In smaller spaces with a tree, or perhaps tree tubs, the context offers the opportunity to talk about how the presence of trees makes you feel, how we nurture and care for seedlings on a day-to-day basis, possibly leading to the design and building of supports, labels, information cards or 'This is my life' books.

Any natural environments containing many different species will extend the affordances of that space. For example, different trees drop their leaves at different times, produce different types of fruits and seeds, and their roots, trunks and branches grow in different ways. The bark and the very essence of trees are so very different. I am reminded of a little boy of three years old, who told me that every tree has a different song. What he had discovered was that his stick created a new sound according to the tree species, its size and age (growth rate). He had not yet acquired the language structure that would explain the different growth rates of species and the effect of climate or that the xylem and phloem inside the tree were acting as resonance tubes, but he did intuitively understand that they were all different because of what lay inside.

The tree features highly in terms of community: the marking of 'place' in public spaces; the meeting point in rural villages; the rite of passage for many adventurous children; the source of materials used for social play such as conkers and ash keys; the shade for picnics in the park. Trees are respected by many cultures and have

Image 6.4   Music on the tree

interdependence with the people that live near them for social connection, but also for herbal remedies, fire wood and sometimes spiritual connection. In some western cultures this has been lost; however, it has been interesting to see children, families and settings and their community coming together with a joint connection to plant trees in outdoor areas, or to recover small areas of community woodland to offer children the opportunity to 'be' in the woods. Perhaps this is because adults do understand the need for a connection to open contexts and the right to play in nature.

Moving forwards

 Things to think about and do

- How can adults create time and space for open-ended investigations about small contexts to support deep-level involvement?

- Discuss the idea of 'play affordance' and how this thinking can enrich your outdoor play provision.

- Create nature spaces with loose materials to act as provocations for creative thinking.

- Explore the consultative strategies you have to find out what purposeful contexts are really of interest to children.

- Create opportunities to record talk through using Flip Mino™ cameras or similar, so that children's voices and motivations are heard throughout the planning procedure.

- Create a landscape area that is naturalistic, reducing the man-made plastic resources inside and outside for the younger children.

⚙️ Key messages

- Through outdoor play, young children can learn the skills of social interaction and friendship, care for living things and their environment, be curious and fascinated, feel awe, wonder and joy and become 'lost in the experience'.

- Children relating to the outside environment can satisfy their deep urge to explore, experiment and understand and become aware of their community and locality, thus developing a sense of connection to the physical, natural and human world.

Further reading and resources 📖

Chawla, L. (2002) 'Spots of time: manifold ways of being in nature in childhood', in P. Kahn and S. Kellert (eds), *Children and Nature*. Cambridge, MA: MIT Press.

Warden, C. (2010) *Nature Kindergartens*. Auchterarder: Mindstretchers.

Warden, C. (2010) *Journeys into Nature*. Auchterarder: Mindstretchers.

24

Classroom Strategies to Develop Talk

Smith, J.

Chapter objectives

By the end of this chapter you will have considered:

- **how to encourage productive talk in your classroom through the principles of dialogic teaching in group, paired and whole-class talk;**
- **the value of Kagan structures and other approaches to co-operative and collaborative learning;**
- **ways to improve questions and answers in your classroom;**
- **the use of Bloom's Taxonomy to encourage high-level thinking;**
- **the use of Drama and role play to stimulate productive talk;**
- **strategies for working with bilingual children.**

This will help you to make progress towards these Professional Standards for the award of QTS:

Q1, Q4, Q5, Q7a, Q8, Q10, Q18, Q19, Q25a, Q25c, Q30

Introduction: improving the balance of talk in the classroom

What does dialogic teaching look like in the classroom?

You will remember that Chapter 3 ended with an introduction to the powerful notion of dialogic teaching, an approach to classroom talk currently strongly advocated by many educationalists, notably Robin Alexander (2008). Dialogic teaching is a pedagogy which aims to help teachers provide more opportunities for high-quality talk in their classrooms by improving the balance of strategies that teachers use. It offers you the opportunity to create sound foundations in your classroom practice upon which a range of other good practices can be overlaid. Alexander suggests that, as we look at the approaches to talk which teachers adopt, we should look out for five key features which collectively mark out a particular style as dialogic teaching. He says that:

> *[i]n a nutshell ... dialogic teaching is:*
> - collective: *teachers and children address learning tasks together, whether as a group or as a class, rather than in isolation;*
> - reciprocal: *teachers and children listen to each other, share ideas and consider alternative viewpoints;*
> - supportive: *children articulate their ideas freely, without fear of embarrassment over 'wrong' answers; and they help each other to reach common understandings;*
> - cumulative: *teachers and children build on their own and each other's ideas and chain them into coherent lines of thinking and enquiry;*
> - purposeful: *teachers plan and facilitate dialogic teaching with particular educational goals in view.*
>
> (Alexander, 2008, p28)

You should notice that Alexander's criteria relate as much to teacher attitude and classroom ethos as they do to teaching styles. He is not suggesting that there is only one model of talk which would satisfy these criteria and observes that skilful teachers develop a repertoire of strategies which they can select from in the different circumstances they find themselves. Based on extensive international studies in classrooms, Alexander identifies the following five strategies (Alexander, 2008).

Five classroom strategies

In Chapter 3 we described the commonly observed exchange of questions and answers, such as the routine sometimes described as the IRF (see page 29). This strategy is the first identified by Alexander and is known as *recitation*. A second familiar routine is an approach described by Alexander and others as *rote*. This is the kind of teaching that might occur during a maths lesson, for example, when the teacher wishes the children to practise a number table. The third strategy which is commonly found in classrooms is *instruction* or *exposition*. There are many situations in which this approach might be in evidence, such as during lessons in art, PE or science, when the teacher is guiding children towards a new skill.

Even though the first three strategies described provide fewer rich opportunities for the development of children's talk than other approaches might, all three have their place in the good teacher's repertoire. What is vitally important if you wish to improve your teaching, however, is to make sure that the fourth and fifth of the strategies Alexander has observed – *dialogue* and *discussion* – are integral parts of your teaching. These, Alexander suggests, are the strategies most likely to be missing in the British primary classroom. There is some overlap between these last two approaches in that both describe situations in which children's contributions are built upon to develop constructive thinking. We will deal here with dialogue in relation to whole-class teaching and with discussion in relation to groups later in this chapter.

PRACTICAL TASK PRACTICAL TASK **PRACTICAL TASK** PRACTICAL TASK **PRACTICAL TASK**

The purpose of this exercise is for you to audit your current approach in order to evaluate the opportunities which children currently have to engage in talk during the whole-class periods in your teaching. This is, of course, hard to do and your memory is likely to give an incomplete picture. You should therefore ask a colleague with whom you have a good working relationship to observe you teaching a lesson and feed back to you honestly, using the following questions as a guide.

- Roughly what was the balance of questions asked by you and by the children?
- Were the children's questions (if there were any) about significant content issues or were they mostly procedural (about the correct layout of their work, for example)?
- Did all of your questions require simple recall of facts or did some of them require more considered answers?
- Did you allow much thinking time before children answered?
- Were there long periods when you were speaking without interruption, periods which sounded like monologues?

What did this analysis reveal? You may have been pleased by the results or you may have discovered that you dominated the classroom exchanges and offered only restricted opportunities for children to contribute. Over the next few pages we will consider a few strategies which should help you to adjust this balance.

Better questions

You have probably recognised already that questions are vitally important for teachers. Many professionals use questions but they do not all use them in the same way. Consider the different ways that these three professionals would use questions in their work:

- a barrister in a court of law;
- a doctor in the surgery;
- a teacher in the classroom.

Let us first consider the barrister and the doctor. While the doctor uses questions to assist in diagnosis ('How long have you had these pains?'), a barrister uses questions to establish the truth – or, perhaps more accurately, the barrister's preferred version of the truth – for the benefit of the jury ('How was the defendant behaving when you entered the room?'). For obvious reasons, the barrister can encounter considerable reluctance to answer questions, whereas truthfulness is assumed in the doctor's surgery. (There are exceptions to this, of course, such as the responses which might be given to the doctor's question 'How much do you drink?') The doctor's questions are genuine searches for information, whereas, in general, the barrister is already aware of the answer which a witness is likely to give but wishes this answer to be publicly stated.

Generally, the teacher, like the doctor, does not know the answer that will be given to a question although, like the doctor, professional expertise allows the teacher to anticipate a range of potential answers that children may give and the clues these answers will give about their understanding. The teacher will also ask questions in order to encourage children to participate actively in the lesson. Clearly, the type of question asked affects the answers which can be given. An important distinction which you have probably come across before is between open questions and closed questions. Open questions allow for a range of answers, like this one:

> Question A: How do you think the main character felt when his mother was taken prisoner?

Closed questions, on the other hand, invite a much narrower range of answers, often only one, as in this question:

> Question B: What is five times three?

The distinction between open and closed questions is more complex than it seems at first sight, however. There are questions which, although linguistically closed, do in fact invite higher-level thinking and are therefore equivalent to open questions, for example 'Should people eat meat?'. A good indicator of such a question is that it often leads to an initial response like 'That would depend...'. It should be apparent, though, that open questions like Question A generally demand a higher level of thinking than closed questions like Question B and you might therefore imagine that you should only ask questions of this kind. The evidence from research, however, challenges this common-sense assumption. Askew and Wiliam analysed a range of classroom research (Askew and Wiliam,1995) from a maths teaching perspective (though these findings seem generalisable across the curriculum) and they identified a number of points which you should bear in mind when you are considering your use of questions.

- A blend of higher-level and lower-level questions is generally better than just asking questions of the same type. Lower-level questions can test children's recall while higher-level questions can test their understanding.
- Adjusting the length of time you pause before taking an answer, something referred to as 'wait time' or 'thinking time' (the second term is used in this book), can have very significant effects on the quality of responses to a question and can allow more children to participate. Research suggests that most teachers pause for less than one second before taking an answer. Extending thinking time to just three seconds, after asking a question which requires high-order thinking, can make a significant difference but you should avoid leaving such a pause after every question as this can actually *decrease* engagement.
- Posing a question as a statement can be a very useful strategy. In a maths lesson for example, rather than asking a question like 'Can you have two rectangles with different areas but with the same perimeter?' you might say, 'A child in another class said that you couldn't have two rectangles that had the same perimeter but different areas. Talk to your partner and decide whether you agree with her.'

(Summarised from Askew and Wiliam, 1995)

At an even more fundamental level, if you would like your teaching to move closer to Alexander's picture of dialogic teaching, you should consider the hidden assumptions in your class about who can pose questions, answers and other contributions. Mercer and Dawes suggest that the implicit ground rules which often exist in classrooms include the following.

- *Only a teacher can nominate who should speak.*
- *Only a teacher may ask a question without seeking permission.*
- *Only a teacher can evaluate a comment made by a participant.*
- *Children should try to provide answers to teachers' questions which are as relevant and brief as possible.*
- *Children should not speak freely when a teacher asks a question but should raise their hands and wait to be nominated.*

Children who call out an answer without being asked are breaking a rule, and their contribution may thus be treated as 'invisible' until they have been formally asked to speak.

(Mercer and Dawes, 2008, p58)

Of course Mercer and Dawes are not suggesting that teachers set out to create this set of rules. As you have probably realised, however, the processes by which classroom ethos and teacher expectations are created are subtle and you should always be alert to the conditions which may have evolved in your classroom without your being aware of them. Working to change such norms within classrooms is a central part of what Alexander and others are arguing for when they advocate dialogic teaching.

Improving answers

We will turn our attention now from questions to answers. Although you can never control children's answers to your questions, you can do a lot to ensure that these are of as high a quality as possible. As well as considering the hidden norms and expectations in your classroom, as you were advised to do in the previous section, you should think about the ways in which children are given opportunities to answer. We have already noted the impact that adjusting thinking time can have but the way in which you accept answers may be more patterned than you think. The default strategy for most teachers is to encourage children to raise their hands when bidding to answer. This strategy has its place but it has limitations too. Without realising it, you may be inviting more responses from girls than boys (or vice versa) or from those children you perceive to be more able or more confident. The 'hands-up' strategy also prevents you from gaining a picture of the answers that are not selected. There are many alternatives which you should consider, including the following, and a mixture of strategies is likely to be best.

1. Use of small whiteboards and pens so that children's answers and other exploratory ideas can be written, displayed and then erased. (Some schools have technology such as voting pods or tablets linked to an interactive whiteboard which achieve similar results.) 'Show-me' techniques such as these have become particularly popular in maths lessons in recent years, some examples from that curriculum area being place-value cards, number fans, number operation cards and so on. Equivalents can be used in other curriculum areas too. You might, for example, give children cards marked from A to D for multiple choice responses to a particular set of questions, problems or challenges. These techniques have the advantage of letting you know what a range of children are thinking, rather than just the child who is selected to answer in the 'hands-up' system.
2. Writing every child's name on a card and drawing out a name at random when an answer is needed. This technique has the advantage that children's turns all come around periodically. You can increase the likelihood of this by not replacing names in the pack once drawn out. If you do this too often, though, you may lose the attention of the earliest children to be picked.
3. Making fun selections by saying something like: 'I'll take an answer from someone... whose birthday is in June/who supports Football Club X/whose first initial is between A and G, etc'. You need to know your class well before adopting this third approach and you should take care that criteria are not problematic or unduly sensitive but, like 2. above, it will allow you to randomise the responses you select.

REFLECTIVE TASK

Think about your response to children's answers. Does your current teaching style match any of the portraits below?

Teacher A is very keen to hear a particular answer to each of his questions. He is determined not to allow his lesson to be thrown off course by answers which will divert the class from the direction he has set. He dismisses answers which are not the ones he is looking for with responses like 'No, that's not it' or 'Anyone else?'

Teacher B takes up and pursues most of the answers her children offer and she takes pride in how much she values their contributions. There is a lack of direction in her lessons as she zig-zags her way through a series of disconnected responses.

Teacher C is complimentary in the extreme and praises every response a child gives with words like 'Wonderful!' and 'Excellent!'

Did you recognise any of your own classroom habits as you considered these portraits? They are a little caricatured but the features highlighted are common and demonstrate that there are a variety of ways in which this aspect of class management can be mishandled.

So what are the problems with each of these styles? You probably recognised immediately that Teacher A has too narrow a view about the sorts of answers he should allow. He pays no respect to children's answers unless they are in his script and the children will quickly become disaffected in his lessons. Questions in Teacher A's class are rather formulaic and his children are unlikely to feel that they are taking part in a dialogue during his lessons. The problems with the styles of Teacher B and Teacher C are harder to spot since both are clearly much keener to recognise and value the responses their children give and their styles therefore seem to embody some of the core values of dialogic teaching. Unfortunately these good intentions are insufficient on their own and the children in both of these classes are likely to feel frustrated (in Teacher B's class) by the lack of direction or patronised (in Teacher C's class) by praise which is given so indiscriminately that it ceases to have value.

Let us turn these observations into advice for you in your classroom.

- You should of course allow and encourage children's responses and recognise that many of them will be completely unexpected. (It is often useful to remind yourself that they have not read your lesson plan.) We can never predict with certainty the responses of any group of children or adults and sometimes an 'off-the-wall' comment or answer can bring a class to life, if handled appropriately.
- Remember, though, that the responsibility for steering the dialogue in the lesson is largely yours. Children cannot be expected to keep time or to keep their contributions moving in the direction that you have planned. Teacher A was so keen to maintain this power that he did not allow any response that he had not anticipated. Teacher B, though, allows so many responses to be aired and followed that she has effectively sacrificed any hope of keeping the lesson moving in a satisfactory direction. Although good communication in a classroom can feel like a conversation, a lesson as a whole is very different from an everyday conversation in which the participants can negotiate the direction from moment to moment. You will therefore need to decide which avenues suggested by children can be explored and which should be avoided, at least during the lesson in which they arise. Deal with the latter sensitively, 'That's an interesting point, Jack, and perhaps we can come back to it in another lesson. For now, though, I want us to follow up Rashida's point.' In the same way that you should respect children's contributions to the lesson, they should, and generally will, respect yours which, despite everything that has been said here about power-sharing, includes your right as the teacher to decide on the pace and direction of the lesson.
- Children's responses should always be treated with courtesy and respect and with an appropriate level of appreciation. It is impossible to specify what 'appropriate' will look like in every situation and you must develop your own style in the particular contexts in which you work. Some general guidance may be useful though. All children need praise and encouragement and, sadly, some do not get enough of these, either outside or inside school, but it is easy for teachers to overcompensate for this and hence to devalue the currency of their praise. Children are astute judges of sincerity. Try to avoid the extremes of either never praising or over-praising so that children can come to trust you, to recognise that you value what they say and to know that when you praise their efforts, you really mean it. A further point to make here is that you can show that you like and value children's company in the classroom in many ways. As well as praising them for the quality of their work, remember that this should not be judged against a universal standard. A creditworthy standard of work by one of your children, for example, might be a mediocre or half-hearted standard for another. Knowing your children and their capabilities is crucial since this allows you to give realistic feedback which should sometimes, though not always, include praise. You should also try to comment favourably upon your children's attitudes to their work and to the care and consideration they show towards others in the class and school community.

As we move towards the conclusion of this section, remember what was said at the beginning of this chapter about the mixture of styles that comprise dialogic teaching. The message here is a subtle one. There is a place for authoritative, teacher-directed communication alongside more open dialogue with children. (Notice the difference between the words 'authoritative' and 'authoritarian'.) Phil Scott (2008) describes an extremely useful way of looking at this in the context of science lessons. Scott suggests that communication can be analysed on two different dimensions. One dimension specifies whether the communication is *dialogic* or *authoritative* while the other specifies whether it is *interactive* or *non-interactive*. We might easily imagine that an approach that was authoritative and non-interactive would be a poor teaching style and one that ran counter to the principles of dialogic teaching but this would be a mistake. Scott's analysis reminds us that we should choose the style we use according to the needs of the children in that situation. In a science lesson there will certainly be the need for children to have the chance to explore their current ideas and to exchange these freely. There will also be the need, however, for the teacher to introduce a more expert interpretation of the situation to help the children move on in their learning. (Remember the ideas of Vygotsky and others which were considered in Chapter 3.) Scott gives the example of how *everyday* and *scientific* views differ when children consider the topic of *forces*. If the children had no input other than their own ideas they would struggle to discover the science that underlies apparently straightforward phenomena like how a bottle stays on a shelf or why a ball falls to the ground. The skill of the successful teacher lies in scaffolding children's learning and, in the case of a science lesson, providing bridges for them to move from everyday to scientific understanding (Scott, 2008). Similar needs occur elsewhere in the curriculum.

Something should be said here about listening, the mirror of talk. Clearly, for talk to be effective, there is a need for good listening and educationalists often refer to 'listening skills'. However, as with talking skills and thinking skills, it is not quite as clear what we mean by this as the words might suggest. This issue was raised in Chapter 2 and, while the use of the word skill when applied to talking, thinking, listening and so on does seem entirely legitimate, caution about these matters is never a bad thing and leads us towards greater clarity. We might, then, be specifying the behaviours that a good listener displays when we refer to listening skills, but we are all familiar with situations where this behaviour has become separated from what we understand by listening. Children who simulate good listening as a cover for a lack of attention to the speaker – a phenomenon to be found in every classroom at one time or another – for example, or, by contrast, children who stare at a television screen for the whole time that they are being spoken to but who can afterwards recount every word that has been said to them. Clearly, therefore, we do not want the surface appearances of listening on their own. Although behaviour can be a useful cue, therefore, we need to direct children's attention to the inner processes that underlie this behaviour, processes which involve thinking.

A useful distinction, which most children can eventually appreciate, is between simply hearing and listening. As I write these words, I can hear traffic and a power tool somewhere near my house. Occasionally an aircraft passes overhead. It is only when I consciously shift my attention to these sounds and listen actively to them, though, that they cease to be sounds that I hear, almost subconsciously, and become the objects of my listening. There are some excellent materials by Mercer, Dawes and Wegerif which can be used to help children develop skills in these areas (Mercer *et al.*, 2004). Listening, then, like looking (which pairs with seeing in a similar way to listening/hearing), is a matter of shifting our attention.

Bloom's taxonomy: a model to develop higher-level thinking

Working on the issues raised so far in this chapter should help you to adjust the conditions for talk in your classroom so that children can participate in a less inhibited way and feel that their contributions are valued. You can then begin to work on the tasks that you set children in order to adjust the cognitive level that these require of them. A very useful model for judging the cognitive level of tasks has been drawn from the work of educational psychologist Benjamin Bloom. Bloom argued many years ago that cognitive tasks like identification and recall were low level by comparison to tasks that required students to demonstrate understanding. Higher still in Bloom's Taxonomy of Educational Objectives were tasks like application and analysis and the highest-level tasks involved synthesis and evaluation. Bloom's Taxonomy is outlined briefly below, with lower-level tasks at the bottom of the list and with some examples to illustrate each of the six major classes. (Many more are given in the original versions of Bloom's work and in the work of subsequent writers using Bloom's Taxonomy.)

- Evaluation: *appraise, compare and contrast, judge, give arguments for and against, assess;*
- Synthesis: *bring ideas together, build upon, reorganise, combine, join up ideas;*
- Analysis: *classify, suggest reasons for, investigate;*
- Application: *use, apply, manipulate, transfer;*
- Comprehension: *understand, interpret, explain, define;*
- Knowledge: *recall, label, identify, name.*

(Based on Bloom, 1956)

PRACTICAL TASK   PRACTICAL TASK   PRACTICAL TASK   PRACTICAL TASK

Make five copies of this list and use one each day for a week while you are in a teaching role. Try each day to identify some examples of questions you have asked or tasks you have set children which encourage thinking at various stages in Bloom's Taxonomy. Do not attempt to cover every possibility and be aware that there has been some dispute over the years about the levels assigned to particular tasks. (To explain something as a teacher, for example, might be regarded as a higher-order task than Bloom's Taxonomy suggests.) Try to ensure, though, that there are some opportunities for children to develop higher-level cognitive skills as well as those from lower in the list. Do you notice a tendency to ask mainly recall questions or do some tasks require evaluation or synthesis, for example? You will have to adapt this exercise to suit the situation you are in, taking account of the age of the children you are working with, but you should find that this reflection sharpens up your interactions with children and makes you more aware of opportunities that exist to raise the cognitive level of both planned and impromptu activities and interactions in your classroom. Hopefully, your lists showed more evidence of higher-order thinking as the week progressed.

Developing talk in groups

As we noted in Chapter 3, classroom researchers have known for some time that simply putting children into groups does not ensure that they will work as groups. Fortunately, however, there are approaches you can adopt which can lead to children working collaboratively and co-operatively. Valerie Coultas (2007) describes a wide range of approaches to oracy which can be used in (as her title puts it) *challenging classrooms* and across every school age range. She describes the challenge posed by group work extremely well.

> *Group work can be a frightening concept for some teachers. They may see it as an opportunity for pupils to get out of control, talk off task and generally muck about. If the group task does not really require group work this can be the result. The key test for a group task is that the group has to cooperate: the task* must *involve a group decision, negotiation or consensus of some kind, and have a real purpose.*
>
> (Coultas, 2007, p 53; author's emphasis)

At this point I should make an important point about some of the classroom approaches which we will consider in the chapters to come. To understand any of these approaches thoroughly and fully integrate them into your classroom teaching, you should attempt to obtain some further training by specialists in this area, since a book like this one can only offer a brief introduction. If attending training is not a practical option for you, you should read as many printed and online resources as you can, again taking care to select reputable sources. At the end of this chapter and the ones that follow, some links will be offered so that you can follow up the approaches which most appeal to you at present. Having said all of this, the introduction that follows should give you a good idea of what these approaches entail and a few practical ways that they can help you in the development of talk and co-operative learning in your classroom.

Collaborative learning

In Chapter 3 we saw how the *Bullock Report* (DES, 1975) had helped teachers recognise that oracy was inextricably linked to literacy – one could not develop without the other. From that time onward, approaches have been developed which have treated language development holistically. Some good examples are those which can be used in the teaching of reading and these have been used effectively in classrooms in the decades since Bullock. Some examples are cloze, sequencing and group prediction techniques which require children to work together in pairs or groups to solve a problem involving text which is in some way incomplete. Sequencing and group prediction require children to reassemble sentences from a text into the correct sequence (sequencing) or to predict what will happen next as short extracts from a story are presented to them (group prediction). You may not have come across the word 'cloze' before but this is another common and extremely useful technique involving the systematic omission of words from a text. Here is an example of a cloze text.

> Darren was unhappy that morning. It was his birthday and he had already had his presents from his mum and his sister but there was no sign of a present from his dad. Not even a card. As he got ready for school he looked down the ____ for the postman. All he could see though ____ a few cars, one or two tired-looking people ____ off to work and the bus that chugged its way through the ____. Then, as he was eating his cereal in front of the ____, Darren heard the click of the gate and the ____ of heavy footsteps as the postman came along the ____. After a few moments he heard the sound of mail being stuffed ____ the letter-box and the snapping shut of the flap. ____ was almost quick enough to catch the mail before it ____ the floor and he flicked through the envelopes ____. A gas bill, a couple of those glossy leaflets ____ bank and phone companies sent and a ____ for his mum wrapped in plastic. He threw them ____the mat and walked sadly away.

As you can see, words have been omitted and the children's task is to decide on words which would be suitable to fill the gaps. The first couple of sentences are left intact to allow children to get a sense of what the passage is about and then words are deleted regularly. In this case the gaps are about every ten words but this pattern has been modified a little to allow a variety of words to be omitted. The intervals between gaps can be adjusted, as can the reading level required and the difficulty of the text in terms of style and subject matter. (David Wray's book in the *Learning Matters* series (Wray, 2006) will tell you more about these approaches.)

There are two important points which should be made about these kinds of approaches. The first is that the process is far more important than the product, a distinction made in Chapter 2. You should therefore be much happier with a well-argued case for a word which is not the missing word from the original text than with a quickly decided correct answer. In the example above, children might quite justifiably argue for different words to describe how Darren flicked through the envelopes: eagerly perhaps (which was the word in the original text) or anxiously, even angrily. (Notice that children will probably bring their own emotional experiences and reactions to the discussion.) The value of the exercise lies entirely in the process of articulating reasons why some words would fit while others would not. Notice, too, the gains in terms of children's grammatical understanding. The recognition that an adverb is required to fill this gap is likely to emerge much more powerfully through such discussion than it might from an exercise in a grammar lesson which offered only a decontextualised definition.

The second point to be made is that these techniques involve children in talking and thinking through discussion and such discussion is one of the elements which you need to develop in order to make your teaching more dialogic. If activities such as these are successful, children will have collaborated with one another in the process of completing them. It is possible for children to attempt such activities alone and at times this will be appropriate. If they are never offered as pair or group activities, though, then valuable opportunities for collaborative learning will be lost. For further ideas and resources you should visit the Collaborative Learning Project website (see page 68). This project is an extremely useful point of contact for any teachers wishing to pursue this kind of work. Set up by English teaching specialists with a commitment to the development of oracy, the project website contains a great deal of useful information and downloadable resources relating to various age groups and curriculum areas and, at the time of writing, access to these resources is free of charge.

Kagan structures

During the 1970s, an American educationalist named Spencer Kagan recognised the difficulty that researchers have consistently found with group work, the difficulty which Valerie Coultas described very well in the quotation on page 60. Kagan decided that children needed structures to encourage them to co-operate. The development of these 'Kagan structures', as they are known, has become a worldwide educational project and significant numbers of schools in this country now adopt these approaches. Kagan structures are all designed to create the conditions which will encourage co-operative learning and they incorporate four principles which Kagan describes as: *Positive Interdependence*, *Individual Accountability*, *Equal Participation* and *Simultaneous Interaction* (Kagan, 1994). (You might usefully consider whether authors are likely to mean the same thing, or something slightly different, when they refer to 'co-operative' as opposed to 'collaborative' learning.)

Kagan structures are content-free and can be used with the whole class, pairs (we will look at some examples of these later) or groups and, when working in groups, Kagan recommends that, where possible, four children should work together. (When class teachers or whole schools follow Kagan structures in a comprehensive way they will usually adopt his recommendations about the make-up of these groups, which are carefully constructed to mix abilities. There is insufficient space here to explore the rationale for this but it is worth noting the importance attached to inclusion in the Kagan approach.)

A useful example of a Kagan structure for use with groups is called *Numbered Heads Together*. A group talks about a particular problem, question or task and feeds back its collective response to the rest of the class. Here, however, a very useful device is used to maximise the chances of interdependence and accountability among group members. The device is to ask group members to number themselves from 1 to 4 and then a child is selected to feed back to the larger group, using a randomly generated number (using a spinner, adjusted die or computer program, for example). Returning to Kagan's principles, every child remains accountable, all participate equally and there is an interdependence among all of the group members and among the groups in the class. What this device counters is the tendency for some group members to sit back and disengage from the group activity, through shyness or apathy, for example, and for others to push themselves forward or to be selected by the teacher disproportionately often (as we considered earlier in this chapter). If children know that they may have to feed back on behalf of the group, their involvement in the group task is likely to be high: there is therefore a much greater chance of genuinely co-operative learning. Try this approach as an alternative to self-selected spokespersons in groups and you should see a noticeable difference in engagement. We will return to Kagan structures later in this chapter and in Chapter 8.

CLASSROOM STORY

A highly experienced teacher has seen very significant improvements in her teaching and her children's learning since she began to use Kagan approaches. The content-free nature of Kagan structures allows her to use them across the curriculum and in helping her mixed-ability groups to build a sense of identity and belonging. She has also found that putting children into groups of four facilitates talk since (using Kagan terminology) the children can talk to their *shoulder partners* (the child beside them) or their *face partners* (the child opposite).

Other group approaches

There are a wide range of other techniques and approaches to group work which you might also consider. Making radio programmes (as mentioned in Chapter 3 and clearly on a non-professional scale) can be a useful way of helping children to focus upon an audience (this could be another class or year group) and making a very short news, documentary or entertainment programme for them. Television programmes offer similar opportunities. If circumstances require a more easily managed activity, however, the larger scale of television programmes can, at times, be harder to handle and the sound-only nature of the radio broadcast creates more of a focus on talk.

A range of useful techniques are gathered together in the Primary National Strategies materials *Speaking, Listening, Learning: working with children in Key Stages 1 and 2* (see page 69 for the website address from which you can download these materials). Two very useful examples follow.

Jigsaw games

These activities involve children rotating around the classroom as experts from their original groups and sharing their expertise with other groups, and generally rejoining the original groups at the end. (Valerie Coultas (2007) describes this activity). So, for example, five or six groups at the beginning of this activity might each focus on one character from a story and become the 'experts' about this character. Then, through a series of group reorganisations, they share their expertise with others in order to complete a task which requires all of this expertise. (Many schools use a related, drama-based approach called *The mantle of the expert:* see page 69 for website details.)

Statements game

This activity requires children to rank a set of statements in order of importance and to place them on a triangle or diamond as shown below. The more important the statement is judged to be, the closer to the apex of the triangle or diamond it will be placed. An example might be a set of statements giving reasons for having laws.

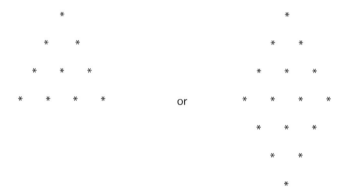

As with any activity of this kind, a focus on the justification of children's choices, in the debriefing session, is likely to improve the level of their thinking. Debriefing is another example of metacognition.

PRACTICAL TASK   PRACTICAL TASK   PRACTICAL TASK   PRACTICAL TASK

The following activity will allow you to investigate the valuable resources on the Collaborative Learning Project website (see page 68 for web address) and to practise using the Kagan structure Numbered Heads Together. It will also allow you to see whether your interactions with your class have improved since the analysis you made at the beginning of this chapter.

Go onto the Collaborative Learning Project website and find a group activity to suit the age group of a class you are working with. Download the relevant resources and plan a lesson or a series of lessons in which to embed the activity. As an example you can think about how you could use the activity connected to T S Eliot's poem 'Macavity – the Mystery Cat', an activity which is probably most suitable for children aged seven or eight. Use the Kagan technique of Numbered Heads Together to choose a spokesperson from each group to justify their reasons for their decisions. (Tip: if you use a spinner or other device to choose a number, do this each time a group reports back not just once at the beginning.)

Use this example as a guide to structure the activity you use. There are many examples so choose one you feel comfortable with. Ask the children to undertake these activities in groups of four (clearly you will need to have one or two groups of three or five unless your class size is a multiple of four).

Note how the children responded to these activities. Did all of them participate at every stage? Was there evidence of higher-order thinking in the children's contributions? (When evaluating this, think of words from Bloom's Taxonomy like: *compare and contrast, judge, give arguments for and against; bring ideas together, build upon, reorganise*.)

Working in pairs

Pairs are very powerful units for talking and thinking. They offer children the security of talking time with just one other person, rather than the more daunting challenge (for many children) of speaking aloud in a group or in the whole class. They also offer a great deal of time for each child because of what Kagan calls *Equal Participation* and *Simultaneous Interaction*. These are very important points to recognise. Imagine a two-minute section of your lesson in which (rather unusually) two children talked, one after the other, for a minute each. Two children out of perhaps thirty would have had this opportunity. Now imagine the situation restructured so that the children worked in pairs. Using a Kagan structure called a *Timed Pair Share* (Kagan, 1994 and 2009), each child could have one minute of speaking time and one minute of listening time and at the end of two minutes all thirty children would have had these opportunities, rather than just two.

Asking children to work in pairs in this way is not just a Kagan approach but is now common practice in many classrooms. A term that you will often hear is 'talk partners' (although other phrases are in use) and you may have already encountered this arrangement in a classroom you have worked in. It is an approach that can be used in many curriculum areas. Kagan structures can be used to make these paired sessions more productive. For example, another Kagan structure for use with pairs is the *Rally Robin* (Kagan, 1994). 'Robin' in Kagan terminology indicates a talking activity (think of a chattering robin) and 'Rally' here conjures up the image of a rally in tennis when the ball rapidly passes from one participant to the other. In a Timed Pair Share, each participant has a designated time, say a minute, to talk without interruption and this will be appropriate when lengthy reflection or analysis is required (for example, 'In the Timed Pair Share talk to your partner, for one minute each, about the things that you learned during our visit to the old mill yesterday.') A Rally Robin is better suited to quick exchanges of information (for example, 'With your partner in this Rally Robin, try to think of as many ways that we use plastic as you can. You have one minute.') Spencer Kagan describes the ways in which the Rally Robin structure can be used with different age groups.

> *Younger students might do a RallyRobin to name colors or to create or devise possible alternative endings to a story. Older students might RallyRobin prime numbers, inert elements, possible causes or consequences of an historical event, or literary techniques. Because, like all Kagan Structures, RallyRobin is content free, it is used at all grades with a very wide range of academic content.*
>
> (Kagan, 2009, p3)

Pairs can be joined together to form groups of various sizes and this can offer children the opportunity to pool the information they have acquired at each stage of an activity, with further opportunities to negotiate the nature of this information and to prioritise its importance. If children are using the Kagan Timed Pair Share or Rally Robin pairings, they could then be combined into groups of four for Numbered Heads Together. The Primary National Strategy materials, mentioned earlier, describe groupings called 'Think-Pair-Share' which work on the same principle and the activity known as 'Snowballing' which progressively combines pairs into fours, eights and so on until the whole class is involved.

You should note that using any of these strategies once only will probably lead to little benefit. Like all of us, children need time to get used to new routines so build them in regularly and monitor the results which, hopefully, will be impressive.

Drama and role play

Drama is a subject which is harder to pigeon-hole in the primary curriculum than, say, science or PE. It is closely associated with English but it can also be used to support learning across the curriculum. Another complication is that the word 'drama' can suggest large-scale productions, either in or out of school, and much smaller, classroom-based activities. The former clearly has a great deal to offer children but it is essentially the latter which we are concerned with here.

There are a wide range of drama and role-play techniques which you can use to develop children's talk. Used regularly and matched to your curricular objectives, these can help children to become more confident and to make increasingly appropriate judgements about the audience for, and the purpose of, such communication. They can also encourage them to use their imaginations to explore issues and themes arising from the subjects and topics they study.

One common and very effective example is a role-play technique called 'hot-seating'. This involves a child, yourself or another adult playing the part of a character who is central to whatever curriculum area you are involved with at the time. It may be a historical or a fictional character, but whoever is playing that character should be able to answer questions plausibly in role. These questions, asked by children in the class, can afford deeper insights into the character's emotions and motivations. Clearly, as in all unscripted drama, the responses will be improvised but you should try to steer both questions and answers to be as evidence-based as possible.

Related to hot-seating is the 'freeze frame' technique which involves groups of children becoming silent and still (as the name of the technique suggests) while representing critical moments in any event – real or fictitious – that your class is studying. Like hot-seating, the freeze frames should be evidence-based. In the debriefing session after these representations, children can explore the inner reality of the event as experienced by the characters they modelled. A variation on freeze framing is to ask for 'photographs' of these events – an old camera can be a very useful prop for you to wield. In the debriefing session, a photograph album or slide show can be shown. It is surprising how much thinking, memory and emotion can be contained kinaesthetically through the use of such techniques. Freeze frames, hot-seating and a range of other approaches of this kind are featured in the Primary National Strategy materials (see page 69).

Teaching bilingual children

Many classrooms include bilingual children who speak English as an Additional Language (EAL) and it is important to consider the special attention to language development which these children need. The Nuffield Languages Inquiry (2000) strongly suggests, however, that we can easily underestimate the language resources which bilingual children and adults possess and we should therefore avoid taking a deficit view of their abilities. A good way of exploring this topic is to consider another important aspect of language use which is its functional nature. Language is often designed to make something happen in the world. A useful term introduced by philosophers some decades ago to describe this is 'speech act' (see, for example, Austin, 1962). In order to understand what is meant by this term, consider the use of the words 'It's cold in here'. While someone might say these words on entering a room simply as a comment on the temperature, they would often be used as an indirect request for someone else to turn up the heating or to close some windows. Similarly, to answer the question 'Have you got the time?' with 'Yes, thanks' would be thought rather cheeky. Words like this are potentially rather ambiguous and confusing unless you are a very competent speaker of English.

A less proficient user of English might understand the literal meaning of words but miss the speaker's real intention in saying them. An important implication of this for the teacher working with bilingual children is to be careful not to use too much idiomatic and indirect language when this might not be understood. Bilingual children can become quite mystified by expressions like 'What are you up to?' or 'What was the writer trying to get across?'. (Indeed, some speakers of English as a first language might find language like this harder to understand than you might imagine.) You should not attempt to simplify your language to the point that all of its richness and word play is lost since, as we have already noted, your language is an important model and reference point for children. You should, however, monitor your use of language and try to make sure that it is intelligible to as many children as possible.

All teachers have to develop the ability to switch registers, or ways of speaking, in order to communicate in particular ways. Think, for example, of the differences in the ways you would speak to your class during a whole-class lesson, to the parent of a child in your class and to a colleague during a coffee break. Having bilingual children in your class can help you to do this as their linguistic needs will often be more acute than those of other children (at least initially) and their understanding of what you say might be more literal than you intend.

Bilingual children's use of English is likely to be different from that of speakers of English as a first language in two ways. The most obvious way is that they may lack some proficiency in English. We have already considered how skilled in English (or any mother tongue) children generally are, even before they reach school. If bilingual children come to this country with little or no English, or come to school having a different mother tongue to English, then they will have a great deal of skill to acquire in English in order to fully access the curriculum and to interact with their peers. The good news is that with appropriate support bilingual children can make remarkably rapid progress.

The second way in which bilingual children's language is likely to differ from that of their peers is through the influence of their mother tongue. There may be subtle difficulties that children experience in English because of the ways that English differs from their mother tongue. One example is that speakers of many languages from India, Pakistan and Bangladesh have difficulty mastering what we term the 'definite article' in English – the word 'the' – since there is no direct equivalent of this grammatical item in many of their mother tongues. It pays class teachers therefore, to have some knowledge of the mother tongues of bilingual learners in their class. Clearly this is likely to be quite limited, especially if there are a range of mother tongues spoken and if your time in the classroom is brief, but some teachers do not even know which mother tongues children in their classes speak and this is clearly an unsatisfactory state of affairs. By contrast, being able to say even the simplest phrase in a child's mother tongue is likely to be much appreciated by the child and by any family members who come to hear of this.

Community languages such as Urdu, Punjabi and other languages introduced to this country as new communities have arrived, often lack the status they deserve in the wider community. Bilingual children themselves can therefore feel that their own languages are in some way inferior to English and other European languages. Children and their families frequently have remarkable multilingual skills which can be unappreciated in school as we have already noted. Try to encourage respect for these accomplishments in your class. Making a positive feature of the enrichment which the mother tongues of bilingual learners and their families bring to your classroom makes a powerful statement of support to children who can easily feel marginalised and who can even fall victim to racism within school. The idea that one particular language is superior to others is a myth which surfaces from time to time and it is important to recognise that there is no linguistic evidence to support such claims.

Other useful strategies that you should consider when teaching bilingual learners include good use of audio-visual aids to support teaching and learning. There should be encouragement for children to contribute orally in the ways suggested in this chapter but without such contributions being forced upon bilingual children (or any children for that matter). An extended silent period, while children soak up the new language around them as they prepare to speak independently, is entirely normal and children should not be hurried into speaking before they are ready as this may jeopardise their long-term development and confidence in using English.

A final point to remember is that it is easy to underestimate bilingual children's ability and the level of work that they may be capable of. Although bilingual children will benefit from the assistance of any specialist EAL teachers and mother tongue speakers who are available, such support is often limited and the class teacher plays a key role. Try to help bilingual children overcome the language barriers they face without removing the cognitive demands in the work you set them. It should be clear from this brief review that good teaching for bilingual children is in many respects the same as good teaching for all children. If you would like more background information on these matters, you might find the work of Jim Cummins useful (for example, Cummins, 2000).

A SUMMARY OF **KEY POINTS**

> **The dialogic teaching approach advocated by Robin Alexander is an extremely useful model if you wish to make your teaching more oracy-based. Alexander suggests that dialogic teaching has five elements. Three of these – recitation, rote and instruction/exposition – are more commonly found than the other two – discussion and dialogue – and so you should work hard to develop this pair in your classroom.**

> The way in which questions and answers are handled in your classroom is crucial. You should work on techniques to improve these and examine the ethos in your classroom about who can contribute and how.

> A range of approaches to collaborative and co-operative work, based on purposeful discussion, have been considered. The Kagan approach offers many useful structures to develop co-operative learning. Focused group work is vital, as is the use of pairs such as talk partners.

> A variety of approaches from drama and role play can enhance your teaching and you should explore these with your class.

> Bilingual learners have particular needs with regard to the development of their oracy skills. A classroom which is well-run for bilingual learners is likely to be a good classroom for all children to learn in.

REFERENCES REFERENCES **REFERENCES** REFERENCES REFERENCES REFERENCES

Alexander, R J (2008) *Towards dialogic teaching*. (4th edition). York: Dialogos.

Askew, M and Wiliam, D (1995) *Recent research in mathematics education 5–16*. London: HMSO/ OFSTED.

Austin, J L (1962) *How to do things with words*. Oxford: Clarendon Press.

Bloom, B S (1956) *Taxonomy of educational objectives. Book 1 Cognitive Domain*. New York: David McKay.

Coultas, V (2007) *Constructive talk in challenging classrooms*. Abingdon: Routledge.

Cummins, J (2000) *Language, power and pedagogy: bilingual children in the crossfire.* Clevedon: Multilingual Matters.

DES (1975) *A language for life*. London: HMSO.

Kagan, S (1994) *Cooperative Learning*. San Clemente, California: Kagan Publishing.

Kagan, S (2009) *The instructional revolution*. Kagan Publishing & Professional Development. 1(800) 933-2667 1(800) 266-7576 Accessible at: www.kaganonline.com/KaganClub/FreeArticles.html

Mercer, N and Dawes, L (2008) 'The value of exploratory talk' In Mercer, N and Hodgkinson, S (eds) *Exploring talk in school*. London: Sage.

Mercer, N, Dawes, L and Wegerif, R (2004) *Thinking together. A programme of activities for developing speaking, listening and thinking skills for children aged 8 to 11*. (2nd edition). Birmingham: Questions Publishing Company.

The Nuffield Languages Inquiry (2000) *Languages: the next generation.* London: The Nuffield Foundation.

Scott, P H (2008) Talking a way to understanding in Science classrooms, in Mercer, N and Hodgkinson, S (eds) *Exploring talk in school*. London: Sage.

Wray, D (2006) *Teaching literacy across the primary curriculum*. Exeter: Learning Matters.

Useful websites

The Collaborative Learning Project at www.collaborativelearning.org contains an extensive range of oracy-based materials which can be downloaded. Strongly linked to the Collaborative Learning Project is the London Association of Teachers of English (LATE) at www.late.org.uk. A very useful site dealing with the teaching of bilingual children is www.naldic.org.uk.

To find out more about the Kagan approach, visit www.kaganonline.com. In this country, the sole source of Kagan accredited training is Teacher to Teacher (UK) Limited and you can access their website at www.t2tuk.co.uk. Another useful site is www.Kagan-UK.co.uk.

You can download the Primary National Strategy materials *Speaking, Listening, Learning: working with children in Key Stage 1 and Key Stage 2* at:
www.nationalstrategies.standards.dcsf.gov.uk/node/84856.

You can find out more about the approach known as *The mantle of the expert* at:
www.mantleoftheexpert.com.

What Makes a Creative Teacher?

Desailly, J.

Learning objectives in this chapter:

To understand the key knowledge, skills and interactions that a teacher needs to teach effectively both creatively and to foster creativity, including:

- To model creative working processes yourself
- To be able to identify creativity in others
- To be able to foster creativity in others
- To be able to encourage creativity in others
- To have and to enhance the personal attributes that enable you to identify, foster and encourage creativity in others
- To identify and foster in yourself the pedagogic skills necessary to identify, foster and encourage creativity in others

Many teachers claim that they themselves are not creative. They sincerely believe this but what they usually mean is that they are not talented in the arts. In the preceding chapters we have seen that to be creative is far wider than having talents and expertise in arts subjects and that creativity is a human characteristic that we all share, although it will manifest itself in different ways in all of us.

The importance of your own creativity

Understanding your own creativity and being prepared to model your own creative working processes with the children is one of the cornerstones of helping them to recognise and make the most of their own creativity.

 Personal thought and reflection

In what ways are you creative? You began this process in Chapter 1. After what you have read so far can you identify more areas in which you could consider yourself to be creative?

Think about:

➤ Tactics in team games: are you a creative playmaker?
➤ Cooking
➤ Designing (invitations, displays, home décor, fashion)
➤ Music (playing or singing yourself but maybe you put together amazing playlists)
➤ Photography
➤ Computer solutions
➤ Finding personal solutions for your own or others' problems
➤ Solving or working on puzzles, logic problems, patterns and sequences
➤ Choosing just the right present for people

This is just the start of the list of possibilities. How many other areas can you identify and how many of them would you place yourself in? You might even want to score yourself on a scale of 0–10 and identify the areas where you consider yourself most or least creative. Are there areas where you have potential but could do more to develop?

Sharing and modelling your own creativity may take many forms. We have already discussed how teachers can 'speak aloud' their thought processes in terms of decision making and assessing alternative courses of action. If you have skills yourself as, for example, an artist, dancer, gymnast or musician then would you be prepared to share that expertise with the children? You might explain and explore the way you work and the choices you take. Why did you decide to take some photographs in black and white rather than colour? What difference did it make? How could you play a piece of music differently? How much scope is there for interpreting a composition in terms of tempo, ornamentation or dynamics? This is closely allied to modelling the learning process yourself.

Guy Claxton comments, 'One of the problems with conventional schooling is that it delivers knowledge to the students after all the interesting learning has taken place, and all the uncertainty, disagreement and trial-and-error has been squeezed out of it' (Claxton 2002: 97). He goes on to suggest that children would learn better if they could see all the first drafts or initial observations that went into the works of art or scientific and mathematical theories they study. Teachers can help here. If you write poetry or songs or stories why not show your class the multiple drafts you generate before you are satisfied? Guy Claxton suggests teachers could set up their own science experiment in the classroom and talk through what they are trying to do. Perhaps you are involved in a mini action-research project, maybe about the children's learning, and could share your thinking and research methods. The possibilities are endless. The process need not take long but making sharing of that type a regular feature of your classroom will really help children to see what a creative person and a successful learner does. You do not have to be an expert in order to do this, in fact it may inhibit children if they are overawed by your prowess. Just showing your interest, enthusiasm and process is enough.

Identifying creativity

The NACCCE report identified three different tasks in teaching for creativity: identifying, encouraging and fostering. As we examine these three elements it is important to apply them to your own creativity as well as to that of the children you teach.

When you tried to identify in the Activity above how you yourself were creative, you began by looking at particular domains such as photography or music for, as we have seen, creativity expresses itself through such domains, you cannot be creative in a vacuum. However, certain personality characteristics have been identified by various research projects which can be seen as characteristic of creative individuals. These are quoted by Anna Craft in her book *Creativity in Schools: Tensions and Dilemmas* (Craft 2005: 56, 57) and are reproduced here:

- achievement within a domain of knowledge
- seeking of order
- curiosity
- assertive, self-sufficient, dominant or even aggressive
- tendency to be less formal, less conventional, to reject repression and to be less inhibited
- tendency to like work, to be self-disciplined and to be persistent
- independence and autonomy

- capacity to be constructively critical
- tendency to be widely informed
- openness to emotions and feelings
- personal judgement influenced by the aesthetic dimension
- capacity to adopt values that fit with the wider environment
- capacity to manifest masculine interests if female and vice versa if male without inhibition
- tendency not to require social interaction
- self-fulfilled and self-realised

The above list was collated by Stein (1974) and the following by Torrance (1965):

- having the courage to hold a strong opinion
- curiosity and search approach
- independent judgement
- intuition
- capacity to become preoccupied with tasks
- unwilling to accept things without being convinced with evidence
- idealistic and visionary
- risk-taking approach

And Anna Craft added her own list:

- goal directedness
- fascination for a task
- orientation toward risk-taking
- preference for asymmetry and complexity
- willingness to ask many (unusual) questions
- capacity to display results and consult other people
- a desire to go beyond the conventional

Obviously a creative individual would not display all the above characteristics and some might seem contradictory, but looking out for these characteristics in others can help you to identify where creativity is manifesting itself. It is also evident that some of the characteristics are those that do not necessarily endear you to others or make you easy to get on with. As teachers we will have to foster the creativity but help individuals to handle their personality traits in socially acceptable ways without stifling their individuality.

Personal thought and reflection

Think about people you know or have known whom you consider to be creative. This might be friends, family, colleagues or children you have taught. Which of the above personality characteristics do they exhibit? Have these characteristics caused them any problems with relationships? If so, was this more likely with peers or with authority? Have these individuals had to make changes to accommodate others or do other people tend to accommodate them?

Teachers need to be able to identify creativity in many different situations. Christopher Bannerman, writing on 'Creativity and wisdom', reminds us that these creative expressions might be 'vibrant and overt, or secret and personal'. They may appear completely unexpectedly. Bannerman cites the example of 'individuals experiencing a sudden unleashing of creative energies, which appeared to be entirely hidden previously, through contact with a new context or discipline' (Bannerman 2008: 140). Most, if not all, teachers will have recognised this phenomenon. It most often happens when a child is working with an outside agency visiting the school or a learning experience outside the classroom. The unusual working methods, different relationships with the teacher/facilitator and different setting seem to stimulate responses in some children which were unexpected and surprising. When this happens and the teacher notices the engagement then they can find ways to encourage and foster that spark of creativity in the future.

Encouraging and fostering creativity

For a teacher in regular contact with their class and with more established and necessary practices and procedures it can be harder to provide experiences that will allow for expressions of creativity to be stimulated than for an outside facilitator. The creative teacher needs to steer a course of balance through their days and weeks. They will need to balance structure and security in regular classroom procedures with innovation and flexibility. This can be difficult to achieve, particularly in the early stages of a teaching career, and teachers should give themselves space and time to develop the skills and confidence they will need and to develop within the children they teach the skills and confidence to work in this way. It should be a slow and steady process for all parties.

Classroom idea

To help children feel comfortable and confident in working in different ways be sure to make very clear to the children exactly what your expectations are: 'In this activity I want you to move around and talk to as many people as you can until I ring the bell.' 'In this activity I want you to sit still and quietly in your seats and think the problem through on your own before we share our ideas.' If you are very clear about the type of activity and the expectations of behaviour during that activity the children will not find you inconsistent and will be secure in what is required. You may, of course, have to stop them and reinforce sensible behaviour and working practices until they are used to working in a range of different ways, but if you are consistent in this they will soon respond.

A creative teacher needs to be comfortable themselves with flexibility and able to change routines where appropriate. However, flexibility leads to uncertainty and this is an integral part of creativity. 'Problem-solving at all levels requires people to face uncertainty,' says Leslie Safran, 'to be open to all sorts of solutions and to be uncertain about the answers they are looking for' (Safran 2001: 88). Some people are much happier about open-ended activities than others and, as a teacher, you will have to balance the need to address certain areas of learning and to plan for particular outcomes while allowing (or even planning for) the unexpected to happen.

 Classroom idea

Begin by planning for expected outcomes. Have a clear 'route' that you want the lesson to take. Notice when children suggest ideas, solutions or different avenues that you had not anticipated when you planned. Record these on paper and commend the children for their responses. Say you will come back to these ideas in subsequent lessons but for now you want to pursue a particular route. Display the ideas on your 'working wall' or noticeboard and plan ways to address them in the future.

Once you are comfortable that you can plan lessons that go where you want them to and fulfil the objectives you planned for you can then try planning a more open-ended activity where you are less sure of the outcomes.

You may also want to take advantage of the unexpected stimulus that can appear in school: a windy or snowy day, something a child has brought in, an occurrence in the news, the ceiling suddenly leaking. In these situations you have to make decisions quickly as to the educational value they will offer. It might simply be that the excitement they generate gives the children motivation to create good descriptive phrases to use in their writing, going out to experience the weather, touching and looking at the shells or bird's nest can prove an immediate stimulus that engages the children. In changing the direction of your Literacy lesson it will be quite easy to substitute the learning objectives you will achieve from this activity for what you had planned. You will later have to find an opportunity for your original learning objectives to be achieved. Sometimes, though, the potential of the unexpected stimulus might impact on more than one lesson. What if the leaking roof leads to a whole possible investigation into waterproof materials, water containers and materials that absorb liquid or the bird's nest to questions about flight and feathers and wind resistance or insulation? Here you will have to make more difficult decisions. You will need to think about:

- Are these areas that would have been on the curriculum this year anyway?
- Have they already had experience in learning in these areas? Or will they in the future?
- What generic skills will be generated? (e.g. research skills, using the Internet or non-fiction books; close observational drawing)

If you can identify areas of the curriculum that you would have covered in other ways at a different time during the year then addressing them now while the children's interest is excited might be a very sensible thing to do. If they have already addressed learning in that area you could build on what they have already learned, reminding them of past learning, making connections and extending their thinking by applying it in new circumstances. If you identify generic skills that can be addressed now in an authentic situation rather than creating a situation for them at another time, that is obviously worthwhile too. The most difficult situation is likely to be launching into studying, for example, waterproof materials and absorbency when you know they would cover this next year. Your decision in that case will have much to do with how the school works and your relationship with other teachers. Many teachers would be happy to know what prior experience the children have had, will assess what they already know and understand and tailor what they teach accordingly. We will look more closely at the planning process in such cases in subsequent chapters but it will be seen that in encouraging creativity a creative teacher must balance being able to recognise the potential for enquiry and to take advantage of the moment the children are motivated to learn in a particular area with their responsibility for teaching certain curriculum areas during the school year.

Making these kinds of decisions requires a teacher to have good subject knowledge in the whole range of National Curriculum subjects. They will need to understand the progression of skills inherent in each subject and the range and breadth of the areas of learning. They will also need to have enough confidence in what they are teaching to be able to be flexible. As Margaret Boden, writing on 'Creativity and knowledge' (2001: 101) says, 'The teacher who lacks the relevant knowledge, who thinks in rigidly prescribed fashions, who cannot try to make their intuitions explicit and who lacks the self-confidence to say "Let's try this!" or "I don't know" will feel helpless and threatened if asked to teach in the ways sketched above.' She outlines three different types of creative thinking: combinational, exploratory and transformational. As their names imply these correlate with the key elements of creativity outlined in Chapter 1 of this book. Boden makes the point that all these types of creative thinking are 'grounded in previous knowledge, but the way this knowledge is used differs in each case. It follows that the way to encourage them – or to smother them – differs too' (Boden 2001: 96).

Combinational creativity refers to combining ideas in different or unexpected ways and Boden makes the point that in order to do this a person needs a rich 'memory bank' of ideas to use and the confidence to apply them: 'The more diverse types of knowledge (concepts, not just "facts") a person acquires, the richer their mental source for making novel combinations of ideas' (2001: 96). So, in order to encourage this type of creativity a teacher has to provide a broad and rich curriculum and encourage their class to enjoy and use the knowledge they have acquired. It also helps if children experience knowledge without it being rigidly compartmentalised.

 Classroom ideas

- Put words in a hat and ask the children to draw out two. They should then find a way to combine the two words, perhaps by putting them both into a sentence or stating three ways in which they are similar and three ways in which they are different.
- Enjoy and analyse puns and jokes that rely on word play. Use homonyms and homophones to create jokes: e.g. 'When is a door not a door? When it's ajar.'

(Adapted from Boden 2001: 100)

Exploratory creativity assumes that a person has learned a certain amount in a particular domain and can then explore or 'play around' with the 'rules' or ideas. This might take the form of a musician improvising on a particular chord sequence or a mathematician using knowledge in one area to prove something else. Again we meet the need to allow children the time to explore ideas in different areas, to challenge them with 'what would happen if' and encourage them to ask that of themselves. It needs to be acceptable to try these approaches even if there turns out to be nothing to be gained. Blind alleys teach you where there are blind alleys and that this is knowledge gained, just as much as finding a route to something new and exciting.

Sometimes exploratory creativity may lead directly to transformational creativity where the 'rules' of a domain are changed or seen to be different. This is the type of creativity that leads to new inventions or discoveries. Transformational creativity will always break some of the norms or 'rules' of a domain. Think of the proof that the earth was a sphere, or the theory of evolution and how these ideas shocked established thought and beliefs; how abstract painting shattered accepted ideas about representation. When established rules are broken many people will deny the value of the new idea and it is genuinely difficult to establish whether a revolutionary idea or style is a groundbreaking creative insight or complete nonsense. In the classroom there will be the same issues. A child cannot break the conventions of a subject area creatively and with purpose unless they understand them in the first place. For example, changing a fairy story so that we have sympathy for the giant, or so that the wolf is the misunderstood hero or the princess refuses to marry the prince, loses its impact if you do not know that this is not how conventional fairy stories usually go. You cannot make an impact by changing a rhyme scheme or the structure of a limerick unless you understand the normal conventions and have made the changes for a particular purpose. So, teachers need to have confidence in their own subject knowledge and yet the flexibility to recognise when and how 'rules' and conventions can be altered or ignored, and they need to teach children the conventions within different disciplines but to encourage children to 'play with' those conventions and to see what effects that has and what they think of the results. The ideal would be to understand the conventions but not be conventional.

 Classroom idea

Discuss and question the children's attitudes to different styles and representations, e.g. in visual arts, music, literature, architecture, food. What do they like and why? What is being achieved and how? Does everyone like the same things? How does it make them feel? Make sure they are aware that people have very different tastes and ideas and may hold these views strongly, and that we can disagree while respecting the other person's right to hold that viewpoint.

Margaret Boden concludes, 'the "freedom" of creative thought is not the absence of constraints, but their imaginative – yet disciplined – development . . . Creativity is not the same thing as knowledge, but is firmly grounded in it.

What educators must try to do is to nurture the knowledge without killing the creativity' (2001: 102).

Personal attributes and pedagogic skills

Many of the personal attributes and pedagogic skills that will enable a teacher to teach creatively and to identify, encourage and foster creativity have already been evident in this and previous chapters but the list is long and there are more aspects to consider.

If teachers are to recognise and encourage their pupils' creativity they will have to be able to appreciate ideas that they might not themselves have thought of and be able to see different ways of doing things. They need to have the empathy to recognise that what works for them might not work for others. Ken Robinson comments on an 'assumption in the Western worldview, the idea of linearity' (2001: 85). He points out that we tend to expect learning to move in a logical sequence with new learning building on previous learning 'like bricks in a wall' but that this is not always the case. Learning can sometimes be more random than that and a 'jigsaw' approach where individual pieces come together to make a whole picture can sometimes be the way that children make sense of new and established learning. Encouraging children to use mind maps to see and plot the relationships between things and lists and timelines to examine the linearity will all be key in encouraging different kinds of thinking.

In encouraging and fostering creative responses teachers need above all to have and show respect for the individual learner. A put down, however unintentional, or ignoring an idea because it doesn't fit with your view of the progression of the lesson may give messages to the child that you do not appreciate their contributions and they may stop contributing. Bill Lucas (2001: 40) has compiled a list of ways in which a teacher can encourage rather than stifle children's creativity:

- being respectful rather than dismissive
- encouraging active not passive learning
- supporting individual interests rather than standardized curriculums
- engaging many learning styles not one
- encouraging and exploring emotional responses
- posing questions not statements
- offering ambiguity rather than certainties
- being open-ended rather than closing down
- being known as surprising rather than predictable
- offering many patterns rather than a standardized model
- moving the 'classroom' to varied environments
- recognizing multiple intelligences

- including visual representations as well as auditory ones
- including tactile and experience-based activity
- stimulating social as well as private learning

 Individual or group activities

1 Rank the above statements in the order you think they impact on encouraging children's creativity. If you are working with others discuss your reasons as you do so.

2 Identify any statements you think you would find personally difficult to fulfil, that you do not agree with or that you think might present problems in the classroom. Note down or discuss why you feel this.

3 Think of an experienced teacher whom you consider to be good at encouraging creativity in their pupils. Which of the above statements would be true of their practice?

4 Discount any statements you identified in activity number 2. Of the remaining statements which do you feel are already part of your practice as a teacher? Which would you like to develop next? Set yourself a couple of individual targets to work on in the classroom.

It is important not to expect that you can do all of these things straight away. Guy Claxton uses the phrase 'mayonnaise model' (2002: 89) as he says, 'Setting yourself clear targets, one at a time, is a very good way of blending ideas into practice and preventing them from curdling.'

A teacher who manages creative learning skilfully is going to be able to manage time successfully. The demands of the curriculum mean that there are constant decisions that have to be made as to how much time can be allocated to certain activities. To allow time for children to think and reflect and to explore, play and investigate possible avenues of enquiry and outcomes will be a constant balancing act. In 2003 an HMI report was published called *Expecting the Unexpected – Developing Creativity in Primary and Secondary Schools.* They concluded that 'Creative work also often needs unbroken time to develop. Primary schools which maintained sufficient flexibility in their timetables for lessons to be blocked or extended to accommodate planned events or just to provide more time for creative activities, found it easier to enable this kind of development' (HMI 2003: 12). Deciding what to do if one or two children are deeply involved in a really fruitful activity while the rest of the class is ready to move on will be difficult too.

So, what can you do to make and manage the time successfully? We will look at this in more detail when we look closely at planning in Part Four, but for now think about:

- Not all work has to be done to the same depth. Identify which activities are the most important and allocate them more time, early on in the term. Later, if there is not time for everything you want to cover, give different activities or areas of enquiry to individual groups to work on and then get them to report back on their research or findings to the rest of the class.
- Work with parallel learning objectives in two or three subjects where possible. So, learning note taking can be practised with reference to research in geography, organising the findings, drawing conclusions and writing them up can incorporate learning in both the geography and non-chronological writing. Position areas of learning that link well with others carefully on the timetable so they occur when they are most useful to you, e.g. data handling when you will need to do a survey in geography or generate data in science.
- Find a key text or texts that you can use in literacy which enhances the context of the themes being studied and allows for thought and discussion in these areas.
- Block work where possible. So, for example, use three afternoons in a week on multidisciplinary work without needing to break and change from subject to subject.
- Plan time (maybe on a Friday) for extended work, applying learning from earlier in the week or pursuing long-term projects. Have shorter challenges available for those who finish before others until you need to pull findings together and move on as a class.
- Sometimes work a 'carousel' of activities so that the best use of targeted support and resources can be made.

A teacher who is successful in identifying, fostering and encouraging creativity in their pupils will be able to step back, observe and analyse the learning that is happening in the classroom. They will need to be able to reflect on what they have observed and to make decisions to balance the needs of the class, different groups and individuals. We have seen how they will need the ability to promote the culture and ethos that supports children in working creatively, be able to put all children at their ease but also make them feel safe by being firm, consistent and fair. They are also going to be prepared to learn from others, including their pupils, and be good team players, relishing opportunities to team teach or work in collaboration with others. All of this means that a teacher who is successful in this area will have a strong core identity, being confident in themselves so that they are prepared to take risks and to be flexible but reflective and analytical so that their decisions are taken in the best interests of the children's learning. Mathilda Marie Joubert says, 'Experience has shown that creative teachers constantly reinvent themselves and adapt their teaching styles and strategies to different situations as required . . . If teachers remain firmly rooted in terms of their identity and core principles it allows them to feel free to use flexibility in terms of what they do' (2001: 22). In the early days and years of a teaching career that core identity is still developing, as are the skills to support it, but small steps can lead to significant results even during a teacher's training, and working creatively brings benefits to the teacher as well as the children. Joubert puts it succinctly: 'This is a difficult but exciting and rewarding process, which could prevent stagnation and mental starvation' (2001: 22).

 Personal thought and reflection

Above we used the phrase 'core identity'. Imagine you are about to retire after a long and successful teaching career. A trusted colleague will make a speech about your strengths as a teacher. What would you want them to say about you? Jot down the points you would want to hear about yourself. Now think about the teacher you are at present. Obviously you lack the experience of the 'retiring' teacher but which of the points you jotted down are developing already in your practice? Can you sum up your 'core identity' as a teacher at present in fifteen words or less? Record it somewhere and date it (perhaps inside the cover of this book) and return to this activity in the future and see how or if that 'core identity' has changed.

Chapter summary

In this chapter we have looked at the importance of recognising your own creativity and using it to model creative processes for children. We have seen how examining our own creativity can lead to us understanding better the creativity of the children we teach. We have looked at ways to identify creativity in others and how to foster and encourage creativity once identified. We have discovered many of the personal attributes necessary to be a successful creative teacher and begun to identify the skills that need to be mastered to encourage and foster creativity in the children we teach.

Further study

Critical reflection: Activity 5

Allow an hour for this activity.

You have just *identified* your core identity. Choose one aspect of this that you believe flourishes in your role as a primary teacher. *Synthesise* the evidence that leads you to believe this.

Choose one aspect of your core identity that is less well developed. How could you use the strength identified above to develop this aspect of yourself? *Identify* the first steps you need to take to make progress on this journey.

Now, look from the perspective of the children you are teaching. *Identify* a child whom you think is not achieving as much as s/he could. *Identify* one of the child's creative aspects which s/he seems to enjoy. *Analyse* how you think you could use this aspect more fully to enable the child to progress.

  Further reading

Craft, A., Gardner, H. and Claxton, G. (eds) (2008) *Creativity, Wisdom and Trusteeship: Exploring the Role of Education.* Thousand Oaks, CA: Corwin Press.

HMI (2003) *Expecting the Unexpected – Developing Creativity in Primary and Secondary Schools.* HMI 1612. London: Ofsted.

Robinson, K. (2001) *Out of Our Minds.* Oxford: Capstone.

Creativity: Meaning-Making and Representation

Wright, S.

Figure 1.1 Lifting Off from Earth (boy, 6.6 i.e. 6 years, 6 months)

At the completion of this chapter, you should be able to:

1. Describe the important role of drawing in promoting creativity and meaning-making in young children,
2. Understand graphic, narrative and embodied aspects of children's meaning-making and representation, and
3. Reflect on how the content of a child's drawing is closely related to the form in which it is created.

Art and learning

The imagination is energetically deployed and reaches its peak in children's early years of life, however, it gradually declines as children grow order. Yet as Egan (1999) urges, imagination is precisely what is needed to keep us intellectually flexible and creative in modern societies. Most notably, the arts 'play to the imagination' (Gadsden, 2008, p. 47). Gadsden elaborates that the arts:

> allow individuals to place themselves in the skin of another; to experience others' reality and culture; to sit in another space; to transport themselves across time, space, era in history, and context; and to see the world from a different vantage point. (p. 35)

Arts education and early childhood education in general have emphasized important principles that have increasingly found their way into more recent studies on multimodality and new literacies. Such studies have opened up debates about what 'counts as a text and what constitutes reading and writing' and have extended our notions of creativity (Hull & Nelson, 2005, p. 224). For decades, early childhood educators, artists and arts educators have recognized that the arts draw upon a variety of modalities, such as speech, image, sound, movement and gesture, to create multimodal forms of meaning. Such experiences are fundamental to the fluidity and flexibility of human thought and learning. Art provides young people with authentic meaning-making experiences that engage their minds, hearts and bodies.

This book focuses on how young children's creativity is surfaced through the act of meaning-making within the medium of drawing. As will be illustrated through many examples of children's works, drawing is an imaginative act which involves a range of creative forms of sign production and interpretation. Like all areas of learning, becoming competent in drawing generally requires exposure, participation and practice. It is when there is refined mastery of an art medium, combined with high levels of creativity and talent, that breakthroughs can be accomplished, such as in the case of Picasso. Picasso was an outstanding individual who showed exceptional artistic ability at an early age (Gardner, 1993a), and continued to develop his expertise throughout his life.

In a sense, every instance of representation through art is new and creative. Although drawing involves a 'set of rules', children never just mechanically apply rules when they make an artwork. Generally, each artwork is different and requires adaptation to the circumstances at hand. This is why composing through art is such an important and fundamental form of creativity.

Creativity

Several authors have written extensively on the topic of creativity. This literature will not be described in detail here, as the focus is on illustrating how creativity is demonstrated in young children's art-making processes. However, some fundamental issues are featured at this time, and examples throughout this book will illustrate these, with a particular focus on meaning-making and representation through drawing.

Let us begin with a brief definition of creativity. Creativity is the process of generating ideas that are novel and bringing into existence a product that is appropriate and of high quality (Sternberg & Lubart, 1995). Everyone has at least some creative potential, but they differ widely in the extent to which they are able to realise that potential. In addition, as Gardner (1983, 1993a, b) pointed out, people tend to be creative or intelligent in some specific domains but not necessarily in others. For instance, we might be good at art, but not music; or be good at science, but not maths.

This is because creativity is a cognitive or *mental trait* and a *personality trait* as well. Some personal qualities include (Wright, 2003a): a valuing of creativity, originality, independence, risk-taking, the ability to redefine problems, energy, curiosity, attraction to complexity, artistry, open-mindedness, a desire to have some time alone, perceptiveness, concentration, humour, the ability to regress and the possession of childlike qualities. These personality traits are linked to thinking styles, which involve: visualization, imagination, experimentation, analogical/metaphorical thinking, logical thinking, predicting outcomes or consequences, analysis, synthesis and evaluation. In addition, intrinsic motivation and commitment are important personal qualities that are fundamental to the development of creativity.

Creative individuals were once widely seen as receiving divine inspiration for their ingenuity, and as needing nothing or anyone to excel. The stereotype is of a born genius whose innate talent does not require further honing or the support of others. Yet, in reality, the role of others is crucial throughout creative individuals' development (Perkins, 1981). Creative activity grows out of the relationships between an individual, his/her work in a discipline and the ties between the individual and other people (or institutions) who judge the quality of his/her work (Csikszentmihalyi, 1988).

Hence, teachers, parents and the community influence children's participation and development, and can support (or alternatively thwart) their creativity. Indeed, the decision to encourage or limit creativity is related to the attitudes of the significant people who shape children's environments – whether they value creativity and are tolerant of the children's ideas or products, even if these may challenge their own viewpoints or digress from conventional thinking and behaving.

Creativity is closely tied to personal connection, expression, imagination and ownership. It involves problem *setting* as well as problem *solving*. It comes out of explicit probing into meaningful issues, and constructing meaningful interpretations. Meaningful art-making reflects the ways of thinking of young artists – the makers who actively interact with the artwork. John Dewey (1934/1988) suggests that art offers multiple entry-points into the aesthetic experience, combining creation and appreciation. Indeed, children's early representational drawings often emerge as a result of a dialogue between production and perception (Thompson, 1995; Thompson & Bales, 1991).

The imagination of the child can transform a blank piece of paper into something very real. Young children are careful planners during the creative process of drawing. They often decide in advance what content is to be included and where to locate it on the page. Frequently they review their work-in-progress and make additions or corrections. Golomb (2004, p. 191) emphasizes that composition in art is an ongoing process of revision, of 'monitoring the performance, planning actions, inspecting the outcome, deciding on its merits and flaws'.

Although there are numerous ways in which creativity can evolve, some key processes are described in Table 1.1, along with an illustrative example of how these might apply to the medium of drawing. I am somewhat reluctant to introduce a range of technical terms, because these may seem to merely serve as a list or be viewed as being exhaustive rather than illustrative. Rather, the aim is to aid debate; by labelling some of the distinctive features of creativity in relation to drawing, allowing some security in the discussion. For a more extensive elaboration on some of these issues, readers may like to refer to some of my earlier works, particularly *The Arts, Young Children and Learning* (Wright, 2003a).

Artistic creation, through the medium of drawing, enables children to improvise. In the process, they develop a sense of arrangement and structure while transforming their graphic content on the blank page. This creative process is liberated through open-ended composing.

Table 1.1 Creative Processes, Descriptions and Examples

Creative process	Description	Example
Problem finding and solving	Finding and exploring alternative goals and approaches to a problem	Blending yellow, orange and brown to create the desired colour for a drawn dog's fur
Flexibility	Taking different approaches to a problem, thinking of ideas in a variety of ways or viewing a problem from another perspective	Changing a daytime scene into night by scribbling out a drawn yellow sun
Fluency	Producing many free-flowing ideas for an open-ended problem or question	Illustrating different unfolding events that flow in and out of the overall plot scheme of the drawing
Elaboration	Adding details to an idea, which includes developing, embellishing and improving the idea	Verbally explaining how a drawn object, such as a car, 'moves' across the page to get to the other side, or adding a wavy line to show the path of the movement
Transformation	Changing one object or idea into another by adding, subtracting, substituting or transposing	Noting that a drawn cloud looks like a shark, and adding details to make it into a 'flying shark'
Objectivity and selectivity	Going beyond generating ideas to distinguishing which of these ideas are the best and worth pursing	Choosing the 'best' colours, shapes or lines to depict something and deciding where to locate it on the page
Aesthetic appreciation	Striving for something which has purpose, results and high standards	Carefully detailing graphic content so that it communicates clearly and elegantly

Composing through drawing

Bresler (2002, p. 172) described Child Art as 'original, open-ended (in at least some aspects) compositions which are intended to reflect students' interpretations and ideas'. While composing, children are comfortable with altering their artworks to suit their purpose. They feel at liberty to improvise structures as they dialogue with the materials, such as changing birds to butterflies, scribbling out a dead figure or turning grass into water. A number of things may stimulate a child to improvise in ways such as these, which may include:

- changing the identity of a *character* (e.g., deciding that a prototypic rock star in a drawing should be the artist himself)
- altering the *plot* content (e.g., modifying the structure of the plot by introducing a new theme, scene or event)

- modifying the *genre* of the narrative (e.g., shifting from factual to fictional)
- adjusting the *time* frame (e.g., shifting between the present, future or past)
- varying the *place* (e.g., turning a house into a hotel)
- confronting a challenging *schema* (e.g., leaving 'Daddy' out of a family scene because the artist does not know how to draw men's clothes), or
- seeing another *image* in what has been drawn (e.g., thinking that a drawn dog looks more like a bear, and adding salient content to refine the image).

Most children seem to find composing through art an appealing process, perhaps because it is not strictly *rule-bound*. Children are at liberty to experiment and to represent ideas and actions in whatever form they choose. Hence, my intention is to feature not just the *content* of children's artworks, but to also emphasize how the *form* of this content is meaningful. I want to highlight how children's art making is an active, meaning-making experience. Like Kress (1997), I take the position that children's visual narrative texts have structure, and that the structure that is given to these texts is done so through the interests of the text makers. It is a transformative process. The signs that children make are different from adult forms, but nonetheless, they are fully meaningful.

Art allows children to 'say' and 'write' what they think and feel, usually without adult intrusion. Through such open-ended experiences, children develop a repertoire of marks, images and ideas. They refine these through practice and skill and through exposure to the art of other children and adults. In the process, children experiment with 'the language' of the materials and develop a 'grammar' of communication. As mentioned above, they decide not only on the *content* to be depicted, but also the aesthetic *form*, or the manner in which content is presented. The artwork's compositional component is a vital element of the child's communication. It is the organizational force used to project ideas and to illustrate relativity and relationships. Composition not only makes the content accessible, it also heightens the young artist's perceptions and stimulates his or her imaginative involvement.

When composing through drawing, children combine graphic, narrative and embodied signs. Dyson (1993) noted that at around the age of two, children often use drawing as a prop for storytelling, complemented with dramatic gesture and speech. These multimodal texts involve drawing, gesture and talk – they stem from visual, linguistic, aural and tactile modes to make meaning. Indeed, the marks that children make are often the 'visual equivalent of dramatic play' (Anning, 1999, p. 165).

Because of the play-oriented, compositional component of drawing, I believe art is essentially the *literacy par excellence* of the early years of child development (Wright, 2007b). As many have noted, infants and very young children generally draw *prior* to the acquisition of the skills of reading and writing written text (i.e., letters, words, phrases, sentences). Gunther Kress, in his book *Before Writing* (1997, p. 10), describes the social, cultural and cognitive implications of the 'transition from the rich world of meanings made in countless ways, in countless forms, in the early years of children's lives, to the much more unidimensional world of written language'.

Indeed, the act of representing thought and action while drawing actually strengthens children's later understanding of literacy and numeracy. Unfortunately, however, many traditional systems of schooling suppress children's *free composing* through drawing in favour of *teaching* children the more rule-bound, structured symbol systems of numeracy and literacy. This is because schools often perceive writing letters, words and numbers as a 'higher status' mode of representation (Anning & Ring, 2004). Yet, as Pahl and Rowsell (2005, p. 43) noted, many children are constrained by a literacy curriculum that only allows writing. They asserted that a multimodal approach 'lets in more meaning'.

To focus too strongly, too soon, on a literacy curriculum distracts children from the ability to compose using pictorial signs, which in many ways are developmentally more meaningful to young children. When picturing and imagining within the 'fluid' boundaries of art, children are in control of *what* they want to say and *how* they want to say it, in a free-form way. The less rule-bound system of drawing offers children freedom of 'voice'. When this co-exists with the learning of the more structured symbol systems, children engage in creative meaning-making in an assortment of ways.

Composing through art, like play, is a fundamental function of early cognitive, effective and social development. Through art, children actively *construct* understandings of themselves and their worlds, rather than simply becoming the passive recipients of knowledge. To suppress and replace artistic play with formal teaching not only denies the voice of children, but overlooks the significance of composing in the act of meaning construction.

Yet, Kress emphasized that, perhaps in the absence of strong theoretical descriptions and explanations of art, drawings and images of most kinds are thought of as being about expression, rather than about information or communication. Hence, art is not usually subjected to the same analysis for meaning, or seen as being as important a part of communication as language (Kress, 1997, p. 35). Kress adds that if the makers of the artworks are children, the question of 'intentionality and design becomes contentious' (Kress, 1997, p. 36).

The goal of this book is to overcome some of these misconceptions by providing a theoretical foundation for understanding and appreciating the artworks that stemmed from the participation of over 100 5–8-year-old Australian children. The children were asked to draw and talk about what the future will be like, on a one-to-one basis, with a trained interlocutor, who interacted with each child throughout the process (an aspect which will be described in greater detail in Chapter 2).

The topic 'Futures' was chosen to inspire children to break out of the common schemata (e.g., trees, houses, the sun) that often are inherent in self-selected, rehearsed drawings. Indeed, it was found that this topic stimulated children to mentally manipulate and organize images, ideas and feelings about complex subjects, and to engage in a rich amalgam of both fantasy and reality. It inspired children to speculate on futures yet to come – to consider multiple interpretations, to generate new meanings and to expand existing ones. Such thinking involves a high-order consciousness (Slaughter, 1994b). It also appeals to children's interest in things that are far from what they know firsthand, such as aliens, spaceships, force-fields and virtual reality.

This propensity of children to engage in such unfamiliar topics is featured in the foreword to Kieren Egan's book, *Children's Minds, Talking Rabbits and Clockwork Oranges* (1999), in which Elliott Eisner comments that:

> it is faulty to assume that youngsters do not have the capacity to understand and find interest in ideas and practices that are not already in their midst. It is precisely the capacities of very young children to exercise their imagination that should be sustained rather than diminished in school. (p. xi)

Eisner adds that educational systems often cultivate 'a logocentric conception of mind that diminishes the imagination and romantic side of human nature' (p. xi). Imagination is seen as frivolous and less important because it is associated with fantasy and play and, 'as we all "know", play is the opposite of work ... play and imagination are at best questionable and at worst a distraction from what really matters' (p. xi).

Through the numerous examples of children's work in this book, I aim to illustrate how imagination, creativity, fantasy and play are fundamental components of young children's art and meaning-making. Art involves imagining possibilities. The contents of children's imagination can be realized through the art they make and the meaning that this communicates.

Meaning-making

Without the arts, the history of cultures throughout the world would be very different. Indeed, the arts have always played a significant role in humans' creation and sharing of thoughts and feelings. As Rabiger describes it: 'in every period and in every part of the world, art has supplied a surrogate experience to exercise hearts and minds' (Rabiger, 2008, p. 178).

Our representational practices serve a basic human need – to explore and understand the world in meaningful ways, no matter which medium is used to do so (Danesi, 2007). Chandler (2002, p. 17) described meaning-making as an innately driven characteristic of humans: 'We seem as a species to be driven by a desire to make meanings: above all, we are surely *homo significans* – meaning-makers'.

But, paradoxically, 'by representing the world, we end up changing it, making it virtually impossible for us to distinguish between reality and our representations of it' (Danesi, 2007, p. 122). The famous question by Bertolt Brecht remains: Is art a mirror to society, or a hammer working on it? Does art reflect actuality, or does it change and therefore create it? The answers will vary, but we can say with confidence that representational practices allow us to probe and explore reality and thus 'discover' the elements of reality and the 'hidden principles' that govern human life and the universe (Danesi, 2007, p. 132–133).

Through art, people of all ages make an object of their own contemplation. They use symbols to manipulate images and concepts, which is linked to the creative process of meaning-making. Art allows us to create a symbolic world and to 'shape and reshape, revise and revision' our own 'hidden and subjective' lives (Abbs, 2003, p. 13). Art gives shape to formless ideas. It is a vehicle by which we can express our growing awareness of ourselves and the worlds in which we live. This provides a powerful mechanism for reaching the deepest, richest, most abstract aspects of our existence. The process can engender a sense of freedom, release, fulfilment and wholeness – sometimes to the point of ecstasy – because it connects with deep levels of symbol, meaning and emotion. The arts help us place our objects, our activities and ourselves in a larger existential framework, where we are actually 'touched' through a different way of understanding.

Art making and its narrative description of the here and now (Kellman, 1995), allows children to share the day-to-day details of their lives with others. But beyond the 'here and now', art making also allows children to explore abstract and complex concepts, such as what the future may be like. Because multiple options are available for the future, this topic is an inspiration for creative thought, as it delves into the intangible, the 'what might be'. Kellman notes that art making, coupled with narrative, is a 'means of inventing, a method of thinking, a way of giving life to hopes and dreams' (Kellman, 1995, p. 19). In a similar vein, Rabiger (2008, p. 129) states that, 'to make fiction is to propose reality'.

Art making involves thinking in symbols, which Dewey in his book *Art as Experience* (1934/1988) described as one of the most sophisticated modes of thought. The human child is endowed with ingenuity and symbol-making propensities to go beyond reality as immediate experience. By using the symbolic system of drawing, children manipulate images and concepts, thus joining with others who share a culture, who share the same 'imaginative universe' or 'worlds of possibility' (Dyson, 1993, p. 23). This capacity is at its peak in early childhood.

Early childhood is a time when children's thinking is still imaginative, flexible and linked to fantasy and fiction. Yet, imaginative and fictional qualities are what young children begin to lose as they grow older, and what adults should seek to rediscover. The future-conscious teacher is led to prefer a curriculum that supports these qualities, and encourages thought process that will help children develop concepts that will prepare them for what is likely to happen (Egan, 1999, p. 78). But in addition to exploring *probable* options for the future, pedagogy should also help children explore concepts of *possible* and *preferable* options (Eckersley, 1992, 1999; Slaughter, 1994a).

Future-conscious teachers aim to equip children to become autonomous and active *creators of the future*, through skills such as adaptability, imagination, fantasy, altruism, sensitivity towards others, decision-making, resilience, empathy, an interest in other cultures, and abilities in communication, problem solving and lateral thinking (Wright, 2001). As Egan (1999, p. 78) describes curriculum, it should encourage 'critical thinking rather than knowledge acquisition, problem-solving skills rather than familiarity with past problems, openness to change rather than commitment to a set of ideas and institutions'.

Consequently, meaning-making through drawing is a means for capturing many of these future-oriented values. Through the act of drawing, children's thought, body and emotion unite. Indeed, drawing involves more than simply forming images; it is equated with the capacity to think and to feel (Egan, 1992). Goodman's (1976) reminder is that 'what we know through art is felt in our bones and nerves and muscles as well as grasped by our minds' (in Buckham, 1994, p. 140).

Young children's drawings open a window into their realities and how they shape these. We come to understand the range of a child's thinking and feeling through close observation of the drawing activity itself and the talk that accompanies it. As Cox (2005, p. 124) notes, the constructive process of drawing helps children to 'purposefully bring shape and order to their experience, and in so doing, their drawing activity is actively defining reality, rather than passively reflecting a "given" reality'. The examples of the artworks of children presented in this book demonstrate that, through drawing and talking, children came to not only *know* reality, they *create* it.

Hence, a fundamental component of the work of early childhood educators is to understand what is *meant* by a child's drawing in relation to his/her ideas, actions and feelings. How we may interpret and possibly extend this meaning in our interactions with young children is an important consideration. One approach is through the application of principles derived from the multidisciplinary field of semiotics. Semiotics assigns much weight to creativity and human inventiveness as factors that shape evolution (Danesi, 2007).

To do justice to the topic of creativity, while also providing a context for the value of semiotics in early childhood art education and research, some brief definitions and descriptions will be helpful. These constructs will be revisited several times throughout this book, supported by many examples of children's creations for illustrative purposes. Put simply, semiotics is the study of 'the capacity to create and use signs such as words and symbols for thinking, communicating, reflecting, transmitting and preserving knowledge' (Danesi, 2007, cover note). It provides us with a potentially unifying conceptual framework and a set of methods and concepts for making sense of all kinds of human products, from 'words, symbols, narratives, symphonies, paintings and comic books to scientific theories and mathematical theorems' (Danesi, 2007, pp. 3–4). Semiotics can be applied to the full range of *signifying practices* (Chandler, 2002). These include gesture, body language, facial expressions, eye contact, dress, writing, speech, narratives, the mass media, advertising, drawing, photography, space, cuisine and rituals. In sum, semiotics involves investigating, deciphering, documenting and explaining the *what*, *how* and *why* of signs.

As an approach to communication, semiotics foregrounds how meaning is not passively absorbed, but arises through the active process of sign creation and interpretation. Specific *semiotic modalities* are addressed by such specialists as linguists, art historians, musicologists and anthropologists. But as Chandler (2002, p. 214) points out, 'we must turn to *semioticians* if we wish to study meaning-making and representation *across modalities*' (my italics). Because the act of drawing is multimodal, I aim to make my analytic strategy explicit so that others may apply it either to the examples presented in this book, or to other examples of children's art. Rather than engaging in a debate about various semiotic approaches that might have been applied (e.g., relativism, poststructuralism, traditional structural semiotics), I prefer to adopt a general standpoint that signs are related to their signifieds by social conventions that we learn, and to illustrate some examples of this through the selected presentation of several children's works.

I will focus on how representation, as sign-making, bridges the child's real world 'out there' with his/her inner imagination. Yet I will also foreground how children's drawings represent something according to specific traditions and practices. In other words, representation is not, purely, an open-ended process. It is constrained by social conventions, by communal experiences and by other contextual factors (Danesi, 2007, pp. 122–123). Some of the foundational constructs of semiotics might do with teasing out a little; so let us briefly delve more deeply into signs and how their meaning is communicated in children's drawing texts.

Signs and texts

A sign can be defined simply as 'something that stands for something else in some way' (Danesi, 2007, p. 29). In a broad sense, a sign is anything that communicates meaning. Signs can take many forms. As mentioned above, they can be words, images, sounds, gestures, touch, odours, flavours, acts or objects (Chandler, 2002).

But signs have no intrinsic meaning in and of themselves. They become signs when we invest them with meaning – when we interpret the sign as *standing for* or representing something other than itself. For instance, we interpret a child's meaning when we ask ourselves what is meant by his/her mark on paper, use of a word or gesture, physical action and many other forms of communication. These component parts are what Danesi would refer to as the 'small' signs, which must be seen in relation to the whole artwork and the overall meaning of the child's drawing. In such cases, we are considering the collection of signs as something much 'larger' – as a *text* – and are looking at the text's larger *message* (Danesi, 2007, p. 97).

The child's integrated drawing-narrative-embodied text becomes a single, multimodal communicative act. The constituent parts (the small signs) of speech, image and non-verbal communication (e.g., facial expressions, gesture, body language, expressive vocalizations) are integrated, *holistically*, as a single form. As van Leeuwen (2005, p. 121) metaphorically describes it, multimodal communicative acts such as these, blend 'like instruments in an orchestra'.

Such holistic texts are in stark contrast to texts that are interpreted *linearly* such as numbers in the decimal system, equations and written language. Danesi explains how linear texts are deciphered by means of a sign-by-sign interpretation process. Numbers, for instance, are composed and read in a linear fashion and interpretation is cumulative: 'the value of the entire number (= the text) is gleaned by assessing the values of the individual signs (= the digits in the number)' (Danesi, 2007, p. 98).

By contrast, the component parts of holistic texts, such as drawing and narrative, are not assessed one at a time, but instead, are seen as elements of a whole. Indeed, one element, such as a word, cannot be detached from the accompanying graphic mark or physical gesture without impairing the overall meaning of the text. Susanne Langer referred to meaning creation and communication in art as involving elements, such as lines, shapes, proportions, colours, shadings, perspective and composition, which are 'abstractable and combinatory' (Langer, 1924/1971, pp. 86–89). These elements are as complex as combinations of words, yet they have no vocabulary of units with independent meaning. For instance, there are no items within pictures that might be metaphorically equated to the 'words' of portraiture.

Consequently, compared to 'tight-structured' linear texts, art is a loosely structured and holistic text. This is because the elements of art have so many potential relationships. For instance, the colour pink or a jagged line can have very different meanings according to how they are used within the context of the drawing. Similarly, the placement of an image, such as a bird on the ground versus a bird in the sky, communicates a different meaning. Hence, the range of possibilities of signifying meaning through visual elements, such as colour, or the distance between objects, or the placement of content within a pictorial plane, are virtually infinite.

So we must view children's drawings, combined with their spontaneous running narrative and non-verbal communication, as a single multimodal act. The meaning is constituted by its total effect and understood as a complete whole: as a macro event or a macro sign. As such, the artwork-narrative in its entirety is a *semiotic unit*. Its meaning works at two levels: it is presented not only on the surface level (that which is denoted) but also below the surface (that which is connoted).

Levels of meaning

As a human species, we interpret each other's meaning almost unconsciously, by relating signs to familiar *systems of conventions*. Indeed, we are so used to using the systems of words, pictures, numbers, gestures, touch, sounds and many other signs in our everyday life that we generally don't stop to think about how we do this, how important these sign systems are to human communication, how they have derived or how we have learned them. Humans have invented a number of *sign systems* for representing ideas and experiences, such as language, art, music, maths, physics, dance and history. We use these sign systems to make ideas and experiences a public, shared form of communication that can be understood by others. Indeed, as Eco (1976) states, these systems form the basis for creative and critical thought processes.

Hence, as teachers of young children, our goal is to understand the principles that children use in their representations of the world. Whether this be in relation to mathematics, literacy or the arts, it would be virtually impossible for teachers to communicate the content of education, or to understand the layers of meaning in children's communication, without understanding our shared systems of meaning.

The study of children's meaning and their inherent 'layers of text' is linked to the branch of semiotics called, generally, *hermeneutics*. Danesi (2007) describes the defining methodological features of classical hermeneutics as involving an analysis of:

- a surface (signifier) level consisting of constituent forms (sentences, words, phrases, etc.), and
- a deep (signified) level, which contains its true (sometimes called 'hidden') meanings (pp. 105–106).

The 'smaller' signs, such as words, images (e.g., colours, lines, shapes, textures, composition, etc.) and gestures, are the 'signifiers' in children's visual-narrative texts. They combine in order to communicate some overarching message – or the 'larger signified' – which is the 'something else' for which a physical structure stands (Danesi, 2007, p. 29). So we must 'look behind or beneath the surface' (Chandler, 2002, p. 214) of a child's drawing in order to discover its underlying organization and meaning. This requires noting the child's use of art elements in relation to words, gesticulations, dramatic vocalization, pauses or hesitations, and how art elements are combined with language and movement to carry meaning (i.e., what they 'stand for').

Following on from the work of the visual semiotician Roland Barthes (1957/1973, 1977), layers of meaning are given the terms *denotation* (surface level) and *connotation* (deep level). Barthes (1977) described denotation as the *literal message*, such as the depicted people, places, objects and events, and connotation as the *symbolic message*, such as the broader, abstract concepts, ideas and values being expressed. Abstract concepts, like 'love', 'friendship' and 'justice' are especially high in connotation. Such concepts are understood as culturally shared meanings (Barthes, 1977) and are communicated in visual forms through association. Some examples of connotative associations of *what* the represented people, places, objects and events stand for might include, for instance:

- people's poses (e.g., arms raised heavenwards, which may connote exuberance)
- places (e.g., a playground, which may connote fun and games)
- objects (e.g., a bookcase, which may connote intellectual ideas)
- events (e.g., a running person, which may connote fleeing or freedom).

Hence, connotation is not only about *what* is being communicated but also *how* this is done through the use of aesthetic form, such as the arrangements chosen to visually present the people, places, objects and events. This includes aspects such as:

- techniques (e.g., shading, bold lines, strong contrasts, angle, framing)
- style (e.g., the child's own artistic identity or 'individual stamp' on the artwork).

As a simplified illustration of this, the message of the artwork presented in the opening of this chapter (Figure 1.1) has two layers.

Figure 1.2 Olympic Equestrian Event (girl, 7.9)

At the denotative level, the man standing on Earth, 'planting' a flag in the soil next to Australia (signifier) denotes that he is 'first' or the 'owner' of Earth (signified). At the connotative level, the profile and angle of the spaceship and the astronaut inside (signifier) connotes that the man is taking off from Earth to fly around in space on 'joy rides' (signified).

By way of a further example, some features in the artwork in Figure 1.2, of an Olympic equestrian event (drawn by a girl, 7.9), include judges seated behind dark desks (i.e., the six figures at the back of the stands). The judges stand out from the crowd of smaller, less clearly defined people who fade into the background as 'secondary' figures, compared to the 'primary' figures of the judges. Most prominently, the competitor in the event is large and central – the focus of the content. The art elements of colour, proportion, shading and perspective all function to communicate that the rider is being judged while competing in the Olympics.

Four creative transformations were used by this young artist while improvising her content. Behind the audience is a scoreboard, which indicates that Australia (Aus) is scoring 2001, and New Zealand (New), 991. The artist decided to change the score, so she *deleted* the original scoreboard by blackening it out and *substituted* this by *adding* a new scoreboard below it. Later in the drawing, she *transposed* the grass behind the jump post into water by drawing swirling blue lines – to make the equestrian event more challenging.

As illustrated in Figure 1.2, and relevant to children's meaning-making, our understanding of their communication within the open-ended framework of art requires us to become sensitive to children's *processes of production* and to their *authorial intentions* (Chandler, 2002, p. 210). Such receptiveness surfaces an awareness of *how* things are being represented by children, rather than only *what* is represented. As Eisner (2002) reminds us: 'How something is said is part and parcel of what is said. The message is in the form-content relationship, a relationship that is most vivid in the arts' (www.infed.org/biblio/eisnerarts_and_the_practice_of_education. htm).

Attention to this relationship is key to understanding the holistic meaning of children's artworks. The work is a macro event in which the signs of words, images and actions are unified into one semiotic unit, and the text's meaning is made through its total effect, as a complete whole. Hence, a final component of this chapter will focus on how children's articulation of meaning during the creative act of drawing is multimodal and 'other worldly', and that the structures that children improvise are fluid.

Visual narratives: improvising in 'other-worldly' ways

Golomb (1988) describes children's representational forms as being the outcome of a 'dialogue among the hand, the eye, and the urge to symbolize reality' (p. 234). Indeed, Vygotsky describes drawing as a kind of 'graphic speech' (Dyson, 1982). One cannot, however, over-look the narrative and non-verbal communicative aspects as compelling features of children's meaning-making while drawing. Yet, because of the emphasis on traditional views of narrative (i.e., from a literacy perspective), far more attention within research has been given to oral storying and story writing than to the important role of visual narrative.

When viewed from a semiotic perspective, children's drawings – as macro events or holistic messages – include an expansive range of signs used in highly interactive, fluid and expressive ways. This involves the depiction of content through *graphic* and *body-based action*, while *talking* about aspects of the artwork and/or the processes of its creation through a free-form type of narrative.

This perspective is aligned with a *conception of mind* (Sutton-Smith, 1995) and the prominence of the role of visual narrative in our ways of making sense of the world and of experience. The work of Bruner (1986), Gardner (1983) and Egan (1999) give us a more detailed understanding of how scripts, schemata and stories are deployed in our meaning-making experiences. They emphasize that the function of narrative is a method of thinking, of sharing experience and of assigning meaning. Narrative is as important in the lives of children as it is in the lives of adults.

Children and adults alike use narrative as a means of constructing their interior, psychological worlds (Goodman in Bruner, 1986). The insights and images in a child's world help us to see through the eyes of the child as he/she reflects on life and constructs 'other' worlds (Kellman, 1995). By examining the narrative in children's art as invention, communication and as a method of solving problems, it is possible to come closer to their interior worlds.

The fantasy-filled narratives concocted by young children seek out the rhythms and patterns of the story form. Yet the content and structure of young children's narratives are often different in important ways from that which typically engages adults (Egan, 1988). Children's depictions of imaginary worlds, while dialoguing with the materials (i.e., paper and felt pens), is more akin to play than to story-telling. Their narratives do not necessarily follow the rules or 'universal form' of story-telling, which Egan (1988, p. 3) described as having 'a beginning which sets up an expectation, a middle that complicates it, and an ending that satisfies or resolves it'.

Instead, children's visual narratives encompass processes whereby people, places, objects and events are 'told' through the child's graphic action – mark-making that depicts ideas and feelings in *real time*. It is a spontaneous unfolding of content that moves in and out of loosely structured themes. The themes of children's thinking generally unfold 'radiationally' (Gallas, 1994) rather than sequentially. Indeed, connections within the content are made and re-made as the child describes his/her evolving ideas – in whatever order these may evolve.

This loosely structured type of thinking is associated with the openness of the *configurational signs* (Arnheim, 1969, 1974), such as people and objects, that are used in the medium of drawing. Configurational signs are similar to their natural referents – a child's drawn tree, for instance, resembles what he/she sees in nature. But compared to syntax in language, which is highly rule governed, configurational signs are ever changing. As Arnheim explains, they offer an open invitation to be altered; for children to elaborate upon their forms. Children, for instance, readily add a hat to a drawn figure, depict the person in a different position, or attach whoosh lines to show that the person is running. This is because the non-standard nature of configurational signs encourages the invention of new visual forms.

Consequently, the running narrative that accompanies a child's drawing is, similarly, ever changing and open to alteration. It responsively 'mirrors' the loose structure that stems from the configurational signs that the child spontaneously constructs. The child uses gestures to describe, locate, relocate and 'play' the characters, objects and events. Yet, when 'playing' through drawing, the dialogue generally is not like conversation, such as asking 'would you like to have a cup of tea?'; a type of dialogue which is more common in children's socio-dramatic play, or solitary play with toys. Rather, the playing of characters and events while drawing is more omniscient, descriptive and indexical, such as, 'this is where she stepped on the stones to get to the other side of the river' (this issue will be discussed in more detail in the next chapter).

In addition, because the child's dialogue is intimately linked to his/her graphic action, it is similar in some ways to the dialogue found in film – it is highly succinct. As Rabiger (2008) explains, film dialogue 'must exclude life's verbosity and repetitiousness' (p. 133). He elaborates: 'In real life, little is denoted (said directly) and much connoted (alluded to in a roundabout way). Silences are often the real "action" during which extraordinary currents flow between the speakers' (p. 133). Similarly, character dialogues in children's visual narratives are full of such silences, the meaning of which must be deduced by the young artist's gestures, expressive vocalisms, facial expression and body-based communication. These, accompanied with graphic action, do the 'talking' of the characters.

The loosely structured meaning that is generated is similar to what Egan (1988) described as *causal schemes*, which are more like plots than stories. Causal schemes determine the organization of the narrative, which is similar to how plots develop during children's play. Egan elaborates that such schemes are 'ordered in sequence by causality' as the plot unfolds, which is determined by 'affective connections' (p. 11), such as, 'these events cause these emotions in people which cause them to do these things which cause these results, and so on' (p. 24). One scene follows another, taking their places in the affective pattern, building coherently towards the overall unit.

Egan's view is that causal schemes grow out of the logic of metaphor, and he cites C.S. Lewis's perspective that the real theme of stories is 'like a state or quality' and an 'empathy with characters' through the 'immersion in other worlds' (Lewis, 1982, p. 18). Others have discussed the other-worldly, special frame of mind the child enters when inventing a pictorial reality through art. Golomb (1988), for instance, states that art transforms children's ordinary experiences of the world and allows them to represent it 'on a new and perhaps mythical plane of action and thought' (p. 222).

Young children's other-worldly ideas, as reflected in their visual narratives, demonstrate the intricate link between their affective, imaginative, rational and abstract thinking. Their narratives, coupled with drawing and action, encapsulate into one compact package, ideas, context and emotion. This offers an authentic kind of participation for the child, and a concrete form through which we can observe the workings of the child's imagination and the role of imagery in his/her thinking. Drawing serves as direct documentation of the diverse concepts that children apply to their personal experiences, to more fully grasp their worlds. Most notably, it enables children to imagine new perspectives, new worlds. Drawing is something the child can inhabit or get inside of. Indeed, drawing is something the child *is*.

It is the integration of three modes in consort – graphic, narrative and embodied – that makes visual narrative a powerful source for children's learning, representational thought and creativity. Body and mind intersect as children discover, through exploration and play, the distinctive features of meaning-making that take place within these modes. Table 1.2 provides a description of these modes and their features. Yet, it should be noted that the examples for each feature are illustrative, rather than forming an exhaustive list of possibilities. Throughout this book, several cases of children's work will be used to illustrate these modes and features, and specific chapters will cover these issues in greater depth.

In sum, the graphic, narrative and embodied modes co-exist while children draw. This multimodal, symbiotic relationship increases children's capacity to use many forms of representation. Many authors have discussed how talk, drawing and movement are parallel and mutually transformative processes – they enrich and inform each other (cf. Dyson, 1986, 1990, 2003; Kendrick & McKay, 2004; Kress, 1997; Matthews, 2004; Short, Kauffman, & Kahn, 2000; Thompson, 1995; Wright, 2003a, 2005). Gallas (1994), for instance, demonstrates that the narratives that children create while drawing are paralleled by their oral storying and role-play. This is 'a constructive process of thinking in action' (Cox, 2005, p. 123). As Linqvist describes it, 'children draw pictures and tell a story at the same time; they act a role and create their lines as they go along' (Linqvist, 2001, p. 8).

Table 1.2 Modes and Features of Meaning in Visual Narratives

Modes	Features	Examples
Graphic	Art elements	Marks, lines, shapes, colours, textures, shadings, proportions, composition and perspective
	Symbols	Letters, words or phrases to label characters, places, objects or events, or to title the work; numbers to quantify content or signify sequences; flags, traffic lights, emblems, badges, motifs, logos
	Icons and iconic devices	Speech balloons to 'voice' the characters; whoosh lines to 'move' the objects or figures; dotted lines to show movement trajectories between things
	Spatial relationships	In front/behind, close/distant, above/below, similar, proximal, surrounded, vertical/horizontal axes
Narrative	Non-Fictional	Real, true-life, personal
	Literal	Descriptive, factual, exact, unembellished
	Fictional	Imaginary, unreal, fantastic, illusory
	Metaphoric	Rhetorical, symbolic, allegorical, abstract, which may include: • figures of speech, such as 'heavy music' • rhyming • onomatopoeia (i.e., the use of a word or vocal expression which sounds like the thing or action designated, such as 'frmmmph')
Embodied	Descriptive action	Moving the hand across or outside the page (e.g., to show spatial relationships or movement)
	Expressiveness	Gesticulations, facial expression, body-language, vocalisms (e.g., emphasis through change in pitch, volume or speed of speech) and gestures to accompany onomatopoeia (e.g., flicking fingers to go with the word 'poooooofff')
	Dramatization	Enacting as if being a character or an object (e.g., demonstrating a steering motion to indicate driving a car)

Using play as the vehicle for their explorations, children selectively and frequently move from one mode to another to represent and re-present what they know most effectively. They may choose to draw it, or to tell it, or to show it through their bodies – or to combine these modes. For instance, sometimes the child might talk about an idea and then show this graphically or through physical action; sometimes the child might draw something, and then talk about it or demonstrate its meaning through vocalisms, dramatization or action; sometimes the child might dramatize an idea and then describe this through language or show it through pictorial content; sometimes these processes are concurrent (e.g., the child might draw a squiggly line below a figure, while simultaneously saying 'Aaaahhhh' and gesturing downward, to show that the person is falling).

So, the signs that children make offer the possibility of representing through a multiplicity of means, at one and the same time (Kress, 1997). Children are 'playing with the process of signing' (Cox, 2005, p. 123), and the integrated text of drawing, talking and role playing becomes what Chandler (2002, p. 3) calls an 'assemblage of signs', or what Goodman (1976, 1984) referred to as a form of integrated 'languages'. It is a discourse using the 'mixed-media' of language, image-making and graphic and physical action. Children experiment with the 'language of materials and marks' (Cox, 2005, p. 122) combined with narrative and embodied telling. In the process, they build concepts and become *authors* of an integrated text, using a range of voices of communication.

Summary

Semiotics helps us realize the affordances and constraints of various modes of communication. This helps us avoid the 'routine privileging of one semiotic mode over another', such as the written over the visual, or the verbal over the non-verbal (Chandler, 2002, p. 219). Through visual narratives, children invent worlds in other-worldly ways to create, represent and communicate meaning. These processes are surfaced through the child's imagination while using the open-ended resources offered – a blank page can 'become' anything. The loosely structured use of the configurational signs offered through art, accompanied by narrative, gesture and role play, provide infinite possibilities for symbolic communication. This liberates children to construct and re-construct visual arrangements on the page and to 'speak' through the medium of graphic, narrative and embodied communication. The message of the *macro text* stems from the child's imagination, personal experiences in the world and exposure to a range of things, such as the media, mentors and opportunities.

Art provides a place where negotiation takes place, where new meaning becomes possible and where new worlds can be developed. While drawing, children enter into an interpretive space where they can 'tell themselves about themselves' (Geertz, 1971, p. 26). To be present in that space is to witness the internal worlds that children imagine, investigate and make real through the images of their art.

Indeed, many aspects of the child's discourse can remain invisible unless we witness his/her creation of the text and understand the multifaceted ways that it evolved. Without an understanding of the child's processes, the drawing itself is merely a stagnant artefact – a remnant which may be filed and stored, or alternatively displayed on a refrigerator door of a home or on the walls of a classroom or gallery. Yet rich understandings of the artwork and the creator can arise when we observe the child's various verbal, visual, spatial and bodily-kinaesthetic forms of representation as they unfold in real time, naturalistically. This involves reflecting on the child's creative process of meaning-making: what the content denotes and how this communicates deeper meaning, connotatively.

Children draw to create meaning and to communicate this with others. They demonstrate incredible control of the process of composing through dialoguing with the materials of art. Meaning-making through visual narrative is a highly creative and 'fluid' process, where children become authors using multiple texts, combining graphic, verbal and embodied modes. In consort, these modes increase children's capacity to represent, to mentally manipulate and to organize their thoughts and feelings. Children's meaning can be understood when the following aspects are considered relationally:

- the *content* (i.e., themes, people, places, objects, events), and
- the *form* in which this content is communicated through three modes:

  o *graphic* (i.e., structural arrangements and use of art elements, symbols, icons and iconic devices),
  o *narrative* (i.e., telling the content and the processes of its creation through various forms – non-fictional, literal, fictional or metaphoric), and
  o *embodied* (i.e., descriptive action, expressiveness or dramatization).

However, open-ended, free exploration through creative processes such as problem setting, problem solving, elaboration and transformation can be denied within the culture of classrooms. Instead, precedence in school often is given to 'teaching' the more rule-bound symbol systems of numeracy and literacy. Yet, as argued in this chapter, learning the more loosely structured, holistic discourse of art is a parallel (if not preliminary) form of literacy development. Children learn to arrange elements such as lines, shapes and colours in a visual composition, attending to how the component parts combine, and how the content and form of their meaning function.

Through art, children discover the power of signs and learn to manipulate these as a means towards defining themselves and their connections with the outside world while also creating fantasy worlds.

(Continued)

(Continued)

Future-oriented educators highlight the importance of developing children's fluid thought processes and skills, such as imagination, fantasy, adaptability, empathy and resilience – all of which equip children to be autonomous and active creators. Young children's thinking is still imaginative, flexible and linked to fantasy – qualities that we should seek to retain in children as they grow older.

〰 Reflections

With permission of the child and his/her teacher and parent, photograph or colour photocopy a drawing that has already been made by a child who is between 4 and 8 years of age. Invite the child to tell you about the drawing and take notes of what was said. With permission, video- or tape-record this conversation so that you can revisit this content for deeper understanding.

1. What is the content of the drawing (i.e., what do the signs stand for)?
2. Did separate or combined art elements of the drawing (e.g., line, colour, shape, arrangement of figures) strike you as holding particular significance?
3. What words and/or gestures were used when the child described the artwork?
4. Do you think you may have understood the child's intentions and meanings better if you had been present to witness the child's creation of the drawing? Why?

Bring the child's drawing to class to discuss these questions with your colleagues.

Additional readings

Anning, A., & Ring, K. (2004). *Making sense of children's drawings*. Berkshire: Open University Press.

Gallas, K. (1994). *The languages of learning: How children talk, write, dance, draw and sing their understanding of the world*. New York: Teachers College Press.

Matthews, J. (2004). The art of infancy. In A. Kindler, E. Eisner, & M. Day (Eds.), *Learning in the visual arts: Handbook of research and policy in art education* (pp. 253–298). Canada: University of British Columbia.

Planning for Play

Briggs, M. and Hansen, A.

It is also naïve to think that good play environments can be achieved only through design. (Hart, 2002: 14)

Introduction

In this chapter we look at the issues around planning for play activities with primary aged children and how both adults and children can be involved in the planning and organisation of play environments. It will include discussion of the design and planning of environments, as well as the development of environments through spontaneous events in the classroom and outside as a response to children's interests and ideas. This chapter will typically raise questions about how we stimulate play with older learners and how we allow the element of choice within activities for the children.

To begin we need to revisit what the objectives are of the play that we wish to initiate with the children. The following is a good starting point for any adult beginning to plan for play. In Chapter 2 we outlined six roles for older learners playing and used these to form our play principles for primary aged children. These were:

- child as autonomous learner
- child as creative learner
- child as investigator
- child as problem solver
- child as reflective learner
- child as a social learner.

Additionally, in Chapter 5 the Croftlands Junior School case study showcased how the staff developed their own principles about their play-based approach to learning. Regardless of the play principles you adhere to yourself or in your school, what is crucial is that you are explicitly aware of these when you are planning. By subscribing to your principles, you are more effectively able to provide appropriate conditions for learning.

Making connections with the existing curriculum

This can be seen in two ways. Firstly, there is the existing curriculum from government and then secondly, the curriculum that may already have been planned within school. This partly reflects the first but is about more than merely ensuring that the curriculum is delivered; it is also about personalising or adapting to local needs via medium-and/or long-term planning. Whichever view of an existing curriculum you are taking there can be pressure to ensure that the children are given access to the expected curriculum. As discussed in Chapter 5, teachers can feel the pressures of the existing curriculum and the need to cover it, and are aware of external expectations. This can lead to the view that everything should be planned to ensure specific outcomes. A play-based approach to learning is flexible and therefore addresses children's needs and builds on their strengths (for more discussion of this see Chapter 8).

 Points for reflection

Consider the forthcoming curriculum you have planned for your class and which parts might lend themselves to the development of play activities. How would this approach enhance the learning of the curriculum? Which skills, knowledge and attitudes would play activities offer children the opportunity to practise or develop further?

In addition to considered planning of play opportunities there are also times when you may want to be freer in the planning you undertake. The following section explores this, acknowledging the tensions that exist and offering one possible solution.

Taking account of children's interests

Play is freely chosen, personally directed, intrinsically motivated behaviour that actively engages the child ... Play can be fun or serious. Through play children explore social, material and imaginary worlds and their relationship with them, elaborating all the while a flexible range of responses to the challenges they encounter. (National Playing Fields Association (NPFA), 2000: 6)

This is particularly a challenge for teachers of primary or elementary aged children with a curriculum to teach and, as discussed in the previous chapter, there are always concerns about coverage. However, a period of heavy snow might generate an interest in peoples who live in cold climates and how they construct their home using snow, for example. This could be built on by the teacher by allowing the class to construct an igloo in the classroom or outside using different modelling techniques to show scale and size of the home. Is there room in your own planning to build on serendipitous opportunities such as this? After all, we are reminded that many scientific discoveries were made through serendipitous learning (Spalding, 2000).

Tracking curriculum coverage

When using a play-based approach to learning, you will see children taking their learning beyond or away from the curriculum objectives you originally planned. Depending on your confidence and other external factors, you may encourage the children to pursue this or you may need to refocus the children back to your original intention. What is important is your own record keeping and how you maintain a record of what the children have learnt. This will be discussed further in Chapter 7 but is also a consideration in planning.

One effective way to track coverage of the curriculum in a play-based approach is to use the yearly objective tracking sheets that are used for individual children. By using only one for each subject, it is possible to list the objectives in the left-hand column and use the remaining columns to identify time periods during the year. As planning is carried out and as learning progresses, it is possible to make annotations about the extent to which the objectives are addressed generally by your class. Not only does this format provide a document for you to account for the children's learning you have planned and observed at a whole-class level, it also serves as a key document for planning further learning during the year as you can very easily identify gaps or areas for development. Crucially, it is a map for seeing where you have been as well as identifying possible direction of travel. See Figure 6.1 for an example.

Key learning experiences and activities

Mason and Johnson-Wilder note the difference between (mathematical) tasks and activity. They state:

Music Curriculum Coverage Tracking Sheet: 7-11 years of age

TERM / WEEKS / TOPIC	Controlling sounds through singing and playing – performing skills			Creating and developing musical ideas – composing skills		Responding and reviewing – appraising skills		
	1a sing songs, in unison and two parts, with clear diction, control of pitch, a sense of phrase and musical expression	1b play tuned and unturned instruments with control and rhythmic accuracy	1c practice, rehearse and present performances with an awareness of the audience	2a improvise, developing rhythmic and melodic material when performing	2b explore, choose, combine and organise musical ideas within musical structures	3a analyse and compare sounds	3b explore and explain their own ideas and feelings about music using movement, dance, expressive language and musical vocabulary	3c improve their own and others' work in relation to its intended effect
TERM 1 WKS 1-6 COLOUR				Representing 'colour' through composition (Also *)	Timbre			*
TERM 1 WKS 7-12 SACRED TEXTS	Hymns - one + two parts						Canons	
TERM 2 WKS 1-3 FRACTIONS		Musical notation (Also *)			*	Pitch + duration		

Figure 6.1   Tracking curriculum coverage example: Music

> The purpose of a task is to initiate mathematically fruitful activity that leads to a transformation in what learners are sensitised to notice and competent to carry out. In learners' normal everyday activity, they initiate actions to satisfy their own motives, but educational activity is initiated in response to teachers' tasks. When a task is set, the *teacher's* intention is that the task will promote certain kinds of learning, but the *learner's* motive will depend on how the task is seen. (2006: 25)

Although we have already mentioned the dangers inherent in making all the decisions for children as this can lead to a lack of engagement with expected key learning activities, it is important to have thought about what might be possible key learning experiences that you want the children to gain. Depending on how confident you are within your planning and teaching, you may feel more secure in insisting the children meet particular outcomes. Alternatively, you may plan for these particular outcomes but allow the children to move away from these if it is appropriate. This rekindles the planning paradox (Ainley et al., 2006) introduced in Chapter 1.

It is important to distinguish between outcomes and outputs (Williams, 2011). Outcomes occur through activity whereas output is a tangible product. Often the process undertaken to produce an output has many more outcomes than the product itself shows. This is discussed further in the next chapter on assessing learning through play.

At the end of this chapter Table 6.1 provides a checklist you may find helpful when planning.

Children's involvement in developing the plans

Giving children choice and ownership over their own learning increases motivation and improves behaviour. It also impacts on the likelihood of them wanting to be involved in the future (Xiang et al., 2003). Starting with a 'what do we know and what do we want to find out?' lesson at the beginning of a unit or topic can spark children's imagination and motivation in a new play situation. Using an electronic poster tool such as 'Prezis', which is freely available for educational purposes, can be a very different way of producing linking ideas as part of the planning process. It is possible to track routes through the connected ideas, zooming in and out. This will assist children to choose resources to support the development of the environment. The more that the children are engaged in the overall design of the environment/activity, the more they are likely to remember and learn from the experiences. They are also developing their skills of problem solving and organisation as they work on planning, designing and resourcing the environment. In turn they are drawing on their creative, mathematical, historical, scientific, literacy and geographical skills which might be linked to any given environment.

Another way of gaining children's input could be to start with a resource, for example exploring the initial possibilities of plaster of Paris bandages or wire sculptures as one form of artistic play. Once the children have had a go with the resource then the class can discuss how an area might be developed so that children could explore the resources further. A visiting artist could also demonstrate some of the possibilities which the children can then replicate and/or develop to become their own ideas. We would argue for a co-construction of the play activities with the children informed by the curriculum, the interests and needs of the children as well as reflection upon previous experiences and assessments by the adults plus reflections on their own practice.

Creating the environment and providing the stimulus

Think about the case studies that you have already encountered in this book and consider the range of possible starting stimuli. For example, in Chapter 4 there was a book *The Friends of Emily Culpepper* which stimulated the villagers' meetings, and the playing at being a centurion in the Roman army was part of a topic about invaders and settlers.

There can be dangers in trying to impose pre-planned environments and activities on the children because of concerns about control. Baker-Sennett et al. (2008) discuss the differences between teachers who control and those who engage children in the process of planning. Their research found that not being directive resulted in better outcomes as the children naturally engaged with reading and writing activities as part of their play if they were not told that was what they had to do. As Anning suggests: 'It is unrealistic to argue that education contexts can offer the same freedoms to children's play behaviours as in the home or out of school settings/contexts' but she continues nor is it helpful to shape 'childrens' self-initiated play into a "sanitised" version for educational purposes' (2010: 29).

There can be occasions when the initial stimulus is very clearly planned but the activities that the children engage with and their use of resources is their choice. An example of this is the case study we met in Chapter 5. This can be seen in Baker-Sennett et al. (2008) when they differentiate between 'playplanning' and 'non-playplanning'.

> *'Non-playplanning'* was play-related events that did not involve decisions about the play, such as reading a script provided by the adult, puppet making under the direction of the co-oper, rote rehearsals with no proposals for change, or imitating something already decided ... Planning could occur 'in character' or 'out of character'. (2008: 1003)

They also argue that the children's involvement in planning assists the development of their own planning skills and the co-ordination of plans with others. The latter is a key skill for team work in later life.

The outdoors

When working with older primary or elementary aged children we can learn a lot from the work of early years practitioners and their relatively recent development of using the outdoors as an environment for learning. To begin with we want children to be aware of their surroundings indoors and out, and to look at environmental issues, citizenship and care for the local environment. There are concerns about children's engagement with their environment, as can be seen in the work of Thomas and Thompson when they say:

> Children are losing their connection with the natural environment and their well-being and environmental quality are inextricably linked. The worse a local environment looks, the less able children are to play freely ... (2004: 3)

As a result of the lack of the use of outdoors for activities, with the exception of sport in many schools, children can initially view going outside as an excuse to run around and this can be coupled with Anning's concerns about 'the strategy of using "play outdoors" as a safety valve for boisterous, physical play for girls' and boys' (2010: 29). In order to ensure that children understand what going outside actually means during school time the adults need to prepare the ground rules carefully for the learners and also decide how this might be communicated to parents and carers, who may raise their own concerns about time spent outside the classroom.

Points for reflection

Some schools have small outdoor theatre spaces that can be used for dramatic play or there may be a natural bowl in the school grounds that might work as a kind of auditorium. If these kinds of spaces are available in your school then consider how to make more use of them for play of different kinds.

Planning for access for all

In planning environments consideration must be given to access for children with physical disabilities such as mobility issues or sensory impairment. All areas should be available to all children or variations made available in consultation with the children themselves to ensure that adults are not being even unintentionally patronising towards any child with any additional need. It can be easy to make assumptions that they might not cope with an area that has stairs, for example where the child may view this as a challenge or additional practice in managing that kind of environment. This is best negotiated directly with the children involved so they set the agenda and feel included rather than excluded from any of the decision making. You will also need to consider any cultural issues there might be with understanding the environment being created or specific issues about sensitivities to religious views.

Another way to provide access to all children might be to create an environment where everyone has their sight restricted, say with blindfolds, so that they must use their other senses more carefully to play in the environment. Sensory gardens work on a similar principle emphasising the sense of smell over the other senses, for example. Recreating a coal mine shaft with little light where children worked in dirty conditions could be a way of demonstrating what happens when you have limited sight in a cramped environment. More about play for all children is discussed in Chapter 8.

Differentiation

Differentiation is a necessary component to consider in all planning of learning opportunities. Pedagogical practice impacts on learner identity and social values (Raveaud, 2005) and therefore meeting children's needs through differentiation is as important in play environments as it is in other approaches to teaching and learning. If you plan for the play environment to offer an open-ended task then differentiation by outcome is possible. Managing differentiation through adult or child intervention is another valid approach. Sometimes planning to assign roles to specific children within an environment can challenge and extend their thinking. For example, 'What might you say in a given situation if you were in this person's shoes?' Asking children to research ideas, periods of history, scientific knowledge or other facts that they could use in a role play could provide extension work away from the play environment and inform their role development. Another form of differentiation by support is to consider the resources that are available to children (the use of resources is discussed further in the next section). Finally, peer support is a clear aid to differentiation when children are collaborating in mixed attainment groups during play-based activities.

Besides academic differentiation, your planning should consider other aspects of children's development and differentiate according to this if appropriate. For example, are there children in the class who need specific support when working with others? Who might you pair them up with? Or are you going to encourage them to select who they will work with? Does it matter whether they work with someone else or idependently?

Resources

Many theorists identify the need for children to use various resources and representations to support their learning (for example, Bruner, 1960, 1986; Dienes, 1969; Piaget, 1952; Skemp, 1987) and identify how resources can mediate social construction of knowledge (for example, Cobb, 1995; Vygotsky, 1978).

Collecting resources is a vital part of allowing children to choose and discuss what resources are the most appropriate for a given scenario. If you are not an early years practitioner it is worth visiting an early years setting to see the range of resources that they collect to support play environments. The resources need not be expensive as children can make things to sell in shops from clay, plasticine or junk. Drews explains how 'flexible uses of resources can encourage flexible thinking. This approach can help develop a classroom culture in which it is recognised that there are many paths to reach the same [destination]' (2007: 29).

You will need to think about storage when the resources are not being used and how they will be organised in the classroom. Also think about the extent to which you are going to allow the children to freely choose which resources they can use. For example, will children always have access to the internet, scrap paper or calculators? What limitations, if any, will you put on the resources and why? Turner and McCullouch suggest that allowing children a choice in the resources they use 'enhances the ability of children to apply their knowledge to new situation' (2004:65). Adults in the classroom are also resources – and the most expensive – so in your planning think about how this resource is going to be best utilised!

Thinking about adults' roles

Chapter 5 was dedicated to considering the roles that adults have in play-based approaches to learning, reflecting the importance of this aspect. Not only is it necessary to be aware of your role and the roles of other adults, it is also necessary to keep those roles in mind when you are planning. Will you encourage the other adults you are working with to adopt the role of manager as they organise the time, space and resources that promote play? Will they mediate, or interpret the play that occurs? Perhaps you will ask them to adopt an active role in the play, engaging in parallel play, co-playing or play tutoring (Dockett and Fleer, 2002).

Organisation and management of time

A key part of the planning and organisation is not just the location of the activities, environment or resources but when the children will be able to play in the space. You will need to decide when this occurs based upon your classroom or outdoor space and the organisation of the other activities when this occurs. You might decide that the activities will be available for the whole class every afternoon for a week or in the afternoon of one or two days in the week during the period of this particular project. Will all of the children be involved at the same time? Do all the children have to be involved at all? There are various ways you may group the children to be involved in play-based activities including:

- whole class
- attainment grouping
- self-selected groups
- interest groups
- pairs.

Teachers and trainees can be worried about letting children select their own groups. However, we have observed that when children are given the choice about who they may work with, they often look beyond friendship groupings to work with the most appropriate people for the task in hand. Of course this is often their friends, and what better way to encourage children to learn collaboratively than with children they have already developed highly sophisticated ways of relating to. Behaviour is also often more appropriate when children choose who they work with. Our observations concur with Boyatzis et al. who note using 'self-awareness, self-management, social awareness and social skills at appropriate times and ways in sufficient frequency to be effective in the situation' (2000: 3) shows emotional intelligence.

Reflection

Many teachers now have advanced skills in reflecting on their own teaching and on the children's learning. Afterall, Schön (1983) encourages teachers to take time to deliberately reflect through 'reflection on reflection in action', in order to develop a 'repertoire of knowledge and experience'. While it is important for teachers to reflect during evaluations of play experiences, we want to focus on planning for children to reflect on their own outcomes in a play situation. After all,

> Some have argued that play is children's work but I would say that it is far more than this. Play is their self-actualisation, a holistic exploration of who and what they are and know and of who and what they might become. (Broadhead, 2006: 89)

Supporting children in their ability to reflect upon how their thinking has changed is a critical part of a learning process (Hansen, 2008). Assessment for Learning (AfL) has led to a plethora of activities for helping children during their reflection process. It might be helpful when you are planning for children's reflection opportunities to use the materials provided on AfL websites and documents (for example, www.assessment-frform-group.org/index.html:www.aaia.org.uk/afl). Furthermore, plan for the children to reflect on two distinct parts of their involvement in the play activities.

1   What have you discovered?
2   What have you learnt?

The first relates to the 'hard' outcomes: what the children have found out. What declarative knowledge do they have now that they did not have prior to the activity? The second relates to the 'soft' outcomes: what they have learnt about their ability to carry out a particular task, their relationship with another child, assumptions they made about their own time management and so on.

Reflection on activities can often be reduced to writing about the activities that children have undertaken. Even this can have a very different feel with the use of technology, for example groups' blogs about the activities they have taken part in on a once a week basis over a half term. Robson's research looked at how 3–4-year-old children exhibited metacognitive behaviour. She found that there was a shift during an activity 'from a preoccupation with metacognitive skilfulness and planning and monitoring the activity ... towards more emphasis on displaying metacognitive knowledge in the children's later reflection upon it' (2010: 239).

Although we have presented 'reflection' towards the end of this chapter, be mindful during planning that opportunities for children to reflect are necessary throughout the play experience and should not only come at the end.

Bringing activities to a close, display and presentation

Rather than allowing the play environment to just become unused during the day or for the class to lose interest, it is important to consider how long an environment/activity will be available and how you will close the activity. One way is to have a culminating activity, such as a celebration. For example, the centurion soldiers returning home to their families and a traditional feast would mark the end of the activities linked to Roman soldiers and their way of life. It is then possible to start a new environment/activity which can be advertised ahead of time with a poster which proclaims what is coming soon.

Another powerful way to bring longer periods of play to a conclusion is to create a sense of audience for sharing the outcomes from the play. For example, displays of action photos could form a book, a wall display or a slide presentation on an IWB.

Beyond the wider school curriculum is the United Nations Convention on the Rights of the Child (UNCRC, 1989). In Article 12, point 1 states, 'the child who is capable of forming his or her own views [has] the right to express those freely in all matters affecting [them], the views of the child being given due weight in accordance with the age and maturity of the child'. This is followed up in Article 13 where 'the child shall have the right to freedom of expression; this right shall include freedom to seek, receive and impart information and ideas of all kinds, regardless of frontiers, either orally, in writing or in print, in the form of art, or through any other media of the child's choice'. By sharing findings with others children can feel empowered – which the convention states is their right.

Table 6.1 Checklist for planning

Have you considered?	Resources/issues	Tick/cross
Curriculum objectives		
Location of play environment		
Children's involvement in planning		
Inclusion issues		
Resources available for the children to use		
Trial activities with specific resources		
The overall design of the environment		
Time allocation: time each day, total time span for activities		
Behaviour expectations for the children		
Expectations for the adults of interactions and engagement		
Involvement of other expert adults		
Expected outcomes		
Communication with parents/carers		
Reflections by the children		
How you will assess skills, knowledge, attitudes		
How you will record any assessment		
How you will retain a record of the activities/environment		
How you will close the activities		
How you will evaluate the whole of the activities/environment		

Summary

This chapter has raised some challenges about planning for play activities with primary/elementary aged children. Consider the implications for your own practice by reflecting on the following questions.

1 What concerns do I have about planning for play?
2 How does my understanding of the concerns impact on my practice?
3 How can I give more control of the planning process to the children?
4 What changes might I need to make to my practice?
5 What are the benefits of play for children's learning?
6 What are the benefits for my teaching of using play approaches?

Further reading

Children's Play Council (2006) *Planning for Play: Guidance on the Development and Implementation of a Local Play Strategy*. National Children's Bureau/Big Lottery Fund. Available at: www.playengland.org.uk/resources/planning-for-play (accessed July 2011).

Drake, J. (2005) *Planning Children's Play and Learning in the Foundation Stage*. London: David Fulton.

Prezis details are available at: http://prezi.com/ (accessed July 2011).

Fogarty, R.J. and Pete, B.M. (2009) *How to Integrate the Curricula*. Thousand Oaks, CA: Corwin. Provides ten models of curriculum integration offering a way of addressing the issues of having to 'cover' curriculum objectives. All of the models they identify can be used in a play-based learning environment in primary schools and many address the issue of coverage.

References

Ainley, J., Pratt, D. and Hansen, A. (2006) 'Connecting engagement and focus in pedagogic task design', *British Educational Research Journal*, 32 (1): 23–38.

Anning, A. (2010) 'Play and legislated curriculum', in Moyles, J. (ed.) *The Excellence of Play*, 3rd edn. Maidenhead: Open University Press.

Baker-Sennett, J., Matusov, E. and Rogoff, B. (2008) 'Children's planning of classroom plays with adult or child direction', *Social Development*, 17 (4): 998–1018.

Boyatzis, R.E., Goleman, D. and Rhee, K.S. (2000) 'Clustering competence in emotional intelligence: insights from the Emotional Competency Inventory', in R. Bar-On and J. D. Parker (eds), *The Handbook of Emotional Intelligence:*

Theory, Development, Assessment, and Application at Home, School, and in the Workplace. San Francisco: Jossey-Bass. (pp. 343–62)

Broadhead, P. (2006) 'Developing an understanding of young children's learning through play: the place of observation, interaction and reflection', *British Educational Research Journal*, 32(2): 191–207.

Bruner, J.S. (1960) *The Process of Education*. Cambridge, MA: Harvard University Press.

Bruner, J.S. (1986) *Actual Minds, Possible Worlds*. Cambridge, MA: Harvard University Press.

Cobb, P. (1995) 'Cultural tools and mathematical learning: a case study', *Journal for Research in Mathematics Education*, 26 (4): 362–85.

Dienes, Z.P. (1969) *Building Up Mathematics*. London: Hutchinson Education.

Dockett, S. and Fleer, M. (2002) *Play and Pedagogy in Early Childhood: Bending the Rules*. Australia: Nelson.

Drews, D. (2007) 'Do resources really matter in primary mathematics teaching and learning?' in D. Drews and A. Hansen (eds.) *Using Resources to Support Mathematical Thinking: Primary and Early Years*. Exeter: Learning Matters Ltd. pp 19–31.

Hansen, A. (2008) *Children's geometric defining and a principled approach to task design*. Unpublished doctoral thesis. Institute of Education, University of Warwick. Available at: www.children-count.co.uk/images/PhD%20Final.pdf (accessed July 2011).

Hart, R. (2002) 'Containing children: some lessons on planning for play from New York City', *Environment and Urbanization*, 14 (2): 135–48.

Mason, J. and Johnson-Wilder, S. (2006) *Designing and Using Mathematical Tasks*. St Albans: Tarquin Publications.

National Playing Fields Association (NPFA), Children's Play Council and PLAYLINK (2000) *Best Play: What Play Provision Should Do for Children*. London: NPFA.

Piaget, J. (1952) *The Child's Conception of Number*. New York: Humanities Press.

Raveaud, M. (2005) 'Hares, tortoises and the social construction of the pupil: differentiated learning in French and English primary schools', *British Educational Research Journal*, 31 (4) 459–79.

Robson, S. (2010) 'Self-regulation and metacognition in young children's self-initiated play and reflective dialogue', *International Journal of Early Years Education*, 18 (3): 227–41.

Schön, D. A. (1983) *The Reflective Practitioner: How Professionals Think in Action*. New York: Basic Books.

Skemp, R.R. (1987) *The Psychology of Learning Mathematics*. Hillsdale, NJ: Erlbaum.

Spalding, E. (2000) 'Performance assessment and the new standards project: a story of serendipitous success', *Phi Delta Kappan*, 81 (10): 758–64.

Thomas, G. and Thompson, G. (2004) *A Child's Place: Why Environment Matters to Children*. London: Green Alliance/DEMOS.

Turner, S. and McCullouch, J. (2004) *Making Connections in Primary Mathematics*. London: David Fulton.

United Nations Convention on the Rights of the Child (UNCRC) (1989) 'Convention on the Rights of the Child'. Available at: www2.ohchr.org/english/law/crc.htm (accessed July 2011).

Vygotsky, L.S. (1978) *Mind in Society: The Development of Higher Psychological Processes*. Cambridge, MA: Harvard University Press.

Williams, H. (2011) Review Day at Croftlands Junior School, Ulverston. 12th May, 2011.

Xiang, P., McBride, R., Guan, J. and Solmon, M. (2003) 'Children's motivation in elementary physical education: an expectancy-value model of achievement choice', *Research Quarterly for Exercise and Sport*, 74, (1): pp. 25–35.

Planning

Cockerton, E.

Chapter overview

Making lessons work? It's all in the planning. Much great teaching relies on the bedrock of good planning. While acknowledging that schools and teachers plan in different ways Eleanor Cockerton provides some fundamental principles and guidance on how to plan effectively. She demonstrates how personalising your own planning to the needs of the children you teach can make all the difference.

Introduction

Planning needs to be considered in close partnership with assessment. Reading the previous chapter alongside this one will give you a better view of the process. Planning is a vital part of teaching and it is well worth spending time and effort getting it right. It can be an invaluable teaching and self-assessment tool and it will ensure that you have thought through exactly how the lesson will work for you, the children and any supporting adults. You will then be able to look back and see if it worked as you imagined, whether the children learned what you had intended and anything you did to improve or detract from their learning experience. It takes practice and can be a highly individual process, so do not despair if it takes a while to make it work well. When you are able to plan effectively it will put you in a stronger position in the classroom. You will have a clear idea of where you are going, the timing of different elements and what the learning should look like by the end. It will make you feel more prepared when you are in front of the class, a little like a sophisticated security blanket, and will make your thought processes evident to anyone supervising your progress. It is very difficult to help a prospective teacher improve their teaching when the planning and thinking behind it are difficult to unravel.

Depending on the way your placement school plans, you will be given long- and/or medium- and sometimes short-term plans to work from. This is rather a 'swings and roundabouts' situation as the more the school has done for you, the less you will need to do but the less you will learn about the whole planning process and your individual needs. It is important therefore to make the planning your own. I have always found it extremely difficult to teach effectively using plans which I have not personalised taking into account my children, my teaching style and my resources. You also lose some of the excitement from planning your own learning opportunity or taking a bit of a risk because you think a particular activity will grab your children's interest.

Elements of your planning are likely to be dictated by preset curricula (such as the National Curriculum, Early Years Foundation Stage Guidance or school documentation) but there will be some elements you will be able to make your own. Some schools also use commercial schemes of work as a basis for planning. There may be opportunities to plan cooperatively with colleagues in a parallel age group or you may be teaching more than one age group in your class. Your training establishment will also have its own views on what should be included although these tend to be fairly standard. So, as you can see, there are many variations before you even start to think about how and what might work best for you.

The Early Years Foundation Stage (EYFS) planning takes on a quite different guise from that undertaken in Key Stages 1 or 2 as the children take much greater control over their learning. Long- and medium-term plans will contain ideas, possibilities and a balance between the subject areas devised by the teacher(s) but short-term and lesson plans will have a much greater emphasis on the children's needs and interests. Activities will not necessarily have predetermined learning outcomes and there is a much greater emphasis on observation. The whole process needs to be extremely fluid and adaptable.

In this chapter I aim to help you through the maze of what you might be presented with and how to turn the planning process into an invaluable personal learning resource. I have chosen not to include specific examples of plans as there are so many ways of doing this. Your training institution will have formats of the kind of thing they expect and adapting what you are given using this advice is going to be easier than trying to juggle several different systems.

Long-, medium- and short-term planning

These terms are used within schools and training establishments but can mean a variety of things. They are used to describe the various stages of the planning process but may not all be used in your particular placement school.

Long-term plans

These are generally discussed and planned as a school, or possibly with a subject leader, and may reflect a whole year's teaching or possibly a term's. They give an overview of the learning expectations of each class or age group and enable individual teachers to plan more specifically within these.

They ensure:

- all aspects of a subject are covered
- skills and processes have a logical progression
- equipment and resources, which may be limited, are not being used at the same time in two different areas of the school
- where there are two or more classes of the same age group the children have an equitable experience
- if necessary, they take into account something specific to that school such as a special event.

Long-term plans will contain varying amounts of detail. Some schools will use the same long-term plans from year to year while they remain appropriate, and some will change them on a yearly basis. Schools with mixed-age classes usually consider this stage of the planning in some detail to ensure that all children receive good subject coverage without unnecessary repetitions. Long-term plans may also be formulated where cross-curricular links are identified. This type of learning approach is becoming more common and is explored in detail in Chapter 14, 'Making sense of the curriculum'. Whatever you receive will be individual to the school's needs and ethos.

For younger children long-term plans are usually based around topic areas and possible activities which would meet the Guidance for the Early Years Foundation Stage (DfES, 2007) or other National Curriculum needs for this age group. Visits and visitors as well as any special events would be planned here too.

Medium-term plans

These may be for the length of a topic, a term, half a term or a week depending on the school's or teacher's views and needs. They put more substance into the long-term plans and are usually individual to the class teacher. In a school where there is more than one class of a parallel age group these can be undertaken jointly, or occasionally one teacher will plan one subject area such as maths and another English and ideas are then shared. Almost invariably these will need to have enough room for you to teach in an appropriate way for your own children.

Medium-term plans for you may initially be a week of maths or English lessons where your concerns will be to show appropriate progression with learning objectives, teaching and activities all building gradually on learning from the previous lessons.

Medium-term plans in the EYFS would use information from the long-term plan but would start to incorporate ideas from the children.

Short-term plans

For an experienced teacher these may be presented as a week or a group of lessons but each will have been planned with specific learning objectives, teaching input, activities and assessment criteria in mind. They should be fluid in that the children will not necessarily have reached the point you predicted by the end of the lesson and therefore the next session will need to reflect this.

Short-term plans for the EYFS would set out in detail any adult-led activities with expected outcomes, the deployment of adults, continuous provision, a guide to what might be set out initially in different areas of the classroom and outside area, and observation opportunities, and would be open to change and adaptation according to the children's needs.

As a trainee you will need to plan each lesson you teach in some detail. This will be discussed later.

What do your plans need to show?

Your training establishment will have set out requirements for what you should include but you will undoubtedly be required to provide more details than your class teacher's plans in order to demonstrate your thought processes in a clear and ordered way.

Long- and medium-term planning

Initially you will not need to be part of this process as your individual lessons will build on your class teacher's planning but very soon you will need to consider the bigger picture. What you are given as a starting point varies considerably from school to school and sometimes medium-term plans are devised by a group of teachers during holiday periods, so if your placement stretches across a half term you may find there is nothing in place when you start for a later part of your placement. Try to see this as a positive learning opportunity and offer to join in the planning process. This will give you a chance to see how the other teachers operate and to put forward some thoughts and ideas of your own. If you are working in a paired placement (where you have another student teacher working alongside you in the same class) this is something you can work at together.

However, you may find that very little has been done in this area and it is entirely down to you. This sometimes happens in a summer term placement in year 6 where the testing has finished and the curriculum requirements have already been met. This can also be turned to your advantage. It gives you a real opportunity to embrace the subject knowledge and skills required to teach a topic and although it may not initially be as successful as adapting someone else's plans, you should end up with a much sounder understanding of the whole planning process.

You may have a class teacher who presents you with very full medium- and/or long-term plans from which you can plan very easily.

Whatever you are presented with at this stage I would advise you to talk to the class teacher (and maybe the subject coordinator) about the needs of your children and possible difficulties, what they have covered before, any available resources and how you might obtain them, as well as considering how you might add to the process with your own expertise, materials and preferences. You will undoubtedly need to put more thought and detail into these plans at this stage. You will be more focused about where the learning is going if you think about learning objectives. (What exactly do you want the children to learn in each lesson?) Some possible activities would be helpful although these should not be set in stone and can be changed later. Looking at the available resources or searching the Internet at this stage could give you some real help in deciding what the best activities and teaching resources are which would help the children meet your learning objectives. You could then think about how you might assess learning. (What will it look like at the end of the lesson?) The more thought you put in at this stage the less work you will need to do at the lesson planning stage. I find this part of the process really exciting but have often found that my ideas need a little taming when it comes to writing the lesson plans. If this part of the process is planned effectively it gives you real chance to prepare all manner of things such as collecting equipment or organising a visit or visitor or borrowing a resource from a friend or the library or museum service. The more you put in the more the children are likely to gain from the experience, so it is really worth spending some time and effort at this stage.

Medium-term plans need to be fluid as the process of learning can be unpredictable and areas may need to be revisited or the children may learn more quickly than you thought. I have always found it useful to annotate my plans either in a different colour pen from the original or making handwritten comments on a computer-generated one. This ensures it is really clear to you or anyone else looking at your plans how you have adapted your teaching according to the children's needs. If you find yourself teaching the same topic at a later date this information can be really useful to refine the plans and give you sensible starting points. From your point of view as a trainee it is immediately obvious to your class teacher and/or supervisor that you are reflecting on how your teaching and the children's learning relate to each other.

In the Early Years Foundation Stage you need to show how you intend to implement your ideas for topics by outlining possible activities and how these fit with the EYFS Guidance in the six areas of learning. You also need to suggest how the different areas of the classroom might be used and possible resources. Here again it is a question of reaping what you sow and more time spent on developing ideas here will save you time later.

CRITICAL ISSUES

One of the recommendations of the Cambridge Primary Review is to:

Work towards a pedagogy of repertoire rather than recipe, and of principle rather than prescription. (Alexander, 2010, p. 511)

What do you think of this statement? Read further about these ideas in the chapter on 'Re-thinking Pedagogy'. Reflect on the pedagogy of your school and your own views. How will this influence how you plan for the needs of your children?

Lesson plans

These need to be detailed and show your thought processes. They certainly need to have enough information so that another teacher could use them to teach from if you were suddenly called away or were ill. As I said initially, it is difficult to help a student improve their teaching if their planning documentation is muddled or too brief. Once completed it should act like a written shopping list – even if you leave it on the kitchen table you generally remember what you need to buy because you have reinforced the thought process by writing it down. It is helpful to have it nearby (as with the shopping list) while you are teaching to refer to occasionally, but it should be embedded in your mind firmly enough so that you do not have to hold it in front of you throughout the lesson.

Your lesson plans should include details such as date, time, number of children, year group(s), subject (and maybe the topic this falls within) and length of lesson. They need to set out clear learning intentions or objectives (what they are going to be learning today) and how you are going to assess that learning (assessment or success criteria). Success criteria are discussed in more detail in the preceding chapter on 'Assessment'. Sometimes you may overlap with other curriculum areas, such as in a lesson on writing instructions for making an Egyptian mummy which may be taught as an English lesson but would have developed out of a history topic, and it is helpful to note this. Key vocabulary is useful as a reminder for you and also any other adults in the classroom. Resources and anything else needing preparation beforehand is a part I always tried to write carefully as realising you have forgotten to locate the bead strings in the middle of a maths lesson can be really disruptive. A little bit of forethought here helps to make the lesson run smoothly. You also need to think about how the children are going to access any resources such as whiteboards or art materials. It is well worth observing how experienced teachers manage this and trying some different approaches (see also Chapter 5). I always favoured giving children responsibility for equipment but letting 30 children get up to find whiteboards at once is never going to be an efficient use of time. I had daily monitors and made sure that any regularly used equipment was easy to access. This helps when tidying too.

If we move on to the actual lesson content, the detail needed here is really a matter of personal preference but you do need to ensure that you have thought about every stage of your teaching and the resources required, the way the children are going to be organised, how the other adults are going to be deployed, and how the lesson will begin and end. You will also need to consider the differing abilities and levels of understanding among the children and any children who have other particular needs such as language, behaviour or physical. Although you need to provide for different abilities you should not need any more than three activities, so do not make life more complicated than it needs to be. You may have children for whom these activities do not work but often they can be amended slightly to be appropriate. Sometimes differentiation by outcome will be your preferred option where, for example, the more able children will have done the task in more depth. Your class teacher will be the best source of information initially although as you get to know the children you will soon find you will develop your own ideas. You will also need to consider whether, when and how you might use a plenary session. This is generally used to gather together or assess the learning at the end of a session but can be at any time. The word plenary means 'full' or 'all together' so is purely something the whole class engages in. To begin with it is helpful to have timings for the various parts of the lessons. One of the most common difficulties beginning teachers have initially is overrunning the allotted time and therefore not reaching the concluding part of the lesson – often the 'plenary' where the learning is evaluated or reinforced or skills learned are to be used in a real-life context. There are so many different facets to teaching a lesson, the potential for things to go wrong is great. Even experienced teachers do not escape this although practice and evaluation limit the potential for failure. Every time you begin with a new class you will go through the process of developing plans and activities which work for that group of children, so it is a continual learning process.

The final requirement of your plan will be a space to evaluate your teaching and the children's learning which will be further discussed later in this chapter.

In the Early Years Foundation Stage your lesson plan might be for a short whole-class lesson or a group activity. This could be with just a few children for whom this activity would be appropriate, with the whole class in rotation or with children who choose the activity. Whichever it is, at this stage you will need to include your learning objectives and possible success criteria. These are more problematic with small children as they often take an activity in a different direction from that which you had planned and it can be counterproductive to try to change their course. You soon learn when you can persuade children back to your course and when it will not work.

You need to have a list of resources and equipment so you are fully prepared before you begin and an outline of your activity. Key questions and vocabulary are useful reminders and you need to have considered how you intend to assess the outcome. The key difference from Key Stage 1 and 2 planning here is thinking about the 'next steps'. This gives you the opportunity to note down where you think particular children need to go next with their learning. This will then be carried forward in your general planning. Again, noting down your successes or otherwise is good practice for improving your teaching. Some teachers find that planning in this way for their teaching assistants works well as there is likely to be a much clearer understanding of what you intended than you could establish in a quick chat about sowing seeds or making play dough. As you can see this type of plan is only going to apply to some of the learning for some of the time so more thought needs to be spent on the bigger picture which I will explain in more detail in the next section.

Planning a sequence of lessons

This may seem a daunting prospect to begin with but view it as an opportunity to really take responsibility for the children learning something at a deeper level of understanding.

Begin by looking at the expectations of the learning. This may be outlined in the medium-term plans but you may need to look at documents such as the National Curriculum or other government documentation. Ask you class teacher to help here. You will also need to ask him/her to tell you where the children's expected starting point might be. This will be an approximation as even if the topic is building on work covered as little as a term ago there is no guarantee that the children will have remembered all they had achieved at that point. A little revision or consolidation of skills is therefore good in order to establish current understanding as well as to act as a reminder to the children.

You then need to divide the learning into lesson-sized chunks within the number of sessions your sequence allows for. Consider what your learning objectives will be for each of these stages. Do not make them unnecessarily complex but do make sure they are specific enough to indicate what you are expecting the children to learn during that lesson. 'To name and understand properties of 3D shapes' is a little too vague to be helpful. 'To be able to classify 3D shapes using the terms faces, vertices, edges and curved surfaces' would be much clearer. You might also want to think about how you would explain that to the children in language which would be clear for them. Having established what you want the children to learn you then need to think about what direct teaching, modelling or revision you will need to do and how you will deliver this. In the context of the 3D shape-learning objective you might demonstrate what the terms mean and then play a game to reinforce the learning, or you might have a range of regular and irregular 3D shapes for the children to investigate and sort and then teach the terms that they would need to describe what they had done. There are as many ways of delivering a lesson as there are teachers. Use ideas from what you have observed or ideas from your tutors to begin with and gradually adapt and add to these to suit your particular needs. There is also a wealth of ideas on websites but be careful that what you select meets your learning objective. You do not need to reinvent the wheel for every lesson in your sequence. Often, if you have taught the children a game, it can be easily adapted to move the children on to the next stage. After each lesson an instant evaluation of your teaching and the children's learning will give you an indication of whether the next lesson in your sequence will work or whether you need to adapt it. You need to be reflective and critical but the sooner after the lesson you review the teaching and learning the more detail you will remember. Do not be afraid to go back and teach a concept again. If the children have not understood it will be counterproductive to try to move them to the next stage – *even if it means you will not get to your planned end stage!* No one will thank you for leaving the children in a state of confusion.

I have concentrated rather on a maths context here but in an English lesson it would look much the same. If your end point is going to be 'To write a traditional tale' then you need to consider all the skills the children will need to have in order to do this. Your first lesson might include a chance for the class to tell you what they know already about traditional tales and how they work, although again your class teacher will be a good source of information about prior learning. You might spend time on characters, good beginnings and possible endings. You might use film, drama, still photography, cartoons and animation as well as books as input and to practise the necessary skills. All the time you need to be building up the children's skills so they can reach the end point successfully.

You will need to devise some way of assessing whether the children have met your learning expectations. This is often produced as a written piece of evidence. From the school's point of view this means that there is a collection of written work which shows progression and is usually kept in an exercise book. Parents can see these easily and the results can be discussed. From a child's point of view, producing the same kind of evidence all the time can become tedious and flat and for some children the writing process is a difficulty in itself so you will not see an accurate reflection of their learning. In these days of technology, evidence can be kept as a photograph, a photocopy of notes on a whiteboard, notes taken by a scribe, etc. This was really brought home to some PGCE students I was teaching a history session to. They had spent a while researching their given topic and when feeding back to the rest of the group I asked how they would prefer to present their findings. Out of four groups of 30 students none of them chose to produce a written account! Assessment of learning has been covered fully in the previous chapter.

Planning in EYFS

In the EYFS, planning for continuity, good coverage and individual needs is an area where many students become confused about what is and what is not important. I will outline what you *do* need to have on record. The other adults need to be able to see what is in your mind, as do your class teacher and your supervisor, and you need a record of what was planned and what happened in practice.

1. Starting with your medium-term ideas, on a weekly basis you need to consider the whole teaching space, inside and out. Using what the children have previously shown you, plan for each area and consider what equipment and possible additions

or substitutions could happen during the week to keep these spaces exciting and fresh. Devise a simple planning format which has sections for each of the areas and systematically think through each area. These can and should change as the children use them and demonstrate interests and needs. You may have planned to have mini beast cutters and related extras with dough which you have made, but if the children decide on baking cakes and discussing tea parties instead then you need to provide something for them to cook in and possibly plates, birthday candles, etc. Ask them what they need and involve them in their learning. You can even involve them in the planning process such as in designing a new role play area. When this happens your plans need amending and doing this in two colours, one for your changes and one for those suggested by the children, will give you a clear picture of how much control the children are taking and what they are showing you about their learning needs.

2. A timetable for general responsibilities and activities for the week is also valuable. You need to indicate where direct teaching is to happen and where an adult is there to support rather than lead. Deployment of adults is a key factor and making sure that all the children are adequately supervised while still being able to take control of their play and learning is important. Make sure your adults feed back to you any observations of the unusual, the surprising or general trends so that these can inform your future plans. You also need to allocate some time for observation. Watching closely how children play will help you immensely in planning appropriately for them. The key is to remain flexible. *You will not have achieved everything in your medium-term plan if you have really taken notice of what the children are telling you about their learning needs.*

Using plans to improve teaching

Evaluation

I have always found that evaluating my plans was one of the best ways of improving my teaching. I annotated them at the first available opportunity and encouraged my teaching assistants to make notes either directly onto my plan or on Post-it notes which could then be attached to the plan. Do not do this on a fresh plan on the computer. It is much more helpful when you look back to see what you changed from your original plan while you were teaching;

- any activities which were a real success or failure
- whether particular groupings of children worked well or not
- whether the resources were adequate
- any areas of difficulty
- classroom management points
- uses of any other adults.

It is also useful to have an immediate assessment of which children really struggled and any who achieved beyond your expectations. This is not the same as a considered formative assessment process but will give you an indication of how you might need to change the next lesson for those children. Ask your teaching assistant to make notes of any surprises during whole-class teaching. You may think you will remember but chances are that you will not. Once noted on your plans they will be in the context of your teaching and they can then feed into more detailed lesson evaluations as soon as you have the time.

One of the most effective ways of moving your teaching on is being able to reflect on these findings and consider what it is that you may have done to influence them (see also Chapter 9 on reflection). This is a skill which all good teachers do throughout their careers. I still do this in the context of my PGCE teaching and adjust my plans accordingly to improve the outcome and ease of understanding or to ensure individual needs are met.

What you do not want to do in this process is sink into deep depression because you will never 'get it right'. There will always be room for improvement and the better you get to know your children the more likely you are to feel you have not quite met their needs. If, like me, you have a tendency to focus on your failings, make a list of the good points first and highlight any breakthroughs. These are really important and sometimes one child understanding a concept they have found really difficult is reward in itself.

In the Early Years Foundation Stage evaluation works in much the same way and there will be days when you seem to have achieved nothing you set out to do but there will have been achievements! Ask your teaching assistant to help you here.

Reflection is more fully discussed in Chapter 9.

Refining your planning to enhance learning

Your teaching will be much more effective if you plan to use your strengths. You may find that these change slightly as you progress through your training but consider how you might include the skills you gained before embarking on this course.

Be adventurous. Try some of those suggestions which your tutors have suggested and give them a fair go. Think about the times you remember from when you were at school. There were probably visits or visitors or something different which happened and although you cannot be all singing and dancing every day, variety is going to keep your teaching and the children's learning fresh.

Useful resources

ICT can offer wonderful learning opportunities but using a slide show for every lesson is not going to improve your teaching. What I have often seen happen is that the student teacher is sidelined by the slides which then dictate how the lesson will run. Any text you show needs to be minimal and of a font size which is easily readable. And do not assume that because you have put your learning objective on the interactive whiteboard (IWB) that the children have read and understood it. Many student teachers are hampered by the fact that the IWB is often the only board available to write on in a classroom and there is an expectation that this expensive piece of equipment will be used as much as possible. This is a real difficulty and needs to be considered carefully when planning. Many children spend most of their waking day with a screen of some sort in front of them, especially if the IWB is in use most of the time. Before using the board think whether it will help the children meet your learning objective(s) and what the other options might be: plan for technology failure! What will you do if the Internet is down or you cannot calibrate the board? (see also next chapter on e-learning).

Although *you* are an amazing teaching resource consider what other options there might be. I have used a parent who was a vet to come in with her dog and demonstrate the sort of care he needed. She even clipped his toenails. That was a far superior experience than using a video or a book and the role play and understanding of caring for animals was greatly improved. On another occasion we wrote to the local council when investigating our locality with concerns and ideas for improving road safety outside the school and they sent their road safety officer to discuss our suggestions. This gave a really clear meaning to the children's work. The local religious minister is often willing to come and baptise a doll or bring artefacts. Visiting local places is relatively easy to organise and well worthwhile provided you have given it enough thought at the planning stage. It is surprising what children do not know about their neighbourhood, so do not assume because it is on their doorstep it will not be interesting. These options need to be considered at the medium-term planning stage so that you can plan to maximise the experience and organise it well.

Encouraging independence

The temptation when you begin teaching is to 'float' so that you are able to deal with difficulties before they escalate. Try to gradually wean yourself off this. Plan to focus on one particular group of children to really move them on. This can be in stages at the beginning. Settle the children and deal with any immediate needs, then sit with your focus group. Then, near the end of the session, you could circulate again and check on general progress. The children will soon get used to the idea that you are not always available and such a strategy will enable you to spend more time with a group.

You need to help all your children become independent learners and the way you plan can either help or hinder this. Often the lower achievers sit with a teaching assistant so that they have instant access to help when they need it. This strategy does help with immediate classroom management needs but these children will not learn important independence skills if this is their only working experience. All children need regular opportunities to work independently and the tasks or activities need to be ones which they can access with no help. As you get to know the children better you will be able to work out appropriate opportunities and activities. One of the worries student teachers have with this is how to keep the children engaged while they are working with others. Make them accountable so by the end of the lesson they will need to have achieved something specific which they know you are going to ask them about or maybe they will need to report back to the rest of the class. If they know there will some immediate comeback it will give them more incentive to be successful. You can also give them independence strategies so that they do not bother you at the first difficulty such as 'If you get stuck, think about the instructions, ask the person next door to you, ask a designated reader/helper to help you read the instructions/sort out what you do next' etc. The other side of this is that *all* the children deserve some quality time with you.

Planning opportunities for talk

You also need to plan for opportunities to talk. I always refer to my ability to negotiate around Norwich in a car when thinking about this. I have a vague idea where different parts of the city are in relation to each other but it is not until I am trying to give someone directions that I really get it sorted out. Verbalising your learning really reinforces it, and this needs to be a consideration in your plans: how you might include talking partner opportunities in your whole-class teaching or plenary and what opportunities there might be in group or paired work where this kind of discussion can take place. Sitting and listening is something that none of us do efficiently for very long at a time so breaking up your teaching with opportunities for the children to discuss, reflect and consolidate like this will add to their learning potential.

Using support staff

Planning for your extra adults can initially be quite difficult and there are several things to take into consideration. Find out your support staff's strengths and preferred ways of working from them and/or the class teacher and build on these. Remember that working with the same group of disillusioned or disruptive children is not going to be a fulfilling task day after day so ring the changes. If possible ask them to feed into your planning and help to make them a part of the process. Ask the support staff to feed back to you on how the children achieved but also on the strengths or weaknesses of the activity. Use them to support children in whole-class teaching or to observe for you. Make sure they are really clear about what you intend in your lesson by giving them a clear copy of the plan and explaining which parts they will be responsible for. Some classes have a communications book if teachers and teaching assistants do not have a chance to speak to each other before the day begins. However you do this, do bear in mind that teaching assistants are paid a fraction of a teacher's salary and therefore your expectations must not be unreasonable: remember that, on the whole, they are dedicated, positive and have the children's interests at heart. Working with other adults is discussed more fully in Chapter 16.

Catering for different ages and abilities

Most Key Stage 1 and 2 classes will have some sort of ability grouping already in place (usually for English and maths but sometimes for science) to aid differentiation and help teach the children at an appropriate level. While these groupings have their place there are other ways of organising the children when planning tasks and activities. Where children are conducting an investigation or the outcome is a joint effort, mixed-ability pairings or groups can work surprisingly well. This requires some knowledge of the children as the pairs or groups need to be supportive. Giving a poor writer a more able writer as a scribe to record views or thoughts, especially at a planning stage, can free a child from the constraints of writing so that they can concentrate on thinking and developing ideas. This is certainly worth trying and you may be pleasantly surprised at the results.

Planning for a class where there is more than one age group can be difficult. Your class teacher will be able to offer you guidance here. One of the difficulties is that these children will often be in the same class for more than one year, so it is important that they do not repeat the same curriculum. If there are two year groups together quite often they will focus on the specific subject areas for one of those year groups. What the teacher then needs to ensure is that the teaching covers the skills that both age groups need to acquire. This is really no more than a greater spread for differentiation. I have taught in mixed age classes for many years and have really enjoyed the mix of abilities and the potential to move more able children on and support those who are having difficulties. Mixed ability groupings in this context have the potential to really move the younger children on whilst reinforcing valuable learning for the older ones. In some very small schools you may find reception and Key Stage 1 in one class and all of Key Stage 2 in another. The numbers of children in each class are usually quite small so planning will focus much more on individuals. Again, your class teacher will be in the best position to advise you and there will be as many benefits as disadvantages in the experience.

Planning Independence at Early Years Foundation Stage

In the Early Years Foundation Stage many of these points are also applicable. You need to be imaginative and involve the children as much as possible in planning and organising their environment. If they feel they have ownership of their setting in this way they will then use it more effectively as well as seeing the need to look after it. It is important to foster independence skills at this stage too. Make sure that children can access equipment easily and ensure that they take responsibility for their environment and learn to tidy up. Talking skills can be introduced here. Start simply by getting them to talk about a picture they have drawn or a model they have made so they have some visual prompts. Listening is also a key skill if this is going to work well. The attention span of 3, 4 and 5 year olds is extremely short so even if you manage to keep them sitting on the carpet for 30 minutes do not assume they have absorbed all your words of wisdom. Plan for short sharp whole class sessions with changes in activity and if they are having a day when they cannot do it do not push it! They will however concentrate for quite long periods of time when involved in their own play so also make sure that they have chances to do this.

CRITICAL ISSUES

The Teaching and Learning Research programme identified that,

A chief goal of teaching and learning should be the promotion of learners' independence and autonomy. This involves acquiring a repertoire of learning strategies and practices, developing positive learning dispositions, and having the will and confidence to become agents in their own learning. (Alexander, 2010, p. 303)

How did you develop these necessary skills? Observe how other teachers foster independent learning dispositions. How independent are the children in your class? Decide what your priorities would be for planning to improve independent learning opportunities.

Final thoughts

According to *Children, Their World, Their Education* (Alexander 2010),
  Good teaching:

- Is well organised and planned
- Is reflective
- Is based on sound subject knowledge
- Depends on effective classroom management
- Requires understanding of children's developmental needs
- Uses exciting and varied approaches
- Inspires
- Encourages children to become autonomous learners
- Facilitates children's learning
- Stimulates children's creativity and imagination.

(p. 281)

If you have captured these elements in your planning then your teaching is going to be heading in the right direction!

Summary

- Be clear and focused in your planning. Remember someone else will need to be able to read it and understand your thought processes.
- If learning objectives are used then make them simple and ensure your teaching and any activities or tasks feed into achieving them.
- Use your long- and medium-term planning to think about exciting resources and start to prepare them.

(Continued)

(Continued)

- Be clear about how you are going to be able to tell if your plan was successful.
- Record any observations as soon as possible and use them to inform future planning.
- Try something new. If you stick to the same mould you will not progress to be an exciting and inspiring teacher.

Issues for reflection

- Observe teaching in a different key stage from that you have chosen. What are the different planning implications for this age group? What could you use from this to incorporate in your own planning?
- From time to time (maybe at the end of each placement) look back at your planning notes and evaluations. What were your key breakthrough moments? Is there anything you tried and rejected which you think you might be ready to try again? Are there any continuing areas of difficulty which you really now need to sort?
- Think about all the children in your class. Choose one or two who you really feel you are not reaching and plan some lessons with their needs particularly in mind. Did this make a difference? What have you learned from this about your teaching and the children's learning?

Further reading

Alexander, R. (ed.) (2010) *Children, Their World, Their Education*. Abingdon: Routledge. This is the final report of the Cambridge Primary Review which is a comprehensive examination of English primary education based on extensive, recent research. The chapters on 'Children's Development and Learning' and 'Re-thinking Pedagogy' give particularly interesting information related to the planning process.

Fisher, J. (2008) *Starting from the Child*, 3rd edition. Maidenhead: Open University Press. This looks at the needs of very young children but is a very useful starting point for teachers of any age of child. Especially relevant is the chapter on planning for learning.

Pollard, A. (2008) *Reflective Teaching*, 3rd edition. London: Continuum. This has a very comprehensive chapter on planning as well as useful web links.

Planning

Briggs, M.

Learning Outcomes

By the end of the chapter you will have:
- become aware of the essential components of planning that are undertaken in schools including children's previous experiences, teacher's subject knowledge, vocabulary and resources;
- become aware of the levels of planning that are undertaken in schools;
- looked at the necessary elements of lesson planning in detail including evaluation;
- considered the planning requirements for additional adults;
- considered opportunistic planning and the issues surrounding different locations.

TEACHERS' STANDARDS
A teacher must:

1. Set high expectations which inspire, motivate and challenge pupils
- establish a safe and stimulating environment for pupils, rooted in mutual respect
- set goals that stretch and challenge pupils of all backgrounds, abilities and dispositions
- demonstrate consistently the positive attitudes, values and behaviour which are expected of pupils.

2. Promote good progress and outcomes by pupils
- be accountable for pupils' attainment, progress and outcomes
- plan teaching to build on pupils' capabilities and prior knowledge
- guide pupils to reflect on the progress they have made and their emerging needs
- demonstrate knowledge and understanding of how pupils learn and how this impacts on teaching
- encourage pupils to take a responsible and conscientious attitude to their own work and study.

3. Demonstrate good subject and curriculum knowledge
- have a secure knowledge of the relevant subject(s) and curriculum areas, foster and maintain pupils' interest in the subject, and address misunderstandings
- demonstrate a critical understanding of developments in the subject and curriculum areas, and promote the value of scholarship

- demonstrate an understanding of and take responsibility for promoting high standards of literacy, articulacy and the correct use of standard English, whatever the teacher's specialist subject
- if teaching early reading, demonstrate a clear understanding of systematic synthetic phonics
- if teaching early mathematics, demonstrate a clear understanding of appropriate teaching strategies.

4. Plan and teach well structured lessons

- impart knowledge and develop understanding through effective use of lesson time
- promote a love of learning and children's intellectual curiosity
- set homework and plan other out-of-class activities to consolidate and extend the knowledge and understanding pupils have acquired
- reflect systematically on the effectiveness of lessons and approaches to teaching
- contribute to the design and provision of an engaging curriculum within the relevant subject area(s).

5. Adapt teaching to respond to the strengths and needs of all pupils

- know when and how to differentiate appropriately, using approaches which enable pupils to be taught effectively
- have a secure understanding of how a range of factors can inhibit pupils' ability to learn, and how best to overcome these
- demonstrate an awareness of the physical, social and intellectual development of children, and know how to adapt teaching to support pupils' education at different stages of development
- have a clear understanding of the needs of all pupils, including those with special educational needs; those of high ability; those with English as an additional language; those with disabilities; and be able to use and evaluate distinctive teaching approaches to engage and support them.

6. Make accurate and productive use of assessment

- know and understand how to assess the relevant subject and curriculum areas, including statutory assessment requirements
- make use of formative and summative assessment to secure pupils' progress
- use relevant data to monitor progress, set targets, and plan subsequent lessons
- give pupils regular feedback, both orally and through accurate marking, and encourage pupils to respond to the feedback.

8. Fulfil wider professional responsibilities

- deploy support staff effectively.

Introduction

In order to plan effective lessons and sequences of lessons for any subject in the curriculum there are a number of areas that need to be explored. When a trainee teacher observes experienced teachers teaching, it can appear that they can perform without any apparent planning and very little written down. This can be misleading as it can make you think that this is how you need to operate. The experienced teacher is only able to operate effectively in this way through building up their expertise by initially planning lessons in more detail as this helps with the thought processes needed to plan good lessons. It is tempting to want to shortcut this process as it is very time consuming and it may feel like an unnecessary workload during your training course. However, it is worth seeing this as part of the training process like any other and, although it appears that it is the written plans that take precedence, you will be going through a process which involves a number of other elements. Your teaching of a specific topic within the curriculum could be the only time children are introduced to that area during the year, so it should be well planned, organised and taught. In time you will be able to plan good lessons without the weight of apparent paperwork but you will have still undertaken the cognitive activity of thinking through each lesson or session in detail and it will be no less rigorous as a result. This will include the necessary consideration of elements of contingency planning which may well initially look intuitive to the observer but are skills developed over time.

Essential components of planning

The following areas are the general starting points for all planning regardless of the amount of detail that is actually recorded. Your course will have guidance about the requirements and expectations for planning at each stage of your progress, which will also guide your thinking and your actions.

The National Curriculum

The National Curriculum is the statutory document you are legally obliged to teach. Once you know the curriculum areas and topics you are going to be planning to teach it is worth looking at the National Curriculum and the detail of the expectations for the age group you will be teaching.

Teachers' planning for schemes of work should start from the programmes of study and the needs and abilities of their children. Level descriptions can help to determine the degree of challenge and progression for work across each year of a key stage (QCA, 1999, p.18).

Children's previous experiences

Securing pupils' progress that builds on their prior learning is a central curricular objective. Because progress is goal-related, the goals of learning must be explicit in order to guide planning and teaching, whether cross curricular or focused on discrete subject content (Rose, 2009, para. 35, p.11).

Previous experience of the topic by the age group you will be teaching

This has two elements, the detail of the activities and tasks given to the children i.e. the teaching that has been undertaken and more importantly the assessments of the pupil's learning and any indication of any errors, misconceptions or areas that need to be recapped that occurred during the previous lessons. It is also useful to know how long ago this area of the curriculum area was last undertaken by the group or class and what the lesson was immediately prior to the lesson that you will be planning. With this information you can think about making connections within the subject and across the curriculum for the children. This can be content knowledge as well as skills developed in other lessons. Even when children appear to have had no previous experience of the topic to be taught they will bring their own ideas about the area to the lesson. This can include any preconceptions they may have established when making sense of their world. For example, they may think clouds cry when it rains. Part of the planning process is to allow space in your lesson to explore ideas children may bring to school with them and only then can you begin to use these in your teaching and address misconceptions and errors. If you don't address these they become harder to shift and can create barriers for future learning in any subject.

Teachers' subject knowledge

In order to plan and teach effectively you will need to look at the progression within a specific topic and the links between the topic to be planned and other areas within the subject being taught or between curriculum areas. Once you know what you will be teaching and you have asked your class teacher and/or mentor about the pupil's previous experiences, attainments and misconceptions, you are ready to explore you own subject knowledge. Your course will include sessions on subject and pedagogic knowledge. Look at your notes for the specific topic you are planning to explore the details of the progression. Use these to understand where the lessons you will be planning and teaching fit into this progression. Try to identify any aspects that you may want to revisit in relation to your own understanding. Explain the key aspects to a colleague to try out your approaches and check your understanding. Be honest with yourself at this point as it is possible to make assumptions about your knowledge.

Vocabulary

Your understanding of the vocabulary needed during any unit/session/lesson is a crucial part of planning effective teaching. Think about how you will explain what each of the words means in the context that it is used within the curricula focus particularly if they are everyday words that have a subject specific meaning. Part of your planning will be to have the words available to introduce to the children on an interactive whiteboard, poster, display and/or cards.

> **Activity**
>
> Choose a subject you are less confident teaching. Look at the appropriate National Curriculum expectations including levels of attainment, schemes of work and any long term planning you have access to, and identify the progression of subject knowledge required for the learner and the teacher. Check your understanding of terms, processes, procedures and all other aspects of content.

Resources

What kind of resources will be needed to help you teach the topic? Ensure you are familiar with the resources available in the school you will be working in. Do they use an interactive whiteboard (IWB) to present and manipulate ideas? How can you vary the resources that you plan to use to support different learning styles or different age groups of children?

Levels of planning in settings and schools

There are three levels of planning in settings and schools – long term, medium term and short term. As a trainee teacher, long and medium term planning is the level you are likely to be given by your placement setting/school, and you are not as likely to have access to the staff discussion about this level whilst you are on placement, particularly if it is of short duration. If you do have the opportunity it is good experience to join in the discussions even if you will mainly be listening to the other teachers. It would also be worthwhile talking to teachers about how the plan was developed so that you can gain a sense of the process. Schools evaluate this level of planning through work trawl scrutiny and a review of children's progress in learning across the curriculum in preparation for the next years' teaching.

Long term planning

This planning is usually the focus for the whole setting or school and is designed to ensure continuity and progression for children in a subject. In terms of coverage this level of planning should ensure that the requirements of the Early Years Foundation Stage and the National Curriculum are met for all children.

Medium term planning

Medium term planning is in greater detail than long term planning and usually comprises half term to termly plans. As a trainee you may find yourself being given the existing medium term plan or scheme of work. It can be difficult to work from someone else's plans as you may not have been part of the discussion about the order of topics or the amount of time to be given for teaching those topics. It is worth making these plans your own by looking at the medium term plan for the placement's duration and adding appropriate detail to support your work and to address the specific standards related to planning across the curriculum.

Mixed year group classes

It can be particularly important to gain an overview of what is to be taught when dealing with a mixed year group class. You will need to ensure the subjects of the whole curriculum to be covered by the year groups coincide so that the same areas are being taught at the same time. This will make it easier to plan in the short term and for you to offer a coherent approach to all children. This level of planning is evaluated either by the whole school or by a member of staff who has responsibility for a subject area or teaching and learning and is usually the agenda for a whole staff meeting, year group or key stage, depending upon the size of the school and its organisational structure. On a longer placement, you may be asked to evaluate the planning for a sequence of lessons either within a subject area or thematic approach and here you will draw on individual lesson evaluations in order to make judgements about the effectiveness of learning and teaching across the sequence. You can also draw upon any feedback you have had from observations of your teaching of appropriate lessons as part of your evidence base.

Block plans/unit plans

If your placement school is using the revised National Strategies framework they will focus on blocks of work. When mapping out blocks and units over the term or year the inter-relatedness of the content and pitch of the units needs to be taken into account. There are various ways that the units can be pieced together to provide children with a coherent learning experience and the example provided can be adapted to suit the specific school context and the pupils' needs. This will be based upon previous teaching and assessment of pupil's learning. Some schools produce their own block plans for subjects like science which they allocate blocks of time on the timetable for teaching these areas.

Other starting points

It is possible to think about planning and the starting points for lessons in different ways. For example you could use a book as the stimulus for planning across the curriculum or a topic approach neither of which may cover all areas of the curriculum. The reasons for this are explained in Chapter 2. These cannot detail all the possible activities, but they offer you a starting point to think about your planning from differing perspectives.

Commercial schemes

Some areas of the curriculum may be taught using a commercial scheme which structures the teaching and learning and supports the teacher's planning. This can include pupil books, teacher books, large text books, posters, IWB resources and others. Be sure that you use these only as a guide or loose framework so that you continue to focus on the children's needs and prior experiences foremost as textbooks cannot be written for a specific class and the potential range of needs.

Research Focus

Despite the importance of planning as part of the teaching process there is little research specific to this area. Much of the research looks at the effectiveness of implementing a teaching strategy and how this is planned by the teacher. Beyer and Davis's (2009) research looked at preservice teachers' use of 'educative curriculum materials' for science teaching in Canada. They argue that teachers need to cultivate the capacity to critique and adapt curriculum materials in productive ways and that for new teachers this is challenging task. They found that the lesson-specific nature of the supports made it difficult for the preservice teachers to recognise the principle underlying the ideas in the supports. Thus, most of them did not use the principle within the educative supports to analyse the lesson plan more broadly or analyse other lesson plans, resulting in missed opportunities to further improve the materials beyond the suggestions given in the support' (p.699). This raises questions for how trainee teachers work with curricular materials and the support you may be given to enable you to work with materials more effectively. It also points to trainee teachers being aware that they need to unpack the principles within materials before use with a class.

Activity

When you are on placement, find out which subjects are taught using a commercial scheme. How does this impact on planning? Does this mean that the planning, teaching and learning for this subject is a separate area and that there is no integrated planning with this area of the curriculum? Look at the commercial scheme material available to you on placement for a specific subject.

- Read through the lesson plan and any guidance.
- Adapt the plans to take account of the least and most able children.
- Annotate a copy of the plans to meet your pupil's needs.
- What ideas could you take for activities from the material?
- How could you change the worksheet offered into a practically based activity?
- If you intend to use a prepared plan as part of your planning consider how you will intervene to monitor progress during the lesson and inform and redirect learning when necessary?
- Discuss any use of scheme materials with your school based tutor/class teacher/ mentor.
- How does this compare with the issues raised in the research focus?

Short term planning

Short term planning is the level that you will have most autonomy over as a trainee teacher. The other chapters in this book encourage you to consider many issues related to planning for children, such as meeting individual needs, planning a motivating lesson, the need to plan for assessment opportunities and so on. This section considers the 'nuts and bolts' of lesson planning.

Daily or lesson planning and lesson formats

Most teachers use their weekly or block plans as the main short term planning rather than working on individual lessons, although you may find schools where teachers plan daily lessons. However as a trainee you are likely to be required to plan individual lessons, especially when you are being observed. This will also allow you to gain evidence against a number of standards for QTS.

Below is a list of the typical content you will find required in a trainee teacher's lesson planning proforma. While each course will vary as to its format and precise content, what is important is that your plans include all the key elements that are required to ensure a clear effective plan that will support your teaching and progress in learning in the classroom.

The following list is clearly intended for planning lessons according to the features of a three-part lesson. You will find that some teachers use this lesson format to structure their lessons but others will vary the format according to what is being taught. You will need to consider an introduction at the beginning of the lesson where you make the links to previous learning and connections between aspects in mathematics. Plus a review/plenary at the end of the lesson to assist with assessment and give children time to reflect upon their learning. The lesson can be stopped at any point for a mini review which would allow you to monitor progress, pick up on any misconceptions and extend or redirect learning where needed.

In addition to noting the *subject/theme, date, class*, and *number of children*, you will need to consider:

Children's previous experience: Work to be built on from previous lessons, units, years.

The previous previous lesson: Make notes from evaluations and assessment, including children's errors and misconceptions that need to be addressed in this lesson.

National Curriculum references: Include key statements and where appropriate level descriptors. Also consider the relationship with QCDA schemes of work and/or NS frameworks.

Learning objectives: Should be specific to this lesson and measurable and may vary for different groups of children and say how you will share these with the class.

Possible errors and misconceptions or sources of difficulties: This should show you your awareness of potential difficulties children might encounter.

Assessment: **What** precisely do you want the children to achieve in this lesson? **Who** is to be assessed: individuals, group, class? **How** will the assessment be made e.g. observation during intro, group work questioning; marking work?

Cross-curricula focus: Links with other subjects, themes.

Teachers' Standards: Trainee teacher's personal targets to be addressed during this lesson. Two or three maximum.

Resources: Materials, equipment, ICT, texts.

Safety issues: This could include what you say to the class about the use of potentially dangerous equipment e.g. scissors, compasses or the need for children to wear appropriate clothing if working outside or awareness of allergies if cooking.

Subject specific language: Including introducing and using key vocabulary both by the children as well as the teacher.

Specific expectations for behaviour: (Make clear to children, this could be a general focus on a show of hands or specific targets for individuals or groups.)

Speaking and listening objectives: As appropriate to this subject/lesson.

Introductory activity: Focus on the teacher and the children. Include assessment. May be an oral/mental starter if a mathematics lesson. Include timings.

Introduction to the main activity: Focus on teacher input to start the lesson, what are the key concepts that you want the children to learn. What stimulus will you provide to focus the children's learning.

Main activity: Will include differentiated tasks, including IEPs where appropriate. Include differentiate assessment. Consider mini plenaries where appropriate. What will your role be? The role of other in-class supporting adults? Timings?

Plenary: Key questions to ask/objectives to revisit/areas to discuss; consolidation activity; introduce homework where appropriate; note any errors/misconceptions to address.

Evaluating lessons

In addition to the above aspects to consider, your lesson plan should also provide space for an evaluation of the lesson. Annotate the plan, using a different colour. Add other working notes or changes directly to the plan. After the session consider both the quality of the teaching and whether each of the children really progressed in their learning. Make any relevant notes that will help you plan the following sessions. This may include: comments on timing; the appropriateness of the resources; additional ideas to reinforce the learning; suggestions for alternative organisational strategies.

Did each child really learn what was intended? Remember you can't judge learning just by completion of the work or activities set. Also remember to think about the children's understanding of vocabulary used in the lesson. Make reference to specific children (which may or may not need to go on their records). Make notes on how you might help the children progress in their learning, this can include areas for recap as well as what, where and when with next steps.

In the case study below you will be able to see these headings in practice, in a plan for a Key Stage 2 history lesson planned by a trainee teacher. As you read the plan, think about the extent to which the trainee is responding to each of the areas in her planning.

Case Study: Planning for a history lesson

Subject/ Theme	History – Life in Tudor Times. The Tudor Monarchs
Date:	20th October
Class/year group	**Class:** 5B **Number of Children:** 28
Children's previous experience:	In Year 3: Explored past photos from 1900s as a source of evidence about changes in the local area. Throughout KS2 children have been encouraged to use to exploring different sources of evidence in order to find out about a specific period of history as part of historical enquiry skills
Notes from previous lesson	Last couple of lessons on Who were the Tudors? and Early Tudors Explored pupil's existing knowledge about the Tudors Arranged dates of Tudor Monarchs in chronological order Placed pictures of Tudor Kings and Queens on a large family tree S.N and M.J had difficulty sequencing large numbers in dates (pick up on this in numeracy as well)
NC references	**NC** SU 2 Life in Tudor Times 4a find out about the past from different sources (e.g. contemporary pictures, portraits, costume)
Learning objectives	**By the end of the lesson most children will:** • Know the Tudor family were a family of kings and queens who reigned in fifteenth and sixteenth centuries • Specifically know who Elizabeth I was and key facts about her reign • Have discussed the evidence and bias about the character and images of the Tudor Monarchs as presented in contemporary portraits e.g. *Holbein's portrait of Elizabeth I* • Have made at least one inference based on the evidence contained in the Tudor portraits.
Possible errors and misconceptions or sources of difficulties	Children may have difficulty relating the centuries to the dates e.g. sixteenth century and 1500s

$\rightarrow$

Assessment	**What?** Can the children identify some aspect of the portrait as evidence to make inferences about the life, status or character of the king or queen e.g. *the padded clothes make the queen look big, strong, powerful. Symbolism used in Elizabeth's portrait* **Who?** Orange group (T), T.A to assess J, M, E, S, D and K **How?** Observation/questioning during intro, focus group activities and plenary
Cross-curricula	Art. Artists and portraits. Hans Holbein, Nicholas Hilliard
Focus	Ma. Ordering larger numbers – dates. Group collaboration
Resources	National Gallery posters, postcard – Tudor portraits, http://www.marileecody.com/eliz1-images.html
Safety issues	Manage transitions group by group. Discourage dashing from carpet. Bring back if necessary
Subject specific language	Primary source, evidence, inference, portrait, artist, costume, facial expression symbol, chronological order, family tree
Specific expectations for behaviour	Work as a team. Allocate a person to record your ideas about the portraits. Share your ideas. Listen to others, Encourage everyone in group to contribute
Speaking and listening objectives	En 1. Speaking and listening – expressing ides to an audience Paired and group discussion

(Time: 10 mins)	Introductory activity/Mental Oral:
Teacher: *Manage groups to carpet.* *Review* previous lesson on Tudors IWB. Display large portrait of Richard III *Discuss portraits* Valuable, important source of evidence/ information about people and life in the past *Why no photographers to take their pictures?* ● *Q.A/Partner talk* ● *Who do you think these people are?* ● *What clues are there?* ● *Give one or two examples, e.g. jewellery, background, facial expression* ● *Why might they be made to look stern, wealthy etc.*	**Children:** Gather on carpet **Partner talk.** Review. What do you remember about the Tudors? Two things you learned about the Tudors Children discuss other clues and what they might tell us about the Tudor Kings and Queens as they are presented in the portraits

● **Assessment: Can the children** identify at least one aspect of the portrait as evidence to make an inferences about the life, status or character of the king or queen e.g. *the padded clothes make the king look big, strong, powerful. The map in the background suggests they ruled over other lands*

(Time: 5 mins)	Introduction to the main activity
Teacher: Display portraits of Henry's children in early life and as monarchs so that children can see how children were dressed and any changes once they become monarchs, Edward and Mary and Elizabeth **Explain Task** Use famous portraits of Tudor Kings and Queens Become Time Detectives. What can we discover about each monarch from the portraits? **Model example on flip sheet. e.g. Edward V** **Arrange groups (6x5)** ● Orange to Teacher ● Support group with T.A	**Children:** In groups at tables Each group of 'Time Detectives' discuss Henry's children as presented in the portraits Examine carefully. Describe what they can see Identify what might it tell us? Elect a recorder Use large sheets to record the clues and what it might tell us about the character or life of a each monarch

(Time: e.g. 30 mins)	Main activity:	
Group (TA) **Pomegranate,** With J, M, E, S, D and K To work on carpet **Use IWB** Coronation portrait of Elizabeth Supervise recording or scribe for the children. Record clues and pupil's ideas **Assess each child** as below	**Groups** **Swan,** Edward **Hawk,** start with portrait of Mary Queen of Scots **Red Rose,** Mary Each group to discuss and record clues/evidence and inferences about monarch	**Group (with Teacher)** **(White Rose)** To examine Rainbow portrait of Elizabeth Discuss some examples of symbolism, e.g. serpent, wisdom, dog loyalty etc.
Assessment: Can these children: identify at least one aspect of the portrait as evidence to make inferences about the life, status or character of the king or queen *e.g. the padded clothes make the king look big, strong, powerful? The map in the background suggests they ruled over other lands*	Can these children: identify at least two aspects of the portrait as evidence to make inferences about the life, status or character of the king or queen *e.g. the padded clothes make the king look big, strong and powerful? The map in the background suggests they ruled over other lands*	Can these children: identify at least three aspects of the portrait as evidence to make inferences about the life, status or character of the king or queen? *In addition can they identify some of the symbols and what they might mean? E.g. Crown, orb, serpent?* *Visit website for information.* http://www.marileecody.com/eliz1-images.html

→

Differentiation/target setting including IEPs where appropriate:

A.K – IEP (EAL support) encourage use of vocabulary for everyday items – king, queen, clothes, picture, portrait, costume

Encourage T, W, KM to use of mother tongue where helpful.

Teacher's role during the main activity:

Develop Rose groups' appreciation of symbolism and use internet search if available

Use of in class support, including guidance to supporting adult(s):
See above

(Time e.g. 15 mins)	**Plenary:**

Gather children on carpet

Key questions to ask/objectives to revisit/areas to discuss:
What has each group of Time Detectives learned about their child of Henry from their portrait?
What did they notice about the representation of them as children and then as monarch?
What makes Mary Queen of Scots the odd one out?
Each group to display chart and briefly report
Explore the idea of 'bias' in the pictures
Do you think the portraits are accurate?
Why might an artist's portrait be biased?
What would you do if you were an artist in the time of the Tudors?
Reinforce and praise original or independent inferences drawn from portraits

Consolidation activity
Hot seat an artist
Choose a volunteer to be Holbein or Hilliard
Ask them to describe the monarch they painted
Children ask questions about what they were really like!

Introduce homework where appropriate:
Find other pictures of the Tudor Family which might tell us something of their lives or characters

---

Activity

Use the following lesson plan discussion sheet to evaluate the history lesson above. If possible, talk to other trainees/tutors/your mentor about your findings. What would you alter from the plans?

Lesson Plan Discussion Sheet   Title: _____

            Date: _____

Focus	Yes/no/ partly	Notes and suggestions
Are there clear and appropriate references to the EYFS, NC, relevant frameworks, QCA, School Schemes? Do they match age related expectations? If not why not?		
Are the learning objectives and intended outcomes specific and clearly defined? Is it clear what knowledge, skills, understanding or attitudes the children will gain from the lesson? Are there sufficient opportunities for challenging children? Remember children who find activities either too easy or too hard can become bored, frustrated and disruptive in the lesson. Does the plan indicate how children will know what the objectives for this lesson area?		
Does the plan identify potential errors, misconceptions and difficulties that the pupil's might have with the content or processes?		
Does the plan show that the trainee's knowledge and understanding are accurate?		
Will this be an interesting lesson, set in an appropriate context, relevant to the children's experiences? Remember children who are bored can be more disruptive in lessons.		
Does the lesson plan demonstrate that the trainee teacher is building on an evaluation, assessment and knowledge of the pupil's ability, achievements and needs?		
Does the lesson cater for children with a range of different abilities, SEN, G&T or those with EAL?		
Is there an opportunity to find out what the children already know at the start of the lesson?		

Are there planned opportunities for the children to contribute, talk, interact, communicate and engage in activity?		
Is it clear where and how the class will be organised for the activities, e.g. whole class, group, paired and individual work?		
Are health and safety issues considered?		
Are the activities explained in sufficient detail for another teacher to be able to lead the lesson if necessary?		
Is it clear what both the teacher and children will be doing at each stage of the lesson?		
Have any additional adults in the classroom been planned for?		
Does the lesson have an obvious structure e.g. beginning, middle and plenary? Has the timing of each stage of the lesson been considered?		
Can the outcomes be realistically achieved in the allocated time?		
Have appropriate questions and the introduction of new vocabulary been planned for? Does the plan show how the new vocabulary will be shared with the children?		
Is it clear what resources, including ICT, will be used and how they are to be organised?		
Is it clear who and what is to be assessed and how this lings to the learning objectives?		
Are the activities to be used as opportunities for formative or summative assessment?		
Is it clear what the purpose of the is plenary for this lesson?		
Are there appropriately planned mini plenaries to allow reinforcement of specific issues/ address misconceptions/monitor progress with activities/share feedback with the class group from pairs or small group work?		

One issue you may have considered is the standard ability groups within the plans for the main activity. What other ways are there for organising the learning during this phase of the lesson? You may consider individual work, pairs, small groups but not necessarily by ability, splitting the class into two and whole class working depending upon on the content and focus of the lesson to be taught. You may also notice that one of the aims of the lesson was key facts about Elizabeth yet the main focus was Henry VIII's children. What would you do about this?

Planning for other adults in the classroom

Many classes have other adults in who support the learning and teaching of individuals and groups. They can be supporting children with additional learning needs, English as an additional language, behavioural issues or as a learning mentor. They will need to know what is expected of them during the lesson and you may not have much time to discuss your plans ahead of time. A written plan to support them is helpful for both you and them as everyone is clear about expectations.

Subject/theme	
Date	
Group or set including number of children or individual you will be working with	
Children's previous experience Work to be built on from previous lessons, units, years	
Notes from previous lesson Based on evaluations and assessment: (Include children's errors and misconceptions that need to addressed in this lesson)	
Learning objectives	
Activities here detail the activities to be undertaken with the group/individuals	
Assessment by additional adult **What** the children to achieve are to achieve **What will you be looking for?**	Notes from assessments made by additional adult
Resources **Materials, equipment, ICT, texts**	
Safety issues It is your responsibility as the teacher to indicate if there are any safety issues that other adults working in the class should be aware of in relation to the specific tasks you are asking them to undertake with groups/individuals	
Subject specific language Including key vocabulary	
Any specific expectations for behaviour for group/ individuals	
Speaking and listening objectives	

Activity

Plan for another adult in your placement class and then gain some feedback about the details of your instructions for future planning for other adults with whom you will work.

Alternatively, plan for the additional adult for the previous history lesson.

Research Focus

Panasuk and Todd (2005) describe a method of evaluating lessons a 'Lesson Plan Evaluation Rubric' (LPER) which is an instrument derived from the Four Stages of Lesson Planning (FSLP) strategy and the empirical results that provide the insight into the elements of lesson planning with a specific focus on mathematics lessons. They begin by exploring other previous writers discussing planning e.g. Clark and Dunn (1991) who said that planning is a psychological process of envisioning the future, and considering goals and ways of achieving them. The teacher makes decisions that affect their behaviour and their students. Schön (1983) described lesson planning as pre-active decision-making that takes place before instruction.

OBJECTIVES formulated in terms of students' observable behaviour HOMEWORK matches the objectives DEVELOPMENTAL ACTIVITES reflect the objectives advance development and learning MENTAL MATHEMATICS activates prior knowledge, prepares students for the acquisition of new concepts	ELEMENTS OF INSTRUCTION *Instructional Environment* ● Inquiry-Based Instruction ● Expository/Direct Teaching ● Labs and Projects *Instructional Approaches based on* ● Problem Solving ● Multiple Representations ● Critical Thinking ● Communication ● Connections *Class Arrangements* ● Individual ● Group Work ● Pair Work

Figure 12.1 Four stages of lesson planning (Panasuk and Todd, 2005, p.216)

Each element of the plan was scored for each teacher's plan and the results identified four factors that influenced the effectiveness of the lesson plans for mathematics.

1. *Worked out problems* – this is about working out the answers to questions that the teachers would ask the children and by examining the questions that the children would complete during the lesson the teachers had a better picture of scope of the concepts that were going to be taught.

→

2. *By-products of the Four Stage Lesson Plan (FSLP)* – this was related to the organisational structure of the lesson, not always the same but planned carefully
3. *Lesson Coherence* – this is related to the links between the different elements of the lesson to maximise the learning for the pupils
4. *Representations* – these were the mathematical representations used by the teachers to support the pupils learning

Activity

Look at one of your lessons using this framework and discuss with other trainee teachers on your course and or teachers in school. What can you learn from this research about planning and its importance?

Opportunistic planning

The following extract is taken from the Rose Review of the Primary Curriculum and it sums up the use of opportunities that arise in the classroom which teachers can take advantage of in their teaching.

> **3.58** *As well as planning work, primary teachers are invariably skilful opportunists, always ready to capitalise on the unexpected to build from children's interests. For example, when a 5-year-old announced, 'My new baby brother was born last night', what followed was a lively class discussion covering several aspects of personal development: thinking about the care of babies, how to hold them, why they are weighed frequently, and why milk is better than water for feeding them. This was followed by an invitation to mum and baby brother to visit the class to celebrate the baby's birth and learn more about how to care for him.*

(Rose, 2009, p.75)

Activity

Think about a time when you:
a) allowed an unplanned event to impact on your teaching. How did this affect the children's learning? Or,
b) chose not to follow up an unplanned event and therefore kept following your planned lesson. How did this impact on the children's learning?

Location and planning

So far we have considered planning within a classroom but there are other locations for which you will need to plan. Planning resources for outdoor work is important as you need to consider weather conditions and how you protect recording that children may complete as part of their activities. Outside you can also plan larger scale tasks or use the children themselves as a main resource.

Activity

Walk around the school in which you are on placement. Note outdoor areas including playgrounds, fields, and nature environments. Find out how they are currently used as a location for learning and teaching. Plan in consultation with your school-based tutor/mentor/class teacher to use one of these locations as part of your plans and evaluate the lesson(s).

Learning Outcomes Review

Thinking about the school in which you are currently placed, or in which you most recently undertook a placement, respond to the questions which follow each of the intended learning outcomes, as a means of identifying your knowledge and understanding of the issues covered in the chapter.

- **Become aware of the different levels of planning that are undertaken in schools:**
  - What were the long term plans for the class you were teaching?
  - How were the plans organised? Were they organised in subjects or were they cross-curricula?

- **Consider the required elements of planning, children's previous experiences, subject knowledge, vocabulary, resources:**
  - Identify examples of planning during your placement which shows how you have taken account of:
    pupil's previous experiences;
    your own subject knowledge required before teaching;
    the necessary vocabulary for lessons;
    appropriate resources including the use of ICT to support learning.

- **Become aware of the documentation you need to be familiar with before planning any area of the curriculum:**
  - Show examples of how you have linked your planning to the appropriate statutory and guidance materials for the curriculum and how this has

influenced the decision you have taken in planning learning and teaching activities. This is more than quoting the references in your planning.

- **Look at the elements of lesson planning in detail:**
  - Identify an example of lesson planning during your placement where the lesson was successful in promoting learning and one where the lesson was less successful. Try to identify what the differences were in your planning that supported the more successful lesson and why? What changes will you make to the process of planning as a result in the future?

- **Consider the planning required for additional adults:**
  - Identify an example of planning for another adult during your placement where the activity was successful in promoting learning and one where the activity was less successful. Try to identify what the differences were in your planning that supported the more successful activity for both the children and the other adult and why? What changes will you make to the process of planning for additional adults as a result in the future?

- **Consider how to evaluate planning, teaching and learning and how to use this information to feed into future planning:**
  - Identify examples of lesson evaluations during your placement which show how you have altered elements in the next lesson as a result of your review. Discuss these with another trainee teacher on the course and compare methods of review. Between you can you draw up a list of questions to assist you both in reviewing future lessons?

Further issues associated with continuity and progression will be addressed in Chapter 11, the assessment chapter of this book.

Further Reading

Medwell, J. (2006) Approaching long term and medium term planning. In Arthur, J., Grainger, T. and Wray, D. (eds) (2006) *Learning to Teach in the Primary School*. London: Routledge, pp.81–89.

Medwell, J. (2006) Approaching short term planning. In Arthur, J., Grainger, T. and Wray, D. (eds) (2006) *Learning to Teach in the Primary School*. London: Routledge, pp.90–101.

Superfine, A.C. (2008) Planning for mathematics instruction: A model of experienced teachers' planning processes in the context of a reform mathematics curriculum. *The Mathematics Educator*, Vol. 18, No. 2, 11–22.

Threlfall, J. (2005) The formative use of assessment information in planning – the notion of contingency planning. *British Journal of Educational Studies*, Vol. 53, No. 1, March, pp.54–65.

References

Ausubel. D.P. (1968) *Educational Psychology: A cognitive view.* New York: Holt, Rinehart and Winston.

Beyer, C.J. and Davis, E.A. (2009) 'Using Educative curriculum materials to support preservice elementary teachers' curricular planning: A comparison between two different forms of support' *The Ontario Institute for Studies in Education of the University of Toronto Curriculum Inquiry,* 39:5 pp.679–703.

Clark, C.M. and Dunn, S. (1991) Second-generation research on teachers' planning, intentions, and routines. In H.C. Wanen and H.J. Walberg (eds), *Effective Teaching: Current research* (pp.183–200), Berkeley, CA: McCatehum Publishing.

DfE (2011) *Teachers' Standards.* Available at www.education.gov.uk/publications

Panasuk, R.M., and Jeffrey, T. (2005) Effectiveness of Lesson Planning: Factor Analysis. *Journal of Instructional Psychology.* Vol. 32(3), Sep, pp. 215–232.

Qualifications and Curriculum Authority (QCA) (1999) *The National Curriculum for England at key stages 1 and 2.*

Rose, J. (2008) Independent Review of the Primary Curriculum: Interim Report. Nottingham: DCSF Publications.

Schön, D. (1983) *The Reflective Practitioner.* New York, NY: Basic Books.

30

Values and principles of assessment in the Early Years Foundation Stage

Percival, J.

Chapter Objectives

- To consider why all practice begins with the careful consideration of values and principles.
- To reflect on current policy values and principles in relation to assessment.
- To assert the view that the Early Years Foundation Stage (EYFS) is a framework for regulation but also reflection, giving scope for autonomy.
- To consider how values and principles evolve over time: they are not fixed or given but shaped by our understanding.
- To prompt reflection and evaluation of assessment processes starting from shared principles.

Why is it important to include a chapter about values and principles in a book about assessment? Principles may be defined as a general set of rules or beliefs which guide behaviour. The EYFS (DCSF 2008c) themes and commitments have been the subject of information boards in the entrance halls of many early years settings. How many more focus instead on the six areas of learning, without reference to any underlying principles? Assessment is an integral part of practice and not an additional consideration once provision for care, learning and development has been decided upon. The values and principles you have adopted for your assessment practice should be in harmony with the values and principles that influence your wider work.

The policy context

The overarching aim of the *EYFS: Setting the Standards for Learning, Development and Care for Children from Birth to Five* (DCSF 2008) is to help children achieve the five *Every Child Matters* (DfES 2004) outcomes of staying safe, being healthy, enjoying and achieving, making a positive contribution, and achieving economic well-being. One of the ways in which the policymakers hope this will happen is through the setting of universal standards that all providers of childcare and early education can refer to as a basis for their work. These standards should offer parents reassurance and enable workers across the variety of provision to have a shared professional language. Most importantly, entitlement to quality should not to be dependent on where children live, their ethnicity, culture or religion, home language, family background, learning needs or disabilities, gender or ability.

The commitment to improve the lives of children and young people has been reinforced with the publication of *The Children's Plan: Building Brighter Futures* (DCSF 2007). The theme of this document is that 'services do not bring children up, parents do.' Collaborative respectful partnerships between practitioners, children and families should be a feature of universal services and ensure that in times of need, children are supported to have the best possible outcomes. For responsive, flexible services to be a reality, practitioners must hold certain principles and values in the forefront of their mind. This can be quite challenging.

Both *Every Child Matters* (DfES 2004) and the *Children's Plan* (DCSF 2007) are the focal point for a plethora of initiatives and guidelines. It is not altogether clear how the values and principles will be translated into effective practice. Each layer of decision making must grapple with the values and principles contained within the documents, knowledge of existing resources, and histories of service delivery – along with local and practitioner priorities.

∿ Reflective Activity

Visit the following sites to find out more about two useful documents that you can use to develop your thinking.

- Go to www.info4localgov.uk to find the General Social Care Council (2008) Values for Integrated Working with Children and Young People.

  - What kind of practitioners do children value?
  - What key attributes underpin values-led practice?
  - Within your particular specialism and through integrated working, it is suggested that the values shown in Table 2.1 should underpin practice.

Table 2.1   Aspects of professional practice that exemplify value-led practice

respect	trustworthiness	patience
honesty	reliability	integrity
resilience	supportive	sensitivity
transparency	positive	creativity
listen and take account	clear communication	safeguarding

Could you define these values? Could you cite an example of your practice that exemplifies each value?

- Go to www.everychildmatters.gov.uk/ to find the Common Core of Skills and Knowledge for the Children's Workforce (DfES 2005). Within the Common Core prospectus, communication is seen as central to working with children, young people, and their families and carers.

  - How do your behaviour and your everyday practice communicate your values?
  - Trust, rapport, continuity and engagement underpin effective communication. What do you understand by these terms? Do you think there is a shared understanding, common to the practitioners you work alongside?
  - How can you evidence your thoughts?

The EYFS: designed for reflection

The *EYFS: Setting the Standards for Learning, Development and Care for Children from Birth to Five* is a collection of documents that is made up of five elements. The *Statutory Framework* (DCSF 2008a) sets out the legal requirements relating to welfare, learning and development. The *Practice Guidance* (DCSF 2008b) contains 'essential advice and guidance' for those working with babies, toddlers and young children, from birth until the term after they are 5 years old. There is a pack of 24 *Principles into Practice Cards* (DCSF 2008c) that are designed to be a source of 'best practice'. The *Wall Poster* serves as a 'daily reminder' of some of the needs of children and the principles of the EYFS. Finally, the CD-ROM contains all four documents along with an extensive bank of information and resources.

The EYFS pack (DCSF 2008) seems to have been designed to help front-line practitioners develop practice in particular kinds of ways. All do need to be clear about the basic minimum standards that enable provision to be operational and registered with Ofsted, but this is not all that is offered. Examples of best practice and research are accessible, with a commitment to the updating of the online resource index. Questions to prompt reflection are posed on the cards. Principles are mapped out for all to see. The EYFS became mandatory in September 2008. However, there remains considerable flexibility and choice as to how you use this pack to respond to the uniqueness of each child. Relationships and environments evolve according to the decisions you make. Children's creativity and enthusiasm, confidence, and sense of self-worth are in your hands. How have you chosen to work with the principles?

- Which document from the pack has had the most use in your setting?

- If our practice is a reflection of our values, what does your *use* of the EYFS materials show about your approach to supporting the care, learning and development of young children?

Accountability: a reflective approach to regulations

The implementation of the EYFS is monitored and inspected by Ofsted through a process that begins with completing a self-evaluation form designed around the EYFS statutory requirements and the *Every Child Matters* outcomes. Rules and regulations have long been a feature of working with babies, toddlers and young children. Prior to the introduction of the EYFS in September 2008, the *National Standards for Under 8s Day Care and Childminding* (DfES 2003), the *Birth to Three Matters Framework* (DfES 2002), and the *Curriculum Guidance for the Foundation Stage* (DfES 2000) were used to structure and guide practice. The previous inspection regime for private, voluntary and independent settings (such as private day nurseries, playgroups and independent schools) was based on the

Every Child Matters outcomes and reflective, evidence-based practice was implied.

Currently, practitioners are requested, for example to 'take a critical look at the effectiveness of what you and any assistants or staff do to help children enjoy learning and achieve as much as they can' (Ofsted 2008). Evidence of the impact of practice needs to be recorded along with any plans for improvement. The views of stakeholders, as with any inspection, have to be recorded. It is not enough to have, for example, the appropriate number of practitioners employed, or the appropriate policies in place: in the spirit of the EYFS, practitioners should be working reflectively for quality and equality. This involves each lead practitioner having an understanding of what is being done, when and how, along with why certain practices take place and what the impact of those practices are.

Deciding 'what next', either session by session or through the setting of longer-term goals, requires careful thought. Why choose this course of action? Will stakeholders be consulted? What resources are required? What techniques and behaviours will be important? What will success look like?

The EYFS can be a source of support to help teams to discuss their values and make choices about their practice. Fundamentally, settings and their teams – including you as an individual – are being asked to be accountable for the quality of what you provide. More cynically, you are being asked to account to the taxpayer for any funding, such as Nursery Education Funding or Graduate Leader Fund, that you receive. Are you spending wisely? Accountability is part of professional responsibility.

Families access care outside their own home for their children for very many reasons. They send their children to school, again, for many reasons. To date, rules and regulations have not eliminated the diversity of provision available to children and parents, nor have they led to uniformly good (or, indeed, excellent) provision.

Communicating clearly and purposefully about your work could be seen as a fundamental responsibility. It enables you to demonstrate the basis upon which you do indeed put children at the centre of what you do and practically how it is done. Without a certain amount of evidence gathering, reflection, action and review, could you be certain that you were not basing decisions on personal assumptions and intuition? Reflective processes can also help target driven settings to complement numerical data with richer qualitative data that are more accessible to a wider range of audiences, such as parents and children. Reflect on your values, the aspects of your work you believe are vital for young children to thrive, and the guiding principles that you return to when you need inspiration or support to make a decision. Regulations provide a framework but regulations are open to interpretation. How regulations are played out in your setting is to a large extent in your hands.

Finding a theoretical grounding for your work

Values and principles can be hidden in our beliefs about the children in our care. Along with our personal assumptions and intuition, we are offered a variety of theoretical perspectives upon which to base our decision making and evidence gathering. MacNaughton (2003) challenges practitioners to think critically about their ideas and methods so that they can account for their practice both to themselves and others. Different theoretical positions are grouped according to their fundamental view of the child as a being but also a learner. Table 2.2 has been created through the selection of just one example of a position that sits within each of the three paradigms. When you look out onto the children and the setting you work in, what you see and attend to is mediated by the theories you subscribe to. This in turn impacts on how you assess children and make provision for their well-being and learning.

Table 2.2 Comparing theoretical positions, their implicit values and principles

Child	Practitioner	Assessment
'Conforming' position (e.g. behaviourism) Culture determines learning: behaviour is shaped so that children can conform.		
Starts off unknowing, uninitiated, liable to become bored. Compliant, ready and willing to learn if appropriately motivated, the rules are clear and the rewards/sanctions consistently applied.	Direct the learning through carefully designed programmes with clearly stated goals that can be monitored and measured. Refine, remodel and prepare the child to 'fit in'.	Measures what has been taught, perhaps to the exclusion of other aspects of development and learning. Assessment tasks are designed to complement the instructional programme and can be standardised across all learners. Accountability comes through standardisation and measurability?

Table 2.2   (Continued)

Child	Practitioner	Assessment

'Reforming' position (e.g. constructivism)
The interaction between nature and culture enables thinking to be reformed and improved as the child progresses through stages in development.

Child	Practitioner	Assessment
Learns through the senses as a social being. Builds own understanding but this can be shaped by interaction with and through the physical and social environment. Competent at each stage of development with the propensity to see themselves as active learners.	Carefully design the environment so that children can learn by doing, using open-ended materials and play. Focus on intellectual performance as an indicator of holistic well-being. Facilitate creative thinking. Learning possibilities are identified.	Observes and reflects on how the child operates in the environment (context) provided. Assessment systems are designed to capture the child's interests and dispositions along with the learning process, not just the end product. Curriculum development and assessment opportunities are interwoven and evolve. Accountability comes through the practitioner knowledge of developmental ages and stages and/or the prevailing national policy framework.

'Transforming' position (e.g. postmodern, social constructionalism)
Learning can only be understood within and through the context in which it occurs. Understanding and relationships are transformed or reconstructed through situated interaction.

Child	Practitioner	Assessment
Development implies the child is less formed than an adult, instead the child is seen as a meaning maker, a contributor and influencer from birth. Learning takes place in and through race, gender and class. As social beings, the collective learning is as relevant as the personal learning.	Attention is paid to the values and power relations. Differences are not only acknowledged but explored because learning is 'situated' in different places and times. Planning centres on equity and what is just, and is based on the dynamics of the group as well as children's interests and the collaboratively constructed curriculum.	Is a process shared between practitioners, parents and carers and the child. Responsibility is taken to ensure that the assessment systems. capture how children learn in and through their culture, gender race and disability. Ages and stages (norms) are seen as cultural tools with a limited use for some settings. Accountability comes through: • active participation, the documentation and relationships of those involved; • the application of detailed knowledge of pedagogy across a range of domains of care learning and development along with the prevailing national policy framework.

Source: adapted from MacNaughton 2003.

Being accountable for our practice in an autonomous, professional way relies on being able to identify the source of our beliefs about children, families and our practice. At times we need to challenge our beliefs, discuss them openly, and maybe alter the course of our actions. We need to acknowledge that there are multiple ways of viewing children, but also that children have multiple ways of being themselves.

The EYFS CD-ROM is a well-researched collection of ideas, carefully selected on the basis of growing theoretical knowledge and understanding of a variety of aspects of early years work. It is possible to interpret the inclusion of this resource in the pack as an attempt to take the information to the practitioners in the hope that theoretical concepts and suggestions for effective practice will be more widely disseminated. Perhaps practitioners will be reminded of key concepts covered during initial training? Perhaps leaders and managers will structure time into the working week for professional discussion?

'There's no time for values and principles and besides the EYFS is more or less the same as the other documents it replaced'

Unfortunately, evidence of what has worked before, reported outcomes of carefully designed research and accessible interpretations of theory, can easily be left on the bookshelf. The learning and development grids that look quite like the stepping stones from the Curriculum Guidance for the Foundation Stage (DfES 2000) could be well thumbed. On a weekly basis, practitioners may become more familiar with the grids as they match observations to 'Look, listen and note' statements.

Superficially at least, it seems that the EYFS is being implemented. Unfortunately, without taking the time to consider the values that underpin practice, the following two dangers (at least) may occur:

1. A system is grafted onto existing practice. Confident practitioners, familiar with their effective routines, care practices and rich curriculum, may lose momentum. There are a variety of reasons why they have not been able to reflect on their wealth of skill and knowledge. They have strong values yet these are not clearly articulated: they are not readily to mind to be integrated with new

ideas. This loss of momentum can be disheartening. Less effective practitioners begin to appreciate the need for development so systems and processes are adopted quickly. Some practitioners are not sure why new systems need to be put in place. Without the underpinning rationale, setbacks cannot be explained – the vision cannot be defended. The EYFS becomes just another policy directive that has been found wanting. For some there is a strong feeling that once again they could not match up to the expectations placed upon them. For others, the explanation that policy-makers never really know about the 'real world experiences' of working with young children seems plausible.

2. Practice remains the same (but with different headings on the planning sheet!). Policies say children are at the heart of practice, but practice does not bear this out. The 'folk model' of practice described by Margaret Carr (2007) is perpetuated through the common-sense, gut instinct approach. Values and principles are never explored. Institutionalised, 'one-size-fits-all' routines continue to dehumanise children. Inappropriate learning experiences are repeated and dispositions to explore and solve problems whither. Practitioners know what to do when required. A principled approach to practice passes the setting by.

Values and principles: themes and commitments

The four principles of the EYFS are:

- Every child is a competent learner from birth who can be resilient, capable, confident and self-assured, the *theme* of this principle being the uniqueness of the child.

- Children learn to be strong and independent from a base of loving and secure relationships with parents and/or a key person: the *theme* of this principle is positive relationships.

- The environment plays a key role in supporting and extending children's development and learning: the *theme* of this principle is enabling environments.

- Children develop and learn in different ways and at different rates, and all areas of learning and development are equally important and interconnected: children's learning and development are the *themes* of this principle.

Holistic care & education provides all 4 of these.

Table 2.3   The underpinning values of integrated working and the EYFS commitments

Respect for each human being's capacities and their culture. No child or family is discriminated against	**Trustworthiness** You trust each child to be themselves: they trust you to be genuine and loving	**Patience** Environments, development, learning and relationships do not happen overnight
Honesty Fundamental to building a secure and loving relationship together	**Reliability** Fundamental to building a secure and loving relationship together	**Integrity** Fundamental to building a secure and loving relationship together
Resilience Work with young children is varied, complex, challenging and rewarding! Promoting resilience in children and colleagues enables us to face the challenges of life	**Supportive** Development and learning can be challenging; all children need to build confidence in their abilities – supportive relationships with adults who are generous with their knowledge beat any amount of resources	**Sensitivity** Intimate and personal care carried out sensitively on the basis of a careful review of need is the basis of all work with babies and young children. Sensing when to support children's learning – using your senses in combination with knowledge
Transparency Openness supports secure relationships with babies, children, parents, colleagues and the wider community of professionals – agendas are not hidden – testing does not masquerade as play	**Positive** Enables you to constructively build relationships and environments where children can be seen as capable	**Creativity** Using every resource to flexibly respond to the child's needs and interests Being open to possibilities, different patterns of need and learning, that adult's knowledge can be used flexibly/creatively to meet needs and take learning further
Listen and take account *Time* is made for children, parents and colleagues to express their view, and the environment, care plans and provision for learning reflects this	**Clear communication** Ambiguity is kept to a minimum. Children know they are loved and valued; they know what they are good at and that communication is a two-way process	**Safeguarding** Every child (every person) is potentially vulnerable. Psychological and physical well-being is central for children to become resilient adults

Direct links between the values set out for integrated working and the principles of the EYFS (DCSF 2008) have been made in Table 2.3.

What do these values and principles look like in everyday practice? Given the diversity of the sector, it is only to be expected that they will look different in every setting! The EYFS in some respects is a 'manifesto' of beliefs laid out under the four themes. Working to any principles requires a *commitment* to certain beliefs about children and best practice. There are four commitments for each of the four themes. If you have made a commitment to work in a certain way, try to understand why this might be. If you are studying for a qualification, you are probably using a learning journal to help you reflect on the content of the course and its application to your work-based learning. Mind mapping or simply writing can be a useful starting point for reflection. If you are not sure what you are committed to, now is a good time to get deciding!

A principled approach to practice is not new

Bruce's influential text (1987, first edition) argued for a principled approach to practice that could empower practitioners in their decision making. Table 2.4 compares Bruce's principles with a more recent publication from the series edited by Hurst and Joseph (Brooker 2008). Decades have gone by. Priorities change or are expressed in new ways, and notions of what constitutes quality practice evolve over time.

The highly regarded approach to supporting and documenting children's learning that has been developed by the teams who work in the Reggio Emilia region of Italy is founded on what Rinaldi calls 'a sensitivity to knowledge' (2006: 72) and a richness of questioning. The 'pedagogy of listening' (Rinaldi 2006: 65) helps practitioners to be curious and doubtful, to suspend prejudice and be open to change. A series of values and principles do not provide answers but they do provide an evolving framework for learning about practice, which in turn informs our decision making. The EYFS principles have evolved through the accumulated thinking, provoked by key thinkers (of which Bruce, Brooker, Hurst and Joseph cited here are examples) and the lobbying of practitioners and researchers. In many ways they represent compromise between a host of competing policymaking agendas. However, they do provide space for you to reflect and take ownership of your work; to exercise your senses, to represent not only the thinking of children but also the hundred, if

Table 2.4   Changing principles over time

Ten common principles of early childhood education	Principles for a developmental curriculum
• Childhood is seen as valid in itself, as part of life, and not simply as a preparation for adulthood. • The whole child is considered important. • Learning is not compartmentalised into subject areas. • Child-initiated, self-directed activity is valued because it is an indication of the child's motivation to explore. • Nurture self-discipline. • Receptive periods are characterised by patterns in behaviour that support learning and exploration (such as schemas). • What children can do (rather than what they cannot) is considered first when assessing and planning for the future. • Favourable conditions support children to display their thinking and connect their inner life with the world around them. • Interaction with peers and adults is of central importance. • 'Education is seen as an interaction between the child and the environment, including in particular, other people and knowledge itself.'	• Each child is an individual and should be respected and treated as such. • The early years is a specialism with its own criteria of appropriate practice. • Support for young children centres on their concerns and actively engages them. • The practitioner has the responsibility to counter negative messages and foster positive attitudes. • 'Each child's cultural and linguistic endowment is seen as the fundamental medium of learning.' • Anti-discriminatory approaches are essential for a developmentally appropriate curriculum. • 'All children should be offered opportunities to progress and develop and should have equal access to good quality provision.' • Coherence and continuity in the offered and experienced curriculum is founded on partnership with parents. • Quality provision is linked to democratic relationships.
From Bruce, T. (1987) *Early Childhood Education.* London: Hodder Stoughton (p10).	From Brooker, L. (2008) *Supporting Transitions in the Early Years.* Supporting Early Learning Series. Maidenhead: Open University Press (pp. ix–x).

not the thousand languages, symbols and codes we use when we carry out our work.

Energy and time are necessary but the journey is worth beginning. Your values and principles will evolve, and the way your practice is framed by them will almost certainly never stay the same as each child comes into the setting, each policy imperative looms, or, most importantly, your own understanding or 'sensitivity to knowledge' (Rinaldi 2006) blossoms.

[handwritten margin note: adapts... coincidingly]

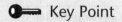 **Key Point**

- Audit where you are before making changes to practice. Incremental (or even whole-scale) changes without reference back to principles and values can lead to disjointed practice: sometimes it seems expedient to do something and yet on reflection it takes you off course (Table 2.5).

Table 2.5 Interrogating our assessment of young children: an audit

Assessing young children's care, learning and development

Question and describe
Who will contribute to this description? Children, families, colleagues?
What is being done to inform our understanding of the child?
When are assessments taking place?
How are assessments being carried out?
What aspects of care, learning and development are assessed?
How is information gained and used?

Question and evaluate
What is the quality of the assessment information we gather?
Have we decided on a rationale for our judgements about quality?
What is the impact of our assessment processes on children?
What is the impact of our assessment processes on families?
What is the impact of our assessment processes on colleagues?

Question and analyse
Why does assessment happen the way that it does?
How are decisions about the assessment processes made?
Whose voice is heard loudest – child, parent or practitioner?
Do our assessments actually have a positive (or negative) impact on our systems, routines and provision?
Can we see our values and principles/the EYFS principles in our work?
If yes, can we document this and celebrate it?
If no, can we begin a process of development so that the uniqueness of the child is supported through responsive relationship and enabling environments?
How will we document our shared learning: children and adults together?

Mary Jane Drummond (2003) has been involved with supporting early years workers to reflect on their practice for many years. Assessment practice can be challenging and a worry for adults and children alike, depending on the type of assessment tools being used. Her experience, supported by her research leads her to assert that

Effective assessment – clear seeing, rich understanding, respectful application – will be advanced by a full appreciation of the value-base from which teachers' choices are made. (Drummond 2003: 14)

Having gathered the data for your audit, you should ensure you have time to *read* and *interpret* and then *recall* and *reconstruct* your understanding (Rinaldi 2006). What activities attract the most time and effort? How do the most time-consuming activities inform your understanding of each child's learning? Are the assessment activities enabling the enriching of the learning experience for each and every child?

The concept of the work-based learner-practitioner (Rawlings 2008) working within a 'community of practice' (Lave and Wenger 1998) is a useful one for all interested in assessing children and provision. Article 12 of the UN Convention on the Rights of the Child encourages adults to ensure that children actively contribute to decision making where matters concern them. Their views should be taken seriously and the child's competent participation should be expected and nurtured (Clarke and Moss 2001; Lancaster and Broadbent 2005). It takes a particular type of listening and a challenging of certain discourses to consider alternative perspectives. The audit is a suggested starting point for understanding what is actually happening in your setting. Definitive answers as to what and how to assess cannot be supplied to fit the needs of every setting. Learning together, building shared understandings, and revisiting actual actions in the light of values and principles can help to keep coherence and quality at the forefront of your practice.

Purposeful assessment

The purposes of your assessment practice must be kept in mind and balanced carefully so that one purpose does not outweigh another. Nutbrown (2006), for example, identifies three broad purposes:

- Assessment for management and accountability.

- Assessment for research.

- Assessment for teaching and learning.

[handwritten annotations: "original source"; "As a teacher should be main focus → focus on individual."]

Implicit in this list of purposes is the need for practitioners to ensure that well-being is accounted for and built into any setting's practice. We assess to ensure equity of practice and delivery of social policy imperatives. We assess to find out more about our practice and its impact on all involved. We assess to celebrate children's learning and so practitioners can select what they might teach next and how they might teach it.

However, the EYFS does not just provide a framework for practice in schools. For many practitioners the intimate care of groups of children must be carefully thought out and organised for extended periods of the day. Children's well-being is a feature of much unrecognised practice in terms of assessment in the EYFS.

> Care was (and to many still is) regarded as second best to education and this tunnel vision has been a serious obstacle in the way of quality provision for very young children. (Lindon 2006: 23)

Tuning to children's sleep patterns or preferences for being comforted and changed, for example, is a vital consideration for many parents and carers but also early years practitioners. It is not that schools do not provide a caring environment – they most certainly do! Practitioners throughout the EYFS should to be open to the need to assess children's well-being so that they can plan appropriately for care that respects each child as an individual. Supporting babies and young children in their development in ways that respond to individual patterns in growth and development takes careful observation and the application of high levels of knowledge and skill. Routines must be carefully planned to ensure that dehumanising systems do not evolve and that each person living in a care-led setting feels first and foremost respected as a person, not just a learner, capable of achieving the Early Learning Goals.

Alongside assessment for teaching and learning should come assessment for care and well-being. Progress that is trackable through the 'learning and development grids' (DCSF 2008b) should be interlinked with a child's fundamental well-being. This is not a plea for additional, specialised assessment techniques, but a valuing of the social, interpersonal assessment that many practitioners carry out and use to inform their daily practice. Closely linked to a child's learning, assessment for care and well-being needs asserting as valuable and purposeful in its own right.

Owning values and principles

Read the following case study. It illustrates how a group of practitioners chose to learn about their own practice so that they could improve their assessment of children's behaviour. They used their beliefs about children and the principles of the EYFS to help guide their choices as to how their practice needed to develop.

 Case Study: a team explore their values and principles, as they search for a way to change practice

An early years professional (EYP) working alongside a team of colleagues discussed how the behaviour of some children was causing concern. Their informal assessments had not been transferred to written observations, as generally, those were only made for significant achievements within the six areas of learning (DCSF 2008a). Negative behaviour was not really something they chose to record, unless part of a particular strategy for particularly inappropriate behaviour. Lots of instances of inappropriate behaviour seemed to be occurring. Various ideas were floated as to how to deal with the situation. The only consensus was that something had to change so that things could settle down again and parents would not feel there was a problem.

The EYP decided to lead a staff meeting, using the work of Louise Porter (2003) to help the team step back from the behaviour and talk about their values and principles (Table 2.6).

There were some very challenging discussions, as the staff were asked to place themselves along the continuum between controlling and guiding children in their learning about their behaviour. Assessments of behaviour were coloured by the views practitioners held about children, their behaviour, and the possible intervention methods. The discussion about rewards and punishments became particularly heated!

When they looked at principles of the EYFS, alongside the work of Porter (2003), it seemed as if they should reconsider their assessment of their children's behaviour. It was decided to follow the current setting policy for the time being, but to jot down instances of the behaviour that caused concern to review at the next meeting.

The team spent 2 weeks making brief observations of instances of behaviour they deemed inappropriate and sharing some short sections from the EYFS and other literature: this gave them some thinking space so that when they met again, they were ready to reflect on values and principles, and consider what the behaviour consisted of and why it might be happening. Their assessments of the children led them to reconsider their provision, but, significantly, they began to formulate some different strategies for responding to children's behaviour, based on the principles behind the guidance style of discipline.

During subsequent meetings colleagues confided that they found it really difficult to work in a guiding way. Sometimes it was more time-consuming and needed such patience! They juggled with making sure that children knew what was unacceptable or hurtful and remaining calm, when sometimes behaviour seemed very challenging.

For the next 6 months, behaviour became a standing item on the agenda. By then the EYP felt able to review the behaviour management policy. The staff decided that the policy needed a new title that reflected the new approaches being taken. Words like control and management were replaced in the document with support and guidance. Staff responded to the unique learning needs of the child through their key person system and talked with parents about their work. They built in time to explore powerful emotions rather than push them to one side. Talking explicitly with children about feelings became an accepted aspect of their work that warranted time, resources, recording and assessment – the curriculum became enriched and assessments acknowledged children's emotional intelligence. The environment became more settled. Values and principles led the development of practice.

Drummond (2003) argues that claiming principles as your own will not bring about the changes that you hope for. She discusses how thinking about practice should be scaffolded so that answers do not come from a policy document with principles, an authoritative text (such as Porter's), or set behaviour management techniques derived from psychological theory (for example, reward systems such as sticker charts). These can only be starting points to prompt thinking. The confidence of the practitioners to make changes in their assessment of behaviour in this case study came from their questioning of what was going on and how it related to their values and principles. This questioning of what is good and worthwhile is central to our autonomy as professionals.

Table 2.6 A continuum of styles of discipline: a copy of the handout that was discussed

Control ◄——— Discipline style ———► Guidance		
Lies *outside* the child: control is in the hands of the 'rule-maker'	**Locus of control**	Lies *within* the child: the child is supported to exercise control over their own behaviour
Obedience and compliance are prioritised through direct instruction Challenging feelings need to be controlled or ignored, not acknowledged and explored	**Goals**	Strategies are used by adults to support children to • be autonomously considerate • develop ways of dealing with (powerful) emotions • cooperate with those around them • have a sense that they too have an impact on the community/ setting in which they live
Perhaps adults have failed to 'reward' appropriate behaviour sufficiently Perhaps inappropriate behaviour has been inadvertently rewarded or gone unchecked	**Causes of disruptive behaviour**	Normal exuberance Normal exploration Lack of coordination and or self-control Natural response to having little autonomy or chance to learn about feelings and actions
It is natural for all children to misbehave Sometimes children are 'naughty'	**View of children**	Children learn to 'behave' at different rates and in different ways Will behave well if treated well
Inappropriate Wilful noncompliance	**View of disruptive behaviour**	An opportunity for scaffolding the learning Some errors are inevitable – we all wish we could have done things differently sometimes!
Rewards Punishments	**Intervention methods**	Acknowledgement (not necessarily agreement!) Problem solving and resolution
Dictator!	**Adult status**	Emotionally intelligent leader

(Source: adapted from Porter, 2003, p18).

Assessment as your opportunity to learn

The questioning was not a comfortable process for the practitioners in the case study. Carr (2007) describes how she was anxious to be seen as the competent practitioner in the face of her local community and the parents. She assumed that readiness for school was the main priority for her and her children in terms of assessment (and in turn for her planning of the curriculum). Niggled by the fact that exciting learning episodes were going unrecognised, she decided to challenge her assumptions and reviewed her assessment practice. The documenting of children's learning that Carr and her colleaques developed has been very well received. The 'learning stories' are purposeful and identify the focus for future interventions for the practitioner, parent and child together. Progression can be seen and authenticity is captured so that parents and children can connect with the learning – it means something to them and they develop the language of learning for themselves, so that they can join in the talk that surrounds assessment. Administrative demands are met through tracking sheets. But the tracking sheets do not stand alone – evidence supports the ticks and highlighted sections. Children are not seen as one-dimensional, following a single pathway because the time and effort goes proportionately into the stories and not just the tracking.

Rights and responsibilities

Value the time you spend exploring your values and principles! You have the right to work in an environment where all are prepared to challenge ideas and existing practice. You have the right make choices about practice. You have the right to have your values acknowledged.

But with your rights, you have responsibilities. When you challenge ideas and practice, you have a responsibility to have a reasoned, researched position. You are responsible for choosing to practise in a way that puts the child at the centre of what you do. You are responsible for implementing the statutory requirements of the EYFS. However, approaching the implementation of the EYFS as a practitioner-learner (Rawlings 2008) with integrity will give you scope for expressing your values and keeping them with you as you work.

Provision for young children in the EYFS must address well-being and learning. Assessments will never be worthy of the child if they do not take account of the powerful and varied ways children influence their world and learn through it. If provision is narrow and unresponsive, assessments will only reveal a partial picture. Accountability, a worry for many practitioners will remain elusive. Reviewing your principles and checking that they drive your decision making can put the child at the centre of your work and in turn ensure that assessments are useful and authentic.

Further Reading

Both the Clarke and Moss (2001) text and the Lancaster and Broadbent (2005) (see references) materials provide practitioners and parents and carers with underpinning knowledge and practice skills to aid listening to children. Suggestions for 'when', 'why' and 'how' to listen are skilfully woven together, making for inspirational reading.

Fleer, M. (2006) 'The Cultural Construction of Child Development: Creating Institutional and Cultural Intersubjectivity', *International Journal of Early Years Education*, 14 (2): 127–140.

- This is a theoretical paper that asks readers to broaden their assumptions about institutionalised practice so that they can better understand children in the context in which they live. This will lead you to consider the work of Lave and Wenger.

Marsh, J. ed. (2005) *Popular Culture, New Media and Digital Literacy in Early Childhood.* London: Routledge Falmer.

- This locates children, with their multiple identities, as competent learners within their culture. The gap between home-based learning and setting-based experiences of new media challenges the possible misconception that the setting is the place where children learn. Our assessments are incomplete when we fail to acknowledge the cultural world in which and through which children learn.

Penn, H. (2008) *Understanding Early Childhood: Issues and Controversies.* Maidenhead: McGraw-Hill/Open University Press.

- Accessible problematising of taken-for-granted understandings and practice, including consideration of the ethics of routine observation (or surveillance) of children.

Seitz, H. and Bartholomew, C. (2008) 'Powerful Portfolios for Young Children', *International Journal of Early Years Education*, 36 (1): 63–68.

- This article makes the case for 'authentic assessments' through portfolios that are constructed by the child, the parent and the practitioner. However, from the start there are clear lines of responsibility for each partner, and time is planned for all to share in the assessment process. The lasting meaningful documentation enables parents and children to understand the learning process more fully and for practitioners to take responsibility for identifying relevant national benchmarks for accountability purposes.

Whalley, M. and the Penn Green Centre Team (2007) *Involving Parents in Their Children's Learning,* 2nd edn. London: Paul Chapman.

- Each person who goes through the doors of this centre for children and families is seen as having the capacity to be self-directing and capable of 'constructive discontent' (Whalley 2007). Are parents viewed as having a reasoned voice that you take account of?

Useful Websites

www.info4localgov.uk/documents/publications [accessed May 2008].

- General Social Care Council (2008) *Values for Integrated Working with Children and Young People.*

www.ofsted.gov.uk/Ofsted-home/Forms-and-guidance [accessed May 2008].

- Office for Standards in Education (Ofsted) (no date) *Early Years Self Evaluation Form and Guidance.*

www.ofsted.gov.uk/Ofsted-home/Forms-and-guidance [accessed May 2008].

- Office for Standards in Education (Ofsted) (no date) *Are You Ready for Your Inspection? A Guide to Inspection of Provision on Ofsted's Childcare and Early Years Registers.*

www.standards.dfes.gov.uk/eyfs/ [accessed May 2008].

- Department for Children, Schools and Families (DCSF) (2008) *The Early Years Foundation Stage: Setting Standards for Learning Development and Care for Children from Birth to Five.* Nottingham: DCSF.

www.ewenger.com/theory/ [accessed May 2009].

- Wenger, E. (no date) *Communities of Production: A Brief Introduction.*

Assessment

Briggs, M.

Learning Outcomes

By the end of this chapter you will have considered:
- what assessment is and its relationship with learning and teaching;
- your role in monitoring and assessing children's progress in learning across the curriculum;
- how to share assessments with children;
- how to feed back to children on their work and/or responses;
- the role of recording assessments;
- the statutory assessments;
- reporting to parents/carers and consultations.

TEACHERS' STANDARDS

A teacher must:

1. Set high expectations which inspire, motivate and challenge pupils
- establish a safe and stimulating environment for pupils, rooted in mutual respect
- set goals that stretch and challenge pupils of all backgrounds, abilities and dispositions
- demonstrate consistently the positive attitudes, values and behaviour which are expected of pupils.

2. Promote good progress and outcomes by pupils
- be accountable for pupils' attainment, progress and outcomes
- plan teaching to build on pupils' capabilities and prior knowledge
- guide pupils to reflect on the progress they have made and their emerging needs
- demonstrate knowledge and understanding of how pupils learn and how this impacts on teaching
- encourage pupils to take a responsible and conscientious attitude to their own work and study.

5. Adapt teaching to respond to the strengths and needs of all pupils
- know when and how to differentiate appropriately, using approaches which enable pupils to be taught effectively
- have a secure understanding of how a range of factors can inhibit pupils' ability to learn, and how best to overcome these
- demonstrate an awareness of the physical, social and intellectual development

of children, and know how to adapt teaching to support pupils' education at different stages of development

- have a clear understanding of the needs of all pupils, including those with special educational needs; those of high ability; those with English as an additional language; those with disabilities; and be able to use and evaluate distinctive teaching approaches to engage and support them.

6. Make accurate and productive use of assessment

- know and understand how to assess the relevant subject and curriculum areas, including statutory assessment requirements
- make use of formative and summative assessment to secure pupils' progress
- use relevant data to monitor progress, set targets, and plan subsequent lessons
- give pupils regular feedback, both orally and through accurate marking, and encourage pupils to respond to the feedback.

8. Fulfil wider professional responsibilities

- communicate effectively with parents with regard to pupils' achievements and well-being.

Introduction

Assessment serves a number of purposes:

- identifying next steps and planning future learning;
- ensuring consistency of standards;
- demonstrating progress;
- accountability.

Assessment is the aspect of teaching that is used for accountability as teachers are judged by the results of the assessment levels their children achieve. As a learner you may still remember the importance given to external assessments made of your work whilst at school. There are two linked aspects of assessment that of attainment and achievement.

Attainment is:

- a 'snapshot' of how a child is doing at a specific point in time;
- linked to National Curriculum Key Stages;
- shown in marks or grades in relevant national tests or examinations or school-based assessment.

Achievement is:

- an assessment of children's knowledge, understanding and skills in relation to their capability;

- reflects the progress they make in relation to children of similar capability;

- a judgement about whether children are doing as well as they can.

There are three main concepts associated with assessment are:

Assessment FOR Learning
This is the assessment that is completed to inform the planning of future learning and teaching. This involved the teacher and child in a process of continual review about progress

Assessment AS Learning
This aspect of assessment has developed from the personalised learning agenda (see Chapter 4), the increased awareness of the learner's role in their own assessment and application of different learning styles to the teaching process. This aspect focuses on reflecting on evidence of learning. This is part of the cycle of assessment where learners and teachers set learning goals, share learning intentions and success criteria, and evaluate their learning through dialogue including self and peer assessment. Learners are able to build knowledge of themselves as learners, and become *meta-cognitive*. In other words, they become aware of how they learn. It also helps learners to take more responsibility for their learning and participate more in the process of learning.

Assessment OF Learning
This assessment provides a summary of the assessment to date. It involves working with the range of available evidence that enables teachers, schools, Local Authorities and government to check on learners' progress and using this information in a number of ways.

Assessment and personalised learning

Associated with assessment is the move to develop a personalising learning agenda. Several of the elements of this agenda are helpful in relation to developing your understanding of current assessment practices. This shifts the focus of assessment from an activity which is 'done to' children to one which is done with children.

Component	Features
Learning how to learn	Giving learners skills, strategies and procedures to enable them to become meta-cognitive and self-managing learners.
Assessment for learning	Developing a wide range of assessment strategies, which place the emphasis on formative rather than summative approaches by engaging the learner in the assessment process
Teaching and learning strategies	Providing learners with a wide range of appropriate options to enable them to learn in the most effective way for them to experience the full portfolio of teaching and learning strategies
Curriculum choice	This involves changing the curriculum experience from the 'set meal' to the 'a la carte' menu. Students are given increasing choice as to what they study and when they study it
Mentoring and coaching	The one-to-one relationship is central to any model of personalising learning – it is the most powerful expression of a commitment to the learning of the individual. Mentoring may be used to monitor academic progress, support meta-cognition and provide focused support for aspects of the curriculum.

Table 11.1 Elements of personalising learning

Research Focus

The Assessment Reform Group (2002) developed the following principles for assessment for learning to guide classroom practice. This will involve all adults working with pupils in schools and early years settings.

Assessment For learning guide to classroom practice: 10 principles

Assessment for learning should:

i)   be part of effective planning of teaching and learning;

ii)   focus on how students learn;

iii) be recognised as central to classroom practice;

iv)   be regarded as a key professional skill for teachers;

v)   be sensitive and constructive because any assessment has an emotional impact;

vi)   take account of the importance of learner motivation;

vii) promote commitment to learning goals and a shared understanding of the criteria by which they are assessed;

viii) give learners constructive guidance about how to improve;

ix)   develop the learners' capacity for self-assessment so that they can become reflective and self-managing;

x)   recognise the full range of achievements of all learners.

(Black et al., 2002)

Planning for assessment

Use of observations, tasks, tests and other activities

Observation is a key skill to develop as part of your teaching skills. You may be asked by your tutors and school based staff to be aware of what is going on all around the classroom at all times, so that you notice if a child goes out of the class without asking or interactions between children become heated. (See Chapter 13 for more on managing behaviour for learning.) This is quite a different observational skill from that needed to make assessments of children. You will not be able to keep track of everything in detail but you will be able to note significant events that will assist all of those working with children to make judgements about progress and achievement in their learning.

By observing young children in play situations you may see them use their knowledge and therefore acquire the evidence upon which to make judgements about their learning. All the adults working with children in the EYFS will contribute to these observations that will be used to compile the profile at the end of the EYFS. There are two kinds of observations of young children. The first will be planned observations which you may plan with the team of adults working in the class and include activities outside as well as indoors and the second will be the spontaneous noticing of significant learning that you will wish to record.

Focused observation can be used with older learners. Although it will give you a wealth of information about their learning, it is time consuming, However you may find this a helpful method of assessment if looking at the use of mathematical skills, knowledge and application when teaching using a cross curricular approach. You may find a sheet like the one that follows as an initial guide to your observations.

Date	Observer	Child/group
Context Related objective and learning outcomes		
Unaided task	Aided task	Practical task
Notes		
Reference to any recording by child/group		
Objective achieved Notes	Objective partially achieved Notes	Objective not achieved Notes
Targets set as a result of observation	Review date	

Figure 11.1 Selecting children for intervention strategies/additional input

Working with a group can provide assessment information that is more difficult to capture in the whole-class context; it provides an opportunity to discuss the mathematics in more detail with individuals in the group. The focused attention given to a group helps to inform future planning and teaching. It also gives children who are not active contributors in the whole class the opportunity to participate more directly, share their ideas and extend their learning within a small group of peers.

(Williams, 2008, p.67)

Although the focus in this quotation comes from a review of primary and early years mathematics the same issues apply across the primary subjects.

The main focus is identifying groups of children for guided group work. You can identify children for a guided group through the following strategies.

- Through day-to-day assessment of children's progression in the lesson.
- Following feedback from a teaching assistant.
- As a result of a **planned assessment** activity with a focus on an identified target group.
- Following periodic assessment to track progress in a specific curriculum area.
- In response to school priorities about the attainment of particular groups of children, where there is evidence of underperformance (target group).

Case Study: Using effective guided group work

Going into her final block placement, Samir had a target to focus on effective guided group work in her teaching. Over the first half of the placement, she began to feel more comfortable using it as a teaching strategy. During her mid-placement review, Samir talked with her mentor about what she had learnt about guided group work.

'In terms of assessment, I see how guided group work helps me to build upon the assessment I undertook previously. It really helps me to target my teaching to the appropriate level for each of the children in the group and I can probe and assess children's understanding far better than when I'm working with the whole class. More generally, I now get that it is pretty fluid and it must respond to the children's learning needs. So, I can't plan for it too far in advance. I'm going to work more on using practical and ICT-based resources, as well as thinking about more appropriate subject specific models to develop children's understanding.'

Marking and written feedback

Marking and giving children written feedback on their work across the curriculum is an important part of the role of a classroom teacher. By marking work you gain a sense of outcomes across the whole class and the range of ability including pupils you may not have worked with directly during a specific lesson. This enables you to feed forward into your planning for the next lesson.

Research Focus

Val Brooks (2009) has specifically researched 'marking as judgment' because she believes that this area of assessment has not received the amount of attention it should, deserve despite its pivotal role. This work raises important issues for primary teachers who work predominantly with criterion referenced assessment, that is, you are matching the work against criteria which are pre-established. These criteria come from level descriptors in the National Curriculum, key objectives from the Primary National Strategy or success criteria linked to the learning objectives for a specific task within a lesson. Brook cites the following research when exploring the use of criteria... 'there is no common understanding of what criteria-based means or what it implies for practice... Additionally, the concepts of "criteria" and "standards" are often confused' (Sadler, 2005, p.175). Brooks goes on to argue that teachers need to be familiar with the criteria before they can use these to mark effectively but she also explores the disadvantages of this as once teachers think they have internalised the criteria they still tend to make judgements on the basis of their memories of how children performed tasks and sought to use the criteria to confirm judgements they have already made. The marker can also suffer from bias as they are likely to be swayed by the neatness of the work and legibility of handwriting. In addition there is the issue of looking at the role of affect – which includes looking for opportunities to give credit. Brook's paper asks us to take another look at the process of marking and the judgements teachers make when completing the task.

Activity

Choose a piece of work from a curriculum area and familiarise yourself with the description of the criteria for the appropriate levels before you mark this work. Jot down what you are paying attention to as you mark and then re-read the passage about Brook's research and try to identify what you were focusing on. Share your thoughts about this process with other trainees on your course.

Oral feedback

There are two different kinds of oral feedback; the planned and the responsive. With planned feedback you will have time to consider how you phrase the feedback for an individual, group or whole class so it is likely to be based upon marking a class set of books or your reflection on a previous lesson in conjunction with your school-based tutor/mentor/class teacher's feedback. This may include general feedback on strengths and areas for development against the objectives that you might give to the class at the start of the next lesson. This can help model feedback for children to use in peer or self assessment situations.

Responsive feedback is usually in the form of comments that you will make during the lesson to individuals, groups and to the class depending, upon the specific activity that is being undertaken. You may find this very daunting as it is part of thinking on your feet whilst teaching. If you are not sure it is worth saying directly to the individual, group or class, then you may want to take away the information and to think about it before you give feedback rather than feeling uncomfortable about the position in which you find yourself. This strategy shows that you have listened and/or observed what is going on and that you are responding. You can then plan a more considered response but you must make sure you follow through with the response and give feedback. Don't forget. It may be an issue that you wish to discuss with your school-based tutor/mentor/class teacher before talking again to the children involved especially if you are new to the class and need guidance on how a child might respond to the feedback given. Don't forget to ensure that all children get some oral feedback, including children with additional needs. For this group you may want to plan your feedback very carefully if it is to be a public feedback. For any pupil negative feedback in a public arena could damage their self-esteem and their attitude to learning. Read Chapter 4 for more on supporting children with additional needs.

Peer and self assessment

Young children are more than capable of making judgements about their own and others' work as part of the process of assessment in schools. Many schools have introduced an approach called 'two/three stars and a wish' and some even produce sheets/templates to put onto children's work.

The idea behind this approach is to get the learners to look carefully at their work and reflect on two or three 'stars' that form the positive feedback and one 'wish' indicating where development could be made. This can be completed as self assessment or can be used to guide peer assessment. The teacher can then talk to the child about how they might work on the area they have identified in the wish category. This approach can be flexible and children can be allowed to give only one star or no wish, or there may be situations where wishes are not appropriate as its overuse could have a negative effect. Children can find it difficult to begin with and focus on holistic areas of their work including the presentation rather than the learning objectives or success criteria agreed for the lesson and the teacher may need to remind them about focus of their feedback for themselves or others. A key element here is that the success criteria are clear and accessible for all learners. Be aware that children can also focus on trying to please the teacher rather than making judgements against the criteria for themselves.

Another approach to self-assessment uses a star diagram where the child is asked to rate themselves against the items indicated. In this case it is some general items in relation to a geography topic on the study of a local area. 1 is a low score and 5 is high. The star can have more arms so more items can be included. You can use the results from individuals to evaluate teaching approaches and plan for future approaches to learning.

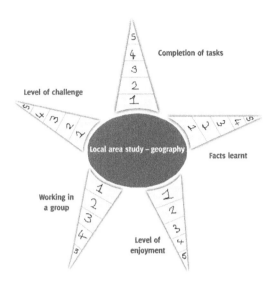

Figure 11.2: Star diagram

Role of peer coaching

Linked to self and peer assessment is the role of mentoring and coaching in the classroom. Mentoring and coaching are terms which are often used interchangeably for two people working together to change outcomes for one of the pair. Sometimes that can be a directive relationship relying on the coach or mentor being a more knowledgeable person than the other where the coach/mentor.

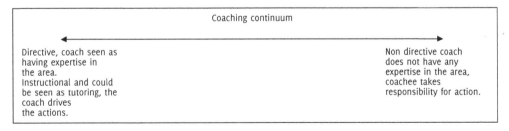

Figure 11.3 Coaching continuum

Children can develop the skills of a coach as Briggs and Van Nieuwerburgh (2010) have shown in their work with Year 5 and 6 children focusing on giving and receiving feedback. Below is an example of feedback given on the drawing of a giraffe and how the child has responded to the feedback in another drawing.

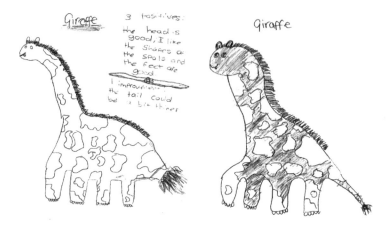

Figure 11.4: Children's drawing of a giraffe pre- and post-coaching

Although the research was carried out with the oldest children in Key Stage 2, in one school a Year 1 teacher had already been working in this way encouraging her class to give and receive feedback.

Record keeping

All teachers keep records of children in their class and these can take a variety of forms from notes scribbled on sticky notes whilst teaching, to in class test results and level assessments against key objectives or attainment targets. What is important about record keeping is that it is useful. You may like to ask yourself the following questions in relation to your own records.

- Can you identify groups of children for whom it would be helpful to work as a group with you on a specific topic they find difficult from your records?

- Does your record keeping help you to compile summary information about children's progress and attainment? If not what other information would you need to collect?

- Would your records allow someone else to be able to pick up and plan for your class rather than trying to assess them all again?

You may have been asked to record information as below to indicate whether or not targeted learning objectives have been achieved in a specific lesson.

Name	Attendance register		Targets achieved		
	Present ✓	Absent ✗			

Figure 11.5 Class record sheet

What kind of information does this give you and is it helpful in identifying specific groups of children for guided group work or for future planning or for summative assessment purposes? What kinds of records would give you more comprehensive information in order to address these questions?

Activity

With a small group of trainees on your course pool any examples of record keeping that you may have collected or been given and see if you can evaluate their effectiveness. See if you can construct a list of the most useful information that you need to keep as a record in the class and why.

Assessing pupil progress

Assessing Pupil Progress (APP) is a voluntary approach to tracking children's attainment. APP is the tracking of children's attainment in English, mathematics and speaking and listening using diagnostic information about individual's strengths and weaknesses. In order to make a judgement about pupil's work you will need to follow a series of steps.

This process begins by needing to plan for the collection of evidence as a teacher in the class. It then becomes a three step process of:

1. Considering the evidence → 2. Reviewing the evidence → and 3. Making a judgement

(National Strategies, 2009)

You can read more about APP in Chapter 3.

Summative assessment points across early years and primary age range

Early Years Foundation Stage (EYFS) profile

The *Assessment and reporting arrangements* (ARA) contains guidance on the early years foundation stage (EYFS) profile curriculum assessment and reporting arrangements. These are updated regularly, so ensure you have the most up-to-date copy.

The EYFS profile is a way of summarising each child's development and learning attainment at the end of the EYFS. For most children, this is at the end of the reception year (Year R) in school. Others may be assessed in settings such as nursery schools, private, voluntary and independent (PVI) settings and by Ofsted-registered childminders. It identifies children's learning needs for the next stage of school, helping Year 1 teachers to plan an effective and appropriate curriculum for each child.

Reporting children's attainment to parents or carers

All EYFS providers must provide parents or carers with a written summary of a child's progress against the early learning goals and attainment within the assessment scales. A copy of the EYFS profile summary scores reported to the local authority must also be provided to parents or carers if requested.

For children in Year R the following must be reported to parents/carers:

- brief particulars of achievements in all subjects and other activities. Comments should be included for each of the six areas of learning, where appropriate;
- comments on general progress;
- arrangements for discussing the report.

For children at the end of Year R there should be a written summary reporting progress against the early learning goals and the assessment scales given to all parents/carers.

Schools must offer parents/carers a reasonable opportunity to discuss the outcomes of the EYFS profile with their child's teacher.

Key Stage 1

Ensure you have the most recent copy of the 'Assessment and Reporting Arrangements (ARA)' as this will give you the most up-to-date information for this age group. The *Assessment and reporting arrangements* (ARA) provides statutory information and guidance on the Key Stage 1 national curriculum assessment and reporting arrangements.

At the end of Key Stage 1, teachers summarise their judgements in relation to the national curriculum level descriptions taking into account the child's progress and performance throughout the key stage, determining:

- a level for reading, writing, and speaking and listening;
- an overall subject level for mathematics;
- a level for each attainment target in science.

The statutory national curriculum assessments must be administered to all children who are working at level 1 or above in reading, writing and mathematics. Their role is to help inform the final teacher assessment judgement reported for each child at the end of Key Stage 1. There is no requirement to report separately the levels obtained from the tasks and tests.

Reporting to parents/carers

Children's overall teacher assessment levels sent to the Local Authority must be reported to their parents or carers. However, for science, only the overall level, not the levels for each attainment target, is reported. For children with special educational needs who are working towards level 1, schools should report progress in the P scales in English, mathematics and science (see below).

Results held by schools as part of an individual child's educational record must be disclosed to that child's parents or carers on request.

For children in Year 1 and above information given to parents/carers includes:

- an attendance record;
- brief particulars of achievements in all subjects and other activities, highlighting strengths and development needs;
- comments on general progress;
- arrangements for discussing the report.

For children at the end of Key Stage 1 this information includes the above plus:

- teacher assessment levels;
- comparative information about the national curriculum levels of attainment of children of the same age in the school and at a national level.

Optional tests in Years 3, 4 and 5

A suite of standardised optional tests provide additional evidence that can contribute to teachers' periodic assessment of their children in Years 3, 4 and 5. They provide schools with an instrument for gathering assessment evidence to support teacher judgements. Schools can use optional tests selectively as part of a range of assessment tools, including the assessing pupils' progress (APP) materials developed by QCDA and published via the National Strategies. The tests therefore present a tool to help schools map their children's progress which schools can decide how to use. They can be used summatively to produce a national curriculum level or used in whole or in part at any point during Key Stage 2 to provide valuable diagnostic information about children's strengths and weaknesses. Teachers may choose to administer the tests alongside written work, class discussions and group activities in a rich variety of contexts. Tests are marked internally and results are not collected or published.

End of Key Stage 2

A recent Review of existing Key Stage 2 testing, assessment and accountability (Bew, 2011) made a number of recommendations that were being addressed (DfE, 2011a) at the time this edition went to publication. Therefore, ensure you have the most recent copy of the 'Assessment and Reporting Arrangements (ARA)' as this will give you the most up to date information for this age group.

At the end of Key Stage 2, teacher assessment judgements for English, mathematics and science are reported with the national curriculum test results. The tests take place on specific days in May and include the following tests for each subject.

There are three English tests:

- a reading test;

- a writing test (made up of a longer task and a shorter task);
- a spelling test.

There are three mathematics tests:

- *Test A* (a non-calculator paper);
- *Test B* (a calculator paper);
- mental mathematics test.

In science, only selected schools participate in sampling tests.

At the end of Key Stage 2, teachers summarise their judgements for each eligible child, taking into account the child's progress and performance throughout the key stage. They need to determine:

- a level for each attainment target in English, mathematics and science;
- an overall subject level in each of these subjects.

Teachers base their judgements on the level descriptions in the national curriculum and use their knowledge of a child's work over time to judge which level description is the best match or 'best fit' to the child's performance, taking into account written, practical and oral work as well as classroom work, homework and the results of school examinations or tests.

Teacher assessment provides a rounded judgement that:

- is based on knowledge of how the child has performed over time and in a variety of contexts;
- takes into account strengths and weaknesses of the child's performance.

Teachers look at the level descriptions of the attainment targets immediately above and below the level awarded to confirm this level is the closest match to the child's performance.

Reporting results of tests to parents/carers

The following information must be reported to parents or persons with parental responsibility each year during Key Stage 2.

- Brief details of achievements in all subjects and other activities forming part of the school curriculum.
- Comments on general progress.
- Results of any national curriculum tests taken during the year.
- Attendance record
- Arrangements for discussing the report.

In addition to the above, the following information must be reported to parents or carers at some point during the final year of Key Stage 2.

- Teacher assessment levels for reading, writing, speaking and listening, English overall, mathematics and science.

- Comparative information about the national curriculum levels of attainment for children of the same age in the school.

- Comparative information about the national curriculum levels of attainment for children of the same age nationally. Comparative information will comprise a national average from the previous academic year for each core subject, at each level.

- A statement confirming the national curriculum levels of attainment have been awarded in accordance with the statutory arrangements.

- Detail of any National Curriculum attainment targets or subject from which the child is exempt.

- A brief account of what the teacher assessment and national curriculum test results show about the children's progress individually and in relation to other children in the same year, drawing attention to any particular strengths and weaknesses.

Parents or carers must be given an opportunity to discuss the report and the report should include details of how to arrange this.

Inclusion issues in relation to tests

A small number of children within this age group may need to be considered for a slightly different arrangement for their tests. Access arrangements are allowed for children who have a long-term illness or have an injury, such as a broken arm, and for children who have limited fluency in English and children with special educational needs. The support given must not result in a change in the test questions, and the answers must be the child's own. When considering these arrangements schools may look at the following groups of children:

- those with a statement of special educational needs as described in the *Special educational needs* (SEN) or a local equivalent such as Individual Pupil Resourcing Agreement (IPRA);

- those for whom provision is being made in school at *School Action* or *School Action Plus* of the SEN *code of practice*, and whose learning difficulty or disability significantly affects their ability to access the tests;

- those who require alternative access arrangements because of a disability;

- those who are unable to sit and work for a sustained period because of a disability or because of behavioural, emotional or social difficulties;

- those with English as a second language and who have limited fluency in English.

Children working below the levels covered by the tests

QCDA has produced a suite of optional tasks covering levels above and below the test levels. The optional tasks provide additional evidence that can contribute to teachers' assessment of their pupils.

P scales

The use of P scales is statutory for children with special educational needs who are working below level 1 of the national curriculum. In this context, special educational needs are defined in the Education Act 1996 as all those on the school's Special Needs Register. Schools will need to use P scales to record and report the achievements of those children in English, mathematics and science. The P scales must not be used to assess children with English as an additional language (EAL) at any age, unless they have additional special educational needs.

For further discussion about including all children, read Chapter 4.

Reporting religious education

Religious education is a statutory subject for all children registered at a maintained school, except for those in nursery classes and those withdrawn by their parents or persons with parental responsibility under section 71 of the School Standards and Framework Act 1998. It is not a subject within the national curriculum and there is no national programme of study. It is a general requirement that schools report children's progress in religious education to their parents or persons with parental responsibility, but there is no required format for national reporting. *Religious education: The non-statutory national framework* provides guidance for schools and local authorities on assessing progress in religious education using two attainment targets and a non-statutory eight-level scale, which may be used for reporting progress.

Information that is exempt from disclosure

Schools must report a child's national curriculum test level to their parents or persons with parental responsibility. A head teacher can disclose the marks awarded to a child in the national curriculum tests or allow their parents or persons with parental responsibility to see, or have copies of, marked test scripts, but there is no requirement in education law to do so.

Tracking children's attainment

Schools make appropriate use of pupil-tracking approaches which include year, class and group curricular targets are set, linked to analysis of assessments.

Teachers:

- use a range of summative assessments to: judge attainment; identify children's progress; inform groupings of children;
- use optional and statutory tests to monitor and assess progress;
- use assessment to establish challenging targets for pupils.

Schools make use of data from the Foundation Stage Profile, end of key stage tests, optional tasks and tests and systems for tracking progress. Other sources of information include tests, tasks, assessing pupil progress (APP) levels and age standardised scores, say, for reading ages.

Tracking can take place across a variety of time periods from across key stages, annually, termly or half yearly, half termly and day to day. With shorter term periods curricular targets, key objectives, progress books and any half termly or termly tests are used as data for judgements made about progress. For day-to-day tracking, teachers use marking, observations, annotations of work and plans, feedback both oral and written and any notes taken as part of lesson evaluations.

Attainment needs to be measured against age-related expectations and progress is measured against the child's starting point. By analysing data teachers can begin to address the following questions.

- How well are we doing? – *Analyse current performance of children.*
- How well should we be doing? – *Compare with national standards and similar schools.*
- What more can we achieve? – *Set clear and measurable targets.*
- What must we do to make it happen? – *Identify and implement improvement plans.*
- What went well?
- What can we do better? – *Take action – review success – start again.*

With the changes to end of key stage assessments, assessment no longer has an end of key stage focus alone. Now there is more emphasis on ongoing assessments and there is a greater need for consistency of judgements

Case Study

As a placement task, Sheila had to find out about the system used in school to track children's attainment and discuss how often teachers add data to this system and the frequency with which they review all the data and what they do as a result. The head teacher showed her a line graph of three children in her class and how they had all increased in levels of attainment over their time at the school.

In addition to this, Sheila was also required to track the attainment of three individuals in her class during the placement. She chose the same three children, but was staggered to find their progress was less than smooth and that the topic being studied had a significant impact on their attainment.

Sheila's mentor explained how, over time, learning may appear smooth, but at any one time, learning is a challenging process and is far from linear. They discussed why assessment was such a crucial part of teaching, reflecting on Sheila's revelation.

You can read more about the process of learning in Chapter 3.

School self-evaluation and target setting

Reporting and Analysis for Improvement through School Self-Evaluation, RAISEonline provides interactive analysis of school and children's performance data. This has replaced the Ofsted Performance and Assessment (PANDA) reports and Department for Children, Schools and Families' (DCSF) Pupil Achievement Tracker (PAT) or any use of Assessment Manager to track the data. This system aims to enable schools to analyse performance data in greater depth as part of the self-evaluation process whilst providing a common set of analyses for schools, local authorities, inspectors and school improvement partners.

The system allows the generation of reports and analysis covering the attainment and progress of children in Key Stages 1 and 2 for primary as well as for secondary and these include the facility to explore hypotheses in relation to children's performance. Optional test results can be added to RAISEonline, the joint Ofsted/Department for Education tool for school self-evaluation and target setting. Contextual information about the school is part of the key information and this in turn then allows comparison with schools nationally and locally. The program allows for question level analysis to investigate children's performance in specific subjects. In addition there is a facility to set targets which supports schools in the process of monitoring, challenging and supporting children's performance. The final part of the system provides the ability to import and edit child-level data and create school-defined fields and teaching groups. This information is then used by schools to set targets as part of their learning improvement plan (LIP) which replaces the school improvement plan (SIP). Further information about RAISEonline can be found at www.raiseonline.org

Consultations with parents

As a teacher you will be in a position to discuss their child's learning, behaviour, attitudes and any other aspects of their education with their parents/carers. This can be quite a daunting prospect for a new teacher so it is an activity you should try to observe and then undertake as a mentored task whilst you are in school.

Learning Outcomes Review

Thinking about the school in which you are currently placed, or in which you most recently undertook a placement, respond to the questions which follow each of the intended learning outcomes, as a means of identifying your knowledge and understanding of the issues covered in the chapter.

- **Consider what assessment is and its relationship with learning and teaching:**
  - Look at your lesson plans to identify how you have used assessment to plan and teach specific curricular subjects. Have you used assessment in different ways for different subject areas? What might you improve for your next teaching placement?

- Consider your role in monitoring and assessing children's progress in learning across the curriculum:
  - Look at your lesson evaluations to identify how you have monitored children's progress over a sequence of lessons in specific curricular subjects. What strategies have you used for monitoring and recording progress? What have you done as a result of your monitoring – for example selecting children for guided group work? What might you improve for your next teaching placement?

- Explore how to share assessments with children:
  - Look at your plans and specifically the success criteria. How have you shared these with the children?

- Consider how to feedback to children on their work and/or responses:
  - Consider examples of the written feedback you have given to children and review any notes you made in preparation for oral feedback sessions. What responses did you get from the children? Could you see any impact on their progress and/or attainment as a result of the feedback?

- Consider the role of recording assessments:
  - Look at the records you have kept. Can you evaluate its usefulness? What might you improve/change for future teaching placements?

- Consider the statutory assessments:
  - Consider the experience you have of any statutory assessment procedures and target any gaps for your next teaching placement. Have you read the current arrangements for primary schools?

- Consider reporting to parents/carers and consultations:
  - Review the experience you may have had of reporting to parents/carers. What else might be helpful experience? Have you attended parents' evenings?

Further Reading

Further issues associated with continuity and progression will be addressed in Chapters 5 and 12 of this book.

RAISEonline. Read about using RAISEonline in Hansen, A. and Vaukins, D. (2011) *Primary Mathematics Across the Curriculum*. Exeter: Learning Matters.

Personalised Learning:
www.standards.dcsf.gov.uk/nationalstrategies/sup4/personalisedlearning

Primary assessment area:
www.standards.dcsf.gov.uk/nationalstrategies/sup4/primary/assessment

Transfer and transition:
www.standards.dcsf.gov.uk/nationalstrategies/sup4/transferandtransition

The Assessment for Learning (AfL) strategy:
www.standards.dcsf.gov.uk/nationalstrategies/sup4/aflstrategy

AfL with APP: Developing collaborative school-based approaches:
www.standards.dcsf.gov.uk/nationalstrategies/sup4/aflandapp

References

Bew, P. (2011) *Independent Review of Key Stage 2 Testing, Assessment and Accountability: Final Report.* London: DfE.

Black, P., Harrison, C., Lee, C., Marshall, B. and Wiliam, D. (2002) *Working inside the Black Box.* London: King's College.

Briggs, M. and Van Nieuwerburgh, C. (2010) 'The development of peer coaching skills in primary school children in years 5 and 6'. Paper presented at The World Conference for Learning, Teaching and Administration. American University Cairo, Egypt (in press).

Brooks, V. (2009) Marking as Judgment, *Research Papers In Education,* 1–18.

DfE (2011a) *Independent Review of Key Stage 2 Testing, Assessment and Accountability: Government Response.* London: DfE.

DfE (2011b) *Teachers' Standards.* Available at www.education.gov.uk/publications

National Strategies (2009) *Getting to grips with Assessing Pupils' Progress.* Nottingham: DCSF.

National Primary Strategy (2010) *Unlocking Progress: helping children achieve their potential.* London: HMSO.

QCDA (2010) *June 2010 Single level tests: Report on development and outcomes.* September 2010, Coventry: QCDA /10/5250/p.

Sadler, D.R. (2005) Interpretations of criteria-based assessment and grading in higher education. *Assessment and Evaluation in Higher Education* 30: 175–94.

Williams, P. (2008) *Independent Review of Mathematics Teaching in Early Years Settings and Primary Schools.* Nottingham: DCSF.

Assessment for Learning

Isaacs, T., Zara, C., Herbert, G. and and Coombs, S. J.

> Assessment for learning is the process of seeking and interpreting evidence for use by learners and their teachers to decide where the learners are in their learning, where they need to go and how best to get there (Assessment Reform Group, 2002: 1).

Assessment for Learning (AfL) was a term made popular in the UK by Black and Wiliam (1998a, 1998b) when locating teacher and student feedback as part of the assessment and learning process. AfL promoted the sharing of criteria with learners, the effective use of classroom 'talk' and questioning, and supported peer and self-assessment as part of the assessment and learning process (Swaffield, 2009). It represented a challenge to the ascendency of summative assessment and a turn (or return) towards the personalisation of learning, in schools in particular. It was further linked to conceptualising curriculum assessment activities (Black *et al.*, 2003) as part of an ongoing formative assessment process.

However, AfL as a formative assessment strategy (Clarke, 2005) goes back arguably as far as John Dewey's (Dewey *et al.*, 1987, 1988) seminal works linking active learning with meaningful experience and motivation.

Indeed, a pedagogical strategy that encourages action learning tasks and assessment strategies is something also suggested by von Cranach and Harré (1982) in their goal-directed activity theory. This concept was further refined by critical theorists such as David Boud (1988) who suggested the benefits and practice of student-centred and autonomous learning that underpins much of the pedagogical aspirations of AfL. Dylan Wiliam (2011) traces the history of AfL from the early 20th century, stressing the importance of individualising instruction, assessment and **feedback** to suit the variety of student needs.

From these ideas, the concept of feedback as an important stage within the human learning process developed, something that Black and Wiliam (1998b) suggested was of vital importance to classroom-based learning. A later publication by Black *et al.* (2003), *Assessment for Learning: Putting it into Practice*, provided a pedagogical rationale that combines the notion of feedback with **self-assessment** and formative assessment:

> an assessment activity can help learning if it provides information to be used as feedback by teachers and their students in assessing themselves and each other, to modify the teaching and learning activities in which they are engaged. Such assessment becomes formative assessment when the evidence is used to adapt the teaching work to meet the learning needs. (Black *et al.*, 2003: 2)

More recently, a group of scholars meeting in Dunedin, New Zealand in 2009 agreed the following definition: 'assessment for learning is part of everyday practice by students, teachers and peers that seeks, reflects upon and responds to information from dialogue, demonstration and observation in ways that enhance ongoing learning' (cited in Crooks, 2011: 71–2).

Citing Brookhart, Wiliam (2011) charts the evolution of formative assessment, which he characterises as nested:

- Formative assessment provides information about the learning process
- Formative assessment provides information about the learning process that teachers can use for instructional decisions
- Formative assessment provides information about the learning process that teachers can use for instructional decisions and students can use in improving their performance
- Formative assessment provides information about the learning process that teachers can use for instructional decisions and students can use in improving their performance, which motivates students (p. 8).

The Assessment Reform Group, which originally commissioned Black and Wiliam's work, defined AfL as 'the process of seeking and interpreting evidence for use by learners and their teachers to decide where the learners are in their learning, where they need to go and how best to get there' (2002: 1). They developed 10 key AfL principles that state that Assessment for Learning:

1 is part of effective planning
2 focuses on how pupils learn
3 is central to classroom practice
4 is a key professional skill
5 is sensitive and constructive
6 fosters motivation
7 promotes understanding of goals and criteria
8 helps learners know how to improve
9 develops the capacity for self [and peer] assessment
10 recognises all educational achievement.

Implementation of the three factors identified by the Assessment Reform Group can take place in a variety of ways: The first, judgements about where learners are in their learning, can be made through diagnostic assessment such as listening to children read and gleaning information from class work or tests. Open-ended 'rich' questions can involve students more deeply, engage them collaboratively in problem-solving techniques and provide opportunities for teachers to ascertain any misconceptions students might have.

The second, moving students forward to what they need to learn, involves a clear statement of learning criteria, building on current learning and explaining why the learning is important. Finally, the best way to achieve this is through feedback and feed forward, most useful when effectively timed and clearly linked to the learning intention. It needs to be part of the understood success criteria, focus on task rather than ego, give clues on how to bridge gaps, offer strategies rather than solutions, challenge, require action and be achievable (Stobart, 2011).

Black and Wiliam (1998a) describe what goes on in classrooms where assessment aids learning. Typically, classroom practices include: observing students and listening to them describe what they are doing and the reasoning behind their actions; using open-ended questioning, which gets students to articulate their ideas; setting tasks that require students to apply skills and ideas; encouraging students to communicate their learning through actions as well as writing; and discussion rather than dialogue.

Further work on AfL, such as that by Mary James and her colleagues (2007), focused on making learning explicit, emphasising learner autonomy and shifting the focus from performance to actual learning (Swaffield, 2009). This means constantly checking the effects of certain practices and turning away from procedure-based activity.

Regarding the validity of assessment for learning, Crooks cites the following variables as being crucial:

- the relevance of the assessment evidence to the intended learning outcomes
- the degree to which the achievement of each learning outcome has been sampled
- how well the evidence focuses on performance at the intended time, or (where progress is the focus) on progress over the intended time period
- the fairness to all students of the processes and judgement during assessment
- the extent to which the evidence coalesces into coherent and meaningful pictures of performance (Crooks, 2011: 72).

Crooks (2011) highlights six key factors in effective assessment for learning: (1) committed, motivated participants – both teachers and students; (2) students' trust, so that they can be comfortable in admitting they need help; (3) students' understanding of the goals to which they are working; (4) learning goals of an appropriate level of challenge; (5) development of students' self-assessment skills; and (6) insight on the part of the person giving feedback (teachers or peers) into the difficulties a student might be having, providing feedback when students are most receptive and excellent judgement in framing comments appropriately, and tailoring them to each individual's needs.

The OECD considers AfL as an important part of a general international education policy to push formative assessment in secondary schools. The OECD (2005) published its findings in a policy brief article highlighting the benefits of formative assessment, in particular, achievement gains and equity of student outcomes. It emphasised that formative assessment builds students' learning to learn skills through: 'involving students as partners in that process' (OECD, 2005: 2). The OECD also identifies the tension between summative and formative assessment approaches and advises national policy makers to avoid 'high visibility summative assessments' as they are a 'significant barrier to formative practice' (OECD, 2005: 6). The challenge is in getting the balance right between summative and formative assessment systems.

Hutchinson and Young (2011) analyse the role of assessment for learning in Scotland, where the government has supported this type of assessment for a decade through its Assessment is For Learning (AiFL) programme. That programme has not been an unmitigated success, partially because Scotland has combined assessment for learning with assessment for accountability. Hutchinson and Young point to the following problems: 'deeply ingrained beliefs about learning and assessment; different understandings of the language and terminology of assessment; lack of mutual professional trust; and reluctance to change practice and take professional risks and responsibility for judgments about learning' (p. 64). They suggest that only through shared understanding of what is important for students to learn, a framework of assessment arrangements, development of professional practice in assessment, adequate feedback to stakeholders and partners, and support from external agencies can assessment for learning truly thrive.

AfL has not been without misinterpretation or critical appraisal. The UK government adopted an Assessment for Learning Strategy (DCSF, 2008) that has been accused of bowdlerising the ARG's 10 principles to promote close focus on only two subjects, English and mathematics, and the frequent in-class 'formative' assessment of levels of attainment students achieved in each (Swaffield, 2009). With its tick-box approach, emphasis on data collection and direct relationship to summative national curriculum assessment, the Strategy's misappropriation of the term AfL undermined formative assessment in schools in England. Coombs and McKenna (2009) also reported that AfL in English schools suffered a patchy implementation due to a lack of any national coordinated and embedded continuing professional development (CPD).

AfL's critics get scant attention, since the concept is almost universally acclaimed. Smith and Gorard (2005) found that the progress of students in year 7 mixed-ability classrooms was less good for those who received formative feedback alone as opposed to those who received marks, grades and minimal comments. While acknowledging that some general practice associated with AfL can be helpful in the learning process, Bennett (2011) argues that with such a wide variety of practices, processes and methods routinely associated with AfL, no overall judgements about its effectiveness can legitimately be made. He questions claims that have been made about the effect size of assessment for learning interventions (between .4 and .7 in Black and Wiliam's famous 1998 analysis [Black and Wiliam, 1998a]) because the studies under consideration were too disparate to be summarised in a meaningful sense. He also believes that certain considerations such as domain specific needs, the amount of support that teachers need to utilise formative assessment effectively and the wider impact on the educational system have not been analysed sufficiently. There are also problems with under-researched issues associated with **measurement** principles, since assessment for learning relies on human judgement and inferences that can be made about student performance, which can lead to measurement error and bias. If the inferences are wrong, the basis for altering instruction could also be wrong; if the inferences are correct, but the changes to instruction are inappropriate, then learning will not be improved. Without a well-defined set of practices, Bennett posits that there will be a wide variety of outcomes from AfL.

In a special issue on formative assessment in Applied Measurement, Robert Shavelson (2008) stated:

> After five years of work, our euphoria devolved into a reality that formative assessment, like so many other education reforms, has a long way to go before it can be wielded masterfully by a majority of teachers to positive ends. This is not to discourage the formative assessment practice and research agenda. We do provide evidence that when used as intended, formative assessment might very well be a productive instructional tool. Rather, the special issue is intended to be a sobering call to the task ahead. (p. 294)

Many researchers, teachers and other stakeholders believe the challenge is worth taking up and continue to explore the efficacy of assessment for learning.

FURTHER READING

Assessment Reform Group (2002). *Assessment for Learning: 10 Principles. Research-based principles to guide classroom practice.* Available at: http://arrts.gtcni.org.uk/gtcni/bitstream/2428/4623/1/Assessment%20for%20Learning%20-%2010%20principles.pdf

Black, P. J., Harrison, C., Lee, C., Marshall, B. and Wiliam, D. (2003). *Assessment for Learning: Putting it into Practice.* Milton Keynes: Open University Press.

Wiliam, D. (2011). 'What is assessment for learning?'. *Studies in Educational Evaluation*, 37 (1), 3–14.

Observation Techniques

Palaiologou, I.

Through reading this chapter, you should understand:

- the most common observation techniques;

- how observations can help you to collect information for each child's assessment;

- how observation techniques can help you collect information for evaluation of the educational programme.

There are a number of observation techniques available to early years practitioners and professionals depending on the purposes of the observation.

Introduction

The Statutory Framework for the EYFS asserts that:

> *ongoing assessment (also known as formative assessment) is an integral part of the learning and development process. It involves practitioners observing children to understand their level of achievement, interests and learning styles, and then shape learning experiences for each child reflecting on those observations.*
>
> (DfE, 2012a, page 10)

It is also stated that all the evidence for children's assessment should have been gathered by observational recordings. Within this requirement there is a necessity for the early years professional to be aware of the variety of observation techniques. This chapter aims to explore these techniques which are there are to help the professionals involved with children.

As explained in Chapter 2, observations should always have a purpose. For the early years professional working with EYFS this purpose is clearly stated. The general and ultimate goal of observations is to collect information to give as complete a picture as possible of the child for assessment purposes. However, in this chapter, it will be stressed that observations can have the important secondary aim of collecting information to enable practitioners to evaluate their own educational programmes, activities and curriculum, and through this systematic evidence, inform future planning. Throughout this chapter, these observational techniques will be explored. It is important to emphasise that each technique has its place and role in the early years sector and, in order to have an effective complete picture of children's learning and development, the early years workforce should master and employ a number of techniques.

Observation methods

There are three types of observation that have been developed from the field of social research and which can be used in early years settings' day-to-day practice. These are: unstructured observations (participant), structured observations (non-participant) and semi-structured observations. The theory focus box and paragraphs that follow describe these methods and their techniques, as well as offering an evaluation of them.

Three types of observation: advantages and disadvantages

Methods	Description	Purpose	Advantages	Disadvantages
Unstructured observation (Participant observation)	The observer is part of the normal daily life of the group being observed. Normally the observer belongs to the group (for example is an early years practitioner). It is naturalistic observation in the sense that events are observed as they occur.	It aims to capture what children do in that setting on a particular day, as they participate in the activity. Notes are kept to be checked afterwards with other team members. The aim is to collect evidence which will support the description of an activity event or behaviour. Other materials may be used such as photographs, videos, drawings or other relevant documents to support the description of the event.	Provides useful insight into activities, behaviours. It is not time consuming as it happens as the events occur. Requires minimum preparation. Captures unexpected behaviours or changes in an activity.	It is difficult to interpret if not supported by other evidence as it relies on memory. It might be based on the perspective of the observer only (lack of objectivity). It can be very detailed and descriptive and it might distract from its significance. It is time consuming. Information collected can be large and messy and requires too much organisation.
Semi-structured observation	The observation has clear aims and objectives but the methods are 'open' so unpredicted events can be captured.	It aims to capture events that cannot be predicted. It aims to discover WHY certain events or behaviours occur.	Provides in-depth information about the context and circumstances of a behaviour, event or activities. Helps you identify problems, good practices, strengths and weaknesses that you might have not considered.	You might miss out events or behaviours you considered normal and to be expected. It is time-consuming as you need to spend time in the setting. It can be messy. It requires careful interpretation and cross-checking with other members of the team or other materials.

Structured observation (non-participant) (all the following techniques are part of the structured non-participant observations)	It is a clear focus observation on exact behaviours, events, activities.	It is mechanistic, as specific techniques are used, but it offers rigour through good information on an activity, event or behaviour.	Evidence collected is normally numerical and easy to be interpreted. Captures sequences of events, behaviours, activities. It does not require a lot of time (including the planning). Information collected can be easily organised and categorised.	Numerical information can be superficial and does not offer an in-depth approach to why certain events, behaviours occur.
Narratives: 1. Anecdotal records 2. Running records	Written description of an event, child's behaviour, activity. Anecdotal: brief narrative describing an event, behaviour, activity. Running: a sequence of written descriptions of a particular event, behaviour, activity.	They aim to record specific behaviours, events, activities and their progress over a period of time. Aim to discover why certain events, behaviours occur.	Offer rich information as the observer records everything that happens. The observer can capture significant, unexpected events, activities, behaviours.	They offer a complete picture of what has happened. They can be messy if not organised carefully. They rely on memory and attention of the individual so need to be cross-referenced with other materials, information. They are time-consuming. They require special training. Observer needs to remove him/herself from the children and this has an impact in the ratio of the classroom.
Sampling: 1. Time sampling 2. Event sampling	Captures samples of events, activities, behaviours. It is concerned with frequency (how often or rare) and duration.	It aims to observe certain behaviours over a period of time or over different activities.	It does not take much time. Children can participate as self-observers. Information can be collected for one child or a group of children at the same time with minimum effort from the observer. Offers useful information on intervals and frequencies.	It does not offer an explanation as to why an event or a behaviour has occurred. It needs to be used in conjunction with other methods. It is limited only to observable behaviours and other behaviours might be missed.

Rating scales: 1. Graphic scales 2. Numerical scales	A scale of events, behaviours recorded before, during or after the event.	It aims to rate the child's behaviour, involvement, participation in a certain activity, event.	Once designed, it does not take time from the observer. It is easy to design. You can observe more than one child at a time. It can be used by several observers for the same child. Children can participate in this method as self-observers.	It is limited only to the focus of the scale. You might miss other behaviours. Scale can be difficult to use if all observers have not understood the rating.
Checklists	They capture a list of behaviours or developmental steps.	They aim to identify whether or not a child or children has/have acquired certain behaviours or developmental characteristics.	Offer an overview of the development of a child or group of children. Once designed, they can be used again. They can be used by several observers. They can be used by children who can participate in self-observations.	They focus only on certain developmental characteristics or behaviours. They do not offer a rationale of why certain characteristics or behaviours occur. They need to be cross-referenced or supported by other methods.
Diagrammatic: 1. Histograms 2. Tracking 3. Sociograms 4. Bar charts and pie charts	This is a purpose-specific technique and captures a certain behaviour or aspect of development.	It aims to observe whether a certain behaviour or developmental aspect has or has not occurred.	It can be used by children as self-observers. Once designed, it can be used again for another group of children. Offers an overview of a behaviour or aspect of development.	It is limited to only one aspect of behaviour or development. It does not offer an explanation of why a behaviour is occurring. It needs to be cross-referenced with other methods.

Table 3.1   Three types of observation: advantages and disadvantages

Participant observation (unstructured)

As it is part of the daily routine, participant observation is well known within the early years profession. When early years professionals work with children they either record an event by writing down quick notes at the time of the event, or later after the event. These brief and immediate notes are part of an ongoing daily practice. The event is recorded when the professional is working with the children directly and he or she does not withdraw in order to observe. These recordings are usually brief comments about a child's behaviour during an activity, or are comments on how the activity was implemented.

There are a number of advantages when the professionals are using participant observation. The daily events recorded can provide the practitioner with a useful insight into a child or an activity. Special training is not required, as the professional writes down his/her perception of an event as it occurs. This type of observation is unstructured and observers write down what appears to them to be most interesting and relevant at the time. It does not require planning or organisation, and it is useful as events such as unexpected behaviour or an unexpected change within an activity are recorded.

However, there are obvious limitations to this method. Participant observation will not give a complete picture of the events and requires the professional to rely on memory, as events will be largely recorded after they have happened.

As Devereux (2003) points out, participant observation can be messy and difficult to manage. It should be categorised and filed immediately otherwise useful evidence could be lost. An additional disadvantage to this type of observation technique is that the recorded information could be examined long after an event, thus allowing the potential for an inaccurate and biased interpretation of events.

However, despite the disadvantages of using participant observation, it is a very simple and immediate tool to use in collecting information as events occur, and can be used to capture unexpected events during the day.

ACTIVITY 1

Can you list any further disadvantages of participant observation?

There are ways to help limit the disadvantages of this type of observation. Professionals can have pre-prepared forms to quickly record occurrences. The following information can be included:

> Name of the observer: _____
> Name of the child: _____
> Date of observation: _____
> Starting time: _____ Finishing time: _____
> No. of adults present: _____
> Area of observation: _____
> Description of the activity observed: _____
> Additional comments: _____
> I think _____ (In this section you add your thoughts that occurred during the observation, that they might help you later to interpret your recordings.)

Note: it might be helpful to create in-trays: one for activities, one for events and one with each child named in your setting where you put the observations recordings for activities, events, or named children. This way helps to categorise and organise observations and limit the messy factor of participant observation.

This obviously speeds up the recording process and facilitates the filing of recordings. Therefore, when the recordings are re-visited, all the information will be included, making retrieval and interpretation much easier.

Kenzie is four years and eleven months old. He has been absent from many of his classes. The aim of the observation is to identify whether or not these frequent absences are affecting his ability to make and sustain friendships.

Aim: to look for evidence of social play and participation.

Observation 1

Name of the observer: Emily (EYP)
Name of the child: Kenzie, 4 years and 11 months
Date of observation: 09/07/11
Starting time: 10:30
Finishing time: 10:34
No. of adults present: 1 adult
Area of observation: free play outdoors

Description of the activity observed:
It is an outdoor play time and Kenzie is in the corner of the playground kicking leaves that have fallen from a tree. He is on his own, smiling and his arms are waving freely as he kicks the leaves. Liam, who has been playing with a group of three other boys, approaches Kenzie and says 'Come and play. It's me, Jack and Tommy'. Kenzie drops his head, looking towards the floor and his arms and legs remain still whilst Liam is speaking to him. Liam returns to his group of friends without Kenzie, who continues to droop his head and remain motionless.

Additional comment:
Prior to Kenzie being approached by his peer, he was involved in play. Kenzie appeared to be joyfully content with solitary play and there was a definite change to his body language when Liam joined him. This event seems to support the concerns raised as Kenzie refused to answer Liam and preferred not to make any eye contact.

Observation 2

Name of the observer: Emily (EYP)
Name of the child: Kenzie, 4 years and 11 months
Date of observation: 09/07/11
Starting time: 11:40
Finishing time: 11:45
No. of adults present: 1 adult
Area of observation: writing area

Description of the activity observed:

Kenzie is sitting at a table with three other children. There is a tub of wax crayons close to him on the table and he has a picture of a lollipop lady in front of him which he has been asked to colour in. He is looking down at his lollipop lady picture and his tongue is moving from side to side as he holds a red wax crayon to the paper. Toby says to Kenzie: 'I need a green, can I have a green crayon?'. Kenzie remains silent and lifts his head to face Toby. Kenzie reaches out his left arm towards the tub of crayons, scoops the tub in the crook of his arm and pulls it towards his body. His eyebrows are lowered and his lips are puckered tightly.

Additional comments:

Kenzie is choosing not to communicate with Toby. He is capable of expressing himself and could well have asked Toby to wait until he had finished with the green crayon and put it back into the tub or give it to Toby. He does not want to share (something that he did earlier in the sand area as well). He makes eye contact on this occasion.

Observation 3

Name of the observer: Emily (EYP)
Name of the child: Kenzie, 4 years and 11 months
Date of observation: 11/07/11
Starting time: 11:15
Finishing time: 11:20
No. of adults present: 1 adult
Area of observation: outdoors play

Description of the activity observed:

During outdoor free play, Kenzie is sitting on a tricycle. He is pedalling, raising his head and 'La-La-ing' a tune loudly. Tommy and Claire run over to Kenzie and Tommy shouts excitedly, 'We are playing trains! Come and make a big, long train'. Kenzie stops pedalling and whilst Tommy is talking, Kenzie is looking and smiling at Tommy, as he is getting off the tricycle. Both of his arms are up in the air and he is shouting, 'Yeah, big train, yeah!' The three children run off together and form a line by standing one behind the other. They are all running around in a line, laughing and making: 'Woo-hoo' noises.

Additional comments:

Since the last observations, it appears that there is progress in terms of making friendships. Other members of staff report that he seems to have settled in well and engages in most activities. He has a lot of free play with Tommy. He has even started to bring items to the Show and Tell time at the beginning of the morning session, which also demonstrates an important social step forward.

In your early years setting, undertake at least three participant observations. Share your observations with a more experienced colleague or a fellow student. Was it difficult to find time to observe events and, if so, how did you overcome this?

Remember:

- be factual and objective;

- record when and where it happened;

- record what was said and done;

- record facial expressions, body language, tones of voice, gestures.

Non-participant observation (structured)

This type of observation is systematic and requires a number of techniques as described below. Non-participant observation requires the professional to step outside the role of practitioner – and not be involved in interacting with the children – acting instead as an objective observer of the child or an activity.

Preparation and organisation are required for non-participant observation and it needs to be planned in advance. It is statutory within the EYFS to provide a profile in the form of a portfolio for each child at the end of the EYFS:

> In the final term of the year in which the child reaches age five, and no later than 30 June in that term, the EYFS Profile must be completed for each child. The Profile provides parents and carers, practitioners and teachers with a well-rounded picture of a child's knowledge, understanding and abilities, their progress against expected levels, and their readiness for Year 1. The Profile must reflect: ongoing observation; all relevant records held by the setting; discussions with parents and carers, and any other adults whom the teacher, parent or carer judges can offer a useful contribution.

> Each child's level of development must be assessed against the early learning goals. Practitioners must indicate whether children are meeting expected levels of development, or if they are exceeding expected levels, or not yet reaching expected levels ('emerging'). This is the EYFS Profile.

(DfE, 2012a, page 11)

For the early years professional to be able to meet the requirements of the EYFS and be able to complete the EYFSP, a systematic preparation towards this type of observation is crucial. The following sections aim to offer a detailed account of all different types of non-participant observation techniques available to early years workforce.

Preparing for non-participant observation

To become a systematic observer of children, you must first step out of the role you normally hold. Once you have decided when your observations will take place, you must withdraw from your role in the class and take on instead the role of the systematic observer. You should position yourself close to what you want to observe, but not interfere with the child/children in question or with the activity you are observing. Your presence as an observer should be discreet. You must not announce to the children that you are doing an observation and the children should be left alone. If children have been involved in the observation planning then there is no need to announce this each time. Sit closely, however, so that you can see and hear what happens. However, if a child interrupts your observation, it is better to stop rather than gather patchy and inaccurate information.

The best time to undertake observations will be determined by the aims and objectives. For example, an investigation of activities popular with children on arrival will be conducted. If you wish to observe children's language development, this could be done through a variety of observations at different times of the day.

Similarly, the type of activity to be observed should relate to your aims and objectives. You may, for example, wish to investigate the social interactions of a child during story time.

However, there will be cases where the type of activity to be observed is not always implicit in your aims and objectives. For example, your aim could be to observe social skills and your objective is to investigate whether or not the child in question forms good relationships with peers. In these instances it is important to refer back to the initial team meetings and reconsider the planning notes.

Preparation of the observations is crucial as it speeds up this process. The systematic way of recording your observations will become effective as you categorise, file, retrieve and then analyse them.

The observation techniques are explained in the following sections and include an evaluation of each one.

Written observations or narratives

This is the most common observation technique used by early years professionals and practitioners. It is a written record of an event as it occurs. The usual process is for observers to remove themselves from the activity, and observe from a discreet distance, avoiding interacting with or interrupting the children or the activities. Each observation is brief (no more than five minutes) and requires an accurate recording of exactly what happens at the time. This is written in the present tense. As discussed in the participant observation section, it is helpful to have forms already prepared. Again, these will include:

Name of the observer: _____

Name of the child: _____

Date of observation: _____

Starting time: _____ Finishing time: _____

No. of adults present: _____

Area of observation: _____

Description of the activity observed: _____

Additional comments: _____

I think _____ (In this section you add your thoughts that occurred during the observation, that they might help you later to interpret your recordings.)

It is helpful to add comments immediately after the observation has been completed, but care should be taken not to include any of your own comments during the observation itself. It is worth reiterating that observations should only include what *actually* occurs. Initial thoughts about what has been observed will give a good basis for later interpretation and analysis.

ACTIVITY **3**

Look at the following photographs and write down what you have observed.

Share your recordings with a fellow student or a more experienced colleague. Have you recorded the same information?

Figure 3.1   Children drawing

ACTIVITY 3 *continued*

Figure 3.2   Children playing

CASE STUDY

Name of child/children: Vicky
No. of adults present: 1
No. of children present: 2
Activity: cooking
Area: writing area
Date of observation: 04/02/12
Start time of observation: 13:45
Finishing time of observation: 13:50
Aim: Social development
Objective: To what extent Vicky has developed her ability to play successfully with others
Observation:
Two children (Vicky & Zara) and the early years professional (Maria) are in the writing area
and they write down a recipe on a sheet of poster paper.

Maria: *So, we need one glass of olive oil and do you remember what else we wrote?*
Zara: *Sugar?*
Maria: *Can you remember how many glasses of sugar we need?*
Vicky: *Three and four glasses of that . . .* [she points to the water]
Maria: [pointing to the word 'water'] *Here, it says 'water'. We need four glasses of water.*
Maria: *What else did we say?*
Vicky: *Two glasses of that.*
Maria: *What is it?*

Vicky: I don't know.
Zara: Is this semolina?
Vicky: . . . semolina.
Maria: And how many glasses of semolina do we need?
Vicky: . . .two?
Zara: Where does this say 'two'?
Vicky: [points to the poster] Here.
Maria: Yes. If you look here, we need two glasses of semolina.

Comment: (a brief comment may be added here).
The children were working together with Maria in order to make sense of the recipe. Zara was helping Vicky, and with the help of the practitioner, they were trying to cook. The children show some evidence of working together towards a common purpose.

Evaluation of written observations

As this is an unstructured observation, the observer records anything and everything that happens (such as dialogues, movements, emotions) and this offers rich evidence of the children's behaviours or the implementation of activities. Some advantages of this technique are that the recordings are:

* accurate;

* complete;

* comprehensive.

However, as the observation proceeds, the information recorded can be taken out of context and is open to biased and inaccurate interpretations. A further disadvantage is that the observer may have omitted some relevant information, thus presenting an incomplete and patchy picture of the event. In a busy environment, where the observer is an integral part of the team, it may not always be possible or practical to release the team member in order to undertake an uninterrupted observation.

In your early years setting, undertake at least three written observations. Set clear aims and objectives for undertaking these. Be clear with yourself at what point of the day you anticipate undertaking them.

Evaluate the process, for example:

* *Have I included all the relevant information and details?*

* *Have I included any judgements or comments?*

* *Could I have missed significant events?*

Rating scales

Rating scales can be a valid technique for recording certain behaviour or aspects of development. This is a helpful technique as each behaviour is rated on a scale of a continuum from the lowest to highest (or vice versa) and it is marked against certain points along the scale. The observer makes a judgement about where on the scale a child's behaviour is. The most common rating scales in early years settings are the Ferre Laevers scales of involvement and well-being, as will be explained later in this section. There are two main types of rating scales: graphic and numerical. These scales are simple to make. Firstly you should identify the behaviour you want to observe, then you draw a line and mark off a number of interval points along the line. Normally we use five interval points. Although creating rating scales is a simple technique, the observer should know the children very well in order to be able to make judgements and to interpret children's behaviours. This technique can be used by children as well, if it is designed in a way that children have participated in the designing process so that they too fully understand. Children are normally the best judges of their behaviours if they are given the opportunity to express themselves.

Examples:
Graphic scale
Aim: Social development
Objective: Children wait for their turn during play

Always: Child always waits for his/her turn Often: Child often waits for his/her turn Sometimes: Child sometimes waits for his/her turn Rare: Child rarely waits for his/her turn Never: Child never waits for his/her turn

So you can have the following graphic scale for one child :

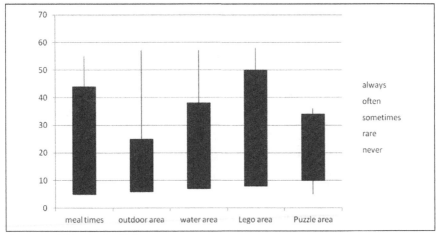

Figure 3.3 Child waits for his/her turn

Alternatively a child self-observation graphic scale can look like this:

👪   Objective: Wait for my turn

☺   always

😐   often

⧗   sometimes

🕐   rare

☹   never

It is important that these symbols would be very carefully explained to children before their use.

Numerical scales

These are normally used where certain behaviours or aspects of development are scored. For example, if you want to investigate children's feelings towards a certain activity, this can be done numerically.

☺   This activity made me happy (smiley face scores high: 10)

😐   This activity was OK (smiley face scores medium: 6)

☹   This activity did not interest me (scores low: 1)

Again these symbols would be very carefully explained to children prior to use.

Using this information, you can obtain an overall picture (in bar chart form) of whether children liked a certain activity:

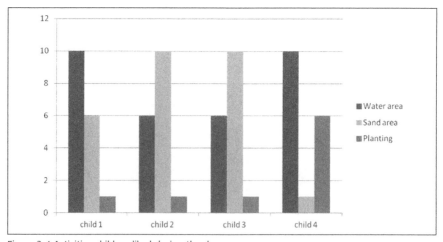

Figure 3.4 Activities children liked during the day

A commonly used and popular type of rating scale is the Ferre Laevers scale of well-being and involvement (Laevers, 1997, 1998, 1999, 2000). The work of Ferre Laevers is concerned with the question of quality in early years education. In an attempt to understand what makes an educational setting a quality one, he proposes that the activities offered and the children's involvement in the activities are key factors of quality. Consequently, along with Moons, he has developed rating scales for well-being and involvement around Ten Action Points, as an inventory of ten types of initiatives that will between them measure these two factors (Laevers and Moons, 1997).

The Leuven Scale for well-being

Signals:

1 Extremely low

The child clearly shows signs of discomfort such as crying or screaming. He or she may look dejected, sad, frightened or angry. The child does not respond to the environment, avoids contact and is withdrawn. The child may behave aggressively, hurting him/herself or others.

2 Low

The posture, facial expression and actions indicate that the child does not feel at ease. However, the signals are less explicit than for level 1 – or the sense of discomfort is not expressed the whole time.

3 Moderate

The child has a neutral posture. Facial expression and posture show little or no emotion. There are no signs indicating sadness or pleasure, comfort or discomfort.

4 High

The child shows obvious signs of satisfaction (as listed under level 5). However, these signals are not constantly present with the same intensity.

5 Extremely high

The child looks happy and cheerful, smiles, cries out with pleasure. He or she may be lively and full of energy. Actions can be spontaneous and expressive. The child may talk to him/herself, play with sounds, hum, sing. The child appears relaxed and does not show any signs of stress or tension. He or she is open and accessible to the environment. The child expresses self-confidence and self-assurance.

The Leuven Scale for involvement

Signals:

1 Extremely low

Activity is simple, repetitive and passive. The child seems absent and displays no energy. He or she may stare into space or look around to see what others are doing.

2 Low

Frequently interrupted activity. The child will be engaged in the activity for some of the time he or she is observed, but there will be moments of non-activity when the child will stare into space or be distracted by what is going on around him or her.

3 Moderate

Mainly continuous activity. The child is busy with the activity but at a fairly routine level and there are few signs of real involvement. He or she makes some progress with what he or she is doing but does not show much energy and concentration and can be easily distracted.

4 High

Continuous activity with intense moments. The child's activity has intense moments and at all times he or she seems involved. He or she is not easily distracted.

5 Extremely high

The child shows continuous and intense activity revealing the greatest involvement. He or she is concentrated, creative, energetic and persistent throughout nearly all the observed period.

Adapted from Laevers (1994, 2005 and 2009); Laevers and Moons (1997); Laevers, Bogaerts and Moons (1997).

Adapted by Ferre Laevers (ed.) Well-Being and Involvement in Care Settings. A Process-oriented Self-evaluation Instrument Research Centre for Experiential Education. Leuven, Belgium: Leuven University.

Checklists

Checklists are a very useful observation technique. It is a relatively difficult technique compared to narratives, as careful planning and preparation are required. Checklists can be used to record the activities of a single child or a group of children. They can also be used to record the progress of an activity for evaluation purposes. They are a useful tool for the early years professional, offering specific information and providing a starting point for planning activities for individuals or for groups of children.

The EYFS assessment scales provide a helpful starting point in creating a checklist. However, they cannot stand as an independent comprehensive checklist and should not be used as such, so they need to be developed further. The assessment scales in the EYFS can become objectives of your checklists but not the checklists themselves (see discussion on aims and objectives in Chapter 2).

Designing a checklist is not an easy task. Things to keep in mind when you create one include:

- length – keep it short;

- include items that are representative of the particular behaviour under study;

- include items that are representative of the age of the children you are observing;

- ensure that it can be understood by the whole team.

Example

Look at the checklist below, which attempts to record a child's behaviour during storytelling time.

- Which of the items below capture listening behaviours?

- Are there any additional items to be added to the list?

- In what ways is this a useful tool for the early years workforce?

    Name of Child:

    Date:

    No. of adults present:

    No. of children present:

    Activity: Story time

    Area: carpet

    Aim: Language development

    Objective: Listens and responds

    1. Looks at teacher directly

    2. Child pays attention

    3. Facial movements:

    3a) Smile

    3b) Impressed

    3c) Apathetic

    4. Uses body language:

    4a) Movement

    4b) Direction

    4c) Emotion

    4d) Relaxation

4e) Interest

5. Asks questions

6. Joins in discussion

7. Answers questions

8. Predicts events from the book

ACTIVITY 5

Using the EYFS learning goals as your guide, create a checklist for social development. How are you going to tackle in your checklist the objective works as part of a group or class by taking turns and showing sharing fairly? Consider the timing of your observation and specific items to include in your checklist.

In the literature, a key element on observation process and planning is children's participation. The early years workforce needs not only to involve children in the process of observation planning but also to involve them in the actual observations. As illustrated in Chapter 2, the Mosaic approach has demonstrated a way of involving children in the observation process, but by using videos and cameras.

Involving children like this can be done in two ways: self-observation and observing others. In both cases, a number of observation techniques (see theory box) are available. Self-observation by children provides a way of recording in detail children's views and opinions about themselves. A number of techniques can be used, for example, drawings, digital media, photographs, videos, sketches made by children. However, if the techniques are designed in a way that is accessible to children, they are capable of using a number of observation techniques as will be demonstrated in the sections below through examples and case studies.

Checklists can become a useful tool for children who use them for self-observation, if they are developed in collaboration with the children.

CASE STUDY

Pictographic checklist

Aim: To assess children's social development during free play

Objective: Interactions during outdoor play

Social play	Pictographic presentation of items	Child self-evaluation
Prefer to watch others when they play		
Prefer to play on my own		
Prefer to have my own toys		✓
Prefer to play with others		✓
Prefer to join in when others have organised the play		
Prefer to be part of organising the play		✓
Prefer to share toys		✓

Table 3.2   Child self-evaluation checklist

Note: When pictographic lists are developed to be used by children, all images need to be very carefully explained to them.

Evaluation of checklists

Observation checklists can be quick, easy and efficient tools if they are carefully constructed. Checklists can be re-used and adapted – gaps in the checklist may be identified, children may demonstrate unanticipated behaviour, or the setting may have particular needs to be incorporated into it. Observation checklists can be used discreetly when the child is present. A number of different observers can use the same checklist to ensure that the information gathered is consistent, accurate and reliable. However, no checklists will be comprehensive and they should always be subject to additions and modifications. Finally, they can become a participatory tool for children to observe either themselves or others, so it increases the participation of children in the daily life and routines of the early years setting.

A major disadvantage of using a checklist is that, if an unforeseen event occurs during an observation, an important piece of information about a child or an activity may not have been covered by it. As this method requires knowledge of and expertise in child development, the participation of children and parents in its preparation may be limited. Although checklists provide a breadth of information, they may lack a depth of detail. It may be best to use them in conjunction with other techniques, to ensure that enough information is gathered.

Diagrammatic

This is a focused and purpose-specific observation technique and it includes a number of different methods:

- tracking;
- the use of sociograms;
- the use of histograms;
- the use of bar charts and pie charts.

Tracking

Tracking is used to record the amount of time a child spends on an activity of their choice or an activity that they have been asked to do. It does not explain *why* a child spends time on an activity or what a child did – it focuses only on time.

It is a useful tool when you want to:

- observe children's attention span;
- investigate the play areas preferred by children;
- assess how many times children visit an area;
- keep track of the use of different areas within the classroom.

Tracking can offer quantitative evidence of the above. However, it does not help you to explain why a particular behaviour has occurred. For example, you may want to observe

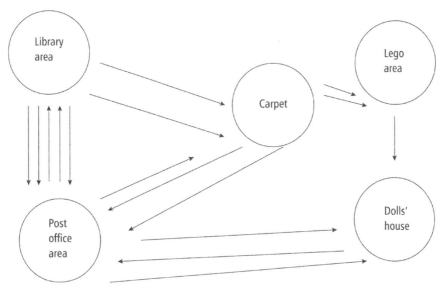

Figure 3.5   Diagram of tracking technique

the physical development of children, so you can use tracking to investigate in what ways children are active during the day. You can track where they go (e.g. tunnel area, playground etc). Children can participate actively in this. For example, in each area you can put a sack and different coloured stones or Lego pieces. Children each have their own colours and when they are using an area they add their coloured stone or Lego piece into the sack. At the end of the day you can count how many times a child has used each area. However, there is always the risk that children might forget to do this or are not putting more than one stone or Lego piece in each time, so early years practitioners or professionals should monitor this during the day.

Example

You are planning to change the learning areas of your class. You want to investigate which areas are the most popular among the children during free play so that you can enrich these. Areas not used by the children can subsequently be removed or replaced. You plan to carry out observations for one week and you are going to use tracking to do this. On completion, the findings show that the Lego area was the least popular among the children, so you decide to alter this area and enrich it with other construction materials instead (see Figure 3.5).

Sociogram

The focus of this technique is social development. It is a helpful tool to investigate how children interact with others during the day. It investigates the child's relationships with other children or adults and can demonstrate the child's popularity with other children.

Table 3.3   Examples of the sociogram technique

Children	Gregory	Alison	Gren	Raj
John	☺	☺	☺	☹
Katie	☺	☺	☺	☺
Mathew	☺	☹	☺	☺
Eric	☺	☺	☺	☺
George	☹	☺	☺	☺
Ahmed	☺	☺	☺	☺
Alia	☺	☹	☹	☹

The main advantage of this technique is that it speeds up the process of observing social development. However, in the same way as tracking, it does not explain the reasons *why* something happens, and can only tell us *what* happens. Sociograms can also offer misleading information as children's relationships can rapidly change.

Example:

The aim of the observation is to investigate how children form relationships with adults and peers. The specific objective is to investigate which children have formed smaller groups of friendships within the bigger class group. You show children three pictures: a smiley face, a sad face and a neutral face. The children are then asked to choose a picture that describes how they feel when they play with other children.

ACTIVITY 6

From this sociogram, can you make any interpretations?

Can you identify which child has most friends among the children that were asked?

Can you identify which child has the least friendships among the children that were asked?

Histograms

Histograms are a helpful technique to follow the development of a child for a long period of time. Histograms are a special form of bar chart where the information gathered is represented continuously rather than in discrete categories. This means that in a histogram there are not gaps between the columns representing the different categories. The main advantage of histograms is that you focus on a child's particular behaviour over a longer period of time.

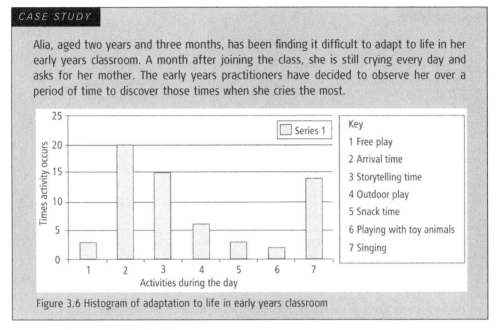

CASE STUDY

Alia, aged two years and three months, has been finding it difficult to adapt to life in her early years classroom. A month after joining the class, she is still crying every day and asks for her mother. The early years practitioners have decided to observe her over a period of time to discover those times when she cries the most.

Key
1 Free play
2 Arrival time
3 Storytelling time
4 Outdoor play
5 Snack time
6 Playing with toy animals
7 Singing

Figure 3.6 Histogram of adaptation to life in early years classroom

Bar charts and pie charts

These can both be useful as techniques for collecting information about both groups of and individual children. They can be produced to offer a visual presentation of the results from your observation recordings – how children come to the early years setting, for example. Others might include what children eat in school, which areas boys prefer using during the day, which areas girls prefer during the day, or what boys do during outdoor play.

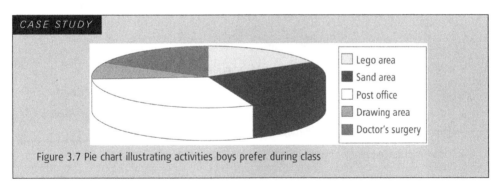

CASE STUDY

Lego area
Sand area
Post office
Drawing area
Doctor's surgery

Figure 3.7 Pie chart illustrating activities boys prefer during class

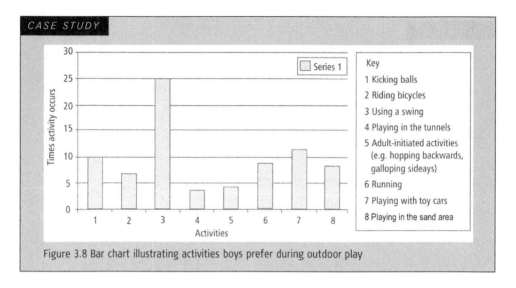

Figure 3.8 Bar chart illustrating activities boys prefer during outdoor play

Sampling

The aim of sampling is to identify how and when a particular behaviour occurs. The emphasis of sampling is on the duration of a particular behaviour. For example, you may want to investigate how long a two and a half-year-old child pays attention and focuses on storytelling or how often a three-year-old visits the sand area.

Time sampling

The observer records whether or not certain behaviours occur over a period of time. The focus of time sampling is on the duration of a particular behaviour. As time sampling records behaviours over a period of time, the frequency of the chosen behaviour is highlighted.

The main advantages of time sampling are:

- it takes less time and effort than other techniques;

- it helps you to remain objective as you know the behaviour that you are looking for;

- you can collect data on a number of children or a number for behaviours at the same time, and it provides information at intervals throughout a given period of time;

- it shows the frequency of behaviour.

However, time sampling is not open-ended. You may miss important behaviours as you are merely recording their frequency and not actually describing the behaviour. Time sampling is thus limited to observable behaviours that occur frequently. This usually focuses on a type of behaviour and may therefore give a skewed view of the behaviour of a child.

There are concerns that Val demonstrates some aggressive behaviour. The early years practitioners have decided to observe her, in order to find out how frequently Val demonstrates inappropriate behaviours that caused some distress among other children.

In preparing for the time sampling, it is important to define what inappropriate behaviour is. So the EYP, with reference to the EYFS, highlights some specific behaviours that can be easily observed and measured:

1. turn-taking;

2. taking toys from other children before they have finished with them;

3. hitting other children;

4. pushing other children;

5. shouting at other children.

To make the process faster, you can give a key to your chosen items. For example, you can use numbers or you can use the first letter of each item. It is up to you to decide how best you are going to code your items. Then you will need to decide when to record them - for example, departure time, outdoor play, literacy activities, etc. The emphasis on this observation is to record *when* Val demonstrates inappropriate behaviour.

Activity	Time	Behaviour observed
Departure time	8:45 a.m. 9:15 a.m.	1 4 5 2 3
Outdoor play	11:15 a.m. 2:20 p.m.	5 5 4 3 3 3 1
Storytelling	10:30 a.m.	1 3
Drawing area	3:00 p.m.	3 5 4 2 2
Dancing activity	11:45 a.m.	4 4 4 4 4 5

Table 3.4   Example of time sampling technique

Event sampling

The observer records a specific, pre-selected behaviour. Event sampling is used to study the conditions under which particular behaviours occur. It may be important to learn what triggers a particular kind of behaviour, e.g. biting.

Event sampling helps you to keep the event of the behaviour intact. This can make analysis easier and is objective, as behaviour can be defined ahead of time. It is also helpful to record infrequent behaviours. However, it can take the event out of context and, as it looks at specific behaviours, it can be lacking in detail.

Behaviours	Departure time	Outdoors play	Storytelling time	Gardening activities
Turn taking	**	*		****
Hits other children	****	********	****	***
Pushes other children	*******	*****		**
Shouts at other children	*	****		*

Table 3.5   Example of event sampling technique

Event sampling can help you to investigate what behaviours occur during different times of the day and with time sampling it is possible to determine how many times that occurs. In this way, you can develop strategies to either encourage certain behaviours or discourage others.

Digital media

With a variety of accessible electronic media now widely available, the early years team can use a number of techniques to improve the observation process. The digital camera or the digital video recorder can be used to add another dimension. The photographic evidence or tape/video recording evidence cannot replace the traditional observation techniques such as narratives, checklists sampling and diagrammatic methods, but they can be used as additional tools in the observation process. They offer accurate information about events as they capture everything objectively. The Mosaic approach (mentioned in Chapter 2) provides an excellent example of how media techniques were used as a useful method of gathering information about children's progress through the activities. In the Mosaic approach, it was demonstrated how media techniques became a powerful tool to encourage children's participation in contributing to data collection. They adopted media techniques as *participatory techniques* for use with children to enable them to be actively involved in the observation process (Clark and Moss, 2001).

However, when using digital techniques, we might want to consider that, for some children and early years practitioners, photographs or videos can make the observation intrusive as they might object to being photographed or videoed. It also eliminates the anonymity and confidentiality factor and might affect behaviour, and spontaneity might be lost. It is also worth mentioning that digital media for observation serve as representation of a narrative and we cannot ignore the fact that that they illustrate a narrative sequence; their interpretation is subject to individual experiences. Pink addresses this in the following extract:

> [. . .] *visual research methods [in our case visual observation techniques] are not purely visual. Rather they pay a particular attention to visual aspects of culture. Similarly, they cannot be used independently of other methods; neither a purely visual ethnography nor an exclusively visual approach to culture exist.*
>
> (2007, page 21)

ACTIVITY **7**

Try to evaluate the different observation techniques. Your evaluations should aim to answer the following questions:

1. *Does this observation technique help me to gain rich information in order to investigate/answer my specific observation aim/focus/objective?*

2. *What are the advantages of using this technique? (They always need to be linked with your observation aim/objective/focus.)*

3. *What are the disadvantages of using this technique? (Again, they must be linked with your observation aim/objective/focus.)*

SUMMARY

This chapter discussed the most common tools that the early years workforce can use to observe children and to evaluate the education programme and its activities. The two dominant observation methods are participatory observation and non-participatory observation. The non-participatory observations include:

- *written observation;*

- *rating scales;*

- *checklists;*

- *diagrammatic observation;*

- *sampling.*

The next chapter aims to discuss how we record and analyse observations

FURTHER
READING

For extensive examples on observation techniques, see the work of:

Riddall-Leech, S (2008) *How to observe children* (2nd ed.). Oxford: Heinemann Educational Publishers.

Salaman, A and Tutchell, S (2005) *Planning educational visits for the early years.* London: SAGE.

Smidt, S. (2005) *Observing, assessing and planning for children in the early years.* London: Routledge.

Summary

The chapters in this part should have given you a good grounding in how to develop as a professional and enhance your teaching and learning. The end of your university studies does not mean the end of your learning journey. As a reflective practitioner you will be responsible for your own professional development with support from your school. You should seek out opportunities for enhancing your own subject and pedagogical knowledge as well as carrying out practitioner based research to enhance your own professional practice. This will help you in developing your own classroom ethos and philosophies for teaching and learning as well as ensuring that you are up to date with the latest developments and advancements. Having your own classroom allows you the opportunity to try out new practices and strategies in line with our overarching theme of innovation. Look for exciting and innovative ways to enhance your teaching and give them a go!

Student activities
- Carry out some peer observation. In one lesson ask your peer to observe the teaching and then, in a subsequent lesson to observe the learning. What do you notice about how one impacts upon the other?
- Think about your own classroom! What do you want it to be like? How do you want the pupils to feel? What will it look like? How will an observer know that effective teaching and learning is taking place? Think about philosophies and strategies that will help you to achieve this.
- Look at the National Curriculum document and choose any objective or skill. Now think about how you could approach this in your placement in a creative way. What will you do? What will the pupils do? How will you know they have achieved?
- Think about classroom practices you have observed. Which strategies encouraged higher order thinking skills and why? What could you use to enhance your own practice?
- Observe two children playing – what assessment data can you take from this?
- Over the course of a day in school make a note of all the assessment opportunities that you observe in a classroom; both informal and formal e.g.: marking, dialogue, show me whiteboards...

Top tips
- Don't be afraid to try out new practices and strategies in class – even if it does not work you can still learn from it. The key is to recognize that it is not effective and find something that is!
- One size does not fit all – just because something worked for one class of children it does not mean it will work for another! Your practice needs to constantly change and evolve in light of the pupils you teach.
- Assessment needs to be manageable, always ask yourself if this will improve the learning of your pupils – if not then why?

- Assess what you teach – do not teach what you assess. Teaching to tests is not inspiring, innovative practice!
- Play does not stop in the early years and it is not something that only occurs in the playground! Children of all ages can learn from play!

Additional readings

The Reflective Teacher

Bolton, G. (2010) Reflective Practice: An Introduction. In *Reflective Practice: Writing and Professional Development*. London: Sage.

The Classroom Environment and Ethos

Evanshen, P. and Faulk, J. (2011) *A Room to Learn: Rethinking Classroom Environments*. Lewisville, USA: Gryphon Press

Stewart, N. and Moylett, H. (2011) *How Children Learn: The Characteristics of Effective Early Learning*. London: British Association for Early Childhood Education.

Hodgman, L. (2011) *Enabling Environments in the Early Years: Making Provision for High Quality and Challenging Learning Experiences in Early Years Settings* (Early Childhood Essentials) Salisbury: Practical Pre-School Books.

Creativity and Play

Bruce, T. (2011) *Learning through Play for Babies, Toddlers and Young Children*, 2nd edn. London: Hodder.

Moyles, J. (2010) *Thinking About Play: Developing a Reflective Approach*. Maidenhead: Open University Press.

Wilson, R. (2012) *Nature and Young Children: Encouraging Creative Play and Learning in Natural Environments*. Abingdon: Routledge.

Anthony Wilson (Ed) (2009) *Creativity in Primary Education* (Achieving QTS Cross-Curricular Strand Series), 2nd edn. London: Learning Matters.

Planning

Barber, J. and Paul-Smith, S. (2012) *Early Years Observation and Planning in Practice: Your Guide to Best Practice and Use of Different Methods for Planning and Observation in the EYFS*. Salisbury: Practical Pre-School Books.

Kerry, T. (2010) *Cross-Curricular Teaching in the Primary School: Planning and Facilitating Imaginative Lessons*. London: Routledge.

Male, T. (2012) *The Primary Curriculum Design Handbook: Preparing our Children for the 21st Century*. London: Continuum.

Woods, A. (2013) (Ed) *Child-Initiated Play and Learning: Planning for Possibilities in the Early Years*. London: Routledge.

Assessment and AfL

Brodie, K. (2013) *Observation, Assessment and Planning in the Early Years: Bringing it all Together*. Maidenhead: Open University Press.

Spendlove, D. (2011) *Putting Assessment for Learning into Practice* (Ideas in Action) London: Continuum.

PART 6 — BEHAVIOUR AND BEHAVIOUR MANAGEMENT

Overview

Behaviour management has been the focus of considerable research, publication and professional development in the field of education and consequently, there is a plethora of information and strategies to inform those involved in teacher education and school development. In spite of this, pupil behaviour remains an area of concern for trainee teachers and teachers. During your school placements you will observe numerous behaviour management strategies but the key to managing behaviour is developing an understanding of the reasons for and the cause of the behaviour. There is no definitive answer to managing behaviour effectively; what these readings aim to do is to support you in shaping and refining your own behaviour management strategies. Using these readings in conjunction with your reflections and observations you will begin to build up a repertoire of ideas and strategies for developing professional practice.

This section begins by providing an overview of the issues surrounding behaviour in schools. The section moves on to a chapter by Kate Adams outlining the general issues of how behaviour can impact the effectiveness of teaching and learning in the primary classroom.

Alan McClean then discusses the motivations behind different behaviours and introduces the 3As: affiliation, agency and autonomy as well as discussing energizers and drainers for motivation. He moves on to highlight the five personality traits and how schools can shape and develop these in children as well as their emotional intelligence.

The importance of whole school approaches are reviewed; analysing the benefits and assumptions of a collegiate approach to behaviour management.

The next part of this section explores the notion of pro-social behaviour and how this is exhibited by children in the classroom and how children process social information as well as the impact that social information processing can have on behaviour.

Finally there are chapters offering some practical suggestions for trainee and newly qualified teachers, aiding you in reflecting upon behaviour management strategies and techniques observed in practice as well as considering how your own behaviours can impact upon the behaviour of the children in your class.

Behaviour: Why you need to care

Adams, K.

Chapter objectives

By the end of this chapter you should be able to:

- **describe the types of behaviour you might encounter in primary schools;**
- **understand that behaviour and learning are linked;**
- **know the three key components of the Behaviour 4 Learning approach;**
- **understand that the concept of Behaviour 4 Learning applies to you as well as to children.**

This chapter addresses the following Professional Standards for QTS:

Q2, Q10, Q30, Q31

Links to: Every Child Matters (ECM); Primary National Strategy; spiritual, moral, social and cultural development (SMSC); personal, social and health and citizenship education (PSHCE); special educational needs (SEN); inclusive education.

Introduction

Excitement and anticipation are prevalent when details of placements are publicised. Crowds of students hover around the noticeboard and typical comments overheard include: 'Oh that is such a lovely, friendly school, you are so lucky', 'I can't go there, the children are so badly behaved, I'll never control them' and 'That's a fantastic school, the children all work really hard and get great results'.

Many factors will affect your response to the school you have been placed in – how far you'll have to travel, whether the school has a good reputation or not, if you know anyone who works there or has had a placement there. You will inevitably be concerned about the school's standing, whether it be based on information gleaned from the 'grapevine' and/or through research into their Ofsted reports and place in league tables. One of the key factors underlying your reaction is likely to be the school's reputation for children's behaviour. If the school has a large number of children with challenging behaviour, you may be apprehensive about how this will affect your performance in the classroom.

Your concern about children's behaviour is shared by many other trainees and newly qualified teachers (NQTs) alike. The Association of Teachers and Lecturers (ATL) surveyed students and NQTs and discovered that 94 per cent of student teachers and 97 per cent of NQTs identified pupil discipline as the most important issue for them (ATL, 2006). This is understandable – after all, if children are misbehaving, you cannot teach effectively and they won't learn.

Hopefully you will feel prepared to face the challenge of the children's potential misbehaviour before you arrive at school. However, Ofsted's report *Managing challenging behaviour* (2005a) states that NQTs often report that their initial training contained little specific guidance on understanding and managing children's behaviour. Ofsted (2005a) acknowledges that training in this area requires more than one or two sessions and should be part of a longer-term strategy which continues to support you over the course of your career. Fortunately, the Training and Development Agency for Schools' (TDA) annual survey of NQTs shows that the teaching of behaviour management in initial teacher training (ITT) is improving. Their report of those who successfully completed their initial teacher training in England in 2005/2006 shows an increase in the number who rated their training for this area positively. During that period, 71 per cent of the 11,000 respondents rated this aspect of their training as good or very good – compared with 59 per cent in 2003 (TDA, 2007a). While this provision still has considerable room for improvement, this is encouraging news.

Behaviour: why you need to care

Children's positive behaviour is important for a range of reasons. Firstly, and possibly of most immediate concern to you, is that in order to achieve qualified teacher status (QTS), you will be required to meet a set of standards laid out by the TDA (2007b). Three of these include explicit reference to children's behaviour. Trainees are required to:

- *Demonstrate the positive values, attitudes and behaviour they expect from children and young people (Q2)*
- *Have a knowledge and understanding of a range of teaching, learning and behaviour management strategies and know how to use and adapt them . . . (Q10)*
- *Establish a clear framework for classroom discipline to manage learners' behaviour constructively and promote their self-control and independence (Q31)*

The QTS standards are underpinned by five key outcomes identified in the government's *Every Child Matters: change for children* (ECM) policy (DfES, 2004), which were subsequently laid out in the Children Act 2004. ECM arose following the death of Victoria Climbié in 2000. Victoria was an eight-year-old girl who lived with her great aunt and her aunt's partner in London. Her aunt and partner tortured her, and despite previous involvement of social workers, doctors and police, the horrific abuse led to Victoria's death. ECM built on existing plans to strengthen preventative services to protect children (DCSF, undated). ECM has five key outcomes for all children, which are:

- *Be healthy*
- *Stay safe*
- *Enjoy and achieve*
- *Make a positive contribution*
- *Achieve economic well-being*

(DfES, 2004, page 10)

Anti-social behaviour beyond the school gates

In the Every Child Matters agenda, behaviour is a focus in the two outcomes 'stay safe' and 'make a positive contribution'. It aims to keep children *safe from anti-social behaviour in and out of school*, and help them *engage in law-abiding and positive behaviour in and out of school*. It also aims to prevent them from engaging in bullying behaviour (DfES, 2004, page 10). These outcomes draw attention to further key reasons for caring about behaviour – issues of safety both within and outside the school, self-respect and respect for others.

The emphasis on behaviour beyond the school gates is a sound reminder that your role as a teacher carries positive influence on children out of school hours. Further, their behaviour outside of school can also be reflected in the classroom. Part of many trainees' apprehension about managing children's behaviour will have stemmed from the media. For example, high-profile cases such as the fatal stabbing of 10-year-old schoolboy Damilola Taylor on his way home from school in 2000 show the tragic consequences of extreme anti-social behaviour among teenagers. Following Damilola's tragic death, Southwark council in south London began a scheme in which some schools had police officers on their premises. By 2003, police officers were on the premises of 100 schools in London, Manchester and Birmingham (Hackett, 2003).

We need to care about behaviour because children and young adults need to be safe, and feel safe, on the streets as well as in school. That right to be safe, of course, also extends to you and legislation is in place to support that right. For example, the Crime and Disorder Act 1998 introduced Anti-Social Behaviour Orders (ASBOs) which ban recipients from acting in a public place in the manner which gave rise to the Order. Schools can be named as a public place in an ASBO. Fortunately it is only the minority of young people who will be given ASBOs or be the perpetrators of violent behaviour. It is important to acknowledge that behaviour is not simply an issue for trainees and teachers – it is also a concern for children, young people and their parents (DCSF, 2007), as well as for all other members of the community. Inevitably, then, behaviour is also an issue for teacher trainers and policy-makers (EPPI, 2004). In short, every-one in society is a stakeholder in the behaviour of young people.

In essence the education system has a significant role to play in nurturing children to become responsible citizens who can make informed choices in their lives. The non-statu-tory guidelines for personal, social, health and citizenship education (PSHCE) are followed by many primary schools, which helps give children the knowledge and skills they need to make healthy choices, manage their feelings and deal with moral and social issues that arise. Alongside PSHCE is the statutory requirement for the spiritual, moral, social and cultural (SMSC) development of children, which underpins the National Curriculum. Together, PSHCE and SMSC can contribute to helping children act responsibly and morally, in turn creating a safe environment.

Let's return to the classroom and take a closer look at your role in it, the types of behaviour you may encounter, and explore another crucial reason for caring about behaviour: the link between behaviour and learning.

Behaviour and learning

It may be tempting to think that the management of behaviour is an 'add-on' to your teach-ing, but this would be a mistake. In fact, another key reason for ensuring positive behaviour in school is its link with learning. Behaviour and learning are inextricably linked, as will become clear throughout this book.

The link between behaviour and learning has long been recognised. In 1989 a committee of enquiry was set up to explore behaviour in schools, which resulted in the Elton Report, entitled *Discipline in schools* (1989). This report still has much relevance today. It stated that children can learn well only if they have a purposeful and peaceful classroom environment in which to work. Similarly, in 2002, the government appointed a panel of experts to again enquire into discipline in schools, resulting in the Steer Report – a series of four published from 2005 to 2008. The first, entitled *Learning behaviour*, (2005, page 2) subscribes to the view that *the quality of learning, teaching and behaviour in schools are inseparable issues*. Government policy also emphasises this link – the Primary National Strategy, launched in 2003 through the document *Excellence and enjoyment – a strategy for primary schools* (DfES, 2003a, page 4), aims to focus on raising standards, but combines this with *making learning fun*. If teachers can enable children to enjoy their learning, it is increasingly likely that their behaviour will be positive.

Similarly, Ofsted (2005a, page 15) endorses this link, commenting that in their own inspections, *effective teaching and learning is a key to encouraging good behaviour and engaging with those pupils who have the most difficult behaviour*. Ofsted recognise that the poor behaviour of some children affects not only their learning but also the learning of others.

The government actively seeks to improve children's attendance, behaviour and learning through its policies. For example, they spent £470 million on the Behaviour and Attendance Strategy, and their Improving Behaviour in Schools Programme recognises that staff, parents and pupils all have a role to play in ensuring positive learning environments for all who attend school.

REFLECTIVE TASK

Consider the range of behaviours you have observed in the classroom. What kinds of positive behaviours have you seen that supported children's learning? What kinds of behaviours have you seen which inhibited learning? How did one child's disruptive behaviour affect others' learning?

Behaviour, learning and special educational needs

For some children, particularly those with special educational needs (SEN), difficulties in learning can lead to frustration which manifests in poor behaviour, while children with social, emotional and behavioural difficulties (SEBD) can exhibit behaviour which prevents their own learning as well as that of their classmates. The government's policy on inclusion has increased the number of children with such difficulties in mainstream schools (Garner, 2005). Westwood (2006) states that broadly, inclusion refers to the right of every child, irrespective of gender, ethnicity, social class, ability or disability, to be educated within a mainstream classroom. There are, however, differing conceptions of inclusion (Farrell and Ainscow, 2002) and you are directed to the literature on this topic for a more in-depth consideration of the history and theoretical underpinning of this important area.

For members of school communities, the impact of inclusive education has been significant. Many have welcomed the drive to educate all children together (irrespective of whether or not they have special educational needs) because it works towards social justice. However, others have raised concerns that mainstream classrooms are not the most effective place for educating children with severe SEN (Westwood, 2006). In extreme cases, violence is a major concern for staff and pupils alike, albeit as Ofsted (2005a) state, they are rare and carried out by a very small proportion of pupils. Chapter 6 explores SEN and SEBD in more detail.

Managing behaviour

Throughout the course of your training you will become extremely familiar with the term 'managing behaviour'. It is the theme of countless books written to support trainees and NQTs, an essential section in every book on how to be an effective teacher, and of course as you have already seen, a term used in the QTS standards. But what does the term actually mean?

CASE STUDY

What does 'managing behaviour' mean?

Emma was a reasonably confident trainee who was about to embark on her final placement. In her previous placements she had successfully engaged children in learning but was nervous about her final one because of the reputation of the bad behaviour exhibited by a group of children in her Year 6 class. As she talked through her anxieties with her tutor, it appeared that she had taken the term 'managing behaviour' to mean that she had to gain control over children who were not behaving.

Emma is not alone in her misunderstanding. The EPPI-Centre report (2004) noted concern that too often teachers perceive behaviour management to mean establishing control over disruptive pupils. If you share this view, such a perception can place significant but unnecessary stress upon you while you are training, partly because you cannot anticipate and prepare for all pupil responses that you may experience in school. The term 'managing behaviour' involves different components and is more wide-reaching than simply stopping bad behaviour.

A large component, detailed in the next chapter, relates to the provision of practical techniques for the prevention of challenging behaviour, rewarding positive behaviour, giving sanctions for negative behaviour and implementing strategies to deal with different types of misbehaviour. No trainee can survive without such strategies and knowledge, and all trainees and experienced teachers alike use them on a daily basis. However, the word 'management' also relates to your provision of a strong ethos of mutual respect which also supports learning. It is important for you to know that, throughout your career, you will have a wide range of support to help you achieve positive behaviour in the classroom. This support is an important aspect of government policy which recognises that *behaviour is a critical issue* and helps schools in teaching positive behaviour through the Primary National Strategy (DfES, 2003a, page 8). The full range of support will be identified throughout this book, and explored in detail in Chapter 8.

Managing behaviour, therefore, consists of different components and is not simply about controlling disruptive children. Prior to exploring those components in depth in the following chapters, we will first consider the forms that disruptive behaviour is likely to take.

The nature of disruptive behaviours in the classroom

While it is natural for you to be anxious about your ability to support children in their learning, including achieving positive behaviour to enhance that learning, official documents are keen to reassure you that overall, highly challenging behaviour is found only in a minority of primary schools. Ofsted (2005b, page 3) judged that behaviour was at least satisfactory or better in 90 per cent of primary schools in 2003/2004. In their report for 2006/2007, Ofsted (2007) combined their primary and secondary judgements to declare that behaviour is good or outstanding in 88 per cent of all maintained schools. They observed that only 8 per cent of primary schools had behaviour which was 'just satisfactory', compared with 29 per cent of secondary schools.

The Steer Report (2005) supports the view that the majority of pupils work hard and behave well. It acknowledges that there are exceptions where serious misbehaviour, including violence, occurs, but emphasises that these are rare and often take place in schools which have major failings in other areas, as defined by Ofsted. Similarly, Ofsted (2007) observes that behaviour is rarely inadequate across a school as a whole. More recently, the third part of the Steer Report (Steer, 2008) emphasises that the number of schools with serious behaviour problems is at the lowest level ever recorded. So, what kinds of behaviours are you likely to encounter in schools?

Low-level disruption

The Elton Report (1989) noted that the most frequent forms of misbehaviour were low-level disruption. Interestingly, this situation has not changed over the years, as more recent reports have similar findings. Ofsted (2005a,b) note that low-level disruption is still the most commonly reported type of misbehaviour in schools. The term refers to behaviours which are generally inoffensive, do not hurt others, but can be frustrating and distracting. These include talking while the teacher is talking, leaving one's seat, calling out or not having equipment (Rogers, 1998). Others frequently encountered are tapping an object on a table, leaning back on a chair, giggling instead of concentrating and making silly comments at inappropriate times (Hayes, 2003). For the teacher, such behaviours can be frustrating. Significantly, these minor behaviours can also disrupt other children's learning.

Garner (2005) and Rogers (1998) point out that defining inappropriate behaviour or rating it as 'low' or 'high' is not necessarily straightforward because of the subjective elements. One teacher may be able to ignore a child's tapping of a pen against the table, while another teacher may find it extremely annoying. Further, a teacher's level of frustration can also be affected by other factors such as their mood or the time of day, so on Monday morning they might be tolerant of pen tapping but by the end of term, at the end of a day of indoor playtimes, their patience might be considerably lower.

CASE STUDY
The frustration of low-level behaviour

Tom, a trainee, was undertaking observations in a Year 4 class on the types of low-level disruptive behaviour that occurred over a week. He indicated surprise at the number he noted. In order of frequency they were: calling out, looking for a pencil, asking to go to the toilet, deliberately making noises, playfully hiding other children's possessions, distracting other children and answering back. Tom commented that while none of these caused distress to other children, nor seriously impeded the progress of a lesson, they were a constant source of frustration to the teacher and the TA. *There are days*, the teacher told him, *when I feel exasperated. All I want to do is teach but I seem to spend so much time dealing with minor interruptions*.

High-level disruption

While the majority of misbehaviour in primary schools is low-level, there are cases of high-level disruption in some schools. Visser (2000), Rooney (2002) and Westwood (2006) state that children with emotional and behavioural difficulties (EBD) present a significant challenge to schools becoming inclusive settings. As Rooney (2002) notes, many parents and teachers have expressed concern that children with very challenging behaviour not only disturb the learning of others but can also be a threat to the safety of others.

REFLECTIVE TASK

Have you encountered violent children in any of your placements? What form did their behaviour take? Why do you think they behaved in this way?

A major area of concern for children, teachers and parents alike is bullying, which involves a range of unacceptable behaviours, some of which are physical, but not all. Oliver and Candappa of the Thomas Coram Research Unit conducted research into children and young people's views of bullying for the charity ChildLine (DfES, 2003b). They discovered that bullying was widespread, with 51 per cent of primary school children questioned believing that it was either a 'big problem' or 'quite a problem' in their school. More Year 5 children (51%) reported being bullied that term, than did pupils in Year 8 (28%) (DfES, 2003b, page 3). However, the research showed that bullying did not occur equally in every school. Further, while schools have anti-bullying policies, the children in this study appeared to be receiving mixed messages about bullying and the authors argue that policies need to take into account children's social worlds. Policies, they suggest, should begin with pupils' experiences and should consider the consequences for children of telling someone they are being bullied.

The government acts against bullying and has launched different initiatives to help schools and their children. For example, the DfES (2000) provided a pack entitled *Don't suffer in silence* which includes a video, to support schools in establishing a whole-school policy that explores the nature of bullying, children's views, methods of detection, and how to work with victims and families. In 2003 an Anti-Bullying Charter was launched which offers practical advice for schools, and the DCSF website hosts information pages for pupils, teachers and parents (see www.dcsf.gov.uk/bullying/index.shtml).

A final growing area of anxiety in some parts of the country is the increasing number of children bringing alcohol, drugs or weapons onto school premises. While secondary schools are the main focus of these concerns, primary teachers in these localities are particularly alert to these potential threats to the safety of those in their schools. In the third part of Steer's review of behaviour (Steer, 2008), there are recommendations that the power of search for teachers be extended to include a broad range of items, not only weapons. Fortunately, for most of you working in primary schools throughout the country, instances of children bringing alcohol, drugs or weapons into school will never be an issue.

The Behaviour for Learning (B4L) approach

The misbehaviour of some children in a primary classroom is inevitable, even if it is mainly of a low-level nature. Given the importance of positive behaviour for the reasons outlined above, the TDA is active in helping you to meet the standards required. The TDA supports

ITT Professional Resource Networks (IPRNs) which are expert groups. One such IPRN is Behaviour4Learning – B4L – which helps you to foster a classroom ethos of behaviour for learning. So, what is meant by the phrase 'behaviour for learning'?

In 2004, the Evidence for Policy and Practice Information and Co-ordinating Centre (EPPI-Centre) at the Institute of Education, London, published a report which presented a systematic review of studies which explored the theoretical links to learning behaviour in school contexts which had been published between 1988 and 2002. The review had three components:

- *To examine how researchers use theories to explain learning behaviour;*
- *To explore what is known about children's learning behaviour in school contexts;*
- *To examine the utility of the review's conceptual framework for end users.*

(EPPI, 2004)

B4L conceptual framework

At the heart of the B4L approach is an emphasis on the influence of relationships upon children's learning behaviours. EPPI-Centre (2004) offers a diagram depicting their conceptual framework. See Figure 1.1.

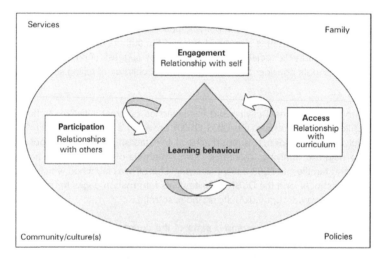

Figure 1.1. The Behaviour for Learning conceptual framework
Diagram taken from the EPPI-Centre Report (2004)

As Figure 1.1 shows, and this book explores in depth, the complexity of the variables which can affect learning behaviour is considerable. For example, relationships with self do not develop in isolation from relationships with others and relationships with curriculum. This complexity makes a definitive definition of 'learning behaviours' difficult. However, this chapter seeks to highlight the main features of a potential definition. Further, the book will take you through the different components of relationships with self, others and curriculum in separate chapters to help you gain a fuller understanding of them and how they can affect behaviour for learning.

Children's learning behaviour

The term 'learning behaviour' was described by the studies in the EPPI-Centre review (2004) in different ways, which further highlights the difficulty in offering a precise definition. However, the studies tended to suggest that behaviour which indicates learning reflects that learning in school contexts is influenced by the interaction of a range of individual, curricular and social variables.

REFLECTIVE TASK

Recall a lesson which you have seen or taught, where children exhibited positive behaviour for learning. What were the children doing which indicated that they were learning? What personal traits were they displaying while working?

EPP-Centre's review (2004) recorded the terms used in the studies to describe learning behaviours and found that most terms used were positive. The most common was 'engagement', found in 43 per cent of the studies. Other terms were 'collaboration', 'participation', 'communication', 'motivation', 'independent activity', 'responsiveness', 'self-regard', 'self-esteem', and 'responsibility'. For the 5–10 years age group, the most frequently observed learning behaviours were engagement, collaboration and participation. Compare these with your list compiled in the practical task above.

EPPI-Centre's review (2004) also explored the types of theories included in the studies. The researchers classified them as social (21 referents), cognitive (18 referents) and affective (17 referents). Generally, the use of these types of theories suggests that researchers were interested in the interplay of feeling, thinking and doing/interacting. However, researchers tended to link cognitive and social theories together more frequently than they linked cognitive with affective. The relevant theories are detailed in Chapters 3 to 6 in a way which also shows the usefulness of the underpinning conceptual framework in depth – showing how the interplay of different relationships can have a marked effect on shaping a child's behaviour for learning. This approach will help you to see how the theory has practical applications for you in the classroom, and will also give you guidance on how to develop your practice further.

Your behaviour for learning

Until now, the discussion about behaviour and learning has largely focused upon children. However, before you continue reading this book, pause for a moment to consider how your own approach to your placement – your behaviour – affects your learning and vice versa. As QTS Standard 2 states, you will need to *demonstrate the positive values, attitudes and behaviour [you] expect from children and young people* (TDA, 2007b, Q2).

Approach this task with as much honesty as you can. Your tutors and mentors won't need to see your answers.

PRACTICAL TASK PRACTICAL TASK **PRACTICAL TASK** PRACTICAL TASK **PRACTICAL TASK**

Read the statements below and tick the appropriate box to indicate your response to them.

		Strongly agree	Agree	Not sure	Disagree	Strongly disagree
1	I'll do everything needed to pass my placement with high grades					
2	I'll do what I need to in order to pass					
3	I want to be involved in extracurricular activities on placement					
4	I want to learn much more about specific areas of teaching					
5	I'll be happy to do whatever the teacher asks me to					
6	I will be proactive and seek tasks to assist the teacher					
7	The targets I have set myself are very challenging					
8	I'd like to help at the school fete on Sunday but I don't have the time					

Tutors, lecturers and mentors see a variety of approaches to learning in students. The vast majority of trainees are highly motivated and conscientious and this attitude is exhibited in their behaviour. Essentially, they arrive at school early with fully prepared lesson plans; if the teacher is busy they use initiative to utilise their time efficiently; they engage with children and other adults in the school to begin to build relationships with them; they stay late to prepare the classroom or take part in extracurricular activities; they seek opportunities to learn, whether it be to ask questions of staff, read policies, or find their own resources. In short, their conscientious approach is exhibited in their behaviour: they are keen to learn and display behaviours which not only reflect that desire but also facilitate learning.

If you rated questions 1 and 3–7 as 'strongly agree' or 'agree' then you are most likely to be in this category. As the descriptions for positive behaviour for learning above suggest, you probably exhibit at least some of those characteristics: you were fully engaged with tasks; collaborated with colleagues; participated in a range of activities; communicated well with children and staff; remained motivated; worked independently; were responsive to situations and suggestions and took responsibility. You are also likely to have positive self-regard and good levels of self-esteem.

Conversely, students who are unmotivated to learn convey less positive behaviours and often admit that they are undertaking training because they didn't know what else to do. It is difficult to hide a lack of commitment on an ITT course. Frequent indicators include: trainees who leave school as early as possible; do not have their file up to date; complain that their teacher has asked them to do jobs which they consider to be menial; and who claim that they are not certain of their remit because 'things were not explained properly' by the lecturers (i.e. passing the blame). Fortunately these trainees are in the minority – and cannot meet the QTS Standards. I also suspect that they are not reading this book.

For the motivated student, it is not sufficient to simply recognise the aforementioned positive qualities in yourself. In order to gain a deeper understanding of learning behaviours, you also need to examine the factors which have shaped and affected them.

REFLECTIVE TASK

What enables you to exhibit positive learning behaviour on your course? Consider the following potential factors and assess their relevance for you. Do you have high levels of motivation? Where does this motivation originate? Who or what influences your motivational levels? How do you sustain levels of motivation in times of difficulty?

Our approach to learning is affected by many things, particularly our relationships with self, with others, and with the work we are doing. While this book focuses primarily on behaviour for learning in the primary school, it will continue to ask you to reflect upon aspects of yourself. These are timely reminders that as an adult you must also be conscious of your own attitudes towards learning and how your behaviour corresponds to those attitudes – and how your approach is affected by other influences. Such insights into yourself will develop your role as a reflective practitioner, as detailed in Chapter 9. Further, your insights will deepen your understanding of children's behaviours, making you more empathic when trying to understand why a child is misbehaving.

A SUMMARY OF **KEY POINTS**

> Children's behaviour is a widespread and valid concern for most trainees.

> The majority of poor behaviour in primary schools is low-level disruption.

> Behaviour and learning are closely linked.

> The B4L approach has three major components: relationship with self, relationship with others and relationship with curriculum.

> B4L is as relevant to you as it is to the children.

MOVING *ON* > > > > > > MOVING *ON* > > > > > > MOVING *ON*

During your induction year, you will need to meet the core standards laid out by the TDA (2007b). Some of these relate specifically to behaviour management strategies, which are set out for you at the end of Chapter 2 in its 'Moving on' section. The Standards do, however, specify that your knowledge and understanding of learning and behaviour management strategies are kept up to date (C10). For that reason it is advisable that you maintain your understanding of the behaviour for learning approach, which you can do through reading, consultation of the B4L website, and if possible through attendance at continuing professional development (CPD) courses.

As a trainee you are very busy juggling study, placements and personal life. You know that you need to manage the children's behaviour effectively and because of demands on your time you need some strategies to help you achieve this. The following chapter provides you with a basic repertoire of strategies, but also encourages a critical approach, which will prepare you to explore the behaviour for learning approach in depth for the remainder of the book.

FURTHER READING FURTHER READING **FURTHER READING** FURTHER READING

Behaviour4Learning (available from www.behaviour4learning.ac.uk). In addition to covering the theoretical components of the B4L approach, the website provides a range of useful resources and links.

DCSF hosts a website on behaviour and attendance. It includes links to reports and projects and also offers guidance on a range of topics including truancy, exclusion and parenting contracts. The latest reports and strategies on behaviour are posted on the site. (The website is available at: www.dcsf.gov.uk/behaviourandattendance/index.cfm)

EPPI (2004) *A systematic review of how theories explain learning behaviour in school contexts*. The report details the key findings of the review. (You can download it from www.behaviour4learning.co.uk)

Every Child Matters: change for children (2004) London: DfES. ECM expresses the government's aim for every child and young person, from birth to age 19, to have the support they need to be healthy, stay safe, enjoy and achieve, make a positive contribution and achieve economic well-being. (Available from: www.everychildmatters.gov.uk)

Steer Report (2005) *Learning behaviour: the report of the practitioners' group on school behaviour and discipline*. This report details the findings of the enquiry and also lays out recommendations for future practice, (which are available from www.dfes.gov.uk). This is one of a series of four reports. At the time of writing, the second and third have been published (see below). By the time of this book's publication, the fourth will have been released.

REFERENCES REFERENCES **REFERENCES** REFERENCES REFERENCES REFERENCES

ATL (Association of Teachers and Lecturers) (2006) *Poor behaviour is an ongoing problem, ATL survey finds*. Available from www.atl.org.uk

DCSF (2007) *The Children's Plan: building brighter futures*. London: DCSF

DCSF (undated) *Background to Every Child Matters*. Available at www.everychildmatters.gov.uk/aims/background, accessed 9 June 2008

DfES (2000) *Bullying: don't suffer in silence*. London: DfES

DfES (2003a) *Excellence and enjoyment: a strategy for primary schools*. London: DfES

DfES (2003b) *Tackling bullying: listening to the views of children and young people. Summary report*. London: DfES

DfES (2004) *Every Child Matters: change for children*. London: DfES

Elton Report (1989) *Discipline in schools. Report of the committee of inquiry*. London: HMSO

EPPI (2004) *A systematic review of how theories explain learning behaviour in school contexts*. Available from: www.behaviour4learning.ac.uk, accessed 5 January 2008

Farrell, P and Ainscow, M (2002) Making special education inclusive: mapping the issues, in P Farrell, and M Ainscow (eds) *Making special education inclusive*, pp 1–12. Abingdon: David Fulton

Garner, P (2005) Behaviour for learning: a positive approach to managing classroom behaviour, in S Capel, M Leask, and T Turner (eds) *Learning to teach in the secondary school: a companion to school experience*. Abingdon: Routledge

Hackett, G (2003) Education: tackling violence in schools. *Times Online*, 9 February 2003, (available at www.timesonline.co.uk/tol/news/article869695.ece). Accessed 4 June 2008

Hayes, D (2003) *A student teacher's guide to primary school placement: learning to survive and prosper*. London: Routledge

Ofsted (2005a) *Managing challenging behaviour*. London: Ofsted. Available from: www.ofsted.gov.uk/Ofsted-home/Publications-and-research/Care/Childcare/Managing-challenging-behaviour(language)/eng-GB, accessed 20 October 2008

Ofsted (2005b) *The annual report of her majesty's chief inspector of schools 2003/2004*. London: Ofsted

Ofsted (2007) *The annual report of her majesty's chief inspector of education, children's services and skills 2006/2007.* London: The Stationery Office

Rogers, B (1998) *You know the fair rule.* Harlow: Pearson Education

Rooney, S (2002) Inclusive solutions for children with emotional and behavioural difficulties, in P Farrell and M Ainscow (eds) *Making special education inclusive,* pp 87–100. Abingdon: David Fulton

Steer, A (chair) (2008) *Behaviour review, paper 3.* Available from www.teachernet.gov.uk/docbank/index.cfm?id=12743, accessed 10 September 2008

Steer Report (2005) *Learning behaviour: The report of the practitioners' group on school behaviour and discipline.* London: DfES

Training and Development Agency for Schools (TDA) (2007a) *Results of the newly qualified teacher survey 2007.* London: TDA

Training and Development Agency for Schools (TDA) (2007b) *Professional standards for teachers.* London: TDA

Visser, J (2000) *Managing behaviour in classrooms.* London: David Fulton

Westwood, P (2006) *Commonsense methods for children with special educational needs: strategies for the regular classroom.* Abingdon: RoutledgeFalmer

most recent standards?

Motivation and Self-Esteem

Beckley, P.

Learning objectives

- Awareness of a range of communication strategies for children and adults
- Knowledge of ways to promote children's perseverance
- Understanding of planning for personalised learning
- Ideas to celebrate children's achievements

This chapter considers what motivation and self-esteem are. It describes communication strategies for different ages and needs. Ways to encourage children's perseverance while responding to their particular interests are addressed. Links are made to planning and personalised learning based on individual interests and experiences. Consideration is given to sharing children's achievements while encouraging them to understand the next steps in their learning.

SELF-ESTEEM

Self-esteem considers the value the child places on his or her own worth. It covers the child's self-image, the stage the child feels they are at and the ideal self, what the child would like to be. If the child is happy with their progress then positive self-esteem will be evident.

MOTIVATION

Motivation stems from emotions and the feeling that we want to do something, we are motivated to do it. There are intrinsic and extrinsic motivators. Intrinsic motivation comes from inside the person. It is a personal desire to achieve the goal the person has set themselves. It is meaningful to them and gives them pleasure in doing it. This is evident in children's pastimes at playtimes in school when they carefully work on a project that has relevance to them. Extrinsic motivation comes from others. It is to please them or gain some reward for achieving something. In an early years setting or classroom this can take the form of a school reward or form part of a progression of rewards, gradually building in perceived worth.

 Case Study

Tom was a well-loved child whose parents had full time employment. He attended day-care daily. This provision was also attended by four girls and the practitioner's son. Tom was popular with all the children and they played well together and enjoyed each other's company. After a summer break one of the girls left to go to school and her place was taken by a young boy, Toby, who was bright and easily made friends with Tom. Surprisingly Tom's motivation began to wane and he did not want to go to the daycare. When asked about his feelings he said that everyone was very kind there but that Toby was obviously much brighter than he was and he felt he could not do anything anymore. Toby could run faster, write, read and was learning to count. Tom's self-esteem had plummeted because he was comparing himself unfavourably to what he perceived he would like to be. He needed to be reminded of the qualities and strengths he possessed to help him come to terms with differences of ability and achievements and be aware of his own self worth.

There needs to be the right amount of challenge for children to be motivated and feel they can succeed. The goal cannot be out of their reach or too easy or they give up, feel it is not worth trying or become upset. A child might try to avoid an activity rather than be faced with a challenge where others might think them silly for being unable to do it.

A child's previous experience might influence the response given in a particular situation. If a child has been brought up in a household with adults he/she might have difficulties making social relationships or be motivated to participate with peers. Conversely a child may be at ease with his/her peers but feel nervous and uncomfortable when speaking to an adult. A child with a low self-esteem may not give of his/her best because it is felt it is already decided that the outcome would not be good.

To support children develop a positive self-esteem it is beneficial to help them have an awareness of their personal achievements and of themselves. In this way they can have a realistic view of their ideal self, one that is achievable and that they can work towards.

BABIES AND YOUNG CHILDREN

Babies respond to those around them and closest to them. They develop their concept of themselves from birth as they respond to how others see them. Bowlby's attachment theory recognised the importance of contact between a child and his or her mother to develop an attachment bond. This was felt to be particularly important in the first six months of a child's life. Failure to achieve this was felt to possibly lead to irreparable damage. These conclusions, which Bowlby later considered did not completely reflect the nature of his research, did however, raise an awareness of the importance of a young child's first experiences and relationships. Bowlby's work is further discussed in Chapter 2 which looks at theories of learning. 'Positive and close relationships with adults are crucial for all children – indeed for all human beings' assert Nutbrown and Page (2008: 21).

 Case Study

A baby accessing daycare is observed and records kept of his development and progress. This provides an excellent means of sharing his activities during the day and milestones in his personal development with his parents who can talk about it to grandparents and friends.

Wednesday 12 January, Cameron 1 year 2 months
Arrive: 7.45am, Depart: 5pm
Nappies: 11am, 4pm; sleep: 10.30am–10.55am, 2pm–3pm; milk: 11.05am; dinner: 12.15pm

Cameron settled straight away at the daycare provision and played with the transport toys until it was time to go to take the older children to school. When we got back we had a music session and Cameron used the shakers. He then played with stickle bricks and building blocks. After a sleep Cameron played with another boy and used inset trays. Cameron pointed to the pictures and said cat and dog. He played with the shape sorter until his mother came to pick him up.

Thursday 13 January
Arrive: 7.45am, Depart: 12 noon
Sleeps 9am–9.30am

Cameron played with the transport toys and the wooden train track set. After going to the school we went to the childminders' meeting. Cameron and his friend made some painting prints. He liked the feeling of the paint on his fingers. He also played with stickle bricks, cars and garage and looked at some books. He joined in the group music session and clapped his hands when the others did.

(Continued)

(Continued)

Figure 5.1 Cameron enjoys painting and feeling the paint on his fingers

Friday 28 January
Arrive: 7.45am, Depart: 2.15pm
Nappies: 10.10am, 2pm; sleep: 12.15–12.50pm; milk: 10.30am; lunch: 11.45am

Cameron settled straight away and went into the tent with his friend until it was time to go to school. After walking to school Cameron enjoyed playing in the soft play area, musical instruments and playing outside at his playgroup. He had lunch with his friends at the playgroup. In the afternoon he played with wooden stackers and transport toys.

The childminder keeps an account of Cameron's activities and interests to provide a record of his achievements and development and a means of sharing his progress with his parents. His routines are established. From this safe base he is able to be sociable with his friends and he enjoys new experiences. His interests are evident. He likes the transport toys, but has also started to look at books on his own. From these records Cameron's parents and the practitioner can share in his interests and build on them to support him in his next steps.

Children become aware of the effects of their presence on those around them. Children who feel safe and secure and have a positive self-esteem are prepared to take risks and explore their surroundings. They are able to communicate through non-verbal expressions and make known their wants and fears. When children are in their second year they recognise themselves in pictures and photographs. There world is peopled with adults they are familiar with and they will refer to themselves as 'me'. The term daddy could be a generic term used for anyone's daddy and they progress through a stage of calling any man 'daddy' until they learn to differentiate individuals and the specific concepts that are appropriate. Through language children have a growing awareness of the world around them and increasingly distinguish elements, forming new concepts as they learn them. They enjoy make-believe and role play events that might happen in life or imaginary scenarios, where hopes and fears can be acted out in a safe environment.

THE KEY PERSON

This secure and safe relationship with an adult can be continued in early years provision. According to Nutbrown and Page (2008: 21) 'the development of close and safe relationships is never more important than for young children who spend time in day care – away from their own homes and parents'. A key person in a setting can provide a crucial link between home and the provider for the child. Records can be kept, like the one described above in the case study, to provide a record of progress and a point of reference for discussion when sharing views on the activities and interests of the child. This can provide invaluable information to help parents and practitioners plan the next experiences for the baby or young child and enhance the relationship formed between those concerned for the benefit of the child. In this way planning continues to be appropriate, relevant and sufficiently challenging for the child, stimulating interest and motivation to explore and investigate. A range of ways of sharing information can be used, such as photographs, written observations, paintings, drawings or models, and could take the form of shared experiences, for example when growing plants.

CHILDREN AS INDIVIDUALS

Practitioners are responsible for devising an appropriate setting for the children in their care. Consideration of factors to support this can include provision of opportunities for children to investigate, create, practise, repeat, revise and consolidate their learning in enjoyable ways. Children show their involvement with the tasks they or an adult have devised by looking and listening intently, asking questions and taking part enthusiastically in the range of activities in the setting. They can feel sufficiently confident in their own abilities and the responses received in the setting to initiate their own activities that promote learning and help them to learn from each other. They are able to take considered risks, make mistakes and time is available for them to become engrossed in tasks through periods of time in sessions. In this way, they can make links in their learning and try out new ideas in a variety of ways, for example acting out personal or devised experiences or using newly acquired language. They respond well to the boundaries of behaviour set, and show self-discipline and consideration for all others in the setting.

To foster this approach to the setting practitioners should show a good knowledge and understanding of the principles underpinning national guidelines, for example the Early Years Foundation Stage framework and the rationale for it. They should be technically competent in teaching phonics and other basic skills, especially using language work to promote children's thinking and understanding. However, these aspects can be greatly influenced by the emotions and feelings of the children and adults working in the setting.

Children can be encouraged to develop a positive self-image through activities to celebrate the individual strengths and achievements of each person in the setting. Children's self-esteem can become low after feelings of security at home change. Divorce, separation or changes in circumstances can affect all family members but could influence a young child through low self-esteem. Lawrence (2006: 43) states that:

> whatever changes occur in a family's circumstances or its structure, it is the way that the whole family reacts to the changes, the emotional support they give one another and their expectancies for the future that are the prime influences on the child's developing self-concept.

MASLOW'S HIERARCHY OF NEEDS

Maslow's hierarchy of needs is a theory in psychology, proposed in his 1943 paper 'A Theory of Human Motivation'.

Maslow identified a series of needs, starting at the foundations of the pyramid, which can be met (see Figure 5.2). It starts with physiological needs, where factors for human survival are apparent, such as food and breathing. These need to be met before other forms of needs can be considered:

- *Safety* – With their physical needs relatively satisfied, the individual's safety needs take precedence and dominate behaviour.
- *Love/belonging* – This concerns a human need to belong to groups such as family or friends. If these supportive networks are absent anxiety and depression can arise.
- *Esteem* – Esteem presents the normal human desire to be accepted and valued by others. People need to engage themselves to gain recognition and have an activity or activities that give them a sense of contribution, to feel accepted and self-valued. Maslow noted two versions of esteem needs, a lower one and a higher one. The lower one is the need for the respect of others, the need for status, recognition, fame, prestige and attention. The higher one is the need for self-respect, the need for strength, competence, mastery, self-confidence, independence and freedom.

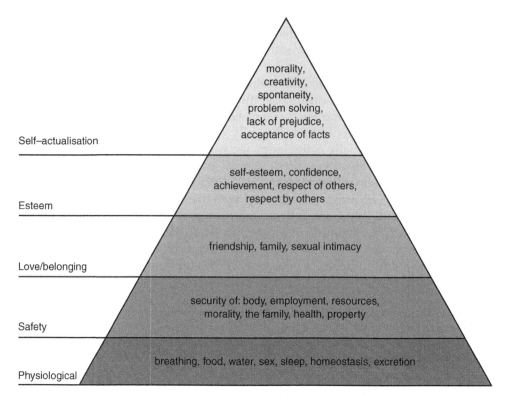

Figure 5.2   Maslow's hierarchy of needs (Maslow 1943)

- *Self-actualisation* – This level of need pertains to what a person's full potential is and realising that potential. Maslow describes this desire as the desire to become more and more what one is, to become everything that one is capable of becoming.

According to Woolfolk et al. (2008: 108):

> over 100 years ago, William James (1890) suggested that self-esteem is determined by how successful we are in accomplishing tasks or reaching goals we value. If a skill or accomplishment is not important, incompetence in that area doesn't threaten self-esteem. Learners must have legitimate success with tasks that matter to them.

GENDER

Gender identity comes from birth and is apparent when a baby is born. Gender is affected by gender stereotypes, which are commonly held beliefs about males and females in society. These beliefs are affected by cultural values. Gender issues might arise when a person does not 'fit' into the gender stereotype of the culture he/she belongs to. Culture can affect self-esteem. The culture in a child's locality could be different from the one where he attends early years provision. Practitioners would need to ensure an inclusive atmosphere was established to negate this factor. Parenting styles could also affect self-esteem. A child might live in a household which is authoritarian or laissez-faire. If they attend provision which requires independent thinking of the children or has a structure and routine, the child could find the adjustment difficult.

UNDERSTANDING YOUR EMOTIONS

It is possible to experience a range of numerous emotions. It is how we deal with them in the early years setting that matters, in order to promote a positive, empowering environment for children and adults within it. Children might be experiencing positive feelings, such as enthusiasm or friendliness, or negative feelings, for example anger, unhappiness or a desire to withdraw from the environment. These emotions can be recognised by the practitioner and accommodated and supported in an appropriate way. Assessment of a child's state of well-being can be noted at the beginning of the session and consideration made of whether it is important to intervene, or simply observe the situation to channel or celebrate reasons for positive behaviour or outlook, or whether, and what type of, further support is needed if the child is experiencing a negative emotion. It might be that the child can be observed to see whether coming to the setting changes the emotion and whether when they have seen their friends their negative emotion disappears. It might be that a child requires a more proactive approach and a few well chosen words are needed to encourage the child to participate in the atmosphere of the setting. Negative emotions might be understandable when the circumstances are known, for example the death of a pet, and can be acknowledged and the child supported. Negative emotions might be too deep seated and more support for the child might be needed, for example in cases where they are an indication of abuse.

Some emotions can be positive or negative, for example contentment. A child could be content and happily develop their learning, whereas another might be content to do nothing or get into trouble with another child!

Both children and adults need to be engaged in a setting which values all in the setting and incorporates an appropriate ethos, where occasional happenings which result in negative emotions can be seen to be supported, and children helped through difficult times.

THE EMOTIONAL LEARNING ENVIRONMENT

Adults and children need to feel emotionally safe in order to learn and achieve. There are times when emotionally stressed or anxious people tend to behave in a different way than they would normally. This could include such behaviour as talking too much or too little, having an inability to 'take in' instructions or listen carefully to others. It is extremely unpleasant to be anxious and can result in conditions such as panic attacks for the child or adult, if the anxiety is severe. Again, if the condition is too severe the child or adult may need further help to address a debilitating and overwhelming emotion and find out why it is occurring.

Practitioners should be aware of possible events or happenings which might trigger negative emotions in some children and consider controlling the situation before it becomes one where a child might be anxious.

 Case Study

A child who had previously had an unhappy home situation had recently changed schools to live with a new foster carer. He entered the classroom at his new school quietly and had difficulty concentrating on any of his work. When there was any change from the movements to or from the classroom he could not contain his emotions and screamed, kicked and shouted. This happened in a number of situations during the day, such as playtimes or a lesson change to the next lesson. He found school assemblies particularly challenging and would suddenly scream, kick and shout in the middle of the quiet communal time. The teacher could not cope with him in her large, busy class so he was sent to another class which was less formal. Here the child was emotionally supported and allowed to come to the teacher if he felt anxious. He was aided during the change of sessions and his outbursts declined, then ceased. He was taken to the assembly hall and shown there was nothing to fear in the large open area. Eventually, he successfully participated in assemblies and was helped to gain sufficient confidence to return to the class where the rest of his age phase were.

 Questions for Discussion

In the early years setting how can children's self-esteem be promoted?
Are strategies clearly in place to do this?
Can the provision for this aspect be improved? If so, in what ways?
Is the importance of this aspect of provision appreciated by all adults working in the setting?

Some situations could be challenging for a child, yet sufficiently so to provide a welcome experience for the child to positively achieve, for example a problem-solving activity in which the child or a group of children feel challenged in a safe learning environment where they know they will be accepted whatever the outcome of their deliberations. It is important to plan for situations that might be emotionally challenging for a baby or young child. This could include moving from hospital to home, home to daycare or nursery provision, nursery class to reception class, Foundation Stage to Key Stage 1, and so on. Events happening during this time can also be challenging, for example the change of a key worker, assistant or teacher or a move to a different area in the setting. Emotional challenges can occur throughout the day, such as the absence of a friend or a change in routine or an unexpected event when things happen, for example the roof leaks or the boiler breaks.

Events at home can be challenging too. They might be serious, such as divorce or changes in financial circumstances, or minor, for example the car breaking down. The child observes and responds to emotions the adults around them are experiencing and reacts accordingly. They may well be upset because a parent is upset and not know why!

CIRCLE TIME

Strategies can be devised in an early years setting to promote self-awareness, the needs of others and positive self-esteem. With babies a calm, kind, reassuring voice can sometimes be sufficient to soothe a child. Discussions with young children can be enlightening and they will invariably tell the listener the truth about how they perceive a situation, what happened and what might happen. Further reflections from the child can be encouraged with such activities as circle time. Children sit in a circle with adults present and take turns to talk on a specific subject. This can begin with themes such as:

I am happy when …
I am sad when …
I am frightened when …
I enjoyed going to …

This can be developed to promote empathy with others in the group. For example, starting points such as those listed can be used but the child talks to a partner about it. He/she then feeds back to the group what the partner thought. Children can sometimes disclose child protection issues during such times. These need to be reported to others in the hierarchy of the provision.

If a child is reluctant to speak in the circle you can tell them to tell you if there was anything they want to say later. This usually only occurs once or twice before the child gains sufficient confidence to speak in the group. The circle time can be used to enhance self-esteem with such themes as:

I like [name] because …
[Name] can …

To promote a child's self-esteem they need to become aware of themselves and others. Goleman categorises Emotional Intelligence as:

- Self-motivation
- Empathy
- Reflection
- Impulse control
- Optimism
- Understanding relationships
- Self-awareness

This spells the word SERIOUS (cited in Burnett 2002: 57).

Children may continually choose the same area of the provision. This is useful to develop their understanding of the resources available in this area and scenarios for play. However, it may become a comfort zone and children can be encouraged to explore all areas to try out different experiences.

STORIES

Careful use of selected stories can promote discussions of valuing individual strengths and supporting others. These can be used within the framework of the provision to enhance the areas of learning and development. They can cover all areas of the framework and provide a stimulating focal point for shared consideration between children and adults. Such books are plentiful and can be picture books or contain written text. Books from Neil Griffiths' Storysack collection are useful.

Other forms of expression can be useful if a child is experiencing low self-esteem. Art, music, physical activity can all encourage children to respond in different ways to their emotions.

HOW WE COMMUNICATE

There is much literature on the importance of spoken communication and developing language to interact with others. Alongside this there are other ways of communicating in an early years setting which are just as important, if not more so, in carrying meaning, particularly for very young children. Yet possibly far more attention is given to what we say than to other elements in communication. We can possibly all think of instances where a statement is said, for example 'that's lovely', but the expression and the tone of voice seem to mean the opposite! You may well have noticed such instances occurring in an early years setting, for example when a practitioner says to a child that the work achieved 'looks interesting' while the practitioner has not looked at the work and is not paying attention to the work or the child.

It is thought that we respond to a speaker in the following proportions: to their facial expression 55%, to the tone of voice 35%, and to the words merely 10%. Young babies and children seem to be able to pick up clues from our body language and facial expression particularly readily. Perhaps you have noticed when a parent with a new baby suggests that she does not know what is wrong with the baby – he/she has been changed, fed, kept warm. One of the reasons could be that the mother herself might be experiencing difficulties or have doubts about her own capabilities and the tense way she is holding the baby is being communicated to the young child who is responding appropriately to the anxiety. It is useful occasionally to model managing difficult emotions by explaining how you will cope, for example 'I might look a bit fed up this morning because my car broke down on the way to school, but I am sure when we have read the next part of this brilliant story I will start to feel a little better…'.

Children might demonstrate their body language and communication in three ways.

- *Aggressive* – rude, unpleasant, arrogant
- *Assertive* – polite, pleasant, confident
- *Submissive* – humble, servile, timid (Lawrence 2006: 104).

High self-esteem is shown through confident politeness where children are content with their self-image and have nothing to prove. Low self-esteem could result in timid behaviour or aggression, where a child is covering feelings of low self-worth by being rude. A child might have an inflated perception of themselves and be arrogant towards others. If a child is bullying others it is important, therefore, to find out why as it could be because the child has a low or an inflated self-esteem.

The role of the adults in the setting is crucial to sustain feelings of self-worth with the young children. Interactions can be powerful tools to affirm a child's sense of personal value. As Trevarthen (2002: 17) notes: 'A child's pride in knowing and doing must be recognised and supported too. Shame of not understanding, or of not being understood, is destructive of learning. The child who is proud to learn, and whose pride is recognised with admiration, will learn.' (cited in Nutbrown and Page, 2008: 32).

PRAISE

To receive praise is a motivating experience but what do we praise children for? It is important as early years providers to consider that praise not only concerns the child's achievements but addresses a positive affirmation of the child's worth as a human being, for example, 'thank you for those kind words', 'that was thoughtful of you', 'well done for being such a good friend'. High-achieving children may also believe that they are only worthy when they do something well. They need to feel valued not just for academic success or they might find it hard to cope in the future if they get something wrong.

Sometimes individual children may feel uncomfortable receiving praise from an adult in the setting as they might not be used to praise and not know how to respond, or they might feel it is not 'cool' to receive praise. Praise can be adjusted to respond to their needs, for example a quiet word to them when something is good, a smile or a thumbs up when no one else is particularly paying attention.

Praise plays an important part in a child's self-esteem. Lawrence (2006: 21) states: 'whilst there is a place for genuine praise in self-esteem enhancement, this has to be realistic praise, otherwise the child will be in danger of developing a faulty self-image'. He continues 'sustained high self-esteem in the child is not dependent on internal factors such as feelings of confidence and personal integrity and not on external factors such as praise'.

A negative word or look can be demoralising for any of us and can start a wave of emotions that takes a while or a positive happening to dispel. How often have we felt 'out of sorts' and it is not until we have thought about it and tracked down why we feel that way that it becomes apparent that it began with a frown or a cross word earlier. A simple word of praise or even a smile can make such a difference to a person's emotional outlook and can brighten the start of a day. Imagine what an effect a practitioner has on the feelings of well-being of the children in the setting.

Further Reading

Roberts, R. (2002) *Self-esteem and Early Learning*. London: Paul Chapman.

Useful Website

www.nasonline.org
This website provides useful information about aspects of motivation and self-esteem in young children.

References

Burnett, G. (2002) *Learning to Learn.* Carmarthen: Crown House Publishing Ltd.

Lawrence, D. (2006) *Enhancing Self-Esteem in the Classroom.* London: Sage.

Maslow, A. (1943) A Theory of Human Motivation. *Psychological Review* 50: 370–96.

Nutbrown, C. and Page, J. (2008) *Working with Babies and Children.* London: Sage.

Woolfolk, A., Hughes, M. and Walkup, V. (2008) *Psychology in Education.* London: Pearson Education Limited.

36

What Pupils do to Motivate Themselves

McLean, A.

What is personality?

 Stop and think

What aspects of your personality do you like and dislike?

Our personality is how we adapt to different situations. It is our personal organizer that influences how we think and feel about ourselves. Pupils share the same emotions and needs. Their individuality comes from their unique personality that shapes the different ways each pupil tries to meet their needs.

Differences in pupils' personalities become apparent early in life and have pervasive influences upon and throughout their school career. From the young person's perspective, personality is their identity, who they are, shaped in terms of how they adapt to the demands of school and other aspects of their lives. From the teachers' and peers' view, personality is the young person's reputation, what kind of pupil they are, defined in terms of traits, such as helpful and calm. Reputations describe pupil behaviour and identity explains it.[1]

Personality traits and the learning stances

It is our personality traits that make us unique and consistent.[2] Individual differences in personality traits exist in degrees. Traits are stable over time and situations, and they let us predict how people are likely to behave.[3]

Personality is organized in a hierarchy, with broad traits at the highest level, for example, extraversion, and more specific traits at lower levels, for example, sociability, that are made up of particular behaviours, for example, being talkative. Pupils express their personalities in classrooms through the behaviour they exhibit in a given situation, that is, their learning stances.

Personality does not predict academic achievement very well. Personality types (how we categorize people who share similar personalities) have been found to be better at predicting achievement than personality traits (the main labels we use to describe personality). Personality type at the start of primary school predicts later behaviour problems.[4] These associations, however, are small.[5]

Achievement is more closely related to individual pupils' approaches to learning than to their personality, such as learning styles (and learning stances) that are a learned component of pupil personality.[6,7] Approaches to learning are changeable over time, which explains why they may be better predictors of achievement than personality.[8]

Research has identified five broad traits that we use to describe personality. The traits, known as the 'Big 5', are described below. Each of the traits is bidirectional, for example, agreeable–disagreeable.

1   Extraversion

Extraversion and introversion reflect how people are energized. Extraverts are energized by interacting with the world, while introverts draw from their inner world. Introverts avoid too much external stimulation because they are already stimulated enough. Extraversion is shown by being communicative, optimistic, cheerful and assertive. Extraverts are drawn to competitive sports and enterprise.[9] Extraversion is reflected in pupils' sociability and positive activity.[10] Extraverts tend to be better at doing more than one thing at a time and are more resistant to distraction on verbal tasks. They have good conversation skills because they can think up topics of conversation and speak fluently. Extraverts are also advantaged when speed is more important than accuracy. These factors make extravert pupils likely to adopt the energetically engaging stance.

The downside of extraversion includes

- impulsivity
- excitement-seeking
- recklessness
- poor tolerance of monotony and boredom
- overconfidence
- a tendency to be self-important.[11]

Extraverts find it harder to think deeply and may be better equipped to handle stimulating environments, whereas introverts cope better with monotony and boredom. Introverts perform better when attention needs to be sustained or when reflection and caution are required. Introverts are perhaps more likely to adopt the quietly engaging stance.

2   Agreeableness

Agreeableness involves being respectful, co-operative, empathic and trusting.[12] It is a key trait for getting on well at school and predicts the positive stances, particularly the harmoniously engaging stance. It is linked to being likeable. Even the biggest rogue in the class can be 'forgiven' if they are likeable. Agreeable people, however, may be less ambitious. When stressed they tend to self-sacrifice rather than try to outdo others.

A lack of agreeableness is reflected in being

- antagonistic
- dominant
- competitive
- selfish.[13,14]

It is also marked by a tough-minded, self-reliant and impatient approach. Low agreeableness will often be linked to the opposing reaction. An early childhood precursor of low agreeableness is a frequent and intense expression of negative emotions.

3   Conscientiousness

Conscientiousness refers to determined efforts to succeed, including being efficient, predictable and purposeful. It is crucial for the internalization of values and rules. It is an important contributor to long-term achievement, independent of ability.[15] It has been termed the 'will to achieve'[16] and is an asset that encourages positive learning stances.

While some elements of conscientiousness relate to achievement, others relate to dependability, that is, orderliness, conformity and high need for structure. Conscientiousness may be constraining when linked to an excessive need for order. Another downside is when highly conscientious people are short on agreeableness; they can be inflexible and unreasonably demanding.[17]

4   Emotional stability

Emotional stability is the tendency to experience positive emotions. It is reflected in a calm, assertive and optimistic approach along with a keenness to take the lead and seek autonomy. The opposite tendency to experience negative emotions leaves the individual vulnerable to stress. Pupils low in emotional stability tend to be pessimistic and unsure of themselves and so dislike decision-making and become nervous presenting themselves. Low emotional stability damages both self-belief and self-esteem[18] reflecting a lack of perceived control. It leads to passive and emotion-focused ways of coping.[19]

Anger and fear are emotional tendencies that are separable by the end of a child's first year. Fear is related to later shyness, while anger is linked to later aggression.[20] These two kinds of negative affect predict these two types of behaviour problems in the early school years. Fearful pupils turn in on themselves, common in the hiding reaction, while pupils who show irritable distress turn in on themselves but also against the world, typical of the alarming and draining reaction. The alarming and draining reaction reflects how anger and fear gradually merge later into the broad trait of emotional instability.[20]

5   Openness to experience

Being 'open to experience' is being reflective, creative, unconventional, willing to question authority and champion change. People high in openness are intrinsically motivated, idealistic and find rules constricting. They are commonly found in the harmoniously engaging stance.

Openness is linked to, but broader than, intelligence[21] and includes receptivity to one's feelings. It is similar to interpersonal intelligence.[22] Achievement is correlated with openness.[23] Openness is a mixed blessing as it can lead, through high sensitivity, to distress as well as happiness. Low openness reflects a conforming, risk-averse, cautious person who adapts to convention.

Stop and think

What are the demands that school makes on pupils' personalities?
When and how do you take pupils' personalities into account?
When can pupils' personalities become a barrier to engagement?
When can pupils' personalities become an asset to engagement?

How our needs shape our personality

> To get a big reputation in this school you need to be tough and popular. (George, 11 years old)

Pupils learn in peer groups structured in terms of status hierarchies and this creates two main drives, namely to get along, that is, to seek affiliation, and to get ahead, that is, to seek status through agency.[24] They also have to seek acceptance and be allowed to participate, that is, to seek autonomy.

Achievement may be the desired outcome for our curricula but, as articulated by George, the energizers within many peer groups (and political parties) are popularity, acceptance and toughness. Motivating teachers manage to align these energizers to their learning goals.

How our personality traits help us meet our 3A needs

Affiliation
Agreeableness is the personality trait that most significantly shapes how pupils meet their needs for affiliation. Affiliation also benefits from a high degree of emotional stability and conscientiousness, making pupils easy to get on with.

Agency
Getting ahead benefits from high levels of emotional stability, conscientiousness and openness to experience. These traits help to instil confidence, ambition and an eagerness to learn. Striving for status is also linked to extraversion, which makes pupils keen to excel and to achieve rewards.[25]

Autonomy
Autonomy, the capacity to balance our motives to get along and get ahead, is nurtured by all five traits, but in particular by emotional stability and openness.

Traits as pointers to preferred environments

 Stop and think

Does your personality make you more comfortable in particular settings?

Personality traits help us to thrive in particular kinds of environments and, as such, are pointers to our most suitable environments. Low emotional stability, for example, leaves pupils vulnerable to anxiety in evaluative settings.[26] It is especially draining to be exposed to threat to your self-worth in social settings.[27] All teachers will know anxious pupils who are distractible in stressful circumstances and who do better when the environment is reassuring.

The traits consist of helpful and unhelpful aspects. For example:

- Extraverts are more useful to have around when a rapid response is needed but introverts perform better when reflection is required.
- The sociability of extraverts helps teamwork but their impulsivity can make them over-competitive.
- Extraverts prefer competitive climates whereas introverts prefer co-operative climates.[30]
- Extraverts seek excitement and group involvement, whereas introverts prefer environments with lower stimulation and cope well with working alone.[31]
- Extraverts respond best to fast pace, novelty, rewards and competition, while introverts prefer order and set their own pace.
- Agreeable pupils are popular but they can be disadvantaged in competitive, pressured or conflict situations, because of their tendency to be deferential or dependent. Agreeableness leads to distress following conflict.[28] High agreeableness together with emotional instability creates dependency.[29] Highly agreeable pupils will therefore be better suited to co-operative than competitive group work.
- Conscientiousness is essential for achievement but can stifle enterprise and creativity.
- Low emotional stability can be problematic but it can also help keep us alert to threats.

The advantages and disadvantages of extraverts compared to introverts are summarized in Table 3.1.

How schools develop pupil personality

Many education systems see personality development as an important purpose of the curriculum. For example, the Standards in Scotland's Schools Act, 2000 states that

> The purpose of education is to encourage the development of the *personality*, talents and abilities of pupils to their fullest potential.

Table 3.1   Introverts and extraverts: who has the edge in school?

	Introverts	Extraverts
Advantages	find it easier to think are seen as more mature are quieter, more reflective are conforming are good listeners show good concentration do not need much feedback persevere are creative think independently cope well with monotony enjoy routine seek order and precision approach tasks carefully focus deeply	perform better in public are more sociable and enjoy groups are confident communicators express themselves easily enjoy action concentrate on results are enterprising are happier have more influence over others are better at dual tasks are better at verbal/symbol processing are better if speed is needed

Disadvantages	find it hard to think in groups
	struggle in groups
	are less outgoing
	are less rewarding to teach
	can become isolated
	cope badly with public
	   class tests
	are indecisive and risk
	   aversive
		are poor listeners
		are on 'transmission only'
		are high maintenance
		need a lot of attention
		can lose self in frenzied activities
		are easily bored
		enjoy socializing over learning

Stop and think

What does developing personality mean?
What aspects of personality development can a school influence?
Is there a tension between the role of education in personality development
and its role in socialization?

Paradoxically, personality has been somewhat ignored in educational think-ing, probably because of the widespread assumption that it is hard-wired and there is little we can do about it. But we need to understand the significant role personality plays, see it in context, and support young people to adapt and make the best of their personality. Developing personality means helping to bring out the best in pupils. Motivation becomes more stable as people age but it is far from fully crystallized, even by late adolescence.[32]

Young people's sense of progress influences how their personality develops. Success or failure at one stage is likely to shape the mastery of later tasks, and repeated failures may pave the way for later problems.[33] For example, pupils with low achievement and high levels of antisocial behaviour experience increasingly high levels of negative emotionality as they grow older.

Pupil personality develops through their two-way interactions with the class-room. Just as we as adults shape our jobs to suit ourselves, pupils mould their classroom into environments that suit them.[34] Their personalities also elicit distinctive reactions, thus continually reinforcing their qualities. For example, teachers of overactive pupils may become hostile to them, while easily engaged pupils evoke more positive responses. Pupils also seek out peers who are like themselves. Friends resemble each other because we choose to mix with people like ourselves. Aggressive pupils, for example, choose to mix with other aggressive pupils.

Childhood personality has been found to predict early adult competence in coherent ways.[35] For example, conscientiousness and agreeableness predict success in adulthood. Pupils high (or low) on these traits eventually reached better (or worse) attainment than would have been predicted based solely on their childhood attainment.

However the correlations between childhood and adult personality are moderate. Continuity estimates suggest some degree of stability but much less than that found in adults, suggesting personality is only beginning to stabilize in childhood.[36] Substantial change takes place across the years. Personality is dynamic and responds to environmental changes.[37] For example, pupils with family risk factors are more likely to change from being resilient to impulsive.[38] Extreme negative emotions, caused, for example, by protracted bullying can also trigger personality change.[39]

Adaptation, and therefore personality, is never permanent. There are always new challenges, vulnerabilities and strengths emerging.[40] Personality integrates our well-being, therefore it must be open to change to allow us to profit from experience.[41,42]

The classroom provides the context in which pupils express their personality through their learning stances. Pupils should be helped to function within the best part of their personality. Personality development is a journey towards increasing autonomy.[43] As such, schools are well placed to support their pupils' personality development.

Pupils express their personalities differently as a function of the degree of support for their needs, particularly autonomy. This is because support for autonomy is all about support for being oneself.[44] The more autonomy-supportive the climate, the more pupils will express their personality and be more extraverted, agreeable, open, conscientious and emotionally stable. The more they feel controlled, the more they become closed, less caring, less outgoing and energetic, and more tense and unstable.[45]

Late adolescence offers possibly the greatest potential for transformation and the first real opportunity for individuals to take charge of their lives.[45] Sexual maturity changes pupils' identity and motivates young people to evaluate themselves. Adolescents' competence at meeting their needs creates the possibility for them to move away from their childhood relationships and choose the environments in which they will develop. This creates the opportunity for self-directed change, and the emergence of abstract thought makes self-realization a real possibility.

Stop and think

Which aspects of school life resonate with and make the most of your personality?

Which aspects of school life clash with or drain your personality?

Children's Social Relationships

Wardle, G.

Key ideas explored in this chapter are:

- The definition of prosocial behaviour
- Prosocial behaviours demonstrated by children
- Theoretical explanations of prosocial behaviour
- Children's social information processing
- Prosocial behaviour in the classroom

As teachers strive to promote a culture of engagement in quality learning for all, they frequently ask how they can improve social relationships among their pupils. Part of the answer to this question lies in developing an awareness of how pupils relate to each other. This chapter will explore some aspects of children's peer social interactions, relevant to teachers because of the educational benefits of a calm and effective learning environment in schools. First, we focus on what is understood by the term 'prosocial behaviour', taking into account children's own perceptions of what constitutes normative peer prosocial behaviour. We then move on briefly to consider theories of developmental psychology which have informed our understanding of children's prosocial development, then investigate how children themselves may interpret, or misinterpret, the motives behind their peers' prosocial behaviour. Finally, we consider ways in which the development of a prosocial atmosphere in the classroom can help to empower learners and promote real social justice in the classroom.

What is prosocial behaviour?

People may engage in prosocial behaviour for different motives; for instance, to achieve some benefit for themselves (egoistic) or for others (altruistic). To complicate matters, different authors may apply slight variations in the precise types of behaviour which they define as 'prosocial'. So, for the purpose of clarity throughout this chapter, the definition of 'prosocial behaviour' adopted will be the definition used by Grusec et al.: 'any intentional action that produces a positive or beneficial outcome for the recipient regardless of whether that action is costly to the donor, neutral in its impact, or beneficial' (2002: 458).

Thinking point 8.1

- Can you think of instances where children have demonstrated kindness to their peers?
- How did the other children – and teachers – respond?

Prosocial behaviours are often categorised as being either 'relational' or 'practical'. Relational behaviours are those behaviours, such as caring for others, and including others in activities or games, which may be seen to foster relationships. Practical behaviours are usually described as involving sharing or helping activities. Interestingly, children place greater value on relational prosocial behaviours in peer interactions, and they consider practical prosocial behaviours to be more salient when directed towards adults (Greener and Crick, 1999; Wardle, 2007). It seems, then, that the motives behind relationship-building prosocial behaviours directed towards peers differ from the motives behind adult-directed prosocial behaviours, which tend mainly to demonstrate cooperation or obedience. When asked to identify which types of prosocial behaviour they consider to be normative, older children generally cite behaviours designed to sustain peer relationships, for example, inclusion, whereas younger children tend to cite behaviours such as sharing (for example, Greener and Crick, 1999).

 Case study 8.1

A typical example of children's inclusive behaviour is illustrated by the actions of Joe, aged 8. A new boy, Zach, had arrived in school from overseas and was quite shy during on his first day in school. During break, some of the boys were playing football in the playground, and Zach was standing at a distance from the others, looking lonely. Joe stopped playing, went over to Zach and asked him to come and join him in the game. Although shy, Zach joined in and felt included and more welcome in the new school.

In recent years, although there has been an increase in the number of studies examining prosocial behaviour as one of the components of social competence, the volume of research undertaken on prosocial behaviour remains less than that in the area of antisocial behaviour, perhaps not surprisingly, due to the problems posed globally for society by a perceived increase in levels of antisocial behaviour.

The philosophical background

Enquiry into prosocial behaviour has focused both on human nature itself, and on the notion of what constitutes appropriate behaviour towards others. The historical view of prosocial behaviour has considered the role of innate goodness (for example, Hume, 1957), the ability to understand the perspectives of others (for example, Smith, 1853), and the role of reason (for example, Kant, 1895). The contemporary paradigm accepts that a wide range of environmental and psychological factors influence the individual's prosocial development. The scope of this chapter, however, does not allow for consideration of all these factors, so we shall narrow the focus, by considering psychological theories of prosocial development.

Psychological theories

In evolutionary terms, behaviour intended to benefit others may be regarded as necessary for the survival of both the individual and the group. In the absence of caring behaviour by another member of the species, human infants would not survive; and customs which protect individuals may be regarded as fundamental to the functional operating of society (Radke-Yarrow et al., 1983).

Theories of developmental psychology tend to agree that instances of children's prosocial behaviour increase with age. The behaviourist approach suggests that children learn to act prosocially through a process involving modelling and reinforcement (for example, Bryan, 1971): typically, children will copy observed behaviour, and on being rewarded for their good behaviour, are inclined to repeat it, thus establishing patterns of positive behaviour. Cognitive-developmental theorists, on the other hand, often regard development as a type of progression through a series of stages (for example, Eisenberg, 1986; Kohlberg, 1969; Piaget, 1965). Stage theories of moral development argue that a capacity to reason that behaviour is 'right' or 'wrong' develops along predetermined lines in children of different cultures, and that evidence of these universal stages may be seen in the prosocial behaviour of children in culturally diverse societies. Although stage theories have much in common with each other, they differ in slight, but important, details.

Piaget (1965) regards the progression through the stages of moral awareness as the child's development from a stance of having little concept of ideas such as fairness, justice and authority, to a more mature understanding of these principles; an understanding which the child can employ in social interaction. Kohlberg (1969) claims that children progress through three levels of moral reasoning; the *preconventional (up to approximately 10 years of age)*, the *conventional,* and the *post-conventional* levels, with each level having two stages. As individuals progress through the stages, their reasoning changes from being based on considerations of rewards and punishments and the needs of others (stages 1 and 2), to the awareness of existing social arrangements, role obligations and respect for the legitimated rules of the social system (stages 3 and 4), and then to considerations as to what is 'right' and 'wrong', determined by mutual respect and contractual agreements (stage 5), and ideas of welfare, justice, and rights (stage 6) (Kohlberg, 1981).

Eisenberg (1986) claims that children progress through five levels of pro-social moral reasoning. The first level, *'Hedonistic'*, is seen in pre-school and young school-aged children, and is characterised by a self-focused outlook, illustrated by concern for self-oriented rather than moral considerations. At the second level, *'Needs of others'*, also evident in pre-school and young school-aged children, children express concern for the physical, material and psychological needs of others, even though those may conflict with one's own needs. At the third level, *'Approval and interpersonal orientation and/or stereotyped orientation'*, evident in pre-adolescents, the child is able to use stereotyped images of good or bad people and actions in order to justify positive or negative behaviours. The fourth level, *'Self-reflective empathic orientation'*, seen in adolescents, is distinguished by judgements which show self-reflective, sympathetic responding, and guilt or positive affect resulting from one's own actions. This is followed by a *'Transitional'* level, when behaviour may be justified because of internalised norms and values, concern for society, and the rights or dignity of others. The fifth level, *'Strongly internalised'*, is seen in people of high-school age and older, and reasoning at this level is distinguished by internalised norms, values, responsibilities, individual and societal obligations, dignity, rights and equality (adapted from Eisenberg and Mussen, 1989). Eisenberg stresses the importance of the environment and the emotions in the development of children's prosocial behaviour. These stages define children's development in the capacity to reason about issues of right and wrong, yet they are highly relevant to the classroom as they help to explain developmental changes in children's capacity to reason about issues of 'right' and 'wrong', and to understand the views of others.

Are girls really more prosocial than boys?

Research findings do not seem to support the view that girls are more prosocial than boys. The meta-analysis undertaken by Fabes and Eisenberg (1996) concludes that overall, findings appear to suggest that girls are slightly more prosocial than boys. However, importantly, these modest differences seem to depend on the particular type of prosocial behaviour involved and the methodology used in the studies. In terms of the type of behaviour involved, girls were found to be more inclined to show kindness or consideration, but not to engage in sharing, comforting or helping behaviour. Regarding methodological differences, girls were more likely to be regarded as prosocial when self-reports or other-reports were involved, as opposed to observational methods. Sex differences favouring girls were also found to be more likely when the recipient of the prosocial behaviour was an adult rather than a child; a point which may be seen to support the notion of greater compliance, or a willingness to please on the part of girls rather than boys. As a result, it is important that teachers do not have lower expectations of boys' than girls' behaviour, but understand that both sexes are equally capable of prosocial behaviour; however, as adults, teachers may be the targets of more prosocial behaviours from girls than from boys.

A wide range of important factors – biological, environmental and psychological – can influence children's engagement in prosocial behaviour, and the picture of prosocial development is by no means simplistic. Hay et al. (1999) identify many complex associations, other than emotional and cognitive maturation, between prosocial behaviour and psychological adjustment. These include factors such as early peer relationships, family structure and the social dimensions of the child's background. The fact that evidence of these associations may be seen in the first three years illustrates the important and formative nature of early childhood experiences. It is crucial that teachers, striving to facilitate individualised effective learning to meet the needs of the whole child and to foster social justice, are aware of the factors beyond their control which may impact on the learning environment in their classrooms.

Teachers continually seek to establish learning environments which are physically and emotionally secure for their pupils, in which children can interact purposefully and form effective peer social relationships. An important insight into children's relationships is the way in which children interpret – or misinterpret – the social cues of their peers. If children effectively interpret peers' intentions, then they may be able to respond appropriately, in a socially acceptable manner. However, if children misinterpret the motives behind their peers' behaviour, they may choose to act in ways which are inappropriate and unexpected, thereby beginning a chain of events which may result in aggression or hostility.

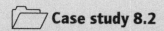 **Case study 8.2**

Nicola is a quiet, serious 9-year-old girl, who usually works well in class, but she seems shy and lacks confidence in social situations. One day, just as she was walking to the front of the class to hand in some completed work, she tripped up on the leg of a chair, which had been inadvertently pushed back by another girl in the class, Lynn, who had been about to stand up, not noticing that Nicola was behind her. Nicola, too intent on reading over the written work she was about to hand in, had not noticed that Lynn's chair was being moved. In frustration, Nicola kicked out, hitting Lynn's leg, whereupon Lynn kicked back. The teacher then intervened and Nicola explained that she had thought Lynn deliberately caused her to trip. The teacher established that it had been an accident, and both girls apologised. This had been a classroom incident where one child had misinterpreted the social information she was receiving from another, and there had been potential for the situation to escalate.

Social Information Processing

The way in which children process social information, or cues, during interactions with others, has been shown to follow a sequence of six key stages. According to the Social Information Processing (SIP) model, children are seen to enter social situations with different biological abilities and sets of personal past experiences, which form latent mental structures, stored in long-term memory. These latent mental structures influence children's online (that is, in the moment) processing in social interactions (Crick and Dodge, 1994; Lemerise and Arsenio, 2000). Although children's online processing is believed to occur quickly, it is claimed that this happens in a sequential process. Lemerise and Arsenio (2000) describe the steps in the process as follows:

> *Steps 1 and 2: Encoding and interpretation of cues.* The relevant stimulus cues from peers' behaviour are encoded and interpreted. For example, a child may get hit by a ball while walking across the playground, and must then work out what happened (encoding), and why it happened, that is, was it an accident, or deliberate action? (interpretation).
>
> *Step 3: Clarification of goals.* The child must clarify his or her goals in the situation. For example, the child may wish to maintain a friendly relationship with peers, or may wish to show that this type of intrusion will not be tolerated.
>
> *Steps 4 and 5: Response access or construction and response decision.* The child evaluates possible responses to the situation in terms of goals and self-efficacy. For example, the child may think about retaliating, but may then decide against this because he or she does not want the situation to escalate; or, the child may be afraid that he or she is not physically able to throw the ball hard enough.
>
> *Step 6: Behaviour enactment.* The child selects the most positively evaluated response (in terms of goals, anticipated outcomes and self-efficacy), and acts accordingly (Crick and Dodge, 1994; Lemerise and Arsenio, 2000).

At each step in this model, the child's response is determined by his or her understanding, or misunderstanding, of the initial situation, in addition to past experiences stored in long-term memory. However, the child's emotion processes and cognition also both contribute to the child's responses (Lemerise and Arsenio, 2000). Anger, in particular, has been shown to be associated with hostile attributions of the behaviour of others, less friendly goals and social behaviour (de Castro et al., 2003); so, if a child is angry for some reason, he or she is more likely to think that another child's actions were deliberate rather than accidental. Importantly, it has also been shown that children who attribute hostile intent to the behaviour of others are more likely to respond aggressively (Dodge and Frame, 1982; Erdley and Asher, 1996). On the other hand, it has been shown that prosocial children are more likely to put on 'rose-coloured glasses', and to give peers the benefit of the doubt in potentially provocative situations (Nelson and Crick, 1999). Misinterpretation of another child's motives at any stage may result in a breakdown of the sequence, and may provoke potentially antisocial responses. The relationship between psychological understanding and prosocial and antisocial behaviour is therefore a complex one.

Interestingly, Arsenio and Fleiss (1996) suggest that proactive aggressive children lack, not the cognitive ability in one (or more) steps in the social information processing model, but the understanding that hurting others for personal gain is morally wrong. This claim has been supported by the findings of Menesini et al. (2003), who demonstrated that, compared with victims, bullies stressed positive personal advantages to be gained from bullying behaviour, and denied or distorted the consequences for the victim.

Thinking point 8.2

What types of motives are you able to attribute to children's prosocial or antisocial behaviour which you have witnessed? Why do you think this?

What should practitioners do to help foster prosocial behaviour?

In current curriculum guidelines in the UK, the importance of fostering healthy social relationships is clearly recognised. In the National Curriculum for England and Wales (1999), it is stressed that children should be encouraged to value themselves, their families 'and other relationships' (Woolfolk et al., 2008), while in Scotland, one of the four capacities identified in *A Curriculum for Excellence* (2008) requires that children develop into confident individuals who can 'relate to others and manage themselves'. Classroom activities, such as roleplay and group discussion, can be used to develop children's interpersonal understanding, to minimise the occurrence of misunderstandings and misinterpretations, and to develop awareness of how their actions affect the feelings of others. Similarly, it is important that children learn to appreciate the perspectives of, and to empathise with, their peers. Woolfolk et al. (2008: 486) cite evidence of the importance of collaborative and cooperative learning in developing children's empathy, friendships and self-confidence (Solomon et al., 2001). A wide range of helpful resources, designed to develop social skills and emotional literacy is now commercially available, and activities which help to increase pupil self-awareness, self-esteem, and confidence, can be used to foster a non-threatening learning environment.

Summary

Insight into children's peer relationships can help educators as they aim to improve the behaviour and learning culture in schools. However, there are some key points to keep in mind. First, each child is unique, and children vary in terms of their ease of social interaction with peers: some children may encounter difficulties in social interaction which are difficult to address at classroom level. Second, teachers do not teach in isolation, and it is important to remember that children come to school with a vast array of previous influences from life outside school, and that the effects of these may impact on children's social behaviour. Some children are fortunate in that they have supportive home backgrounds, and parents or carers who foster a positive approach to the social and learning environment in school; other children are not so fortunate, and for them, the school environment may present more of a challenge. As society strives to address inequality and social issues such as deprivation, antisocial behaviour, substance abuse, and crime, professionals who work with children on a daily basis cannot deny that evidence of these problems is seen in schools. However, schools, although not in a position to provide a panacea for all society's ills, very often do play an integral role in addressing the problems. Since the development of positive relationships and classroom culture can help foster children's self-esteem and develop confidence in their learning, it is important that professionals involved in education acknowledge the benefits to be gained from initiatives designed to help develop prosocial reasoning and behaviour in children.

 Key questions for discussion and reflection

- How do young children relate to antisocial or aggressive peers?
- Why might the study of young children's prosocial behaviour help address problems of antisocial behaviour in adolescence?
- How far do you think it is reasonable – or possible – for teachers to be responsible for children's behaviour towards each other?
- What are the implications for the curriculum of initiatives designed to improve behaviour?
- Can you identify any appropriate activities which class teachers of young children could provide in order to develop reasoning skills?

Further reading

Eisenberg, N. and Fabes, R. A. (1998) 'Prosocial development', in W. Damon and N. Eisenberg (eds), *Handbook of Child Psychology*. Vol. 4. 5th edn. New York: Wiley. pp: 701–78. This chapter provides an excellent meta-analysis of studies in the field of children's prosocial development.

Greener, S.G. and Crick, N.R. (1999) 'Normative beliefs about prosocial behavior in middle childhood: what does it mean to be nice?', *Social Development*, 8: 350–63. This is an interesting paper which investigates children's own perceptions of what constitutes peer-directed pro-social behaviour.

Grusec, J. E., Davidov, M. and Lundell, L. (2002) 'Prosocial and helping behavior', in P.K. Smith and C. Hart (eds), *Blackwell Handbook of Childhood Social Development*. Oxford: Blackwell. pp: 457–90. An accessible and comprehensive chapter which is informative for the reader interested in exploring the topic of children's prosocial development.

Pollard, A. (2008) *Reflective Teaching*. London: Continuum. This very readable text contains an excellent chapter on classroom climates and interpersonal relationships, with the focus on the teacher's relationship with pupils.

Warden, D. and Christie, D. (1997) *Teaching Social Behaviour*. London: David Fulton. A text which offers a good range of practical classroom activities designed to foster children's prosocial behaviour.

38 Handy Behaviour Management Strategies

Bullock, E. and Brownhill, S.

Resource:	'Behaviour Binoculars'

Explanation

'Behaviour Binoculars' are simply a set of binoculars (these could be real binoculars, a set of toy binoculars or a pair made out of a cardboard tube and a piece of string) which 'look out' for good behaviour in children. The practitioner/teacher is encouraged to wear them around their neck throughout the day and look through them, either to 'spot' a child who is behaving well on their own or within a group context. This is an excellent resource for managing the behaviour of children both inside and outside; 'Behaviour Binoculars' can also be used to develop observational behaviours as practitioners/teachers can encourage children to look for birds, specific colours and different types of trees or interesting cloud formations.

Handy Hints

- Use the behaviour binoculars during children's learning experiences, both indoors and outdoors.
- Make a point of 'looking' for children who are being well behaved as opposed to those who are behaving inappropriately.
- As opposed to verbally acknowledging your use of the binoculars, simply raise them to your eyes – children quickly learn that you are looking for good behaviour once you have explained their use to them.
- Make the binoculars 'distinct' so that they are different to other binoculars in the setting by decorating them, painting them or accessorizing the strap.

Advantages

- Children react very quickly when practitioners/teachers bring the binoculars to their eyes – this can help to eradicate inappropriate behaviours with speed and efficiency.
- Behaviour binoculars are a cheap and easy resource to make and use in the setting.
- Support staff and parents can also be encouraged to use behaviour binoculars in the setting and at home with support.

Adaptations

For older children, practitioners/teachers could use a monocle or a large magnifying glass (think Sherlock Holmes!).

For those practitioners/teachers who would like to keep a record of which children they spot being well behaved, their names could be recorded on a large pair of laminated binocular lenses displayed on a board in the setting.

Questions for Consideration

When would be an appropriate time to introduce this resource to the children in your setting – the start of term? The end of a week? Why?

Should the children be involved in the decorating of the behaviour binoculars? If so, why? If not, why not?

Linked Resources

Make-Me-Smile Board – See page 101
Wow Card – See page 34

Shaker

Resource:	'Whistle or Bell' (Helen Wilson)

Explanation

The use of a whistle or bell is a very effective way of getting everyone's attention. You can use either the whistle or the bell as a signal for stopping or starting an event or activity very quickly. A short blast on a whistle or sound of a ringing bell easily cuts through a noisy environment and can be used as a very effective signal of event/activity change, especially in an outdoor environment.

Handy Hints

- Make sure all of the children know and understand the significance of the signal.
- Do not overuse the whistle/bell. Sound the bell or whistle for a short time and then wait for the desired effect using praise to reinforce the children displaying the desired behaviours.
- Always use the same signal – for example, one short use of the whistle means stop what you are doing, while two short whistles signal carry on.

Advantages

- The bell and whistle are both very simple and effective tools that don't require the use of a loud voice to get attention.
- They can be used in a variety of environments to signal a change in expectation of behaviour.
- They can be used gently in a more enclosed environment to bring attention to something positive.

Adaptations

Get the children to devise the signals so they have more ownership of the strategy.

As a reward, allow one of the children to be in control of the signal.

Use the signals at the start of an activity as well as at the end of an activity, especially if it is 'fun', so the signal is not always attributed with stopping an activity.

A quietly chimed bell could be used to signal a particular session – for example, a story or music session or to signal a particular event, behaviour or activity that has been performed with a desirable outcome.

Questions for Consideration

Is there a right and a wrong time/place to use a piercing whistle or bell?

Does the sound of a whistle or bell upset anyone working in your setting?

Linked Resources

Midday Supervisors – See page 43
Outdoor Area – See page 64

Resource:	'10cm Ruler'

Explanation

The 10cm ruler is really a metaphor for helping to manage the noise levels children make, either when they are inside the classroom/setting or outside in the play area/playground. Some children have a tendency to shout and scream or talk loudly – the 10cm ruler allows practitioners/teachers to gently ask children to lower their voice by using their '10cm voice', i.e. one which is quiet and calm. To support children in understanding what this means, practitioners/teachers can model the modulation in their voice by talking quietly or indicating 10cms on a ruler. Consider how children would change their voice if they were asked to use their '30cm voice'? *Put your fingers in your ears for that one!*

Handy Hints

- Actively model what you mean by a '10cm voice' so that the children understand what you expect in response to this polite request.
- Clearly indicate 10cm on a ruler using paint, coloured paper or an arrow so that it is visually clear for children to see where 10cms appear on the ruler.
- Indicate on the ruler where you think that the children's voices were when you asked them to use their 10cm voice – show them how this has changed as they lower the volume of their voices by sliding your finger/a cardboard arrow down the ruler.

Advantages

- This is a very quick and easy way to get children to lower the volume of their voice.
- For children who are very 'visual' in their learning, having an actual ruler is a power indicator of the volume their voice was at and how this changes when they lower it.
- For many children, showing them the ruler instantly has an effect on the volume of their voice as they recognize that they were being too loud.

Adaptations

Younger children and those who have special educational needs may not understand the concept of centimetres. Practitioners/teachers could use linking cubes as a visual aid so that children are encouraged to use their 'little tower' voice as opposed to their 'skyscraper' voice.

For older children, it is useful to use a large ruler as a visual aid as opposed to a small ruler as the larger ruler will have more visual impact for the whole class.

Questions for Consideration

Do you think it would be better to have your 10cm ruler visual aid displayed on a display board or kept in your pocket? Why do you think this?

Which particular children do you work with would respond positively to using this resource to manage their loud voice?

Linked Resources

Noise-O-Meter – See page 104
Whistle or Bell – See page 31

Resource:	'Referee Cards'

Explanation

Referee cards are one of the simplest and most effective strategies we have used in the settings we have worked in. The cards work in a similar way to those used by referees who oversee football matches – the practitioner/teacher has about their person two cards, one of them is green and the other is red. When they see a child behaving in an appropriate and sensible way in the setting/classroom, the practitioner/teacher will show the child the green card as an indication that their behaviour is 'good'. If the child is shown a red card, this indicates that the child is currently doing something which displeases the practitioner/teacher; this should highlight to the child that they need to stop whatever it is which the practitioner/teacher is unhappy about seeing. Once this happens, the practitioner/teacher should show the child the green card to indicate that they made the right choice in behaving appropriately.

Handy Hints

- Some practitioners may consider the red card to be rather 'severe', especially when you consider that in football a player would be sent off the pitch; are you prepared to send children out of your class if you show them a red card? Consider changing the colour of the red card to yellow.
- For whole-class teaching opportunities, prepare a larger set of referee cards for the children to see.
- Ensure that your teaching assistant/colleagues have a set of referee cards themselves so that they can use them with groups of children, thus reinforcing the use of these cards as a consistent strategy in your setting.
- Use facial expressions to accompany the displaying of the different cards to reinforce the message, e.g. a smiling face with the green card and a surprised/frowning facial expression when you have to use your red/yellow card.

Advantages

- This resource provides an instant visual indication as to whether a child's behaviour is good or 'not so good'.
- The cards are relatively easy to carry around and use in any context, e.g. indoors, outdoors, hall, corridors.
- Boys respond positively to this idea due to its links to football.
- The cards are simple to make and can be used by any adult working with children, e.g. teachers, practitioners, parent helpers, teaching assistants, student teachers/practitioners.

Adaptations

Consider changing the colour of the red card to yellow *unless* you are prepared to send children out of your class.

For older children, it is useful for them to discuss with you what behaviours will result in a green and a red card being given; consider devising a chart so that when the children are shown a card they can record its colour on the chart – what will happen when children receive five green cards in a row?

Questions for Consideration

What would you give a red card to children for in your class? What about a green card?

How often would you give a red card out in your class each day?

How will the children know which behaviours will yield a green or red response from you?

Linked Resources

Traffic Lights – See page 102
Numbered Cards – See page 37

Resource:	'Wow Card'

Explanation

This is a simple strategy that can be used to manage low-level disruptive behaviour without interrupting activities or whole-class input. The idea is that a series of cards, one green, one red and one with 'Wow' written on it are used as a non-verbal, visual support to encourage children to take responsibility for managing their own behaviour.

The practitioner/teacher uses the set of cards as a management tool during teaching time or whole-class work. When used as intended, they will allow sessions to continue to run without disruption.

If children are displaying low-level disruptive behaviours such as talking to friends, bothering other children or calling out, the cards can be shown as a series of warnings. The green card is to let children know that they are showing good behaviour, the red card is shown if the children are disrupting sessions. The 'Wow Card', which is the most fantastic thing for any child to see, is shown to let a child know that they are displaying outstanding behaviour.

Handy Hints

- Consider using the cards in different ways to make the resource more flexible. They could be put on a chain that can be worn around your neck, they could be used as flash cards, or as enlarged versions that you can place photographs of the children onto.
- Put a child in charge of the 'Wow Card' so that sometimes they can show others that they recognize good choices.
- Make some stickers saying 'Ask me why I got shown the "Wow Card" today' so the children are able to share their achievements with their parents.
- Make sure you use the green card as much as the warning card, to reinforce positive behaviour.

Advantages	**Adaptations**
- The 'Wow Card' recognizes the children who make good choices the whole time. - This is an easy resource to make that can be used in a variety of settings and can be easily adapted. - It is a quick visual tool that can be used without disrupting teaching to support children in managing their own behaviour. - The children will feel very special if they are shown the 'Wow Card'.	For younger children, the 'Wow Card' could be converted to stickers so that others are able to see the children who have made good choices throughout the day. The effectiveness of this strategy may be short-lived for older children. To ensure the children are still motivated by the cards, encouragement can be given by sending e-mails to the children/parents of children who are shown the 'Wow Card'. Another worthwhile strategy could be to allow the children to re-name the 'Wow Card' with a name they prefer.

Questions for Consideration	
How could you use the 'Wow Card' with a larger group of children, for example in an assembly or outdoor play setting? Do you think that the 'Wow Card' would be more effective for an individual child, a small group or for a whole class/group of children?	

Linked Resources

Referee Cards – See page 33
Stop and Go Cards – See page 35
Traffic Lights – See page 102

Resource:	'Stop and Go Cards'

Explanation

'Stop and Go Cards' are a very simple management tool. One card is green showing the word 'Go' on one side and is plain green on the other and the other card is red showing the word 'Stop' on one side and is plain red on the other. These cards can be used to start and stop children during activities and can also be used to prevent bad behaviour. The children need to recognize the importance of the cards and to immediately stop what they are doing and face the practitioner/teacher or begin/continue with a task when shown the cards. The red side of the stop card can also be used in whole-class teaching and can be shown to particular children who are making the wrong choices to manage behaviour. The green side of the go card can be used in a similar way to show recognition of positive behaviour.

The cards can also be used outside of the classroom to manage behaviour, for example during PE lessons and assembly time, and could easily be used on trips away from your setting.

Handy Hints

- Make the cards large enough for the children to be able to see.
- Choose a child who has impressed you with their behaviour to be in control of a reduced size set of the cards that they can wear around their neck. Involve this child in choosing when to use the cards alongside you.
- Perhaps use a flashlight or try saying 'Stop' or 'Go' with the stop or go card if the children struggle to notice.
- The cards can be used as part of a wider reward scheme, for example if the children are shown the go cards as a reward then you may award them a sticker or a house point.

Advantages

- The cards can be an excellent way to manage low-level disruptions.
- During whole-class buddy chatting, the cards are very effective in controlling the length of discussion.
- The cards can resolve behavioural problems quickly before they get out of hand.
- The cards can be used to praise positive behaviour and warn children who are showing poor behaviour.
- The children easily associate stop and go with the colours of the cards.

Adaptations

In an open-plan setting, the stop and go cards could be simultaneously flashed onto multiple interactive whiteboards. In this large version, they could also initiate tidying away.

A coloured light could be used instead of the cards for older children, or perhaps even a gesture or action.

The cards can be used for many reasons; to manage noise, to prevent low-level disruptions, to initiate or end an activity, or to praise children.

Questions for Consideration

Can you think of a situation in your setting where the stop and go cards might be particularly effective?

What noise could you use to accompany the cards in a busy situation?

Linked Resources

Referee Cards – See page 33
Traffic Lights – See page 102

Stickers

Resource:	**'Stamps'** (Helen Wilson)

Explanation

Using an ink stamp is an easy and very effective way to encourage and reward positive behaviour in our early years settings/classrooms. They are an instant response to reward and recognize positive behaviour. You can use a stamp on a piece of work, a chart or even on the back of a child's hand. Stamps can be used to encourage particular positive behaviours in individual children which can in turn have a positive effect on the behaviour of other children. By rewarding and reinforcing positive behaviour, you are likely to witness repetition of the desired behaviour. Using stamps can also help build confidence and self-esteem in the child in a particular subject or topic area.

Handy Hints

- Make sure that the type of stamp used appeals to the individual child. Find out about their interests so the stamp has real appeal; for example, a smiley face stamp might not be received with as much delight as a dinosaur.
- Display the stamps on a chart so there is an audience for the achievement – a stamp on a page in a book is often forgotten.
- Focus on one behaviour at a time so the child is clear on which positive behaviour you are looking for.
- Make sure all adults are clear on which positive behaviour is being targeted or rewarded.
- Don't over-use them or they may lose their impact.

Advantages

- This provides a very easy and immediate reward system.
- If used consistently and carefully, the stamps can result in very positive behaviour changes quickly.
- There is a large variety of stamps and ink colours to choose from, from cartoon characters to favourite storybook characters.
- Stamps are easily transferable to home so parents can be involved too!

Adaptations

Stickers are also a very useful and effective alternative to stamps.

Create a chart to display how many stamps are collected.

Use different ink colours for different desired behaviours.

Use a target number of stamps to aim for a special treat!

Stamps can also be used to reward behaviours such as concentration, helpfulness, tidying up.

Questions for Consideration

Would stamps work as rewards for all children? You must really get to know what works for individual children in order to achieve a change in behaviour.

Linked Resources

Positive Praise – See page 12
Stickers – See page 52
Reward Charts – See page 110

Resource:	'Numbered Cards'

Explanation

Numbered cards are a very simple and easy resource to make and use with children to manage their behaviour, both indoors and outdoors. The practitioner/teacher has about their person a number of cards, some with the number 1 on them, some with the number 2. As the children are playing/working, the practitioner/teacher will give a child who is behaving particularly well a card with the number 1 on – this child must then go and post it in a box marked '1'; for those children who are not behaving well, the practitioner/teacher will give these children a number 2 card which needs to be posted in the '2' box. At the end of the session/day, the practitioner/teacher counts out the number of cards in each box – *have more 1s been given out*? If there have been more 2s issued, the practitioner/teacher can ask the children what this means about the behaviour throughout the session/day.

Handy Hints

- Ensure that the cards are different colours (green for 1s and yellow for 2s); ensure that the boxes that the children post the cards into are the same colour as the respective cards.
- Avoid making a 'big thing' about giving the card to the child – place it near to them with a smile (1s) or a surprised look/slight disappointment (2s) so that it does not interfere with their learning, particularly those who receive a 1 card.
- Regularly review the meaning of the 1 and 2 cards with the children as a whole group and individually so that they are clear as to what behaviours they will get each card for.
- Keep a written log of the cards that you give out so that each child is given a card during the session/day.

Advantages

- Young children like to know that they are behaving well – they will quickly get used to wanting and working hard for a 1 card.
- Peer influence helps to manage the behaviours of those children who receive a 2 card – we have seen children helping those who have had a 2 card to think about their behaviour and what they could do to get a 1 card.

Adaptations

The age of the children determines the number of cards used – young children should only be given 1 and 2 cards; with older children you could extend this to numbers 3 and 4 if you feel this is appropriate.

The numbers on the cards could relate to specific behaviours, depending on the age and abilities of the children, e.g. 1 = positive *manners*; 2 = positive *working behaviours*; 3 = positive *relationships with peers and adults*.

The numbers could be changed for letters or words, e.g. A and B; *Positive! Think! Well done! Reflect!*

Questions for Consideration

Which colours do you intend to make your cards out of? Why have you chosen these?

If a child gets a 1 card, can they get *another* 1 card in the day? What would you do if a child in your setting gets three 2 cards in a row?

Linked Resources

Referee Cards – See page 33
Stop and Go Cards – See page 35

Resource:	'Raffle Tickets'

Explanation

The idea behind raffle tickets is that the children earn the tickets as a kind of token. On any occasion the child does something particularly kind or special, if they produce pleasing work or demonstrate good behaviour, they are given a ticket. The tickets can be given by any adult in a setting. After receiving a ticket, the child's name is written on the back and the ticket is put into a box in the setting. What happens next depends on how you want to reward the children – this can be done in a number of ways. I would recommend for younger children that the draw is done weekly or even daily but for older children a draw could be done every 2 weeks or even at the end of a half term. The reward could be; a small prize, a certificate, an activity for one child or a reward for a group of children whose tickets are drawn, for example, extra play or a small party.

Handy Hints

- Advertise the prize before the draw to motivate the children.
- Make a feature of the raffle ticket box – you could ask the children to decorate the box in the first week in the setting.
- Invite a member of the senior management team to the draw.
- You could send a letter home for the children that are recognized so parents are aware that their good behaviour/hard work has been acknowledged.
- For every draw, remember that there are lots of children who earned tickets that will not be mentioned. Congratulate the whole class before carrying out the draw.

Advantages

- The children receive instant recognition with the raffle ticket.
- The scheme is easy to apply across a whole setting rather than in one class or unit.
- The draw is something all children will look forward to every week/day.
- The strategy will remain effective as you can keep it exciting by changing the rewards regularly.

Adaptations

Involve older children in the planning of the rewards. Allow them to create posters to advertise the weekly prize. Encourage the children to collate the tickets and do the draw for the rest of the class.

Rather than using numbered raffle tickets for the younger children, use small laminated photographs of the children or cards with their names on so that they can be more involved in the draw and have a better understanding of the tokens.

Questions for Consideration

Would you acknowledge the children who had a significant number of tickets in the box at the end of a week even if they did not win the final prize? How?

Could you involve the children in the draw? How?

Linked Resources

House Points/Table Points – See page 112
End of Term/Year Awards Assembly – See page 81

Resource:	'Behaviour Dust'

Explanation

Behavioural dust is a versatile resource which can be adapted and used in any situation with any children of any age, both at home and in the setting. The dust can be used at any time, either to address behavioural issues or to pre-empt behavioural issues and stop them before they start. The dust only works when practitioners/teachers sprinkle their children with 'behaviour dust' at the start of the session/lesson to make the children 'well behaved'; if there are individuals who are behaving inappropriately then practitioners/teachers can speak to the child/children and sprinkle behaviour dust over them which will encourage them to make better choices regarding the behaviours they exhibit.

Handy Hints

- The behaviour dust can be *imaginary* or it can be *real* – consider using fine glitter or very soft coloured powder (we have found that no dust works best!).
- Behaviour dust can be kept in the practitioner's/teacher's pocket or in a special bag; always have it to hand!
- The dust can be sprinkled over the head of the child or over a particular part of their body, e.g. their hands or their feet, which is not behaving appropriately (they might be exhibiting punching or kicking behaviours which need to be managed).
- To maintain the idea of the behaviour dust having 'magical powers', ensure that only practitioners/teachers administer it.

Advantages

- Young children really 'buy in' to the idea of the dust being magical; use your story-telling skills to present the mystical and powerful effect that the dust can have on children's behaviour.
- This resource can be very cheap (i.e. it could cost nothing) or it can be very expensive if you use lots of dust on the children!
- The dust can be used on individuals, groups of children or the whole class, depending on the situation and the behaviours being exhibited.

Adaptations

Older children can be encouraged to rub the behaviour dust over a part of their own body which they recognize as misbehaving, e.g. their lips and mouth (if they use inappropriate words); their fingers (if they constantly fiddle with things).

Behaviour dust can be 'distributed' using a black and white magic wand for the boys or a pink sparkly star wand for girls.

Children can create their own container for their own behaviour dust if they wish to manage the behaviour of their peers.

Questions for Consideration

Who would the behaviour dust work best on in your setting?

Would you use imaginary or real dust? Why?

How often do you think you would use the dust with your class over one day? Why this amount?

Linked Resource

Whistle or Bell – See page 31

Thinking about Students with Challenging Behaviour

Roffey, S.

Part A – Thinking about students with challenging behaviour

Students who don't 'fit' the system

Although there is now an emphasis on personalised learning (DCSF, 2008) this is more about tracking the achievements of all children in meeting the same curriculum targets rather than valuing diverse abilities. It is possible that great strengths are lost because of an insistence on a 'one size fits all' provision. Some of the greatest men and women, such as Einstein, did not shine at school because their abilities lay in a specific direction. One Nobel Prize winner nearly didn't get to university at all because he had not been able to pass a language exam. Someone created some flexibility in the system and ultimately let his specific talents shine. There are many stories of individuals classed as 'behaviour problems' in school who had creative or entrepreneurial skills that brought them great acclaim in later years.

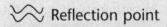 Reflection point

Do you know anyone who has achieved success in life even though they were often in trouble in school? Can you find out if there was someone who believed in them and gave them a chance?

Risk and resilience

Many of our most challenging students who do not 'fit the system' have experienced disadvantages or trauma, such as loss, abuse or neglect. For some this is a temporary situation, for others this is their whole life. Children who have multiple adversities are more at risk from negative outcomes (Werner, 2005). They often behave in ways considered unacceptable in school, which then reinforces rejection and disadvantage. This spiralling cycle of social exclusion can either be set in stone in school or broken by a different approach. It may be that for some of our children there is nowhere else to make a difference. This chapter expands on what a 'different approach' might mean and how to put this into operation.

Resilience is promoted by factors within the child but also within their environment – including what happens in school. The three most important things a teacher can do are:

- Show students you think they are worth your effort – that there is something special and lovable about them. You may have to dig deep but nearly everyone has positive qualities – even if well hidden.
- Expect the best in all situations and let students know you are not going to give up on them but do everything you can to enable them to shine – this means identifying their strengths
- Give pupils opportunities to participate, have a say and a place in the class. They are important members of the school and it matters that they are there.

Do you label students *as* problems or see them as young people *with* problems?

Teachers may see their role as attempting to fit these square pegs into round holes – a difficult and thankless task. Trying to 'make' others fit our own expectations is rarely easy and can become a battle of wills, the struggle for power and control. The alternative is not to condone unacceptable behaviour but to create flexibility in the system to celebrate the individuality of each student. Holding on to a view of pupils as whole people, with qualities as well as quirks will enable you to find those elements you can work with. Seeking out the glimpses of good and re-conceptualising students in terms of their competencies and resources will help. There is a meaning to everyone's behaviour, even if we cannot initially make much sense of it ourselves.

 ## Case study

On Sunday, 11-year-old Matthew spent the day with his Dad, who had recently been separated from his Mum. Together the two of them made jam and spent the evening delivering pots as gifts to friends and neighbours. When Matthew got home late his Mum was angry with him and with his Dad because his homework wasn't finished. Matthew went to bed feeling confused and upset. On Monday, he was suspended from school for an episode of violence when he banged a classmate's head against a wall.

The behaviour was unacceptable and sanctions appropriate, but labelling Matthew as 'violent, cruel, a bully or a monster' puts him in a position which offers little escape. It acknowledges only one aspect of who he is as a person and also leads to self-fulfilling prophecies. We all tend to live up to the labels we are given. Reframing Matthew's behaviour as a sign of distress paints a different picture of him. He can be said to be behaving like a monster but if he is acknowledged as a person rather than a problem there are things to build on. In all interactions with students it is essential to make it clear that it is their behaviour that is unacceptable – not them. Acknowledging the 'whole person' also makes it easier to work with families (see Chapter 6).

 ## Activity

Issues of loss, including family breakdown, may lead to feelings of anger and confusion as well as sadness. Sometimes parents are so distressed themselves they are not emotionally available to their children at a time when they need it most. Children below the age of 7 often believe the break up was their fault in some way or that Dad would have stayed if they had been 'good enough'. Pupils may be distracted and feel insecure which affects their learning.

What might schools do to reduce the impact of families splitting up on children's learning and behaviour? Research the following:

- Programmes dealing with loss and change in school
- Helping parents talk with children about separation and divorce.

Do you see children as monsters or behaving like monsters?

Figure 7.1

Focusing on solutions rather than problems

We have a problem-saturated society. When we try to identify positives people often seem to prefer to jump back into negativity. They are not used to doing it! An increasingly influential force in school psychology is solution-focused thinking (Ajmal & Rees, 2001). This switches conversations around to a different focus. If we were dealing with a challenging student a solution-focused approach would ask questions such as:

focuses on the positive.

- What is working well?
- When does the student behave well?
- What are the circumstances of any positives – for example, with which teacher or adult is the behaviour most appropriate? What is this person doing that seems to work?
- Does this student have any supportive relationships?
- What strengths does this student have?

- What are they are able to manage?
- What have they learnt?
- What helps them cope?
- What comforts them and makes them feel better?
- What helps them calm down?
- What has worked well in the past?
- What can this pupil be proud of?
- How does the student visualise life without the problem?
- What can we build on here?
- What can we put in place so the student knows they are being successful, being supported, being valued?
- What would the student see as solutions for themselves? They might be the only person to know what the real options are (Berg & Steiner, 2003).

Thinking about behaviour itself

[handwritten margin note: Means ch probably have the exp. behaviour sometimes]

Behaviour only has meaning within a context. There is virtually no behaviour that does not have an appropriate context somewhere. Screaming and yelling is what you are supposed to do at a big match if your team scores: screaming and yelling in the classroom is seriously frowned upon. It helps students to succeed at school if they are taught in a structured and supportive way what is appropriate behaviour in a classroom. They also need to know what is not acceptable and why. In the first place it may be more constructive for teachers to assume ignorance rather than defiance or disobedience. This is particularly important for transitions into a new school or new class (Dockett & Perry, 2007; Roffey & O'Reirdan, 2001).

[handwritten margin note: This creates a situation where]

Sitting still and writing, not talking, obeying school rules, wearing the 'right' uniform and so on are not about being 'good' but being part of a social order. These behaviours have no moral quality, neither are they particularly 'natural' for lively young people. Expectations are on pupils to ensure a controlled environment. Most students take up this position of being a 'good student' in the same way as you take up the behaviours of what you understand as a 'good teacher'. Students in fact have few real choices. Even though sometimes we offer choices and consequences to maintain 'appropriate' school behaviour these are controlled by the power of the institution. Acknowledging this may help us see how much even the most defiant students accept what is required of them, even if they don't manage it sometimes.

School demands and expectations do not always make sense to some pupils and may undermine their need for a sense of agency. If they have little choice over much that happens in their lives they are going to try and control what they can, actively or passively. If you give pupils choices and where possible the right to have a say in what concerns them – whilst showing them that what they do or don't do matters to you – this is more likely to gain their cooperation. If you try and tighten control for the sake of it you are in for a battle you are unlikely to win.

The meaning of behaviour for students

It is useful to have some idea of what certain actions mean for students. Many behaviours, for instance, can be interpreted as 'coping mechanisms'. Meanings are often hidden, not deliberately but because the triggers are deeply buried in past experiences.

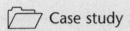 Case study

One young girl displayed difficult behaviour with one male teacher only – and only at certain times. For a long time no one could understand why. Careful analysis revealed that the distressed behaviour only occurred on days he was wearing a blue check shirt. It was then discovered that the girl's abusive father, with whom she no longer lived, used to wear a similar shirt. The teacher wearing a blue check shirt brought back painful memories of home that triggered emotional upset. When he stopped wearing the shirt the behaviour improved.

Sometimes it requires only a good relationship, a suspension of prejudice and a moment of listening to have a way of understanding. Being prepared to do so may be linked to how the student is positioned by the school in the first place. Psychological survival is a motivation for many behaviours, and underpins emotions that are associated with fear and defence. Young people who have had difficult experiences may construe the world as a hostile place and see demands, expectations and social interactions as potentially threatening. No one needs to tell you to f-off unless they interpret what you are asking as a threat. We live in a society that is increasingly based on competition, fear of failure and wariness of others. This may account in part for the numbers of young people who need to protect their sense of self by whatever means is at hand. Making an effort to understand what a student's behaviour means for them gives us more chance of working together to change it.

You can help to discover meanings by looking at patterns in behaviour, by talking to children about the pictures they draw, sometimes just by asking indirect and open questions and listening – for example: 'You seem a bit bothered lately, what's up?'. You may only get a useful answer if the student feels safe with you and does not feel interrogated. It works better if you are doing something together, like tidying up or walking around the playground rather than in a face-to-face encounter.

Should you find yourself in a situation where a student discloses abuse you must make it clear immediately that you are obliged to tell someone whose job it is to protect children. Check out the child protection procedures in your school and which staff member has responsibility for this.

Sometimes you can 'reframe' behaviour for a student which interprets its meaning in terms of qualities rather than deficits. For example, young students sometimes explode at the taunt 'Your mum is a …' even before the sentence is finished! If the student is given credit for loyalty they may then listen to why it is not necessary to punch the perpetrator on the nose!

Managing the Behaviour of Boys

Sousa, D. A.

WHY A CONCERN WITH BOYS?

Almost every veteran teacher will admit that boys present many more disciplinary challenges in the classroom than girls. Boys fall behind girls in literacy in the earliest years of school and never really catch up (Newkirk, 2006). As for behavior, many educators suspect that the misbehavior demonstrated so much more frequently by boys stems, in part, from academic deficits and perhaps even from the very instructional methods and materials used in the traditional classroom. For example, some educators have noted that young boys seem to require reading materials that are more oriented to "heroes and superheroes" using "superpowers," but few basal reading programs include stories of this nature. Perhaps boys have a distinct preference for these reading materials because their stories manifest clear distinctions between good and evil. In contrast, young girls seem to prefer reading materials that emphasize the more subtle aspects of relationships and friendships (King & Gurian, 2006; Tatum, 2006).

> *Although the strategies suggested in this chapter are particularly effective for boys, they can be effective for girls as well.*

For these reasons, many educators have begun to pay particular attention to the educational and disciplinary needs of males in the classroom. Consequently, in this chapter we will discuss some possible genetic, biological, and psychological reasons why boys misbehave in school more often than girls. We will also suggest some strategies that are particularly effective for handling boys' misbehavior, although these tactics are effective for girls as well.

GENDER DIFFERENCES IN BEHAVIOR

Genetic and Environmental Factors

For decades, the physical, emotional, social, and behavioral differences between males and females have fed the story lines of many a television comedy series. They have spawned a variety of parlor games, and generated some popular and undying myths. Yet buried in all this hype are a few scientific findings that shed light on why males and females often behave differently in the same situation.

Behavior is the result of genetic and environmental (social) factors. The genes that now underlie the behavior differences between males and females must have been selected because they improved the chances that an individual of that gender would survive and reproduce. If we accept the theories about the different roles that our male and female ancestors played, then it becomes possible to understand why their behavior and associated cognitive skills developed differently.

Development of the Male Brain

Males were the hunters, builders, and defenders of their tribes. Successful hunters needed to make weapons that would kill the prey before the prey killed the hunters. They had to be good trackers, throwers, and archers. They had to determine what kinds of materials would make a shelter waterproof and able to withstand strong winds. They also had to learn how to defend themselves against invading tribes seeking to expand their territory. Eventually, as communities grew larger, a social hierarchy had to be devised. Those individuals who were the most aggressive very likely became leaders. Aggression is an effective strategy for establishing social dominance and resolving social conflict. In short, males who were good at making weapons and tools, as well as aggressive and socially dominant, were more likely to survive and win the favor of females to mate.

Development of the Female Brain

Females stayed close to home and raised the children. Childcare is a challenging task. First, deciding why an infant is crying requires making educated guesses about what is wrong. The children of females who were good at this were more likely to survive. Females who created a community of friends could help each other watch and care for the other's children when necessary. Building friendships made for a more stable and watchful community where children could be safer and less likely to be attacked by ever-present predators. Making friends and keeping a partner, however, required that she be mindful of the feelings of others (especially her mate), be ready to compromise, and be a good listener. Such strategies reduced the chances of conflict and aggression within the family and community. In short, females who were good at empathizing, child-rearing, and working toward a community consensus were more likely to survive and reproduce.

Social Brain Has Changed Little

Modern day humans behave much like their ancestors. Although the social environment of Western societies has changed dramatically during the last 200 years, the social brain is essentially the same as it was thousands of years ago. Of course, the brain has *learned* and participated in these social changes, but how it emotionally *reacts* to them has hardly changed at all. Hurling an insult at someone provokes the same inflamed emotional response today as it did in our ancestors in the cave. Granted, the contemporary legal consequences might discourage a violent reaction in most of us, but the strong emotional feelings still emerge, nonetheless.

Impact of Biology

Along with genetic influences, biology plays a role in explaining the sex differences in behavior. Male babies typically have higher levels of the sex hormone testosterone in their blood than female babies. As we discussed in Chapter 2, a high level of testosterone does not in itself cause aggressive behavior, but it does increase the likelihood that certain misbehaviors will be expressed if the genetic inclinations are present and the situation provokes it (Booth, Granger, Mazur, & Kivlighan, 2006). On the other hand, research studies indicate that low levels of testosterone (common in females) lead to higher levels of language, better communication and social skills, and increased eye contact (Baron-Cohen, 2003). These advantages suggest that females are more likely than males to resolve conflict by resorting to face-to-face communication and talking the matter through.

Structural Differences in the Male and Female Brain

It is important to recognize that neither the male nor female brain is better or worse than the other. Their genetic composition has been selected to successfully support entirely different roles. In addition to initiating and monitoring biological processes, genes influence the growth and development of brain structures. Because the mix of genes is somewhat different in males than in females, it is no surprise that there are gender differences in the anatomies of several brain structures, some of which are believed to be associated with behavior. These brain regions include areas that have been associated with memory, social behavior, and emotional processing and response (see Table 4.1).

Table 4.1   Gender Differences in Brain Regions Thought to Be Associated With Behavior

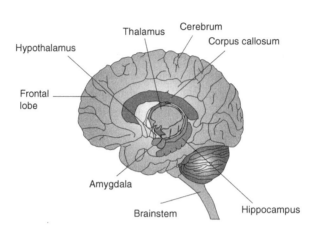

Brain Region	Males	Females	Implications
Amygdala: Attaches emotional significance to stimuli and generates emotional responses	High response activity when looking at photographs of fearful faces	Lower response activity when looking at photographs of fearful faces. More active when figuring out what another person is thinking or intending.	Males may respond aggressively before taking time to find out the other person's intent
Corpus callosum: Thick cable that transfers information across the brain's two hemispheres	Proportionally smaller	Proportionally larger and thicker, leading to better interhemisphere communication, language fluency, and emotional processing	Females more apt than males to resolve conflict with language than with physical attack
Hippocampus: Active during learning and memory, including spatial memory	Grows faster in young males and is proportionally larger than in females	Grows slower and is proportionally smaller than in males	Males more likely to feel their personal space invaded and respond aggressively
Hypothalamus: Regulates mating behavior, reproduction cycles, and circadian rhythms	Area regulating mating behavior is about twice as large as in females	Area regulating mating behavior is about one-half the size as in males	Males more likely to respond aggressively if another male appears interested in mate

Sources: Adapted from Baron-Cohen, 2003; Bishop & Wahlsten, 1997; Cahill, 2005; and Suzuki et al., 2005.

Amygdala. As we discussed in previous chapters, the amygdala is the brain's gateway to emotions. Brain scans indicate that the amygdala in male brains shows far greater activity than in female brains when looking at photographs of fearful faces. This response difference is probably linked, once again, to survival. The man was the family's defender. Seeing a fearful or hostile look on another's face could be the warning sign of brewing conflict. The quicker an individual's brain processed an emotional response to the face and generated a defensive posture, the more likely that individual would survive.

The female amygdala, however, shows higher activity (along with parts of the frontal lobe) than the male's when looking at photographs of eyes and trying to figure out what a person is thinking or intending to do. Thus, the female is more apt to plan her response to an emotional threat through communication and reason. Furthermore, the amygdala of both genders is rich in testosterone receptor cells. Because males generally have a much higher amount of testosterone than females, the male response to an emotional threat is more likely to be: act first, talk later. The opposite is true for females.

Corpus Callosum. Another structure to consider is the *corpus callosum,* a thick bundle of nerves that connects the brain's two hemispheres and allows information to flow between them. Although the female brain is typically about eight percent smaller than the male brain, the corpus callosum in women is proportionally larger than in men. The larger size is due to a greater number of nerve fibers connecting the hemispheres. Consequently, on tasks that would benefit from the rapid transfer of information between hemispheres, such as analyzing intent and communication, females should do better, and numerous studies have shown this to be the case (Bishop & Wahlsten, 1997; Cahill, 2005).

Hippocampus. We discussed in Chapter 1 the importance of the hippocampus in encoding information into long-term memory. It is particularly important in recording spatial memories, such as knowing your way around your home in the dark, or driving a specific route to work each day. It also influences an individual's personal space. Although the size of one's personal space varies among cultures (e.g., closer for Mediterranean cultures, further back for North Americans) there is a minimum distance in all cultures within which an individual feels threatened. In young males, the hippocampus grows faster than in young females (Suzuki et al., 2005). It seems then that young males establish their personal space sooner than females and are thus more likely to feel threatened and respond aggressively when others come too close.

Hypothalamus. Near the hippocampus is a small but important structure called the *hypothalamus.* This collection of nuclei work together to maintain the internal stability of the body's systems. Two areas of the hypothalamus, however, have clear differences in male and female brains: the *suprachiasmatic nucleus* and the *preoptic area.* The suprachiasmatic nucleus is important in regulating circadian rhythms (e.g., light-dark cycles for sleep) and reproduction cycles. The main difference between males and females in this nucleus is shape: spherical in males, elongated in females. Researchers are now trying to determine if the difference in shape influences the connections that this area makes with other areas of the brain.

The preoptic area is involved in mating behavior. In males, this area is more than twice as large as in women and contains twice as many cells. This size difference becomes apparent after a person is only four years old. Most young males, then, typically begin to demonstrate mating behaviors sooner and more intensely than young females of the same age. One of these behaviors is the aggressive response that arises if a male believes his current mating relationship is being threatened by another male's actions (Cahill, 2005).

Some Research Findings on Behavioral Differences

Evidence of this persistence in behavioral differences shows up in research studies. For example, to solve conflicts, boys are more likely to use *physical* aggression while girls are more likely to use *verbal* aggression (Calvete & Cardenoso, 2005). Girls tend to get better grades in school because they are more self-disciplined than their male peers. Throughout elementary, middle, and high school, girls earn higher grades than boys in all major subjects. However, girls do not outperform boys on achievement or IQ tests. Researchers suggest that this disparity may be because girls are more self-disciplined, and this advantage is more relevant to report card grades than to achievement or aptitude tests (Duckworth & Seligman, 2006).

Male and female teachers often display differences in their disciplinary approaches to male and female children. One study explored these differences, examining the connection between an educator's gender and method of disciplining urban, elementary school-aged children. Given surveys that contained eight behavioral scenarios (four scenarios with boys and four with girls), elementary school teachers were asked how they would react in order to discipline the student involved. Responses for each scenario were listed in random order and ranged from most assertive to least assertive disciplinary action.

> *Male and female teachers display differences in their disciplinary approaches to male and female children.*

Although there were many similarities between male and female teachers' discipline responses, male teachers were significantly more likely than female teachers to select a more aggressive disciplinary approach toward boys. Both male and female teachers chose more often to ignore the boys' misbehavior if no aggression was involved. Female teachers were slightly more consistent with their disciplinary responses for both boys and girls (Rodriguez, 2002). More findings from research are included in the following discussion of how to translate the research on gender differences in behavior into instructional and management strategies that work.

USING RESEARCH-BASED STRATEGIES

Research studies over the years support the notion that differences in certain brain structures in males and females lead to differences in behavior, including their responses in social situations. Because attending school is a major opportunity for social interaction, teachers need to understand these differences and be prepared to deal with them effectively. For the foreseeable future, we can assume that boys will continue to be the source of more behavior problems than girls. So let's move on to some research-based strategies that we suggest teachers consider when handling the misbehavior of boys. Remember, these strategies can also be adapted for use with misbehaving girls.

Movement-Based Instruction and Classroom Management

Importance of Movement In Learning

The emerging research on brain-compatible instruction has highlighted the importance of including instructional activities that include movement. Called *movement-based instruction,* this powerful classroom technique has been shown to encourage appropriate behavior because some students who may be hyperactive will have some of their need for movement addressed in the context of the lesson. Because physical movement has long been associated in the human brain with survival, brain imaging studies show that movement stimulates long-term memory and recall. Remember that time you were at your desk and your mind stopped working while you were trying to balance the checkbook, do a tax return, or plan a lesson? You took a break, and after a short walk you were able to return to the desk and complete the task. What happened during that brief walk? Moving activated long-term memory sites, allowing you to recall the information you needed for the task at hand.

Figure 4.1 explains what happened. When sitting for more than 30 minutes, blood begins to pool in your feet and in your seat, decreasing the amount of blood flowing through the brain. The arrows in the diagram on the left of Figure 4.1 show the frontal lobe accessing long-term memory sites to gather data for solving a cognitive task. When we get up and walk around, two beneficial things happen: First, the movement

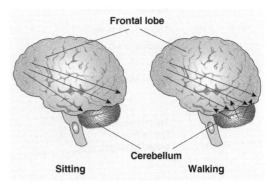

Figure 4.1 The arrows in the diagram on the left represent the frontal lobe accessing long term storage sites near the base of the brain. The diagram on the right shows how walking stimulates the cerebellum to activate additional long-term sites, thereby increasing the information available to solve a problem.

breaks up those pools and sends more oxygen-rich blood to the brain. Second, the cerebellum, which controls our walking is stimulated and it activates additional long-term storage sites. As a result, you now have more memory sites contributing information to help you solve the task at hand.

Most students enjoy movement-based learning activities because it is more natural to move than to stay still. Movement stimulates the flow of oxygen-rich blood and brain chemicals, such as noradrenaline and dopamine, that are natural motivators and serve to maximize cerebral energy levels. Thus, curriculum content that is associated with frequent movement will likely be learned and remembered for a much longer time than if presented in the traditional fashion whereby the teacher talks the sitting students through the content. What research is telling educators is that, whenever possible, content should be associated with repetitive movement (Bender, 2008; King & Gurian, 2006; Sousa, 2006; Tate, 2003).

Incorporating movement into a lesson does not have to be complicated. One simple example of movement-based learning for the upper elementary grades involves associating the parts of a business or personal letter with parts of the human body (Chapman, 2000). Note in the example pictured in Figure 4.2 how movement logically flows from the top of the human body to the legs, as the organization of the various components of a letter follow from top to bottom. This type of activity, repeated frequently during a two-week unit of instruction on letter forms can greatly enhance learning and retention.

Although teachers of younger students have used movement in their teaching for years, researchers are now advocating the use of movement across all grade levels, particularly to teach

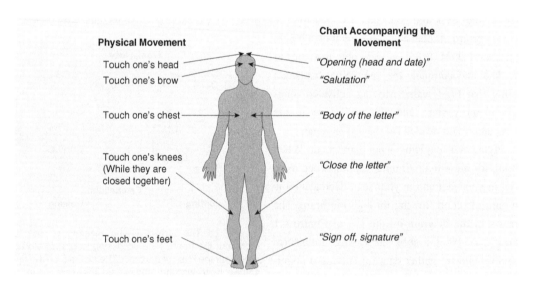

Figure 4.2 This diagram illustrates how easily movement can be incorporated into a lesson. Here, the students touch a part of their body while singing a chant that helps them associate the body part with the part of a business or personal letter.

Source: Adapted from Chapman, 2000.

content in the subject areas in secondary school. For example, imagining one's body superimposed on a map, and then associating various body parts with locations on the map can assist students in learning where the continents are on the globe, where individual states are located, or where various cities or rivers are within a single state (Chapman, 2000).

Many other examples of movement-based learning exist in the literature. Moving students along a large number-line on the floor assists in mathematical measurement activities or in operations with positive and negative integers (Tate, 2003). Arranging cards on the classroom floor that depict both the words and the punctuation for a sentence is much more interesting to students than teaching the same grammar and punctuation lesson merely using a worksheet. This "card on the floor" movement activity serves as both an effective instructional technique as well as an enhancement to class management for boys, since the male students are less bored than they would be sitting at a desk with a worksheet on the same content (King & Gurian, 2006).

Ways of Using Movement

There are two distinct ways to use movement for teaching content. In the previous examples, each student is acting independently (i.e., a student touching his/her body parts to represent parts of a letter). Another option is to ask several students to move together through a representation of the content, perhaps representing different roles. When this type of activity is repeated over time, students are more likely to learn and remember the content.

Given this overall emphasis on movement, teachers in the upper grade levels should consider using some movement-based learning activity during every learning episode. For example, making lines of 3, 5, and 7 students can be used to illustrate a bar graph, or semantic webs can be constructed with students holding a poster to represent their position on the web. However, rather than using several different movement activities each day during an instructional unit, teachers should develop a unified movement activity that represents the essence of the whole unit (see the "cell wall" example that follows). Merely adding different content to the same movement simplifies matters for the teacher yet enhances the instructional impact of that movement for the students. Again, the general guideline for teachers across all grade levels is simple: Try not to let a learning episode go by without some type of movement-based learning activity.

> *Try not to let a learning episode go by without some type of movement-based activity!*

Movement-Based Instruction in a Lesson

With this emphasis on instructional movement in mind, we can now consider how to use movement in a lesson so that it not only serves as an instructional tool but controls undesirable behavior as well. For many male students with attention-deficit hyperactivity disorder (ADHD) or opposi-tional defiant disorder (ODD), distraction or hyperactivity are fundamental characteristics of their learning difficulties. This is not to suggest that young females do not display similar problems. However, many more males than females are identified as hyperactive and defiant, as research studies and most experienced teachers will confirm.

Across the grade levels, many of these male students cannot control their impulse to move. Consequently, these students will move around the classroom regardless of what the teacher does. These students do not move around because they are spiteful, evil, or meanspirited individuals who intentionally plan to disrupt the instructional activity. Rather, most of them move at inappropriate times in the classroom because everything in their mind and body is shouting: "You have to move right now!"

For teachers of these students, providing some movement options in the classroom is a must for survival, and building movement into the content-based teaching is the most efficient way to do that. It also has the added result of enhancing the effectiveness of one's teaching. Frequently using movement-based activities while learning content reduces the unscheduled moves of hyperactive male students because they will have some of their urge for movement met by the activity. Movement-based instruction is not only a very effective instructional strategy for young males, it is also an effective classroom management technique. Here are other examples.

Movement-Based Instruction in Biology: An Educator's Idea

Ms. Susan Jasper was teaching at Jackson County High School in a ninth/tenth grade biology class. The lesson was the first lesson focusing on cells and came the first day of a two-week instruc-tional unit on that topic. Ms. Jasper was using a diagram on an overhead transparency that depicted a cell wall as a circle enclosing the cell. Both bacteria and food enzymes were represented by exter-nal arrows impacting on the cell wall, and while the cell wall kept the bacteria out, the food enzymes penetrated the wall. The diagram showed that the main functions of a cell wall are two-fold: keep bacteria out and let food in.

Although the transparency showed this process graphically, the class seemed uninvolved with this lesson. Several students were getting physically restless and two were whispering in the back of the room. Suddenly, Ms. Jasper stopped talking about the overhead diagram and asked five male students to stand up and lock their elbows together in a circle to represent the cell wall. Ms. Jasper explained to the class that the cell wall was very strong—like those young men. That comment captured the interest of these males since they were being described as "strong" in front of their peers. Ms Jasper then asked a female student to pretend to be a bacterium, and told her to "Get into the cell!" Ms. Jasper explained that tickling above the waist was allowed, but no touching was allowed below the waist. The males in the cell wall were told to "Keep out the bacterium!" Ms. Jasper then shouted "Go!"

After a few moments of tickling and fun, Ms. Jasper shouted, "Freeze! What does a cell wall do with the bacterium?" The class answered loudly in unison, "Keeps it out!" Next, another female was selected as the food enzyme, and the males forming the cell wall were told to "Make her work for it, but then let this food enzyme in." Both the bacterium and food enzyme began to tickle the cell wall, and within a few seconds the food enzyme got into the center of the cell. Ms. Jasper again shouted "Freeze! What does a cell wall do with a food enzyme?" The class answered, "Let's it in."

In this simple example, Ms. Jasper cleverly used a sexual allusion to get the students' attention—a tactic that usually works with high school students, but is not always wise or appropriate. Still, it worked wonderfully in this case because Ms. Jasper knew which of these students would cooperate without letting the activity get out of control. She subsequently reported that, because the secondary students loved that movement-based example, she used it each day during the ten-day instructional unit. She added content throughout the unit to enhance the movement model of the cell. Within a few days, other types of cells (e.g., cells featuring a cell membrane rather than a cell wall) were discussed along with other internal structures, such as the nucleus.

Although this example reflects excellent teaching in a secondary class, it also represents a classroom management strategy. Whenever the students appeared bored or distracted during the two-week unit, Ms. Jasper introduced a movement-based activity related to the content that the students enjoyed and that quickly brought them back on task. Further, she reported that throughout the unit, she often asked, "How can we incorporate this new cell structure into our movement model?" Finally, the students enjoyed the movement so much that Ms. Jasper now develops at least one such movement example for each instructional unit she teaches. She also noted that every single student in the class knew the function of the cell wall—keep bacteria out and let food enzymes in.

Boy-Friendly Instruction and Discipline

The gender-based differences in the brains of boys and girls that we discussed earlier in this chapter suggest that some instructional tactics might be more appropriate for boys. For example, males seem to participate more in discussions when the literature they read has clear delineations of good and evil, heros and villains, or right and wrong. Boys tend to be more boisterous in the classroom than do girls, and this may be misinterpreted as "hyperactive" or even "behaviorally disturbed." Implementing instructional tactics that target these differences seems to result in making boys less disruptive in the classroom overall, and at least one school credits such "boy-friendly" teaching with closing a significant achievement gap between boys and girls in their elementary school (Allen, 2006; King & Gurian, 2006).

These brain-compatible classroom tactics have been featured in a wide variety of instructional methods books, and are generally being well received by educators today. Our point here is that, whenever possible, teachers should use techniques that capture the energy and attention of the males in their classes, in order to indirectly reduce disciplinary problems with those students. Although many instructional suggestions have been suggested, the following are directly related to the learning capabilities and difficulties of males.

Instructional Tactics to Motivate Males and Decrease Behavior Problems

Here are five suggestions based on the research literature for strategies and techniques that have been shown to motivate male students and decrease their misbehavior.

- **Use more visual representations.** Because the brains of males generally have more areas dedicated to spatial-mechanical functioning, using dynamic visual representations often results in increased attention, which will, in turn, result in less misbehavior.
- **Use dynamic, moving models.** Because the male optical and visual processing systems rely more heavily on cells that detect motion, using a physically moving example of a concept is likely to engage males in the learning task more so than static graphics. In many cases, computerized instructional packages can make traditional charts and graphs dynamic. For example, in biology class, rather than merely presenting a series of overhead transparencies depicting growth of a fetus over time, a computerized presentation would generate a video of a growing fetus.
- **Build learning activities around team competition.** Boys are naturally more aggressive than girls, and while overt aggression can sometimes cause problems, team competition can channel those aggressive tendencies toward productive learning experiences, and thereby reduce inappropriate aggression. Team competitions that involve running from one location to the next to identify a question for the team, can result in increased attention for young boys.
- **Use role play activities.** Because boys are less likely to be as highly attuned to various social situations as girls, providing learning opportunities that offer the option of acting out the learning content can be effective. Although girls also benefit from role play activities, boys are more likely to understand the social implications of the learning content in actual role play situations, certainly more so than when a teacher merely asks the boys to reflect on content.
- **Use music to enhance memory.** Although music can be used to facilitate memory for all students (consider the "ABC" song so frequently used to teach the alphabet), music coupled with movement may be particularly appropriate for young males. Here is a mathematics chant using the rhythm of "We will, we will rock you!" for teaching about circles (Bender, 2005).

> *This is circumference, all around the side.*
> *Next comes the radius, middle to the side.*
> *Next is diameter, all the way through!*
> *All of that's a circle, I'll show it to you.*

In using this chant, students can walk in lines into the various components mentioned above. For example, while chanting the first line, six to ten students march into an open space in the classroom, making a circle. While chanting the second line, three to four students enter the circle and form the radius. During the next line, six to eight students enter the circle again, forming the diameter. In this fashion, both music and movement are coupled to represent the components of the circle.

A Case Study: Using Music and Movement to Curb Inappropriate Behavior

Ms. Lovorn was teaching mathematics in her fourth-grade class and noted that each time she began the lesson, Eric would begin to misbehave. Sometimes he tossed his books on the floor, or he called other students names to provoke an argument. During the next few weeks, Ms. Lovorn noted that he was more likely to do so when the mathematics assignment involved multiplication and division. Subsequently, a few observations of Eric's mathematics skills confirmed that he had never mastered the times tables. Apparently, Eric was misbehaving whenever he was confronted with a mathematics problem requiring multiplication facts.

Almost every veteran teacher has encountered students whose misbehavior was caused by a deficit in prerequisite knowledge. These students are essentially using misbehavior to avoid work that they know they cannot do successfully. Although the times tables were included in the third-grade curriculum, Ms. Lovorn noted that several other students had not mastered the threes, fours, sixes, sevens, eights, and nines times tables. Apparently, the only times tables that all students had learned were the simpler ones: the ones, twos, fives, and tens. For that reason, Ms. Lovorn felt comfortable spending a brief time each day on the times tables with the entire class, but she also wanted to intervene to curb Eric's inappropriate behavior. She decided to combine these two needs into one plan.

Initially Ms. Lovorn collected some baseline data on Eric's misbehavior during mathematics. She found that over four days she had reprimanded him more than 30 times for his misbehavior during the daily 50-minute mathematics class. She then decided to use a music and movement-based intervention that the students would enjoy because it would be more interesting while enhancing the likelihood of remembering the content. At the same time, it would teach Eric his times tables and likely decrease his misbehavior. To focus on Eric, she made him the "Times Table Leader." His job was to lead the class in a chant of the multiplication facts known to the class while "slapping out" the times tables.

Initially the class focused on the three times table only. Each day, Eric was presented with a times table chart that represented all of the equations in the three times table set: $3 \times 1 = 3$, $3 \times 2 = 6$, and so forth through $3 \times 10 = 30$. Eric was taught to read the equations aloud while leading the class in reciting the times tables to the rhythm of "We will, we will rock you!" The class participated by calling out the times tables and slapping out that rhythm on their desks. During that one sentence, the students should be able to chant the first two equations. The next time they repeat the sentence, they chant the next two equations, and so on. Ms. Lovorn participated as the class chanted the equations using that rhythm, and each day the class recited the entire set several times before moving on into their other mathematics work. The entire recitation for any given day lasted only about two minutes. After two weeks, the class moved to the four times table for two weeks, and then to the sixes, and so on.

As they progressed through the times tables over the next several weeks, Ms. Lovorn noted that students at their desks doing other work appeared to be "slapping out" the rhythm and reciting times tables in order to find a multiplication fact that they needed. Ms. Lovorn told Eric and all the other class members that if they needed a multiplication fact for a times table set that they have *not* practiced using the rhythm, she would gladly provide the answer. However, if a student needed a multiplication fact for a set they had previously practiced, Ms. Lovorn would gladly "slap out" the times table with the student for that particular set. This provided her with opportunities to remind the class that while they may not have practiced the seven times table, they did know some of it because they had previously practiced the threes and fours, and that 7×3 was the same as 3×7, and 7×4 was the same as 4×7.

> Using music and movement together helped this teacher redirect a student's chronic misbehavior to leading productive classroom activities.

Many students in the class appeared to be learning their multiplication facts and were retaining that information for use in other work. However, the most impressive results were shown in Eric's behavior. Over a period of only five days, his behavior during mathematics instruction improved dramatically, and by the end of the project, his misbehavior was all but eliminated. As the data in Figure 4.3 show, his occurrences of misbehavior during mathematics were reduced to an average of less than one misbehavior per day in the last two weeks of the intervention period. Ms. Lovorn shared this intervention with the principal and school counselor, both of whom were impressed. However, the real payoff came when she shared this with Eric's parents at the next parent-teacher meeting. Eric's mother almost came to tears while saying quietly, "I'm so glad you've noted Eric's love for music, and used that to make him behave. Most of his other teachers could not figure out how to make him behave in class. Everyone in my family has always loved

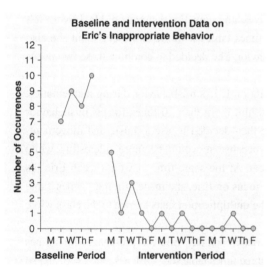

Figure 4.3 This chart shows frequency of Eric's misbehavior before (baseline) and after the music and movement intervention during his mathematics lessons.

music, and I know Eric does. He listens to his MP3 player for hours on end, and if music can help him behave better, all the better. Thank you for seeing that in him, and for caring."

Targeted interventions to improve behavior do require that the teacher take some extra time for planning, as Ms. Lovorn did in this example. The payoff includes more successful learning and a more enjoyable class. Sometimes, too, these interventions make a critically important difference in a student's life.

The Responsibility Strategy

Males frequently seek attention in the classroom in very inappropriate ways. Although females also need attention during their childhood and adolescent years, males seem to require more of their teacher's time. Unfortunately, some males get attention through oppositional or defiant misbehavior. From the perspective of the male student, attention for a negative behavior is still attention. Furthermore, during an episode of misbehavior, the offending student often captures the attention of his peers and, thus, feels empowered. At the same time, the teacher needs to address the student's misbehavior. This results in unfortunate situations where the student, through his misbehavior, has the attention of his peers and the teacher, and the lesson is at a standstill. Now the student is in a powerful position, and many oppositional students intentionally seek their recognition by creating and misbehaving in situations such as these.

In some cases, a cycle begins in which the only recognition these students receive stems from their own misbehavior, and given the desire of most young males to receive attention (some might say, "show off"), more misbehavior follows. One way to effectively counter this negative, self-feeding cycle is to provide positive attention for *appropriate* behaviors. Specifically, teachers should seek ways to empower male students by having them perform a classroom responsibility that the students will take seriously and be proud to do (Tournaki & Criscitiello, 2003).

The term "Responsibility Strategy" was first used by Bender (2003), though the idea is certainly not new. The essence of a responsibility strategy involves empowering male (or female) students by providing them a way to earn positive attention for necessary and appropriate behaviors. Through this strategy, students are encouraged to identify their unique contribution to the "society" of the classroom, and to meet those responsibilities to the teachers, the classmates, and the school, thus gaining the positive attention that they seek. Using these students for individual responsibilities allows them the opportunity to "show off" in an appropriate way, and, for many males, that is sufficient motivation to participate in a responsibility strategy intervention. Moreover, the tasks done by these students should be selected so that they assist the teacher and others in the class.

> *Responsibility strategies work because they give otherwise disconnected students opportunities to make meaningful contributions and to feel valued as a member of the school community.*

One critical factor in this behavioral intervention is to ensure that the task gives *meaningful* responsibility to the students—one which they wish to take and that allows them to receive positive attention. Such responsibilities not only fill the attention needs of the students, but also positively affect the students' relationships with the teacher and others in the classroom. If students who are aggressive, defiant, and oppositional can find ways to demonstrate their personal authority and power in productive ways, they will not need to demonstrate their power in disruptive ways.

Note that a responsibility strategy intervention is different from the more common "reinforcing appropriate behavior" strategy. In using responsibility strategies, the opportunity to perform the task should not be contingent upon appropriate behavior. Rather, the message the students need to glean from the responsibility strategy is that their responsibility is so essential for the class that they must do that task daily, even if they misbehave on any particular day. The intent here is to convince the students that (1) their task is essential, (2) their responsibility task is their contribution to the society of the class, and (3) they are meaningfully integrated into the class. Here are several examples.

Light Bulb Monitor: An Educator's Idea

Dr. Bob Brooks, who was principal of a locked-door school unit in a psychiatric hospital for difficult kids, often tells of a student who broke every light bulb he could reach within the school. All lights were fair game, and he really didn't care what disciplinary measures were used as punishment for breaking light bulbs, since he was going to break them anyway. He clearly derived a great deal of pleasure from this destructive and bizarre behavior.

To Dr. Brooks' credit, he reflected on that student's relationship to the class and the school in general. He decided to provide a positive behavioral opportunity and a responsibility for this student that was directly related to the student's interest in light bulbs. Dr. Brooks made that student the "Light Bulb Monitor" for the entire school. Dr. Brooks explained to the student that each day the student was expected to go from room to room and assure that every light bulb was working properly. If a light bulb was out, the student had the responsibility of reporting the problem to Dr. Brooks' office. Naturally, the student loved going into a room of his peers each morning, filled with his own sense of self-importance, and switching on the lights several times while the teacher checked attendance or attended to other business. His peers saw that he was given special privileges along with his unique responsibility. That peer recognition made a positive difference in this student's behavior. At the same time, this particular responsibility strategy ended the light-bulb-breaking incidents. More importantly, this student had assumed a responsibility, and was making a meaningful contribution to the school, perhaps for the first time in his life.

Reverse Role Peer Tutoring: Another Responsibility Strategy

Peer tutoring has long been shown to be an effective learning strategy. A variation described here involves role reversal and has been useful in curbing undesirable behavior. Reverse role peer tutoring is another example of providing a serious responsibility to students with behavioral problems. In reverse role peer tutoring, students with behavioral problems and other disabilities serve as tutors rather than tutees, and research over several decades has confirmed that this tactic will curb the inappropriate behavior of students with emotional problems (Maher, 1982, 1984; Tournaki & Criscitiello, 2003).

Charles Maher was among the first to develop this concept. He reported on several research studies in which adolescents with terrible behavior records were used as tutors for students with mental disabilities in lower grade levels. Initially, this tactic may seem frightening for an experienced educator. Imagine selecting a group of adolescent males who have been identified as violent or aggressive, and using them as tutors of younger students! In a very real sense, this took considerable courage because these aggressive adolescents could have victimized their younger tutees. Fortunately, the research results demonstrated just the opposite.

In several controlled studies, the behavior of the socially maladjusted students used as tutors improved dramatically, compared to another group of similar students who received only peer counseling (Maher, 1982; 1984). The number of disciplinary problems for the tutors went down, their attendance improved, and their tutoring even assisted them academically. Anecdotal notes across these studies suggested that the *responsibility* of tutoring seemed to be the deciding factor. By virtue of reverse role tutoring, these students with disabilities were seen as "leaders," a role they had rarely experienced.

Anecdotal reports on this intervention were particularly enlightening. These behavior-problem adolescents began to protect their tutees on the playground and began to relate to them as younger siblings. Clearly, reverse role tutoring gave these behavior-problem students a responsibility for others and established a meaningful connection that greatly improved their own behavior. Other studies that used students with behavior problems as tutors have had similar positive results (Lazerson, Foster, Brown, & Hummel, 1988; Tournaki & Criscitiello, 2003).

One key indicator in using a responsibility strategy is the frequency of the behavior problem. Many students act up from time to time, but when teachers or administrators have a student who demonstrates disciplinary problems frequently, one might conclude that punishment options are not working. For many male students who seem to be constantly in the principal's office for misbehavior, implementation of a responsibility strategy would be appropriate. The same is true for students who feel disconnected with the school environment or with others within that environment. In that case, the responsibility strategy is well worth considering (Blankenship & Bender, 2007).

> *Despite its atypical approach, reverse role peer tutoring has been shown to be an effective technique for curbing chronic misbehavior in students.*

This strategy should be used when teachers and administrators have exhausted all other options. In such cases, a specific set of responsibilities individually selected for the student may result in reconnecting the student emotionally to the school, establishing a basis for positive relationships, and improving behavior. The responsibility strategy is appropriate in situations where students are angry, aggressive, or oppositional. After the immediate behavioral concern is over, the teacher talks with the student about how the student can assist in the class, using his leadership skills.

Implementing a Responsibility Strategy

For students who are frequently in trouble, address an immediate behavioral disruption through other strategies because the responsibility strategy is a long-term intervention. Figure 4.4 shows the seven steps involved in implementing a responsibility strategy in your class.

Step 1. Disengage from the immediate behavior problem. Walker and Sylwester (1998) suggest that teachers disengage from the situation rather than escalate to a power struggle with the offending student. For example, inform the student in a soft voice that he (or she) will need to schedule a conference about the misbehavior. Then turn away from the student and attempt to get the other students to refocus on the class work at hand.

Step 2. Reflect on the misbehavior and gather baseline data. Next, reflect on the student's relationship with everyone in the class and school. Understanding the motivation of a student is important and one initial step for this intervention is reflecting on what actually motivates the student to misbehave. Ask yourself: "How have I invited this student to positively contribute to this class today?" This statement is phrased very carefully. Note the phrasing, "How have I invited . . .?" Has the student been *invited* to demonstrate his capabilities, talents, or leadership skills? Has he been directly and personally invited to present a positive contribution to the class?

In some cases, the answer is probably that the student has not been effectively invited to make an appropriate and meaningful contribution. This does not suggest ineffective teaching, a lack of caring, or a lack of attention to student needs. Rather, this simply reflects the reality that teachers often face: Attending to the diverse emotional and behavioral needs of 20 to 30 or more students in the class at the same time. Still, this brief reflection can motivate teachers to find ways to involve the student and to make him feel special by inviting him to contribute in a more appropriate way. Also, at this point, a baseline count of problem behaviors is begun. Generally, a minimum of five days of baseline data is recommended.

Step 1: Disengage from the immediate situation.

Step 2: Reflect on the misbehavior and gather baseline data.

Step 3: Select a contribution or responsibility.

Step 4: Consider the implications of the responsibility.

Step 5: Meet with the student to jointly choose a task.

Step 6: Discuss the responsibility with the student and principal.

Step 7: Monitor the student's behavior during the intervention.

Figure 4.4 These are the seven steps that teachers should take when implementing a responsibility strategy.

Step 3. Select a contribution or responsibility. Next, select a responsibility for the student, based on careful consideration of the student's interests, capabilities, and desires. You may wish to talk with the student about his interests. In some cases, particular misbehaviors can provide a clue to student interest, as in the case of the light bulb monitor we described earlier. Does the school need to take photographs for a particular event? Could you use someone to report gang graffiti? Might adjudicated delinquents, supervised by teachers, take some responsibility for notifying teachers about verbal fights on the playground? If planned appropriately, any of these tasks could represent an effective contribution to the school and a positive responsibility for troublesome students.

The actual task assigned for the responsibility is unimportant and almost any necessary task will serve the purpose. However, two things are critically important:

1. The student must feel that he is truly given an opportunity to contribute. In other words, the student must have impressive "bragging rights" along with the task.

2. The student must believe that the task is important to the class. He must be made to feel like he is a contributing partner in a task that he values.

Step 4. Consider the implications of the responsibility. In selecting the responsibility, consider the implications should the student choose to undertake the responsibility. This involves obvious issues such as the student's confidentiality, privacy, safety, and legal liability. For example, no student's responsibility should require that he leave the campus or get involved in physical altercations that have already begun between other students. The principal, because of training in school law and policy, should be contacted when considering responsibilities that involve students leaving the classroom. Also, supervision should always be available for any student completing his responsibility, particularly when the student is having a challenging day behaviorally.

In addition to routine supervision, remember that students may need to be more closely supervised the first few times they try out their responsibilities. In implementing the tutoring intervention described earlier, consider how and what type of training to offer the tutors. How much supervision will be necessary for those tutors, and what types of reinforcement can be offered to them? For example, do they get to leave the classroom a few minutes early to go to tutoring? Leaving the classroom takes place in front of peers and indicates a great deal of trust, thus providing substantial reinforcement, even for students with serious behavior problems. However, you should carefully consider implications of this type of responsibility in advance.

Step 5. Meet with the student to jointly choose a task. After gathering the baseline data, meet with the student and discuss the responsibility strategy options. The student should be allowed to choose which option he would like as his contribution to the class. Again, the student must feel that the task is important and that choosing it is critical to his ownership of this responsibility. Thus, you should present several choices and be prepared for a discussion which may generate others. After the discussion, you and the student select a responsibility task. The student writes a one-paragraph agreement, including a description of the task and specific statements about how it is to be done. Both you and the student sign the agreement.

Step 6. Discuss the responsibility with the student and the principal. If the student's responsibility involves duties outside of class, the intervention is discussed with the school administrator. Involving the student in this discussion will highlight the importance of the task for the student as well as inform the principal as to why the student is doing tasks around campus.

Step 7. Monitor the student's behavior during the intervention. With baseline data already collected, it is now necessary to collect data on the student's behavior during the intervention period. The data will provide an assessment of how well the responsibility strategy worked.

Why Give a Student This Responsibility?

Some teachers may question the wisdom of providing a responsibility for students who are known to frequently misbehave. Is it realistic to hope that students with a history of misbehavior will take any responsibility seriously? Surprisingly, the research cited earlier suggests that even students with fairly severe behavioral problems will take some responsibilities seriously, although the manner in which students are approached with the responsibility is crucial. If a responsibility or task is unilaterally announced to students with behavior problems, they will probably not participate willingly or actively. However, thorough reflection on the individual student and on potential responsibilities, coupled with an invitation to contribute, results in most students with behavioral problems taking and fulfilling their responsibilities seriously.

Most teachers remember being helpers around the class when they were students in school. Tasks such as dusting erasers, cleaning the blackboard or dry-erase board for teachers, and doing other classroom jobs often result in fond memories. These teachers might also remember how special, and how important and involved, those mundane tasks made them feel. Students with behavior problems in our classes today have rarely performed those jobs, because those tasks were usually reserved as privileges or rewards for good behavior. Perhaps this is one reason why the research has shown this responsibility tactic to be so effective, even with hard-core students with serious behavior problems. For some students, this might be just the ticket to turn negative behavior into positive behavior, and thereby improve the student's relationship with the teacher and with others in the class and school.

> *Research studies confirm that even students with serious behavioral problems can take and fulfill their responsibilities seriously.*

The Class Production Assistant: An Educator's Idea

Here is another example of a responsibility strategy related by Wendy Williams, a teacher at Taylor Elementary School, in Lawrenceville, Georgia.

My student, Shanta, has mild autism as well as certain overt behavior problems. Wherever he was in school, he always seemed to get into trouble. He would draw on everything within reach, turn off the CD player while I was using it during the lesson, and touch all of the levers and buttons on the school bus. Clearly, Shanta was fascinated by electronics and he loved to draw, but his behavior was inappropriate.

I decided to try several things with him to curb these behaviors. First, I made him the "Class Production Assistant" during circle time in my room. During that time, I typically play easy-listening music on the CD player and either read a story or discuss one of the lessons with the class. The musical selections I use are fairly long, and when a song ended, I made it Shanta's job to turn off the CD player. I explained to him that he would need to stop turning off the player unless the song ended, but that he could touch that button when the music stopped. As my production assistant, he gets to sit beside me in the circle, with the CD player between us, and he now automatically turns it off each time he is supposed to.

In addition, I made a personal file folder for Shanta with lots of drawing paper for him to use in his drawing. I used paper that included space for a drawing and some lines at the bottom for writing a description of the picture. Now, each day Shanta is supposed to "make book pictures" for me, and each time he draws a picture, we put it in Shanta's "picture book" (the picture book is a three-ring binder that holds all of Shanta's former pages). We call the picture book, "Shanta's Picture Book."

Finally, I showed him how to clean the room with a spray cleaner and rag (mostly cleaning the dry-erase boards in the class), and each time he gets those clean, he is offered five minutes for one of his preferred activities. He usually chooses to draw more for the picture book. He will also pick up any trash on the floor around the room because he knows he will get the reward at the end. I've let him know that these things are very important for our whole class and that no one else has the right to earn time for their preferred activity by cleaning the room. These strategies worked for Shanta, and he has gone from being very disruptive to being a real sweetie. Now I really enjoy having him in the class.

Giving responsibility to misbehaving boys may seem odd, but there are many situations where this approach can be successful.

And What About Girls?

We made clear at the beginning of this chapter that many of the strategies used here could be readily adapted for use with girls who misbehave. We also explained that a girl's brain is different in some ways from a boy's brain, especially in the early development of communication skills. Consequently, girls are more likely to settle disputes verbally rather than physically. It takes a lot to provoke most females to physically attack another female. But when the anger level gets to the breaking point, the confrontation can be extremely vicious and result in serious injury.

Disciplining girls will probably be more effective when the approach takes into account gender differences. When using strategies to address misbehavior in girls, including those in this chapter, consider adapting them with the following thoughts in mind:

- **Talk it over.** Girls' language and communication skills develop faster than boys. They also have more brain regions involved in language processing and are very good at it. As a result, they are more apt to talk about what provoked them to misbehave. Encourage them to discuss whether they understand the consequences of their actions and what would be appropriate steps to take to curb that behavior in the future.
- **Focus on feelings.** We noted earlier in this chapter that female brains are more attuned to how others feel and are better at empathizing. Ask the girl to think about how her misbehavior made others feel, and how she would feel if the misbehavior were directed toward her.
- **Shift to perception.** After talking about her feelings, shift to discussing how others perceive her. Females are more sensitive than males to what others think about them. Describe how her misbehavior may negatively affect what other students think of her.
- **Use delayed gratification.** Females are better than males at yielding to delayed gratification. Discussing a potential future reward may be enough to moderate or eliminate her misbehavior.

When educators have a deep understanding of how boys' and girls' brains differ, they can make more informed decisions about which strategies are likely to be effective for dealing with misbehavior.

THE RISE OF CYBERBULLYING

It may seem odd at first glance to include this topic here. But put simply, boys are more apt to be school bullies than girls. And bullying of all types is becoming a major and persistent problem in schools. Much has been written about bullying in recent years and many Internet resources are available to help teachers, administrators, and parents deal with the issue. Our purpose here is not to deal much with traditional bullying. Rather, we want to raise awareness of how technology has raised bullying to a new and insidious level and to suggest some actions that schools can take to prevent it.

Bullying Versus Cyberbullying

Educators have been concerned with bullying for a long time. But a new threat has emerged in recent years as an increasing number of students gain access to cell phones, personal digital assistants (PDAs), and the Internet. This threat, called *cyberbullying,* is the intentional and repeated harm inflicted on someone through electronic devices. Believing they are anonymous, cyberbullies engage in cruel and harmful actions that embarrass and demean fellow students without fear of discovery or facing the consequences for their behavior. Some students have committed suicide because they could not take the harassment any longer. Because the problem occurs in the hidden online world, its effects can be similar to, but also different from, traditional bullying. Table 4.2 compares traditional bullying with cyberbullying.

Bullying is often categorized as direct and indirect. Common forms of direct cyberbullying include denigration, exclusion, harassment, and masquerading. Denigration occurs most frequently by students against school employees, usually teachers and administrators. Angry students may establish a Web site to ridicule their victim and post harmful, untrue, or cruel statements. The primary purpose is to damage the victim's reputation. Online exclusion occurs when victims are rejected by their peer group and omitted from technological communications with the group. A victim of harassment may receive persistent hurtful or offensive messages through various forms

Table 4.2 Comparison of Traditional Bullying With Cyberbullying

	Traditional Bullying	**Cyberbullying**
Description	Can be categorized as direct or indirect. Direct bullying is more physical than indirect and includes shoving, hitting, verbally threatening, tripping, and stabbing. Both direct and indirect bullying include spreading rumors, blackmailing, and excluding from a group.	Can be both direct and indirect. Flaming is an indirect form that consists of an argument between two people that includes rude and vulgar language, threats, and insults. Direct forms include denigration, excluding, and harassment.
Extent of problem	Nearly one-half of middle/junior high school students report being victims of traditional bullying.	About one-fourth of middle/junior high school students report being victims of cyberbullying.
Gender differences	Male bullies are likely to engage in direct bullying, while female bullies are likely to engage in indirect bullying.	Males are more likely to be cyberbullies than females, although the gap is much narrower than in traditional bullying. Female cyberbully victims are more likely to inform adults than their male counterparts.
Identification	The bully intentionally and repeatedly harms individuals or groups through power, age, and physical strength. Identifying the bully is usually easy.	The cyberbully may hide in anonymity, making identification more difficult. This anonymity also raises the fear factor.
Effect on victims	Victims experience academic, personal, and social problems, including withdrawal and depression.	Victims often withdraw from school activities, and become ill, depressed, and suicidal.

Sources: Chibbaro, 2007; Crawford, 2002; Li, 2006; Quiroz, Arnette, & Stephens, 2006; and Willard, 2006.

of technology. Masquerading is pretending to be someone else and sending material that makes that person look bad or puts that person in danger.

Cyberbullies who are often overlooked are the "social climber bullies." These bullies are upper social class students who bully within the context of the "in-crowd," teasing those who want to be part of the in-crowd (the wannabes) and insulting those who are excluded from the in-crowd (the losers). They are overlooked because they are looked upon with favor by teachers and administrators. Furthermore, the losers and the wannabes don't report the cyberbullying to school personnel because to do so would bring retaliation to the losers and ruin the wannabes chances of gaining their desired social status (Willard, 2006). Cyberbullying victims, in general, are often reluctant to tell adults because they fear the bullying will become more intense and they worry that the adults will take away their access to the communications technology.

Dealing With Cyberbullying

Schools must develop strategies for preventing and intervening in cyberbullying that should include the following (Beale & Hall, 2007; Chibbaro, 2007; Harris & Petrie, 2003; Ribble & Bailey, 2006; Willard, 2006):

- There should be a clear, updated written policy stating that all forms of cyberspace harassment, both during and after school hours, will not be tolerated. Many schools have adopted an Accepted Use Policy (AUP). Some secondary schools have integrated a short curriculum unit that teaches students about how to use technology appropriately. Components include etiquette, responsibility, rights, safety, and security. The instruction is designed to make the students technologically literate and give them an understanding of proper use through guided practice and modeling.
- A range of punishments should be in place for cyberbullies, including loss of computer privileges, detention, suspension, and expulsion. In some areas, law enforcement authorities may need to be notified.
- Students should have a means of reporting cyberbullying anonymously.
- School personnel should carry out awareness campaigns to alert teachers, students, and parents about cyberbullying. Because cyberbullying frequently occurs away from school, parents should be reminded to monitor their child's online activities. The Center for Safe and Responsible Internet Use has published a parents' guide to cyberbullying and cyber threats. See the **Resources** section for more information on this site.
- Ask the local police department if they have cyber experts who can speak to parents and students about proper Internet use.
- Conduct professional development workshops so that teachers and administrators can be trained in the nature of cyberbullying and its effects, how to respond if it is detected, and how to report it.

- Student training should include learning how to identify cyberbullying at school and away from school, providing students methods of reporting it, and discussing school policy.
- Increase supervision of school areas where cyberbullying is likely to occur.
- Counseling and support programs should be in place for both the victim and the cyberbully. Victims could be offered training in developing a more positive self-concept, increasing assertiveness skills, reducing social isolation, and practicing behaviors that will reduce the risk of further victimization. Bullies could be counseled and trained in improving their self-concept, recognizing the legal and personal consequences of cyberbullying, increasing social problem-solving, developing anger management skills, and increasing the ability to empathize with their victims.

Despite the convenience of communications technology, its misuse by students creates new challenges for teachers, administrators, and parents. Cyberbullying is on the increase. Thus, school personnel must take all the necessary steps to design and implement prevention and intervention programs that protect students from the negative effects of cyberbullying.

SUMMARY

Differences in biology and brain structures between the two genders lead to differences in their behavior. These differences become apparent in social environments such as schools. Females tend to be more socially aware, communicative, and likely to resolve conflict through language rather than physical aggression. Males, on the other hand, tend to be more physically aggressive, mobile, and protective of their personal space than females. When teachers understand the nature of these gender differences, they can select strategies that are more likely to be successful in curbing the misbehaviors of males in the classroom.

Thus, by using movement (perhaps coupled with music or chants), appropriate reading materials emphasizing clear hero roles, and responsibility tactics that allow students opportunities to "show off" for good behavior, teachers can reach the young males in their classes and, at the same time, make the class a much more enjoyable place for all.

The threat of cyberbullying is real, and schools need to develop programs to curb and eliminate its negative effects on the school community.

Summary

By now, you should have developed an awareness of the importance of a consistent approach to behaviour management and begun to feel more confident about your role in managing pupils' behaviour. Thinking again about the overarching themes of this book – Communication, Innovation and Participation – we can draw links to the importance of using dialogue and the language of positive praise to pre-empt possible behaviour issues; listening for clues and cues to divert and distract children's attention. You should be on the lookout for innovative and active lessons which engage pupils therefore helping to prevent inappropriate behaviours from arising. Variety and change will enliven your lessons for yourselves and your pupils. Developing individual relationships with all pupils will ensure that you can develop a good understanding of individual and group dynamics as well as identifying potential triggers for behaviour. Knowing which strategies will work for who is dependent upon a good rapport with all members of your class – children need to feel valued and supported regardless of their behaviour and ability – your job will be to recognize this and realize that 'one size does not fit all'. Adapt and accommodate!

Student activities

- On your next teaching placement obtain and read a copy of the school's behaviour management policy and summarize its key points. How is it applied in practice? Are you adhering to this policy consistently across every phase? Which strategies do you find effective and ineffective for you, personally?
- Examine the behaviour of one child in detail – how do they respond to different behaviour management strategies? Can you identify any triggers? What motivates them?
- Think of a child you have taught/observed who consistently displayed inappropriate behaviours. Try to consider possible factors affecting these behaviours. What are the reasons for their poor behaviour? How could this be managed effectively?
- Write the names of a number of children that you have taught or observed on individual post it notes. Rank them in order of levels of motivation. Why do you think these children are in these positions? Think about all the potential contextual factors which may influence their position in the ranking? Do they change position dependent on subject, area of learning or activity type?

Top tips

- Establish routines for behaviour management from the first day.
- Begin to think about your 'teacher persona' – be aware of tone of voice, body language and eye contact.
- Be well prepared.
- Have a clear system of rewards and sanctions that are personalized, meaningful and age appropriate and be consistent in their application.

- Establish a positive classroom ethos where pupils feel confident and valued, able to try, fail and succeed on their learning journey without fear of retribution or ridicule. All pupils need to feel that their contributions, feelings and opinions are valued.
- Prevention is better than cure with regards to behaviour – use non-verbal cues, tactical ignoring and distraction.

Additional readings

Year One and Two
Belvel, P. and Jordan, M. (2002) *Rethinking Classroom Management*. California: Corwin Press Inc.
DfES (2003) Primary National Strategy *Developing Children's Social, Emotional and Behavioural Skills*. HMSO: Department for Education and Skills.
Dreikurs, R. (1972) *Discipline Without Tears*. Hawthorn Books.
Galvin, P. (1999) *Behaviour and Discipline in Schools*. London: Fulton.
Glasser, W. (1990) *The Quality School*. New York: Harper Row.
Goleman, D. (1998) *Working with Emotional Intelligence*. London: Bloomsbury.
Higgs, M . and Dulewicz, V. (1999) *Making Sense of Emotional Intelligence*. Berkshire: NFER.
Maslow, A. H. (1954) *Motivation and Personality*. New York: Harper Row.
Metcalf, L. (1995) *Counselling Towards Solutions*. New York: Centre for Applied Research in Education.
Rogers,W. (2000) *Classroom Behaviour*. London: Books Education.
Sharp, P. (2001) *Nurturing Emotional Literacy*. London: Fulton.
Weare, K. (2004) *Developing the Emotionally Literate School*. London: Paul Chapman Publishing

Year Three [B]
Hayes, D. (2012) 'Managing Classroom Discipline', Chapter 12 in *Foundations of Primary Teaching*. 5th edn. London: Routledge.
Pollard. A., Anderson J., Maddock M., Swaffield S., Warin J. and Warwick P. (2008) 'Behaviour: How are we managing the class?', Chapter 11 in *Reflective Teaching*, 3rd edn. London: Continuum.

PGCE
Hayes, D. (2008) Chapter 8 in *Foundations of Primary Teaching*, 4th edn. London: Routledge.
Arthur, J. and Cremin, T. (2010) Chapters 3 and 4 in *Learning to Teach in the Primary School*, 2nd edn. London: Routledge.

Early Years
Adams, K. (2009) Chapters 1 and 2 in *Behaviour for Learning in the Primary School*. Exeter. Learning Matters.
Dreikurs, F. (2004) *Discipline Without Tears: How to Reduce Conflict and Establish Co-operation in the Classroom*. Chichester: John Wiley.
Gerhardt, S. (2004) *Why Love Matters: How Affection Shapes a Baby's Brain*. Hove, Sussex: Brunner Routledge.
Papatheodorou, I. (2005) *Behaviour Problems in the Early Years: A Guide for Understanding and Support*. Abingdon: Routledge Falmer. Read Part 1, Understanding Behaviour Problems, pp.1–46.

PART 7 | SPECIAL EDUCATIONAL NEEDS, DIVERSITY AND INCLUSION

Overview

In this part you will be given an introduction to the concept of Special Educational Needs (SEN) and what the implications are throughout the UK for you as practitioners. Hodkinson and Vickerman will begin by contextualizing the term SEN within the primary classroom. You will then be given an overview of the term inclusion and what this looks like in practice with a view to 'becoming an inclusive teacher'.

The following chapters cover a wide range of special educational needs as well as issues that children in your classroom may face. These include EAL and bilingual learners; race, culture and ethnicity, traveler children, refugees and asylum seekers (LAC) and gifted and talented pupils.

A key area when looking at issues of diversity and inclusion is the role of other professionals and parents which is looked at in the wider context and their role in supporting children to develop as learners.

This part concludes with a chapter on how to create an inclusive learning environment which aims to give you ideas on how to accommodate the needs of all learners.

Introduction to Special Educational Needs

41

Hodkinson, A. and Vickerman, P.

This chapter will introduce you to the concept of SEN. It will include definitions of SEN and special needs and will outline the scale of the issue in England and Wales. It will also provide you with a number of case studies which will help you to develop a better understanding of these key concepts. The final section of the chapter suggests additional reading and offers practical activities that will further develop your knowledge and understanding of SEN and inclusion.

DEFINING SEN IN ENGLAND

A child has special educational needs if he has a learning difficulty which calls for special educational provision to be made for him. A child, for the purposes of the SEN provisions, includes any person under the age of 19 who is a registered pupil at a school. (Education Act 1996 [DfEE, 1996] and SENDA, 2001 [DfES, 2001b, section 312])

Following a formal assessment under section 323 of the 1996 Education Act, a local authority may issue a Statement of Educational Needs. This is a legal document which describes the SEN of the child and states how these needs will be met.

The term SEN was coined by the Warnock Report of the late 1970s (DES, 1978). Previously, children had been labelled by employing ten categories of 'handicap' as set out in the regulations of the 1944 Education Act (DoE, 1944) (see Chapter 4).

The ten categories of 'handicap' as defined by the 1944 Education Act were:

- blind
- partially sighted
- deaf
- delicate
- diabetic
- educationally subnormal
- epileptic
- maladjusted
- physically handicapped
- speech defect.

The Warnock Report in 1978 (DES, 1978), followed by the 1981 Education Act (DES, 1981), radically altered the conceptualisation of special education by emphasising that a child's educational need should be prioritised first and not their individual learning disability or impairment. Today, in the context of educational provision, the term SEN has a legal definition which refers to children who have learning difficulties or disabilities that make it more difficult for them to learn or access education than most children of the same age.

In terms of current government legislation children require special educational provision if they:

- have a significantly greater difficulty in learning that the majority of children their age
- have a disability which either prevents or hinders them from making use of educational facilities of a kind generally provided in schools
- are under the age of five years and are (or if special educational provision were not made for them) likely to fall within either of the above sections when over that age
- are over two years of age and receive educational provision which is additional to, or different from, provision made generally for children of the same age in local schools; or
- are under the age of two years and receive educational provision of any kind. (DfEE, 1996)

The 1996 Education Act (DfEE, 1996) offers guidance that is intended to help teachers and other professionals make accurate decisions in relation to deciding whether a child has a SEN or not. For example, the law states that children do not have a SEN if they have a learning difficulty because of the language or form of language of their home background. In addition, under the terms of the Act, pupils who are considered to be gifted or talented, or very able, would not be classed as having a SEN either, unless they had an associated learning difficulty. Furthermore, section 7:52 of the Special Educational Needs Code of Practice (DFES, 2001a) provides practical advice to local authorities, maintained schools and Early Years education settings on how to identify, assess and make provision for children's SEN. The Code of Practice recognises that there are no hard and fast categories of SEN and that there is a wide spectrum of SEN that are frequently inter-related. The Code does however indicate that a child's needs and requirements may fall into at least one of four areas:

- communication and interaction
- cognition and learning
- behaviour, emotional and social development
- sensory and/or physical.

To enable the government to collect detailed information on a child's educational requirements a broad set of categories is employed, which define types of SEN and special need. These categories sub-divide into:

(A) Cognition and Learning Needs

- Specific Learning Difficulty (SpLD)
- Moderate Learning Difficulty (MLD)
- Severe Learning Difficulty (SLD)
- Profound and Multiple Learning Difficulty (PMLD).

(B) Behaviour, Emotional and Social Development Needs

- Behaviour, Emotional and Social Difficulty (BESD).

(C) Communication and Interaction Needs

- Speech, Language and Communication Needs (SLCN)
- Autistic Spectrum Disorder (ASD).

(D) Sensory and/or Physical Needs

- Visual Impairment (VI)
- Hearing Impairment (HI)
- Multi-sensory Impairment (MSI)
- Physical Disability (PD).

Defining Special Educational Needs

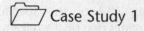 Case Study 1

Specific learning difficulties

Asif is an eleven year old child who is a pupil in a Year 6 class in a small rural primary school. He is a very articulate child who is a well liked member of the class. Asif, however, has difficulties in any activities that involve reading, writing, or spelling. Despite several attempts Asif's teacher has been unable to help him make progress with his school work. Recently, Asif has become more and more frustrated with his inability to keep up with the rest of the class, especially in his English lessons. In light of Asif's continuing difficulties he was referred to an educational psychologist for an assessment of his needs. After completing several tests the educational psychologist detailed that Asif was some 36 months behind in his spelling and reading ability compared to that which might be expected for a child of his age. It is interesting to note that, when questioned, Asif's father stated that he had had similar difficulties with his English work when he was at school.

In terms of government legislation it may be observed that Asif will require SEN provision because he has a 'significantly greater difficulty in learning' than other children of the same age. If we examine the categories box on page 5 above we can see that Asif's needs would be considered under Section A (those of cognition and learning) and that his SEN would be described as a specific learning difficulty.

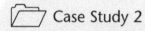 Case Study 2

Behaviour, emotional and social development needs

Natasha is a five year old pupil who is a member of a reception class in a large urban primary school. Natasha is very immature for her age and as a result has found difficulty in making friends. She is often to be found playing by herself both in the classroom and in the school playground. Unlike the other pupils Natasha has found difficulty learning to sit still and is also unable to share toys with other people.

Although Natasha is mainly well-behaved there are periods during the day when she exhibits challenging behaviour. These outbursts are intense and severe and they often disrupt the learning of the other class members. During these outbursts Natasha has tantrums and displays physical aggression towards other pupils and teaching staff. When she does not get her own way she will fall to the ground and scream loudly. Despite the best efforts of the teachers and her parents the school has been unable to improve Natasha's behaviour.

Natasha is presenting with significant behaviour and emotional difficulties which are a barrier to learning. In terms of the legislation, Natasha's behaviour is so severe that she would be classified as having a SEN.

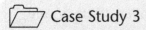 Case Study 3

Sensory needs

Joanne is a very happy, polite and well motivated pupil who is due to sit her GCSEs next year. She has a very wide circle of friends and is often to be found at the centre of any playground games. She is an avid reader and likes nothing better than reading her favourite stories to her friends. She is an extremely well liked pupil and her teachers had expected her to do very well in her forthcoming exams. However, recently Joanne's handwriting had become very untidy and she was becoming increasingly slower at copying work from the board during lessons. Her teachers had also noticed that she been finding it more and more difficult to navigate around the school. At a recent hospital assessment Joanne was found to have a deteriorating eye condition. With this knowledge the school has begun to make adaptations both to Joanne's classroom and to her curriculum. The teachers have made sure that she always sits at the front of the class in lessons that involve reading from the board. They have also provided Joanne with large print books and with these she has rediscovered her love of reading.

For the purposes of the Code of Practice (DfES, 2001a) Joanne would be classified as having a SEN that is sensory in nature. This is because her deteriorating eyesight is adversely affecting her ability to learn and her educational progress is therefore being restricted because of this.

SEN in Scotland, Northern Ireland and Wales

Within the United Kingdom the educational provision for children with learning difficulties broadly operates under similar legislative systems, although England and Wales are perhaps closest in terms of the operation of their legal and organisational systems. It is important to remember, however, that aspects of the Northern Ireland and especially the Scottish system can differ substantially from those observed within English schools. Whilst this book will mainly focus on England and Wales it will, when relevant, make reference to those systems currently operating within Northern Ireland and Scotland.

For further, and more detailed, information on the organisation of SEN support in Scotland, Northern Ireland and Wales, you will need to access the following links:

Scottish Executive
www.scotland.gov.uk/Publications/Recent

Northern Ireland Department of Education
www.deni.gov.uk/index/7-special_educational_needs_pg.htm

Welsh Assembly
http.//wales.gov.uk/topics/educationandskills/policy_strategy_and_
planning/ schools/127044211-wag/%3Flang%3Den

Scotland

Until fairly recently, special education in Scotland was governed by a legal framework established within the Education (Scotland) Act 1980 as amended by the 1981 Act. These acts organised SEN provision in a broadly similar way to that observed in England. However, in 2005 the legal framework in Scotland substantially changed with the implementation of the Education (Additional Support for Learning) (Scotland) Act 2004, as this abolished the employment of the term SEN and replaced it with a much broader definition – that of 'additional support need'. Additional support need, as defined by the Act, refers to any child or young person who would benefit from extra help in order to overcome barriers to their learning.

The Act stipulates that some children and young people may require additional support for a variety of reasons, such as those who:

- have motor or sensory impairments
- are being bullied
- are particularly able or talented
- have experienced a bereavement
- are looked after in social care surroundings
- have learning difficulty
- are living with parents who are abusing substances
- are living with parents who have mental health problems
- have English as an additional language
- are not attending school regularly
- have emotional or social difficulties
- are on the child protection register
- are young carers.

Northern Ireland

The organisation of special educational provision, and the definition of SEN employed in Northern Ireland, are similar to those which operate within England. Special education in Northern Ireland is governed by the legal framework established within the Education (Northern Ireland) Order 1996 as amended by the SEN and Disability (Northern Ireland) Order 2005 (DoE, 2005). These orders place a statutory duty for the provision for children with SEN upon the education and library boards and the boards of governors within mainstream schools. SENDO (DoE, 2005) increased the rights of children with SEN to attend mainstream schools and, for the first time, introduced disability discrimination laws for the whole of the education system in Northern Ireland. Similar to Scotland, Wales and England, the Department for Employment and Learning in Northern Ireland offers advice and guidance on how to operate a system for identifying and assessing children with learning difficulties. This guidance is contained within a Code of Practice which came into effect in Northern Ireland on the 1 September 2005.

Wales

The organisation of special educational provision in Wales and the definition of SEN are exactly the same as those which are to be found in England. The legal framework for the provision of special education is governed by the Education (SEN) (Wales) Regulations 2002. Wales, however, does have its own Code of Practice which became operational on the 1 of November 2001 and schools have had to observe this since April 2002. The Welsh Assembly has also provided additional advice to teachers and local authorities on how to operate the SEN Code of Practice for Wales, with a handbook entitled 'Good Practice for Children with SEN'.

SEN – The Scale of the Issue

In 1978, the Warnock Report (DES, 1978) initially estimated that as many as 20 per cent of children, during their time at school, might experience a SEN that would necessitate additional educational provision to be made. The report also estimated that around 2 per cent of all children and young people of school age may have an educational need that was so severe that they would require a Statement of Educational Need. Nearly thirty years later, data from the Department of Education and Skills (DfES, 2007a) continue to show that approximately one in five children is currently identified as having a difficulty with learning that requires extra help to be given in class (see Chapter 7 for a further analysis of the legislation). The data also reveal that the figure of 2 per cent initially provided by the Warnock Committee in relation to children who would require a Statement vastly underestimated the numbers of children and young people who would need the highest level of special educational provision.

In 2007, government data (DCSF, 2008) indicated that 16.4 per cent of all pupils had a SEN and that an additional 2.8 per cent also had a learning difficulty that was so severe that they would require the provision of a statement (see Figures 1.1 and 1.2 following). These data represent an increase of 15.7 per cent in the incidence of SEN over the previous year. Additionally, in 2007,

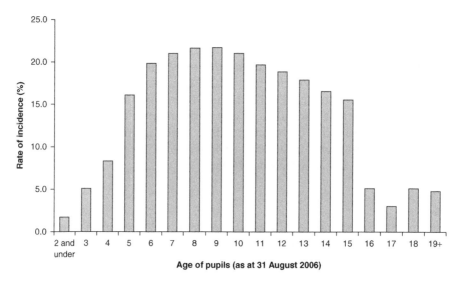

Figure 1.1 Rate of incidence of pupils with SEN without statements in maintained primary and secondary schools: January 2007 (DCSF, 2008)

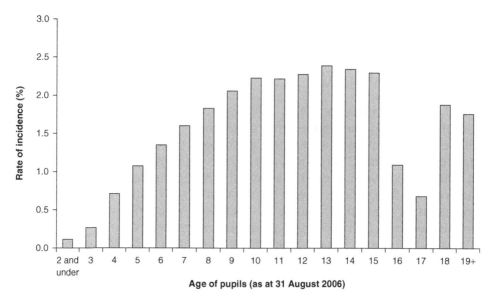

Figure 1.2 Rate of incidence of pupils with statements of SEN in maintained and secondary schools: January 2007 (DCSF, 2008)

there were 1,293,000 children of school age who had a SEN, and 229,100 had a Statement of SEN (DCSF, 2008).

Government data (DCSF, 2008) also indicated that the incidence of children with SEN who did not require a Statement was higher in primary schools (17.7 per cent) than it was in secondary schools (16.2 per cent). Furthermore, it was interesting to note that the incidence of SEN was greater for males (1 in 5) than for females (1 in 8). Moreover, in 2007, nearly 95,000 males had a Statement (1 in 40) as opposed to 35,800 females (1 in 100). An overview of the data also revealed that the majority of statements in mainstream primary schools were categorised within the area of speech, language and communication (23 per cent) and within secondary and special schools around 25 per cent of the statements issued were maintained, by local authorities, for children who had moderate learning difficulties.

- A mainstream school is one that provides an education for all pupils, including those with SEN and disabilities.
- A special school is normally one that provides an education for some children who have a Statement of SEN.

SEN – A Contested Concept

In relation to individual children and the implementation of government legislation deciding what is, or is not, a learning difficulty and what counts, or does not count, as a SEN can be difficult. For example, Terzi (2005) argues that the concept of SEN itself is theoretically difficult to specify and in practice is unworkable. Indeed, OFSTED (2004), in its review of special educational provision, found wide variations both within local authorities and within schools themselves in the numbers of children specified as having a SEN. It is also interesting to note that their investigations revealed an inconsistency as to how SEN were defined within schools in England. Moreover, OFSTED expressed a concern that some schools were employing the term SEN to refer to those children who simply displayed low attainment or were 'below average' on their entry to school. It thereby seems apparent that for some schools SEN are not defined solely in relation to children who have a learning difficulty.

In recent years, it has also become apparent that educational professionals have been subject to increasing difficulties and confusion in establishing the differences between disability/special needs and the definition of SEN itself (see Education and Skills Committee, 2006). A child, for example, may have a special need but might not actually have a SEN in terms of the 1996 Education Act. Additionally, it might be the case that a child has a SEN but might not have a special need or disability in terms of the Special Educational Needs and Disability Act (DfES, 2001b) or the Disability and Discrimination

Act (DDA, 2005). Many people do confuse SEN and special needs and this can result in serious consequences (Frederickson and Cline, 2002). For example, this form of confusion may lead to low expectations of achievement for all children whose first language is not English. In addition, difficulties in defining special needs and SEN may lead to confusion in planning educational support; for example, expecting the same staff to have an expertise in teaching English as a second language as well as teaching children with reading difficulties (Frederickson and Cline, 2002).

Special Needs or Special Educational Needs?

> A child has a special need if they 'come from a social group whose circumstances or background are different from most of the school population'. (Frederickson and Cline, 2002: 36)

A special need may relate to any child, at any time, during their school career. So, for example, a child could have a special need if they have emotional or physical challenges not normally experienced by their peers; or if they have a history of physical abuse; or if they are a member of a religious or cultural group. The key difference between this concept and that of SEN is that a special need does not necessarily manifest itself as a barrier to learning. As such, a child with a special need would not normally need access to SEN as detailed within the 1996 Act.

 Reader Reflection: Special Need or Special Educational Needs?

Using the information given in each of the case studies below and the detail offered above in relation to special provision, decide if each child has a SEN, a special need, or both.

Case Study 1

Ben (aged 10) employs a wheelchair to aid his mobility around his school. He enjoys learning about history but he does not like having to learn his times tables in his numeracy lessons.

Case Study 2

Maria (aged 12) migrated to England with her family a month ago. She has a hearing impairment and has had difficulty in learning English in the time she has been in school.

Case Study 3

Paula (aged 10) really enjoys primary school. She always comes first in the class in any test that her teachers set. Paula does though sometimes find it difficult to complete her homework because she is the main carer for her mother who has a disability.

In examining the cases studies above you may have found that defining special needs and SEN can be a difficult thing to do.

In the first case study, Ben would be considered as having a special need because of his reduced mobility. Yet while he might not enjoy his 'times tables', this would not be classified as being a barrier to his ability to learn.

In the second case study, Maria presents quite a different and rather interesting case, as she perhaps could have a special need as a result of being from a minority cultural group. In terms of the 1996 Act, though, Maria's employment of English as a second language would not constitute a SEN. What is interesting here is that Maria's inability to learn English is being complicated by her hearing impairment. If you examine the categories box on page 5, it is clear that a hearing impairment would indeed be considered to be a SEN.

In Case Study 3, Paula clearly has no issues with learning in class, indeed, she often comes first in any test that the teacher sets. Paula's home background, though, means that she is often distracted from her homework because she is the main carer for her disabled mother. While in this case Paula does not have a SEN, she is however still subject to a special need.

A further issue with the employment of the term SEN is that it has been argued that the definition itself is negatively linked with a medical view of disability. Terzi (2005) suggests that the concept of SEN is inscribed within the medical model of disability, and rather than moving away from the notion of categorising children as Warnock (DES, 1978) envisaged in reality it does nothing more than introduce a new category – that of SEN! As such, any difficulty a child may have with learning may be seen by the professionals involved as resulting from personal deficit and difference and not from the barriers created by such things as inaccessible buildings, inflexible curricula, inappropriate teaching and learning approaches and school organisation and policies (we will discuss these ideas more fully in Chapter 2). This form of labelling, it has been suggested, is not only disrespectful and hurtful to the individual child but also has repercussions for the manner in which their learning is supported (CSIE, 2005). Despite these arguments it is important to remember that the term SEN has, within the context of the English and Welsh educational systems, a legal status, and that as such it is a term that is commonly employed in the vast majority of state and independent schools.

Conclusion

Within this chapter the definition of SEN was considered in terms of the legislation that governs England, Scotland, Northern Ireland and Wales. The difficulties professionals sometimes have in deciding whether a child has a special need or a SEN were also discussed. The final section of the chapter determined how many children in England and Wales were considered to have a SEN and how these figures showed that males have a greater prevalence of SEN than do females.

 Student Activities

1. With another student, discuss the definition of SEN as outlined in this chapter. Use the internet to contrast and compare definitions of SEN in England and Wales with those available in other European countries.
2. Read section 9 of the Education and Skill Committee Inquiry into SEN memorandum evidence submitted by the Centre for Studies on Inclusive Education (see CSIE – September 2005). Make a list of the reasons why the CSIE disagrees with the employment of the term SEN. (Document available at http://inclusion.uwe.ac.uk/csie/campaigns.htm)

 Suggested Further Reading

Clough, P. and Garner, P. (2003) 'Special Educational Needs and inclusive education: Origins and current issues'. In S. Bartlett and D. Burton (eds), *Education Studies: Essential Issues*. London: Sage. pp. 72–93.
   The first few pages of this chapter offer a good overview of what is actually meant by the term SEN.

DfES (2001) *Special Educational Needs: A Guide for Parents and Carers*. (Available at www.teachernet.gove.uk/_doc/3755/Parents%20Guide.pdf).
   Pages 1–5 of this text offer a concise but wide ranging discussion of the definition of SEN.

Early Identification

Mathieson, K.

> Working in partnership with parents is something which needs to be worked at and continually developed as a two-way relationship. Observation and assessment procedures can be used effectively to meet all children's needs. Using structured 'can do' statements can provide a positive starting point for realistic target setting. The adult role is crucial and needs to be planned for in as much detail as the next steps.

What do we mean by early identification?

Early identification and early intervention for children with additional or special needs are talked about a lot these days, but I'm not sure we are always clear about what we mean by either phrase. In order to help all children make the most of their learning opportunities it is the role of the adults who care for them to look for ways to help make it easier for them to make sense of the world around them. In the first instance, at home parents care for, spend time with and provide interesting activities for children. These activities of talking to babies, showing them toys, tuning in to their needs, likes and dislikes are very important in supporting future learning. Parents are the adults who know individual children best and are their first educators. All children develop at different rates and in different ways. For example, we don't all walk or talk at the same age. However, generally speaking there are stages of development which roughly map out a child's progress in those early years. The Birth to Three Framework (Sure Start, 2002) gives good indications of the developmental progress of young children. All practitioners working in day nurseries and pre-schools will also have their training in child development to guide their view of children's development. As well as this general knowledge it is important that we use our knowledge of the individual child to identify progress and ways to help. One of the best ways to make sure that this view is accurate for each child we are working with is to share our evidence and thoughts with parents from day one of our involvement with the child. By working alongside parents from day one we gradually build up a picture together of the children as individuals and personalities. We can then plan together to use the children's developing interests and skills to help them explore and learn from the environment around them.

To enable this positive and proactive relationship with parents it is useful to review the information we provide for parents before their child joins us. Whatever we provide leads the parents to have expectations of what we can offer to them and their child as well as the way we will react to both them and their child. Sometimes it is helpful to decide as a staff group what impression you would like to make on parents during that first communication. Once you have agreed your priorities you can then improve your current information and contact with parents by focusing on how to communicate your priorities. Every opportunity you can find to get feedback from parents, both those who go on to place their child with you and those who decide not to, will help you to ensure that your setting is welcoming to your local community. Inviting parents into your setting for a variety of reasons and at a variety of times will help to keep you in touch with their views about your setting and support the continuation of positive relationships. It is such a powerful message for children to see their parents and caregivers from the setting working and communicating together in a positive way.

This establishment of an open, positive relationship with parents which is developed through mutual care and interest in the child is the most supportive context for a child's learning and development. In the context of this relationship it is possible to celebrate achievements, identify next steps for learning and share evidence of achievement. You may not always agree on every issue, but you have a context in which to have a professional and purposeful discussion with the mutual goal of the child's best interests at the centre of the relationship.

Good practice in early years settings is based on observation, assessment and planning for children's learning experiences. Good practitioners are able to evidence children's current learning and to link this evidence with planning for the child's next steps in learning. Clear systems are in place to document the observations for individual children and the ways in which their learning experiences are being supported. Sharing this information and talking through how and why decisions have been made ensures that parents have confidence in the practitioners caring for their child. It also helps to link opportunities for learning at home with current next steps in the setting. Sharing information about the child's responses to situations, new toys, relationships, etc. at home and at the setting can help parents and practitioners to celebrate and problem solve together as appropriate. In order to make this effective the routines in the setting need to be flexible enough to provide place and time for sharing information, ideas and concerns. Making such discussions a regular and frequent part of the child's and parents' experience of your setting helps to confirm confidence in the fact that everyone is working together for the child's best interests and that even if things are not going as smoothly as we would like, we can work together to suggest and try different ways to help.

As information about the child's achievements and development builds up, a pattern will begin to emerge about the personality and likes and dislikes the child has in a variety of contexts. This will build from special toys, music, ways of being cuddled as a baby through to ways in which the child communicates their needs and wants. Finding out about the child's communication and being able to identify their needs quickly and effectively will help to ensure that the child will feel secure and relaxed with you. Checking out this information and sharing this knowledge and understanding with colleagues makes sure that everyone has the opportunity to respond consistently and supportively to the child even if their keyworker is not present.

Which of your children prefer to learn outside?

From this bank of knowledge and information, the adults involved will begin to predict how children will react in certain situations. They will develop shared expectations of what children will like as an activity, preferred ways of communicating if they don't want something and who they will like to be with at a particular time.

There is sometimes a feeling that if we don't voice our concern about a child's progress, then we won't need to do anything about it; if it is that important, someone else will do something about it. This view usually comes from either uncertainty about what to do or fear and anxiety about the reaction we may get from parents. The easiest ways to counteract these barriers are to have frequent conversations with colleagues about different concerns which are identified, clarify the procedures in the setting which need to be followed if you have a concern, and most importantly to attend local training. By attending local training as an individual you will become more confident and knowledgeable about the local support and advice which is available and how this support can be accessed.

The fear and anxiety which is experienced by practitioners with regards to talking to parents about concerns relating to children's progress can be broken down on an individual and setting level. On an individual level it is a significant part of our role in caring for children to establish and maintain positive relationships with all parents. Inevitably there will be some parents with whom we find this easier than with others but by taking on the professional role of working in childcare we must accept the responsibility to take the lead in the relationship with parents, for the benefit of the children in our care. The characteristics of this relationship are crucial and need to be regularly reviewed with opportunity for feedback from parents about ways in which we can improve. To be effective the relationship needs to be based on professional priorities. Being friends might make things easier on a day-to-day basis but can mean that we find it harder to initiate more difficult conversations. The relationship needs to be explicitly two way: parents can bring concerns to us as well as us sharing concerns with them. The ideal is to have clear opportunities for extended discussion in an appropriate place, with the professional setting the tone of a joint problem-solving approach to the discussion. Basic things which can help to build this context and relationships with parents are to:

- ask current parents for feedback about their first experiences of the setting

- ask for suggestions of ways to make the setting information more accessible

- check that the first contacts with parents invite further discussion and involvement

- check through the year's events in the setting calendar and have parents and families identify ways in which they could be more involved

- discuss with staff concerns and anxieties about talking to parents, identifying ways in which these can be addressed either through training, mentoring or changes in setting practice

- identify what you consider to be good practice in relationships with parents and families, sharing this with parents and asking for feedback and suggestions about ways to improve and make the experience more consistent

- review the ways in which building positive relationships with parents is included in your induction for new members of the staff team

- review as a staff team everyone's expectations of individual responsibilities in working in partnership with parents and families.

The starting point for some of these discussions with staff could be to consider that every relationship with parents and families should begin with the expectation that at some point in the future there will be a need for a difficult conversation. If we start out thinking everything is always going to go smoothly, we often begin to make assumptions about how others think which are based on very little real information. These assumptions then become a reason for not keeping parents involved, for example thinking parents don't have time to talk, don't want to talk, don't spend enough time with their children, don't know enough about their children, have an unrealistic view of their children. These assumptions are often 'don't' or 'can't' phrases and tend to be statements which enhance our own role by implication: where parents can't or don't we think we can and do. If these assumptions begin to characterise discussion in the setting about parents generally or individually, this is a danger sign that our relationships are not being maintained in an effective way. Trying to see things from a parent's perspective can be very difficult if our personal experience is quite different from the parent concerned. However, there are some key ideas which may help:

- Parents want the best for their children.

- It is a difficult decision to choose a childcare setting which is convenient, affordable and somewhere you feel able to leave your child.

- Parents are likely to experience feelings of guilt and a sense of missing out on elements of their child's development.

- In the current climate parents will have concerns and doubts about what their child is doing and the quality of the care being provided for their child.

It is inevitable that at first you and the parent will be talking about a different child. It is impossible for the parent to see their child in a group situation with 'new' adults without being present. The child is having to learn about and cope with a huge range of new situations and relationships which you will observe but the parent is unable to see directly. Parents are the best advertising for your setting so it is worth your investment in ensuring that they are involved in the development of your policies and procedures. Needless to say, having established these policies and procedures, they then need to be implemented effectively and reviewed with staff and parents regularly.

Developing a quality learning environment for all children will be based on a variety of elements, including our knowledge of:

- child development
- Birth to Three Matters, the Foundation Stage Curriculum and associated guidance
- providing quality learning opportunities
- the role of the adult in supporting children's learning
- relationships between the children in the group.

With adult help

On my own!

There are several ways in which we establish and build on each of these elements. Our initial training should provide the basis for our future learning about our role in the lives of the children for whom we provide care. Anyone who considers that completing minimum qualifications to get a job in childcare is sufficient to maintain an effective and satisfying career needs to think carefully about their motivation and professionalism. Through training we learn about using observation to evidence children's current learning and what we need to provide to identify and help them achieve next steps. The quality of these observations is crucial to the effective identification of children's learning. These observations form the basis of our shared knowledge of the children's progress with their parents. Being clear about the next steps for a child's learning gives us the opportunity to involve parents and families in their children's learning experiences. In turn, this gives us the chance to have ongoing discussions about a child's rate of progress which is often one of the first indicators of concern surrounding a child's particular needs.

There are many sources of support and information about observation and planning effectively. First, the principles of good practice at the beginning of the Foundation Stage Curriculum (DfES/QCA, 2000, pp. 11–31) set the context. Secondly, *Seeing Steps in Children's Learning* (QCA, 2005a) and *Observing Children – Building the Profile* (QCA, 2005b) give examples of observations, ways to support children's learning and possible next steps. There are also several books available which work through the issues related to both observation and assessment and the essential links between them.

For our purposes the key elements are that our observations are done frequently and regularly, have sufficient detail to make assessments and are recorded in a positive way.

Over time our observations should have representation of a variety of learning situations, including:

- child-initiated play

- group play

- group activities

- practitioner-led activities

- planned activities which are set up for children to experience and carry out independently.

(*Observing Children – Building the Profile*, QCA, 2005b)

They should also cover the range of curriculum areas. Whatever the format of observation, they can be effectively enhanced with the addition of photographic evidence which is dated and annotated. This also provides a very effective way of involving parents in their children's experience of the setting.

Through our collection of observations and planning for next steps in children's learning we gradually build a picture of the child's individual learning pattern, likes, dislikes, strengths and learning needs. This information is then available for us to use to inform what adults need to do to support the child in a variety of ways and situations. By looking collectively at the evidence for all the children in the group, we can begin to evaluate the effectiveness of the learning environment we are offering. The activities we offer should be clearly indicated through our observations and next steps; therefore if children's learning does not seem to be progressing effectively, we should firstly consider the learning activities we are providing. Equally, the impact of the adult role cannot be underestimated. Over the past twenty years there has been a significant shift in our understanding of the importance of the role of the adult in a child's learning. This could perhaps be described as a move from a passive 'delivery of activity' role to a proactive 'companion in learning' role. This is also mirrored in some of the ways in which society generally has changed in the collective thinking about what is best for children. We no longer expect that children should be seen and not heard but neither is there acceptance that children should be able to do exactly as they please. As childcare workers we need to be clear about our expectations of children and our justification in current guidance for these principles. From these principles the expectations of the role of the adults in the setting will be established. As individuals we often have some difficulty in translating the knowledge we gain through training, reading and experience to what we actually have to do and say when we are with the children. Again this is a topic which can very usefully be used for discussion at staff meetings, during appraisals and as part of the induction process. The more opportunity there is for us to clarify our understanding of the role we can play in children's learning, the more confident we will feel in approaching our interactions with individual children. This is particularly true where there is a focus on an agreement about what good practice would look like in a particular situation.

Within this context of working in partnership with families and explicitly identifying good practice, we have the best possible chance of recognising when we have a concern about a child's progress. We are therefore in a position to be able to have a positive discussion with parents and to plan effectively for the child's learning.

What do we mean by early intervention?

Practitioners often feel that they need to do something very different or special for particular children. This is seldom the case if a view of the child's needs are seen in the context of their learning in all areas.

Observation and planned, supported learning opportunities are part of current practice for all children. Once we have identified a concern through our usual observation process and discussed this with parents, our next step is likely to be more focused observation in order to gather further detail of our concern. With this further level of detail we can then construct a selection of 'can do' statements which clearly identify the child's current level of achievement in this context. There is much talk about getting the balance between being 'too positive' about a child's abilities and not clearly communicating areas of difficulty. I would argue that if the following structure for 'can do' statements is used, a practitioner should be able to see not only that there is a need for support but also the extent of the need. The structure I would suggest has the following three elements:

1 description of observable behaviour

2 context in which behaviour occurs

3 length of time the behaviour continues for.

These elements then fit into a clear statement as follows:

Ebony can share a picture book with an adult in the book corner for five minutes.

Having focused on the detail of our observations we now need to look for the adult role in moving Ebony's learning forward. If our ultimate aim is to help Ebony to be part of a group story-time, we need to think about what our first step on the way might be. From our 'can do' statement we know that Ebony can share a book with an adult for five minutes. To change this to a target we need to decide which of the three elements we will change. We could change the context to either sharing a book with an adult and a child or extend the time from five minutes to seven or eight minutes. We would not decide to change more than one element at a time. Our target could, for example, become:

Ebony will share a picture book with an adult and one other child in the book corner for five minutes.

Setting a target does not, however, change a child's behaviour but it should change the adult's behaviour. Having decided on the appropriate target our next task is to identify what we can do to give Ebony the best possible chance of achieving this next step. These can often be covered with the following four 'Ps':

■ Practise – the opportunity to practise some of the elements which will be needed to achieve the target, for example highlighting times when Ebony sits with an adult and one other child involved in any activity.

■ Prepare – reflect on previous success and what made it successful.

- Prompt – use particular phrases, gestures, signs which help Ebony to approach the situation with the best possible chance of success.

- Praise – use the form and level of praise which is most effective for Ebony.

This process can be used for any next step for learning, including behavioural learning which we often find most challenging to think about. As a process it also consolidates the positive relationship with parents and focuses on the current achievements of the child.

 Key points

- Partnership with parents provides a foundation for positively supporting all children's learning.

- Staff teams need to clarify their ideas of good practice which are used in training, appraisal and induction processes.

- In developing relationships with parents staff need to be clear about their responsibilities and the roles of other team members such as the Special Educational Needs Co-ordinator (SENCO), Room Leader, Deputy Manager, Manager.

- Using a structured 'can do' statement can help to communicate clearly progress children are making and what could be worked on next.

Suggestions for learning about children with their parents

The usual initial information, such as name, address, contact details, emergency contact, ethnicity, dietary requirements and medical information, is fairly standard in admission procedures for all settings these days but it is useful to review how the information is collected. Ideally the first gathering of information will set the tone of the future relationship with parents by taking place in a conversational context rather than a pure question and answer session. By phrasing questions carefully those involved are able to expand on the basic answer.

What other information might we want?
How would you phrase the question to make it conversational?

- What situations do you think your child will really enjoy about being at this nursery?

- How do you think your child will show their enjoyment of situations?

- How would you like us to let you know about these enjoyable times?

- What situations do you think your child will find more difficult about being at this nursery?

▶

- How do you think your child will show their anxiety or distress?

- What do you do at home when your child feels this way?

- Compare with the way practitioners in the setting would respond and talk about any differences.

- In what ways does your child communicate that they are hungry, thirsty, tired, needing the toilet?

- What is your child's usual experiences of meal times – eating alone, with one other, whole family together; sitting at a table, on the floor, watching television, talking, etc. Compare with the routine in the setting and explain how you will help the child to learn about the new expectations.

- What is your child's experience of nappy changing, toileting? Are there any special routines which could be used in the setting, e.g. particular songs, particular phrases which are used, order in which things are done, ways in which the child can be involved in the process such as collecting the wipes/cream, etc.?

- How does your child respond at the moment if they are asked to let another child play with the same toy/game? Which things does your child find easiest to share, most difficult to share?

These sorts of questions lead to more of a discussion and a finding out about the child, as an individual. The information gathered can then form the basis of a respectful relationship with the child, taking an interest in their needs, likes and dislikes. The first few days of a relationship between a child and their keyworker and the family and keyworker can be considerably enhanced if the child recognises similarities between home and the setting. It will also reduce the anxiety of both parents and practitioners in those early discussions so making the 'settling period' for the child easier.

It is also really helpful to review with parents what their feelings were about your initial procedures after the child has been with you for a couple of months.

The photocopiable sheets that follow provide a summary of key points covered in the chapter. These can be used as handouts to help practitioners review the aims, ideas and any action which has been discussed or agreed.

Identifying next steps

'Can do' statements can give a clear indication of a child's current achievements and provide the basis for identifying next steps.

To be effective the 'can do' statement has to have three key elements:

1 description of observable behaviour

2 context in which behaviour occurs

3 length of time the behaviour continues for.

Our target could, for example, become:

Ebony will share a picture book with an adult and one other child in the book corner for five minutes.

Adult role

Once the 'can do' statement has been identified it is important to be specific about what the adults will do to enable children to achieve the next step.

The four 'Ps'

The four 'Ps' give a clear structure to help clarify what the adults need to do. Thinking about the example of Ebony:

- **Practise** – the opportunity to practise some of the elements which will be needed to achieve the target, for example highlighting times when Ebony sits with an adult and one other child involved in any activity.

- **Prepare** – reflect on previous success and what made it successful.

- **Prompt** – use particular phrases, gestures, signs which help Ebony to approach the situation with the best possible chance of success.

- **Praise** – use the form and level of praise which is most effective for Ebony.

Becoming an Inclusive Teacher

Rose, R. and Howley, M.

Overview

This chapter will address the following issues:

- defining educational inclusion
- teacher influences upon inclusive learning
- individual pupil needs within whole-class contexts.

Introduction

The term 'inclusion' has been generally accepted as common parlance within today's education system and indeed in wider society. The inequalities of the past often led to the exclusion and isolation of individuals who were perceived as different and sometimes inferior by dint of their needs, abilities, social class, race, gender or culture. As a commitment to the endorsement of policies which promote equality has been achieved, so has it been recognised as wholly inappropriate to provide a school curriculum that provides, for example, experiences to boys from which girls are excluded, or the teaching of literature or music based solely upon a monocultural interpretation. Such were the practices of the past, and it has taken many years to begin to break down those barriers, which denied so many pupils an opportunity to fulfil their true potential. This is not to suggest that the struggle to provide a more equitable education system has been fully won. Indeed, it would be naive in the extreme to suggest that prejudicial attitudes to individuals and groups do not persist to some extent even today in our schools (Barton, 2003; Helavaara Robertson and Hill, 2001). Marginalisation continues to sour the educational experiences of a significant number of pupils within our society, and teachers must accept the challenge of addressing this issue in order to promote a more equitable

however many barriers have been broken down

education system. The majority of teachers demonstrate a daily commitment to ensuring the well-being and improving the educational opportunities of all pupils in their class. This does not detract from the need to be vigilant in ensuring that teaching approaches and attitudes in the classroom demand that the needs of all pupils are recognised and appropriate steps taken to enable every pupil to learn.

The whole tenor of inclusive education has been founded upon a recognition that much remains to be achieved in providing schools which meet the needs of all pupils regardless of need, ability or cultural heritage. The attention given to this issue in recent years has been extensive, but would not have been so had there not been a clear recognition of the denial of opportunities for learning experienced by some sections of our population. Inclusion has become a topical issue, but one that continues to bring challenges to teachers and policy makers alike. Our understanding of an education system that fully addresses the needs of all pupils has developed considerably over the past 20 years, but remains far from complete. This is not to deny the commitment which teachers and others in schools have given to this complex matter, but it more likely reflects the difficulties of fully understanding the ways in which we can create learning environments that are truly inclusive for all learners. In this chapter, we will examine the challenges which teachers are attempting to address on a daily basis, and will consider what is known about promoting more inclusive practice through a review of teaching. This can be achieved only if we consider the definition and nature of inclusion early in a discussion of the critical aspects of pedagogy, classroom management and attitudinal influences that can support or deny greater access to learning.

Seeking a definition of inclusion

Florian (1998) has identified a significant number of definitions of inclusion from both the UK and further afield. Each of these definitions has in common a commitment to enabling pupils who have been marginalised, including those with special educational needs (SEN), to receive improved social and learning opportunities alongside their peers. In particular, the notion of pupils with SEN being provided with the opportunity to be educated alongside those who are not labelled in this way is seen as a priority. However, Florian acknowledges an important factor here in recognising that, for many teachers, pupils with significant SEN will continue to pose a challenge requiring careful planning and in some cases the adoption of teaching approaches specifically aimed at meeting individual needs. Inclusion is not simply about placing pupils with SEN in mainstream classrooms. Once located within this environment, pupils must be afforded opportunities to learn at an appropriate pace and level and be enabled to socialise with their peers whilst taking their place as equal members of the school community. In some instances, this will demand the use of strategies and approaches which are directly aimed at encouraging positive interaction and fostering learning for all pupils. It is simplistic in the extreme to believe that pupils will learn simply because they are placed in a mainstream classroom. Teachers have a duty to consider how each pupil will access learning, and to identify how individual learning needs and preferred learning styles can best be addressed. It is now largely recognised that teachers who are able to adapt their teaching approaches in order to address the learning difficulties of one pupil, often benefit others in the class (Ainscow, 1999) and that flexibility is a critical feature of inclusive classrooms.

Some teachers and parents express an understandable anxiety that pupils with SEN may detract from the learning of others in the classroom. In particular, those pupils who exhibit difficult behaviours may be seen as making inordinate demands upon teacher time. Teachers do need to be aware that when planning lessons particular attention will need to be given to ensuring that the work provided is at an appropriate level to meet the needs of all pupils. Disruptive behaviours often occur as a result of lessons that place either too much or too little demand upon pupils. Lessons that are interesting, stimulating and differentiated to meet a range of needs and abilities are less likely to be subject to disruption. Similarly, the careful organisation of classroom groups and the provision of appropriate resources and levels of support will have a direct impact upon the ability of pupils with SEN to participate fully in lessons.

Even the best organised and most effective teachers occasionally have difficulties in managing some pupils with SEN. Indeed, there are a few pupils whose behaviour or learning difficulties are so complex that even with support they appear difficult to maintain in a mainstream classroom. It is not our contention that in today's educational climate every school will be able to educate successfully every pupil. Currently, there remains a need for highly specialist provision for some pupils that will most likely be found in a special school or unit. Despite the need for specialist provision for some, many pupils with SEN are now educated in inclusive mainstream settings. Class teachers have a clear responsibility to all pupils in their class to explore different teaching approaches and strategies and to manage their classrooms in ways that encourage pupil participation and full access to learning. There will be times when all teachers need to call upon the additional expertise that exists in school, possibly from the SEN coordinator (SENCO), or to seek assistance from outside agencies that can offer specific advice. When this is necessary, teachers should not regard this as a display of weakness or failure to perform at a required level, but should rather consider it a necessary part of working to support a pupil within a multidisciplinary regime. Indeed, the *Every Child Matters* agenda, which has encouraged the development of greater integration within services to children, is already influencing moves toward greater coordination of multidisciplinary responses to the needs of individuals. All teachers can do much to promote the inclusion of pupils with SEN, and the majority will succeed most of the time. It is important that all teachers learn from their experiences of working with such pupils and demonstrate an ability to adjust their teaching practices and seek solutions to the learning difficulties experienced by some pupils.

Key questions and issues for reflection:

- How does my school define inclusion?
- How do school policies influence expectations of pupils with SEN?

Inclusive teaching

All effective teaching begins from a positive attitude and a desire to achieve what is best for all the pupils in a class. Barnes (1999) has emphasised the impact of positive thinking and attitudes upon the management of successful classrooms. He suggests that, when confronted by challenges in the classroom, teachers need to develop powers of objectivity to enable them to recognise the difficulties that they face and take logical steps to addressing them. Some teachers enter the classroom with less than positive attitudes toward individual pupils. If pupils have been given a label, such as behavioural difficulty or ADHD, this can increase teacher anxiety and lead to a lowering of expectation. It is essential that we remember that such labels are no more than broad descriptors. There are no 'typical' pupils with ADHD, Down's syndrome or any other condition, and therefore our expectations should be governed by the actual performance and needs of the individual pupil rather than by some mythological generalisation of need based upon a somewhat dubious system of labelling. Positive teachers expect all of their pupils to learn, and they try to enable them to reach their optimum levels of performance. This, of course, does not imply that all pupils will learn at the same pace or that they will have similar aptitudes, interests or needs. However, as a starting point, teachers must recognise that their primary responsibility is to address the needs of all pupils in the class, including those who offer the greatest resistance to learning. Jupp (1992) suggests that teachers need to develop a child-centred personal philosophy that begins with the belief that all pupils can learn and that the skill of effective teachers can enable any pupil to do so. This is certainly a philosophy that we endorse. Other researchers (Ellins and Porter, 2005; Wilkins and Nietfield, 2004) have similarly demonstrated how different teacher attitudes can affect the learning outcomes of individual pupils described as having SEN. It is up to all teachers to begin with an expectation that pupils will learn rather than to make assumptions that they will fail.

In recent years, there has been a debate about whether there is a specific form of pedagogy that is most appropriate for pupils with SEN (Kershner and Florian, 2004; Lewis, 2000; Lewis and Norwich, 2001). Most of the researchers engaged in this debate suggest that, whilst there are certainly teaching approaches which have been developed by teachers of pupils with SEN, these are likely to benefit all learners and are not only of specific value to selected groups of pupils. Many teachers who have considerable experience of working with pupils with complex needs, including those working in special schools, have devised approaches and adopted techniques to promote greater access to learning or have attempted to overcome specific barriers for some pupils. Examples of this may include the use of an augmentative system of communication, such as Makaton (a form of sign language) or a symbol system to support pupils who have difficulties with language. Similarly, the use of structured teaching, which has found favour with many teachers of pupils with autistic spectrum disorder (ASD), or kinaesthetic approaches for learners with dyslexia have often proved successful for specific groups of learners. However, in a review of teaching strategies and approaches for pupils with SEN, Davis and Florian (2004) concluded that whilst many strategies and approaches are being adopted for teaching pupils with SEN, there has been insufficient investigation into their efficacy in order to reach definitive conclusions about many of these. This conclusion suggests that teachers should give greater consideration to assessing the impact of the strategies that they develop to address the needs of pupils who challenge their conventional methods.

All teachers should consider two important points when contemplating the methods that they may adopt in working with pupils with SEN. Firstly, there is little evidence to support a belief that one model of teaching will address the needs of all pupils. Joyce, Calhoun and Hopkins (2002) have demonstrated how different learning situations and individual learners benefit from a range of teaching approaches. Whilst some learners, including those with SEN, will feel most comfortable when working within one model, learning becomes most effective when they can adapt to a range of different models. Similarly, the teacher who feels at home with one approach to teaching and sticks to this is unlikely to be addressing the needs of all learners in the class. Effective teachers learn to adjust their teaching to address particular teaching situations and the needs of their classes.

A second point relates to the nature of many of the specialist approaches that are seen in use with pupils with SEN. Many of these are used to provide effective access for learners. The use of augmentative communication as described above would be one particular example of this. For pupils with speech and language difficulties, the use of signs and symbols to augment the spoken word may afford them opportunities to participate in class which would otherwise have not existed. The use of technological aids, such as computer access switches or adapted keyboards for pupils with physical difficulties or sensory impairments, is another example of providing access to enable participation. These particular actions may not in themselves constitute a means of promoting learning, but, as Kershner (2000) points out, without the provision of effective access, opportunities for learning may well be denied.

When considering the implementation of a specialist teaching approach, you need to ask a series of questions which will ensure that the management and effectiveness of the approach can be secured.

What do I anticipate the pupil will gain from this approach?

You need to feel confident that the approach to be adopted will genuinely afford the pupil better opportunities for learning. When feeling concerned that a pupil is making insufficient progress, teachers will sometimes grasp at straws and reach for any resource or approach that seems to provide an alternative. This can at times lead to frustration when a newly adopted approach fails to yield results or benefits. It is important that teachers consider carefully why they are choosing to use an approach and identify intended learning outcomes for the pupil. If possible, it is advisable to discuss specific approaches with teachers who have used them before. The SENCO can be a critical point of contact here, should be able to provide advice and may even help with monitoring. Consider also how long it may take before any effects of an approach may be seen. When a new technique or method is adopted, it will take time for the teacher to gain confidence in its use and for the pupil to adapt to materials. When pupils are having difficulties with learning, they need time to adjust to new ideas and will need extra support and coaching until they gain confidence.

How manageable will this be in the general teaching situation?

You will need to manage whole classes, and whilst the introduction of innovative methods or materials may have major benefits for an individual, it is important to consider the impact upon the whole class. Often teachers find that materials or approaches that they introduce for one pupil have benefits for others in the class. It may be worth considering the adoption of an approach for several class members who will then be able to share in activities and discussion of their work. It is important to estimate how much additional time will be needed to support individual pupils who are using a resource that is different from that available to their peers. It may be possible in some cases to allocate a teaching assistant (TA) to work with a pupil in this situation. However, if part of the intended outcomes of learning for the pupil is to gain in independence and confidence, the teacher will need to ensure that dependency is not being created through allocation of a TA to an individual pupil for an excessive amount of time. The teacher will also need to consider factors associated with distraction. To what extent does the resource provided for one pupil detract from the learning of others? Such a factor might determine where the pupil is located in the class and when specific resources are used.

How will I transfer this approach to other teaching and learning situations?

Consistency and application of learning are important factors in determining the success of pupils. If an approach is introduced in one subject in order to provide access to or support for learning, the teacher must ensure that this is generalised throughout the teaching process. For example, if a pupil with learning difficulties has difficulties with reading and writing and a decision is made to introduce an augmentative communication system, such as the use of symbols, as a primary mode of communication, this must be consistently applied. Making use of symbols only in English lessons and then depending upon traditional orthography in, for example, geography would not be of great benefit to the pupil. When considering the introduction of any specialist approach, teachers must review the whole teaching process across the timetable in order to be sure of the implications of such a move. This also, of course, means involving other staff who may come into contact with the pupil at different times of the week. Pupils who receive specialist support through equipment often report their frustration when a successful approach is available only at limited times or when supported by specific members of staff.

Who else needs to be aware of what I am doing, and what is the implication for them?

Everyone who comes into contact with a pupil needs to know if particular approaches or resources are being used. Unless individuals are familiar with the requirements to use specific approaches, they cannot be expected to support the teaching and learning of the pupil. In some instances, this will mean communicating beyond the teaching staff to involve other colleagues, such as lunchtime supervisors, who may come into contact with a pupil. For example, pupils who are provided with a visual timetable to assist them in knowing what to do at specific times may become frustrated if adults are not aware of this and do not allow the pupil enough time to consult this important supportive material.

Contact with parents is clearly important when considering innovation with an individual pupil. If parents feel that their son or daughter is being treated differently without an adequate explanation of why decisions have been made, they may disapprove and feel that the school is not keeping them informed. Most parents welcome the introduction of specific approaches which are designed to help with access and learning, but it is essential for teachers to ensure that a clear explanation and justification of methods is provided.

Are there resource implications in using this approach?

The introduction of any new teaching approach is likely to have resource implications. If you give a commitment to using a new approach, such as the introduction of 'social stories' for a pupil with ASD, or the use of an overlay board to access a computer, this is likely to make demands upon time both within the classroom and in preparing materials. Pupils and teachers will become frustrated if a system is introduced and then fails because it is not adequately resourced. The introduction of a teaching approach that falters because of the lack of availability of necessary materials will damage the confidence of all involved in the learning process. You must be organised and plan ahead either for the production of more materials or the introduction of supportive approaches.

How will the approach be introduced to the pupil?

Pupils who are aware of their own difficulties with learning need to feel confident that new ideas introduced by the teacher are designed to be supportive and are well focused on individual needs. Awareness of intended outcomes is essential. You need to communicate clearly to the pupil why an approach has been introduced and how support will be provided. The pupil needs to be confident that this is an intervention which will make life easier and have definite learning benefits. It is necessary to spend time explaining how an approach is intended to work and what the pupil can do to assist in this process. It is equally important to protect the pupil's self esteem. If individual pupils feel that they are being singled out for treatment different from that afforded to their peers, they may feel self-conscious or embarrassed. Often it is best to involve other pupils in the introduction of new approaches and to ensure that the pupil does not become isolated as the only person using a piece of equipment or other materials. Some pupils will enjoy being singled out by a piece of equipment or approach. For example, a pupil who requires an adapted keyboard in order to access a computer because of a physical disability may well like to demonstrate its use to others in the class and could well be perceived by other pupils as having specific skills that they do not have.

Before introducing any innovation, the teacher should discuss it with the pupil, who will be able to advise the teacher on how to approach this situation. Pupils are very conscious of the efforts of teachers to provide additional support and will value being consulted at the earliest stages. Similarly, any TA or other adult who is to be involved in this process needs to be engaged in discussion at an early stage in order to ensure confidence in the materials and the requirements of the teacher.

Are there professional development implications?

Some specialised teaching approaches can be introduced into classrooms with minimal requirements for training. However, some, such as the use of signed communication or the introduction of an electronic communication device, will require the development of new skills and understanding. For example, the introduction into a class of a deaf pupil who is dependent upon British Sign Language would require the support of a skilled signed communicator in order to ensure that the pupil gains full benefit and access. Whilst, in this case, the teacher may not become a fully qualified signer, a basic understanding which enables social interaction with the pupil is desirable. When considering the introduction of an approach or new teaching materials, teachers should spend time prior to their introduction familiarising themselves with the materials and their workings. Pupils will lose patience and confidence if teachers appear to lack an understanding of what they are doing. For example, the teacher who introduces a software package to help a pupil overcome a maths problem and then spends half of a lesson trying to read a manual or sort out an access difficulty will quickly lose the confidence of the pupil. Sometimes it may be effective to examine new materials with the pupil and to discuss how these will be introduced and used.

Do I see this as a long-term measure or one from which I hope eventually to move the pupil forward to the approaches commonly used in the class?

Some specialist teaching materials may be introduced to overcome specific problems with the anticipation that they are only a short-term measure. If this is the case, you must consider how to make the transition to the approaches in common use in the class. Short-term measures must be used in a way that does not create dependency. You should produce an exit strategy which identifies when the specialist approach or materials will have served their purpose and how to reintroduce the pupil to the generally used methods.

For some pupils, strategies and approaches will be long term, and through these, pupils will be included in learning which would otherwise be denied. This may well be the case with augmentative forms of communication or the use of technology. Where such long-term implications exist, you must ensure the careful transition from one class to another and in some instances from the primary to the secondary school. This will require careful communication with receiving colleagues well in advance of the pupil's move. Time must be allowed for teachers and other colleagues receiving pupils to have training, and there may be a need to plan for the transfer or acquisition of essential resources. Pupils need to feel confident that interventions upon which they have become dependent and through which they have benefited will continue to be there as a critical form of support.

Inclusive teaching requires that teachers ensure that all pupils in a class are able to access learning. This means not only planning to address individual needs, but doing this in the context of a whole-class situation and with due regard to the impact of any actions upon all learners. The term 'differentiation' has become familiar to most colleagues working in today's classrooms. Planning to address a wide range of needs within a single class requires that teachers be able to provide work at different levels, deliver this at a variable pace and use a diversity of resources according to the needs of individuals (O'Brien and Guiney, 2001). Whilst differentiation is clearly important and can enable teachers to be confident that they are addressing the needs of a wide range of learners, there is a need to exercise some caution with regard to its management and delivery. Good practice in differentiating teaching and learning requires a detailed understanding of the needs of all pupils in the class. Simply giving a pupil with SEN work that is less demanding than that given to others is not adequate. The work needs to be tailored to the individual needs, preferred learning style and current level of learning of the pupil. It also needs to provide sufficient challenge to enable pupils to progress and not remain static in their current learning. At times, what passes for differentiation is no better than discrimination. If all that is achieved is the presentation of work to pupils, that keeps them occupied but does not advance their learning, we are not providing an adequate service to the individual. Learning occurs when pupils can do something or know information that they could not do or did not know before the teaching process was undertaken. All pupils must be challenged to learn regardless of need or ability.

Lewis (1992) identified 12 forms of differentiation which teachers may use in order to support learning:

Differentiation of content: e.g. pupils in a group all work toward a single aim, such as reading competence, but use several different reading schemes to get there.

Differentiation by interest: e.g. all pupils are producing graphs, but their graphs represent different data according to personal interest.

Differentiation of pace: all pupils work at the same task, or with the same materials, but the teacher has different expectations of the time required for completion.

Differentiation of access: materials or methods of working are different for individual pupils. E.g. whilst one pupil writes with a pencil, another uses a computer and another produces pictorial work.

Differentiation of outcome: e.g. one pupil writes a story, another draws a picture to tell the story and another records the story on audio tape.

Differentiation of curricular sequence: pupils enter the curriculum at different points or take part in the curriculum in a different order from that of their peers.

Differentiation of structure: some pupils work on step by step (task analysed curriculum) whilst others work on 'chunks'.

Differentiation of teacher time: the teacher gives more time to some pupils during specific tasks in order to ensure access.

Differentiation of teaching style: e.g. some pupils may require individual instruction whilst others can work in small groups or pairs.

Differentiation of level: all pupils work through a similar sequence, in maths for example, but at a variety of levels.

Differentiation by grouping: the teacher groups particular pupils together for specific activities. Pupils act as supporters, or work with peers with whom they are comfortable or confident. (Lewis, 1992, pp24–5)

Each of these approaches can prove useful in the armoury of the teacher, and you should expect to consider these in respect of both the individual pupil and the context in which teaching is taking place. When planning to address individual needs, teachers should contemplate how their actions will be viewed by all pupils in the class. High expectations of all pupils are essential. When presenting work to pupils that is different from that provided for their peers, it is necessary to ensure that this is not seen as a soft option or a form of favouritism. Whenever possible, it is advisable to give several pupils the same work in order that they can discuss this, share ideas and feel that they are part of the group. Work differentiated for one pupil will often benefit others in the class. By bringing pupils together to work, it is possible to encourage peer support and even peer coaching, benefiting both pupils with SEN and the more able pupils who need to think through ideas as they provide support. In an inclusive classroom, all pupils feel that they have a part to play, and differentiation is viewed as a way of ensuring that everyone participates. Where work is prepared solely for an individual pupil, if this is not effectively managed, it may result in isolation or feelings of resentment.

Andy is a teacher in a Year 6 class in a primary school. In his class, he has two pupils who have SEN. Sharon is a wheelchair-user who has cerebral palsy. She has limited use of her hands and poor control of her limbs. However, Sharon is one of the most academically able pupils in the class and is a very responsive learner. Callum has general learning difficulties and finds it hard to concentrate for more than a few minutes. He is often apprehensive about the introduction of new ideas and is very conscious that he finds learning more challenging than his peers.

In an English lesson today, Andy is working with his class on writing a report of a visit which they recently made to a local museum to visit the collection of Egyptian artefacts. During the visit, each member of the class was asked to choose an object to research and to produce a picture of the selected item to take back to school. Most of the class were provided with coloured pencils and paper to produce their pictures. However, Sharon has difficulty controlling a pencil, so Andy provided her and two of her classmates with a digital camera to take some pictures. Sharon's lack of control meant that taking pictures with the camera required the use of a tripod to obtain a steady image. Her two friends assisted her in positioning and stabilising the tripod, whilst Sharon selected an Egyptian statue of the god Horus to photograph from different angles. Callum enjoys drawing and has no difficulty with completing a picture. However, in order to make notes about this, Andy allows him to dictate his ideas and the findings from his research to Mandy, a parent who has joined them on the trip.

In the English lesson, the pupils are writing their accounts. Sharon uses a computer with an adapted keyboard which has large keys and a guard to prevent her hitting the wrong keys when writing her report. This is a slow process and Andy is careful to tell her how much he expects her to write. He pairs her with the two classmates who worked with her at the museum, and the three pupils negotiate what they are going to write so that at the end of the lesson they can combine their work.

Callum is paired with a more able pupil, Mark. He has the notes from the visit which he dictated to Mandy. The two pupils discuss what Callum had found out, and they work together to write their report. Callum's partner does most of the writing, but Andy insists that Callum also writes his section. This is achieved by making a game in which Mark writes sentences, leaving out a word from each sentence. Mark reads each sentence to Callum, who has to guess the missing word and then write it in.

In the preceeding case study, the teacher has demonstrated an awareness of the challenges which the pupils with SEN in his class face in accessing learning. He has planned effectively to differentiate activities for the needs of both pupils in a way which ensures that learning is a social activity and fully includes the individuals within their class. In the terms set out by Lewis, above, Andy has used differentiation by *access, outcome, structure* and *grouping* in order to ensure that Sharon and Callum are fully included in the lessons. Andy has also encouraged and made effective use of peer support to ensure that these two pupils feel that they are fully engaged with their classmates.

Key questions and issues for reflection

- How does planning to meet the needs of one pupil affect the learning of others?
- What processes are in place to assess the effectiveness and potential impact of specialist teaching approaches?
- How are professional development needs identified before implementing specialist approaches or using specialist resources?
- How can best use be made of the SENCO in securing advice about addressing individual needs?
- How many forms of differentiation are being regularly deployed in the class and how are judgements made about which approaches to use?

Conclusion

Becoming an inclusive primary schoolteacher is dependent first of all upon a belief not only that all pupils have an entitlement to learn, but also that they are capable of so doing. However, attitude and belief alone are insufficient to enable the teacher to become effective. Teachers need to ensure that their commitment to inclusion is supported by an understanding of how pupils learn and enhanced by an appreciation of the approaches and resources which are proving effective with a diverse pupil population. There are many resources, schemes and systems available commercially which claim to have benefits for pupils with special educational needs. Some of these are well substantiated through many years of successful use by teachers. Others require greater caution and should be examined in detail before committing to them. The advice of the SENCO and more experienced teachers, or of those working for support services, may be crucial in making the right decisions. However, in the early stages of teaching, all teachers have a preferred approach to teaching and need to identify those resources with which they personally feel comfortable. As teachers gain in confidence, they should ensure that they expand their personal teaching styles and become responsive to teaching in a variety of ways which suit changing circumstances. Teachers who adhere to a narrow set of teaching approaches are unlikely to thrive in an inclusive primary school. Effective teachers are responsive but not reactive. They contemplate the challenges faced by pupils, try to analyse these in respect of both their own experience and the perspective of the pupil, and plan actions on the basis of this analysis. Becoming skilled in this way takes time, and all teachers, even the most experienced, need to seek the advice of others when confronting new challenges. Schools will be inclusive only at the point when teachers feel that they are equipped to meet the needs of all pupils in their classes. This will inevitably take time, but it must begin with a commitment on the part of individual teachers to gain the necessary skills and understanding to support a diverse range of pupil needs.

What is your Culture?

Baldock, P.

This chapter:

> Outlines the nature and importance of cultures

> Uses a fictional example to demonstrate that people do not belong in an uncomplicated way to cultures that have clear and unchanging boundaries

> Invites you to consider your own cultural identity as a way of underlining some of the key issues

> Discusses, in particular, the question of 'Englishness' as a form of cultural identity

---

I was sitting in on a staff meeting at a fairly large nursery, listening to a discussion about the steps they would take to improve the setting following a recent review they had conducted. One of the decisions was to purchase more 'cultural playthings'. I knew what they meant, of course. They were talking about playthings that came from, or at least reflected, cultures other than the white British one to which all of us present belonged. However, the implication that the climbing frame, the copy of *We're Going on a Bear Hunt*, the toy farmyard and the runaround toy in the form of Noddy's little car had no cultural connotations at all was rather odd.

Behind the phrase 'cultural playthings' there lay an unspoken assumption: 'We are normal and some other people have cultures'. Cultures might, of course, be very colourful and interesting – worth more than a quick look. The way they are described might, in other words, sound very positive. It remains the case that they can be seen as exotic, abnormal, something unusual that it requires a particular effort to understand.

The word 'culture' has a number of meanings. On the one hand, it refers to higher forms of refined sensibility and their products in the forms of art, music, literature and comparable activities. On the other hand, it is now used frequently to refer to the rules and habits that bind a particular society together. More recently, there has been greater interest in the academic world in cultural products – popular fiction, fashion, the mass media and so on – that may not aspire to the status of great art but are also important as reflections and developers of values.

The idea of culture as the set of practices that keep a society together and allow its members to find meaning in their lives was first articulated in the studies conducted by social anthropologists from the late-19th century onwards. Much of this research was undertaken among remote peoples whose ways of life were very different from those of Europe. It may have become a term we apply to ourselves as well as to peoples whose lives are significantly different from ours, but for some people the idea that the word 'culture' refers to the exotic remains. To have a culture is to be different, and what those who have a culture are different from is 'us'.

The complications of cultural identity

Life is a bit more complicated than that. Take the (fictional) case of a particular individual.

Mary is a woman in her thirties working as an early years practitioner in a Sure Start Children's Centre in the north east of England. She is married, with two young children. She and her husband are practising Roman Catholics. Already busy, she still finds time for her hobby of painting pictures.

So far, the story sounds fairly simple. Let me now add that Mary and her husband are both Hakka-speaking ethnic Chinese from Mauritius who came to the UK soon after their marriage.

What has been added is not just another bit of information. Mary does not have a Hakka/Chinese culture in the way that she might have, say, a nice fitted kitchen. It is not a simple possession. Perhaps she brings to the care of her own children values and practices she learned growing up in Mauritius. Perhaps her paintings are influenced by Chinese brush painting. However, it gets more complicated than that. Her religion (Roman Catholicism) was introduced to the Far East in relatively recent times and was seen for centuries in England, where she now lives, as an alien and threatening religion (much as Islam is seen by many people today). How does she see her religion fitting in with her Hakka culture or her British nationality? Her understanding of her faith may have been influenced by other parts of her life. Aspects of her background may have brought her to see her professional work with children in a slightly different light from that of her colleagues. Her work in the Sure Start Centre may have brought her into contact with a wider range of beliefs and attitudes and experiences in ways that have led her to re-think aspects of her faith.

Mary is neither just another early years practitioner more or less like any other, nor is she merely a representative of Hakka culture. She is someone living her life and trying to make sense of it with a variety of tools drawn from a variety of cultural influences – Hakka society, the north east of England, her church and her professional training among them. She has in some ways a culture of her own. It is not so much that she has a particular culture as that everything she does is shaped by a complex interaction of cultural perspectives drawn from all the aspects of her life so far.

The best of the early social anthropologists would have had little difficulty in recognizing this. People such as Franz Boas (1858–1942) described particular cultures as accurately as they could, but recognized that cultures were products of history and changed with changes of circumstance, including interaction between different societies. It was not so much that people were governed by a culture to which they belonged as that they had to develop cultural norms in order to interact effectively with those around them. Cultures might be conservative because the very purpose of their existence was to make social interaction as predictable as possible, but social anthropologists recognized that they always have the capacity to change.

The importance of the cultural dimension of our lives can be difficult to acknowledge. For example, the study of child development was until recently usually based on what happened in middle-class Anglo-Saxon communities. Assumptions that were made about what is natural and biologically determined were, in fact, derived from observing the culture of such societies in action. However, it is clear that the young child's response to the 'strange' situation of the child development laboratory where she is left by her mother or encounters unfamiliar figures is going to depend significantly on the extent to which care in her everyday social circle belongs primarily to a maternal figure and how often she encounters unfamiliar people. The need for security is built into her. What security means to her in practice will depend on the culture in which she is being raised. In other words, a child's responses may be based on biological need, but they can only be expressed through culture (Cole, 1998, especially pp. 22–6; Super & Harkness, 1998; Robinson & Jones Diaz, 2001).

In spite of this, there is still a strong tendency to see what happens in middle-class Anglo-Saxon society as natural and other forms of behaviour as oddities that have to be explained by understanding other cultures. Similarly, when dealing as an early years practitioner with families from a different cultural background, it can be very easy to see their culture as a special explanatory factor of a kind that does not come into play if children are white British.

The case of Mary demonstrates something of the complexity of cultural identity. Her situation demands of her that she reconciles various ways of being in the world that have come to her from her ethnicity, her religion, her profession, her roles as a wife and mother, her whole personal and family history. It is not that she is an individual in the sense that she was born with a fully developed personality or has simply invented the type of person she wants to be. All the 'scripts' she uses (consciously or unconsciously) to form her identity were largely written before she came along. On the other hand, the 'scripts' are many and in using them she is also modifying them. In this respect her situation is the same as that of all of us today.

Identifying your own culture

If you were asked to identify your own culture, you might find this task easy or difficult. You might be inclined to deny that you had a particular culture. Alternatively, you might identify yourself quite readily with a nationality, ethnicity or some other grouping. People whose lives involve periods in different countries may have alternative identities. Uwins (2008, p.43) speaks of one early years practitioner who 'considers herself to be black British when she resides in Britain and black African when she is in Nigeria'. Some people have the opposite reaction, speaking proudly of their original cultural or national identity while in Britain, but becoming aware of how British they are when visiting the homeland of their ancestors. The cultural identity that someone develops will be an adaptation to circumstance – perhaps quite unconscious in the case of someone who stays in more or less the same society all her life, much more self-conscious in the case of someone who chooses to live elsewhere or is for one reason or another an exile from her place of origin.

The two activities that follow are intended to get you thinking about your own cultural identity.

 Exercise

What aspects of your life help to determine your identity? In answering this question you can take into account:

- your family roles (partner, daughter, son, parent)
- your family's history
- your profession
- your social class

- your nationality
- the part of the country in which you live
- your affiliation to a religion (if you have one)
- your ethnic identity
- your interests, your taste in music, reading and so on
- anything else that is important to you.

How far has thinking about those things made it possible for you to identify your culture?

You can do this as an individual exercise or get all the members of a group to do it and then share what they have written down.

Quite possibly, answering all those questions has still left you uncertain of what to say about your cultural identity. Part of the reason for this may be that you are uncertain of what to say about some of the elements listed above. Take the case of nationality. You may be a British citizen, but wish to identify yourself as black British or Welsh or in some other way. Are you then saying that your culture is British, but that you belong to some specific sub-section of a wider British culture?

If you can identify your nationality without any question, do you feel comfortable with everything that seems to be implied by that? For example, I would say that I am English and that this is a key element in my identity. However,

- I do not drink tea very often
- I am not a member of the Church of England whose participation in church services is, nevertheless, restricted to weddings and funerals
- I am not interested in cricket
- I speak more than one language
- I rarely use an umbrella.

In other words, there are several ways in which I do not match the stereotype of what many people in other countries, and even other Englishmen, would think of as typically English. (In other respects, of course, I fit the stereotype more neatly.)

Have another stab at discerning your cultural identity by tackling the next exercise.

Exercise

Imagine that there has been a major disaster. The economy and public services are in serious disarray. It has been decided that, in order to cope with the situation, the majority of those fit to travel will have to be evacuated to other countries that have agreed to take them as refugees. This exercise is being organized by the United Nations.

You and your immediate family are to be evacuated to another country. Because of the gravity of the situation, you have no say on the matter of your destination. The emergency will last for some time, so you must expect your stay to be long-term, perhaps permanent.

Write down:

- five things you would want to take with you. These can be of practical or sentimental value. You should be able to fit all five plus some changes of clothing into a small suitcase.
- five things you would want to continue doing once you arrive; examples might include wearing British-style clothing or working in the same occupation.
- five things you would be willing to do in order to fit in with the society you are about to join; examples might include learning a local language, studying a citizenship course and so on.

You can do this as an individual exercise or ask members of a group to write down individual responses and then share them. Some people might be reluctant to share some of their answers with the whole group. For example, the objects someone wishes to take might include one whose significance is so personal that she is reluctant to discuss it in the whole group. That is fine. The object of the exercise is to help each participant focus on what she or he finds important. Sharing that information is optional.

Do not worry too much about the feasibility of the scenario. The point is to get people thinking about what is important to them and what this indicates about their identities.

I have not identified the country to which you are being sent. If someone in your group comes from or is reasonably knowledgeable about a particular country, you might decide to select that as your country of refuge and ask that person questions which might influence some of your responses.

Doing this exercise might help people to see the situation of asylum-seekers in a new light. If so, that is all to the good. However, the key purpose is to help people think about what is important to their own identities.

If you have undertaken the exercise on your own, ask yourself how far the objects you have chosen to take reflect your cultural identity. They may seem to be about your personal life or tastes, but still reflect your cultural background. Taking a wedding ring or some other token of a significant relationship will itself say something about how relationships are seen by people of your cultural background. It may just happen to be the case that you like marmite or thick–cut marmalade, but many people would see these as typical of a peculiarly English taste in food. You can also ask yourself how far your answers to the second and third question help you name those aspects of your identity that are so important to you that you would be unwilling to abandon them, however flexible you wished to be in your new circumstances. If you have run it as a group exercise, encourage participants to share as much as they are happy to share about their answers and look at some of the common features and those where there are differences.

Has this exercise taken you much further forward in defining your own culture?

The particular case of Englishness

There is always a tendency to think that the way we do things is normal and that deviations from that pattern are oddities requiring explanation. This is a key factor in the way in which cultures other than white British may be seen. There is, however, an additional complication in the case of the English. For a long time – and still to a great extent today – the terms 'British' and 'English' were seen (by the English at least) as interchangeable.

Scottish, Welsh, Irish or other forms of national identity were seen as mere regional variations, no more significant than being from Yorkshire, Devon or Kent. It is still possible for a serious report to speak of something being true of the United Kingdom when it is true only of England. Clark & Waller (2007, p.5) describe an example.

This situation has been altered by the process of handing over aspects of government to new assemblies in Scotland, Wales and Northern Ireland and the pressures that led to that constitutional change. People in other parts of the United Kingdom are now much less likely than the English to identify themselves as British. The saints' days of St Patrick, St Andrew and St David are celebrated in a way that St George's Day is not. The decline in the military and political power of the United Kingdom and the recognition of much that was wrong with the establishment and administration of the British Empire have undermined the ability of people to feel pride in the British identity. At the same time there remains a further uncertainty about pride in being English.

This situation has led to the publication in recent years of a range of books that approach the English identity in different ways. Some are content to list and praise the more attractive places in the country. A few pamphleteers take an assertively nationalist stance. Bragg (2006) celebrates the progressive strand in English history and sees this as the basis for a different form of patriotism. Miles (2005) traces the ethnic mix that has led to the English nation. Paxman (1999) observes his fellow countrymen with the sardonic detachment of a journalist. Fox (2004) is also humorous, but also brings to the subject her skills as a social anthropologist. Ackroyd (2002) uses history, literature and other arts to describe the nature of England in ways that may surprise many. Jones (1998) moves even further from the conventional, seeing England not as the 'Protestant nation' many would have described in the past, but as having its real foundations in the Catholic Middle Ages. The vast differences of approach and understanding among these authors illustrate the uncertainty as to what it means to be English.

The complication of national identity is brought out by the fact that many black and Asian people living in England are happy to fly the English flag during the World Cup or other international sports competitions, but would shun the Union flag, which the far right has taught them to see as a symbol of racism (Bagguly & Hussain, 2005). At the same time, many white English people are suspicious of English nationalism and prefer to speak of Britishness. There have also been cases of those in authority trying to prevent the flying of the English flag on the grounds that it might offend black people.

You may have your own views on Englishness. Whether or not you are English yourself, try the following exercise as a way into defining what you think English culture might be.

 Exercise

The following statements are taken from a discussion among people from a small town in the middle of the country about the way they see their cultural identity and national heritage.

How many of these statements would you be prepared to describe as typically English? Can you construct some kind of picture of English culture from them?

- Our patron saint is St George and you often see representations of him on public buildings etc. but I don't think he means very much to most people. He is not an important symbol.
- The flag is very important. It is a symbol around which everyone can rally. I think it has become more important in that sense in recent years.
- Conquering Everest was a big step for us. It made us feel we had literally 'made it to the top'.
- What really distinguishes us from other countries and their people is our common sense.
- There may be examples of intolerance, but basically we are a very tolerant society. We make people welcome as long as they meet us halfway. I think that is the value that distinguishes us from many other nations.
- We are very practical and pragmatic.
- When people talk about 'cultural heritage' you think about grand buildings etc. but other things are just as significant. Lavatory jokes, for example. People might say they disapprove of them, but they always raise a laugh.
- It is in doing the ordinary, simple things that you feel our common heritage – like decorating the tree at Christmas.
- Our old churches are part of what makes us feel part of a nation. People might not go to church very often, but they have strong feelings about the great cathedrals.

(Continued)

(Continued)

- If you really want to know what it means to belong to our nation, you have to go to the countryside. The cities are big, anonymous places and with so many international retail outlets you could be anywhere in the world a lot of the time. It is the country that represents what is best about our society. We have to defend it.

You can undertake this as an individual exercise or in a group. The composition of a group will have an obvious impact on the degree of consensus it is possible to reach and on what that consensus will be. A group of English people might come up with different responses from a more mixed group.

If you undertake this exercise as the facilitator of a group, wait until the discussion is over before revealing that the 'town in the middle of the country' is Sabadell. If that name is unfamiliar, it is because the discussion did not take place in England at all, but in Catalonia, a region of Spain, which has its own language and where the regional government has a considerable amount of devolved power. To the extent that many of the statements sounded true of England, or at least as though they were the sort of thing that English people might say about themselves, this exercise shows up how problematic the idea of a unique national identity can be. I have cheated, of course. Catalonia is in Western Europe and has many features in common with England as with other West European countries. I have also suppressed some of the things that were said when this conversation took place because they would have given the game away. The exercise does, however, raise questions about claims to the uniqueness of any given national culture.

Summary

In all our dealings with other people we rely on habits, conventions and rules that we may help to modify but which came from outside us. We can (with some effort) change the cultural context in which we operate. We cannot hope to operate outside any cultural context at all.

However, this is about culture as a means of understanding the world and making effective relationships. It does not mean that any of us belongs to quite specific cultures with closed boundaries and unchanging natures. All cultures are subject to the historical process of change. All of us operate in a number of cultural spheres determined by our nationality, preferred language, religious faith or secular values, profession or a number of other things to which we belong and which give us ways of deciding how to live our lives and to seek significance for ourselves.

Any approach in an early years setting or elsewhere to people whose cultural background is significantly different from our own depends on our understanding of this fact. It is in this light that we can consider the broad question of multiculturalism or the specific questions that arise from daily practice.

Further reading

You may want to look at some of the books mentioned in the chapter. Siraj-Blatchford (2000) *Supporting Identity, Diversity and Language in the Early Years* is a particularly good book on this topic. Fox (2004) *Watching the English* offers a light read on the question of the English character, but is underpinned by some very clear thinking.

I have deliberately avoided saying a great deal about social anthropology, but that academic discipline lies behind much of what has been said here. Hendry (2008) *An Introduction to Social Anthropology* is a readable text for those who already know something about the subject as well as for newcomers.

The topic of the cultural dimension of child development is covered in Smidt (2006) *The Developing Child in the 21st Century*.

45 Understanding EAL Learners: Theories of Learning and Language: Introduction to Bilingual and EAL Learners

Conteh, J.

Learning Outcomes

This chapter will help you to achieve the following learning outcomes:

- develop understanding of the importance of recognising and reflecting on your own views on language diversity and ethnicity for you as a primary teacher;
- gain awareness of the history of language and cultural diversity in England;
- develop awareness of the diverse range of experiences and knowledge that bilingual and EAL learners bring to their primary classrooms in England.

Introduction

This chapter introduces you to the children you will be teaching who come under the umbrella term of 'EAL learners'. It raises questions about how we define and label attributes such as 'ethnicity' and challenges you to consider your own views and perceptions of these issues. It begins by providing some background information about the cultural and language diversity of British society. Then, through a set of vignettes of individual children, you will gain a sense of the rich diversity of the social and cultural experiences that many bilingual and EAL learners bring to their mainstream classrooms. One of the main aims of this chapter is to help you, as a beginning teacher, to understand the importance of recognising and valuing all the knowledge and experience that your bilingual and EAL learners bring with them to school. This is crucial, if you are to help them become successful learners in the mainstream system. Interspersed through the chapter there are questions and activities to help you to think further through the ideas that you will read about, as well as begin to think practically about their implications for your own practice in different classrooms. There are some suggestions for further reading at the end of the chapter.

These are the main sections and subsections of the chapter.

1. Defining difference
- Behind the facts and figures
- 'Superdiversity' in England

2. Who are 'EAL learners'?
- Advanced bilingual learners – Yasmin
- New to English children – Stefan and Jan
- Asylum-seekers and refugees – Umaru
- Isolated learners – Radia

• Sojourners – Hamida

3. Language diversity and learning – some myths and misconceptions

1. Defining difference

1.1 Behind the facts and figures

> ### Research Focus
>
> Since 2009, the Department for Education has collected information about the languages spoken by children in schools as part of the annual schools' census data. In 2011, the figures showed that about 16.8% of children in mainstream primary and 12.3% in secondary schools in England were identified as learners with 'EAL' (English as an additional language). It is not easy to find a figure for the total number of languages currently spoken by children in schools in England, but it is thought to be about 350 (BBC, 2007). The proportion of ethnic minority children is different from those defined as 'EAL'; currently this is 21.4% for primary schools and 25.5% for secondary schools (Department for Education, 2011a). The data on ethnicity come from the national census, which is done every ten years. The most recent census was undertaken in 2011, and the categories for ethnicity used are shown in the box below. The national census has never collected information about the languages that people speak.

The percentages for ethnic minority children are much higher than those for language diversity, so it is clear that there are many ethnic minority groups in England for whom English is *not* an additional language. But it is also clear that many children can be defined as *both* EAL and ethnic minority, because they belong to an ethnic minority group and also speak another language besides English. It is important to understand, especially for children such as those in this second group, that language knowledge and cultural knowledge are interlinked. This idea is discussed further in Chapter 2, as well as the implications for teaching. There are also children who would ethnically be part of the 'white' majority but who could actually be defined as 'EAL', because they do not have English as their first language and their families are from Europe or other parts of the world.

Activity 1.1
Who are you?
These are the categories of ethnicity used in the 2011 national census. Look at them and think about the following questions.

1. Did you complete the most recent census? If so, which category did you place yourself in? If not, which category would you place yourself in?

2. Could you place yourself into more than one category?
3. Do you find it difficult to place yourself, and if so, why?
4. Would it be difficult to place anyone you know?
5. Would it be difficult to place any children you teach or have worked with?
6. How do you think these categories were arrived at?

A. White
- British
- English/Welsh/Scottish/Northern Irish/British Irish
- Gypsy or Irish traveller
- Any other White background

B. Mixed/multiple ethnic groups
- White and Black Caribbean
- White and Black African
- White and Asian
- Any other Mixed

C. Asian/Asian British
- Indian
- Pakistani
- Bangladeshi
- Chinese
- Any other Asian background

D. Black/African/Caribbean/Black British
- African
- Caribbean
- Any other Black/African/Caribbean background

E. Other ethnic group
- Arab
- Any other ethnic group

Despite the ever-increasing numbers of children from different ethnic and language backgrounds in our schools, the vast majority of teachers in England are still from 'white British or English' backgrounds and do not speak other languages besides English. This means that most teachers who have children in their classes who speak other languages do not share those languages. This can sometimes feel like quite a challenge, on top of everything else you need to know about and be able to do as a teacher. Vivian Gussin Paley, in her book *White teacher*, describes her experiences as a 'white majority' teacher in a school with increasing numbers of children from diverse backgrounds. She soon realised that, in order to understand their needs and make the best provision for them, she had to understand more about her own identity and how it influenced her attitudes to her pupils. She concludes:

Those of us who have been outsiders understand the need to be seen exactly as we are and to be accepted and valued. Our safety lies in schools and societies in which faces with many shapes can feel an equal sense of belonging. Our children must grow up knowing and liking those who look and speak in different ways, or they will live as strangers in a hostile land.

(pp. 131–2)

Ethnicity is a very hard concept to define, and because we often talk about 'ethnic minorities' we sometimes think of it as a term only relevant for people who are different from ourselves and can be thought of as belonging to a 'minority' group. Of course, the reality is that we all have ethnicity. We all belong to different ethnic, cultural and social groups. But ethnicity is only one part of what makes us who we are. In thinking about your role as a teacher, it is more helpful to think about the notion of **identity**, and all the personal and social attributes that this entails. As suggested in Chapter 2, it is vital that you understand how your personal identity is an important aspect of your professional identity as a teacher, especially when you are teaching children from different language and cultural backgrounds to yourself. You need to understand the importance to you of your own ethnicity, language knowledge and other aspects of your personal makeup in helping you understand the needs of the children you will be teaching. As Gussin Paley argues, in this way, you will be able to develop positive, trustful relationships with the children you teach and with their families.

The following activity will help you to think about your 'ethnicity' as part of your identity – in other words, who you are.

Activity 1.2
How does it feel to be different?
You can do this activity on your own. But it would be better if you could do it as a group discussion task, with some of your fellow trainees, or colleagues in a school setting.

- First, think about how you would define your identity. Is it enough just to think about your 'ethnic background' as defined in the categories of the census? What other aspects of your identity are important to you? Where your family comes from might be an important part of your identity, but what else might count for you?
- Make a list of 6–8 attributes that you would say were important aspects of your identity.
- Can you think of a time when you were made to feel different and that you did not belong? This could have been when you were a child, or as an adult in a work situation or in a social context. What did you feel was different about you? How would the quote from Vivian Gussin Paley reflect your feelings? Write a few sentences about how it felt to feel different and perhaps excluded.

1.2 'Superdiversity' in England

In about 120 AD, soldiers from the Roman Empire built a fort on the river Tyne and named it Arbeia (see Arbeia Fort, 2011). Some historians think they named it after their homelands in what are now Syria, Libya and Spain. Britain has always been multicultural and multilingual – a small island which has experienced successive waves of migration from all over the world. The English language reflects this, as it contains words from all the languages of the people that have come to this island and enriched its vocabulary over the centuries.

Over recent years, with the growth of the European Union (EU) as well as more global events, the population of England has changed greatly. The addition to the EU of the 'A8 accession countries' in 2004 and more recent changes have meant that people travel much more than they used to. It has become quite normal for people from Poland, the Czech Republic, Slovakia and other eastern European countries to come to England to work, and then return to their countries of origin or move on elsewhere. This has been described as 'circular migration', and is a worldwide phenomenon. In many British cities now, there are what have been called '**superdiverse**' communities. People with vastly different languages, histories, cultural and social backgrounds and religions live side by side. Sometimes, new migrants arrive and join with communities from their countries of origin that have lived in the city for generations.

Case Study: A superdiverse corner shop

This photo of a corner shop in a Yorkshire city shows clearly the effects of 'superdiversity' on everyday life in a typical community.

Figure 1.1 Shop front in a 'superdiverse' city

→

> A Lithuanian heritage family-owned the shop from the 1950s until they sold it to a Pakistani heritage family in the 1980s. A few years ago, this family sold the shop to a Polish man. He put up a new sign, covering the old Lithuanian name. He kept the small '**halal** meat' logos from the Pakistani heritage owners at the edges of the sign to show that he still provides meat for the local Muslim community. He also sells phone cards to customers from all over the world. He placed a bright yellow banner in the shop window (at the bottom right of the picture) to show how he catered for the changing community around the shop: 'Everyone welcome English, Arabic, Kurdish, Polish, Slovakia', it says. There are now many multilingual communities like this in cities all over England, where many of our EAL children live.

Also, as we see below, an increasing number now also live in towns or villages where they may be very few other bilingual children.

Activity 1.3
Language and cultural diversity in school

If you have a placement in a school where there are children learning English as an additional language, try to find out the following information.

1. How many children in school are defined as 'EAL learners'?
2. How many different languages are spoken by children in the school?
3. How does the school find out about and record the languages?
4. Does the school have a policy for EAL or language diversity?
5. How are EAL issues managed in the school?

If you cannot undertake this activity in your placement school, see if you could arrange a visit to a school where it would be possible to do it.

2. Who are 'EAL learners'?

Sometimes the term 'EAL' is applied only to children who are actually better thought of as 'new to English'. In reality, 'EAL' is an umbrella term for many different groups of children who bring a vast range of experience and knowledge of languages, cultures, schooling and literacies to their mainstream classrooms. The title of this book refers to 'bilingual and EAL learners' to make the point that we cannot think of the children whose learning we are considering as one, uniform group. Different terms have been used over the years in policies and strategy documents to describe the EAL learners you may meet in your classrooms. Here is a list of them.

- Learners who are second and third generation members of settled ethnic minority communities (advanced bilingual learners).
- Learners who are recent arrivals and new to English, some of whom have little or no

experience of schooling, and others who are already literate in their first languages (children new to English).

- Learners whose education has been disrupted because of war and other traumatic experiences (asylum-seekers and refugees).
- Learners who are in school settings with little prior experience of bilingual children (isolated learners).
- Learners whose parents are working and studying and are in England for short periods of time (sojourners).

Activity 1.4
Thinking about bilingual and EAL learners
Before you read the vignettes that follow, think about the children in your current class, or one you have recently taught. Do you think any of them would fit into any of the groups listed above?

Write a list of the names of the children, and identify which group you think each would belong to.

What follow are five vignettes that will help you to understand something about the children that belong to each of the groups listed above and to develop your understanding about who could be defined as 'EAL learners'.

2.1 Advanced bilingual learners – Yasmin

Yasmin, is eight years old and in a Year 3 class in a large, multilingual primary school in a city very like the one where the photo above was taken. Most of her classmates are from similar backgrounds to herself. She represents the biggest group in our list of different categories of EAL learners. She was born in England, the granddaughter of a man who arrived from the Kashmir area of Pakistan forty or fifty years ago to work in the woollen mills in the city. Yasmin is multilingual. English is her dominant language, so 'EAL' is not really a helpful way to describe her. As well as English, she speaks Punjabi and Urdu. She is also **multiliterate** (Datta, 2007). With her sisters and female cousins, she is learning the Koran in Arabic from a Muslim teacher who visits her home. Her brothers go to the local mosque, which is in a converted cinema close to their house. Her mum is teaching her to read and write Urdu, their heritage national language. All these languages have important, but different, roles to play in her life. While English may be the most important, there is no sign that the other languages are fading away. Indeed, the signs are that they will continue to be important for Yasmin and her community (see Chapter 3). Punjabi is the foreign language most commonly spoken by British people, with over half a million speakers. Children whose families originate from Bangladesh would have very similar histories, with Bengali and Sylheti as their community languages. Bengali is the second most commonly spoken foreign language by British people (Wikipedia, 2011).

Yasmin is doing very well in school so far. She is very talkative and keen to answer questions. At the end of Year 2, in the KS1 **Standardised Attainment Tasks (SATs)** she attained level 2 in English and level 3 in mathematics. Her dad helps her a lot in mathematics at home, teaching her the multiplication tables in Punjabi. Her mother and aunts do a lot of sewing, and Yasmin is very good at this and other practical activities. When she was younger, her grandma told her and her siblings lots of stories from Pakistan, in Punjabi. The children loved this and knew many of the stories by heart. Yasmin's reception teacher found out about this, and encouraged the children to tell the stories in school, with the bilingual teaching assistant helping to interpret for her. This had a big benefit for Yasmin's literacy, as it helped her to understand story structures and the kinds of language found in stories, which is different from spoken language. Children like Yasmin are exactly those whom Deryn Hall describes as 'living in two languages' (Hall et al. 2001), and who are discussed in Chapter 3.

2.2 New to English children – Stefan and Jan

Stefan and Jan are both ten years old, and in the same Year 5 class in a small Roman Catholic school in a big city in the north of England. They have both been attending the school for a couple of years, having arrived from Poland at almost the same time with their families. About 40% of the pupils in the school are from Pakistani-heritage backgrounds, and the numbers of children from Poland, the Czech Republic and Slovakia are steadily growing – currently it is about 10%, that is 2–3 children per class. Stefan and Jan's class teacher is a bit puzzled by the two boys. She checked the school records, and noticed that, since coming to the school, both new to English, their progress has been very different. They seemed to start off from a relatively similar position in relation to their knowledge of English. Both have become fairly confident and fluent in spoken English over the two years they have been in the school. They can answer questions in class, hold conversations with their teachers and their peers and take part in social activities in school. But, while Stefan has made good progress with reading and writing and is beginning to perform in assessments at similar levels to his peers, Jan is struggling. He has taken part in various intervention activities, but never seems to be able to catch up with Stefan or his other classmates.

The class teacher is considering what can be done to support Jan to help him catch up before he encounters the KS2 SATs in Year 6. She wonders whether yet another intervention activity is the answer. In studying part-time for her MA, she comes across the work of Cummins (see Chapter 3) and other writers on bilingualism. She finds their ideas about the links between languages in children's learning very intriguing and decides to find out a little about Stefan and Jan's knowledge of other languages, especially their home language, Polish. To her surprise and interest, she finds out that Stefan is an accomplished reader and writer of Polish, and that he regularly attends the Polish Saturday school in the city, where children study Polish to GCSE and A level. Jan, on the other hand, can only read and write a little Polish – his early schooling in Poland was disrupted because of his family situation. He went to the Saturday class for a short while, but then dropped out.

As an experiment, the teacher asks Stefan if he can bring some of his Polish books into school and tell the class about some of the things he does in the Saturday school. Stefan's dad comes along too, and tells the class a story in Polish, which Stefan translates into English. The visit is a huge success. Afterwards, the teacher notices how Jan seems much more enthusiastic and motivated. So she decides to give the children opportunities, from time to time, to work together in same-language groups where they can discuss things with each other, using their home languages and then report back or write in English (see section 2 of Chapter 4 for more information about planning and organising groupwork). As time goes on, Jan's reading and writing slowly begin to improve, while his confidence steadily grows.

2.3 Asylum-seekers and refugees – Umaru

Umaru is eleven years old and in Year 6. He came to England as a baby with his mother, Jenneh, who had had to escape from her home town in Sierra Leone, when it was overrun by fighting during the civil war that ended about ten years ago. His father was a solicitor and his mother an administrator in a large secondary school in the town. At first, Umaru and his mother lived temporarily in bed and breakfast accommodation in London, and after 18 months they moved to a small town in the north-west of England where Jenneh had a friend. Other friends helped with accommodation and Jenneh found a job in a supermarket. They settled fairly well, although they were the target of racial abuse for a while. But they had lost touch with Umaru's father because of the unsettled situation in Sierra Leone. Jenneh applied for political asylum and, after a long struggle, she gained it.

Though they had been in their new home for two years, by the time Umaru began school, their future was still uncertain. Events in Sierra Leone had calmed and Jenneh had made contact with her family, but Umaru's father had died. All the problems she faced were a great strain on Jenneh and she became depressed. The school was a fairly small, Church of England school with very few non-white pupils. At first, Umaru was a well-behaved little boy and he made a good impression on his teachers. He was very polite and spoke good English, as Jenneh had been careful to teach him because English is the official language of Sierra Leone. However, the teachers knew nothing about his home country apart from the awful events that were sometimes shown on television. This made the teachers feel sorry for Umaru, and they did not push him very hard in his work. There were other ethnic minority children in the school, but none from Africa. As time went on, Umaru's attendance at school was sometimes irregular as he had to stay at home to look after his mother when she felt unable to go to work. His school work suffered and he did not make many friends. He did not do well in the KS1 SATs at the end of KS1, and was placed in a SEN group, where he became very withdrawn. He got further and further behind in his work, and his behaviour also began to suffer as his anxiety about his mother grew. No one at school knew of his home situation. Now that he has reached Year 6, his prospects of attaining level 4 in the SATs look slim. His work in school is clearly not meeting expectations, nor is it reflecting his true ability.

2.4 Isolated learners – Radia

Radia is in Year 4 in a primary school in a village near to a small city in the south west of England. The family have been living in England for five years altogether. She has been attending the school for two years, after moving to the village with her family when her father began a job at the local university, where he had recently completed his PhD. When the family first arrived in England from their home country, Algeria, they lived in the city, near the university. Radia attended a large, busy, multilingual primary school where she had some friends whose parents were also students. She did very well and was happy. When the job offer came, Radia's parents decided to move to the village in order to have a bigger house and garden and – they hoped – better schooling for their three children, of whom Radia is the eldest.

All is not going as well as they hoped. Radia's mother is finding it lonely living in the village with no Algerian friends nearby. Although her neighbours are very pleasant, none of them visit her as regularly as she would like, and she often spends days alone with her young child. She takes the two older children to school every day and would like to be able to talk to their teachers more than she does. But she never seems to be able to engage them in conversation. Radia has not settled very well into school. She misses the friends she made in her old school, and has not really made any new friends in the village school. She is the only 'EAL' pupil in her class, and one of only eight or ten in the whole school, all of whom are from well-educated, middle-class backgrounds, some from Islamic countries in the Middle East and others from China. Their parents are either students or former students, like Radia's, or professionals working for companies in the city.

The school has taken steps to find out how to support their new pupils – one teacher has been given responsibility for their induction, and went on a training course, which was part of the *New arrivals excellence programme* (Department for Education, 2011b). But she did not find anything very relevant for the pupils coming to the village school. They all seem to be very fluent in English so language does not seem to an issue for them. One of the strategies recommended on the course was to form good relationships with the children's parents, and she would like to be able to do this. But when she meets them as they bring their children to school and come to collect them, she finds it difficult to think of ways to generate conversations with them. She has not had much prior experience of people from different cultural backgrounds. She raises this in a staff meeting, and this leads to a long discussion. One of the outcomes is a decision to organise a social event to give parents an opportunity to meet their children's teachers and see something of the work they do in class. This proves a great success, and greatly helps the processes of communication in the school.

2.5 Sojourners – Hamida

Hamida is five years old and in Year 1 in a large, mainly white school in a prosperous city in the south of England. She arrived with her family from Saudi Arabia in the city at the start of the school year. Her father is doing a PhD at the university, and her mother also has plans to study, once childcare arrangements are made for Hamida and her two younger brothers. Hamida speaks Arabic, and is also learning to read and write it in a Saturday class run by the wife of another Saudi Arabian student. Her parents are very concerned that she maintains her skills in Arabic, as they will be returning home in three or four years' time. They are also very keen that she learns to speak English – indeed, this was one of the main reasons why they decided to bring her to England with them, rather than leaving her at home with relatives, as other students have done with their children. They want her to learn 'proper' English so that she speaks as far as possible with a **Received Pronunciation** (**RP**) accent, which will afford her high status in Saudi Arabia. They also, quite naturally, want her to retain her Muslim identity, and hope that the school are aware of, and sensitive to, Islamic rules and practices.

The class that Hamida has joined comprises mostly 'white British' children, though there is one other bilingual child, whose parents are students, like Hamida's. He is from Indonesia and – like Hamida – his family is Muslim. Both children are new to the school, and so have not been through the Foundation Stage in the English system. The class teacher is very positive and enthusiastic about having them as her pupils, but is having to work hard to find relevant background information and resources such as stories and information books from their home countries. She is a little wary of the anticipated requirements related to the children's Muslim identities but willing to find out and to be flexible in her teaching. She is very keen to establish good relationships with the children's families as she sees this as a support for her in meeting the needs of their children.

Activity 1.5
Understanding diversity

Each of the five children in the vignettes have particular experiences and knowledge that can be seen as strengths as they benefit their learning in mainstream school, and particular gaps in their experience that may create issues for their progress and their achievements. Make a chart like the one below and, in discussion with other trainees or colleagues in your placement school, list what you think could be seen as each child's strengths and needs, from the vignettes. There are some suggested answers at the end of the chapter on page 19.

child	strengths	needs
Yasmin		
Stefan		
Jan		
Umaru		
Radia		
Hamida		

3. Language diversity and learning – some myths and misconceptions

This brief, final section is intended to begin to raise some questions in your mind about the best approaches to teaching children with EAL. You may already have experience of teaching English to children or adults in other countries, which is normally defined as **English as a Foreign language (EFL)** teaching, and you may even have done a **Teaching English as a Foreign Language (TEFL)** course. There are parallels between EFL and EAL learners and some ideas from TEFL teaching can be very useful in EAL. But, there are also important differences, as the case studies in this chapter show. Some ideas from TEFL teaching may seem like common sense, but they can become myths and misconceptions when working with bilingual and EAL learners. They may not seem to be so helpful when you understand something of the complexities of the experiences of many bilingual and EAL learners. You will read a lot about theories of language, learning and bilingualism in Chapters 2 and 3, which will develop your understanding of the needs of bilingual and EAL learners. They will also help you to see how these myths and misconceptions can sometimes be unhelpful. So, here are my 'myths and misconceptions' – we will return to them at the end of the book, in Chapter 7.

- Languages should be kept separate in the classroom, or learners will become confused *(this is sometimes called 'language interference')*.

- Children will 'pick English up' naturally in the classroom; they do not need to be explicitly taught *(this is sometimes called 'immersion')*.

- Language diversity is a 'problem', and it is better if children speak English all the time in classrooms.

- It is impossible, or very difficult, to learn a new language beyond a young age *(this is sometimes called 'the critical period')*.

Learning Outcomes Review

This introductory chapter has provided you with background information about the children who are categorised as bilingual and EAL learners, and their families and communities. This should have helped you gain awareness of the history of language and cultural diversity in England, and the diverse range of experiences and knowledge that bilingual and EAL learners bring to their primary classrooms. One of the aims was to help you think about the importance of recognising and reflecting on your own views on language diversity and ethnicity for you as a primary teacher.

Self-assessment questions

1. In what ways do you think your own identity might influence your views and perceptions of the children you teach? Think about specific situations where this may have happened.

2. Why do you think it is important to understand something about the family backgrounds of the children you teach? (you will read more about this in Chapter 3).

3. Think about the teachers mentioned in each of the vignettes in this chapter. Following what you have read in this chapter, if you had been the teacher for any of the children described, would you have responded in the same way, or might you have done something different?

4. Think of a group of bilingual and EAL learners you know. Which of the categories introduced in section 1.2 would your learners fit into? Write a brief vignette of one of your learners, along the lines of those in the section.

Suggested answers
Activity 1:5 – understanding diversity

child	strengths	needs
Yasmin	• Strong speaking and listening skills • Supportive home and community • Diverse experiences of learning at home	• Sustained support in developing writing skills in English
Stefan	• Strong literacy in home language • Opportunities to develop expertise and take exams in home language	• Continued support in developing writing skills in English
Jan	• Teacher who is interested in understanding the problems he is facing • Positive attitude in class to recognising children's home languages	• Personalised provision to develop his skills in English
Umaru	• Good level of English language • Loving relationship with mother • Sympathy and caring environment in school	• Understanding (on the part of his teachers) of the broader cultural background of Sierra Leone • Personalised provision to help him catch up
Radia	• Supportive home and family background • Positive attitudes in school towards EAL children	• Improved communication between home and school
Hamida	• Supportive home and family background • Positive attitudes in school towards EAL children	• Greater awareness on the part of the school of cultural and religious factors underpinning Hamida's experiences

Further Reading

Gussin Paley, V. (2000) *White teacher*, 3rd edn. Cambridge: Harvard University Press.
This a personal account of teaching in a school which becomes increasingly diverse. Paley reflects on the way that even simple terminology can convey unintended meanings. She vividly describes what her pupils taught her over the years about herself as a 'white teacher'.

Hayes, D. (2011) Establishing your own teaching identity. In: Hansen, A. (ed) *Primary professional studies* (pp. 118–33). Exeter: Learning Matters.
This chapter encourages readers to think about their own values, motivation and self-identity, and the impact these have on becoming a teacher.

References

Arbeia Fort (2011) http://en.wikipedia.org/wiki/Arbeia (accessed 12 February 2012).

BBC (2007) *Multilingualism* www.bbc.co.uk/voices/yourvoice/multilingualism2.shtml (accessed 21 February 2012).

Datta, M. (2007) *Bilinguality and biliteracy: principles and practice,* 2nd edn. London: Continuum.

Department for Education (2011a) *Schools, children and their characteristics: January 2011* www.education.gov.uk/rsgateway/DB/SFR/s000925/index.shtml (accessed 12 February 2012).

Department for Education (2011b) *The National Strategies: New arrivals excellence programme: CPD modules* http://nsonline.org.uk/node/113690 (accessed 12 February 2012).

Hall, D., Griffiths, D., Haslam, L. and Wilkin, Y. (2001) *Assessing the needs of bilingual pupils: living in two languages,* 2nd edn. London: David Fulton.

Wikipedia (2011) *Languages of the United Kingdom* http://en.wikipedia.org/wiki/Languages_of_the_United_Kingdom (accessed 12 February 2012).

Educational Disadvantage in the Early Years: How do we overcome it? Some Lessons from Research

Siraj-Blatchford, I.

Introduction

The central aim of the five year longitudinal Effective Provision of Preschool Education (EPPE) study has been to explore the effects of preschool education on children's attainment and social/behavioural development at entry to school and beyond[1] (Sylva et at 1999a). High quality ratings, on the environmental rating scales applied to the 141 pre-school settings that were involved in the study, were found to be good predictors of the children's achievement. When correlations were sought between the children's achievements and the scores recorded on the eleven individual subscales that made up these rating scales it was found that the quality practices related to the subscale 'Diversity' were associated with as many as five of the nine cognitive and social/behavioural attainment outcomes. Surprisingly, this was higher that for any of the other sub-scales including 'literacy'. In this paper Gidden's theory of the duality of structure will be applied in an attempt to explain why this might have been the case. In doing so, the paper identifies opportunities available to both parents and professional educators to overcome the structural inequalities associated with underachievement in terms of socio-economic class, gender and ethnicity.

Source: *European Early Childhood Education Research Journal*, 12(2) (2004): 5–20.

Social Inequalities and the Preschool

A wide range of studies have shown how children can be disadvantaged on the grounds of diversity in ethnic background, language, special needs, gender and socio-economic class in both intentional and in unintentional ways at all levels of education (Siraj-Blatchford, 1994; Troyna & Hatcher, 1992; Gillborn, 1995; Ball, 2003; Ladson-Billings & Gillborn, 2004).

The results of standardised assessments show that, as a group, boys underachieve in terms of basic literacy from an early age (Programme for International Student Assessment (PISA)(2000)[2]. But while girls, as a group, underachieved for many decades in subjects such as science and mathematics, the progress they are currently making in these subjects at school is superior to that of boys (DfES, 2003)[3]. The case of girls in science and in mathematics education in the UK is especially important as it reminds us that none of these inequalities are either natural or in any way inevitable. In time, changes in the taken-for-granted everyday cultural practices of homes, schools and workplaces in our societies *can* be effective in transforming structural inequalities.

A major question for the *Effective Provision of Preschool Education* (EPPE) study was whether preschool experience could reduce social inequalities. The study applied multi-level modelling to investigate the separate effects of personal and social and family background, and the quality of the home learning environment from the quality of the learning environment of the preschools themselves. The EPPE study applied the revised Early Childhood Environmental Rating Scale (ECERS R) (Harms, Clfford & Cryer, 1998) to measure the quality of the environmental provisions and pedagogic practices that led to more effective practice (in terms of child academic and social outcomes). The revised ECERS-R has 43 items, which are divided into 7 sub-scales. These sub-scales are space and furnishing, personal care routines, language and reasoning, activities, social interactions, organisation and routines, adults working together. Each item is rated on a 7-point scale (1 = inadequate, 3 = minimal/adequate, 5 = good, 7 = excellent). As the ECERS was developed in (and for) the USA, a rating scale was also specifically developed to suit the English Foundation Stage, which was developed for children 3–5 (ECERS-Extension, Sylva, Siraj-Blatchford and Taggart, 2003).

The ECERS-E was devised after wide consultation with experts and piloted extensively. The word 'environment' in the new 'extension' rating scale continued to be taken in its broadest sense to include social interactions, pedagogical strategies and relationships between children as well as adults and children. The construction of this scale also provided an opportunity to address the issue of the quality of provision for inclusion and diversity more fully than ever before. A copy of the ECERS-E Diversity Sub-scale that was developed for this purpose is included as an Appendix to this paper. In reporting on the associations found between the qualities of provision made by the 141 preschools for diversity, and the children's cognitive and social outcomes, EPPE has provided the very first evidence of the overall effectiveness of these curriculum approaches.

All of the ECERS ratings were carried out by fully trained, reliable research officers. Each of these research officers had been assessing children in a centre for at least 6 months prior to carrying out the observations and ratings. Kappa inter-rater agreement was found to vary between .83 and .97. In-depth qualitative case studies were conducted in 12 out of the 141 settings. These were identified as good to excellent in terms of child developmental outcomes and this qualitative work was further extended through the Researching Effective Pedagogy in the Early Years (REPEY) project (Siraj-Blatchford, et al, 2002).

A total of over 2,800 three and four year-old children from 141 preschool centres as well as 300+ 'home' children were involved in the EPPE study. They were assessed at entry to the study (age 3.0 years to 4 years 3 months), and then at entry to reception class (beginning of primary school when most children are four plus) and then at the end of reception at 5, in Year 1 at age 6, and in Year 2 at age 7. The standardised assessments included elements of the British Ability Scales and instruments were applied to record social and behavioural development in terms of cooperation/conformity, peer sociability, anti-social or 'worried/upset' behaviour. Six local authorities and 141 Preschool centres had been randomly selected to include the full range of English contexts and group care and education providers[4] as opposed to family daycare.

The effectiveness of each of the preschool settings was determined by calculating the value added residuals that were left between the actual child outcome results and those that were predicted when controlled for prior-attainment and significant child, parent and home learning environment characteristics. EPPE found that the quality of the preschool centres (as measured by ECERS-R and ECERS-E rating scales) was related to better intellectual/cognitive and social/behavioural development in children.

EPPE also found that most early childhood settings provide a relatively low quality learning environment for children in terms of diversity (from Sylva et al, 1999b). The quality of diversity provision was highest in combined centres (those that fully integrated care and education) and in some nursery schools where the overall ECERS scores were also higher.

Yet in terms of outcomes, strong patterns of association were found between the ECERS-E subscale for Diversity and children's attainment in Early Number ($r = 0.18$, $p < 0.05$) and Non-verbal reasoning ($r = 0.27$, $p < 0.001$). A positive relationship with Pre-reading was also verging on statistical significance. To fully appreciate the predictive quality of the Diversity sub-scale in terms of the cognitive outcomes it is instructive to look at the overall pattern of the correlations that were found across the full range of attainments and subscales after controlling for the child, parent, home environment and other preschool characteristics.

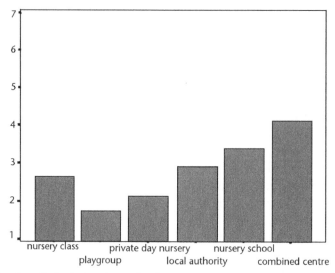

Provisions for diversity by types of preschool type

	Pre-reading	Early number concepts	Language	Non-vebal verbal reasoning	Spatial awareness
ECERS-E					
Average total	positive*	positive		positive	
Literacy	positive*	positive			
Maths				positive	
Science/Environment				positive#	
Diversity	positive#	positive		positive	
ECERS					
Average total					
Space and furnishings					
Personal care					
Language & reasoning				positive#	
Activities					
Interaction		positive			
Programme structure					
Parents and staff	positive#				

* When change of centre is not in model   # verging on statistical significance

In terms of social/behavioural outcomes, high scores on the Diversity sub-scale were also found to be weakly correlated with 'Independence' ($r = 0.16$, $p < 0.05$), and (not quite significantly) with 'Co-operation and conformity' ($r = 0.16$, $p < 0.06$). 'Diversity' was therefore found to be associated with as many as five of the nine attainment outcomes. This was higher than for any of the other sub-scales.

In the struggle to produce an adequate explanation of this finding, another key finding from the EPPE study was found to provide an important clue. This was related to the quality of the Home Learning Environment (HLE) (Melhuish et al 2001) that was provided by parents.

The Significance of the Home Learning Environment

As previously suggested, in order for EPPE to explore the effects of pre-school education and to provide a fair comparison it was important to take into account (or 'control for') the children's prior attainment, and for family and home factors. On their child's entry to the study, over ninety eight per-cent of parents were interviewed based on an 11 page interview schedule. When compared with the child outcome data, the analysis of this child/parent/ home data identified a range of indicators of disadvantage:

In terms of child characteristics children tended to be disadvantaged where English was not their first language, where they lived in large fami-lies with 3 or more siblings or were born prematurely, or with a low birth weight (below 2500 grams).

In terms of parent characteristics, children were disadvantaged where:

- the mother had no educational qualifications;
- the father was semi-skilled, unskilled, never worked, or absent;
- the mother was aged 13–17 at birth of child;
- one parent was unemployed;
- they were brought up in a single parent household.

In addition to the general demographic questions seven types of home learn-ing activities (we asked about many more) were found to be very important to the HLE in the parental interview:

- frequency reading to child;
- frequency of library visits;
- frequency child paints/draws at home;
- frequency parent teaches letters/numbers;
- frequency parent teaches the alphabet;
- frequency parent teaches songs, nursery rhymes, etc.

From the answers given in the interview each activity was rated on a scale 0–7 where 0 was 'not occurring' and 7 was occurring very frequently. These ratings were then combined to form a Home Learning Environment index (HLE). Home learning environments scored at the bottom quartile of the scale were found to significantly predict lower child outcomes at entry to preschool.

But it was found that the quality of the learning environment of the home (where parents were actively engaged in activities with children) promoted intellectual and social development in children. This impact of the home learning environment (HLE) could be assessed either individually for each component or in terms of the overall index. Whichever strategy was chosen similar results showing powerful effects on cognitive, language and social development were found.

The following table oveleaf shows the HLE scores and the percentage of children identified as 'at cognitive risk' (defined in terms of being one standard deviation (sd) below the national average) at the end of their first year at school (age 6 yrs) Siraj-Blatchford and Sammons, 2004):

	All children	Primary reading risk	Mathematics risk
Mean HLE score	23.6 (sd = 7.5)	19.8 (sd = 7.5)	20.2 (sd = 7.5)
0–13	8.4	19.4	18.7
14–19	20.9	29.3	26.7
20–24	23.6	22.3	22.4
25–32	31.9	21.0	24.0
33–45	12.4	5.1	4.0
Unknown	2.9	2.9	4.3
Chi-square	–	93.391, p < 0.001	104.129, p < 0.001

Although the parents' socio-economic status and levels of education were related to child outcomes, the quality of the home learning environment was found to be more important. At age 3 yrs and onwards a strong association was found between poor cognitive attainment and a less stimulating HLE. By comparison there was only a moderate, positive association between the HLE and parents' socio-economic status and qualifications (r = 0.3). For example, the children of parents who reported that they regularly taught/played with the 'a,b,c' had pre-reading scores 4.5 points higher than children whose parents did not teach/play the 'a,b,c'. This could be compared to the impact of social class where the difference between lowest class (IV and V) and highest (I) was only 2.4 points. *In other words; EPPE found that it is what parents did that is more important than who they were* (Melhuish et al, 2001).

This would appear to support Gidden's (1991) theory of the *duality of structure* where structures of inequality are seen as both the medium and the outcome of social practices.

The Duality of Structure

According to Giddens, people shape structures but structures also tend to determine what people can do. Structures are both the rules and resources implicated in the reproduction of social systems. So Giddens has argued that all structures are ultimately enabling, and give the 'knowledgeable' agent the capability to work within them in creative and formative ways. Dual structures are not therefore inescapably determinate, and the effects of structural inequality may be escaped.

Following Sewell (1992) we can consider the rules that Giddens (1991) identifies as cultural schema, with the home educational practices that include reading to children, taking them to the library etc seen as educational schema that only some working class parents currently have a 'knowledge' of. Resources, not least in terms of time, are significant but it is also important to recognise here that the knowledge that working class parents require includes a recognition of the power that they have in providing these educational experiences.

If we apply these principles to the question of explaining the effectiveness of settings in providing for diversity we can see that the improved cognitive and social outcomes achieved by the children may be partly the result of the practitioners having higher expectations. The Diversity sub-scale records provision and planning for *individual* and *cultural* needs, and for the provision of positive role models. High scores on the subscale reflect a recognition of the importance of having high expectations for all children regardless of socio-economic class, ability, gender or ethnicity. If early education practitioners lack a knowledge and understanding of these principles and/or remain unaware of their effectiveness in supporting the achievement of disadvantaged children then the cycle of deprivation and underachievement, which currently exists, will continue.

The experiences and values that young children hold are shaped and constructed from the views of parents and their educators, as well as by their peers, media images etc. In the absence of strong and positive role models some children are often left with negative perception of people like themselves. This bias can start from birth. Many parents and early childhood practitioners may conclude from children's behaviour that they are incapable, without considering their own contribution to the children's socialisation, or considering the impact of role modelling. Of course even the youngest children play an active part in all of this and mutual adaptations of behaviour occur between children and the adults who care for them. Children, for example, often encourage early childhood practitioners, through their behaviour, to play out the social games that they have learnt in the home. Early childhood practitioners may therefore quite inadvertently find themselves taking up the role of a dominating parent or sibling. Early childhood practitioners may therefore lower their demands, and provide children with too much help, giving away answers to problems or questions rather than encouraging and supporting them to come up with answers for themselves.

Dweck and Leggett (1988) categorised learners as 'mastery oriented' or 'helpless' according to their response to failure or difficulty. 'Helpless' children tend to be less persistent, they give up easily as they worry about their lack of ability. But when 'mastery oriented' children experience a setback;

they tend to focus on effort and strategies instead of worrying that they are incompetent. These dispositions to learn are very powerful and are associated with the development of positive personal and social identities. Positive dispositions provide resilience (Werner & Smith, 1982, Claxton, 1999) and lead to positive lifelong 'learning trajectories' (Gorard et al, 1999).

A child may be classed, gendered or 'racialised' (special needs and language status is also important here) in more than one way. Stuart Hall (1992), for example, discussed not only the discourses of identity but also those of difference *within* ethnic groups. In terms of race and ethnicity, Hall argued that there are often contradictions within these categories as well as between these and other categories such as sexuality, class, dis/ability. The way we perceive identities is very much shaped by how they are produced and taken up through the *practices* of representation (Grossberg, 1994).

Making use of the metaphor of a *kaleidoscope* in understanding identity based on a range of inequalities, Bailey and Hall (1992) have argued that there will be individual differences within any identity forming category, such as race, language, gender and social class. For instance, in Britain, an Indian woman who is a first generation immigrant, and working in a factory, will have a different identity to her daughter who is second generation British-Indian, and has become a teacher. Their experience will vary because of how others perceive the combination of ethnic background in relation to their gender, socio-economic status, dress, language, even age and so forth. Others will certainly not treat mother and daughter in the same way even though the two women have some shared experiences.

It is apparent that certain confounding identities, for instance, black/ working class/male, can lead to lower outcomes (in the UK and many other societies) because of expectations held by the children, adults and peer group around them. In asserting their masculinity in the preschool, working class boys might choose gross-motor construction activities over reading or pre-reading activities. Similarly, some girls may identify more strongly with home-corner play and favour nurturing activities over construction choices. Class, gender, ability and ethnicity are all complicit here and while the permutations are far from simple or even consistently applied, it is clear that they do exist and that they do often lead to underachievement. The answer is partly to avoid stereotyping children's identities but this also requires educators to take an active role in planning for, supporting and developing individual children's identities as masterful learners of a broad and balanced curriculum (Siraj-Blatchford, 1998).

In the active construction of their learner identities, just as with every other aspect of identity, children distance themselves from 'others' (Siraj-Blatchford, I. and J., 1999). As one little boy was overheard in a playgroup saying to another boy "Why do you just sit reading? Girls read – boys play football!" The issue is therefore to show children that they are mistaken in

Table 3:

HLE score	Boys	Girls
0–13	206 (13.3%)	102 (7.0%)
14–19	381 (24.6%)	284 (19.5%)
20–24	376 (24.3%)	351 (24.1%)
25–32	463 (29.9%)	497 (34.1%)
33–45	122 (7.9%)	224 (15.4%)
Total	1548 (100.0%)	1458 (100.0%)

associating these 'others' exclusively with particular areas of learning. Early childhood pedagogues can extend children's identity as learners and break down the stereotypes. Boys need to disassociate literacy from 'girls' stuff, and be presented with strong male role models that value literacy. Work with fathers may be particularly relevant here but the importance of educators working with families in developing the home learning environment for all children really needs to be emphasised.

It is important to recognise that the implications of all of this for families are as significant as they are for early years practitioners. The EPPE study found that some parents with high family socio-economic status (SES) and qualification levels provided a home learning environment, which was low on the home learning environment (HLE) index. Conversely there were parents low on SES and qualifications that provide a home environment high on the HLE index. There were also significant gender differences in the reported HLE, which suggests that parenting styles differ for boys and girls. The following table (Table 3) shows the extent to which parents can be seen to provide quite different HLEs for boys and girls (Siraj-Blatchford & Sammons, 2004).

While 37.9% of boys experienced a HLE that scored below 20, only 26.5% of the girls were disadvantaged in this way. Even more significantly the number of boys experiencing a HLE rated under 13 is nearly twice that experienced by girls. A great deal has been written about boys' underachievement in recent years. But historically in the UK, middle class, white boys have over-achieved in schools, and the underachievement of working class girls has always been more significant than any underachievement of girls as a whole regardless of the subject area. Similarly, children from some minority ethnic groups perform poorly in significant areas of the curriculum while other minority ethnic groups achieve particularly highly (Gillborn & Gipps, 1997, *DfES, 2003*).

The EPPE study has shown that preschool education does make a significant difference in terms of attainment for all children when compared to having no preschool education. EPPE also found that while ethnic minority children tended to enter preschool with significantly lower attainment scores in pre-reading they made more progress than ethnic majority (white) children in these terms. The effect of preschool can therefore he seen to be especially significant for minority ethnic groups. But a recent survey of the parents of three and four year-olds has suggests that only 88% of minority ethnic children had recently attended preschool compared to 99% of the ethnic majority (Fitzgerald et al, 2002).

Children with similar levels of HLE were two to three times more likely to be identified as 'at risk' if they had not attended preschool:

	Preschool sample			Home children		
HLE	GCA risk	Pre-reading risk	Early number concepts risk	GCA risk	Pre-reading risk	Early number concepts risk
0–13	46.8	39.0	45.7	76.9	64.0	65.4
14–19	23.3	21.5	24.0	49.1	43.9	56.1
20–24	13.2	16.9	14.5	39.6	31.3	31.3
25–32	9.9	11.6	13.2	35.0	33.0	36.8
33–45	3.6	6.4	5.2	0.0*	0.0*	9.1*

* Only 11 home children were in the highest HLE group so this statistic shown should be treated with caution (Siraj-Blatchford and Sammons, 2004)

EPPE found that while the scores for language attainment for nearly all minority ethnic groups on entry to school were significantly lower than for the ethnic majority children, African-Caribbean children recorded significantly higher non-verbal reasoning scores (Sammons, et al, 2003). The methods applied in school baseline assessments may therefore have important equity implications – and the facts of inequality in education are far from black and white . . .

After taking into account the impact of child, family, home environment characteristics EPPE also found that:

- Children from high quality preschools had in general higher academic attainment at the end of year 1.
- The duration of attendance is important with an earlier start (between 2 and 3) being related to better intellectual development and improved independence, concentration and sociability.
- Full time attendance led to no better gains for children than part-time provision.
- Children from preschool centres with high quality showed fewer conduct problems two years after school entry.
- Disadvantaged children (and those 'at risk' of SEN) in particular can benefit significantly from good quality preschool experiences, especially if they attend centres that cater for a mixture of children from different social backgrounds.

Conclusions

Although I have been concerned here with the structural inequalities which create an over-representation of some groups in disadvantaged conditions, I have cautioned elsewhere (Siraj-Blatchford, 1996) against the assumption that all members of a structurally oppressed group (e.g. *all females*) are necessarily oppressed by those members of a structurally dominant group (e.g. *all males*). Because of the interplay between social class, gender, ethnicity and dis/ability, individual identities are multifaceted. I therefore argue that children can hold contradictory individual positions with respect to the structural position that their 'group' holds in society. Interactional contexts and *agency* (with adults and with peers) are also often highly significant.

The failure of parents and early childhood practitioners to recognise the power that they hold, as well as the sexism, racism and other prejudices that are endemic to our society, explain why at a structural level certain groups of people continue to be disadvantaged in education. But as educators engaging on a day to day basis with young children we should be critically aware of the danger of stereotyping and should always focus upon individuals and individual needs. This is not to suggest that we should ignore structure, far from it, we need to engage in developing the awareness of both adults and children through policies and practices, which explain and counter group inequalities. The effects of gender, class and other formative categories overlap in often very complicated ways, to shape an individual's identity. In fact identity formation is an extremely complex process that is never completed. It is therefore essential for practitioners to avoid treating individuals as if they have had an entirely homogeneous experience with others of their 'type'. As Roberts (1998) argues, the process by which all children develop their self-esteem and identity rests very heavily upon the type of interactions and relationships adults form with them. In this context it is important to recognise that minority ethnic workers are currently much better represented in social services type daycare and combined centres than in other early childhood sectors (Taggart, et al, 2000). Managers and staff in preschool settings need to be challenged by such data, to think about how this has come about and indeed how it might be changed.

A number of publications related to the development of children's personal, social and emotional education provide very useful strategies for supporting the positive development of children's personal identities. Yet few writers relate this work specifically to ethnicity, language, gender or class.

Parental involvement in education is crucially important. There are a range of activities that parents might undertake with children birth to five that could be expected to improve children's cognitive development and learning i.e. have a positive educational effect. As we have seen, such activities include reading to children, library visits, painting/drawing, teaching/playing with letters, teaching/playing with numbers and teaching songs/

poems. All of these activities can be regarded as markers for a parental orientation towards developing their child's learning.

Curriculum approaches focused on equality and diversity, that is, strong differentiation in planning for children's learning, have been shown to be effective in terms of children's cognitive, social and behavioural development.

Notes

1. The study has recently been extended to explore these effects to age 11 see: http://www.ioe.ac.uk/eppe
2. http://www.pisa.oecd.org/
3. http://www.standards.dfes.gov.uk/genderandachievement/understanding/analysis/
4. For a complete account of the methodology and the instruments employed in the study see Sammons et al 2004 and/or the EPPE project website:

References

Bailey, D. & Hall, S. (1992) (Eds.) Critical Decade: Black British Photography in the 80s, *Ten-8* 2, 3.

Ball, S. (2003) *Class Strategies and the Education Market: The Middle Classes and Social Advantage* (Routledge Falmer, London).

Claxton, G. (1999) *Wise up: The Challenge of Lifelong Learning* (London, Bloomsbury).

DfES (2003) Analysis by Gender, Gender and Achievement. Available online at: http://www.standards.dfes.gov.uk/genderandachievement/understanding/analysis/.

Dweck, C. & Leggett, E. (1988) A social-cognitive approach to motivation and personality, *Psychological Review*, Vol. 95, No. 2, pp. 256–273.

Fitzgerald, R., Finch, S., Blake, M., Perry, J. & Bell, A. (2002) *Fifth Survey of Parents of Three and Four Year Old Children and Their Use of Early Years Services* (DfES, RR351).

Giddens, A. (1991) *Modernity and Self-identity. Self and Society in the Late Modern Age* (Cambridge: Polity Press).

Gillborn, D. (1995) *Racism and Antiracism in Real Schools: Theory, Policy, Practice* (Open University Press, London).

Gillborn, D. & Gipps, C. (1997) *Recent Research on the Achievements of Minority Ethnic Pupils* (London: HMSO).

Gorard, S., Rees, G, & Fevre, R. (1999) Patterns of Participation in Lifelong Learning: do families make a difference? *British Educational Research Journal*, Vol. 25, No. 4, pp. 517–532.

Grossberg, L. (1994) 'Introduction: Bringin' It All Back Home – Pedagogy and Cultural Studies', in: Giroux, H. & McLaren, P. (1994) (Eds.) *Between Borders: Pedagogy and the Politics of Cultural Studies* (Routledge, New York).

Hall, S. (1992) Race, Culture and Communications: looking backward and forward in cultural studies, *Rethinking Marxism*, 5, pp. 10–18.

Harms, T., Clifford, M. & Cryer, D. (1998) *Early Childhood Environment Rating Scale, Revised Edition* (ECERS-R) (London, Teachers College Press).

Ladson-Billings, G. & Gillborn, D. (2004) *The Routledge Falmer Reader in Multicultural Education* (London, RoutledgeFalmer).

Lang, P. (1995) The Place of PSE in the Primary School, in: Siraj-Blatchford, I. & Siraj-Blatchford, J. (Eds.) (1995) *Educating the Whole Child: Cross-curricular Skills, Themes and Dimensions in the Primary Schools* (Buckingham, Open University Press).

Melhuish, E., Sylva, K., Sammons, P., Siraj-Blatchford, I. & Taggart, B. (2001) *The Effective Provision of Preschool Education (EPPE) Project: Technical Paper 7 – Social/Behavioural and Cognitive Development at 3–4 Years in Relation to Family Background* (London: DfEE/Institute of Education, University of London).

Roberts, R. (1998) Thinking about Me and Them: Personal and social development, in: Siraj-Blatchford, I. (Ed.) *A Curriculum Development Handbook for Early Childhood Educators* (Stoke-on-Trent, Trentham, pp. 155–174).

Sammons, P., Sylva, K., Melhuish, E. C., Siraj-Blatchford, I. & Taggart, B. (2002) *Measuring the Impact of Preschool on Children's Cognitive Progress Over the Preschool Period Technical Paper 8a* (London, DfEE/Institute of Education, University of London).

Sammons, P., Sylva, K., Melhuish, E. C., Siraj-Blatchford, I. & Taggart, B. (2003) *Measuring the Impact of Preschool on Children's Social/Behavioural Progress Over the Preschool Period Technical Paper 8b* (London, DfEE/Institute of Education, University of London).

Sewell, W. (1992) *A Theory of Structure: Duality, Agency, and Transformation* (Chicago, University of Chicago).

Siraj-Blatchford, I. (1994) *The Early Years: Laying the Foundations for Racial Equality* (Stoke on Trent, Trentham).

Siraj-Blatchford, I. & Siraj-Blatchford, J. (Eds.) (1995) *Educating the Whole Child: Cross-curricular Skills, Themes and Dimensions in the Primary Schools* (Buckingham: Open University Press).

Siraj-Blatchford, I. (1996) Language, Culture and Difference, in: Nutbrown, C. (Ed.) *Children's Rights and Early Education* (London, Paul Chapman, pp. 23–33).

Siraj-Blatchford, I. (1998) (Ed.) *A Curriculum Development Handbook for Early Childhood Educators* (Stoke-on-Trent, Trentham).

Siraj-Blatchford, I. & Siraj-Blatchford, J. (1999) Race, Research and Reform: The impact of the three Rs on anti-racist preschool and primary education in the UK, Race, *Ethnicity and Education*, Vol. 2, No. 1, pp. 127–148.

Siraj-Blatchford, I., Sylva, K. & Taggart, B. (2003) *Assessing Quality in the Early Years: Early Childhood Environment Rating Scales Extension (ECERS-E) Four Curricular Subscales* (Stoke on Trent, UK and Stirling, USA Trentham Books).

Siraj-Blatchford, I., Sylva, K., Muttock, S., Gilden, R. & Bell, D. (2002) *Researching Effective Pedagogy in the Early Years* (London, DfEE/Institute of Education, University of London).

Siraj-Blatchford, I. & Clarke, P. (2000) *Supporting Identity, Diversity and Language in the Early Years* (Buckingham: Open University Press).

Siraj-Blatchford, I. & Sammons, P. (2004) *Social mobility: The role of Preschools and Parents: Evidence from the UK, DfES funded EPPE Study*. Paper Presentation prepared for HM Treasury Conference on Social Mobility, London, March 30, 2004

Sylva, K., Sammons, P., Melhuish, E. C., Siraj-Blatchford, I. & Taggart, B. (1999a) *The Effective Provision of Preschool Education (EPPE) Project: Technical Paper 1 – An Introduction of EPPE* (London: DfEE/Institute of Education, University of London).

Sylva, K., Siraj-Blatchford, I., Melhuish, E., Sammons, P., Taggart, B., Evans, E., Dobson, A., Jeavons, M., Lewis, K., Morahan, M., & Sadler, S. (1999b) *Technical Paper 6 – The Effective Provision of Preschool Education (EPPE) Project: Characteristics of the Centres in the EPPE Sample: Observational Profiles* (London: DfEE/Institute of Education, University of London).

Troyna, B. & Hatcher, R. (1992) *Racism in Children's Lives: A Study of Mainly White Primary Schools* (London, National Children's Bureau and Routledge).

Werner, E., & Smith, R. (1982) *Vulnerable but Invincible* (McGraw-Hill, London).

Appendix

Diversity subscale (from Sylva, Siraj-Blatchford and Taggart, 2003)

Item 1: Planning for individual learning needs. Ask to see the records kept on individual children.

1 – inadequate	3 – minimal	5 – good	7 – excellent
1.1 All children in the setting are offered the same range of materials and activities, rather than having activities matched to their age or aptitude.	3.1 Some additional provision is made in terms of developmental stage, or for individuals or groups with specific needs such as learning support or English language support.	5.1 The range of activities provided enables children of all abilities and from all backgrounds to participate in a satisfying and cognitively demanding way, e.g. showing children the different tasks they can attempt with a toy or game.	7.1 The range of activities provided, together with the organisation of social interaction, enables children of all abilities and backgrounds to participate at an appropriate level in both individual and common tasks, e.g. pairing children of different ages and ability for a certain task.
1.2 If planning occurs it does not take account of specific groups or individuals.	3.2 Some of the planning shows differentiation for particular individuals or group, e.g. simple peg puzzles up to complex jigsaws, fat paint brushes and watercolour brushes.	5.2 Day to day plans are drawn up with the specific aim of developing activities that will satisfy the needs of each child either individually or as groups.	7.2 Planning shows attention to adult participation to individual/paired/group tasks and to the range of levels at which a task or activity may be experienced.
1.3 If records are kept, they describe activities rather than the child's response or success in that activity, e.g. ticked checklists or sampling of children's work.	3.3 Children's records indicate some awareness of how individuals have coped with activities, or of the appropriateness of activities, e.g. 'needs bilingual support' 'could only manage to count to 2'.	5.3 Children are observed regularly, and individual records are kept on their progress in different aspects of their development.	7.3 Children are observed regularly and their progress is recorded and used to inform planning.
	3.4 Staff show some awareness of the need to support and recognise children's differences, praising children of all abilities publicly.	5.4 Staff regularly draw attention of individuals to differences in a positive and sensitive manner.	7.4 Staff regularly draw the attention of the whole group to difference and ability in a positive way, e.g. celebrating bilingual ability,

Item 2: Gender equity and awareness

1.2 Most books, pictures, dolls and displays portray gender stereotypes.	3.1 Some books, pictures and displays include images which do not conform to gender stereotypes, e.g. father looking after baby or female police officer.	5.1 Many books, pictures and displays show men and women in non-stereotypical roles e.g. female doctors or plumbers.	7.1 The children's attention is specifically drawn to books, pictures, dolls and displays that show males and females in non-stereotypical roles and specific activities are developed to help the children discuss gender, e.g. reading and discussing stories like *The Paperbag Princess, Mrs Plug the Plumber* which challenge traditional role-models.
1.2 The staff ignore or encourage stereotyped gender behaviours, e.g. boys are rarely encouraged to work in the home corner, girls are praised for looking pretty or boys for being strong.	3.2 Children's activities and behaviour sometimes cross gender stereotypes, e.g. boys cooking or caring for dolls in the home corner, girls playing outside on large mobile toys.	5.2 Children are explicitly encouraged to participate in activities which cross gender boundaries, e.g. all children are expected (not forced) to join in construction and gross-motor play	7.2 In encouraging both boys and girls to participate equally in all activities, staff are confident in discussing and challenging the stereotypical behaviours and assumptions of children. Are there specific times when certain things can be done **only** by girls or by boys?
		5.3 Dressing-up clothes encourage non-stereotyped cross-gender roles, girl **and** boy nurse or police outfits and non-gendered clothing e.g. cook hat/apron, dungarees.	7.3 Male educators are employed to work with children, where this has not been possible men are sometimes invited to work in the centre with the children. way, e.g. celebrating bilingual ability.

(Continued)

Appendix Table (*Continued*)

1 – inadequate	3 – minimal	5 – good	7 – excellent
Item 3: Race Equality			
1.1 Books, pictures, dolls and displays show no or little evidence of ethnic diversity in our society or the wider world.	3.1 The children sometimes play with toys and artefacts from cultures other than the ethnic majority.	5.1 Children play with artefacts drawn from an extensive range of cultures, e.g. dressing-up clothes used in dramatic play, cooking and eating utensils. Constant messages that all children do similar everyday things, e.g. go to the park, attend weddings.	7.1 Staff develop activities with the express purpose of promoting cultural understanding e.g. attention is drawn to similarities and differences in things and people, different cultures are routinely brought into topic work, and visitors and performers reflect a range of cultures.
	3.2 Books, pictures, dolls and displays show people from a variety of ethnic groups even if the images are insensitive or stereotyped, e.g. other nationalities portrayed in national dress, African shown in traditional rural setting, black dolls with white features.	5.2 Some books, pictures, dolls and displays show people from a variety of ethnic groups in non-stereotypical roles, e.g. scientists, doctors, engineers.	7.2 The children's attention is specifically drawn to books, pictures, dolls etc. that show black and ethnic minority people in non-stereotypical roles.
		5.3 Some images/activities show the children that they have much in common with people from other cultural groups, e.g. stress similarities rather than only the differences, e.g. of rituals; also of physical similarities.	7.3 Specific activities are developed to promote understanding of difference, e.g. paints are mixed to match skin tones to visibly show subtlety in differences.
		5.4 Staff intervene appropriately when child or adult in the setting shows prejudice.	7.4 In multi-ethnic areas ethnic minority educators are employed in the centre. Elsewhere, black and ethnic minority people are sometimes invited into the setting to work with the children.

Race and Ethnicity: Teachers and Children

Warner, D. and Elton-Chalcraft, S.

By the end of this chapter, you should be able to:

- comply with (and seek to go beyond) the legal requirements that concern diversity and promote social cohesion

- understand the impact of your own ethnicity and attitudes towards diversity on your role as a teacher

- reflect on research which investigates cultural awareness among primary children and student teachers

- develop teaching and learning approaches which challenge intolerance and promote equality.

Introduction

This chapter will outline the current picture of racial and ethnic diversity in the UK for new and upcoming classroom practitioners, including statutory requirements and non-statutory guidance. Through consideration of your ethnicity and recent research into children's and student teachers' attitudes towards cultural diversity, you will be able to critically appreciate the importance of developing pedagogic approaches which are culturally responsive and challenging for you, your learners and the school community.

We are all racial and cultural beings, whether we belong to the majority or minority cultures and this affects the way we think, act and interact with one another. Culturally responsive teaching understands this and also recognises that racial and ethnic groups are vibrant and to be valued and cherished. This type of teaching also recognises that such groups are diverse within themselves, rather than being homogenous units. Therefore, recognising children as both individuals and inheritors of a particular cultural dynamic will promote positive self-esteem, racial equity and social justice.

UK classroom statutory requirements and national guidance for teachers

The UK has been an ethnically diverse group of countries for centuries but it is in the last few decades that large groups of peoples, from the Caribbean, Asia, the African countries and more recently those from the European Union, have arrived. Varying reasons for this demographic range from economic change to military and political unrest abroad, leading to the need for employment, refuge or asylum. The 2001 Census identified a Black and Minority Ethnic (BME) population of 8 per cent which it mainly categorised into: Mixed, Asian, Black and Chinese.

In maintained primary schools, 12 per cent are from BME groups (see www.education.gov.uk/ and look at 2007), their spread reflecting the concentration of BME populations in urban areas. Some schools in these areas have 100 per cent of minority ethnic children, while some in rural or suburban areas will have none. Most schools lie on the spectrum somewhere between.

Characterising this diversity of cultures in the UK are: religion, language, customs and values, and often a strong sense of community. However, the 2001 Census alerts us to the fact that minority ethnic groups are varied:

> different groups share some characteristics but there are often greater differences between the individual ethnic groups than between the minority ethnic population as a whole and the White British people. (www.ons.gov.uk/census/index.html)

These differences reflect their histories as well as current social phenomena. Pakistani Muslims in Lancashire, for example, may share many values and practices with

Somali Muslims in West London, but there will be cultural and religious differences too, based on their past and how and where they live now. Alternatively, those whose heritage combines two or more racial backgrounds, for example, a Caribbean-English or Irish-Chinese child, will be of both cultures and represent a new culture, which will develop as they develop and express themselves.

Race Relations Amendment Act (2000)

Teachers have to abide by legislation. The Race Relations Amendment Act states that a body, like a school, must have 'due regard' to:

- eliminate unlawful racial discrimination
- promote equality of opportunity and good relations between people of different racial groups.

In addition, it places specific responsibilities on schools to help them meet the general duty and improve the educational experience for all children, in particular those belonging to minority ethnic groups. It should not be a bureaucratic exercise. These specific duties are to:

- prepare a written statement of the school's policy for promoting race equality, and to act upon it
- assess the impact of school policies on pupils, staff and parents of different racial groups, including, in particular, the impact of attainment levels of these pupils
- monitor the operation of all the school's policies, including, in particular, their impact on the attainment levels of pupils from different racial groups
- take reasonable steps to make available the results of its monitoring.

Schools have a duty to eliminate unlawful racial discrimination and to promote equality of opportunity and good relations between people of different groups.

Community cohesion

From September 2007, schools have been under a duty to promote community cohesion in three main areas:

- **Teaching, learning and curriculum** – to teach pupils to understand others, to promote common values and to value diversity, to promote awareness of human rights and of the responsibility to uphold and defend them, and to develop the skills of participation and responsible action.

- **Equity and excellence** – to ensure equal opportunities for all to succeed at the highest level possible, removing barriers to access and participation in learning and wider activities and eliminating variations in outcomes for different groups.
- **Engagement and ethos** – to provide a means for children, young people and their families to interact with people from different backgrounds and build positive relations, including links with different schools and communities locally, across the country and internationally.

(DCSF 2007)

The community cohesion agenda aims to eliminate racial discrimination and promote positive race, cultural and faith relations in society, including schools. This involves developing understanding, reflection and challenges for teachers and learners to share common experiences and values, build identity and self-esteem and rightfully assume responsibilities for positive diversity. This agenda relates to all schools, from those with mid to high racially diverse populations or mainly white schools. The Teacher Net website is a good source of information and supporting material (www.teachernet.gov.uk/wholeschool/communitycohesion/).

 Reflective task

Use the interactive map on the Multiverse website to find out the ethnicity of primary school children in the area where you grew up, where you now study or work, and another part of the UK where you might have another personal or professional link (www.multiverse.ac.uk/attachments//PrimaryPupilEthnicity/index.html).

1 Examine your own attitudes to the communities in these areas. Why do you think this?
2 How does this relate to legal requirements, your geographical position and your future plans?

Teachers and children: attitudes and approaches

Having considered the legal requirements and begun to think about cultural identity, we now invite you to consider the approaches to multicultural education you have seen in schools and begin to recognise good practice. We also ask you to consider your own mindset and evaluate how you can make a positive contribution to schools in the area of diversity. In this section, we draw on our own research to highlight how race, ethnicity and attitudes towards these, can impact on teachers' and children's world views and behaviour. As you read, consider your own culture, those whom you might teach and the dominant cultural perspective expressed in the curriculum in primary schools today.

Children's awareness of race

Research in both predominantly white and also diverse schools found that the majority of 10-year-old children displayed anti-racist attitudes but nevertheless had internalised the prevailing Western white privilege mindset, whatever their own ethnicity (Elton-Chalcraft 2009). While recognising that the sample was comparatively small (about 80 children from four schools), it became apparent that most children in the multi-ethnic schools who were reasonably knowledgeable about their own culture and other cultures displayed anti-racist behaviour and attitudes (Figure 11.1, Quadrant A). Many children from all four schools were anti-racist even though they displayed limited knowledge (Quadrant B). A handful of children, mainly white boys from a low socio-economic background and in the low sets for maths and literacy, expressed racist comments. In this example, Bart, a white boy, and Kurt, a boy whose mother is white and whose father is of Jamaican heritage, discuss people of different cultures:

Kurt: They're ugly. [giggles]
Sally: They're ugly – so you think people who aren't the same culture as you are ugly?
Kurt: Yeah.
Sally: Why do you say that?
Kurt: Because they've got funny eyes and different to ours – ours are like that, theirs are bozeyed. [making facial gestures]
Bart: Yeah but Heidi [Kurt's girlfriend] is a different culture to you and everyone else in, and some people in, this thing, in this school, has [a] different culture to you but you like 'em – you're friends with 'em. So I don't know what you're pointing that for – ugly … And so if Heidi's got a different culture to you are you gonna dump her?
Kurt: [embarrassed giggle] Nnooo.
   (Elton-Chalcraft 2009 p. 114)

This interchange is interesting because Bart, who had himself expressed racist sentiments, was criticising Kurt's remarks. Thus, Bart and Kurt display racist attitudes towards a particular group but anti-racist attitudes towards a particular individual whom they dissociated from that group (Elton-Chalcraft 2009 p. 114; Troyna and Hatcher 1992). As a beginning teacher, are you aware of the stances towards different cultures held by the children in your placement schools? Is there an ethos of mutual respect or white Western privilege?

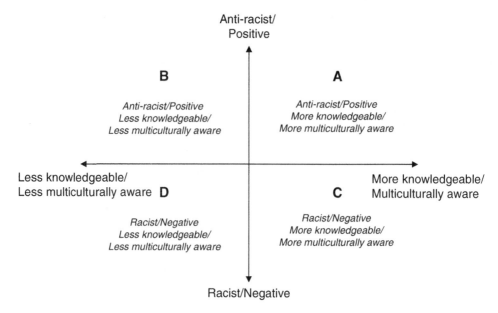

Figure 11.1   The range of children's attitudes and knowledge (Quadrants A, B, C and D)
Source: Elton-Chalcraft 2009

A small number of children in the research were deemed to be knowledgeable about their own and other cultures but still displayed racist viewpoints (Quadrant C). These children were either expressing disgust at an unfamiliar culture, while in the main expressing anti-racist sentiments towards numerous cultures, or they exhibited racist behaviour which they almost instantly regretted. Rachel, a girl of Caribbean heritage, also made a gesture with her eyes but instantly said, 'I shouldn't have done that', possibly because I asked her why she was making a gesture with the corner of her eyes. Many children from one of the multi-ethnic schools described one Muslim boy's racist name calling. However, Roy was described as a bully who dominated both Muslims like himself and other children (Elton-Chalcraft 2009 pp. 110–11).

Schools may attempt to be inclusive, refrain from stereotyping and promote community cohesion and anti-racism. Yet there may still exist within schools a white Western privilege outlook which assumes that the dominant culture of white Western mindset is superior (Dadzie 2000; Elton-Chalcraft 2009; Gaine 2005).

Multicultural stances in schools

The previous section invites you to consider the children's awareness of race but there is a need to understand the school's 'institutional body language' too (Dadzie 2000).

Table 11.1 Types of multiculturalism (Elton-Chalcraft 2009 p. 82, adapted from Kincheloe and Steinberg 1997)

1	Conservative multiculturalists (mono culturalism)	are 'tokenist'. They attempt to address multicultural issues but, deep down, they believe in the superiority of Western (white) patriarchal culture.
2	Liberal multiculturalists	are dedicated towards working to 'one race'. They attempt to gloss over differences in an attempt to make everyone equal and the 'same' ('they' are the 'same' as 'us' – they just happen to be a different colour).
3	Pluralist multiculturalists	believe pluralism is a supreme social virtue, where diversity is pursued and exoticised. There is cultural 'tourism' where 'they' (as opposed to 'us') live in an exotic parallel world. For example, Hanukkah is the Jewish Christmas (an example of neo-colonialism).
4	Left essentialist multiculturalists	are extreme in promoting the minority culture, to the extent that the dominant culture is seen as 'bad' and the marginalised as 'good'.
5	Critical multiculturalists	believe in the promotion of an individual's consciousness as a social being. They promote an awareness (self-reflection) of how and why his/her opinions and roles are shaped by dominant perspectives. They appreciate that there are differences within, as well as between, cultures.

The table above offers a rudimentary tool to consider how well a school (or class) approaches issues of diversity, ranging from tokenistic to critically multicultural. Where would you place yourself, schools you have visited or individual teachers?

The aim is for schools to adopt a 'critical multicultural' stance; however in their journey to this goal, many schools may still find themselves at the starting line – with a commitment to merely adhere to legislation. In practice, this could be use of a limited range of multicultural resources such as a welcome poster in different languages, an annual Hindu dance event or a Caribbean storyteller. The lesson ideas at the end of the chapter provide examples of anti-racist approaches which fulfil the critical multicultural stance.

Teachers seeing and understanding race and culture in the classroom

Recent research among 40 student teachers showed both a deep desire to meet all children's needs alongside a lack of racial and cultural awareness (Warner 2010). This lack of awareness, in their thinking and attitudes, caused them to make automatic responses and assumptions that were based on their own cultural heritage. Reasons for this cannot be easily pinned down and neither would it be right to simplify what is a complex area, but the research identified factors which could be seen as useful starting points for everyone, whatever your cultural background. These were family, schooling and community and the social context of one's upbringing. Such factors can be seen as highly influential aspects of our identity formation and affect, in some way, how we see others.

Nearly all of the students in the study were of the majority ethnic group of the UK, i.e. White British. One had a part-European heritage. All had been educated and lived in white communities, and were currently studying at a mainly white university. It is pertinent to consider what values and assumptions they might have already formed about cultures, resulting from this mono-cultural focus of their backgrounds, and think about how much this applies to all of us. Townsend (2002) describes this as a 'chain of entrenching, white-privilege practices', while Ambe (2006) speaks of 'deep-rooted patterns' which are part of our unconscious being.

Cultural starting points

The students acknowledged their mono-cultural backgrounds, with one stating, 'you simply draw on what you know'; while another, who had lived in the countryside as a child, explained:

> I'd never seen anybody of a different colour; you just knew people in the village. You didn't even think there was an outside world.

Commenting on the use of multicultural children's literature in the classroom, one stated:

> I understand why we have multicultural books because we have a multicultural society, so obviously we need to but I do feel sometimes that by making a book specifically for reading that is on an Asian subject matter, I think that can also make it more of an issue than it actually is.

Other students were worried about appearing ignorant of other cultures and religions, particularly while on placements in racially diverse schools. One commented:

> In 100% Asian school I might see it as more of a challenge because you are not as aware of the culture and beliefs; you're more of an outsider in some ways. Because you're not fully aware of their culture or beliefs I think I'd be more worried that I'd do something that'd offend them or be seen as wrong.

King (2004) suggests that a wariness of approaching cultural differences can result in following known attitudes and approaches, which only affirm the high status of the prevailing cultural majority, and the lower status of minority cultures. This 'avoidance' approach allows the side-stepping of the issue of how far we see minority cultures as subsidiary and unimportant, and therefore raises questions over teaching for equality of opportunity. Anti-racist legislation, community cohesion and school policies and curricula are important markers in this.

In contrast, the student teachers in the research displayed and discussed areas of their lives which resisted a white privilege mindset and displayed a deep desire to teach with equity and understanding. Recognising his own cultural position and the desire to teach with equity, Will, part Ukrainian and part English, articulated his difference:

> My granddad was dark skinned and my mother was a single teenage mum, so although I did not know it at the time, I grew up understanding what it meant to be different.

His later employment in a firm which employed many Black and Asian peoples, also affected his outlook:

> You want school to reflect what's life. The reality is that you might grow up in a white area … but that's not how the world is … As educators we have the opportunity to make sure that children experience as many opportunities as they can and as diverse [sic] as they can.

Helena became more aware of societal attitudes towards difference and disadvantage because of her mother's job as a care worker with learning-disadvantaged people. As a teenager, seeking to become a teacher herself, Jessica often visited the school of her aunt, head teacher of a multiracial West Midlands primary school, noting that the multi-cultural displays and signs in other languages provided important modelling of other cultures to the children. Lou, who lives in the white part of a racially segregated Northern town, has been able to hold on to her existing positive beliefs about racial diversity. While on placement at a white school, an incident, involving the negative reac-tion of some parents about a new Asian child, jarred against Lou's sensibilities and understanding about teaching children equitably.

> We need to reduce ignorance and provide models to help children know they are important and reduce feelings of isolation. Some say 'teaching's teaching', but I think it's [racially-aware teaching] important … It brings a different experience and that's important.

Becoming a culturally responsive teacher

The openness of these comments reveals that alongside personal cultural histories, the potential to re-shape attitudes is present. Participants in this research had begun to recognise that they did not exist in a cultural vacuum but that they were coming from the cultural majority and white privileged position. As both of these influence the way we teach, educators should aim for the 'critical-multiculturist' position, stated earlier, by questioning the underlying cultural assumptions of the curriculum and developing anti-discriminatory, inclusive pedagogies.

Initial teacher training and ongoing CPD are important catalysts in replacing entrenched ideologies and self-satisfied thinking and actions with challenging and trans-forming practices which reflect the complex and shifting nature of our multicultural society. Embracing more multi-faceted understandings, and encouraging this with chil-dren, dismantles blind simplicity and makes difference positive. Teachers need to present opportunities to replace unquestioned attitudes with informed, intellectual, reflexive and ultimately transformative beliefs and principles.

Reflective task

Consider a critical incident in school which presents a challenge with reference to issues of diversity, e.g. racist name calling in the playground.

1 Situate yourself in that position. What is the most appropriate response and why?
2 Consider why the incident took place – what is the 'institutional body language' of the school? Is this an isolated incident or a typical occurrence? What steps could a school take to ensure a critical multicultural approach?

Further scenarios can be found on the Multiverse website at www.multiverse.ac. uk/ViewArticle2.aspx?contentType=2&menu=29795&ContentId=15658

Teaching and learning for cultural and ethnic diversity

Being aware of ourselves as racial and cultural beings is an important position and enables an authentic and viable teacher–pupil relationship. This is a valuable attitude to foster in all schools to avoid a 'colour-blind' approach, an approach which comes from a failure to acknowledge race and ethnicity, or an uncertainty about how to notice it and then avoidance of the issue (Gaine 2005; Pearce 2005). Jones (1999) also suggests that there can be an attitude of professional indifference and lack of interest in the subject. This type of stance can lead to the formation of negative racist attitudes in children because, according to Pearce, 'unthinking racist insults and unintentional stereotypical racial references' are not linked to racism and therefore not challenged (p. 35).

The following two examples of classroom practice will provide ideas and stimulate thinking for further teaching and learning in the area of valuing and raising awareness of racial and ethnic diversity.

Using Persona Dolls: an early years foundation and KS1 approach
Brown (2001, 2008) gives practical advice on how to use Persona Dolls in the early years to combat discrimination. Her ideas can be extended for KS1 and KS2 children, particularly within RE lessons. Used alongside other approaches, Persona Dolls can provide a rich resource for learning 'about' and learning 'from' a particular religion/culture/way of life which is a requirement of many RE syllabi (QCA 2004).

Introducing Jeetinder   Introduce the Persona Doll and encourage your class to enthusiastically engage with the doll by asking lots of questions.

Name: My name is Jeetinder Singh. I am a Sikh which means … *What's your name?*

Language: I speak Punjabi and English. *Do you speak other languages?*

Family: My sister's called Manjit Kaur. Girls often have Kaur after their name and boys often have Singh. But in this country that is sometimes a problem because of the use of first names and surnames so sometimes girls use Singh as a family name. Manjit is 14 and goes to secondary school. She is doing a GCSE in Punjabi (it's the language of many Sikhs who live in the Punjab – north-west India and south-east Pakistan where my grandparents came from). Manjit and Tejpreet, my brother, go to Punjabi school on Sundays; I'm going to go when I'm a bit older. *What are your brothers and sisters like?*

My family came to Britain in 1970, when my Dad was 10. (Show children where the Punjab is on the map). Manjit and my elder brother, Tejpreet, who's 11 and I, were all born in this country. *Where were you born?*

Food: I like eating vegetable curry and dahl made from lentils. I also like fish and chips, especially from the chip shop round the corner from where we live. *What is your favourite food?*

Morning routine: In the mornings, I get up, wash, have breakfast and get ready for school. My mum used to help me tie my jurra (top knot) but I can do it myself now. (Children may ask *Why do you have a top knot?*) In the Sikh religion, we believe it is important to keep our hair long. But actually my cousin Jagdeep and his dad have cut hair but they are still Sikh. In my family, the men have long hair and my dad wears a turban which takes him a while to put on! *How do you get ready in the mornings?*

Playground: On my way here, I went on the slide and swings at the playground just down the road from your school – my favourite is the slide. *What's yours?*

Religion: I sometimes get teased by older children for wearing a top knot. I don't get teased in the infants. *Have any of you been teased? What did it feel like? What did you do? What can I do?*

 A problem, like the one above, would be introduced at the end of the first lesson or in the second, with use of the Persona Doll to demonstrate the problem-solving technique. For this and further ideas, visit the Sage website: www.uk.sagepub.com/cooper

The Island *by Armin Greder (2007): a KS2 approach*

This picture book provides an unusual and challenging resource and stimulus for teachers to enable children to engage with issues of cultural diversity and difference. The story follows a lost and desperate man, washed up on an island where he is confronted by forbidding walls and hostile islanders. He is allowed to stay but because he is different he is treated as an outcast. He is finally set adrift in his burning raft and the islanders return to their heavily fortified, narrow existence. It includes themes of:

- racial and cultural difference
- racism

- effects of immigration, including refugees and asylum-seekers
- human responses and the role of community.

The suggested teaching plan (full details on the adjoining Sage website) covers five sessions, although it could easily be extended to cover a two-week period. This length of time allows for a development of understanding of diversity through the effect and appreciation of the narrative and linked activities designed to draw learners towards greater awareness and knowledge of how we should live together. It uses a cross-curricular approach, which includes Literacy and PSHE, particularly providing significant time for children to share ideas and views and to know how to listen to and accommodate one another. When using the plan, teachers should also think about the cultural, linguistic and ability needs of their pupil groups so that it can be suitably adapted.

1. Preparatory activity   Ask children to think of between two and four aspects of their lives at home, school and in their communities that they really like and wouldn't want to be changed by anyone new coming in. Provide them with 'bricks' made from brown sugar paper to write their ideas on. Stick the bricks on a large display board, or hang them from a line suspended across the room, to symbolise a wall. This 'wall' will later be dismantled as the children discuss and discover positive ways of embracing change and difference.

2. Introducing the book   The book contains powerful black and white images which will elicit thoughtful discussion, so a good way of sharing it is to scan each page into a computer program to project onto a whiteboard. Look at the front cover; ask for predictions and responses. Read the first part of the story and talk about the children's initial feelings. In pairs, children should discuss the man and his feelings. Write these on one side of the wall.

3. Beginning to explore the story and its messages   Use drama activities to explore the actions and motives of the villagers. These could include:

- freeze frames – the children adopt the pose and view of a villager
- hot-seating – the teacher adopts the role of the man, taking questions from the 'villagers'. Give children time to work in groups to think of questions which reflect how their village might feel. Encourage thoughtful questions and ensure there are no racially negative or inappropriate questions through giving some examples and by appointing a group leader to guide and monitor the others.

4. Reflecting so far   Link the children's responses back to the wall, emphasising that although these are natural responses, they may not be helpful and supportive. Discuss and take predictions about the ending of the story.

The complete plan continues the children's journey of understanding and can be found at: www.uk.sagepub.com/cooper

---

Summary

In this chapter, we have enabled you to begin to appreciate and understand what it means to be a racially aware and anti-discriminatory teacher. This includes the suggested ways in which you can adhere to, but also go beyond, the legal requirements for promoting community cohesion, tackling racism and discrimination and valuing and celebrating children's cultural and racial heritages. You have been challenged to consider the impact of your own ethnicity and attitudes towards diversity on your role as a teacher and have been offered the opportunity to engage with current research which discusses white privilege, colour blindness and teacher mindset.

Teachers are always on a journey of discovery where constant re-evaluation of attitudes and ways of seeing the world becomes a key characteristic of learning for themselves and their pupils. This involves questioning, observation, engagement in dialogue and examination of one's thoughts and actions and the effect on other people. It also involves understanding your school's interaction with its community and intersecting with the pupils' different cultural and social identities, through home–school events, visits and meetings with parents and carers.

Even if the pupils appear to be of a similar cultural position, it is important for teachers to dismantle notions of perceived social norms of race and class, which may characterise children as 'cultural others', who don't quite 'fit in'. Teaching instead should centre on a more accurate picture of the existing pluralistic society of the UK and enable what Townsend (2002) calls 'culturally-responsive pedagogy', whereby behaviours, paradigms and judgements are altered. Teachers therefore need to draw on culturally plural modes of teaching which recognise, celebrate and raise the status of minority cultures; and on anti-racist modes which challenge the power imbalance experienced by minority-ethnic pupils by engaging in teaching which builds identity and gives pupils a sense of playing an equal part in building and sustaining their school and community. These attitudes and practices, alongside a critical multicultural approach, should be adopted by teachers in both multi-racial and white schools, so that our pedagogies are transformed.

Questions for discussion

- Look at school policies on anti-racism, community cohesion, cultural diversity: how is policy demonstrated in practice? What could your contribution be at a whole-school level?
- Within your own classroom, what changes would need to be made to reflect a positive 'institutional body language'?
- What steps would you introduce to challenge children's thinking (through planning, cross-curricular activities, through a story or poem) in adhering to a critical multicultural approach?

References

Ambe, B. (2006) 'Fostering multicultural appreciation in pre-service teachers through multicultural curricular transformation', *Teaching and Teacher Education* 22(6): 690–9.

Brown, B. (2001) *Unlearning Discrimination: Persona Dolls in Action*. Stoke-on-Trent: Trentham Books.

Brown, B. (2008) *Equality in Action: A Way Forward with Persona Dolls*. Stoke-on-Trent: Trentham Books.

Elton-Chalcraft, S. (2009) *It's Not Just About Black and White Miss*: *Children's Awareness of Race*. Stoke-on-Trent: Trentham Books.

Dadzie, S. (2000) *Toolkit for Tackling Racism*. Stoke-on-Trent: Trentham Books.

DCSF (2007) *Duty to Promote Community Cohesion: Draft Guidance*. Available at www.dcsf.gov.uk/consultations/downloadableDocs/Duty%20to%20Promote%20Community%20Cohesion%20Guidance%20FINAL.doc

Gaine, C. (2005) *We're All White, Thanks: The Persisting Myth about White Schools*. Stoke-on-Trent: Trentham Books.

Greder, A. (2007) *The Island*. Crows Nest, NSW: Allen & Unwin.

This publisher's web page will provide further details on *The Island* and more teaching ideas: www.allenandunwin.com/default.aspx?page=94&book=9781741752663

Jones, R. (1999) *Teaching Racism or Tackling It: Multicultural Stories from White Beginning Teachers*. Stoke-on-Trent: Trentham Books.

King, J.E. (2004) 'Dysconscious Racism: Ideology, Identity and the Miseducation of Teachers', in G. Ladson-Billings and D. Gillborn (eds) *The Routledge Falmer Reader in Multicultural Education*. Abingdon: Routledge Falmer. pp. 71–83.

Kincheloe, J.L. and Steinberg, S.R. (1997) *Changing Multiculturalism*. Changing Education Series. Buckingham: Open University Press.

Pearce, S. (2005) *You Wouldn't Understand: White Teachers in the Multi-ethnic Classroom*. Stoke-on-Trent: Trentham Books.

QCA (2004) *Religious Education: The Non-statutory National Framework*. London: QCA.

Townsend, B. (2002) 'Leave No Teacher Behind', *Qualitative Studies in Education* 15(6): 727–38.

Troyna, B. and Hatcher, R. (1992) *Racism in Children's Lives*. London: Routledge.

Warner, D. (2010) 'Moving into the Unknown', *Race Equality Teaching* 28(3): 39–43.

Race and Inclusion

Devarakonda, C.

Chapter overview

This chapter discusses the role of race in inclusion and exclusion and how race is addressed in early childhood contexts from the perspectives of children, their parents or carers and practitioners.

Race has always been considered to be a complicated concept. Some children from ethnic minority groups may be confused about their identity – as one 4-year-old Indian girl asked her mum: 'Am I going to be an English lady or an Indian lady when I grow up?' Further, when students on a BA Early Childhood Studies course were asked the question: 'How would you like to describe yourself?' it was considered to be a thought-provoking question to answer by almost everybody, irrespective of their background being white, black, mixed heritage, or other. Some students preferred to refer themselves as English, Scottish or Welsh or British or European. On the other hand, people who migrated from other countries, and in spite of having acquired British citizenship, were still comfortable to refer to themselves as belonging to their original country of birth.

This chapter explores the concept of race and inclusion in early childhood settings – from the perspectives of children, practitioners and parents. The concepts of ethnicity and race have always been used interchangeably and sometimes confused, with some links made to religion, especially in the case of Jews and Muslims. Some of the terms related to race and ethnic minorities are explored in relation to their appropriate meanings, the problems around the usage of these terms and the terms preferred. Several issues around race have been contested, such as the concept of race, self-identity, and little or lack of awareness of other ethnic groups. Are some terms – ethnic minority, minority ethnic or black – used to refer to people who are labelled black or is the word 'black' used to denote everybody other than those who are 'white'? People do not prefer to be labelled as black in spite of being non-white. Skin colour may be differently described as white, black, brown and yellow.

A conversation on race:

> In a multi-cultural setting, a group of 4-year-old children consisting of a Korean, Pakistani, Nigerian and English were engrossed in a conversation about race. They were overheard illustrating and analysing the concept of race by relating to differences and similarities. They concluded that there were four different types of people in the world whose skin colour was black, brown, yellow and white. They commented that although skin colour, hair and facial features are different, there are similarities too in terms of colour of blood (red) and teeth (white).

Statistics

The UK is becoming ethnically diverse, it has been predicted that in the 2011 Census, the population of ethnic minorities in the UK will increase from 7.9 per cent to 15 per cent. As a result of failing political and economic situations in certain countries in the past, in Somalia, Kenya, Uganda and, recently, Afghanistan, Iraq, Egypt and Libya the native population have been forced to seek refuge in other countries for their own safety. As a result of moving to a new country with different cultures and constructions of childhood, children and their families have to familiarise themselves with the expectations and may also have to deal with being stereotyped or discriminated against.

The BBC (2009a) reported the Office for National Statistics projecting the UK population to rise from 61 million to 71.6 million by 2033. If current trends in growth continue, just over two-thirds of this increase in population is a result of migration directly or indirectly.

It has been estimated that the ethnic minority population will double in the next 50 years. In one BBC (2010) report it has been predicted that 'Groups outside the white British majority are increasing in size and share, not just in the areas of initial migration, but throughout the country, and our projections suggest that this trend is set to continue through to 2051'. In this situation it is highly likely that there will be many children from ethnic minority families accessing the early childhood settings and so it will be extremely important to ensure that all children and their families feel included.

Census 2011

Wallop (2011) reported a 2.5 million increase in population as a result of migration and a higher birth rate in families from ethnic minorities. Rogers (2011) reported in the *Guardian*, that the non-white British population has grown from 6.6 million in 2001 to 9.1 million in 2009. The non-white British population has grown by 4.1 per cent owing to the influx of Eastern Europeans as well as people migrating from Australia and New Zealand to the UK. The report also highlights an increase in the number of people identifying themselves as mixed population by almost 50 per cent and this is not due to an increase in birth rates but is as a result of 'the population is mixing more'. The 2011 Census (ONS, 2011a) added new categories such as Welsh, English and Cornish in addition to the Gypsy or Irish Traveller families and Arabs added as 'any other ethnic group'.

Definition and terminology

Black refers to children of Black Caribbean; Black African; mixed White and Black Caribbean and mixed White and Black African heritage. Practitioners should find out about individual children's backgrounds from their families because the various terms used to identify black children incorporate a range of different heritages, histories, and experiences.

Asians – this term has been interpreted in various ways in different countries. In the UK, the term 'Asian' is referred to people belonging to South Asian origin – Indians, Pakistanis, Bangladeshis and Sri Lankans. In the UK census forms, 'Asian' and 'Chinese' are recorded as separate. This term has connotations in different countries.

The census form in 2011 introduced some new categories such as Welsh, English and Cornish.

Contexts of inclusion and exclusion

Race is characterised by physical characteristics, such as colour of skin and colour and shape of eyes and hair. How and why do children get excluded by children and adults on the basis of their skin colour, nationality or religion? Is this blatantly visible or covert? Is this evident through their attitudes, behaviour, language used or using appropriate resources, providing access to environment? Are people with fair skin at an advantage because society assigns them power and control? Do children with fair skin from other European countries living in England face any issues around exclusion?

Race and ethnicity are always considered sensitive issues as everybody prefers to be thought of as politically correct so that they do not offend anybody by using offensive language. Jane Lane warns that when referring to terminology around race there is no right or wrong terminology, but intentions not to offend the individual. 'It is sometimes difficult to know what terms/words to use when we are talking about issues around racial equality and to be confident about using them. Some people may feel anxious or unsure about using the "correct" or "right" word or term and, consequently, may try to avoid using them at all' (Lane, 2006b).

What are the ways in which children get excluded? Are adults more inclined to exclude because of their rigid notions of stereotypes? For example, an experienced practitioner from a predominantly white community may express reservations about their ability to meet the needs (especially, language, food, cultural) of a young 3-year-old Asian child starting at nursery. Questions around race have always been debated from the perspective of their identity and relating to inclusion or exclusion of children. A child, parent/carer and a practitioner may be included or excluded depending on the attitudes and experiences of the people who are in a setting. The attitudes of young children towards difference are influenced by their experiences including the behaviour of adults in their home or in the setting.

Children in predominantly white areas struggled to accept black (non-white) children either by trying to place themselves away from these children or by declaring openly that they do not want to play with them because they may become dirty. On the other hand, an English child brought up in India realised the difference in skin colour, 'Why am I not the same colour as my friend – I was born in this country too?' Irrespective of their physical features, all children prefer to look like their friends and be respected and accepted (Targowska, 2001).

The notion of colour representing positive and negative aspects in a culture has been embedded in all countries. Representation of white as positive and black as negative has been a norm for several communities through generations. It has always been highlighted in children's literature, princes and princesses are illustrated with fair skin and positive roles and the negative, evil and disgraceful characters are portrayed in black colour. For example, angels are white and devils are black. However, there is evidence of raised awareness in contemporary children's literature that is depicting characters in a non-stereotypical way. The constant exposure to negative stereotypes from a wide range of sources, such as family, peers, films and media, may place a child in a dilemma and they may be tempted to emulate a close relative and use the same language and attitude. This attitude might pervade into several activities in the setting, for example, the role-play area, and the child might find it difficult to accept a different perspective from their peer or even a practitioner.

However, an adult in their role of a practitioner or a parent may already have been influenced by the stereotypes and may have impressions from their childhood resulting in their discrimination against children from families belonging to ethnic minority groups. Is this one of the prime reasons for a high rate of exclusions of children from ethnic minority groups? The highest rates of exclusions were found among Gypsy/Roma children, who were more than three times as likely to be excluded, followed by black Caribbean pupils. White, working-class pupils have serious problems in terms of underachievement, but black pupils remain three times more likely to be excluded than white. Several reports indicate that teachers had low expectations of black children (Maylor et al., 2009).

Is prejudice always experienced by people from ethnic minority groups and who are discriminated against by the majority groups? No, discrimination is reported from all over the world. Prejudice against ethnic minority groups has been prevalent in all the communities around the world. The hierarchy of power may be translated into how affluent families are considered to be powerful and how weak and disadvantaged families may be the victims of discrimination. However, globalisation has extended the borders and enabled people to travel inside and outside the country. This has led to relationships across borders and cultures, resulting in mixed heritage families.

Children of families with a mixed heritage are born in the UK with their parents belonging to different races or ethnic minority backgrounds. A major study reports 1 in 10 children are from mixed race families. Young people are six times more likely to be of mixed race than are adults. The proportion of children who face prejudices will increase in future generations and they will struggle to be accepted by both parents' communities as a result of not inheriting any specific physical features such as skin colour, hair colour or facial features that are prominently seen in others.

Do the resources used by the practitioners in early childhood promote inclusion or encourage children and their parents to feel
included? Do the practitioners empower parents of children in their
care to become involved in activities in the settings with children?
Are practitioners from ethnic minority groups respected and valued?

What are the ways in which children are subject to prejudice and
stereotyped because of their race? Parents and practitioners show racist
attitudes and behaviour due to their prejudices and stereotypes. Children are influenced by their parents' and teachers' attitudes that are
reflected as a result of their behaviour and use of negative language.
Further lack of positive role models in their immediate environment
may lead to negative perceptions of themselves. 'Children do not enter
early childhood programs as empty slates but rather bring with them a
myriad of perceptions of difference that they have taken up from their
families, peers, the media and other social sources and negotiated in the
representations of their own identities' (Robinson and Diaz, 2006: 4).

Milner (1983) reports that children pick positive and negative role
perceptions towards different racial groups from a very early age. He
suggests that children as young as 3 are aware of racial hierarchy 'in
line with current adult practices' (ibid.: 122).

Early childhood practitioners may use a wide variety of resources
that promote diversity in the setting in a positive way. This will
benefit children and their families.

Theoretical base

Race is a contested and controversial term. People are categorised
into specific groups on the basis of their skin colour and physical
characteristics, with no scientific basis for this explanation. The Race
Relations Act (1976) defines racial group as making references to
race, colour, nationality, citizenship or ethnic or national origins
(Jews, Sikhs, Romany Gypsies and Irish Travellers).

The first person to coin the term 'race' to connote categories of
people was François Bernier in 1684 in his paper 'A New Division of
the Earth' (Stuurman, 2000). For Bernier, race was referring to people
who looked different physically being categorised as belonging to
different races. Charles Darwin in *Descent of Man* (1874) argued that
stronger races replace weaker races. European races were supposed to
be superior to other races leading to colonisation of several countries
around the world and oppressing the indigenous population in

Australia (Aboriginals), first nations (Canada) and Native Americans in America.

The concept of race is contested as socially constructed as opposed to being a biologically based label. So, in order to demonstrate this, race is sometimes presented in inverted commas.

Origins of racism – racism has been prevalent for the past 500 years all over the world. People are discriminated against by others on the basis of their colour, physical features, religion, culture, language, region and/or background.

At what age are children aware of their racial identity? Do children believe that they will belong to the same race when they grow older? Do children develop their stereotypes and prejudices from a very early age?

MacNaughton and Davis (p. 17) have cited this quote by Park (1928) illustrating the long history around debates on the issue of young children's racial awareness and identity:

> Racial consciousness, is ... as far as observation goes, an acquired trait, quite as much as the taste for olives or the mania for collecting stamps. Children do not have it. They take the world of human beings in which they find themselves as part of the order of nature and respond to a black or yellow face as readily as they do to a white, depending on the character and intimacy of the association. (Park, 1928: 16, cited in MacNaughton and Davis, 2009: 17)

Lasker challenged this notion that children are colour-blind and without 'race consciousness' in 1929. He suggested that children can form racial attitudes from a young age. Since then several studies have refuted Park's contention. Lasker argued that children's attitudes were formed by what adults taught them; their experiences of children's segregation on the basis of their race in addition to biased knowledge acquired from the curriculum shaped their knowledge of race.

Clark and Clark (1939), Criswell (1937, 1939) and Horowitz (1939) conducted early research on young children's 'racial' awareness and self-identification, examining the pre-school children's awareness of physical markers such as skin tone, hair colour and texture. One of the key findings of Clark and Clark (1939) was that children were aware of the racial differences at between 3 and 4 years of age.

Goodman (1964) mentioned that development of racial awareness occurs in three phases: phase 1 (2–3 years) children notice racial differences; phase 2 (4–5 years) children are able to express their orientation (positive and negative) towards specific racial groups; phase 3 (7–9 years) children express stereotypical and prejudiced attitudes.

Aboud and Skerry (1984) suggest that racial awareness begins at 4 years old and is able to relate to own group, awareness of being similar to own group, recognising being similar or dissimilar to others and being able to classify or label others based on their race.

Cognitive development theory described how children have an innate need to understand their world by sorting and classifying items around them and finding similarities and differences. Hirschfield (1995) referred to children using physical markers of 'race' (skin tone, facial feature and hair type) and to other characteristics (positive and negative) of 'race'.

In the UK children aged between 5 and 7 years of age were able to relate to their ethnic identity accurately (Davis et al., 2007). As children grow older, they are able to relate to social norms of racial prejudice being unacceptable. However, all children irrespective of their ethnic background were prone to show positive bias towards whiteness and negative bias towards blackness.

Social identity development theorists believe that children develop a sense of belonging to a specific group in three stages: (1) classification of people into different social groups, (2) differentiating the groups as having a positive or negative bias, and (3) developing their self-esteem based on the group to which they belong.

Ethnicity is often confused or is synonymously used with race. When referring to different groups of people who share common features (such as language, religion and culture) it is more appropriate to refer to people with different ethnicities rather than different races.

Critical race theory (CRT) originated in the 1970s in the USA and relates to racial reforms and deep-rooted racism. According to CRT, racism is deep-rooted in society and adopts a social constructionist approach to race. Delgado and Stefancic (2001: 162) believed 'CRT begins with a number of basic insights. One is that racism is normal, not aberrant in American society. Because racism is an ingrained feature of our landscape, it looks ordinary and natural to persons in the culture'. They further explain:

> Races are categories that society invents, manipulates, or retires when convenient. People with common origins share certain physical traits, of course such as skin colour, physique and hair texture … But these constitute only an extremely small portion of their genetic endowment, are dwarfed by that which

we have in common, and have little or nothing to do with distinctly human higher order traits such as personality, intelligence and moral behaviour. That society frequently chooses to ignore these scientific facts, creates races, and endows them with pseudo-permanent characteristics is of great interest to critical race theory. (Delgado and Stefancic, 2001: 7)

This theory emphasises the power of whiteness and that racism is permanent and embedded in education. However, CRT endeavours to make racism visible, as it is so entrenched in our society that it looks normal. Critical race theory encourages people of colour to articulate their experiences of racism in an explicit way.

Racial hierarchy – enlightened thinkers believed that all humans were considered to be equal, in principle; however, in practice society does not reflect this philosophy. Black and white are emotionally loaded concepts that are polarised. For example, white represents pure and good, and black has negative connotations. This also relates to skin colour of people which justifies people who are white to be powerful and those who are not white to be powerless, resulting in exclusion and disadvantage.

How do children develop racial awareness – are children 'colour-blind', leading them to be unaware of race and racism around them? Are children influenced by adults (parents and practitioners), media, resources (books, stories, displays) used in the early childhood settings?

Legislation

The legislation around race and inclusion has been presented from both the UK and international perspective. Race relations legislation makes it a duty to eliminate unlawful racial discrimination and to promote equality and good relations between people of different racial groups. All early years settings will have developed an equal opportunity policy that will enable all the staff employed in the early childhood setting to adhere to the policy.

The Race Relations Act 1976 defines a racial group by its race, colour, nationality, citizenship or ethnic or national origins (Jews, Sikhs, Romany Gypsies and Irish Travellers are covered, among others). The Race Relations Act 1976 and amended version in 2000 makes it unlawful to discriminate against anyone on the grounds of their race, colour, nationality, religious beliefs and national or ethnic origins.

However, all the legislation around discrimination has been covered by new legislation: the Equality Act 2010 that came into force in October 2010. All settings have responsibility and an obligation not to discriminate against people with a 'protected characteristic' under previous equality legislation. Race is constructed as one of the protected characteristics of the Equality Act 2010. The Equality Act 2010 (DfE, 2010) is a single legal framework that tackles disadvantage and discrimination from different perspectives. Single equality laws around race, disability and gender were combined under the equality law in 2010 to reduce bureaucracy. This change was effective from April 2011. Early childhood settings are not allowed to unlawfully discriminate based on race and ethnicity. This is applicable to children, their parents or carers, as well as practitioners.

The United Nations Convention on the Rights of Children 1989 (UNCRC) was an international agreement that was ratified by the UK in 1991. The UN convention includes a series of articles that describes the rights of children and young people up to age 18 years. The UNCRC articles challenge discrimination relevant to race. These are Articles 2, 14, 20 and 30 that recommend that the government should ensure all children can access their rights and challenge discrimination of children's rights and opportunities based on their race and religion.

> Article 2: Children must be treated without discrimination of any kind irrespective of the child's or his or her parent's or legal guardian's race, colour, sex, language, religion, political or other opinion, national, ethnic or social origin, property, disability, birth or other status.
>
> Article 14: Children have the right, according to their capacities, to form and express views and to have freedom of thought, conscience and religion.
>
> Article 20: Children who cannot be looked after by their own family must be looked after properly, by people who respect their religion, culture and language.
>
> Article 30: Children of ethnic, religious or linguistic minorities shall not be denied the right to enjoy their own culture, religion or language.

The Children Act 2004 places a duty on services to ensure that every child, whatever their background or circumstances, has the support they need to achieve the five Every Child Matters (ECM) outcomes (DfES, 2003).

The Early Years Foundation Stage (EYFS) is a statutory framework

(DCSF, 2008b). All settings providing access to learning, development and care of children from birth to 5 are required to follow EYFS. 'Inclusive practice' is one of the commitments to the EYFS principle of 'A unique child'. This refers to children's entitlements – their right be treated fairly regardless of race, religion or abilities. The EYFS states explicitly – both within its statutory requirements and guidance – that no child should be disadvantaged by their ethnicity, culture or religion, home language, family background, disability, special educational needs, gender or ability. 'All children, irrespective of ethnicity, culture or religion, home language, family background, learning difficulties or disabilities, gender or ability should have the opportunity to experience a challenging and enjoyable programme of learning and development' (EYFS).

Government initiatives

Building Futures: Believing in Children – a focus on provision for black children in the Early Years Foundation Stage – provides additional guidance for settings on how to include children from Black African and Black Caribbean heritage or any mixed black background. Practitioners are encouraged to reflect on their prejudices and challenge attitudes, and endeavour to provide quality provision.

Black History Month (BHM) or African History Month (AHM) is celebrated to commemorate significant events and notable people in black history. This is held every October in Britain and February in USA and Canada. During this month, knowledge of black history and cultural heritage is promoted to raise awareness and disseminate information on positive contributions of black people to these societies.

Tickell (2011) reviewed EYFS and made strong recommendations based on the feedback from the practitioners to retain key elements of EYFS, especially 'Unique child' endorsing the inclusiveness of the foundation stage curriculum.

Examples of good practice

Mac Naughton and Davis (2009) believe that 'developing anti-racist pedagogies requires educators to locate and name the effects and implications of "race" in children's lives and in their own lives'. So, it is essential for an early childhood setting to explore the concept of race from a child and an adult's perspective.

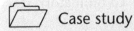

Case study

Every Friday during circle time, all children are allowed to ask a question followed by discussion with rest of the group. A 3½-year-old child asked the practitioner, who is from an ethnic minority group: 'Why do you look different? Why is your skin dark?' The practitioner asked all the children: 'I am different because I am special. Wouldn't it be boring if everybody looked the same?' All the children agreed. Another boy commented: 'My hair is curly; your hair is straight.' After several other comments from other children, the practitioner asked another question: 'What cake did you have for your birthday last week?' The girl excitedly replied, 'OOOH, I had a beautiful chocolate cake with Dora the Explorer on the cake!!!!'

Other excited children joined in claiming to love chocolate cake. The practitioner then explained that as there are different types of cakes – chocolate cake, cream cake and so on – that have different colours, so there are people with different skin colours. But, irrespective of different skin colours, everybody is a human being and 'loves different types of cakes'. This led to more discussion, when children started to compare their skin colour, hair colour, with tan, with spots, without spots, and so on.

Settings must:

1. Offer a rich learning environment in which all children and their families feel welcome, respected and valued. This should include establishing opportunities for all parents to communicate their child's needs to the practitioners; and ensuring practitioners have the knowledge and understanding to support children to freely explore their culture, heritage and faith without feeling stigmatised or self-conscious.

2. Use appropriate resources to raise awareness of differences in culture, religion, background, circumstances and issues that may lead to exclusion of children due to prejudice or discrimination.

3. Challenge stereotypical attitudes and change attitudes of practitioners and parents. Adults may prefer to isolate and exclude themselves from the mainstream and avoid being proactive rather than be discriminated against and excluded. Settings must endeavour to understand the needs of children and their families, so that every family experiences the setting as inclusive.

In order to enable inclusion, early childhood settings and schools should:

- Be committed to inclusion by having a named member of staff (named equality co-ordinator or inclusion co-ordinator) responsible for race equality.

- Provide a welcoming environment with approachable staff enabling all families to access the setting.

- Have accurate information about all the children in the setting, such as ethnicity, religion and naming systems. Be aware of how to spell and pronounce names correctly.

- Identify the need for training around race irrespective of the ethnic make-up of the setting and surrounding areas.

- Encourage practitioners to gain confidence to challenge orthodox practices and attitudes that are discriminatory. Ensure all staff employed in the setting are able to access training to raise their awareness of diversity.

- Ensure all staff have a basic understanding and knowledge of faiths and cultures to ensure that everyone is catered for. Respond to children's questions on race and ethnicity honestly, sensitively and openly.

- Check that resources reflect cultural and ethnic diversity in a positive manner. For example, ensure dolls and puppets have accurate and realistic skin tones and facial features and that story books avoid portraying characters conforming to stereotypes. Show and tell activity – all children and members of their families can be given opportunities to share their resources and culture with other children and the practitioners in the setting.

 Case study

Colour-blind or colour aware?

Ben, a 4-year-old boy in an early childhood setting in Manchester, was found scrubbing his hands vigorously, by an early childhood practitioner. When Ben was asked the reason for scrubbing, he replied saying that he was cleaning himself properly so that he can be clean and white like other children.

A white child but different from majority

Another 4-year-old child living in India with his white British parents, ran into his house screaming 'Mum, why am I not brown in colour and not like my friends Nitin, Ravi and Manish, although I was born in India like them?'.

Challenging children's ideas

A 4-year-old boy tried to clarify his ideas with an Indian visitor.

Continues

Continued

> Child: Are you Indian?
>
> Visitor: Yes, I am.
>
> Child with quizzical face: Are all Indians violent?
>
> Visitor: No, not really, why?
>
> Child: I saw this film with my mum and dad. They showed Indians using bows and arrows. My dad said all Indians are violent.
>
> Visitor: They are not violent. Indians use bows and arrows to protect themselves. There are two types of people who are called Indians: Native Americans who live in America and those who are from India.

Some reflections

- Children are aware of the differences irrespective of where they live.

- It is important to challenge children's views, especially if they are discriminatory, and clarify the ideas in a sensitive manner.

- Children and their parents should be provided with opportunities to raise their awareness of children from different races and their characteristics in a positive manner.

As a practitioner and parent how would you respond to empower and enable these children to accept their skin colour and be proud of their background?

Think tank – inclusion is not being tokenistic:

> A setting may claim their inclusiveness by displaying posters with people from different races displayed on the walls in the classrooms or corridors. Unless these posters are discussed by the practitioners with the children with questions such as why are these people different to each other, where do they come from, what might the background of these people be, and so on, children may not make any sense of these posters. These discussions may encourage children to understand the posters and relate to anybody from their acquaintances, friends or from the media or literature.

Metaphors

Melting pot versus a salad bowl – these metaphors have been used to compare how settings accepted people (children and their families) as in a melting pot, whereby everyone was mixed together to become one single product, expecting all to conform with the majority. Salad bowl, which is considered to be a better metaphor, refers to different vegetables of different colours, tastes, textures and flavours mixed together in a large bowl which will look attractive and colourful, retaining its original character of individual vegetables.

This is reflected in a popular poem titled 'British' by Benjamin Zephaniah. In this poem Zephaniah refers to all the people from different countries entering into Britain who are assimilated into the melting pot of British society. He is comparing British society to a salad bowl. People from different cultures, races and ethnicities are encouraged to keep their culture alive and are not expected to give up their identities while becoming part of British society.

Debates and controversies

- We do not have any children from different races. Is that a good reason for practitioners not to raise awareness of children about diversity? Children would benefit from being aware of differences and learn to be tolerant and accepting in their later life. So, settings must provide opportunities to extend knowledge and understanding about different races and their backgrounds.

- Who am I? What issues might impact the children, their parents and early childhood practitioners who are from ethnic minority groups? Several young children from ethnic minority groups are confused about their identity, so they may attempt to be like the majority children irrespective of geographical location.

- Are black and ethnic minority groups a homogenous group? How are they different?

- How much training can practitioners receive to raise their awareness about the ethnic minority groups?

- Is it possible for a practitioner to be realistic in including children and their families from different minority groups? Is inclusion tokenistic? Is training provided to practitioners on meeting the diverse needs of children and their families belonging to different races and ethnic minority groups?

- Do positive black role models (for example, Barack Obama, President of the USA) significantly impact on the self-esteem of children from ethnic minority groups?

- Who is superior? Do children believe that specific groups of children are more able and confident, which becomes a self-fulfilling prophecy?

- Are practitioners from different minority groups encouraged to participate in the recruitment process? Do employers publicise their recruitment campaign to a wider society, enabling practitioners from diverse communities to apply for jobs and make the recruitment process fair?

Discussion point

How do settings ensure children are provided with positive role models through resources in the role-play area, books and stories, displays, games and toys and inviting guest speakers from different countries and cultures? How would you ensure these resources are not used in a tokenistic manner?

Implications

Early childhood settings must ensure they promote positive attitudes to differences between people and enable children to unlearn any negative attitudes. This is to ensure feelings of superiority among white children and inferiority among children from ethnic minorities are tackled. Settings need to be familiar with the need to understand the concept of racism, and encourage early childhood practitioners to access training to understand racism and its implications for children and their families. They should ensure staff of early childhood settings are provided with opportunities to discuss issues around racism in an open forum and honestly.

Children

- When children are valued and respected they develop positive self-identity and develop to their potential.
- When young children are exposed to children from diverse families, raising their awareness, they learn to respect and celebrate difference from an early age.
- A wide range of resources that portray positive images of children belonging to all races needs to be used to create awareness.
- Provide opportunities for children to express themselves without any inhibitions, and involve them in resolving any issues sensitively.

Parents

- Access to services should be available for all parents, irrespective of their background or race.

- Parents and practitioners need to be able to respect and accept differences mutually.

- Parents can be involved in organising activities and in some decision-making in the setting.

- Parents should be encouraged to access settings. Settings should have an open-door policy encouraging parents to share their culture – unique ways of celebrating festivals, recipes, antiques, stories from the past (especially from grandparents), and so on.

Practitioners

- Recruitment of practitioners from different minority groups will raise the profile of the setting.

- Raise awareness about the needs of children and their families from different ethnic minority groups.

- Provide training to create awareness and develop positive attitudes towards people from different races.

- Use a sensitive approach as well as an open mind (without making assumptions) while communicating with parents.

- Political correctness may force early childhood settings to acquire appropriate resources, however, practitioners need to ensure the resources are used in such a way that children learn to accept and respect differences.

Research issues

The key areas explored to research inclusion from the perspective of race can include:

- Awareness of racial differences in children.
- Children's perception of their identity.
- Strategies used by practitioner to include children from different races.
- Attitudes of children and their parents/carers towards black practitioners.
- Resources used to raise awareness of race.
- Strategies used to involve parent of children from ethnic minority families.
- Practitioner's attitude to education and achievement of children from ethnic minority families.

Continues

Continued

- Explore stereotypes embedded in children, parents and practitioners around race in the current context.

The self devaluation study by Clark and Clark (1939) is one of the key researches that have been conducted to see the impact on young children of the shift in the political ideologies as well as raised awareness due to the presence of positive role models. They reported that children as young as 3 are aware of racial differences. They conducted an experiment with 253 African American children where they presented four dolls (two brown with black hair and two white with yellow hair). These children were asked questions about colour and identity. When asked to hand in the doll of a specific colour more than 90 per cent of the children identified the doll's colour appropriately. When asked if the doll resembled an African American child or a white child, again the choice of more than 90 per cent was accurate. However when asked to hand in a doll that looked like themselves, 66 per cent picked a brown doll while the rest chose a white doll. When asked which doll looked best, which one was bad and which doll was the nicer colour, the results seem to indicate that they have devalued their racial identity. Sixty-six per cent referred to white dolls as best while 59 per cent described brown dolls as bad and 38 per cent believed brown dolls to be a nicer colour.

When this experiment was repeated with a much smaller sample (21 black children) 65 years later in the USA, by Davis (2005) using similar questions about a black and a white doll, 71 per cent of these children preferred the white doll – although the sample size is small, the results are significant. After the victory of Obama in the presidential elections, *Good Morning America* asked 19 black children aged 5–9 from Norfolk, Virginia, which doll did they like best and which doll looked most like them. Responses indicate that boys seem to prefer both or neither dolls and 88 per cent perceived that the black doll looked most like them. With regard to their preferences of dolls, 42 per cent liked playing with black dolls while a majority chose both. Some of the rationale for the results indicates that choice had little to do with race. It is worth noting that these children were older than those children in the original study. These choices could have been influenced by factors such as positive role models, the civil rights movement and more awareness of differences.

- What are the key findings of this research?

- List the strengths and limitations of this study.

- What is the relevance of this study in the UK and in the current context?

- How can you change this study using different methodology, using qualitative perspective?

Connolly et al. (2002) in 'Too young to notice?' studied 352 children aged 3–6 years from Northern Ireland in a survey. This report explored the cultural and political awareness of young children. The children were shown some common objects and photographs related to events and symbols related to Protestant and Catholic communities, and were asked whether they were aware of and understood their ethnic preferences, ethnic awareness, ethnic identity and ethnic prejudice. The children's responses were coded and statistically analysed. Children aged 3–6 years were aware of parades (49 per cent), flags (38 per cent), Irish dancing (31 per cent), conflict-related violence (21 per cent), football shirts (21 per cent), the terms Catholic and Protestant (7 per cent) and colours (5 per cent).

- What are the key findings of this research?
- Explore how your setting (employed or in placement) will include children from different backgrounds.
- List the strengths and limitations of this study.
- Can this study be repeated in a childcare setting in your area?

An unpublished small-scale study explored young children's perceptions around exclusion. Children aged around 3 and 4 years in the nursery class of a school were included in the discussion. Children were shown pictures of six children belonging to the same age range but to different backgrounds in relation to their race, gender, culture, ability, and so on. The children were told that in an imaginary situation, all these virtual children were going to join their group and they were instructed to pick one of the six children as their friend. Children started picking different children as their friend. It was realised by the researcher and the children that one of the six children was not chosen by any child in the group. As the last child declared his choice, all the children expressed their disappointment vociferously as a group for ignoring one of the six children. All the children were very conscious of the situation although it was an imaginary situation. Every child in the group wished and provided alternative solutions to ensure this child was included. Some of the solutions offered were 'Can we pick more than one friend?' or 'Everybody can take turns to befriend this child'. From this experience it is clear that children are aware of the implications of exclusion and illustrated feelings of empathy towards other children's feelings. This illustrates children's awareness of differences in addition to their eagerness to respect the differences. This small-scale project shows that children are aware and are able to empathise with a child being excluded, and this needs to be supported by adults with their positive role models and examples.

- What are the key findings of this research?
- Explore how your setting enables children to accept and respect each other.
- List the strengths and limitations of this study.
- Can this study be repeated in a childcare setting in your area?

Further reading

Gilborn, D. (2008) *Racism and Education: Coincidence and Conspiracy.* Abingdon: Routledge.

Lane, J. (2006) 'Some suggested information/resources that may be helpful in working for racial equality in the early years', www.childrenwebmag.com/articles/child-care-articles/racial-equality-information-for-early-years-workers.

Lane, J. (2008) *Young Children and Racial Justice: Taking Action for Racial Equality in the Early Years – Understanding the Past, Thinking about the Present, Planning for the Future.* London: National Children's Bureau.

MacNaughton, G.M. and Davis, K. (eds) (2009) *Race and Early Childhood Education: An International Approach to Identity, Politics, and Pedagogy.* New York: Palgrave Macmillan.

Robinson, K. and Diaz, C. (2006) *Diversity and Difference in Early Childhood Education: Issues for Theory and Practice.* Maidenhead: Open University Press.

Useful websites

Department for Education, http://www.education.gov.uk/.
Runnymede Trust, http://www.runnymedetrust.org/.
Pre-school Learning Alliance, http://www.pre-school.org.uk/.
Britkid, http://www.britkid.org/.

Gypsy, Roma and Traveller Children in the UK

Parker-Jenkins, M., Hewitt, D., Brownhill, S. and Sanders, T.

This chapter looks at:

■ traveller family, community and gender issues

■ admissions

■ anti-bullying and anti-racism

■ behaviour, communication and the peer group

■ the curriculum

■ attendance.

I think all travelling children should go to school, they will learn a lot more than staying in one place and not getting out. They need to get an education because the world is changing. They need to know how to read and write, so they can deal with people every day (Father of Gypsy/Traveller children, Bhopal 2004: 54).

These are positive words but this community has been described as 'probably the most deprived group of the country' (DES 1967). In 1996b OFSTED said that as many as 50,000 children between the ages of 5 and 16 years were registered in school at that time, whilst 10,000 were not. In a follow-up report in 1999a OFSTED also explained that Gypsy, Roma and Traveller children were amongst the least achieving groups.

Look at the following questions to reflect on your own knowledge and attitudes towards the Gypsy, Roma and Traveller community.

Activities – First thoughts

Explore your intial ideas on Gypsy, Roma and Traveller children:

■ Do you have any of these children in your school?

▶

- What do you know of their community and culture?

- What are the best ways to support and teach Gypsy, Roma and Traveller children?

- Why is the achievement of Gypsy, Roma and Traveller children poor in some schools?

Background

O'Hanlon and Holmes (2004) explain that the terms 'Gypsy' and 'Traveller' are used to cover a range of different ethnic, cultural and occupational groups. In a book for children called *The Travelling People*, Wormington et al. (2003) explain that Gypsies first originated in India around about 1000 AD. In fact the term 'Gypsy' comes from 'Egyptian'. People wrongly thought that the Gypsies came from Egypt.

There are many different groups of people who might be called Gypsies or Travellers, such as:

- Travellers of Irish, Scottish, and Welsh Heritage.

- Romany Gypsies from England and Wales.

- Roma Gypsies from Eastern Europe (Romany people).

- New Age Travellers.

- Bargee Travellers.

- Circus Travellers.

- Showground (showpeople) Travellers.

If you have realized here that Circus and Showground Travellers (showpeople) are an occupational group, then you were right. Many of them prefer the term 'Traveller'. They may originate from the British Isles or could more recently have entered the country as a refugee (for example, the Roma Gypsies of Eastern Europe).

> My children tell me that the other kids call them names. They call them 'dirty, smelly gypos' and that hurts us because we're not dirty or smelly. But that is something we have to put up with, because we're seen as being different. We don't live in houses and people make judgments about us, which are always bad and negative Bhopal (2004: 55).

Everyone has prejudice in them if they are honest. Developing your understanding of Gypsy, Roma and Traveller communities and cultures will help you to identify prejudice in yourself. The first step in supporting Gypsy, Roma and Traveller communities is to understand that they comprise a variety of ethnic groups.

Travellers of Irish heritage, like many nomadic ethnic groups, have usually operated on the margins of the job market: for example, laying tarmac, breaking up cars for scrap and tree lopping. They are largely Roman Catholic, often seeking to place their children in faith schools of their religion (O'Hanlon and Holmes 2004).

Romany Gypsies have many similarities with Irish Travellers. Each group has a language or dialect of its own. You will recognize some Romani words from popular culture. Many have been taken into English (O'Hanlon and Holmes 2004). Irish Travellers use elements of old languages often described as Gammon or Shelter.

Romani Words

dai	–	mother
dadrus	–	father
mush	–	man
kusthi	–	good

Other background issues include:

- Bargee Travellers who live on barges and travel on the canals and waterways.

- Roma Gypsies who come from the East of Europe: the Czech Republic, the former USSR, the Balkans and Greece. They suffered significantly at the hands of the Nazis in the Second World War and whole villages of Roma Gypsies were exterminated in the concentration camps. The English themselves were responsible for persecuting Gypsies long before the Nazis. Edward VI passed a law which required all Gypsies to be branded and made into slaves for two years. 1650 was the last year in which someone was executed 'for the crime of being a Gypsy' (O'Hanlon and Holmes 2004).

- Showground and Circus Travellers have been visiting part of the country for many centuries with fairs or more recently circus shows. Many Roma groups have been associated with theatre and music performance. Django Rheinhart, for example, was a famous jazz musician from the mid-twentieth century who played a guitar with just two fingers on his left hand: the result of a fire in his Gypsy caravan (O'Hanlon and Holmes 2004).

- New Age Travellers differ from other Gypsy and Traveller groups as they cannot be identified by basing this on their ethnicity or occupation. For many, to become a New Age Traveller is a lifestyle choice: rejecting modern and urban ways of living in some cases for a more environmentally friendly approach. New Age families have been particularly affected by recent legislation (O'Hanlon and Holmes 2004). (This is summarized below).

- There are approximately 350,000 people in the Gypsy, Roma and Traveller community, of whom many live in housing. A large number still live a travelling lifestyle: some live on local authority or privately owned caravan sites (Clark and Greenfields 2006). However, about 70,000 Travellers move around the country from one unauthorized encampment to another. Finding somewhere to site a caravan can be a major problem for Gypsy, Roma and Traveller families. In 1968 the Caravan Sites Act required local authorities to provide sites for

Gypsies and Travellers and their caravans but in 1984 the Criminal Justice and Public Order Act repealed this law. New legislation allowed the eviction of unlawful encampments (O'Hanlon and Holmes 2004).

Activities – Teaching Gypsy, Roma and Traveller children

Look at the following statements about the education of Gypsy, Roma and Traveller children. Do you agree with the statements? Do any of these relate to your own experience of working with Gypsy, Roma and Traveller children?

'It can be frustrating for the teacher when families move on unexpectedly.'

'I don't have the specialist knowledge to teach these children.'

'I find that Traveller and Gypsy families mistrust teachers and schools.'

'Gypsy boys can be quick to resort to violence if they feel undermined or are subject to name-calling.'

In fact all of these statements may be true for teachers and the Traveller children they teach. There is no one approach or method of working with Gypsy, Roma and Traveller children which is guaranteed to work, as is the case in so many areas of education. Trust, commitment and understanding are essential qualities for teachers and schools. There has been some research into the most effective approaches and these will be explained later in this chapter.

OFSTED (1996b, 1999a, 1999b) explained how Gypsy, Roma and Traveller children were not making progress in their education. Despite some evidence of improvement in the Primary years, it was said that:

- Attendance generally was still poor: in 1996 as many as 10,000 Gypsy, Roma and Traveller children were not attending school at any one time.

- Progress in learning was still poor in 1999 compared with 1996, especially in English.

- Exclusions of Gypsy, Roma and Traveller pupils were disproportionately high compared with non-Traveller pupils in the evidence collected by OFSTED.

- 74 per cent of Gypsy, Roma and Traveller children were on the Special Educational Needs register.

We can see from this that there was great concern about the educational achievements of Gypsy, Roma and Traveller pupils. Since the late 1990s there has been some research into what really works when helping Gypsy, Roma and Traveller children to do better in primary and secondary schools (DfES 2003b). It can be summarized as follows:

- Developing an approach to induction for newly arrived pupils, which addresses social as well as academic needs.

- Developing an inclusive and welcoming atmosphere by raising the profile of 'race' and equal opportunites in school.

- Involving Traveller parents and the wider community.

- Lifting barries to inclusion by developing a responsive and relevant curriculum.

- Working closely with the local authority's Travellers Education Support Service.

- Systematically monitoring the educational progress of Gypsy and Traveller children and building related targets into a school's action planning.

Traveller family, community and gender issues

In the next section you will find out more about how Gypsy, Roma and Traveller parents and pupils feel about school. Try to avoid the stereotypes which are sometimes associated with Gypsies, Roma and Travellers, one of which is that Gypsy. Roma and Traveller parents are not interested in their children's education. You will see in the following extracts that this is far from the case.

Case Study – Two points of view

Some of the things the children learn, they don't need to know about. Reading and writing, that's all they need. Above that, it's not important. Travelling children stick to their own tradition, my children want to stay with the community. Have you ever known a Gypsy barrister? I haven't. They never get that far and some of them don't need it, they have their own families who can take care of them. Mrs. Kennedy, mother of Traveller children (Bhopal: 53).

Now I've left I miss school. I hated it then. But now with two kids and a missus to scavenge for. At school I had no worries. It was a laugh. The kids took the p*** and all that, called us names. We never took no notice; well, sometimes, if they got too cocky, me and my two cousins kicked their heads in. I don't 'ave any grudges against them. Sorted it out when we were kids … Duke, former pupil and now parent of Traveller family (Levinson and Sparkes 2003: 592).

In the above quotes what do Gypsy, Roma and Traveller parents and children say about the following points:

- Important areas for learning?

- Bullying and ways of responding?

- Aspirations and expectations of success at school and for career prospects?

Keep these thoughts in mind as you read the following pages, which will explain in greater detail Gypsy, Roma and Traveller families and their approach to education.

The above quotes from the Gypsy, Roma and Traveller community illustrate some of their feelings in respect of education. Gypsies, Roma and Travellers clearly differ in their expectations about the importance of education and there is a fundamental tension here for Gypsy, Roma and Traveller communities. This is illustrated in the following diagram:

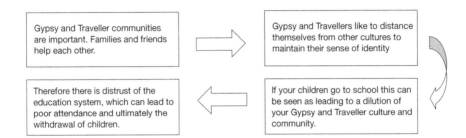

It would be wrong to paint a single view of Gypsy, Roma and Traveller families and schooling. As stated previously there is great variety in the Gypsy, Roma and Traveller communities. One parent summarized the feeling of marginalization and tension surrounding the education of her children:

> A lot of Travellers don't want to send their children to school. They think there's drugs and things out there. The parents are scared themselves because they didn't go to school. I'm glad I went to school and I encouraged my children as much as I could. I'm glad my daughter is going to school. Things are changing now in the Travelling world for the younger ones, maybe they will be going to school. Mrs Lindsay, parent (Bhopal 2004: 53).

Bhopal (2004) explains the unease of the Gypsy, Roma and Traveller community in their own words and it is important that we understand communities from their own perspective. For instance, O'Hanlon and Holmes (2004) explain the rituals and taboos of Gypsy families which are akin to Hindu rules on cleanliness. For instance, even though modern caravans could easily be equipped with modern toilets, many Gypsy families prefer not to have them in the caravan as this is seen as being 'unclean'. Different containers are used for cooking and cleaning so as not to break the rules of 'cleanliness'. Only a handful of Travellers live in a traditional horse-drawn caravan (*vardo*). However, a preference for highly decorated objects, glass and shiney surfaces to make the most of space and light can be seen in more modern caravans or even in the homes of housed Gypsies, Roma and Travellers (O'Hanlon and Holmes 2004).

Time to reflect – Cleanliness in the classroom

♦ Imagine that you are the teacher of a Reception class.

♦ In some Reception classes, there will be easy access toilets adjacent to the class or at the back of the room,

Think about the discomfort that this might cause a young Gypsy, Roma or Traveller child who has been raised in the belief that the toilet and living area should be distanced from each other.

Similarly, as we saw earlier in Chapter 3, issues concerning the use of the toilet may emerge due to language difficulties or cultural connotations.

The family and caravan are central to the lives of Gypsy, Roma and Traveller children. Though space is limited in caravans children are expected to adhere to family rules, which allow life to go on in closed spaces. Outside the caravan they have the freedom to play and explore and Gypsy, Roma and Traveller children often learn alongside their parents and older siblings. The caravan and its site are together a place of informal learning and pupils learn like apprentices even from a young age. This is particularly important for boys (O'Hanlon and Holmes 2004).

Levinson and Sparkes (2003) have done much to enlighten the wider community about the life of Gypsy, Roma and Traveller boys and young men, explaining how and why they act as they do. Learning alongside older brothers, cousins and especially their fathers not only allows boys to develop practical skills, but is very important also in helping them to establish their masculinity. Whereas girls are seen as having a nurturant role within the family, this is not the case for boys. Julie (a 19 year old Traveller) explains the roles of girls:

> I was helping by the time I could walk. By the age of 8, I was doing a lot of cleaning at home. I mean that's natural, like. You can't get a boy to wash up: 'e'd grow up all puffi-fied; woman-like (Levinson and Sparkes 2003: 597).

The important role of women in Gypsy, Roma and Traveller communities is highlighted by a fieldworker in Levinson and Sparke's (2003) research. They state that some Gypsy, Roma and Traveller young men are involved in 'violence, robbery and other criminal damage', ending up in prison. Whilst older men are 'a bit more stable', the result of this is a matriarchal society. However, where a father was present he had the ultimate authority on the majority of issues. Some mothers observe that it is the men who oppose change and find adaptation to changing circumstances more difficult (Levinson and Sparkes 2003).

If men do find change more difficult, perhaps they are the ones who have most to lose if children attend school with the resultant dilution of their culture. Levinson and Sparkes (2003) reported that Gypsy boys in their study sought to demonstrate the qualities held up as being important to Gypsy men. These were:

- Business skills.
- Physical strength.
- Loyalty.
- Sexual prowess and potency.

They also give the example of a boy of 10 years old who once reported to them that becoming a millionaire and demonstrating great sexual prowess (in so many words) were the height of his ambition.

Gypsy boys often develop their business acumen at a young age. Nathan (aged 12) talks in Levinson and Sparkes (2004) of the pleasure he got from exchanging some items from a tip for a CD-music player from a non-Gypsy pupil at school. Nathan took pleasure from doing a good deal and for 'getting one over' on a non-Gypsy. Families frequently explained that these skills were learned at home and not in school:

> They're learning more at home. Why waste time in school? They're going to have to fend for themselves one day. Alfie, aged 30 (Levinson and Sparkes 2003: 590).

Many men and boys also see fighting as a demonstration of masculinity (Levinson and Sparkes 2003). There are many inter-family feuds and as various members of families inter-marry such feuds spread. This is not merely violence for the sake of violence. In and out of school, boys see fighting as a way of establishing the pecking order. Where violence happens in school, this can also be a response to name-calling and racism. Both children and families see the use of violence in these circumstances as legitimate. We looked at gender from the perspective of 'Black boys' in the previous chapter. A question we should ask ourselves here is whether the features we have discussed above relate to being male, being a Gypsy or being a male Gypsy? The following table will help you reflect on this.

Whilst the above qualities may be espoused for boys and men, this does not reduce the threat which many Gypsy, Roma and Traveller communities see in engaging with the wider community by sending their children to school. Bhopal (2004) explains that many families are concerned, especially as children approach their teenage years about the perceived immoralities of non-Gypsy society, in particular the exposure to sex and drugs. It is important therefore that schools make the first contact with Traveller and Gypsy families a positive one. This begins with the admissions policy and procedures.

Admissions

We discussed admissions in Chapter 2 with respect to asylum seeker and refugee children. Here the focus is on Gypsy, Roma and Traveller children. There are great similarities between provision for Gypsy, Roma and Traveller children and others from a diverse background. Admitting and inducting children into the school can be traumatic for children and parents (DfES 2003b). It can set a very positive tone for future relationships or it can lead to distrust, poor attendance, conflict and ultimately a withdrawal from school. These are some of the ways to support children and their parents. In *Aiming High: Raising the Achievement of Gypsy and Traveller Pupils* (DfES 2003b) several approaches are discussed.

Activities – Gypsy boys and behaviour in school

From a teacher's point of view, how can the qualities celebrated by Gypsy males impact on the classroom?

Look at the following table.

■ What strategies from the list might help address each of the areas?

Qualities for Gypsy masculinity	Problems in school	Possible strategies in school
Business acumen	Irrelevance of the National Curriculum	Building a relevant curriculum i.e. links to business in the 14–19 curriculum
Physical strength	Fighting, violence and bullying	Developing an interest in sports
Loyalty	Inter-group fighting	Developing responsibility for younger bothers and sisters
Sexual prowess/potency	Teenage pregnancy	Sex education and support from sexual health services

What other strategies can be added?

The induction and admission of Gypsy, Roma and Traveller children

It helps when:

- Administrative staff are welcoming to parents and pupils and sensitively offer help with filling in forms if this is needed.

- Pupils have a labelled place to put their belongings and a place to keep work in advance of their arrival.

- The headteacher meets parents and pupils and explains school polices and procedures, especially pupil health and safety, bullying and race equality and agrees how the school and family will communicate, such as by mobile phone or through outreach Traveller Education Support staff.

- Pupils are given a buddy who will look after them at break times and explain school routines.

- Pupils are paired with others in the class who will offer peer support for curriculum access if needed.

- Targeted use is made of both Traveller Education Support Service staff and materials and school support staff to ensure that a class teacher is able to offer a pupil access to the on-going curriculum as soon as is possible.

- A key 'named' person is designated for the Gypsy, Roma and Traveller children to contact about any issues which arise for them within or outside school.

- A sanctuary area is identified, to where pupils worried about bullying or harassment or overwhelmed by school pressures can retreat.

- Staff are fully informed of a pupil's situation and informal training may be given.

(DfES 2003b)

The above approaches are judged by members of the Gypsy, Roma and Traveller community to be more effective in developing trust in pupils and parents towards the school (Bhopal 2004).

One parent explained it like this:

> We trust the teachers and the school. They make sure everything's done so that we are happy. The school always involves you. The Gypsy, Roma and Traveller teacher will always get on the phone and tell you what's going on. Being told what's going on and being involved makes a big difference. Then you know they care about you and they care what you think. Their actions show that they care and want to help our children in school (Bhopal 2004: 56).

O'Hanlon and Holmes (2004) explain that the close family relationships of Gypsy, Roma and Traveller children should also be considered when admitting very young children to school. Extended family and older siblings are often involved in bringing up younger brothers or sisters. It might help to reduce family anxiety if older brothers or sisters are allowed to see their younger siblings throughout the day so that both sides are reassured that the other is all right.

Time to reflect – Helping younger children at Admission

At break and lunchtimes a room away from the chaos of the playground can give brothers and sisters at the start of their time in school the chance to acclimatize to the bustle of normal school life.

The experience of children from Gypsy, Roma and Traveller families may be very varied in different schools. Some children may be located in the same area and attend the same school for most of their lives. Others may have a very interrupted experience of schooling, moving from one place to another as jobs dictate: for instance, as is the case for Showground and Circus Travellers.

The Roma Gypsies who have come to England in the last decade provide in some cases a greater challenge as they may have entered the country as asylum seekers or economic migrants (O'Hanlon and Holmes 2004). (Refugees and asylum seekers were also discussed in Chapter 3, and the latter terms were explained earlier in Chapter 2). Depending on their original circumstances, some Roma Gypsies may have suffered great persecution and as a result Roma Gypsy children can be traumatized by this experience. Schools will, therefore, have to consider the emotional and physical needs of these children in addition to their learning needs.

Roma Gypsy children may never have attended a school before. If they have done in the past the experience may have been significantly different, including for example:

- A different language.

- Different areas of learning.

- Different methods for learning.

- Different class routines for behaviour.

It is not uncommon for teachers to be presented with this situation when a Roma Gypsy child is admitted, but all the other competing priorities do not go away! Whilst this is never an easy situation the support of the Traveller Education Support Service can be helpful. They can be contacted via the local authority. If a school has a tradition of admitting and teaching Gypsy and Traveller children, in some cases there may be a Traveller Support teacher or teaching assistant (O'Hanlon and Holmes 2004).

If schools set up and maintain effective relationships at the outset, this can contribute to good attendance on the part of Gypsy, Roma and Traveller children (DfES 2003b). Attendance is, however, a significant concern for pupils from a travelling background. Poor attendance will certainly have an impact on attainment and ultimately the success of these children in future life. This area is explored in the next section.

Attendance

As children approach secondary school age, concerns over racism and behaviour can impact on children's attendance and retention. Derrington (2005) explains in a study of behaviour and exclusion in secondary schools that:

although students' behaviour was perceived to be good by their primary school teachers, problems began to emerge during the first year at secondary school and twenty-four (out of 44) pupils had self-excluded by the age of 14 years. Furthermore, one in three of the students were temporarily excluded on at least one occasion (Derrington 2005: 55).

Derrington goes on to say that the number one factor, which pupils and parents state as a reason for poor attendance, is where schools do not address the problems associated with racism and name-calling. In Derrington's (2005) study, Year 6 teachers predicted many of the problems which Gypsy, Roma and Traveller children went on to experience subsequently in secondary school.

Similarly, in a study of Scottish Gypsy and Traveller families, Jordan (2001) explained that:

the essentially excluding school system and the self-excluding Gypsy or Traveller pupil (condoned by parents) conspired to perpetuate cycles of underachievement and marginalization, confirming their social exclusion with society (Jordan 2001: 117).

Attendance is an important factor in children's achievement in school. Below are what the DfES (2003b) highlights as effective ways of supporting attendance in schools:

Activities – Towards better attendance

- Follow up non-attendance as soon as possible. This conveys the message that a pupil's presence is valued.

- Establish a high level of contact between schools and parents. Developing an effective dialogue helps parents to understand the value of education and their value in supporting the school.

- Provide training for staff on the varied circumstances which pupils face in school and how best to help them.

- Audit curriculum provision, social support, bullying and race equality practice to ensure that these are not factors in poor attendance.

Case Study – Becky's story

Loads of people bully me. It's mostly boys in my class. They say I don't wash and they call me dog or cow. They don't say it to other girls … I used to make up excuses to teachers like saying I was sick when I wasn't.

Becky, KS 3 pupil.
(Derrington 2005: 59)

Becky's response is typical of many children's – if there is a problem, don't go to school. Realistically, this is not just the response of Gypsy, Roma and Traveller children: all children regardless of background, culture or ethnicity may respond in a 'fight or flight' manner when they experience difficulties in school. In Becky's case her school has developed strategies to address some of the difficulties she had been experiencing.

> ## Case Study – Helping Becky
>
> She meets with Jenny [NQT] once a week who is interested in special needs work – we thought it'd be quite nice for Becky to have a young female mentor … she's been doing a lot of work with her looking at self-esteem, working out … 'cos the local community is not particularly tolerant of other people, of 'others' if you like, whatever the other is and she gets a lot of stick in the community and it's difficult for us to deal with it because it's happening outside school or we're talking about people's parents that have said things and it's a very sensitive issue. So Jenny's been working with her trying to help and guide her through that sort of thing and help her solve the problems on her own. Becky's mother (Derrington 2005: 59).

Note how mentors (as previously discussed in Chapter 4) can be useful in supporting children both socially and emotionally which ultimately supports attendance. As schools change and the role of teachers and other adults in the classroom changes also in response to the remodelling of the work-force and *Every Child Matters* (DfES 2006c) there are potential opportunities for a more co-ordinated approach to supporting pupils in this way. It could be a teaching assistant or someone from the Gypsy, Roma and Traveller community who takes on the role of mentor.

O'Hanlon and Holmes (2004) explain that exclusion should be used as a sanction only as a last resort. Excluding children from school only contributes to family perceptions that it is not worth going to school. They go on to explain further a selection of practical strategies for encouraging better attendance:

- Liaison with the Education Welfare Service: for instance, providing transport where families move frequently between short-stay, illegal encampments.

- Provision of effective records: to identify relevant personal information and strategies for supporting individuals, which can then be given to families to take to their next school. This action provides continuity during periods of 'interrupted' schooling.

- Distance learning materials: in some local authorities the Traveller Education Support Service has produced materials which pupils can take with them during periods of absence. Even if pupils are physically not in school the negative impact on their education can be reduced.

Gypsy, Roma and Traveller children have a right to education under domestic law. Do you know the law in respect of Gypsy, Roma and Traveller children? The following will help:

Laws affecting Gypsy, Roma and Traveller children

Parents

Education Act 1996

- All parents have a duty to ensure that their children receive efficient, full-time education.

Local Authorities

Education Act (1996)

- Local authorities have a duty to monitor attendance and take action where necessary
- Local authorities have a duty to provide suitable places for all pupils, even those resident on a temporary basis.

Race Relations (Amendment) Act 2000

From 2003, Gypsy and Roma Travellers and Travellers of Irish heritage were included in the DfES's ethnic categories. It therefore became law for all institutions including schools to monitor the implementation of this law and to take action in cases of racist bullying (O'Hanlon and Holmes 2004).

Human Rights Act 1998

This enshrines the 'right to education' and the right for parents to have their religious and philosophical convictions respected by the state.

The law requires all parents, including those in Gypsy and Traveller families, to send their children to school when they are of compulsory school age (Education Act 1996). Even during periods of interrupted schooling, parents are expected to ensure that their children attend school. Schools for their part are required to provide places for children, even when those children are in the area only for a limited period of time. The DfES has explained in detail the legal issues associated with admissions and attendance (DfES 2003b).

Anti-bullying and anti-racism

The Race Relations (Amendment) Act 2000, highlighted in Chapter 1, places great emphasis on the need to provide for good race relations, to deal with racist incidents and to report them to local authorities. Since many Gypsy, Roma and Traveller children fall within this legislation, schools have a legal responsibility to deal with the one issue which all pupils and parents reported as leading to poor attendance and violence in school – racism and associated name-calling (Derrington 2005).

Tension exists for Gypsy, Roma and Traveller families between the need for an education and the respect that is lost due to such racism, which many of their children suffer personally in school:

> Getting an education is important for everyone, but it's more important for us because we're different. We're Gypsies. If we get an education, then people will respect us and not call us 'dirty, old Gypos'. Mrs Heart, parent (Bhopal 2004: 55).

Reynolds et al. (2003) confirm that the same is true in Northern Ireland where Irish Gypsy and Traveller children were educated in separate schools until a few years ago. Whilst most of these children experienced bullying, name-calling and in some cases physical abuse due to their ethnicity, their families felt unable to approach the school concerned. For most, such experiences go a long way in confirming their attitude that it is 'not worth' going to school'. OFSTED (1996b) said in turn that many of the incidents of exclusion of Traveller children related to physical responses to racism and bullying by non-Gypsy children. Schools do find this difficult as there is a culture of 'non-reporting' of racist incidents. As one boy said:

> All the Traveller children I know have the attitude that if you are not seen to be sorting out your own problems, you are weak. You have failed. (Derrington 2005: 50)

This attitude recalls the cultural aspects of identity and masculinity discussed earlier (Levinson and Sparkes 2003). It is important that all staff in a school look at their own attitudes and also the ways in which they talk to Gypsy, Roma and Traveller pupils. Further, there is a danger that teaching staff can themselves have racist attitudes.

Activities – Avoiding racist comments in school

Read the following comments from a Head of Year in a secondary school.

Think about any comments that you or your colleagues have made which might be seen as being racist.

What can you do to avoid such comments?

> The majority of the staff welcomed them [the Travellers] with open arms, tried very hard with them. But I have to say, and I am ashamed to say it … a very small minority were terrible. As far as they were concerned, they were thieves from the minute they walked into the building, they were vagabonds and they never gave them a chance no matter how many times I took these staff to one side and said you can't. They were unprofessional. I had better not say too much really but they were totally unprofessional in their approach to it … there were certainly times when I witnessed them on a corridor perhaps disciplining them for something they wouldn't discipline another child for because of who they were. I'm ashamed to say that but I have got to tell the truth. Teacher (Derrington 2005: 60).

Bhopal et al. (2000) explain that some schools are very proactive in dealing with racism. Whether it is the headteacher, the Gypsy, Roma and Traveller Support teacher, or a class teacher, in the most effective schools everyone takes racism very seriously. They suggest the following steps to react positively to the challenges of racism:

- All incidents should be recognized, formally recorded and investigated.

- Victims of racism need clear, and if necessary public support.

- Effective sanctions are needed to deal with racism.

- School pastoral systems need to deal with racism sensitively.

As we noted in Chapter 4, racism must be taken seriously. Where racism and bullying are appropriately addressed, this can have a very positive impact on the relationship between a Gypsy, Roma and Traveller family and school. In fact, this can break the circle of distrust that can exist.

Time to reflect – Pastoral support in school

If my son has a problem, he would go straight to the Traveller teacher and the Traveller teacher would then try to sort it out. The Traveller teacher is very good and patient with my son. Sometimes I don't know what my son would do without him. He has helped my son a lot. And what they [Traveller Education Support Service] do is a good thing, because we know that there is someone there who will help us when we have a problem and see things from our side and try and understand what we say and what we are thinking. Mother (Bhopal 2004: 56).

Another secondary school has the following clear sequence in place for responding to bullying (Bhopal et al. 2000):

- Record the incident on a referral form.

- Inform colleagues, particularly if the incident arose out of a situation where everyone should be more vigilant (for example unsupervized toilets).

- Where necessary, tell both sets of parents that the incident is being dealt with.

Jordan (2001) highlights the government's deficiencies in respect of dealing with bullying and racism of Gypsy, Roma and Traveller children. There have been significant developments in legislation and the media has given much attention to this area as a result (for instance, in the case of the Stephen Lawrence Inquiry as we noted earlier in Chapter 4). However, Jordan (2001) points out that there is no mention of Gypsies and Travellers in Scottish legislative developments on housing and social inclusion. Although governmental rhetoric on racism and bullying does not always extend to Gypsy, Roma and Traveller children, you have to start somewhere in addressing the problem. As Reynolds et al. (2003) have said, bullying and racism should not be left to a third party because these are things you do not want to get involved in. If everyone acts to develop an inclusive school and responds constructively to racism and bullying, we will have gone a long way in dispelling some of the reasons for parental lack of faith in schools.

Developing an inclusive approach to different cultures can help to root out some of the negative attitudes which children and families have for people 'who are different'. The displays, topics and content of lessons all have a part to play in developing an inclusive ethos in schools. The overt and hidden curriculum are both important in this respect.

The curriculum

Whilst the overt curriculum (QCA 1999) includes the various levels of planned activities which children experience in school, the hidden curriculum includes all those elements of a school which communicate the school's view of itself and others. Displays are a very good example of this. One parent explained the importance of positive images of Gypsy, Roma and Traveller children:

Case Study – Inclusion in the hidden curriculum

There are some boards with pictures of Travellers, the Traveller Teacher has lots of photos and books in her room. The children made a calendar about our life as well. The school does more than any other school. They've always had Travellers here and know us and do what they can to make sure that we feel included like everyone else is. The Traveller teacher and the Head are always eager to find out about us and learn about our ways. So, this makes us feel welcome and that they care. Mrs. Lock, parent (Bhopal 2004: 56).

Bhopal does, however, go on to say that Gypsies, Roma and Travellers are rarely seen in school textbooks. There are a few notable exceptions. One of these is *The Travelling People* by Wormington et al. (2003). The important point here is that this type of book should be made available to all children, not just those most directly touched by Gypsy, Roma and Traveller communities. How could you incorporate this information book in school? The main contents of the book are outlined in the following table.

The Traveller People

- Contents.
- The Travelling people (introduction).
- Time line (a history of Travellers in Britain).
- Travelling People in Great Britain and Ireland (an overview of groups and terms).
- Gypsy and Roma fact file.
- Irish, Scottish and Welsh fact file.
- New Traveller and Bargee fact file.
- Upper or lower case (terms for different groups).
- Customs and traditions.
- Circus fact file.
- Showmen and Fairground people fact file.
- Where Travellers live.
- Occupations.
- Glossary and bibliography.

(Wormington et al. 2003)

According to one of the Gypsy, Roma and Traveller mothers cited earlier, it gave her pleasure to know that her children and indeed the whole class were working together on a topic about her community. This promotes inclusion through the choice of topic in the curriculum. In primary school, cross-curricular topics in history and geography especially make the development of English skills meaningful when they are combined with a focus on the Gypsy, Roma and Traveller community.

The oral tradition of many Gypsy, Roma and Traveller groups also lends itself to a focus on storytelling. Many stories in Gypsy, Roma and Traveller cultures are handed down through the generations as spoken forms whch have never been written down. In fact this is the origin of most of the traditional tales which are central to our culture. *Little Red Riding Hood* originates from Italy, but was told to Charles Perrault in the South of France during the seventeenth century. Only the interest of Louis the XIV and his court led to the writing down of these tales. Once in print, there is a tendency for tales to be changed according to the teller of the tale (Zipes 1976).

Gypsy, Roma and Traveller tales have much to offer schools in the development of greater understanding of other cultures. Combined with the use of drama, storytelling has much to offer the teacher. It has the dual effective of enlivening the lesson, whilst giving a positive message that tales from all cultures are valued, including those from Gypsy, Roma and Traveller cultures. This can be used to good effect to develop a unit of work in primary schools as follows:

Activities – English unit on Gypsy folk tales

- Use the book *Gypsy Folk Tales* edited by Amabel Williams-Ellis (1973).
- Tell one of the stories from the book.
- Remember, in storytelling it's important to know the main points and signposts in the story. You don't have to retell the story word for word.
- Children can use props to act out key events in the story.
- Read a version and annotate the key features and language on an interactive whiteboard.
- Model to the children your own version of the story.
- Invite alternative characters, settings and storylines from the children using the story, which you then scribe.
- Children can develop a sequel to the story, which they plan and write up during an extended writing session.
- At the end of the unit ask some of the children to read out their stories and others to 'tell' their story without reading.
- Can the children recognize the difference in language between the written and oral forms? This reinforces understanding about the difference between written and spoken forms, dialect and accent: all features of language variation (QCA 1999).
- Can the children recognize words from Gypsy, Roma and Traveller languages and dialects?
- Make a display of the stories and the new words children have learned.

Inclusion of culturally sensitive topics is equally possible in secondary schools. Cross-curricular English activities can be used to develop interesting and purposeful activities between different subjects. Can you think of any other possibilities?

Activities – Cross-curricular opportunities in secondary schools

English	Links to other subjects
Write a report on different dwellings of different peoples.	Geography
Make a time line of a Roma Gypsy from the early 1900s in Eastern Europe to their arrival in England in the 1990s.	History
Make an Irish tale booklet illustrated with Celtic artwork.	Art
Devize a leaflet to advertise the ancient Statutes Fair on behalf of a visiting Showground family.	Business and vocational subjects

It is important to recognize that all children will benefit from activities such as these. In the previous chapter, for instance, you will have been introduced to the difficulties that Black children can face in school. There is evidence that strategies explained in this chapter can be effective in supporting children from minority ethnic communities other than that of Gypsies, Roma and Travellers. Not only will these activities contribute to the development of skills and understanding in English, but they will contribute to the wider understanding of other cultures which is enshrined in the Race Relations (Amendment) Act 2000. By developing an inclusive curriculum, using inclusive materials and teaching methods which promote inclusion, teachers and schools are more likely to avoid some of the poor behaviour and violence which have been explored above. There are some important steps beyond the curriculum which teachers can take in order to encourage positive classroom behaviour and school discipline in Gypsy, Roma and Traveller children.

Behaviour, communication and the peer group

You saw in the preceding sections that masculinity was often reinforced by prowess of a physical nature and that Gypsy, Roma and Traveller boys especially can react unpredictably to name-calling, being quick to resort to violence (Levinson and Sparkes 2003). Similarly, in the previous chapter we discussed the issues of masculinity with reference to 'Black boys'. One teacher summarizes this as follows:

Case Study – One teacher's view of behaviour

I probably shouldn't say this, but they're charming one moment, little devils the next. It's a powder keg, and quite often you know they're playing the system. They know just how far they can go. You wouldn't believe the number of fights some of the boys get involved in, among themselves as well as with other boys, yet somehow it's never their fault. Erica, Secondary teacher (Levinson and Sparkes 2003: 593).

As teachers we should be careful not to generalize based on the reports of a single teacher. However, Derrington (2005) offers an explanation for some of the perceptions held by secondary school teachers, based on the predictions of Year 6 primary school teachers of Gypsy, Roma and Traveller pupils. In addition to the problems of attendance and the lack of a central, trusted adult, Derrington points to the following factors relating to behaviour:

- Hostile exchanges between pupils and teachers as a result of a teacher's arbitrary, hostile or aggressive manner, provoking a pupil to react in a volatile way.

- Direct communication style of pupils misinterpreted by teachers as a sign of disrespect.

- Social and academic grouping of Gypsy, Roma and Traveller children with other children in lower ability groups, whereby other pupils may have low social skills and their own behavioural issues, providing the potential for conflict.

- Peer group approval resulting in 'acting out' behaviours. Alternatively, Gypsy, Roma and Traveller pupils try to establish themselves in the 'pecking order' of the peer group through fighting with others.

Parents of Gypsy, Roma and Traveller pupils often sided with their children when they perceived that the teacher had been aggressive in speaking to them. One mother states:

They [teachers] don't know how to speak to Gypsy children. They shout and tell them what to do but they don't like to be bossed. They don't like to be ordered. If they ask them nicely it's a different thing but if they tell them and boss them they're wasting their time (Derrington 2005: 57).

The direct and open style of communication adopted by some Gypsy, Roma and Traveller pupils is sometimes seen as a very adult quality which can be admired by teachers (Derrington 2005). Others, however, see this as being overly familiar. When looked at in the context of the close-knit nature of Gypsy, Roma and Traveller families and the assumption that these children will take on responsibilities from an early age, then it is easy to see why Gypsy, Roma and Traveller children communicate at such an adult level. Put yourself in their place:

Activities – Talking to Gypsies, Roma and Travellers

Which of these topics would you feel comfortable talking about?

- The football match last weekend.

- The last episode of your favourite soap opera.

- Your holiday from last summer.

- Your first name.

- Your age.

- What you think of some other pupils in the same year.

- Why you have decided to teach a particular lesson.

Some teachers may be comfortable with any of the above topics. Others may recoil at all of these. The important point here is the way a teacher is able to steer pupils away from topics without using an aggressive tone.

As we saw earlier in Chapter 2, knowing two or more languages is an advantage in academic learning. Some Gypsy, Roma and Traveller families speak languages other than English. Not all Gypsies, for instance, speak Romani but most understand some of its words (O'Hanlon and Holmes 2004). Words like *gorja* (a term used for a non-Gypsy) are sometimes used as a riposte to those pupils who call Gypsy children names. O'Hanlon and Holmes (2004) outline a case study in which they encouraged the use of some home language as part of an inclusive approach to Gypsy, Roma and Traveller children:

Activities – Promoting the use of a home language in school

- Raise awareness of commonly used words, which may arise in the classroom situation.

- Explore connections between the home language and English.

- Challenge views that Gypsies, Roma and Travellers are deficient in the use of language: they use language *differently* but not necessarily *deficiently*.

- Dual-language books can be useful, but some parents can be dismissive of 'showing their children up' by using books with home language words in.

Whilst a celebration of the range of languages in a school can help the development of an inclusive whole-school ethos, consistency in the application of a rewards and sanctions system is also very important. Bhopal et al. (2000) summarize the features of an effective school in respect of behaviour:

- They provide a public framework for good behaviour, which is explained carefully to parents and children. For example, in many of these schools the pupil Code of Conduct is displayed in public places throughout the school.

- All staff in the school apply the framework consistently.

- The headteacher has a very important role in setting the tone of relations with both Gypsy, Roma and Traveller pupils and parents. This should be welcoming and supportive. Leadership comes from the headteacher and the school's governing body in this respect.

Any school framework for rewards and sanctions must be applied sensitively. Derrington (2005) explains that teachers should be careful in their expectations for Traveller children in respect of homework. Many Gypsy, Roma and Traveller children have difficulty in finding the space to complete homework. Sometimes parents themselves have poor basic skills and are, therefore, not able to help their children in the same way that some others do. So when a Gypsy or Traveller pupil fails to complete homework on time, it would be wrong to immediately issue a detention in a secondary school, if this is the normal procedure. Where secondary schools encourage dialogue with Gypsy, Roma and Traveller parents this can help to explain and justify school policy on things like uniform and the wearing of jewellery.

Consistency in policy and practice throughout the school is vitally important. Derrington (2005) explains the case of Peter who was excluded for retaliating when another pupil called him names. The other boy was not excluded. Shortly after this incident Peter opted out of school – he was only 12.

Time to reflect

- Have you examined your own beliefs and knowledge about Traveller, Roma and Gypsy communities?

- Has your school developed a positive and welcoming ethos towards Traveller, Roma and Gypsy families?

- Does your school have a consistent policy in place to deal with racism, name-calling and bullying?

- Has your school made constructive links with the Traveller Education Support Service?

- Is your curriculum and teaching style relevant and supportive of Gypsy, Roma and Traveller children?

- Do you monitor the achievement of Gypsy, Roma and Traveller pupils, setting high expectations for all your pupils?

- Are families closely involved in your school to ensure good behaviour and learning in a happy and safe environment?

Reflection and review

- Gypsy, Roma and Traveller communities are varied in make-up and background.

- Look at the diagram below. Ultimately, the success of Gypsy, Roma and Traveller pupils in school is built on the trust that has been developed from the first contact between a family and the school.

- With appropriate support and by maintaining good communication with families, schools are able to help pupils achieve and maintain good attendance, even if their stay at a school is only temporary.

- Gypsy, Roma and Traveller children should no more be subject to 'extreme racism, discimination and stereotyping greater than any other minority ethnic group' (DES 1985).

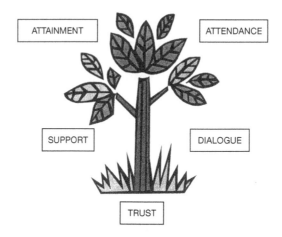

ATTAINMENT ATTENDANCE SUPPORT DIALOGUE TRUST

Key Points

- There is no one approach or method of working with Gypsy, Roma and Traveller children which is guaranteed to work, as is the case in many areas of education.

- Try to avoid the stereotypes which are sometimes associated with Gypsy, Roma and Travellers. One of these is that Gypsy, Roma and Traveller parents are not interested in their children's education.

- Learning alongside older brothers, cousins and especially their fathers not only allows boys to develop practical skills, but is very important also in helping them to establish their masculinity.

- The close family relationships of Gypsy, Roma and Traveller children should be considered when admitting very young children to school.

- As children approach secondary school age, concerns over racism and behaviour can impact on their attendance and retention.

We look next in Chapter 6, at an issue which has emerged throughout our discussions, the importance of working with parents and the local community.

50

Refugee and Asylum-Seeker Children

Knowles, G. and Lander, V.

This chapter explores:

- The distinction between the terms refugee and asylum seeker;
- How the experience of refugee and asylum seeking children may impact on their learning and achievement in school;
- How schools and teachers can support the well-being of refugee and asylum seeker children through understanding the wider needs of their families.

The particular educational needs of refugee and asylum seeking children is an area which is perhaps the least recognized and acknowledged within schools. This could be because the issue may be confined to certain schools in certain areas of Britain, for the simple reason that refugee and asylum seeker families are settled in certain areas. Therefore it is an issue which may be quite removed from the consciousness and experience of many student teachers and teachers. However, the national consciousness is affected by negative headlines in newspapers which indicate that there are too many people in England seeking refuge. It should be noted that people who are referred to as asylum seekers or refugees are not the same as economic migrants. People in the former categories are fleeing persecution, conflict and war, whereas economic migrants will have planned their stay in Britain and will still have a home and safe place to return to in their own country, when and if they decide to return.

That refugees and asylum seekers are, as the term suggests, in fear of their lives in the country they have come from, highlights a number of inter-related issues that impact on the education of refugee and asylum seeker children. For example, there are issues related to their emotional well-being, language, religion and ethnicity which are overlaid by legal issues related to their status and applications to stay in Britain. These issues affect the children and their families. But some children may be in Britain on their own as a result of their families trying to find a better life for their child whilst they may remain in their country of origin which may be affected by war, or by political or ethnic tension and violence.

The needs of these children and their families can also be complex, requiring the support of a number of services such as housing, medical, education and sometimes social services. Most refugees and asylum seekers arrive in Britain with very few possessions and nowhere to live and sometimes no family with them or no family to live with. Their plight is not to be envied but considered with compassion and understanding. For example, fleeing your home country, leaving behind your extended family, house, possessions to become dispossessed is not a decision any father or mother makes lightly. It is only when their freedom and rights are severely restricted or their lives are in danger that they decide there is no alternative but to flee. As one young man said: 'No-one chooses to be a refugee' (http://www.teachers.tv/videos/refugee-kids).

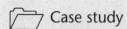 Case study

Abdi is a 14-year-old boy who has just arrived as an unaccompanied asylum seeker. He has just landed at Gatwick Airport, London. The Immigration and Border Control Officers take him to an interview room. Abdi appears tired, confused and bewildered by his surroundings. He was told by his uncle that there would be a better life for him in England. But it has been two months since he last saw his family and his village. It was then that the men with guns ran amok in his village shooting and killing anyone they saw. They murdered his father, mother and big brother. He had seen this all from his hiding place. After the sights he had seen he ran to the next village to tell his uncle. His uncle took him to the capital of Somalia and handed him over to a man. The man took him to Mogadishu airport and put him on the plane. Abdi didn't know he had a passport until then. Now he is in a room with a man who is asking him questions. He seems all right and Abdi can ascertain that he probably wants to know why he has come to England but Abdi can't tell him because he doesn't speak English.

Questions for discussion

What do you think are Abdi's immediate thoughts and feelings? Imagine yourself in his position, or imagine your son or daughter in this position. How would you like to see them supported?

This is how the story of some children's lives as an asylum seeker in England can start. They arrive unaccompanied and sometimes they know why they have left their families behind, sometimes they don't. On arrival another phase of their life journey begins to unfold, a phase that they have very little control over. Every year 3,000 unaccompanied children under the age of 17 arrive in the UK and apply for asylum (http://www.multiverse.ac.uk/ViewArticle2.aspx?Keyword=asylum+seekers+and+refugees&SearchOption=And&SearchType=Keyword&RefineExpand=1&ContentId=15499).

As you can imagine life must be pretty awful for a parent to send a beloved child on such a long and unknown journey and to trust the future of their child to strangers. To develop your understanding of the complex issues faced by these children you are advised to read Benjamin Zephaniah's (2001) book *Refugee Boy*.

History and definitions

The 1951 Refugee Convention was designed to tackle issues of refugees after the Second World War and as such applied largely to a European context rather than a global one. The Convention was modified by the 1967 Protocol which extended its application across the world. It is known that 147 states have signed up to the Convention and its Protocol (UNHCR, 2007). The Convention and its Protocol obliges host states to protect refugees. Although written in 1951 for a very different world situation, 'the Convention has proved remarkably resilient in helping to protect more than 50 million people in a wide variety of situations' (UNHCR, 2007: 9). Can you think of recent situations across the world in which the Convention and its Protocol would apply?

The Convention was the first international agreement to define the basic human rights of refugees. It defines who is and is not a refugee (for example, war criminals are not considered refugees) as well as their right to protection and services from countries that have signed up to the Convention. It defines the rights of refugees, for example, their rights to freedom to practise their religion, to freedom of movement and their right to work and education. It also states that no country should return refugees to the country of origin if they fear persecution. People who are fleeing conflict in one area of the country but stay within the borders of the country, for example, Tamils in Sri Lanka or the people of Dafur in Sudan are referred to as Internally Displaced People. In this situation the Convention and its Protocol do not apply. To be referred to as a refugee you must cross an international border from one country to another. It is interesting to note that one stops being a refugee when you have gained the right to permanently reside in the country in which you first sought asylum. The preferred option is that refugees return to their country of origin when it is safe to do so. This was the case when thousands of Rwandan refugees returned home after the genocide in 1996. It should be noted that under international law no country can return a refugee to their country of origin if they are still in danger of persecution (UNHCR, 2007). The idea promulgated by the popular press of asylum seekers flooding the country is a common myth which deserves to be extinguished. UNHCR (2007) notes that the idea of asylum seekers swamping some countries is not borne out by the facts:

> Countries around the world, including some in Europe, believe they are being overwhelmed by asylum seekers. The global number of asylum seekers did increase in the 1980s and 1990s, but then decreased sharply during the first years of the new millennium. The concerns of individual states are relative. The bottom line is that some nations in Africa, Asia and the Middle East – states with far fewer economic resources than the major industrialized countries – sometimes host much larger numbers of refugees over much longer periods. (UNHCR, 2007: 16)

In fact under 14% of the refugees in the world live in Europe (www. refugeecouncil.org.uk). It may be worth remembering this rather small figure when you read alarmist headlines or negative comments about refugees.

Definitions of the terms asylum seeker and refugee

The two terms are often used interchangeably but it should be noted that in law they are different. In common parlance we do not distinguish between the two terms. But there are differences which teachers and education professionals should appreciate.

Definition of the term asylum seeker

An asylum seeker is a person who has crossed an international border in search of safety and refugee status in another country. The person and dependents have applied for asylum. In the UK asylum seekers are people who are awaiting a Home Office decision as to whether they can remain. (http://www.multi-verse.ac.uk/viewarticle2.aspx?contentId=15422)

As noted earlier, the 1951 UN Convention and 1967 UN Protocol define the rights of asylum seekers. A person can declare themselves to be seeking asylum when they arrive at an airport or port. They can also declare themselves as such when they are in the country. The Home Office has a special department, called the Immigration and Nationality Directorate (IND), which processes all the applications for asylum. The person who has declared themselves as an asylum seeker is required to complete an application which should be supported by evidence. The IND then assesses the evidence and the claim. Rutter (2003) notes that this process can have one of four outcomes:

1 The claimant is assigned refugee status because there is evidence to show that there is a 'well founded fear of being persecuted for reasons of race, religion, nationality, membership of a particular social group or political opinion' (UNHCR, 2007: 6);
2 The applicant is granted 'Humanitarian Protection' but is not given refugee status. This protection covers a period of time and recognizes that if returned to their country of origin the person would be in danger of torture or being killed;
3 Discretionary leave is granted to people who are not granted asylum and cannot be returned to their country of origin. This is often granted to unaccompanied children who have not been granted refugee status and who are under 18;
4 About 80% of applications are refused. Applicants whose claim is refused may have the right to appeal but only 25% are successful.

Forty-three per cent of people seeking asylum come from one of the following countries: Iraq, Zimbabwe, Afghanistan, Somalia and China, and smaller numbers from other countries such as Sri Lanka and the Democratic Republic of Congo. The political situation in each of these countries is widely known and violations of human rights are reported in our news. Most people seeking asylum are men between the ages of 18 and 34. Three thousand unaccompanied children under the age of 18 apply for asylum each year. People who apply for asylum cannot work but require care, support and housing.

Rutter (2003) notes that asylum seekers do not have access to state benefits but children from asylum seeking families can access schooling. The National Asylum Support Service provides financial support and housing. They operate a policy of housing asylum seekers anywhere in the country in an attempt to control the numbers in London and the South East of England. This may sound straightforward but an asylum seeking family can be moved many times to different areas of the same city or region or to different parts of the country. This has the inevitable consequence of adding to their stress and insecurity. The children have to move schools as many times as they move home.

Definition of a refugee

Rutter (2003) notes that the term is more a 'legal construct' which defines a refugee as 'someone who has fled their own country or is unable to return to it owing to a well-founded fear of being persecuted for reasons of race, religion, nationality, membership of a particular group or political opinion' (1951 UN Convention Relating to the Status of Refugees). Under the 1951 UN Convention Relating to the Status of Refugees and its 1967 Protocol, the country in which the person seeks refuge can deem the person to be a refugee. Usually people will seek asylum and make an application, and, if successful, they will be granted refugee status. This status affords people the protection of the state in which they have sought sanctuary and protection from being returned to their country of origin. It also means that people with refugee status can work, have access to benefits, housing, medical care and education. A small number of asylum applications gain refugee status – only 6% in 2003. In 2009 the UK was home to only 2% of the 16 million refugees worldwide (refugee-council.org.uk). The most successful group of refugees in Britain are the Ugandan Asians that were expelled by President Idi Amin in 1972 (www.refugeecouncil.org.uk).

Rutter (2003) explains that whilst in law the status of an asylum seeker and refugee are clear, schools tend not to delineate or know the difference, or even ask. This is because the journey which describes the flight of asylum seekers and refugees from their countries of origin are not straightforward. They can often gain asylum or refugee status in one country and then migrate to another. Remember 80% of the world's refugees are in camps or housing in countries within Africa or the Middle East, countries such as Kenya or Jordan or Syria. So, for example, if you gain refugee status in Sweden as a Somali asylum seeker you may then later come to the UK. In this case the children may speak Somali, Swedish and depending on their age they may also have learnt English in Sweden.

It is estimated that there are 100,000 refugee children in the UK and that about 65% are found in the Greater London area. The largest proportion of refugee children in schools is from Somalia and the numbers indicate that approximately 6% of children in London schools are from refugee backgrounds (Rutter, 2006).

 Case study

Farrah and her mother arrived in Dover after an arduous overland journey from Iraq. Farrah is eight and she is really not sure what has happened to her father. She just remembers being told they were visiting her grandmother and she was put in the car for what she thought was a weekend trip. Her memory is hazy because she was half asleep and half awake as they made their way through the countryside, then on via Syria and other countries to Britain. She hears mum talking to an interpreter and she hears her tell her that they are seeking asylum.

Farrah and her mother are given accommodation in a detention centre where there were many people from around the world. They were then moved to Croydon where they had a small flat. Farrah's mother told her she didn't know how long they would be there but they would try to get her into a school, which they did with the help of a neighbour who was also from Iraq. She was at the school for just half a term and they got moved to North London where it took her mother four months to find a school for Farrah. They spent their days watching television and in that way they started to learn more English. Farrah's mother cried a lot and sometimes she shouted at Farrah, especially if she was messy in this new very small flat. There were very noisy neighbours above who were quite hostile. Farrah is now in her second school in Britain in six months. She asks after her father almost every day and over the course of the days and now the months the answer has moved from 'he will be with us soon', to 'I don't know', and sometimes her mother cries and other times she stares out of the window as if willing him to appear.

 Questions for discussion

As someone who works with Farrah, how would you make Farrah welcome in your classroom?
What would you want to know about her?
How could the school support this family?

This case study provides a very small sample of the issues met by asylum seeker families and their children. They are often families that are emotionally stressed and who are trying to do their best for their children, as any mother or father would seek to do. Schools can support such families by ensuring that they have access to the relevant support services, for example legal, social, medical and English language learning provision for the adults and they can encourage the children and their families to be part of the school community. They also need to be sensitive to the fact that there may not be a lot of money since most people only get £35 or so a week to spend at the supermarket so there may not be enough left over to buy the correct uniform, especially since they may have needed to move schools a few times due to changes in accommodation. Can the school help by providing uniform from spare stock?

The research report by Aspinall and Watters (2010) funded by the Equality and Human Rights Commission to examine the dimensions of equality and human rights as related to the lives of asylum seeking and refugee adults and children, notes that the policy of dispersal leads to uncertainties, disruption and a lack of continuity for the children's education. Yet it is education which can provide these children with stability and help to support their well-being. The policy of moving asylum seeking families to different areas in order to ensure that the resources in one area are not drawn on so much means that the children cannot assume that the first school they enter will be the school they are in the following year or month. The research report notes that schools with places have to admit asylum seeking and refugee children but that this is thwarted by some schools that are not prepared to receive these pupils and others that do not want the admission of these pupils to affect their GCSE results. The report highlights the fact that in one London borough there were 189 children waiting for a school place and 125 of them were asylum seekers.

The report further outlines barriers such as lack of resources in schools and variable practice which hinders the integration and educational progress of asylum seeking and refugee children. The authors noted that varied practice in schools in the admission of asylum seeking and refugee children stemmed from the assumption that this was a homogeneous group and a lack of a nuanced understanding about the needs of different groups. The report (Aspinall and Watters, 2010) highlights research undertaken by the Refugee Council to identify how schools could establish good practice to work with asylum seeking and refugee families and their children; for example by offering extended school provision which educates the children and works more broadly with their families and the wider community; assigning a home–school/community worker who can not only be a tangible link between the school and families, but can also be involved in providing wider specialist support such as inducting families and helping them to access other support agencies; and establishing peer mentors and specific language support in classes, as well as beyond the school day such as in extended provision, or on Saturday mornings which helps other members of the family.

The right to education is a basic human right and asylum seeker and refugee children are entitled to education in the countries in which they seek refuge. In most European countries these children may be sent to centres where they are educated alongside others in a similar position and where they gain proficiency in the language of that country, but in the UK these children are integrated into mainstream provision. What do you see as the advantages or disadvantages of these two approaches?

Schools and teachers supporting the needs of asylum seeking and refugee children and their families

It is important that schools do not see refugee and asylum seeking children as a homogeneous group. They come from a variety of countries for a variety of reasons, as described above. The DfES (2004b: 4) guidance notes that children from the same country may not come from the 'same ethnic or linguistic backgrounds and their families may have different religious beliefs and political observances'. Teachers and schools should also note that children from asylum seeking and refugee backgrounds will have very different experiences of persecution in their countries of origin and their journeys to the country of refuge and varied experiences of being in that country. It is important to note that children will vary in how well they cope with the stresses associated with the change in their lives. In fact many refugees have shown how resilient they can be – an outcome which Anderson (2004) describes as something which emerges from adversity rather than a quality a person possesses or not.

Hamilton and Moore (2004) provide a developmental model which can track the changes refugee children have gone through during the sudden changes in their lives which require adaptation and resilience. Teachers need to become familiar with it as a means of recognizing the factors which may have shaped the lives of these children. The model delineates factors associated with the three stages of transition in the lives of refugee children and the associated tensions resulting from unusual and aberrant life-changing events or conditions. The stages and factors are:

1 **pre-migration factors** – experiencing the events of war or conflict such as bombing or shooting and as a consequence seeing dead and injured people; experiencing the death of or injury to a member of their family, or being injured themselves, witnessing the violent death of a family member through torture; experiencing fear, trauma and panic themselves, but also in other trusted adults; being a child soldier; disruption to their everyday routines like going to school;

2 **trans-migration factors** – suffering the anxiety and tension involved in a long and dangerous journey to escape; experiencing transition through several countries; experiencing life in a refugee camp; being at risk of exploitation and then trying to settle in different countries; the separation from parents or other loved ones;

3 **post-migration factors** – stress amongst children and adults; experiencing anxiety of whether they will be allowed to settle or not; the whole process of application; fear of deportation; the sense of loss of status and dependency on others when once the family were perhaps independent, requiring no support; overcrowded or poor housing; racism and the struggle to access health and schooling.

Richman (1998) states that all these factors impact on the child's well-being and affect their sense of security, self and identity. Inevitably there may be consequences in terms of the child's learning and progress in school, yet, as Richman (1998) asserts, a school's policy and its implementation can have a beneficial effect on the well-being of refugee children. Schools can help children feel safe and help them regain a sense of normality, and each factor sets the climate for learning. Local authorities and schools are obliged to provide full-time education for pupils of school age and to ensure there is no delay in providing schooling for asylum seeking and refugee children; local authorities should have policies and support services to assist asylum seeking and refugee families with, for example, admissions in the middle of a term since the conditions of war and flight from it do not conveniently coincide with the timing of school admissions. Local authorities should assist schools with access to interpreting services or access to Ethnic Minority Achievement Services (EMAS) staff who can assess the child's language proficiency in their first language, and they can then provide subsequent support for the child and the school. For children entering Early Years provision it is vital that the different services work together for the benefit of the child; for example, to ensure that health care professionals such as a health visitor are involved with the family and can provide them with support. Some local authorities have a designated person whose responsibility involves the welfare and education of asylum seeking and refugee children.

A good school will have induction procedures for the parents and children from asylum seeking and refugee backgrounds. The induction process will need to involve initial parental orientation and expectations of schools since schools in the UK differ from perhaps the formal schooling structures of other countries. A well thought out and patient approach to the induction process can provide these families with a sense of security and the beginnings of a trusting relationship can be established between the school and the family. It is advisable for the school staff to undertake some initial research into the conditions within the home country; the communities, languages and history of the country and some research on the schooling in that country. The information gathering process is an important stage for the school and the family but they may not want to recount the tensions that caused them to flee their country of origin. The DfES (2004b) guidance states,

> Specifically, these children need provision that can: meet their psychological needs, by, for example, using play to help a child settle; respond to their language needs; challenge racism and promote an understanding and positive acceptance of cultural diversity; involve parents who may not be confident in speaking English; support families who may be experiencing stress and economic deprivation; address issues of religious belief. (DFES, 2004b: 6)

Schools and teachers need to be aware of the language and the emotional and physical needs of asylum seeker and refugee children. In order to understand these there needs to be staff in-service training which covers such areas as finding out the child's home language, encouraging the maintenance of their home language, deploying the use of bilingual assistants, trying to learn a few key words of the child's home language such as hello and good-bye, for young children knowing the child's words for toilet or hungry or thirsty, having dual language signs and books in the classroom, involving the child in teaching the children in their class words from their home language, providing the child with good language role models who can also be their friends and be supportive – they do not have to be the same ethnicity as the asylum seeking or refugee child, but should be a trustworthy, kind and helpful buddy who can show them the routines of the school and with the teacher's help they can encourage the child to use greetings in English as a start to their development of English. For young children and their families play can provide a welcome return to normality and a means for parents and children being together through a normal childhood activity such as play. It can also help some children as a conduit to talk about their fears and hopes and in this way be therapeutic in helping them cope with the stresses they have endured. The last thing that an asylum seeking or refugee child needs to experience is isolation at school. To be alone in a strange school, in a strange country and not speak the language would instil fear into any person, adult or child; but for these children it would add to the stress and fear they have already experienced as a result of their transit to the UK. This is why schools need to be sensitive to the needs of the child and their family.

 Case study

Grace has just started at your school with her brother. She is 14 and has come to join her father but her mother is still in Zimbabwe. They are an asylum seeking family. Grace starts school in the middle of the Spring term just after half-term. How will her start mid-term affect her work and how can her teacher and the school support Grace to achieve her best. She is keen to become a doctor.

 Questions for discussion

As her form tutor what do you need to know about Grace?
What research do you need to undertake?
How will you welcome Grace into your classroom?

What is interesting about this case study is that it can be tempting to think that children from asylum seeker or refugee backgrounds are from deprived or poorly educated backgrounds. It is correct to think that the children's education may have been disrupted, but, as we can see it is not necessarily the case that all children from these two groups come from backgrounds where they either have not been to school or that they have received minimal education in their country of origin. It is right to consider the child's educational background alongside key facts such as the child's level of language proficiency in their first language; the level of education in their home country and the education or the employment of the parents in their home country. Aspinall and Watters (2010: 42) cite research which found that Somali children perform 22% below the average mean. Rutter (2006) notes that whilst Somali children's performance is below the mean in two local authorities her research found that where schools worked closely with the Somali community the children in those schools outperformed the White students but were still 11% below the national average. There was significant underachievement amongst children from the Congo which Rutter (2006) surmised was due to the 'fragility' of their first language which then in turn impeded the acquisition of English and their subsequent attainment. She found that a relatively new group of refugees from Southern Sudan performed well in school and identified factors such as family status in their home country, level of schooling and education and the fact that English was spoken at home as supportive to their educational success. Her findings showed that where the schools merely worked on homogenized conceptions about asylum seeker and refugee children and failed to recognize the specific needs of the child, that children did not achieve as well.

The duty of schools to promote community cohesion (DCSF, 2007a) should provide schools with a greater impetus to engage and liaise in tangible ways with all the communities it serves. The duty encompasses a number of other statutory requirements, such as the need to promote the children's spiritual, moral, social and cultural education (Education Act 2002) and the duty to promote race equality (Race Relations Amendment Act 2000). The duty to promote community cohesion is designed to be inclusive and to enable schools to prepare children to live in a globally diverse world but also to enable them to appreciate and live in a culturally, ethnically and religiously diverse British society. The duty is a positive attempt to help children wherever they live to value members of their school community, their local community and the global community.

This chapter has explored the distinctions between refugees and asylum seekers and how the experience of flight from their home country and the transition from one country to another can affect children's well-being, their education and their achievement. The chapter highlighted links to the International Convention on Refugees and demonstrated how this can manifest itself in the provision of education for asylum seeking and refugee children. But most importantly, the reader was encouraged to develop a nuanced concept of the children that are part of this group and to begin to understand that their individual stories will illuminate their fears, hopes and needs. Teachers and education professionals need to take time to understand the whole story to meet the needs of the individual child.

Further reading

- Laird, E. (2007) *Kiss the Dust*. London: Macmillan Children's Books.
- Zephaniah, B. (2001) *Refugee Boy*. London: Bloomsbury.

Useful websites

- Equality and Human Rights Commission: www.equalityhumanrights.com
  - o Promotes equality and human rights; aims to create a fairer Britain by providing advice and guidance, and raising awareness of people's rights

- Multiverse: www.multiverse.ac.uk
  - o A website for teacher educators and student teachers addressing the educational achievement of pupils from diverse backgrounds

- Refugee Council Online: www.refugeecouncil.org.uk
  - o The largest organization in the UK working with asylum seekers and refugees offering direct help and support

- Scottish Refugee Council: www.scottishrefugeecouncil.org.uk
  - o Independent charity dedicated to providing advice, information and assistance to asylum seekers and refugees living in Scotland

- Shared Futures: www.sharedfutures.org.uk
  - o A DVD and resource pack that promotes the integration of refugee children and young people in school and the wider community

- Teachers TV: www.teachers.tv
  - o A website with engaging videos, practical resources and an active online community to encourage teacher development

- UN Refugee Agency: www.unhcr.org
  - o Its primary purpose is to safeguard the rights and well-being of refugees. It strives to ensure that everyone can exercise the right to seek asylum and find safe refuge in another state, with the option to return home voluntarily, integrate locally or to resettle in a third country

Gifted Children in the Primary Classroom

Smith, C.

In this chapter we will:

- Help you think about how your own beliefs about what giftedness is can influence pupil performance.

- Offer a circular model to consider giftedness in the primary classroom.

What teachers and pupils believe about gifts and talents

In primary school we have a huge advantage over our secondary colleagues. We see the children every day for whole days at a time. We, therefore, have ample opportunity to build important, long lasting and robust relationships with our pupils. Every primary school teacher recognises that this is vital, not only to create a positive and pleasant working environment, but because it makes a huge impact on how well pupils perform in our class.

The way that we build these relationships is affected by what we believe a 'good' pupil to be. The way that we build relationships, the way that we talk to pupils and the expectations that we have of individuals are deeply affected by how we believe the human mind works[i]. Research[ii] suggests that what we believe about how the human mind works is often built on unquestioned assumptions.

> *Implicit theories…reside in the minds of individuals, whether as definitions or otherwise. Such theories need to be discovered rather than invented because they already exist, in some form, in people's heads.[iii]*

Forming these implicit theories, while often done unconsciously, is essential because they help us to function effectively in life. The way that they help us is by guiding the way we behave; both what we say and what we do. It is not just teachers, however, who hold implicit beliefs. Children in our classes will hold these beliefs too. They are formed as a result of the way that parents and teachers talk to them and give them feedback about their behaviours and achievements.

In the primary classroom, beliefs are particularly important. Pupils are still forming their beliefs and the primary teacher can have a huge influence on how these develop. They are important to think about because what individuals believe about their own and others' abilities:

- can account for differences in achievement between pupils and by individual pupils over time;

- make a difference to the amount of effort a learner might put into an activity;

- can help to explain depressive reactions by pupils (yes, even in the primary school), to bad experiences in learning;

- and can be used to judge and label both ourselves and others.

There are two very different implicit theories of intelligence[iv].

1   Intelligence is fixed.

2   Intelligence is changeable.

What does believing that intelligence is fixed mean for pupils?

If pupils believe intelligence is fixed it means that they are likely to believe that they were born either clever or stupid and that they will stay that way for the rest of their lives. They also tend to believe that school success and school tests are a good indicator of who is clever and who is not. As a result of this they will predict their future success on the basis of today's performance. They will offer reasons for success and failure that are related to personal adequacy or inadequacy. For example, failure may be accounted for by poor memory or low intelligence (I just can't do maths!). Likewise success is because they have a natural aptitude for such things or because their parents were good at them. Such pupils are more likely to show aversion to tasks that they do badly in by saying they are bored or through feelings of anxiety.

Believing intelligence is fixed means that undertaking activities is about performance. Pupils with this belief might worry about how much ability they have or don't have to complete a task. They calculate this by comparing themselves with others. These pupils are more likely to be competitive and can become driven with the need to show that they are the cleverest in the class. They may develop a tendency to choose the easy option and avoid harder tasks that might show them up to be less 'clever' than they thought they were (or that they would want others to perceive them to be). They believe that being clever means that all tasks and activities should be completed very easily therefore having to work hard at something indicates that they are not very clever. Only success that comes easily is valued because this is what indicates high ability.

> ### Questions to consider
>
> - Can I recognise any pupils who might have a fixed view of intelligence?
> - To what extent do I have a fixed view of intelligence of my own learning?

What does believing that intelligence is changeable mean for pupils?

If a pupil believes that intelligence is changeable it means that they are likely to believe that how intelligent they can become is in their own hands. If they work hard they can become better at things and this improvement is an indicator of their intelligence. They rely less on test scores to give them a measure of their abilities and do not believe that test scores and school success will predict their future success or failure. Believing that intelligence is changeable means that failure is more likely to be put down to environmental or temporary contributors such as choosing the wrong topics to study. Equally success is generally attributed to sheer hard work.

Believing in changeable intelligence means that undertaking activities is about mastery. Pupils with this belief strive for personal improvement and so tend to be less competitive. They compete with themselves rather than other people. These pupils may develop a tendency to choose challenging work, rather than easy work, because that means they will learn more. Getting things wrong – within reason – does not bother them because failure is perceived as part of the learning process. These pupils have a belief that if you work hard you can become more able. Trying something really hard and achieving even only part of it shows you that you have improved and have learned new abilities that you did not have before. These pupils are more likely to be able to identify some things that they good at and some things that they are not so good at, believing that people are different and there are lots of ways of being able. These pupils seek to try lots of things because the experience of trying is enjoyable.

Teachers sometimes assume that gifted and talented pupils hold a belief that intelligence is changeable. They can be identified because of characteristics such as willingness to choose hard activities, and willingness to work hard. In fact some gifted and/or talented pupils believe strongly that intelligence is fixed. They will avoid hard work, try to do things with the minimum effort, and can be highly competitive. In this way the idea of implicit theories might help us to understand some aspects of underachievement, disaffection and disengagement.

I have presented here characteristics of the extreme positions that implicit theories can create and these two positions mean very different things for individuals (see Table 1.1). You may have started to recognise a few pupils. We need to be

Table 1.1 *Comparison of pupils' implicit theories*

Questions pupils try to answer	Fixed theory answer	Changeable theory answer
Why am I the way I am?	I was born clever. I am this way because my mum and/or dad is clever.	I work hard to be good at things. I am this way because my mum and/or dad encourage me. Certain things interest me more than others. I get the chance to try different things.
How do I assess my own intelligence?	People tell me I am clever. My results in tests and in class tell me how clever I am. Being first in the class means I am the cleverest in the class. Doing badly in a test tells me I am not as clever as I thought. How easy or hard I find things tell me how clever I am.	How much I improve tells me how clever I am. If I work hard and do well it tells me I am clever. People tell me that I am working hard and am doing well. I can see that I am better today at things than I was the last time I did them.
What does this tell me?	I will always be clever. I am clever at lots of things. I should get things right first time, most of the time. I should always get good results. I should always do better than those who are less clever than me.	The harder I work the better I will do. I might not be clever at everything. I might just be clever at a small number of things. The things I am clever at might not be in school. I might make lots of mistakes but this helps me learn more. I shouldn't worry too much about whom I am better or worse than.
How might this make me act?	I will avoid failure at all costs. I might panic if I start to find something hard. I may cheat rather than fail. I don't like to ask for help because that would be an admission of failure.	I like to try hard things and learn from trying. If I am faced with a really hard problem I will seek out help from others. I need to work hard to make sure that I do well.
Type of learner	Fragile. Sees learning as a competition.	Robust. Sees learning as a personal journey.

careful, however. We don't want to start labelling pupils as one type of theorist or another; labelling has not helped us in the past. Rather let us be aware that believing certain things can impact on how pupils learn in our classrooms and that as teachers we have the power to support or change their implicit theories. Whether we support or change implicit theories of intelligence in a positive way, however, will depend on the theory that we ourselves hold.

Questions to consider

- Can I recognise any pupils who might believe that intelligence is changeable?
- To what extent do I believe that my own intelligence is changeable?

It can be useful to find out a little more about what the pupils in your class believe. Asking pupils the questions on the sheet on page 6 will provide you with some more information.

Think about your own beliefs by considering the questionnaire on page 7.

The more that you have agreed with the statements in the questionnaire on what you believe, the more you are likely to believe that intelligence is fixed. The more you have disagreed with the statements in the questionnaire, the more likely it is that you believe intelligence is changeable. What might this mean for how we teach? The examples below describe the extremes of holding one view or another. Most teachers are – quite rightly – somewhere between the two.

What does believing that intelligence is fixed mean for teachers?

Teachers who believe strongly that intelligence is fixed are likely to believe that some pupils have more innate ability than others. It is the teacher's job to bring out the best in the children; in other words, help them to make the best of what they were born with. These teachers believe that the best way to provide for gifted and talented pupils is to identify which pupils were born with particular gifts and talents and to educate them accordingly. Although they do not believe education can make children more intelligent and that each child has a limit, they do believe that all children can improve their performance.

What am I good at?

1   In school I am good at _____

    _____

2   Outside school I am good at _____

    _____

3   I am good at these things because _____

    _____

4   In school I am not so good at _____

    _____

5   Outside school I am not so good at _____

    _____

6   I am not good at these things because _____

    _____

7   Do you think you could become good at these things? If yes, how? _____

    _____

8   Is there anything that you think you will never be able to do well? If yes, why is this?

    _____

9   What is more important – to be the best in the class or do better than you did
    last week? _____

    _____

What do you believe?

Try answering the following questions.

What do I believe?

1 Gifted individuals form a group that can be identified early in their school career and remains the same over time.

        Agree   Disagree

2 Gifted individuals are born with high intelligence.

        Agree   Disagree

3 Gifted and talented children need different forms of teaching and support from other children.

        Agree   Disagree

4 Because of their differences gifted children need to be educated separately from other children.

        Agree   Disagree

5 Teachers need special training and skills to teach gifted children.

        Agree   Disagree

6 Giftedness is genetic and cannot be changed.

        Agree   Disagree

7 Gifted and talented children need competition to keep them on their toes.

        Agree   Disagree

Belief in fixed intelligence means that intelligence is viewed more as a singular concept, as a general energy (often referred to as 'g') that flows into all that we do. If pupils are intelligent then they are likely to be good at a range of things rather than one very specific area. It is believed that pupils with high intelligence can focus their mental energy (g) towards almost any aspect of school life.

Teachers with this view might be more likely to support the organisation of pupils in or across classes into top, middle and bottom sets or groups. The composition of sets will be viewed as stable because such arrangements reflect the natural order of things in the classroom. Most work required of pupils will be individual in nature and collaborative work will be seen as a way in which 'better' pupils can help out with 'poorer' pupils. Success in school and beyond can be predicted accurately and early in a pupil's school career. In essence this view ascribes to the genetic origins of intelligence as fixed, singular (g), located almost exclusively within the pupil and possible to measure or identify through standardised tests (possibly IQ) and school exams.

A belief in the fixed and general nature of intelligence will support fairly tight frameworks of assessment within schools. Examinations and national testing are seen as good indicators of pupils' abilities. Such teachers might be interested in identifying the strengths and weaknesses that lie within pupils as this is where intelligence resides. They might be less convinced about ongoing classroom assessment because the performance from such assessment may be affected by factors that lie outwith the pupil such as help from parents, other pupils etc.

Teachers who believe in the fixed nature of intelligence tend to encourage performance goals in the classroom. In other words getting things right and performing well is important: mistakes are discouraged and are seen as evidence of a drop in standards. Activities and expectations are tailored to what is perceived to be an individual pupil's intelligence level. Pupils are compared one to another and competition is encouraged within and beyond the classroom as a means of motivating pupils and extending performance. Good work is recognised, valued and celebrated as something for others to emulate.

Believing in fixed intelligence focuses teacher comment and description on the pupils themselves, for example 'you're really good at that'; 'she's very clever'; 'you are a very good boy'. It is also reflected in teachers' expectations of what pupils can achieve. Believing that intelligence is fixed and innate will lead to high expectations of those identified as being born with high intelligence.

What does believing that intelligence is changeable mean for teachers?

Teachers who believe that intelligence is changeable tend to believe that the environment is the most important influence on how intelligent an individual becomes. This means that the teacher's role is to help his or her pupils to become more intelligent through the classroom environment. Whether pupils do or do not demonstrate their intelligences depends on whether or not they are given the appropriate opportunities and encouragement. Every child in the class is a possible gifted pupil.

Because intelligence is determined by the environment it is not possible to group or set pupils by ability successfully since setting and/or grouping can limit opportunities for some pupils. In addition setting, for these teachers, implies that schools can identify capacity within a pupil through school success. For teachers who believe that intelligence is changeable there are no genetic limits or capacities to an individual's intelligences therefore it is not possible to predict success or failure beyond school for any pupil. If circumstances change then much more may become possible for an individual. Conversely, a change of circumstance may limit an individual's progress. All pupils can be gifted and/or talented if they are provided with the right environment and opportunities.

Intelligence is not a singular concept indicating a general energy but much more about separate and distinct areas of ability. Limits cannot be assumed or predicted for individuals nor can intelligences be tested or examined. The role of education is to help all pupils develop and increase their intelligences. This theory is epitomised by the famous quote from Watson[v]:

> ...*give me a dozen healthy infants, well-formed, and my own specified world to bring them up and I'll guarantee to take any one at random and train him to become any type of specialist I might select – doctor, lawyer, artist, merchant-chief and, yes, even beggar-man thief, regardless of his talents, penchants, tendencies, abilities, vocations, and race of his ancestors...*

Teachers who believe in changeable intelligence are likely to prefer classroom assessment rather than examinations and standardised tests as a good indicator of pupils' progress and demonstration of abilities. These teachers will attempt to gather a wide range of assessment evidence that accounts for factors that lie in the environment. The information will be gathered from a wide range of sources and cover a wide range of behaviours.

Teachers who believe in changeable intelligence encourage mastery goals in the classroom. In other words working through a problem is more important than getting a correct answer: mistakes are positively encouraged and are seen as an indicator of the learning process in action. Pupils are encouraged to track their own progress over time and not to compare themselves with others.

Good work is recognised, valued and celebrated but not as an example for others to emulate since everyone has to find their own way of doing things. Feedback and description of pupils will focus on their behaviour or their work, for example, 'I particularly liked the style in which you wrote that piece'; 'did you think that was your best piece of work?'; 'this is a really hard problem to solve but you managed to complete three sections.' Collaborative work is encouraged as this is seen as a way in which pupils can learn from one another. Groups can achieve more than individuals working on their own and all individuals in the group benefit from the collaboration.

Table 1.2 *Comparison of teachers' implicit theories*

Questions teachers try to answer	Fixed theory answer	Changeable theory answer
Why are pupils different from one another?	Intelligence is genetic. Some children are born with more intelligence than others.	Different life chances mean that there are vast differences between pupils' attainment.
How do I sort out who is able to do what?	Intelligence can be identified through a fairly short list of key abilities. If pupils demonstrate these abilities then they can be identified as gifted and/or talented. School work and standardised tests are a good way of sorting out who is most intelligent. Tests of different kinds help to identify capacity in pupils. They can be used to predict who will do well and who will not.	I have to profile pupils across a whole range of intelligent behaviours. I have to provide opportunities for pupils to demonstrate all the behaviours that I would consider an indicator of developed intelligences. I cannot predict who will succeed and who will not on the basis of present performance. I can only offer next steps.
What does this tell me?	I cannot make pupils more intelligent, I can only help draw out what they already have. I can identify who has most and who has least intelligence in my class and then organise them on that basis. Competitions and comparisons are good methods for motivating pupils and giving feedback.	I can help make pupils more intelligent. It is not possible to identify a group who might be considered gifted and/or talented. The combination of strengths and development needs for each pupil will help to tell me what the next steps are. Schools alone cannot identify all the intelligent behaviours that pupils might demonstrate so I need to gather information from elsewhere.

How might this make me act?	I support streaming or setting as a way of organising pupils.	I support mixed ability groups as a way of organising pupils.
	I celebrate and display the best work of the class.	I value collaborative achievement very highly.
	I value individual achievement very highly.	I give feedback to pupils on their work and effort in class.
	I feed back on whether or not the pupil is performing to his or her potential.	I celebrate and display pupils' best efforts.
	I can predict who will succeed and who will not.	
	I will identify those pupils in my class who are gifted/talented.	
System of education created	Exclusive.	Inclusive.
	Based on sifting and sorting.	Based on individual needs.

Is it best to foster fixed or changeable beliefs?

Some of the literature suggests that the 'right' implicit theory for teachers to hold is a changeable theory[vi]. This is because teachers who believe that intelligence is changeable are more likely to encourage mastery orientated beliefs in the pupils they teach. It would appear that mastery orientated beliefs seem to encourage a more positive response to learning in pupils.

Mastery orientated beliefs, then, might be most crucial for those pupils who are turned off from school learning. For pupils to identify with the purposes of schooling they need to gain a sense of belonging. A sense of belonging requires the individual to believe that they are important and are, or at least can be, an active participant in the learning process. Mastery orientated goals, where the focus is not on the adequacy of one's ability but on factors within the control of the individual, are more likely to provide the conditions necessary for this self-perception to be attained[vii]. Unlike mastery orientated goals, performance goals are more likely to separate individuals from their peers on the basis of performance in class and decrease their sense of belonging.

However, even for those who might ascribe to the need to encourage mastery orientation there are some myths around about how this should be done.

1   It is often believed that the more pupils experience success in school the more mastery orientated qualities are fostered. However, from research it

would appear that success in itself does little to boost pupils' desire for challenge or their ability to cope with setbacks. In one piece of research[viii] children who believed in a fixed intelligence theory, even after a string of successes, assigned their one and only failure to a lack of intelligence. They lost faith in their intellect to the extent that they believed that they could not even repeat prior successes.

2   It is believed that praise encourages mastery orientated qualities but we have to be careful with praise. It can matter a great deal: who gives it; when it is given; why it is given and for what it is given. We can cause 'damage' with empty praise[ix].

3   Confidence is a key to mastery orientated qualities. Many so called 'confident' individuals have actually very fragile confidence in their abilities. Their confidence is quickly shaken and they do not wish their intelligence too stringently tested. Such pupils will avoid work that they find difficult and in which they may not perform well.

4   Gifted and talented pupils are mastery orientated: this is untrue. Some gifted and/or talented pupils hold strong fixed intelligence theories and are heavily orientated towards performance goals.

The thing to remember is that a bit of both (mastery and performance) might be the best thing. If we think of Olympic gold medallists like Ian Thorpe (swimmer) or Matthew Pinsent (rower) then it would be best for them to have mastery goals for their training sessions (where they try to improve on their own past performances and pay close attention to their own progress over time) and have performance goals for competitions (where the number one goal is to compare themselves to others with the goals of being first and the best). The questions for teachers are three-fold.

- To what extent do I subscribe to a fixed theory or a changeable theory of intelligence?

- Is this having any impact on pupils in my class?

- Do I think I have the balance right?

But what does this mean for mainstream schools in the meantime? How might schools review their beliefs and practice? Does practice in the school lean towards a particular view of intelligence? Is the range of provision currently available sufficient and suitable? The next section will try to address some of these issues.

A circular model to consider gifts and talents

This model[x] (Diagram 1.1) is based on the idea of identification through provision[xi] and the ways that teachers and pupils interact with one another in the classroom[xii]. It offers a holistic approach to the identification of gifted and talented pupils. The circular process ensures that the identification of abilities is ongoing rather than a one-off test or activity.

The model has four steps.

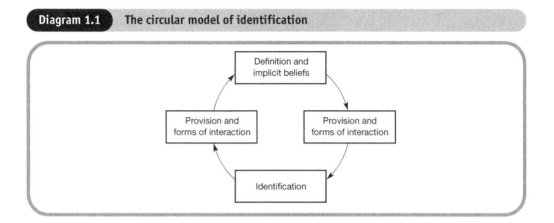

Diagram 1.1 | **The circular model of identification**

Step one: What do I believe about gifted and talented children?

You have begun step one by reading through and thinking about the questions posed in the first part of this chapter. What teachers believe can have a huge impact on whether pupils demonstrate abilities or not. These beliefs help to create particular cultures in schools and classrooms. Some cultures are more helpful in facilitating achievement and motivation than others. There are particular difficulties for gifted and talented pupils if the culture that determines provision rests on the idea that intelligence is fixed, biologically determined and is located wholly within the individual. Such beliefs generate a concentration on performance goals in the classroom that is evidenced by social comparisons and normative evaluations.

Rather than compare one pupil with another it may be more helpful to identify the sorts of behaviours that teachers believe a gifted and/or talented individual should be able demonstrate in the different curricular areas. General lists of intelligent behaviours to be encouraged in all pupils exist. One is provided below[xiii].

- Being open minded and flexible about ideas and solutions.

- Being aware of your own and others' thinking, behaviours and feelings.

- Being able to work with others collaboratively.

- Being accurate and seeking accuracy.

- Being able to monitor and control your behaviour, learning and work.

- Being able to plan appropriately.

- Being able to respond appropriately to feedback.

- Being able to identify and use necessary resources.

There may also be some specific intelligent behaviours that can only be identified when pupils are undertaking particular activities. Such lists, however, should not be seen as a checklist with pupils being identified as being gifted and talented on the basis of a set number of ticks. Rather, it provides a tool to examine the curriculum. This allows us to ensure that the opportunities exist for pupils to demonstrate, develop and learn how to behave in these ways.

There are some key questions that should be considered in step one.

- What definitions of intelligence exist?

- Do I agree with any of these? If not what would my definition be?

- Do I hold a particular implicit theory of intelligence? What does this mean for pupils in my class?

- Do pupils in my class hold a particular implicit theory of intelligence? Is this impacting on their learning in any way?

- Do I identify pupils or sets of behaviour and what criteria do I use?

- Are some criteria specific to particular curricular areas or are they all general?

Step two: What provision currently exists and how do I relate to pupils in my class?

Once some discussion has taken place about what intelligence is and what might be looked for the next step involves an audit of the curricular provision currently available and the pedagogy currently in place. If provision is dominated by a narrow range of opportunities and limited challenge then it will be impossible for pupils to demonstrate or develop anything other than a small range of intelligent behaviours. Opportunities must exist for intelligent behaviours, not only to be demonstrated but to be developed and taught. If gaps exist in the present provision then they require to be filled.

Once the curriculum has been audited for opportunities that match our definitions and understanding of what the full range of intelligent behaviours might be, the next step is to examine our own practices as teachers. The ways in which we interact with pupils (how we phrase feedback, how we support and encourage), the messages we give them (both implicit and explicit) and the media we choose to give deliver messages (written, verbal, and non verbal), in other words the culture we create in our classrooms, all have an impact on whether or not pupils will be able or feel able to demonstrate intelligent behaviours. It may be that a range of opportunities exist but if the culture in the class is dominated by performance goals then some children may feel unable to demonstrate intelligent behaviours that they have already mastered. In fact they may be more comfortable demonstrating these intelligent behaviours elsewhere, for example it takes the demonstration of many intelligent behaviours to plan a robbery and work collaboratively to carry it out successfully.

Some questions that might be posed during step two.

- Do I have high expectations of all pupils in my class?
- Do I provide a full range of opportunities for pupils to demonstrate intelligent behaviours?
- Do I teach the skills necessary for these behaviours to develop in those who are not yet demonstrating them?
- How do I feed back on success and failure?
- Is it safe to fail in my class?
- Is it safe to demonstate intelligent behaviours in my class?

Step three: Who is coping well with the most challenging activities and who might need extra challenge?

Once the opportunities for the demonstration of intelligent behaviours have been identified and put into place the assessment process begins. This process is about recording where and when it is that pupils demonstrate the behaviours that teachers would wish to encourage in all pupils. It is also about asking for help from others to identify where and when a pupil demonstrates them. The pupils themselves should be involved. In this way school starts to reach out into the community and into the pupils' lives for evidence that abilities are beginning to form or have already formed. There are three things to be on the lookout for.

1   The regular and sustained demonstration of intelligent behaviours by individuals.

2   The occasional and sporadic demonstration of these intelligent behaviours by individuals

3   The demonstration of these intelligent behaviours by individuals in contexts other than school.

Step four: What additional provision can I put in place?

From stage three there will be a range of opportunities identified as being possibilities for pupils to demonstrate and learn intelligent behaviours. Pupils will be demonstrating these to varying degrees of sophistication and regularity. There will also be a range of contexts identified where certain individuals can demonstrate intelligent behaviours outwith the confines of the school. It is about designing progress and coherence in challenge so that there are always further challenging opportunities available.

It is necessary to go back to provision and make sure that, for those who are demonstrating such behaviours in a regular and sustained way, there are activities and opportunities to extend their already developed abilities. For those demonstrating sporadically it is about searching for opportunities to help develop these so that they become more sustained and regular.

Stage three will also have provided essential information about pupils who might be demonstrating intelligent behaviours outside of school in other contexts. An analysis of where and when this is occurring might help to identify what it is that the school or teacher can do to help transfer these behaviours into learning based activities in the classroom.

Some questions that might be considered in step four

- Are these the pupils I would have expected to be identified?

- Might there be pupils not currently demonstrating abilities who could if the activities or culture changed in the class?

- For those who are already able to demonstate their abilities in particular areas to a high degree (either before or after tuition) are there sufficiently challenging activities and experiences which allow them to develop their abilities further?

Back to step one: What do I believe about gifted and talented children now?

It is time to revisit out original thoughts about what intelligence means and what it is that we are trying to do.

- Are there new theories or research to think about?
- Does the definition of intelligence require change or amendment?
- How is my theory of intelligence impacting on my class?
- Have I been able to identify pupils in my class with particular views of intelligence?
- Do I need to revisit the criteria I use when assessing intelligent behaviours?
- Does my list of intelligent behaviours require change or amendment?
- Am I collecting information from a wide enough range of contexts?

Conclusion

Points for reflection:

- How much do you think that the beliefs we hold about intelligence make a difference to pupils' achievements and performance?
- To what extent is the model of giftedness in operation in your school linear or cyclical?
- Does the system of identification in your school rest on the performance of individuals or on the provision made available?

The Education Dimension

Cameron, R. J. and Maginn, C.

I've come to the frightening conclusion that I am the decisive element in the classroom. It's my personal approach that creates the climate. It's my daily mood that makes the weather. As a teacher, I possess tremendous power to make a student's life miserable or joyous. I can be a tool of torture or an instrument of inspiration. I can humiliate or humor, hurt or heal. In all situations, it is my response that decides whether a crisis will be escalated or de-escalated and a student humanized or de-humanized.

(Haim G. Ginott, 1922–73, teacher, child psychologist and psychotherapist)

Having made a strong argument concerning central government's overemphasis on increasing the educational attainments of looked-after children in the first two chapters of this book and having followed this with an equally powerful plea for an overdue recognition of the importance of meeting the parenting needs of children and young people in public care and supporting their adaptive emotional development, it may seem paradoxical to be devoting an entire chapter to the 'education dimension' of childcare. However, it would be a major oversight to ignore the potential power of the educational process to enhance (or sometimes constrain) the personal, social, academic and economic outcomes of all children, but particularly those who are in public care. Conversely, we readily recognise that educational underachievement too often reduces life opportunities, can lead to social exclusion, limits their employment prospects and encourages a drift towards a parallel world of alcohol and substance abuse, sexual exploitation and crime.

Of course, the educational system not only provides opportunities for achieving academic outcomes, it is also a powerful force for fostering personal and social development. Hart et al. (1996) have noted some of the subtle dynamics of the educational process, when they claimed that school and college personnel were likely to be among the most reliable sources of compensatory relationships and role models for children who otherwise did not have good relationships or who did not have positive adults in their lives. Further, schools were 'therapeutic environments' in that they promoted achievement and the attainment of pro-social development in children, even when mental health problems and family pathology were present. In his review of education and residential care, Kendrick (1998) mentioned two important, but often overlooked, benefits of a positive educational experience: building up powerful resilience factors in the life of a child, and acting as a source of stability when everything else in the child's life was uncertain.

The power of education as a force for positive change in the lives of young people has also been highlighted by Jackson and McParlin (2006) who wrote that 'each step of the educational ladder is associated with improvements in health, employment, income, housing, family life, the absence of addiction problems and lower risk of involvement with the criminal justice system' (p. 90).

> A high quality education provides the foundation for transforming the lives of children in care. Those who do well in education are more likely to go on to employment, to lead healthier lives and to play a more active part in society. (DfES, 2007, p. 9)

The Attainments of Children and Young People in Care

By now, readers will be only too familiar with the year-after-year information, which reiterates the poor examination results obtained by children and young people in public care. Of the 6,000-plus teenagers who leave care each year, about 60 are likely to go on to university or further education (Sergeant, 2006), a dismally small figure which contrasts sharply with the 43 per cent of the population as a whole who are currently in the higher education sector.

The Department for Children, Schools and Families (DCSF, 2008a) report on attainment outcome indicators for looked-after children did not present evidence likely to lead to future optimism; in fact, their statistics indicated that the gap in examination results between children in public care and their peers had actually *increased* and the following disappointing outcomes were reported:

- Compared with 62 per cent of all children and young people, only 13 per cent of young people in public care obtained five good GCSEs (grades A–C).
- Twenty-eight per cent of the looked-after population had Statements of Special Educational Needs and this contrasted with just under 3 per cent of all children and young people in England.
- More than one in seven looked-after children had missed at least 25 days of schooling and one in a hundred had been permanently excluded from school (DCSF, (2008b) data estimate the number of permanent exclusions in England for all children to be 0.2 per cent).
- At age 16 almost a third of young people in state care had not sat a single GCSE or GNVQ examination (in contrast to approximately 1 per cent of the general population).

Table 6.1 Some of the tensions which exist in the education system today

- The desire to support vulnerable pupils versus the demands for higher attainment outcomes
- The needs of the individual pupil versus the needs of the school population as a whole
- Equal opportunities versus the quest for excellence
- Enhanced choice for pupils in general versus diverting school resources to support disadvantaged groups (including children and young people in public care)
- Inclusion versus special classes/curricula
- Entitlement versus resource management expectations

Important Central Government Initiatives

A complete chapter of the DfES (2006) publication *Care Matters: Transforming the Lives of Children and Young People in Care* is devoted to providing a 'first-class education' for this client group, where it is recognised that, because of the trauma and other difficulties they bring with them they 'approach education at a disadvantage'. To combat such negative antecedents, a number of important improvements for the children in care population are mooted, including: providing local authorities with the power to direct schools to admit those in care (even when the school is fully subscribed); creating a general assumption that children and young people in care should not move schools in Years 10 and 11 (unless it is clearly in their best interests); offering free entitlement to school transport to allow looked-after children to remain in the same school after a placement move; providing funding which should enable schools to offer an 'excellent personalised education' to children in the care of the local authority; creating 'virtual' head teachers to support schools in their work with children in care; providing mandatory training for new principals in further education colleges; and setting up pre-apprenticeship training to help young people gain the skills needed to succeed in an apprenticeship scheme.

Despite their obvious potential for support, all of the above tasks join a long list of requirements and priorities which schools are being asked to take on in today's society. Often it is possible to incorporate such improvements into existing school practices, but frequently many of these demands would appear to compete with one another and produce tensions within both the education and school systems. As a backcloth to this chapter on the education dimension some of these tensions are listed in Table 6.1.

So What Is Missing?

Raising the educational attainment outcomes of children in care which lag so far behind those of the general population clearly needs to begin with early intervention that can avert domestic violence, eliminate the effects of poverty on families, build up positive parenting skills and prevent young people from entering the care system in the first place.

What do young children require to promote positive cognitive development and good attitude towards learning? The Ramey Partnership at the University of Alabama at Birmingham, who are major proponents of early intervention, have carried out research over two decades which has enabled them to highlight the following key parental tasks: encouragement to explore, mentoring in early skills, celebration of achievement, rehearsal and extension of new skills, protection from inappropriate disapproval, and a rich and responsive learning environment (Ramey and Ramey, 1998).

Unfortunately, the majority of children and young people who enter the care system have had a history of rejection, abuse and neglect, so early intervention is not an option at this late stage. In addition, they are likely to be educationally well behind others of the same age and are going to require additional help and support in the classroom, both of which are often recognised as Harker et al. (2003) discovered when they ascertained the children's perceptions of useful and less useful support in school.

The reality for many young people in care is that education is the last thing on their minds: survival is their priority and for them the world is an unfriendly place. It is only when these children are helped through these emotional problems, begin to feel good about themselves, develop a sense of belonging and can have fun that the world becomes an interesting place, full of opportunities – a place to explore. In this new state of mind, children who have been rejected, neglected and abused become able and willing to take advantage of educational opportunities.

Within the context of the children in public care, it is worth reiterating the statement by Howe (2005):

> The more secure children feel, the more time, energy and inclination they have to seek understanding and make sense. Whereas fear constricts, safety expands the range of exploration. This is why the social, emotional and cognitive development of abused and neglected children is so heavily compromised. They don't feel safe; they rarely relax. Fear for these children can be so endemic that exploration is weak, anxious and sporadic. (p. 3)

Despite their disadvantages, however, there is survey evidence which indicates that the majority of children and young people in public care hope to do well at school.

> Children and young people in care tell us that they want to lead normal lives. They want to succeed in education, enjoy a wide range of positive activities

and make a successful transition to adult life. We must help them to reach their potential by providing excellent parenting, a high-quality education, an opportunity to develop their talents and skills and effect the support for their transition to adulthood. (DfES, 2007, p. 5)

What Supports Educational Success?

For the past decade or more, researchers have attempted to identify some of the features of the care and education system that appear to reduce the academic opportunities of children and young people who are looked after. Jackson and McParlin (2006) have singled out some of the more obvious constraints including: the low priority given by some social workers to educational matters; disrupted schooling due to frequent placement changes; the likely lowered expectations of teachers and social workers; the well-documented literacy problems of children in public care; poor access to educational books and conducive conditions for study (especially in residential care); and the often low educational levels of carers (p. 92).

The Jackson and Martin (1998) study focused on the minority of high-achieving young people in the care system and identified the following attainment-enhancing factors, all of which clearly need to go on to the support agendas of all local authorities: stability and continuity in education; learning to read early and fluently; having a parent or carer who valued education as a route to a better life; having friends who are doing well at school; developing out-of-school interests and hobbies; meeting a significant adult who acted as a consistent mentor or role model, and attending school regularly (p. 578).

Disruptive Behaviour in the Classroom

As already mentioned, children who have gone through major traumas and life-changing experiences are unlikely to be able to come into school, sit down, open their books and get on with their class work. Often the disruptive behaviour that they exhibit can be interpreted as a direct, and personal, challenge to a class or subject teacher's authority and can result in the development of a vicious circle where it becomes more difficult for a teacher to maintain a professional attitude to the behaviour and to display more flexibility and tolerance towards the child concerned. Paradoxically, the authoritarian management by the teacher may result in yet more disruptive behaviour from the child or young person who may interpret the teacher's tougher response as 'unfair' and 'personal'.

A helpful publication by Ofsted (2005) entitled *Managing Challenging Behaviour* offers some suggestions on how schools as organisations and local authorities can support improved teaching, an appropriate curriculum for engaging more difficult pupils and consistency among staff when meeting the special needs of children in care. However, the professional challenge of having a difficult to manage pupil in the classroom remains and is likely to require more than the indirect influences of organisational change; providing the teacher with the knowledge and skills to change pupil behaviour becomes a priority task for the applied psychologist.

Miller (2003) has argued that there is a strong tendency for people to make attributions about complex events, like difficult classroom behaviour. The most frequently employed causal attributions of teachers, parents and pupils to emerge from Miller's studies can be summarised as follows:

- Teachers attribute pupils' difficult behaviour mainly to the *children themselves* (for example, need for praise, non-acceptance of social norms, physical/medical problems, and so on) or to *adverse home factors* (for example, parental management of child, violence in the home, and so on).
- Parents attribute pupils' difficult behaviour to *unfairness of teachers' actions* (for example, picking on particular pupils, blaming unfairly and not listening) and *pupil vulnerability* (for example, peer influences and adverse home factors).
- Pupils attribute other pupils' difficult behaviour *to unfairness of teachers' actions and pupil vulnerability* (ibid., 143).

The important point that Miller went on to make about these different explanations offered for the behaviour of children and young people in school was that of their perceived controllability. If teachers view difficult and challenging behaviour as being within the child's control, then they are more likely to be sympathetic to the child's needs, more tolerant and more supportive to the child. So, helping teachers to see more clearly what underpins such behaviour by children in public care becomes a particularly important task for supporting professionals like psychologists.

Obviously, sharing the deeper knowledge of the negative effects of rejection, abuse and neglect (discussed in Chapter 2) will be a good starting point for increasing teacher awareness and with this end in mind, the National Children's Bureau has produced a helpful booklet for teachers to enable them to understand the process of attachment and how secure and insecure attachment can affect the education of all children, particularly those who are in public care (Ryan, 2006). Similarly, teachers need to know that dysfunctional early relationships are also of central importance in the neuronal growth of prefrontal executive functions, which include memory, narrative, emotion representation and states of mind, all of which, as Greig et al. (2008) have pointed out, are crucial for scholastic achievement and social adjustment.

Table 6.2   Pupil behaviours which might alert teachers to the existence of the more subtle emotional needs of the child or young person

- Incessant chattering
- Low-level but persistent and defiant behaviour
- A lack of respect for people in authority
- The use of 'rights' as a weapon for controlling adults' behaviour
- Low motivation to learn
- An expectation that learning should always be easy and effortless
- An inability to deal with failure

Therefore, children and young people in public care may not only be lagging behind in their education because they have missed days at school or have been too emotionally upset to concentrate on their class work, but they may also have an uneven profile of cognitive abilities which make learning more difficult for them.

More pragmatically, the model of behaviour management offered by Dreikurs et al. (1982) which has been discussed in Chapter 4 and in Cameron, (1998) can enable teachers to look underneath the overt behaviour, to consider the underlying message which the child or young person is conveying through such behaviour and to respond with a more empathetic management approach (see Table 6.2).

Ensuring that teachers have a deeper understanding of the relationship between negative early experiences, the resulting emotional pain and confusion, the challenge of the classroom context and their links with disruptive behaviour, does not absolve the pupil from his or her responsibilities. Carers also need to support the rights of teachers to teach, the rights of students to learn, everyone's right to physical and psychological safety, and everyone's right to be treated with dignity and respect (cf. Hook and Vass, 2004). An example of such support appears in the extract from a consultation session in Illustration 6.1.

As discussed earlier, the educational performance of young people in residential care is often poor and while a likely antecedent is the significant factor that relates to rejection, abuse, neglect and other negative pre-care experiences, other factors implicated are likely to be due to the low expectations of carers, a lack of educational continuity, and minimal home–school information sharing and joint planning. All of these often unintentional constraints have important implications for improving and filling existing gaps in the education and social care systems.

Residential and foster carers need to be alerted to the value of education in providing children and young people in public care with much needed opportunities to experience success, to build up self-worth and to increase their life choices and opportunities. (See Gallagher et al., 2004, for their outline of good practice in the education of children in residential care.)

Illustration 6.1 Notes on a staff consultation session on teaching arrangements for Jono

These notes do not refer to one specific young person but are a composite made up from notes on several children.

The problem: Care staff who accompany Jono to his one-hour home tuition sessions with Ms Smith each day reported his behaviour is particularly disruptive during this session and that he is unreasonably rude to Ms Smith.

Likely contributing factors: difficulties in sitting still, limited concentration, general learning difficulties, the effects of a role model of a violent older brother in his previous home environment and anger at being separated from his three brothers and Gnasher, his dog.

Agreed staff action for managing this problem

1. *Reviewing the Jono/Ms Smith relationship*
   Arthur, Jono's key worker, will have a discussion with Ms Smith which includes the following reflective questions:

   - How do you think the current teaching sessions with Jono are going?
   - What are some of the things that seem to be going well?
   - What are some of the things that are not going well?
   - What important elements are missing from these teaching sessions?
   - How can the carers be more supportive to you and Jono?

2. *Agreeing a new format for these one-hour sessions*
   In order to manage Jono's relatively short, on-task behaviour, the following pattern for a one-hour session in the classroom might be more appropriate:

   - A five minute settling-in period.
   - A 15 minute session of sustained and mentored school work.
   - A five minute session talking about the work Jono has completed and how easy or difficult he had found it.
   - A short break which could include an activity (e.g. a board game) in which the attending care staff member could join.
   - Another 15 minute mentored work period and review.
   - A short 'good ending' including a 'looking-forward-to-tomorrow's session'.

   Arthur (Jono's key worker) will draw up an incentive plan for Jono and try to involve Jono in the design/preparation of his plan.
   As far as possible, one or two members of staff should be consistently allocated to accompany Jono at his home tuition session.

3. *Sharing tuition sessions with another child*

   - Considering the possibility of arranging a short, shared period between Jono and Sally (who also receives home tuition in the next-door room).
   - Jono's key worker will try to align some of the work which is going on at the afternoon school session which Jono attends and the morning home tuition session.
   - Displaying some of Jono's best work in the dining room.

4. *Setting out expectations for behaviour in class*
   Arthur will choose an appropriate moment to talk to Jono about his behaviour in Ms Smith's class, her right to be treated politely and the fact that, although he may have difficulty in realising this, she was keen on helping him and was not going to give up teaching him because she considered helping him to learn was too important for Jono when he becomes an adult, to allow him to stop her from teaching.

Building up Resilience

So far the focus has been on improving the beliefs, attitudes and aspirations of teachers and carers to enable them to understand and manage the disruptive, anti-social, sometimes aggressive and occasionally violent behaviour of children and young people in public care. There is, however, an additional and underestimated component of the educational dimension, namely, its contribution to the development of self-worth, well-being and social competence.

In Chapter 4, we discussed the importance of resilience as a powerful influence in people's lives. High levels of resilience can enable people not just to tolerate life's adversities, but to cope with and to manage these: while vulnerability can be viewed as an individual's susceptibility to being emotionally floored by negative experiences, resilience is their ability to get back up, brush themselves down and start all over again! There is little doubt that what happens in the classroom and in the wider school environment can make a major contribution to the development of resilience in children and young people. Indeed, after the family environment, schools are probably the second most effective environments for building up independence skills, promoting self-efficacy and developing the problem-solving skills of children and young people, especially those who have experienced negative life events. (See Dent and Cameron, 2003, for a discussion of the contribution of educational psychology to the enhancement of resilience in looked-after children and Table 6.3 for some low-energy strategies that teachers have suggested could create a school environment, which is more pupil-friendly, valuing and resilience-enhancing.) In both these areas, there can be an important role for the learning support assistant, as Burton (2008) has described in his indirect but important all-round development activities.

For groups of vulnerable or at-risk children and young people, the *Bounce Back* programme (McGrath and Noble, 2003) is a good example of a curriculum-based

Table 6.3 Some examples of small, but important, resilience-enhancing changes which could be introduced into the school or classroom

- After-school homework clubs
- Encouraging friendships between vulnerable children and successful peers
- Noting and encouraging the development of talents and natural skills, e.g. sketching, singing, dancing, dramatic skills, games ability, hobbies, interests, etc.
- Enabling the child or young person to develop strategies for effectively managing potential flashpoints like bullying and name calling, attracting a teacher's attention, apologising, saying 'no' assertively, praising other pupils' work, avoiding being labelled 'a boff', etc.
- Giving feedback in the ratio of three positive comments to one improvement suggestion
- Asking children to reflect upon the skills and knowledge they employed when they have successfully completed a classroom or homework task
- Giving praise unobtrusively (especially in the case of secondary-aged pupils!)

approach to teaching resilience and well-being, which has psychological underpinnings and which concentrates on those personal skills and values of resilience that can be taught, namely:

- pro-social values such as co-operation, fairness, support and concern for others
- optimistic thinking, including the use of humour as a coping tool
- helpful thinking
- the skills that lead to goal achievement, including planning, organising, self-discipline, self-reflection and problem-solving
- skills for understanding and managing emotions
- social skills.

It is interesting to note that self-discipline appears to be a particularly important resilience factor and it as been argued that this factor may predict future academic success more effectively than cognitive ability (cf. Duckworth and Seligman, 2005). Such examples of self-discipline include children's ability to follow rules, avoid impulsive actions and the receipt of instant rewards for later gratification.

Some Subtle Possibilities for Support

In large organisations like schools, it is often difficult to create the *sense of belonging* needed to help pupils to identify with the school (Goodenow, 1993; McNeeley et al., 2002), yet this is an important dimension of school life for all pupils and particularly important for children and young people in public care who may never have felt a sense of belonging to any group or organisation. A sense of belonging is an essential human need, yet many children and young people today appear to have little sense of belonging either to place, community or the country in which they live and can often veer towards cliques or gangs which can meet these needs.

> Increasing evidence shows that when adolescents feel cared for by people at their school and feel like a part of their schools, they are less likely to use substances, engage in violence, or initiate sexual activity at an early age. (McNeely et al., 2002, p. 138)

McLaughlin (2007) has studied school-belonging from the students' perspective and come up with the following characteristics:

- feeling valued as individuals
- feeling accepted and included
- experiencing a sense of personal achievement
- feeling involved and listened to
- experiencing meaningful teaching and learning

- understanding and identifying with the school as an organisation (the congruence factor)
- having a sense of personal efficacy, that is, that things are developing for the better.

These factors, which are likely to make young people identify more closely with the school as an organisation and subscribe more readily to the intentions and aspirations of the school staff, could provide an agenda for the organisational change which could not only create an exciting and learner-friendly social environment for students, but also help to build the kind of student–teacher relationships which are fulfilling for both groups.

While negative teacher attitudes to some looked-after children and young people may be understandable, they not only lower the teacher's expectations of good behaviour, but are also likely to obscure the child's talents and assets. Seligman (2002) believes that each person possesses several *signature strengths*, which are strength of character that a person self-consciously owns, celebrates and (if he or she can) incorporates into such daily activities as 'work, love, play, relationships and parenting'. Although originally designed with adults in mind, a 'Children's Strengths Survey' has been produced by Katherine Dahlsgaard, one of Seligman's research colleagues (see Seligman, 2002, pp. 231–44).

The full list of signature strengths (which includes obvious contenders like a love of learning, fairness, humour and enthusiasm) can be found in Seligman's book, but some of the less obvious ones, which may apply particularly to children in public care include the following:

- *Curiosity and interest in the world*. Curiosity about the world entails openness to experience and flexibility about matters, which do not always fit one's pre-conceptions. Curious people do not simply tolerate ambiguity; they like it and are intrigued by it.
- *Practical thinking*. Thinking things through *and examining them from all sides*.
- *Courage* (this includes both moral courage and psychological courage).
- Integrity and honesty, kindness and generosity, loyalty and teamwork.
- *Discretion* (not saying things impetuously that might be regretted later).
- *Gratitude* (being aware of the good things that happen and never taking them for granted.
- *Spirituality* and a *sense of purpose*.

After an individual has identified and personalised their signature strengths, Seligman's advice on their use is to consider how and in what contexts these can be employed in everyday life. Given young people's ease with information technology it is likely that completing their signature strength questionnaire on-line would be an attraction (at www.authentichappiness.sas.upenn.edu). However, the follow-up discussion is likely to be most effective if it takes place in a discussion between a teacher, a carer and the child or young person him or herself.

While Banks and Woolfson (2008) have reminded us of the importance of teacher expectations, they have also pointed out the powerful influence *of a child's own attributions of success and failure* in school on their academic success and schools: those with fixed, internal and unchangeable attributions (like 'I'll just never be any good at maths') tending to perform more poorly than those with positive attributions. One of the subtle abilities of highly successful teachers is the way in which they can encourage the development of positive, but realistic, attributions for success and their gentle challenging of negative attributions.

Concluding Comments

The Health Education Authority (HEA, 1997) has defined mental health as 'the emotional and spiritual resilience, which allows us to enjoy life and to survive pain, disappointment and sadness. It is a positive sense of well-being and an underlying belief in our own, and others' dignity and worth' (p. 7). In more observable terms, a 'mentally healthy individual' has been described by the Mental Health Foundation (1999) as one who can achieve the following complex life tasks:

- develop emotionally, creatively, intellectually and spirituality; initiate, develop and sustain mutually satisfying personal relationships; face problems, resolve them and learn from them; be confident and assertive; be aware of others and empathise with them
- use and enjoy solitude
- play and have fun
- laugh, both at themselves and at the world.

Our mental health influences how we think, feel, value ourselves, value other people and interrupt what is going on both outside and inside our homes. After the home environment, education is likely to be the second most important influence in supporting the positive development of all children, and for some of the more vulnerable, school can also become a powerful factor in enabling them to achieve these criteria of healthy emotional development.

Time for Reflection

As well as supporting the academic attainments of children and young people, how realistic is it to expect teachers to create a sense of belonging, help children to identify and utilise their signature strengths and challenge their self-limiting attributions for success and failure in school?

Summary

In this part you have had a brief overview of the differing needs of pupils you may encounter on your journey as a teacher. Our society in Britain is widely diverse and evolving and your classrooms will reflect this. Generalizations and assumptions cannot be made and can, in fact be detrimental to your role as a professional. While you cannot be expected to be an expert on all special educational needs or issues for inclusion it is imperative that you know how and where to seek advice and assistance in order to ensure that every child in your class achieves to the best of their ability. This part should have heightened your awareness of the diverse needs of the primary pupil and given you an insight in to how to identify possible barriers to learning. Thinking of our overarching theme of participation the role of other professionals and parents is paramount within this area. You are not working alone and are in fact part of a multi-agency team or work together to provide the best for a pupil with needs.

Student activities

- Find the SENCo in your school and ask if you can speak to them about their role. How does policy link to practice? How do they identify children's needs? What are the procedures? Who supports them and how do they support staff?
- Observe a child with special needs. How do their needs create a barrier for their learning in the classroom? Compare them to another child with differing needs. Are the same issues addressed? Could they be tackled in the same way?
- Look at an individual education plan (IEP) – how do you think this will support the staff who work with a child to ensure their differing needs are addressed?
- Look at what goes on in your school to support children with diverse needs. Who organizes these interventions? Where and when do they occur? Do they have an impact on achievement?

Top tips

- Raise all concerns that you may have about a pupil with another member of staff. They might appear trivial but every comment and observation helps to build up a picture of the child.
- The key word here is diverse! What works for one child will not necessarily work for another even though their needs may appear similar. Every child is unique and will respond to different strategies uniquely too – your job is to find out what works best.
- You are not alone – you are not expected to be an expert. Use all available support and help and speak to the appropriate person to share your thoughts.

Additional readings

Parents

Siraj-Blatchford, I. and Clarke, P. (2000) 'Parents as partners', Chapter 5 in *Supporting Identity, Diversity and Language in the Early Years*. OUP (e-book).

Harris, A. and Goodall, J. (2008) 'Do parents know they matter? Engaging all parents in learning', in *Educational Research*, 50 (3) [available online].

Close, R. (2001) *Parental Involvement and Literacy achievement:The research evidence and the way forward*. National Literacy Trust [available online].

Including all children

Cameron, R. J. and Maginn, C. (2009) *Achieving Positive Outcomes for Children in Care* London: Lucky Duck /Sage.

Dann, R. (2011) 'Look out! Looked after! Look here!: Supporting 'looked after children' and adopted children', *International Journal of Primary, Elementary and Early Years Education*, 39 (5): 455-65.

DCSF (2009) *Improving the Attainment of Looked After Children in Primary Schools: Guidance for Schools* [online]. https://www.education.gov.uk/publications/standard/publicationDetail/Page1/DCSF-01047-2009

Wilkin, A., Derrington, C. and Foster, B. (2009) *Improving the Outcomes for Gypsy, Roma and Traveller Pupils* [online]. https://www.education.gov.uk/publications/RSG/AllRsgPublications/Page11/DFE-RR043

Inclusive environments

Cox, S. (2011) Communities for Learning, Chapter 6 in *New Perspectives in Primary Education*. Maidenhead: Open University Press.

PART 8   WORKING IN PARTNERSHIP

Overview

The first chapter by Gasper is especially useful in setting the idea of partnership into context for you. The idea of multi-agency working is now prevalent in health, education and social services and came about through the death of Victoria Climbie, the subsequent Laming Report into her death and the associated 2004 Children's Act that built largely on his findings particularly in terms of child protection, followed by the accompanying *Every Child Matters* legislation. Therefore, as practitioners we all work in multi-agency teams and often within one classroom at a given time you will find a teacher, teaching assistant, speech and language therapist, educational psychologist, parent helpers, etc.

As well as this type of partnership, as teachers, part of our role is to establish links with parents and carers so that they can feel a part of their child's life in school. There is a well-known phrase that 'parents are their child's first educators' and an understanding of the parents' perspective is always valuable in understanding aspects of a child's learning or behaviour. This perspective is outlined effective in the Grant and Ray chapter.

As teachers, our relationships with the support staff in our classrooms are crucial and this relationship and ideas for successful practice are explored in the Campbell and Fairbairn chapter.

Gasper, M. (2010) 'What Is Partnership Working, Where Did It Come From and Why Is It Important?', Chapter 1 in *Multi-agency Working in the Early Years: Challenges and Opportunities*. London: Sage

Working in partnership with parents and families
Grant, K. B. and Ray, J. A. (2013) 'Engaging Families in Their Children's Learning at School and Home,' Chapter 9 in *Home, School, and Community Collaboration Culturally Responsive Family Engagement*, 2nd ed. London: Sage.

Working with other adults in the classroom
Campbell, A. and Fairbairn, G. (2005) Chapter 11 in *Working with Support in the Classroom* Developing successful Practice with Support Staff. London: Sage

53   What Is Partnership Working, Where Did It Come From and Why Is It Important?

Gasper, M.

This chapter introduces the term 'partnership working', where it has come from, why it holds an important place within government agendas for change and what it means within the context of Early Childhood Education and Care (ECEC) organisation and practice. The chapter explores definitions of associated terms to clarify different ways in which partnerships can be conceived and constructed and what these mean in practical terms to practitioners, families, children and communities.

Chapter themes are:

- What is partnership working?
- Where did partnership working come from?
- What are the associated terms, their definitions, similarities and differences?
- Why is partnership working important?
- How has the move towards greater partnership working developed?
- What is partnership working in practice: benefits, challenges and leadership?

So what do we mean by partnership working (multi-agency working) and what is it all about? Why is it important? Where did it come from and how did it develop into a national policy?

What is partnership working in this context?

Partnership working is a key concept at the core of social and educational policy since the start of the millennium. It is evidence of a shift in emphasis at government, local and setting levels away from a 'top-down' approach towards a 'bottom-up' approach. This shift came from a fundamental change in philosophy which included recognition of the importance of working with service users more closely to help identify needs and how they could be met. This was very different from the previous approach which tended to dictate what would be provided for service users and was based on a view of service organisation and delivery that was separated into and focused on specialism. The previous philosophy took more account of what those in specialist services such as Education, Health and Social Services believed was right for people, rather than listening to what people themselves might say they needed. The more recent definition, organisation and provision of services for children, parents, families and communities by government and local authorities still recognises the need for specialism within service providers but also places a new emphasis on 'joined-up thinking' and working. This change grounded in social theories recognises the value of the principle of including all perspectives, including those who need and use the services, so that what is provided is more relevant and appropriate in matching needs, more efficient in delivery and achieves more effective outcomes. An example of joined-up working in practice is Camden in London and the way they have built their multi-agency team supporting Early Years. The team developed from their original Sure Start Local Programmes (see Useful websites at the end of the chapter). Specialists from a wide range of services including speech and language, midwives, specialist support for the Somali community, librarians and child protection were paid for by the local authority to work as multi-agency support for four days each week and to return to specialist work for the remaining day. The arrangements have been developed to reach and serve a wider community than the original Sure Start areas and professionals have been nurtured who are skilled in planned multi-agency approaches to service provision. The reduction in funding has led to a review to assess how best to continue developing the teams to meet future needs.

Partnership working provides opportunities for needs to be met collectively as well as individually so that the needs of whole families can be addressed in a unified way. Partnership working is embodied in the notion of children, parents, families and communities having access to a wide range of support and developmental services to enable them to:

- identify what their needs are;

- access the most appropriate help from all relevant agencies;

- begin to take greater control of their own lives;

- increase their confidence and self-worth;

- develop their skills and extend their education;

- enable them to live more fulfilled lives and contribute more fully to wider society.

Partnership working is also about professional agencies aiming to improve the way they organise, plan, undertake and reflect on their work jointly as elements of a team, each with their own perspectives and skills but combining effectively as a unified whole. Whereas previously individuals had to attend a range of locations often at some distance, a key principle of partnership working is to reduce this to local sites, initially targeted at areas of high deprivation and then extended, so that children, parents and families can receive the support they need wherever they live. Clearly specialist centres remain – there will always need to be surgeries, hospitals, schools and care centres – but the emphasis is for services to be brought to neighbourhood locations wherever possible. Phrases such as 'joined-up thinking' and 'one-stop shop' capture the emphasis of partnership working.

 Case study

Partnerships developing over time – combining Health, Social Care and Early Years

Ganney's Meadow is a children's centre in an area of high deprivation in the Wirral, housed in part of a refurbished junior school building. In the early 1990s, due to falling rolls, all the primary aged children were accommodated in the adjoining infant building; the local nursery school was relocated into one wing of the empty junior building in line with the local authority's aim of developing their first integrated centre. At this time social care staff rented a couple of rooms and ran a family support group – drop-ins and adult courses which were very low key – in the vacant wing of the building with a locked door between them and the nursery school. These were the first staff that actually integrated with the 'nursery school staff'.

The specialist practitioner nurse role was part of this development of integrated services. One of the governors (a health visitor herself) helped the setting to develop this idea and which led to liaison with the Primary Care Trust (PCT) who agreed to fund the post if the centre allocated a room. The health practitioner on site was and still is funded through the PCT. The salary has never come out of centre budgets.

The refurbishment of the additional space/wing was funded through Early Excellence Centre (EEC) (see Glossary) finance in the late 1990s in order to provide a crèche, training rooms, a family room and a multi-purpose room for a range of groups for 0–3s with their parents. The funding to relocate the local branch library came from the local authority's chief executive and the 0–3s day care came later, funded through the Neighbourhood Nursery initiative.

This example shows how partnership working has developed over time and how different initiatives have been used to develop and extend the organisation, staffing and range of services.

Where did partnership working come from?

To some extent there has always been recognition of the value and importance of joint working and shared information, particularly within organisations. Within Health, Social Services and Education different specialist branches have used joint meetings to evaluate needs and plan actions. Cooperation between pairs of agencies, such as Education and Health or Health and Social Services, have also been well established. For example, hospitals included a welfare department to assist patients and to liaise with Social Services and other agencies. Social Services have been responsible for calling and chairing joint meetings to address child protection issues. Child protection case conferences are focused on the needs of the child. They have brought together representatives from Education, Health, the police, drug and alcohol counsellors and other agencies relevant to specific cases. Within Education the school doctor and school nurse focused on the needs of children with medical needs, alerting the school to specific needs of individuals and linking with Social Services where issues beyond medical needs were involved. Key features of these kinds of cooperation are that they were controlled by the professional agencies, they tended to be in response to a crisis and while they were intended to be supportive and did attempt to allow a voice to the individuals 'at risk', in practice it was often very difficult for the individual or family to make an effective contribution. The increasing emphasis on inter-agency cooperation is illustrated in two successive papers: *Working Together: A Guide to Arrangements for Inter-agency Co-operation for the Protection of Children from Abuse* (DHSS, 1986) and *Working Together to Safeguard and Promote the Welfare of Children: A Guide to Inter-agency Working to Safeguard and Promote the Welfare of Children* (DoH, Home Office and DfEE, 1999). The gradual combining of Health and Social Services and the creation of new government units, such as the Children's and Young People's Unit in 2000, was supported by a series of government papers following the turn of the century. The emphasis changed from departments which dictated to departments and units that encouraged professionals to facilitate and empower families to take responsibility for themselves (Pascall, 1986: 38). The shift in emphasis was also influenced by the growth in understanding nationally and internationally of the interdependence of Health, Social Welfare and Education, supported by research such as the OECD reports *Starting Strong I* and *II* (2001 and 2006).

While this kind of cooperation has continued, what has changed is the 'top-down' emphasis. There has been a growing emphasis on equality and real partnership to allow the true 'voice' of individuals and families to be heard, combined with a clear aim of identifying and addressing need, preferably before reaching crisis dimensions. During the 1990s Social Services established family centres in areas identified as having high social deprivation. These centres were run by a leader from Social Services but aimed to include parents and families in the planning and running of services. This model was later developed and extended in both Sure Start and Early Excellence Centres but is mentioned here to illustrate the shift in thinking and emphasis.

Defining terms

Defining terms in a way that will be clearly understood by all is a challenging task. Each of the key agencies involved in early years care and education partnerships – Community Work, Education, Social Services, Health, Housing, Family Support, counselling services for drug and alcohol abuse – has their own professional language and code, including acronyms, and often employ the same words with completely different meanings. For example, the term for agencies working together is presented in different ways:

- inter-agency

- multi-agency

- inter-disciplinary

- inter-professional

- multi-professional

- multi-disciplinary.

These describe different kinds of combinations, the first two organisationally based practice and the latter three types of organisation (Weinstein et al., 2003). These can be intentional or accidental, formal or informal, structured or loose. The current preferred term is partnership working but even this may not capture appropriately the subtle ethos or underlying desire for new ways of developing and refining the complex warp and weft of professional relationships focused on improvement for families and children. Nevertheless this is the term that will be used throughout the book.

Whittington (in Weinstein et al., 2003) provides the following definitions of partnership and collaboration:

> Partnership is a state of relationship, at organizational, group, professional or inter-professional level, to be achieved, maintained and reviewed.
>
> Collaboration is an active process of partnership in action.

Two other definitions are given by the UK Centre for the Advancement of Interprofessional Education (CAIPE) and quoted by Barr et al. (2005), the first of which emphasises the combination of adult learning principles with collaborative learning and practice, but within the context of a rationale which takes account of all possible combinations including inter-personal, inter-group, organisational and inter-organisational relationships and processes. The second simplifies this to a situation where any two or more professionals share learning 'with, from and about each other' to develop and improve collaborative practice. In other words, the definitions stress the active sharing of professional practice at individual, group and organisational levels in order to improve understanding and collaboration, which Barr et al. refer to as 'interprofessional education', as opposed to 'multiprofessional education' which involves any occasion when people from two or more professions learn side by side but not necessarily with the intention of improving collaboration and the quality of their work.

There does need to be a distinction between the different levels of collaboration and interaction: professionals may be housed together or co-located, which may or may not involve sharing information; they may be working jointly where there is a degree of information sharing; they may be more unified in their approach and working systematically with higher degrees of information sharing, planning and review; or there may be a merging into a single organised unit to achieve agreed common aims. Within a specifically Early Years context this view is supported by Anning et al. (2006) who suggest a hierarchy of terms to describe different levels of partnership which echo this progression (Anning et al., 2006: 6).

Weinstein et al. define the need for successful *inter-professional* collaboration as:

> ... practitioners learning:
> - what is common to the professional involved
> - the *distinctive contribution* of each profession

- what may be *complementary* between them
- what may be in tension or conflict between them

and

- how to work together ...

(2003: 49)

The distinction between learning side by side and learning *about each other* is critical to the underlying theme of this book, which is to improve shared understanding and assist practitioners and researchers alike in raising their awareness of the complexities involved in partnership working.

 Points for reflection

Does this match your experience?

How would you define agencies working together?

What other definitions can you find or suggest?

If defining terms is complex, identifying and finding a common pathway through definitions of practice values, codes of practice and ethics is even more so. Each profession has their own outlook and values and their own priorities. Within a profession different skill areas have their own points of view and stress different aspects, and each has their own way of looking at situations, interpreting them and identifying critical aspects to address. It remains important for each profession and agency to have clear aims and to retain their identity and the ability to make decisions and take actions independently. In addition, however, they must also develop a greater understanding of other professional points of view and cultures and actively improve cooperation and coordination and work towards greater integration. Within complex organisations such as Health, there is a growing understanding of the value and practice of more coordinated and combined approaches (Barr et al., 2005) and greater understanding of how this can be achieved (Freeth et al., 2005).

Why is it important?

During the 1990s a series of research reports pointed to the effects of poverty:

> Children from poorer homes have a lower life expectancy, are more likely to die in infancy or childhood, have a greater likelihood of infections and poor health, a lower chance of educational attainment, a higher probability of involvement in crime and homelessness, and a higher risk of teenage pregnancy.
>
> (Holterman, 1994)

Kelly (2008) also shows the critical importance of housing to child health. This seems to suggest that families in poverty are likely to be involved with a wide range of agencies, for largely negative reasons. It seems entirely logical and necessary, therefore, for agencies to work together to address the effects of poverty in the first instance if they are to break the spiral of deprivation which repeats through generations and as a first step towards reducing poverty itself. Since the late 1990s there has been an increasing emphasis from the government for greater sharing of information and cooperation within and between agencies. The Utting Report *People Like Us – the Report of the Review of Safeguards for Children Living Away from Home* (DoH/WO, 1997) drew attention to the inadequacies of provision for children taken into care. In her summary to the House of Lords Baroness Jay referred to:

> The report presents a woeful tale of failure at all levels to provide a secure and decent childhood for some of the most vulnerable children ... The report reveals that in far too many cases not enough care was taken. Elementary safeguards were not in place or not enforced. Many children were harmed rather than helped. The review reveals that these failings were not just the fault of individuals – though individuals were at fault. It reveals the failures of a whole system. (Baroness Jay of Paddington, statement to the House of Lords, 19 November 1997, Hansard)

This report reinforced the findings emerging throughout the 1990s regarding the consequences of child poverty and served to bring new policies into place to raise standards of health, social care and education for children including those cared for by local authorities, and successive initiatives such as Early Excellence Centre (EEC) Evaluation (2002), the Effective Provision of Pre-School Education (EPPE – DfES, 2004) and the National Evaluation of Sure Start (NESS – 2005 and 2007) have provided evidence of real benefits to children, families and communities where more joined-up working takes place.

In recent times the consequences of agencies not working together have been starkly bleak. There has been powerful evidence from specific cases that we cannot afford to see Early Childhood Education and Care (ECEC) in isolation and need to move towards greater cooperation and coordination of services, especially for vulnerable children and families. The failure of agencies to communicate internally and with each other has contributed directly to dire consequences, illustrated by the tragic case of Victoria Climbié which led to fundamental changes in approach and lent a new urgency to the need for effective inter-agency working. The consequent report (Laming Report, 2003), led to more formal procedures and a government White Paper, *Every Child Matters: Change for Children* (DfES, 2004). The recommendations of this report are still in the process of being implemented and underpin revisions of childcare policy and practice, for example through the Common Assessment Framework (CAF) which has been set in place in an attempt to improve partnership working where children and families 'at risk' are identified. However, the case of 'Baby P' and events in Haringey which came to light in 2008 and Darlington in 2009 serve as a reminder that there is still a long way to go before there can be greater confidence in the systems in place. Perhaps the real need is for constant vigilance.

> The Common Assessment Framework (CAF) is a key part of delivering frontline services that are integrated and focused around the needs of children and young people. The CAF is a standardized approach to conducting an assessment of a child's additional needs and deciding how those needs should be met.
>
> (www.everychildmatters. gov.uk/deliveringservices/caf/)

More recently, in a joint statement in 2007, the professional bodies representing Social Care, Nursing and Education (the General Social Care Council (GSCC), the

Nursing and Midwifery Council (NMC) and the General Teaching Council (GTC)) acknowledged shared values and included recognition of the need to work together:

> Children's practitioners value the contribution that a range of colleagues make to children and young people's lives, and they form effective relationships across the children's workforce. Their integrated practice is based on a willingness to bring their own expertise to bear on the pursuit of shared goals, and a respect for the expertise of others.
>
> (www.nmc-uk.org.uk/aArticle.aspx?ArticleID=2344)

The main benefits from partnership working for children, families and communities can be summarised as follows:

- It is more efficient:

  - There is a better chance for individuals to be heard.
  - Needs are more likely to be identified.
  - Needs can be dealt with holisitically and with regard to the whole family where necessary.
  - Resources are more focused and there is less risk of duplication.
  - Agencies' actions complement each other.

- It is more effective:

  - Individuals are valued and listened to and their confidence and self-esteem is enhanced.
  - The support is focused on empowerment not dependency.
  - Networking between agencies about individuals can reduce bureaucracy and save time.
  - Actions are part of a more coherent shared strategy.

The National Evaluation of Sure Start Summary Report of 2007 noted the following key strategic points:

> What worked at strategic level was:
>
> - systemic, sustainable structures in governance and management/leadership;
> - a welcoming, informal but professional ethos;
> - empowering parents, children and practitioners.
>
> What worked at operational level was:
>
> - auditing and responding to community priorities in universal services;
> - early identification and targeting of children and parents to benefit from specialist services;
> - recruiting, training and deploying providers with appropriate qualifications and personal attributes; and
> - managing the complexities of multi-agency teamwork.
>
> (Anning et al., 2007)

This report did raise additional issues which need to be addressed, particularly in terms of ensuring services reach those in most need and drawing attention to the need for flexibility in organisation, times and availability of services and specific agencies. What it affirms are the underlying advantages and gains from partnership working in identifying and addressing the needs of children, families and communities ...

 Activity

What were the key findings of the Laming Report?

Can you find evidence that the findings and recommendations are being acted upon?

How has the move towards greater partnership working developed?

The short answer is that there was a growing understanding that the service structures and relationships were no longer adequate to meet changing needs, and that this combined with a growing understanding of the consequences of poverty in terms of health, social and educational deprivation. This realisation prompted consultation by government on a much wider basis than previously which helped uncover evidence from examples provided by families themselves and grassroots practitioners of all professional heritages as well as from research findings. Effective lobbying from early years, health and social care professionals and academics reinforced political emphasis on holistic approaches to break cycles of deprivation by developing shared understanding and a more coherent and joined-up practice. Changing theory into practice proved to be complex but has been undertaken in a considered and structured process which has drawn on views from all stakeholders. Baldock et al. (2005: 15–34) and Clark and Waller (2007: 28–33) provide comprehensive histories charting political changes. Figure 1.1 shows some of the more significant changes since 1980.

Many of the new initiatives acknowledged the need for and encouraged the closer cooperation and direct involvement of parents. An example of this is provided by the Early Years Development and Child Care Partnerships (see Figure 1.2).

In 1997 the new government insisted that local authorities establish Early Years Development and Childcare Partnerships (EYDCPs). These groups brought together all those involved in pre-school and early years care and education from the private, voluntary and state sectors (see Figure 1.3 for an example). All had to be represented and their initial aim was to share information, audit what was already in place and identify needs. This then extended to shared organisation, planning and delivery of services to children, including sharing training and development to improve the overall quality of service. The local authority role was meant to facilitate and not to lead within the partnership. Funding for initiatives such as training was made available from government, subject to the acceptance of a successful bid based on a specific plan.

The EYDCPs kick-started a form of partnership working which benefitted the private and independent sector in particular and meant that when stricter registration and inspection was introduced, standards had already been enhanced and there was a supportive body already in place to offer help if needed.

1980	Enabling legislation
As a new head teacher partnership is with school governors and Education, Health and Social Service separately.	
Schools are separated from local authorities.	1989 *Managing Service More Effectively – Performance Review* (Audit Commission)
Increased government emphasis on freedom of choice means parents are encouraged to choose and to take an active part in partnership with schools.	
The profile and voice of Early Years gradually increases. Vouchers are introduced to enable greater access to pre-school education.	1989 The Children Act National Standards for under 8s day care and childminders
1990	
Greater cooperaton developed between Health and Education particularly for children with additional needs.	
Closer cooperative working between agencies exists but depends on informal structures.	
1997	
New Labour – impetus to include all partners in Early Years Development and Childcare Partnerships (EYDCPs).	1998 *Supporting Families: A Consultation Document* (DoH)
Single Regeneration Budget.	2001 *Working Together Under the Children Act* (DoH)
Working family tax credit changes encourage pre-school childcare.	2002 *Integrated Services for Older People: Building a Whole System Approach in England* (Audit Commission) – 'whole systems' approach
Education Action Zones, Health Action Zones.	
2004	
Early Excellence Centres, Sure Start, Neighbourhood Nurseries — make pre-school more widely available, increase quality and encourage agencies to work more closely together.	2004 *Every Child Matters: Change for Children*
Children's Centres.	2004 The Children Act
Parents are seen as equal partners.	2006 The Childcare Act
Multi-agency working in practice.	Pre-school education and care no longer separate EYPS introduced
2008	2007 *The Children's Plan* – EYFS
A Children's Centre available to all by 2010.	

Figure 1.1   The changing face of partnership working

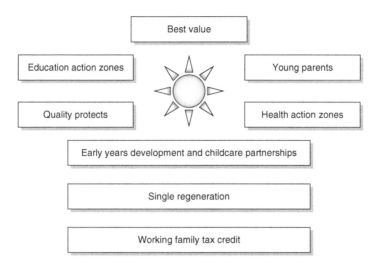

Figure 1.2   Initiatives increasing the emphasis on parental involvement

Nottinghamshire Early Years Development and Childcare Partnership (EYDCP)

We are the Nottinghamshire Early Years Development and Childcare Partnership (EYDCP). We were set up in 1998. We bring together local partners to:

- develop and deliver free early years education for three- and four-year-olds
- develop childcare services for children under 16
- help to deliver Sure Start services.

Our members include childcare providers, maintained and independent schools, local employers, health services, voluntary organisations, Ofsted, Nottinghamshire County Council, Learning and Skills Council and Jobcentre Plus.
Nottinghamshire County Council is responsible for providing leadership, planning services, co-ordinating the way services are delivered and consulting children, parents and carers. It is also responsible for managing our finances and must monitor our performance.

www.nottinghamshire.gov.uk/home/learningandwork/preschool/earlyyearseducation/eydcp.htm

Figure 1.3   An EYDCP example from Nottinghamshire
Reproduced with permission from Nottinghamshire Children's and Young People's Service

In addition three key programmes came into being: Early Excellence Centres (EECs), Sure Start and Neighbourhood Nurseries (see Figure 1.4). Many current children's centres retain their original parent title in their name.

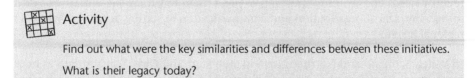

Activity

Find out what were the key similarities and differences between these initiatives.

What is their legacy today?

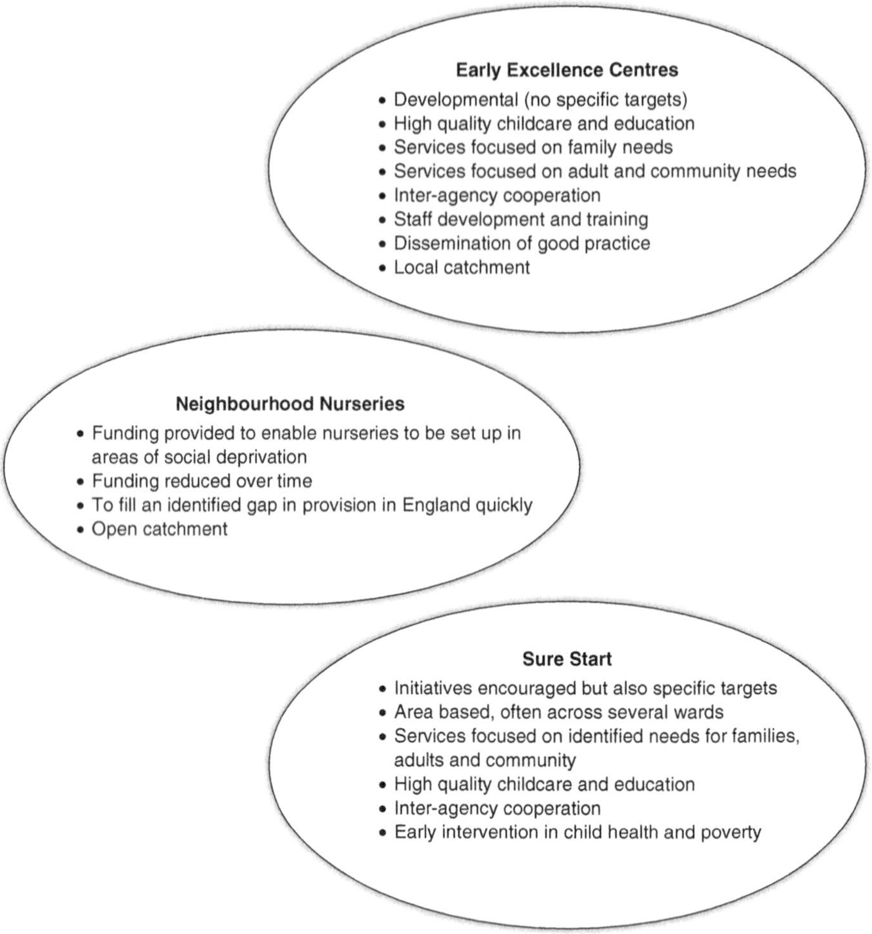

Early Excellence Centres
- Developmental (no specific targets)
- High quality childcare and education
- Services focused on family needs
- Services focused on adult and community needs
- Inter-agency cooperation
- Staff development and training
- Dissemination of good practice
- Local catchment

Neighbourhood Nurseries
- Funding provided to enable nurseries to be set up in areas of social deprivation
- Funding reduced over time
- To fill an identified gap in provision in England quickly
- Open catchment

Sure Start
- Initiatives encouraged but also specific targets
- Area based, often across several wards
- Services focused on identified needs for families, adults and community
- High quality childcare and education
- Inter-agency cooperation
- Early intervention in child health and poverty

Figure 1.4 Key features of Early Excellence Centres, Neighbourhood Nurseries and Sure Start

During the first five years of the New Labour administration, research into these initiatives grew and increased overall awareness and understanding of the need to see professional support more holistically, with Social Services, Health and Education addressing the needs of families collectively. Local authorities in many areas combined Education and Social Services departments under titles more focused on family needs and Community Development grew in importance. Partnerships with private and voluntary sector organisations became increasingly common. There was an expectation that professionals would improve joined-up thinking by consulting more fully, sharing information, working in harmony to identify needs and defining strategies to meet them together. The initiatives called for new models of organisation and communication at setting, local authority and regional levels.

In Wales, Scotland and Northern Ireland Sure Start and Early Years initiatives have been organised differently. The new edition of Baldock et al. (2009) provides a good overview.

There was a clear expectation that service users and the wider local community would be included more equally in identifying their needs and appropriate services to meet them. Critically, funding for these initiatives was available for local authorities through a bidding process.

Change was enabled by the Children Act 2004 which focused on five areas:

- Be healthy

- Stay safe

- Enjoy and achieve

- Make a positive contribution

- Achieve economic well-being.

It emphasised:

- greater public recognition of children's rights;

- greater consultation;

- agencies working more closely together.

It was complemented by the Childcare Act 2006 which placed the lead responsibility for creating and maintaining local care networks on local authorities. There was a new emphasis on ascertaining local needs and of working with and for the community, families, carers and children. In an interview for the BBC in 2006, Gordon Brown referred to the role of government being that of 'servant to the community', encapsulating the shift in relationships.

Research has shown that these experiments in partnership working have had considerable success for children, families and local communities (DfES, 1997–2004; Bertram and Pascal, 2000; Bertram et al., 2002; NESS, 2008; Quinton, 2004). As time has gone on the emphasis has changed. The three initiatives highlighted have been drawn together to form children's centres and there has been a new expectation that services should become 'sustainable' as funding has been reduced. The emergence of Every Child Matters has added a new emphasis and imperative with clear timescales for implementation. Initiatives such as Extended Schools have gained impetus. This is not to suggest a smooth pathway with all loose ends joined up. Not all is plain sailing and not all is for the best. Some of the issues will be explored in the following chapters.

Alongside the national changes, European and worldwide understanding has also shifted and led to statements of principle such as the UN Convention on the Rights of the Child, ratified by the UK in 1991. There was already a European convention dating from 1950, the European Convention on Human Rights, which was a reaction to the Nazi era. In addition, technological advances have accelerated the ability of researchers to communicate and share research findings. This in turn has contributed to the increase in knowledge and understanding of ECEC and the influence of successful approaches such as those developed in Italy in Reggio Emilia and in New Zealand with *Te Whaariki*, which are explored in Chapter 3. The move towards more inclusive and holistic approaches and partnership working is not restricted to the UK.

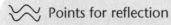 Points for reflection

What are the key benefits of agencies working together?

What challenges face those involved?

What needs to be done to help service users to take an active and equal part?

Partnership working in practice

While Chapters 3 and 4 deal with this in more depth, some indication of practical aspects may be helpful. Partnership working is a way of making the expertise and experience of a wide range of people each with different skills and perspectives available to each other as they come together and find new ways to address needs. The process of sharing involves open dialogue which is a dynamic and creative force: through listening, talking and exchanging ideas, new understanding develops. Dahlberg et al. (1999: 139) describe the difficulty of establishing a culture of critical dialogue and the danger that criticism will be taken personally, stressing the need to treat critical dialogue as 'a way to reconstruct our work'. This is particularly difficult with dialogue between agencies with different professional heritages and languages, especially when the same word can carry a very different meaning.

In addition there are clear gains in terms of more effective use of time and resources if issues are approached jointly rather than separately. The scenario in the case study below is entirely fictional but serves to illustrate some of the potential value of partnership working.

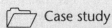 Case study

A family of five

Zac 3 months, Della 2 years 3 months, Wayne 5; mother, Jess 20, suffers with anxiety and depression; partner, Sasha 25, unemployed, is dependent on alcohol. Zac is the only child from the current relationship. Agencies involved currently with members of the family are: School, GP, Health Visitor, Social Services, Drug and Alcohol Counselling Service, Housing.

The family have recently moved into the area and there are no previous records available. They have been housed temporarily in a two-bedroom flat on the third floor of a three-storey block on a large estate with few amenities. Wayne has started school but the reception teacher has observed that he is solitary, listless and never appears to smile. There have been several occasions when Wayne has been late at the start of the day and no one has collected him until well after the end. The health visitor is concerned that Zac is not gaining weight.

If these agencies operate entirely separately or even in small cooperative groups, there is a strong possibility that advice and treatment will only address the immediate issues, not the underlying causes. Advice and help may even be contra-dictory: for example, the school may insist on better time-keeping, unaware that this will add pressure; the GP may prescribe anti-depressants and recommend rest, which may well have side effects including tiredness. All would be offered in good faith and meet the specific aims of each organisation but may not really identify or address the deeper needs of the family. Time constraints and poorly framed target setting tend to lead to short-term approaches. Short-termism tends to be focused on the middle: those at either end of the spectrum of needs tend miss out: they do not 'fit' the system. Partnership working offers a different approach starting from a different set of values. It is based on an approach that is holistic, child and family centred, with the professionals serving needs that children and families themselves have helped define and with solutions that match the children and families rather than the reverse.

If services operate in a more cohesive way and one agency can act as coordinator between them and work directly with the family, all the issues can be aired and the needs of each member of the family assessed and prioritised. In many cases it is children's centres that provide the link and professionals from Health and Social Services are usually part of the core staff team or operate from the same site.

The advantages of partnership working have been known for some time and have been confirmed by research and evaluation. In 2007 Bruce and Meggitt noted that partnership working provided flexibility in the type and timing of services, allowing a balanced mix of families by providing care and education for all, not just those in severe need. Allowing for flexibility has been a key aspect of partnership work-ing, particularly where this is focused on needs identified by families and commu-nities themselves. Where possible, timings are arranged to match need rather than being limited to 'traditional' timings, and this is echoed by the move towards extended school provision. This has the additional advantage of allowing parents to work where this is what they wish. Bruce and Meggitt also comment on the ben-efits in terms of increased quality of both care and education which are echoed by NESS, and which encourage holistic approaches to child development.

By 2002 the evaluation of government initiatives then in process confirmed the positive benefits. In their annual evaluation of the Early Excellence Centre initia-tive Bertram et al. (2002) referred to the benefits of partnership working as enabling individuals 'to have a voice that is heard by all agencies involved' as well as providing easy access to a wide range of agencies and services. In particular Bertram et al. (2002) point to the increased ability of partner agencies to identify needs and jointly plan action to help families move towards greater independence rather than the reverse, thus avoiding duplication and allowing more efficient targeting of resources and greater cost-effectiveness.

Further reinforcement of the benefits were confirmed by NESS (2005) and by 2007 these benefits had become embedded in government thinking and planning, underpinning the anticipated effects clearly stated in *The Children's Plan* (DCSF), 2007). There is a strong emphasis on placing the needs of children and families first and on consultation to ensure that services match the requirements identified by them, rather than by agencies or the state. This change represents a major shift in policy and provides clear expectations of all involved. There is a stated aim to locate services 'under one roof in the places people visit frequently' in order to make them truly accessible. There is an explicit recognition of the need to 'invest in all those who work with children'. The report makes provision for increasing capacity for working across professional boundaries.

The benefits of partnership working are enhanced where integrated centres are established by developing trust through regular contact with parents from an early stage, thus providing opportunities for issues to be raised and discussed sooner. Instead of parents feeling isolated they have access to a key worker who will try to encourage them to recognise their needs and seek help. The professionals are accessible, not distant, approachable, not hidden behind a wall of red tape, and motivated to answer the child's and parents' needs. Chapter 3 sets out case studies which show more detail of the benefits of partnership working.

The context in which partnership working takes place is important and this book explores the way children's centres provide an ethos, organisational structure and physical location for partnership working. In many cases they also provide the leadership essential to successful partnership working.

Leaders of children's centres are currently recruited from a very wide range of professional backgrounds and experience. *The Children's Workforce Strategy* was a consultation paper (DfES, 2003a) which recognised the need to remodel and led to new qualifications becoming available through university programmes. A clearer picture of the skills required has now emerged and is embodied in the National Standards for Leaders of Sure Start Children's Centres. There is now a clear intention for Early Years leaders and others to achieve parity of professional pay and conditions with those in Education and this has been enhanced by the National Professional Qualification for Integrated Centre Leadership (NPQICL), which emerged in 2005 and has equal status with the headteacher's qualification, the National Professional Qualification for Headteachers (NPQH). The leadership is mainly female and there is a wide range of qualifications among those in post, including those whose experience provides sufficient qualification in its own right. However, all children's centre leaders now have to hold the NPQICL. An unpublished study involving 21 children's centre leaders carried out in the summer of 2008 matched some of the findings of Aubrey (2007: 69), revealing that the majority came from a background in education, including pre-school, statutory school, and higher and further education, followed by social work, with significantly fewer from health, including nursing, midwifery and health visiting, or from other management background experience. What this does suggest is that the range of leaders' previous experience is wide, which is also reflected in the evaluations for NPQICL conducted by Whalley et al. (2008). Given the way that children's centres have emerged from Sure Start and the short timescale, it will take some time for training and qualification to catch up. The training provides grounding and opportunities to explore theory linked directly to practice, and also linked with critical reflection and critical dialogue. The groups taking part in training are enhanced by the range of experience as are the settings, and this needs be guarded as a diverse and rich source of potential for innovation and change. There is the potential for children's centre leadership to be free from the constraints of 'established' systems and better able to meet the demands for flexible approaches to identifying and meeting the needs of children, families and communities (NESS, 2007). Many of the leaders have been attracted to their posts because of the challenge and the opportunity to be agents for change.

Partnership working is not easy. Two children's centre leaders made the following comments when interviewed for the research on which this book as based.

> There are huge differences outside of Sure Start and children's centres as to the meaning and way to develop inter-agency/partnership working and it isn't all positive. It cannot be developed from a top-down bureaucratic structure and needs real commitment from all engaged in the process and it constantly changes. Not everyone is suited to this way of working.

> I have found that it takes time, patience and mutual respect to begin to develop partnership working. I found that by making links with other service managers in the area – through 1–1 meetings to talk ideas through – often brings dividends. It is easier to talk through possible issues outside of a general meeting. Managers (including myself) prefer to know in advance what is being suggested. Good coffee always helps!!

This begins to show some of the features of partnership working which will be explored in later chapters.

Since the late 1990s the movement towards more joined-up working, encouraged by government-funded initiatives, has enabled practitioners and families to work creatively together to develop social, health, care, support and educational services which are more closely matched to need, more accessible and more cost-effective. There has been greater opportunity for research and theory funded by government for example the evalutions for the Early Excellence Center programme (Bertram and Pascal EEC Evaluation Reports 2000, 2001, 2002) and the longitudinal studies for Effective Provision of Pre-School Education (EPPE Sylva et al., 2004) and National Evaluation of Sure Start (NESS Sylva et al., 2000 to date) to provide new ways of combining professional support and care and greater attention has been paid to recommendations. Theory has become practice including:

- ECEC which respects and values the child and stimulates natural curiosity, excitement and desire to learn by doing;

- knowledge of the value of emotional well-being which is influencing practice with children, parents, communities and the ECEC workforce and their trainers;

- practice that is truly inclusive and values children and parents as equal partners;

- a growing understanding of 'non-judgemental' approaches and a philosophy which recognises that we learn by making mistakes and by building on the knowledge of experience;

- an improving understanding of the need for flexibility rather than rigidity in ECEC planning and practice;

- a growing understanding and use of reflection, dialogue and research as tools to explore challenges;

- a growing body of skilful practitioners who understand the complexity and demands of partnership working and who are helping to develop and refine new approaches;

- appropriately trained leadership drawn from a wide range of professions and with diverse perspectives, commited to empower others for the needs of children, families and communities to be served.

These are exciting times and partnership working has a great deal to offer. For it to be successful requires understanding of nature of the demands and processes as the following chapters will show.

☐ Summary

The key points to remember from this chapter are:

- Partnership working is beneficial in addressing the needs of children, families and communities more effectively and efficiently.

- When agencies fail to work together there have been dire consequences.

- Partnership working may mean different things to different agencies.

- The same terms may be used to describe different things causing misunderstanding and frustration.

- The increased interest in the Early Years Education and Childcare agendas has grown with the increased understanding of the importance of ECEC in addressing the long-term consequences of poverty.

- Government priorities for addressing the effects of poverty in the new millennium have created an agenda for more joined-up approaches and moved this forward by funding initiatives and research and facilitating dialogue involving all stakeholders.

- Research has shown the value of partnership working in providing more cohesion between agencies and greater involvement of service users in identifying needs and deciding priorities for services.

- The need for a more skilled and qualified ECEC workforce has led to new qualifications at all levels and a national qualification for integrated centre leadership.

- Leadership is important if partnership working is to be effective and currently draws on a wide range of experience.

Further reading 📖

For a more detailed historical overview the following are very useful:

- Bruce, T. and Meggitt, C. (2002) *Childcare and Education*, 3rd edn. London: Hodder and Stoughton.

- Bruce, T. and Meggitt, C. (2006) *An Introduction to Child Care and Education*, 3rd edn. London: Hodder Arnold. This text provides accessible theory and practical advice.

- Clark, M.M. and Waller, T. (eds) (2007) *Early Childhood Education and Care: Policy and Practice.* London: SAGE.

- Quinton D. (2004) *Supporting Parents: Messages from Research.* London: Jessica Kingsley.

Useful websites

For more detail on the aims, background and organisation of service delivery:

- www.victoria-climbie-inquiry.org.uk

- www.everychildmatters.gov.uk/aims/background/

- www.everychildmatters.gov.uk/deliveringservices/caf/

- www.dcsf.gov.uk/everychildmatters/research/evaluations/nationalevalution/NESS/ness publications/

- www.teachernet.gov.uk/_doc/11184/6937_DFES_Every_Parent_MattersFINAL_PDF_as_ published_130307.pdf

For details of children's centres and Together for Children:

- www.childrens-centres.org/default.aspx

- www.togetherforchildren.co.uk/

For other professional perspectives:

Interprofessional education 1: Definition and drivers –

- www.swap.ac.uk/learning/IPE4.asp

Camden Early Years Intervention Team – www.camden.gov.uk then follow the links to: Education followed by Childcare and Contact the Early Years Team.

Engaging Families in Their Children's Learning at School and Home

Grant, K. B. and Ray, J. A.

As the preceding chapters have noted, a sound understanding and appreciation of families is vital for effective family engagement practices. Now, it is time to examine how you can apply your knowledge about families to your classroom practices. In this chapter, you will learn how to engage your students' families in their children's learning and development. Some questions to consider as you learn about this task include the following:

- What should you consider when collaborating with families on academic learning and development? What are barriers to having a full partnership with families?
- How can you help families understand highly technical educational terminology in this standards-based era?
- How can you effectively collaborate with all families on classroom behavioral concerns?
- How can classroom volunteers support students' learning and development?
- What are appropriate homework or interactive home learning activities for children of different ages?

IN THE CLASSROOM: HOMEWORK AND MORE HOMEWORK

Reggie Turner was one of the few male teachers at Kennedy Elementary in Poplar Grove. He was known both for having firm control over his fourth-grade students and for making learning fun. His class regularly conducted scientific experiments, such as testing the properties of the local river water or experimenting with different types of soil for growing plants in the garden behind the school. The class took field trips to the local courthouse, where on one occasion they participated in a mock trial; and recently, they went to the bowling alley, where they not only learned how to bowl but also sharpened their math skills while keeping their score. Mr. Turner had been an athlete in college, and his students clamored for him to play basketball with them at recess, which he only consented to do if they all made A's on a test. He was one of the most popular teachers at Kennedy Elementary, and families often requested that he be their child's teacher.

Mr. Turner was also known for giving homework—lots of homework. His homework assignments were designed to give his students more practice in the skills and concepts they were learning, such as the math worksheet on long division he had given the previous day. He also assigned projects for students to complete over time because he believed that it helped them develop critical-thinking skills as well as a sense of responsibility, which they would need when they went to middle school next year. He knew that the projects were a lot of work, and at his back-to-school meeting with families, he had stressed the importance of their helping their children with homework. He remembered his mom sitting at the table with him, making sure his homework and projects got done, and he knew he owed much of his academic success to her. He didn't have much patience with families who didn't take time to make sure their child's homework got done.

Currently, his class was working on a social studies project relating to their community's history and heritage. His students were researching their family history and relating it to what they had learned about Poplar Grove's history. It was one of his favorite projects because it required his students to interview family and community members, and it helped him learn more about his students and their families. The students had three weeks to complete the project, and he was looking forward to their presentations on Friday.

Shaina stared at the pile of books and the blank poster board in frustration. She had math problems to do, review questions from her science chapter to answer, and her family history poster to make. She didn't know how she was going to get it all done. Her mom's rule about "no TV until homework is done" meant that she rarely watched TV on weeknights. "It just isn't fair," she thought. She considered asking her mom to help, but knew she was busy helping Tyler. Ever since that meeting with Tyler's teacher, her mom spent all her time at night helping him, leaving Shaina to clean up the dishes and try to get Ella to bed. Sometimes she wished that she could live with her dad and Janet. It was a lot more fun at their house, and they let her talk on the phone with her friends as much as she wanted. She wondered if she should put Janet on her family poster, but she knew it would probably make her mom mad if she did. Mr. Turner had told them to put the important people in their family on it and to tell about the history of their family. They were supposed to interview their grandparents, but her mom's parents were both dead, and her dad's mom and dad were divorced and lived out of state. She hadn't seen them since she was six. "Maybe I'll just make something up," she thought, as she got out her math worksheet and started on the problems.

COLLABORATING WITH FAMILIES ON
ACADEMIC LEARNING AND DEVELOPMENT

Parent involvement appears to account for between 10 and 20% of the variance in a student's achievement, and parent expectations of their child's success in school consistently have the strongest relationship with achievement.

—Thorkildsen and Scott Stein (1998)

The recognition that families and communities shape students' learning and development is the cornerstone of family engagement practices. In establishing productive relationships with parents or caregivers, successful teachers first consider the needs and beliefs of the family when planning family engagement activities. That is, they take a family-centered approach, as opposed to a school-centered approach (one based on the school or teachers' needs), in their planning (Foster & Loven, 1992). Think about which approach the teacher took in the following case:

> Second grader Cicely Reid was excited to start school again in the fall. Although she had struggled with reading comprehension during first grade and was placed in the remedial one-on-one Reading Recovery program for 30 minutes, three times a week, she did not receive these intensive services until after Christmas. When her first-grade teacher called her parents to set up a meeting to discuss placing Cicely in Reading Recovery, they were surprised and dismayed to hear this. During the meeting, they said they didn't understand Cicely's reading problems, as they had bought books for her to have at home. They stated they wanted her to do well in school and someday to go to college because that was something they had not had the opportunity to do. The teacher complimented them on realizing the importance of having books in the home, and asked more about their reading habits, such as whether they read and re-read the books with her. The parents described, somewhat defensively, how Cicely often looked at books at night while they watched television after dinner. The teacher went on to explain the importance of actually reading the books with Cicely, identifying the reading skills she needed help with, and gave the parents a sheet of home activities to increase reading interest and motivation. Cicely's parents admitted they didn't realize that reading and re-reading books aloud was that important. They described their busy work schedules and hectic nights with taking care of Cicely and her younger siblings and how their television viewing was a chance for them to relax together for a few minutes. The teacher listened attentively and empathized with them about the difficulties of two working parents with small children. Together, the teacher and parents came up with a plan for one of them to try to listen to Cicely read books sent home by her reading teacher for 20 minutes a night after her younger siblings were put to bed. The teacher promised to send regular updates on Cicely's reading progress and offer further suggestions or guidance. They also agreed to meet again at the end of the school year to share their observations about her reading abilities and discuss some fun summer reading activities. By the end of summer, Cicely's reading skills had greatly improved, and more important, her bonds with her parents were strengthened by the special times she spent reading with one of them each night.

At first, the teacher may have been quick to judge these parents as uninvolved and uncaring, but further dialogue helped her better understand the parents and Cicely's home life. Think about these questions:

- What family strengths did Cicely's parents demonstrate? Did the teacher exhibit respect for the parents' ideas and roles as Cicely's first and most influential teachers?
- What incongruities appeared to exist between the teacher's idea of reading and book usage and the parents' idea of the act of reading? What did the teacher do to help overcome these differences?

- Is there anything that this teacher or Cicely's kindergarten teacher could have done differently to help prevent her reading difficulties before this meeting with her parents?
- How was the teacher able to support the parents in their willingness to work with their child at home? Was the home-school connection enhanced or hurt by this meeting?

Although not all interactions with families will have a positive result, as in this situation, there are lessons to be learned from it. First, it is important not to assume that all parents understand what occurs at each grade level or the academic requirements of a particular classroom. Second, it is also important to suspend judgment while you learn more about families. Third, although you should be prepared with suggestions for help, it is also important to listen to families' ideas and work together with them on a plan for their child's learning. Finally, you should also take notes, or annotate with purpose (the act of taking notes during parental meetings and using those notes to reflect on enhanced student learning), during conversations with parents to later reflect on ways to enhance your student's learning. These notes will provide you with a window through which the student's home learning can be viewed.

Some of the problems with Cicely's reading might have been avoided if her kindergarten and first-grade teachers had made more efforts to share information with her parents about family literacy practices, or the practical things families can do at home that embed reading, writing, and viewing (as well as other domains) into daily life as critical components in the quest for higher literacy. Part of collaborating with families is to share information with them about topics such as these:

- The school's educational mission and philosophy
- Your personal teaching philosophy
- Classroom expectations for academic success
- The everyday academic schedule of the classroom and the supplies students will need to have
- In-school resources that can help students who struggle academically
- Developmental stages common to children at the specific grade level
- Academic concepts, skills, and subjects children will be learning at the specific grade level
- How family members can help their children at home—for example, doing interactive home learning activities together
- How to assess children's progress in both strengths and challenges (Gregg, 1996)

Cicely's teachers also failed to focus with her family on transfer of learning activities, or the application of the reading skills she learned at school to at-home learning activities. For example, her teachers could have made suggestions for home reading activities beyond sharing books, such as reading recipes together while preparing dinner. Woolfolk (2001) suggests inviting parents for an evening of "strategy learning" in which students teach family members a reading strategy they have learned in class. She also suggests that teachers ask family members to include children in at-home projects that require math skills, such as estimation, measurement, and reading word problems. When you create small, family-friendly settings during class meetings, potluck dinners, parent-teacher conferences, or family breakfasts, families may feel more open to discuss the ways in which they interact with their children at home. They may listen more willingly to suggestions about ways in which they can support their child's learning and development (Henderson & Mapp, 2002).

Barriers to Collaboration

Although it is unclear from the short scenario why Cicely's parents had not spent time reading with her, one reason some families may not help their children is a lack of confidence in their ability to make a positive difference in their child's education. A sense of efficacy, or feeling of competence in helping one's child succeed in school, is an important factor in successful home-school collaborations (Hoover-Dempsey & Sandler, 1997). This sense of efficacy is also important for teachers; teachers may be hesitant to encourage family engagement in the classroom for fear of being judged or criticized. Family members' lack of engagement may also be influenced by their experiences as children and by whether their families were extensively involved in school and in home-based learning activities (Mapp, 2003).

As noted in Chapter 1, there are many other barriers to family partnerships from the perspective of teachers and families. Figure 9.1 summarizes some of these common barriers.

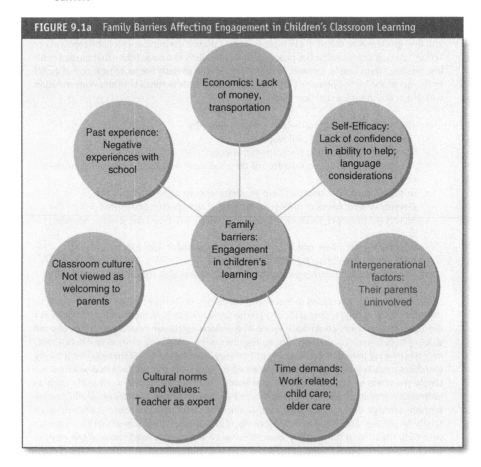

FIGURE 9.1a Family Barriers Affecting Engagement in Children's Classroom Learning

FIGURE 9.1b   Teacher Perceived Barriers Affecting Family Engagement in Children's Classroom Learning

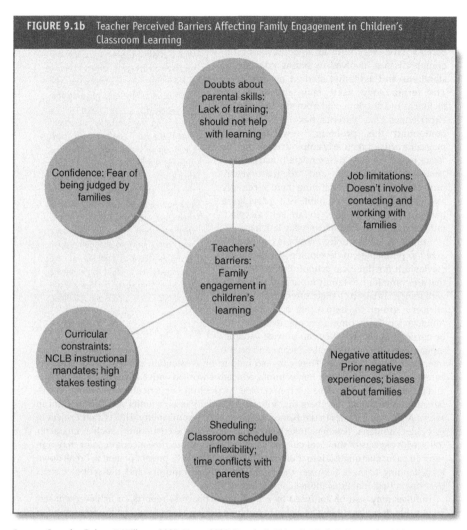

Sources: Gonzalez-Dehass & Willems, 2003; Mapp, 2003; Trumbull, Rithstein-Fisch, & Hernandez, 2003.

COMMUNICATING WITH FAMILIES ON STANDARDS-BASED CURRICULUM

Many times parents do not know the questions to ask or, if they know the questions, may not understand the answers that are provided. Education has its own language, just as medicine and law do.

—Tileston (2006)

In the current atmosphere of high-stakes testing and standards-based curriculum, anxious parents have every right to be confused by the complex issues involved in setting educational standards and assessing student performance. The terminology itself may appear highly technical and disconnected from any educational experiences that parents have ever had. To compound this problem, newspaper and magazine articles regularly employ terms such as "state report cards," "differentiated instruction," "mastery," "subgroups," and "adequate yearly progress" (AYP) without defining them succinctly and clearly for readers. Table 9.1 provides a handout that may be given to families to explain unfamiliar terminology in everyday language.

Family and community members can also be asked to participate in developing standards and curriculum for the local school district. Schools that are committed to family input as they wrestle with standards-based changes often form a parent advisory group to help craft a curriculum. Although family or community members may not be curriculum experts, they can provide valuable input on how their children best learn and on the interests of their children. They can also help to tie curriculum content to community-based resources and culture. For example, educators worked with Native American parents and tribal elders to develop a native-focused curriculum (a curriculum developed in collaboration with tribal members that infuses in its daily lessons/units values important in Native American culture) in the Honor, Respect, and Responsibility (HR2) Grant Project in Box Elder, Montana. Teachers linked particular topics in the curriculum, such as character traits, with aspects of the local culture, such as beliefs about how a certain color may represent a particular quality, into their daily teaching. The HR2 project helped to break down long-standing barriers between the families in the community and the school district (Northwest Regional Educational Laboratory, 2007).

Families may also be confused by report cards, progress reports, or achievement test results that describe student's levels of academic performance based on the attainment of standards with terms such as "proficient," "meets standard," "moderately effective," or "partial evidence." For example, one parent complained in a local newspaper about a school's new report card:

> I am not interested in how my child compares to district or state standards. How does that relate to how my child is doing? . . . I am not interested in comparisons or vague terms like beginning to demonstrate, approaching, meeting, or exceeding district and state levels. Are we afraid to give an F if that's what the student has earned? (Southeast Missourian, 2010).

Guskey (2004) offers valuable advice for teachers working with parents to explain different levels of student performance based on learning goals or standards.

ACTIVITY 9.1

With a classmate, brainstorm how you might eliminate some barriers to family partnerships. For example, on the families' side, how could you overcome the barrier of your low-income families not having transportation to attend parent-teacher conferences? How could you work effectively with families who believe that their role is to raise their child and your role is to educate the child, and that you are not doing your job when you ask them to help their child with school work at home? On the teachers' side, how could you or your school strive to change negative attitudes toward families in the community? How could you eliminate the belief that some families are not capable or do not care about helping their child be successful in school?

TABLE 9.1 Key Terms in Standards-Based Curriculum and No Child Left Behind (NCLB) Legislation

Accountability: As a teacher, I am accountable for your child's learning and academic growth. Furthermore, this state sets academic standards for what your child should know and learn. Your child's academic achievement is measured in different ways throughout the year.

Achievement: This refers to the level of success on an academic task or assessment. As your child's teacher, I look for your child to show academic achievement in many ways during the school year.

Adequate yearly progress (AYP): Adequate yearly progress is the minimum level of academic improvement that our school strives to achieve each year. As a part of that effort, I have goals for each student's academic progress. In a larger way, school districts and states measure and determine AYP and work with schools based on those results.

Alignment: When I prepare to instruct students on new information, my lessons must cover specific concepts I plan to assess students on. I cannot test students on information I have not presented. What teachers teach is in accord with, or aligned with, what the curriculum says will be taught and what is assessed on official tests.

Assessment: As a teacher, I am responsible for measuring what students know based on specific learning goals by assessing how they are able to demonstrate new knowledge. As a parent, you are probably used to tests as the main type of assessment, but there are other types, including observing or watching children, using a checklist, or having them give a demonstration.

Benchmark: This is a standard for judging your child's performance. Some schools name benchmarks to tell what students should know by a particular stage of their schooling. For example, "By the end of sixth grade, students should be able to locate major cities and other important geographical features on each of the continents."

Criterion-referenced tests: In this type of test, children are tested against themselves to show the level at which they know what has been taught.

Differentiating instruction: As a teacher, I strive to provide for the range of student differences in the same classroom by using different learning materials, assigning different tasks, and using other activities, such as children learning in pairs or small groups.

Disaggregated data: In the school, test scores or other data are divided into various categories so that they can be compared. For example, schools may break down the information for the entire student population to determine how different groups of students compare with others.

High-stakes testing: This term refers to state and national testing that occurs in schools and that can determine school standing, according to whether schools have met yearly progress goals.

Highly effective teachers: The goal is for every classroom to have a highly effective teacher as demonstrated through teacher licensing, involvement in district professional development, and other methods.

Mastery: Our school strives to have all students master, or acquire a deep knowledge of each area of a subject before moving to the next level.

Public school choice: A provision of NCLB may allow parents to transfer their children to another public school if their state deems their school needs improvement.

Response to intervention: Our school is using this three-tiered approach to give immediate help to students who are struggling, rather than waiting and letting them fail. All children are in Tier 1, and some children may need small group or one-on-one help with a teacher for specific skills in Tiers 2 or 3.

School district report cards: Each school within a district receives a report card that provides families with specific information concerning the educational success of students in the school.

Standard: These are specific criteria (knowledge or skills) that our students are expected to learn and be able to do.

Standardized tests: These are tests developed by a commercial company to measure how well children perform as compared with others at the same age or grade level or relating to specific criteria.

Supplemental services: Outside tutoring or academic assistance for students that is provided if a school falls within a certain category of need. You can choose the appropriate services for your child from a list of approved providers.

Sources: Tileston, 2006; Association for Supervision and Curriculum Development, 2007; U.S. Department of Education; 2007.

1. *Be consistent in your grading practices and knowledgeable about the grading system:* Parents are used to letter grades as a basis for interpreting their child's progress. They may query you about the grade equivalent and ask questions such as "Does receiving a *proficient* translate to an A or a B, grade-wise?"

2. *Avoid language that compares students:* Parents should revise their perspective from "How is my child doing compared with others in the class?" to "How is my child performing in relation to the learning expectations at this level?" Help them understand how these expectations relate to grades.

3. *Be prepared to present student work samples at various performance levels:* Examples of student work at various levels, illustrating terms such as *beginning, novice, proficient, apprentice, distinguished, or exemplary,* should be displayed and explained to parents.

4. *Be prepared to illustrate other assessment concepts:* Indicators of what students are able to do (quality of work) can be confused with how often they do it (frequency of display). Parents might ask what frequency of display means; be prepared to provide examples to illustrate terms such as *rarely, occasionally, frequently,* and *consistently.* (p. 328)

A back-to-school night early in the school year can offer families an opportunity to explore standards-based curriculum and assessment issues with educators. Regular communication via newsletters, the class website, or personal conversations can help clarify any confusion families have about the standards-based approach.

COLLABORATING WITH FAMILIES ON CLASSROOM BEHAVIORAL CHALLENGES

Parents who know their children's teachers and help with their homework and teach their kids right from wrong—these parents can make all the difference.

—President Bill Clinton, State of the Union Address, 1994

Research has shown that when families get involved in their children's learning, children not only achieve more academically but are also more likely to be better behaved and have a positive attitude about school (Family Involvement Partnership for Learning, 1998). There are numerous ways to collaborate with families to improve children's classroom behavior. Ladson-Billings (1994) speaks of the importance of creating a community of learners (a family-like atmosphere in the classroom that values contributions that each student makes to the overall positive atmosphere of the classroom) (p. 69). Some teachers make discussions and activities about families a regular part of the curriculum. Inviting family members to be a part of the classroom community can help promote family pride as well as classroom cohesiveness and can lessen any alienation that some students may feel. Teachers can also hold class meetings in which students discuss issues relating to learning and behavior and work cooperatively to solve problems. Class meetings have been found to have a positive impact on children's interactions both at school and at home, especially when a family component, such as a parent survey, a student's journal entry, or a discussion of family, has been included in the meetings' agendas (Potter & Davis, 2003).

TABLE 9.2   Student Behavioral Survey

Global Questions: What are your goals for your child's education? How would you like to see your child interacting with other students in the classroom this year?

1. What strengths have you observed in your child at home in the area of behavior and getting along with others?

2. What concerns, if any, do you have about your child's behavior at home?

3. How does your child communicate with you or other adults in the home about frustrations she may be experiencing that may lead to misbehavior?

4. How does your child interact with other children in cooperative settings? Can you give me some examples of incidents that illustrate this?

5. What does the term *respect* mean to your child in the family setting? How does your child interact with siblings or extended family members?

6. How do you praise your child for exemplary behavior as a form of positive reinforcement?

7. What advice could you give me, as your child's teacher, concerning ways in which I could help reinforce positive behavior, communication skills, and goal-setting habits?

One example of a parent survey is the Student Behavioral Survey (Table 9.2), which can be modified to meet the particular needs of the families of students in your classroom. After this questionnaire has been filled in, teachers can have a discussion with families about behavioral concerns or specific behavioral incidents. The questionnaire could be given orally as a part of a parent-teacher conference, or it could be sent home to be returned after a specified period. When families and teachers team up to nurture children's competent classroom behavior, positive results are more likely to occur. An example of a Student Behavioral Survey can be found in Table 9.2.

Collaborating with families about their children's behavior may place teachers in the uncomfortable situation of discussing problem behaviors, which are naturally upsetting to parents. What steps should you consider when confronted with family members who are upset about their child's behavior in the classroom?

1. *Stay objective.* When families are upset, they may struggle to stay composed. You, too, may have trouble staying calm if accusations are leveled. Don't return the anger.

2. *Listen actively.* Allow the child's family to have their say. Try to see their point of view and reiterate it. For example, "I can see why that playground incident last Tuesday would have upset you." Pinpoint the event if possible to keep the conversation specific.

3. *Look for common ground.* If you aim to resolve the problem, you need to be willing to compromise. Taking the high ground and "winning" will stymie your efforts to forge effective partnerships with families. Mutually acceptable solutions can be agreed on. (Truby & Dollarhide, 2006)

As you collaborate with families about behavior, it is also important to implement culturally competent classroom management strategies, or strategies that take into account cultural diversity, in your classroom. Respecting students' cultural diversity is a critical component of effective classroom management (Weinstein, Tomlinson-Clarke, & Curran, 2004). Definitions of and expectations about correct behavior are culturally bound, and teachers of children from different cultural backgrounds may wrongly interpret students' actions. European American teachers generally expect students to listen quietly and then respond individually to a teacher's questions on his prompting. Students from cultures that value interpersonal harmony may be reluctant to compete against others during question and answer sessions. Such students may be seen as not fully participating in class activities (Weinstein et al., 2004). Other cultural groups may respond in ways that teachers with a lack of multicultural knowledge may deem inappropriate or disruptive. For example, students from cultures with more participatory and active styles of learning may be seen as being interruptive. Williams (2007) quotes one parent as saying,

> After a while, black kids want to let the teacher know that they know the answers, so they start shouting out the responses. When they do, the teachers say they're disruptive and need to be in self-contained classes. (p. 254)

Culturally responsive family engagement in the area of behavioral challenges means shared problem solving between teachers and families. Often teachers dictate solutions to families without ever asking for advice; but true collaboration means mutual decision making and a "posture of cultural reciprocity" (Harry, Kalyanpur, & Day, 1999, p. 251), with explicit dialogue with families about differing cultural values and practices in school and in the home. Teachers must never forget that children come to school influenced by their cultural socialization, which shapes their classroom demeanor and attitudes (Williams, 2007).

CLASSROOM VOLUNTEERS

One of the more traditional forms of engaging family members in their child's education has been as a classroom volunteer. By definition, a volunteer is someone who performs a task without pay. In the school setting, volunteers are typically thought of as individuals who come in during the school day and help in the classroom, library, or office, or as field trip chaperones. However, a classroom volunteer can have a much broader definition. The term can include not only those who assist during the school day but also those who support children's learning in any way, at any time (National Network of Partnership Schools, 2006). It can include not only parents but also extended family members, such as grandparents, and community members. Epstein et al. (2002) include volunteering among their "Keys to Successful Partnerships," noting benefits for students, families, and teachers. Student learning can increase with the extra assistance that a volunteer can provide, and students enjoy interacting with volunteers. Families gain confidence in their skills and have a better understanding of the educational process, and teachers are better able to give individual assistance to students with the volunteers' help (DeCusati & Johnson, 2004; National Network of Partnership Schools, 2006). Another important benefit is improved school-community relationships. One study found that volunteers had greater respect for teachers and administrators than they had before volunteering, were more interested in educational issues, and had a better understanding of how schools operate (Brent, 2000). As it is difficult for many family members to volunteer during the school day because of employment, transportation issues, language barriers, lack of confidence, or past negative experiences in the school setting, you should plan for opportunities to involve families not only during the school day but also outside the school day.

Variety of Roles for Volunteers

There are a variety of roles for volunteers to perform both inside and outside the school setting. One study found that the most common role of volunteers in the classroom setting is as tutor for individual or small groups of students. Being a field trip chaperone is another common volunteer task (Brent, 2000). The variety of roles for volunteers is as broad as a teacher's or a volunteer's creativity. For example, one kindergarten classroom volunteer, a stay-at-home mother with a preschool child, assisted weekly for two hours in her son's classroom, helping with clerical tasks, such as restocking the take-home learning kits, making classroom materials, and copying papers. While she was volunteering, her preschool daughter participated in the classroom activities along with her older kindergarten brother. As the year progressed and the mother became more comfortable in the room and with the children, she began helping them at their learning centers, such as assisting with a "green eggs and ham" cooking activity during Dr. Seuss week. By the end of the year, she was suggesting activities that she could do with the children, and she once brought in materials to help the children make kites for a spring unit. The volunteer role changed with time from teacher directed to a more equal partnership. Turner (2000) suggested these different tasks for volunteers who come to school:

- Read stories to children; listen to them read.
- Assist children one-on-one with tasks such as writing, art projects, or computer work.
- Do clerical tasks, such as copying or laminating materials, preparing bulletin boards, typing a class newsletter, or contacting families about upcoming school or classroom activities.
- Gather and/or prepare learning materials, such as learning center games, books on tape for a listening center, or bring library books to class.
- Work one-on-one with students with special needs, such as English language learners, students with learning problems, or gifted students.
- Share information about occupations or teach a skill or hobby to the children.

For those who cannot help during the school day, volunteers might be asked to make materials at home that can be used at school, such as a learning game.

Once family or community members are in the classroom, it is important to be welcoming and enthusiastic about their contributions of time and energy. One way to show your enthusiasm is to have a work area with an adult-sized chair set aside for classroom volunteers. You can be prepared for volunteers at any time by having a volunteer file with folders that are labeled with various tasks for volunteers to do (Inspiring Teachers, 2006). It is also important that you provide clear directions about tasks to be done and information about where materials are located. Monitor the volunteer to make sure there aren't any questions; if volunteers have to ask you repeatedly what to do and where materials are, they may not return (Craven, 2006). For example, if a volunteer is helping a group of children at a learning center, make sure that the volunteer has all needed materials and is comfortable with the activities and noise level of the children. It is also important that you make sure your students treat all volunteers with respect and courtesy and that you do not allow any misbehavior to continue when students are working with a volunteer. Giving the volunteer feedback afterward and checking to see if her experience was positive can ensure that volunteers return to the classroom. A way to make sure that volunteers will have a positive experience is to ask them what their interests, skills, and

Students enjoy interacting with volunteers, and family members can gain a better understanding of the curriculum through volunteering.

talents are in helping in the classroom. You should also use your insights into people as you plan volunteer activities. Giving a variety of tasks so that the job doesn't become boring may be helpful to one volunteer, while another may prefer the security and routine of doing the same tasks each visit. It is important to get to know your volunteers' likes and dislikes for classroom tasks. Finally, it is courteous to recognize volunteers for their time and efforts in some way, such as with a personal thank you note or recognition in your class newsletter. This recognition should include volunteers who help in any way, not just in the classroom.

HOMEWORK AND HOME LEARNING ACTIVITIES

> I didn't know how interested my son is in reading and learning new things until we played those games you sent home with him.
>
> —Parent's note to her son's kindergarten teacher (Barbour, 2010, p. 3)

The subject of homework, the amount assigned, and parental help with homework can easily become a hot-button issue in a classroom. Homework is generally defined as a "teacher-assigned task that students are expected to complete outside of school hours" (Barbour, 2010, p. 19). Research in the area of educational reform has debated whether assigning homework actually enhances student academic achievement; in fact, some schools have limited homework assignments or have banned them altogether. With the push for rigorous state academic standards in the 1990s, homework came back in vogue (Cooper, 2007). One study found that homework has increased in the lower elementary grades, with six- to eight-year-olds now spending more time on homework than in the past (Gill & Schlossman, 2004). Of first graders'

Age-appropriate home learning activities can reinforce the school curriculum.

parents, 38% reported their children did homework five or more times a week, increasing to 51% for fifth graders. Teachers in schools that served high-minority populations expected more homework than teachers in lower-minority schools (U.S. Department of Education, 2008). For many families of kindergarten or elementary students, homework sessions are severely exasperating and cause family strife and anxiety (Shumow, 2001). Yet nightly homework episodes do not have to be horrific!

Research has shown that homework has different benefits, depending on the age of the student. Homework is most effective for high school students and moderately effective for middle school students. Several studies found few or no benefits from some homework, such as preparation for tests for elementary-age children (Cooper, 2001). Although this does not mean that homework is not beneficial for younger children, it does mean that the goals of homework may be different for younger students than older ones. For example, homework may help students make the connection between what they are learning at school and their home, help them become more independent learners, develop responsibility, and give families an opportunity to see what their children are learning and to encourage their learning. It also means that the activities and time required for younger students may be different from those for older students.

Traditional homework assignments typically serve a variety of purposes and come in four basic types:

1. *Practice* homework that reinforces skills already introduced to help students move toward mastery

2. *Preparation* homework that introduces material presented in future lessons

3. *Extension* homework that applies skills already learned to new situations

4. *Integration* homework that applies many skills learned to a single task, such as a report or science project (U.S. Department of Education, 2003, p. 4)

However, a new approach to homework is emerging: interactive home learning activities, or homework assignments that are based upon real-life or authentic experiences and designed so families and children will have interactions relating to what they are learning. Much like parent-education, lecture-based meetings are being replaced by more participatory family events; traditional worksheet homework completed in isolation by students is being replaced by interactive home learning activities that families complete together, encouraging conversations about the assigned curriculum concepts. Barbour (2010) described the characteristics of interactive home learning activities:

- Assignments individualized to students' needs, such as reading books at the child's reading level
- Culturally relevant activities that link schoolwork to the home and real-life situations (e.g., discussing fractions in a recipe while cooking a meal)

- Family members, including siblings, participate in the activity, such as playing a game together
- All materials for activities supplied, with clear directions
- Student confidence built while completing activities, such as interviewing parents or sharing their ideas with family members
- Flexibility in choice of activities and time frame for completing activities

Table 9.3 gives examples of different types of interactive family home learning activities for different subject areas.

Table 9.3	Interactive Home Learning Activities Examples		
	Take-Home Kits	**Family Activities and Games**	**Family Projects**
Language and Literacy	Writing suitcase—variety of writing supplies and paper with suggestions for meaningful writing, such as grocery lists, letters, stories, notes, cards Book backpacks—books, puppets or stuffed animals, laminated pictures from story for sequencing or retelling story, discussion questions, journal	Scavenger hunt—look for items around the house that start or end with certain sounds, or items whose names rhyme Labels—child uses Post-it notes (provided by teacher) to make labels for items around house or adult makes label and child has to find the object; for English language learners, label items in both languages Hangman—play hangman and other word games together, using words on child's reading level	Class cookbook—each family chooses a favorite recipe and completes a recipe form, with child drawing of family meal time; recipes compiled into a book and copies made for each family to try out each other's recipes
Math	Telling time kit—clock with movable hands, stopwatch, hourglass, calendar, books relating to time, suggestions of time-telling activities	Cooking together—read and follow directions from a recipe or box mix, discuss fractions, measurements, (i.e. "how much is needed if we double the recipe?") Estimation jar—fill a clear container with items like macaroni, beans, cotton balls, have everyone guess amount and then count together to see who winner is	Family calendar—provide 12 monthly calendar pages for each family to mark family events, religious or cultural celebrations, and school activities; encourage children to draw pictures on the calendar How many—send home weekly items to count and tally how many are in home, such as, "How many wheels?"

(Continued)

TABLE 9.3 (Continued)			
	Take-Home Kits	**Family Activities and Games**	**Family Projects**
Science	Magnets backpack—assorted magnets of varying strengths and items to test; chart to record results and draw conclusions	Weather watchers—record weather on form each day and discuss how it changes in seasons; draw and label pictures of different types of clouds Nature walk—scavenger hunt to find specific kinds of birds, trees, flowers	Mystery bag—parents help children choose a mystery object to place in bag, relating to science topics being studied; children write three clues about object for classmates to guess
Social Studies	Family history kit–timeline with major historic events marked, writing and drawing supplies, directions for completing by adding family special events	Neighborhood map—take a walk and then draw map of neighborhood; try different routes and add these to map Needs and wants—using newspaper sale ads (teacher provided) and a pretend amount of money to spend, child and family choose items to buy and discuss budgets, needs, and wants	Come visit my town— brainstorm all the good things about the community and create a travel brochure, billboard, or tourism commercial convincing someone to come and visit; include a map with tourism sites marked
Creative Arts	Music backpack—rhythm instruments, books like *My Family Plays Music* (Cox, 2003), activity sheet with ideas to experiment with different sounds, rhythms, patterns Self-portrait kit— multicultural crayons, markers, colored pencils, yarn, glue, drawing paper, mirror; family members look in mirror and draw self-portraits, then compare how everyone is similar and different Home Olympics gym bag— masking tape, bean bags, sidewalk chalk, plastic cups and tennis ball, laminated medals, list of home Olympic outdoor activities, such as 50-yard dash, long jump, bean bag toss or balance, hop scotch, cup bowling	Homemade play dough— using teacher-supplied recipe, create homemade play dough and use to create sculptures Water painting—use a paintbrush (teacher provided) and a bucket of water to paint house, building, sidewalk, fence, etc. Pictionary—create a family list of items to draw; divide into teams and see which team can guess the most objects being drawn Concerts—provide families with list of local free or inexpensive concerts in area to attend together Parks—provide families with list of parks in the area, with suggestions of activities to do together	All about my family—create a family book using templates provided for each page, such as "The People in My Family," "One Special Thing About My Family," and "This is What My Family Likes to Do." Family You've Got Talent show—everyone performs his or her best talent; children sing songs they learned at school; children dance to music family enjoys Copy cats—one person does a certain movement or skill, such as jumping on one foot, bouncing ball with left hand, shooting basketball, or dribbling soccer ball, and rest of family has to try and copy it; see who can come up with skill no one can copy

Source: Learning at Home PreK-3: Homework Activities That Engage Children and Families, Barbour (2010)

When planning your homework program, there are four keys to a successful home learning program:

- Age appropriate homework
- Individualized homework that meets each student's needs
- Communication with families about homework expectations
- Consideration of diverse family views about homework

Although all types of homework can be used with children of different ages, it is important that you choose age-appropriate activities for your students. Young children learn best through hands-on activities, so paper-and-pencil assignments that focus on drill or isolated skills may not be the most effective homework assignment for a kindergarten or first- or second-grade classroom. Younger students also benefit from being able to talk about what they're learning and get support from adults or older siblings. Interactive homework, such as the take home activities or "mobile learning centers" shown in Table 9.3 are effective with preschool and primary-grade children (Trahan & Lawler-Prince, 1999, p. 66). For older students, paper-and-pencil assignments may be more appropriate, although students of all ages will be more engaged in homework that is meaningful and interesting. Older students are also capable of planning and completing long-range homework assignments, such as a science fair project, a report on the community's history that includes interviews with older members of the community, or creating a book of favorite poetry.

The time required for homework should also be set based on the age of the children. According to what is often called the "10-minute rule," 10 minutes per grade level is adequate. This means that for kindergarten and first- and second-grade classrooms, homework should not last any longer than 10 to 20 minutes per day, while homework for third-through sixth-grade classrooms should not require students and families to work more than 30 to 60 minutes per day (Cooper, 2001). Homework requirements should also be flexible for busy families. For example, you may give a weekly homework packet that students complete during the week as the family's schedule permits. If homework assignments are a comprehensive project, consider breaking the project into manageable sections with benchmark due dates.

The second key to effective home learning activities is individualizing the requirements based on the students' needs. Today's classrooms differentiate instruction, based on individual needs, and homework should reflect this individualization. Families are frustrated when children have busywork or have to spend hours completing assignments that are too difficult for their children. If all students are to spend approximately the same time on homework, homework assignments may need to be modified for some children. For example, when sending practice math or spelling homework sheets home, it is appropriate to create a variety of levels and numbers of math problems or spelling words that reflect the student's needs. Homework does not have to be the same for each child.

Two-way communication between home and school concerning homework is also crucial. Although parents may be anxious to help with their child's learning, they may also be unsure about how to go about it and have concerns about the time required for homework assignments (Walker et al., 2004). Remember that homework affects family leisure time, work commitments, and family scheduling of afterschool activities. Make sure that you have an academically valid reason for giving homework. Be prepared for questions that families may pose about homework, particularly on these topics:

1. *Time concerns.* Should it be taking my child this long to complete the assigned homework? My child rushes through the nightly homework in 10 minutes; is this enough time? When my child says something is due in one week, shouldn't he be starting the work well before it comes due?

2. *Homework assistance.* Should I help my child with challenging assignments? Are we supposed to do this activity together? What should I do if I am asked for help and I don't understand how to solve the problem or answer the question? If I provide help with homework in some way, is that considered cheating on my child's part?

3. *Record keeping.* Should my child be keeping a daily assignment notebook to keep track of homework? What if she leaves it at school and can't remember what was due? Is there another way to retrieve the assignment, such as a homework telephone hotline or website list? Should I check my child's assignment notebook daily to ensure homework is completed?

4. *Grading homework.* How do you grade homework? What percentage of the total subject grade is part of the homework? If my child is absent and unable to complete the homework, what is the grading policy then? Are make-up homework assignments given if my child completely misses the point of the homework? Do you formally grade every assignment; if not, how do you manage feedback?

One way to assure that families see their children's homework is to require a signature on it. However, a parent signature gives you little meaningful information from the families. Instead, consider using a standard form that allows families to give you feedback on how their child did on the homework, such as the example from the Teachers Involve Parents in Schoolwork (TIPS) program math homework template in Figure 9.2. The form invites conversation with families about the homework and offers them an opportunity to give you regular feedback on their child's success with home learning activities.

FIGURE 9.2   Homework Signature Form

Dear Family,

Please give me your reactions to your child's work on this activity by checking one of the following:

_____ 1. OK. My child seems to understand this skill.

_____ 2. PLEASE CHECK. My child needed some help on this, but seems to understand this skill.

_____ 3. PLEASE HELP. My child still needs instruction on this skill.

_____ 4. PLEASE NOTE (other comments).

_____

_____

_____

Signature_____Date_____

Source: National Network of Partnership Schools, TIPS Math—Elementary (2006)

The part you expect families to play in your students' homework activity should be reviewed at the beginning of the year. You should elicit collaborative ideas from them. An open house or group parent meeting can give you a chance to discuss home learning activities, answer questions, and get feedback from families about your suggestions for activities that would meet the needs of individual students (Trahan & Lawler-Prince, 1999). You can model or role-play some homework situations that may prove sticky, and you can share homework tips, as well as ask other parents to share suggestions for completing homework successfully.

Don't assume that families know about homework hotlines, spelling lists, writing portfolios, or the participatory nature of interactive home learning activities. Explain and demonstrate everything! Discuss reasonable time expectations for homework completion. Explain when parents should sound the alarm if they think their child is spending too much time on certain tasks. You will also want to send the information home in written form for those families who didn't attend the open house or parent meeting. It is helpful to send ongoing information about home learning activities as a part of your class or school newsletter or other written communication.

Finally, it is important that you recognize and honor that diverse families may respond to home learning activities differently. Past studies have found that Chinese American parents considered the amount of U.S. school homework to be insufficient to boost the academic performance of their children. However, a recent survey of Chinese American parents' attitudes about the amount of homework their children were given indicated that they felt it was appropriate (Li, 2006). Delgado Gaitan (2004) stated, "Homework is not an equal opportunity activity" for all students (p. 47). Although Latino parents routinely express high expectations for their children in the area of homework completion, those who have less experience with school or speak limited English may find themselves isolated from school in helping with homework yet hesitant to contact the teacher; or they may try to assist their children but supply the wrong answers. Some suggestions for improving homework practices with Latino or other non-English-speaking families include the following:

- Organize a public announcement with Spanish radio stations that suggests ways for families to help children with homework.
- Set up a bilingual hotline number that families can call to get advice on helping their children at home.
- Develop individual contracts with families and students, with all three of you agreeing on homework responsibilities. Consider recommending study groups as a form of homework support.
- Open a bilingual homework center along with offering workshops for families and students. (Delgado Gaitan, 2004)

Although non-English-speaking families may be hesitant to contact teachers about homework issues, one study found that low-income African American mothers often used homework as an impetus for contacting the teacher or stopping by school. These parents also monitored their children's progress closely, and they provided routines and structures for homework completion. The researchers found that parents worked hard. As one mother said,

Just getting over the hurdle with this new math about how to make sure that I'm learning it so I can teach it to her and make sure I'm doing it with her right. So that was like the biggest hurdle with this new math. (Jackson & Remillard, 2005, p. 63)

How can teachers help families of students who have special needs with homework? Richards (2004) recommends that parents help their child assemble a homework survival kit at the beginning of the school year. This kit can contain materials necessary for effective studying, starting out with a large calendar for assignments. Richards suggests that parents model strategies, including preplanning, teaching their children to use mnemonic devices (tricks to help memorize something), and creating visual organizers to "pull in processing strengths while compensating for processing weaknesses" (p. 3). Motivational devices such as a reward spinner, a customized game spinner with each section listing a reward (e.g., earning five extra points toward the 20 points needed to go to the amusement park), can expedite the completion of homework. A timer can help parents to monitor children's time on task as well as to meet the expectations outlined on a homework contract. Using some of the previous suggestions of interactive family home learning activities that are highly motivating and individualized for students' needs can be especially beneficial for a student with special learning needs.

As a teacher, you can help your school establish an infrastructure to promote homework success. The organization of a homework club after school with tutors can support students who may not get homework help at night. Offering parent workshops on study skills and homework hints, along with a meal and child care, can encourage families to connect with homework activities. Organizing a schoolwide interactive home-learning program using similar forms, such as recommended by TIPS, can provide consistency across grade levels and be especially helpful for new teachers in developing interactive homework based on specific learning goals (The Center for School, Family, and Community Partnerships, 2001). District policies on homework can vary greatly, with some districts requiring a set amount of homework each week and others leaving it up to the individual teacher. If your district has a homework policy, it is important that families receive copies of the policy, with translation if necessary.

Here are some questions or comments from parents concerning homework. Based on what you've learned about effective home learning activities, how would you respond to these situations?

- You told us at the open house at the start of school that homework would average 20 minutes for each subject. There is no way! What is going on?
- Will there be homework on weekends? Tanya lives with her father on weekends, and it is difficult to check on her finishing it with him in control. I want to make sure she gets things done, but we don't communicate at all.
- Kasey spends so much time completing five addition problems. She has no time for the rest of her reading, science, or social studies homework. It is already past her bedtime. Is this normal?
- You never seem to send home stories that have children who are like Mia or our family. I don't think this is fair, and she doesn't seem to connect with the stories.
- Mario's father and I do not read English so well at this time. When he brings home reading homework and asks us to help him with a word, we have to check in the Spanish language dictionary for the English meaning and then try to draw a picture or somehow get the meaning across. It doesn't work well; how can we help him with homework? (Translated from Spanish)

- I am sick of teachers not knowing how to teach. All they give the kids to do is research papers. I have other things to do than take my child to the library.
- I try to help Sam with worksheets he brings home, but when I do, he gets angry and tells me I am showing him the wrong way to do it.
- Thanks for sending home the writing suitcase. Abby loved writing her grandmother a letter, but was very sad when she had to return it to school. When will she get it again?

Each of these questions represents a facet of homework that you'll want to consider when developing your home learning policies.

SUMMARY

In this chapter, you have learned about engaging families in the classroom. By recognizing families and communities as children's first and most influential teachers, you can collaborate effectively with them to support your students' learning and development through home learning activities. Your role as a teacher also involves helping families better understand the terminology and concepts of the current standards-based curriculum and collaborating with families to address students' behavioral challenges. Partnering with families also means actively seeking and providing a variety of opportunities for volunteers. Successful family engagement includes both understanding and appreciating families *and* implementing supportive classroom-family engagement practices.

REFLECTION QUESTIONS

Reread the In the Classroom case study presented at the beginning of the chapter and reflect on these questions:

1. Are Mr. Turner's homework practices family friendly? Why or why not?
2. Evaluate the appropriateness of the family history project. What are the advantages and disadvantages of a homework assignment like this? Who might have difficulty or be unable to complete this homework assignment?
3. What are appropriate examples of homework for different age students, such as kindergarten and first, second, third, and fourth grades?

WEBSITES

¡Colorín Colorado! http://www.colorincolorado.org/families/.

A bilingual site for teacher and families; the family section offers suggestions for families to help their child learn to read and succeed at school, as well as how to build strong parent-teacher relationships.

Parental Involvement: Title I, Part A, www.ed.gov/programs/titleiparta/parentinvguid.doc.

The purpose of this guidebook is to assist state education agencies, districts, and schools in administering the parental involvement provisions of Title I, Part A of the Elementary and Secondary Education Act (ESEA).

Parents Toolkit, www.ed.gov/parents/landing.jhtml.

This site, sponsored by the U.S. Department of Education, offers help in explaining the No Child Left Behind legislation to families, along with tips on monitoring homework and helping children learn to read, with a special toolkit for Hispanic families.

Teachers Involve Parents in Schoolwork (TIPS) Interactive Homework: http://www.csos.jhu.edu/P2000/tips/index.htm.

This site offers guidelines for interactive homework, with examples for language arts, math, science, and social studies, as well as blank templates to use for creating activity sheets.

STUDENT STUDY SITE

Log on to the student study site at www.sagepub.com/grant2e for additional study tools, including the following:

- eFlashcards
- Web quizzes
- Web resources
- Learning objectives

Developing Successful Practice with Support Staff

Campbell, A.

In this chapter I identify and discuss key issues and features from the previous chapters in the book, from research done for a recent dissertation (Randall, 2004) and from the current debates around workforce reform. They will provide guidance and support for developing successful practice when working collaboratively with voluntary support assistants, learning mentors, nursery nurses, students, teaching assistants and special needs assistants. The chapter draws conclusions and hopefully suggests a set of practices that bring together ideas developed in each of the chapters about roles, responsibilities and ways to develop collaborative practice.

●●● Let a thousand flowers bloom?

One of the major issues arising from this book is the need to understand the complexity and range of support roles in schools and classrooms. This book could therefore have been subtitled 'Let a thousand flowers bloom', indicating the plethora of named support roles. Nomenclature is a major area of controversy. What support workers are called is important but, due to the previous use of different job titles such as nursery nurse, classroom assistant, teaching assistant and learning support assistant, can also be confusing. Complicating the area even more are the differing training, status, conditions of service, job descriptions and pay of the various support workers in school. Nursery nurses arguably have had good cause to be aggrieved when their title and status were changed to teaching assistants, as they were the group of support workers who had the longest and most vocationally orientated training while others, such as classroom assistants, could be parent helpers with no formal training. Conversely some classroom assistants, are very well qualified, some having degrees including highly relevant degrees in education studies, early years studies or psychology as well as a qualification for support assistants. Similarly, learning support assistants for children with special educational needs have varying levels of qualifications, expertise and experience. Learning mentors pose similar issues. Many learning mentors have degree-level qualifications in relevant areas such as social work, community studies and education and are paid at entry to teaching level of salary.

As many LEAs have found as they embark on trying to construct job descriptions and pay scales for the diverse workforce of school support workers, this is a minefield, fraught with histories of past roles, varying customs and practices in schools, residential care and private and voluntary sector involvement. As can be gleaned from the two headteachers in Chapter 10, there are varying practices across different LEAs with regard to job descriptions and pay scales. This makes the national picture complex and difficult to manage centrally.

It has been useful in this book to map and explore the development of roles and functions of people other than qualified teachers in classrooms. The term 'support worker' has been used throughout this book as a general term but it covers the following roles: the now defunct nursery nurse; the member of the community; the parent or grandparent helper; the learning support assistant for children with special educational needs; the learning mentor; the teaching assistant; the student teacher; the bilingual support worker/teacher/instructor depending on his or her qualifications; and, arguably in the near future, possibly the most controversial of all the roles, the large number of higher-level teaching assistants (HLTA) to be employed in schools. In the future all support workers will be called teaching assistants. As pointed out in Chapter 10, there are two distinct strands to the roles: those teaching assistants who are covering and taking the class; and the teaching assistants working alongside the teacher. Other distinctions are emerging too. Do teaching assistants support the teacher or the child? Or is the important distinction support in the classroom or across the school? Or is it all these? The main areas of support can be listed as: curriculum support as in literacy, numeracy and ICT; behaviour support as linked to learning mentors' work; administrative support (e.g. for photocopying and dinner-money collection); classroom support (such as mounting displays and cleaning art and technology areas and tools); and pupil support for children with special educational needs or for specific group activities. The importance of definition of role is an important one which, as recognized in many of the chapters, normally requires individual, personalized negotiation. Not every teaching assistant will want to take a class, and the teacher has got to be the one who specifies the work within the National Curriculum

The role of the nursery nurse serves as a good example to explore the impact of changes in government policies on support workers in schools in the last ten years. Nursery nurses have seen substantive changes in their role over the last decade, ever since they were no longer solely employed in the Nursery. Supporting children across the 3–7 age range and beyond became the norm for many of them. Sometimes they were based in one class but often they spent time in a variety of classes each week. It was possible to visit several schools in the same district (as the author has) and see very different organizations and a variety of roles undertaken by nursery nurses. In some cases nursery nurses were almost like the teacher, involved in joint planning and teaching, undertaking many of the same tasks as teachers. In another school visited, the nursery nurses undertook mainly menial tasks such as laying out materials, cleaning up messy areas, mopping up after children, giving out milk and snacks, doing the photo-copying and taking more of a care role with children. In many cases in the past, the wishes and capabilities of the post-holder would determine the role rather than any school management edict.

The name itself has connotations of days gone by when nurseries were perceived as 'safe' places with a cosy, soft and unchallenging atmosphere, somewhere to sleep and rest and listen to nursery rhymes. The development of practice and the advent of Sure Start early years provision, the integration of care and education for children up to 5 years old in centres such as Early Excellence Centres and now Children's Centres and, of course, the Foundation Stage developments have changed the nature and environment of early years settings to make them more vibrant and intellectually stimulating. This has meant a review and reconceptualization of roles, resulting in what Anning and Edwards (1999) termed 'the new professionals'. Further complications arise when we widen the lens to include the private and voluntary sector settings in the early years. There are few qualified teachers in the private and voluntary sector and many of the support workers have only the most basic qualifications, such as Level 1 National Vocational Qualifications in childcare. It will be interesting to monitor the effects that workforce reform and the regrading of posts in the state sector have on the private and voluntary sector. Will HLTAs appear in private nurseries?

●●● Working together and partnerships

To collaborate with some is often to shape up to confrontation with others. For collaboration is limited to those parts where good faith exists. (Fletcher and Adelman, 1981: 23).

Good faith is an essential component of collaborative working, and the openness and quality of relationships are of great importance to the success of any team. As identified in all the preceding chapters of this book, working together, collaboration, team working, partnerships and connecting with the other people in the classroom or school feature as key issues for successful support working in classrooms. Collaboration is not easy. It takes time, thoughtfulness and skill from all participants. Collaboration does not just 'happen'. As well as the tone of interpersonal relationships, the environment and 'hidden curriculum' send out messages. Bignold (in Chapter 2) stresses the importance of ethos and the physical layout of schools as having positive effects on both those who inhabit the space and those who visit. This may be a challenge for some people as this may mean a change in attitudes, beliefs and behaviour. She also highlights the need to value all those who contribute to children's learning and she identified the benefits of having support workers in school, whether voluntary or paid, who:

- foster children's self-esteem;
- acknowledge the cultural and linguistic backgrounds of all children;
- value what boys and girls can do equally (or men and women as in this example);
- foster an awareness of diversity in class, gender, ability and culture;
- promote respect for similarity and difference;
- challenge bias and prejudice;
- promote principles of inclusion and equity; and
- could provide a model for the community which supports the participation of the parents in children's learning (and other family members).

Benefits are also identified in Chapter 9 and it is strongly suggested that they need to be visible and celebrated in the school. Chapters 9 and 10 demonstrate how the voice of pupils or students about support for learning can be important in both understanding the roles and in supporting collaborative learning. Many support workers in schools have a 'history' with their school, as parent, relative or even as former pupil. Many educationalists extol this 'history' as a virtue. Hughes (in Chapter 4) illustrates how a learning mentor who is a member of the local community has 'street cred' with pupils and makes a valuable contribution to children's educational experience. Bignold (in Chapter 2) documents the value of a local community resident as a support worker in children's development in valuing diversity. There are, however, important ethical considerations in using local community, voluntary helpers or teachers and teaching assistants who are the parents of children at the school and who live in the local community. Having access to information about individual children's abilities, achievements, behaviour, special needs or other sensitive information through records and test results, classroom observation, staffroom or classroom discussion requires a professional code of behaviour. Where is this training for professional behaviour undertaken? This needs to be addressed in all forms of training for anyone who works with children in a voluntary or paid role. It also needs to be addressed in the settings themselves through clear policies and practices for all childcare workers, support workers and teachers. It is not difficult to imagine situations where the personal and professional interests collide to create ethical dilemmas for those who both work and live in the local community.

The DfEE guidance (2000: 24) regarding the effectiveness of the teamwork of teachers and teaching assistants emphazises the need for sharing plans and 'consultation over their execution'. Randall (2004) identified a general lack of quality time between teachers and teaching assistants in planning in her school. The problem that emerged was linked to the paid hours of employment of the teaching assistants and the workload of the teachers. Some teaching assistants may have timetabled preparation time when the teachers are not free. Releasing teachers to meet with their assistants during the day involves someone covering the class. Randall's further discussions with teachers involved in the action research project have indicated that they would rather plan with their assistants before or after school, but the assistants are not employed to work then. Relying on 'the goodwill of teachers and teaching assistants in meeting informally for planning and discussion' may not be good enough in the busy atmosphere of most schools.

In Chapter 7 the nursery nurse plays a significant role in the children's learning. The tensions inherent in a situation where an experienced and confident nursery nurse or support worker who has a high level of context-specific knowledge encounters a newly qualified teacher are illustrated, and these tensions demonstrate the complex issues about status, experience and collaborative work.

The importance of forming a good collaborative partnership between teacher and support worker is explicitly demonstrated in this tale. This scenario highlights the need for beginning teachers to work co-operatively with other adults and suggests teachers need to take the lead role in managing the involvement of other adults in the classroom. It also highlights the need for initial teacher education courses to accommodate training for this role even though the prescribed teacher education curriculum is arguably already over full.

●●● Role definition and description

The need to stress the importance of the clarification and development of the teaching assistants' role, [Moyles and Suschitzchy (1997)] is a finding corroborated by Randall's (2004) research. In her study, Randall asserted that there was total agreement about the need for clarification and development of the role of teaching assistants by the teacher and teaching assistant participants. The stages the teaching assistants went through in defining their role in terms of support for the pupil, teacher, curriculum and school revealed an overlap, confirming that the roles are 'not separate but interdependent' (DfEE, 2000). However, the guidelines, while adequate, fail to capture all the possible roles, concentrating on teaching rather than classroom support. This emphasizes the need to personalize job descriptions, allowing for the particular skills and abilities of the assistants. Randall's involvement with this process led her to concur with the DfEE that careful consideration needs to be given to the development of job descriptions with the associated implications of time and personnel.

Both headteachers interviewed in Chapter 10 emphasize the importance of clear, negotiated job descriptions for support staff. This, as they document, is not as easy as it may first seem. It is proving to be messy, inconsistent across the regions and difficult to understand and manage by unions who are centrally organized. The division of labour in educational contexts is arguably not as straightforward as it has been in the medical profession, although there are some who would argue differently. Issues of who does what are still being discussed, and the controversial area of whole-class 'teaching' by HLTAs still sits uneasily in most teachers' minds. They remember the 'Mums Army' debates of the past.

One of the thorny problems, which may cause more bureaucracy in schools, is having a teaching assistant with a variety of roles or job descriptions. For example, it would be possible to be a part-time support worker for children with special educational needs and a part-time HLTA, taking classes to release teachers for their PPA time. Or it could involve moving around the school in a support role for a particular subject such as ICT or sport. If a school had a number of these, the timetable arrangements would be complex indeed. Several flexible solutions to facilitate joint planning times are evident in Chapters 9 and 10: having a whole-school club afternoon run by teaching assistants or flexible starting times for teaching assistants so they can plan after-school hours with teachers. Creativity and flexibility are the order of the day for many schools as they strive to implement and develop collaborative support strategies. The current position with the various unions involved is also complex, with UNISON awaiting news of better pay and conditions for its members and headteachers' unions awaiting news of more money for schools. The position of the NUT has remained constant throughout: they have not signed up to the agreement. At some point this could potentially divide schools and destroy the collaboration needed to make remodelling of the workforce work. Good working relationships, as discussed above, are necessary to develop and implement policies and practices in schools. Bubb and Earley (2004) support good leadership and management strategies to facilitate a good work-life balance and workforce well being as essential to the success of schools in the future.

●●● Support for curriculum subjects

As stated in Chapter 6 and to a lesser extent in Chapter 8, confidence and competence in subject areas is an issue when teaching assistants are required to support children's learning. Subject knowledge has been for some time now a key issue for teachers themselves. The most common areas in primary schools are literacy, numeracy and ICT, although teaching assistants supporting children with special educational needs might find themselves supporting across the whole curriculum. Hall (in Chapter 3) lists the required abilities for teaching assistants, ranging from lateral thinking to patience and the ability to observe and evaluate progress. Although discussed in the context of special educational needs support, these seem suitable for all teaching assistants in schools.

Personal and pedagogical subject knowledge is key when working with individual or groups of children. What level of subject knowledge is required for teaching assistants? The answer is not clear. HLTAs must have English and maths GCSE-equivalent qualifications, but other teaching assistants need not. What kind of training in teaching numeracy and literacy will be the baseline for teaching assistants? Will there be curriculum specialist teaching assistants who only do ICT, for example? Clearly there is a huge training agenda.

●●● Professional development and training

In times of change and the development of new roles, it is important to consider support for professional development and training for those involved in the changes. Throughout the book this issue is addressed in different ways. Bignold (in Chapter 2) suggests that schools might like to organize whole-staff training to discuss and develop guidelines for welcoming 'special guests' from the community into school to support children. Certainly, the issue of Criminal Records Bureau clearance is one that she suggests has to be dealt with sensitively.

Hall (in Chapter 3) identifies greater reliance being placed on the use of teaching assistants and suggests that training and career development should be essential. However, Ofsted found that fewer than half of all LEAs provided relevant training for teaching assistants (www.inclusive.co.uk). Hall also suggests that all in-service workshops and sessions that seem relevant to the role of the teaching assistants should be available to them, or they should have regular in-school feedback from the teachers attending. She cautions that, if some teaching assistants attend courses and others do not, it is possible that a double layer of teaching assistants is created with a certain amount of prestige going to those who have attended.

In Chapter 4, Hughes refers to a National Training Programme for Learning Mentors, which was established in 2001. Materials for this programme have been updated and revised each year. Importantly, the programme provides learning mentors with a formal qualification.

In Chapters 5 and 6 (which focus on support for mathematics and ICT), knowledge of the subject matter is of great importance. Teachers and teaching assistants need regular subject updating and need to keep abreast of the pedagogical aspects specific to the subject in which they either teach or support children. Cronin and Bold in Chapter 5 do actually teach teaching assistants as part of their role and suggest a mind-mapping exercise to help understand the purposes of learning mathematics. They also suggest that teaching assistants need to explore and understand the frustration for some children in learning the subject and suggest shared planning as a good way to do this. Crowley and Richardson (in Chapter 6) think liaison with the ICT co-ordinator is essential to ensure continuity and to develop confidence. In their section on professional development they highlight the value of collaborative work and, in general, suggest many useful, practical activities.

Chapter 8 emphazises how teachers and student teachers need to learn together. Smith and Hewitt identify mentoring as a very worthwhile source of professional development for teachers and identify scenarios for student professional learning. There has been much research into mentoring (see Kerry and Shelton-Mayes, 1993; McIntyre *et al.*, 1993; Edwards and Collison,1996; Campbell and Kane, 1998), but still there is a need to explore the impact of mentoring on teachers' professional learning and development and the actual benefits for schools who are in partnership with teacher education institutions.

In Chapter 9 the voices of pupils and students provide a salutary reminder of the importance of consulting and listening to those who are supported and taught. They have a surprisingly clear view of what teachers and support workers do and should do. The headteacher in this chapter displays a good understanding and extensive experience of supporting and leading professional staff development. This serves to remind us of the importance of good leadership that is inclusive and that invites participation from all staff and from the pupils themselves.

The two headteachers interviewed in Chapter 10 have been involved in training as participants and as leaders of training for teachers and teaching assistants. They identify training as a key factor in the success of the workforce remodelling initiative and highlight the complexities of providing support and training for a diverse group of people. There are some difficult issues as the government's plans roll out. For example, what will the training for HLTAs finally look like and will it be sufficient for a role akin to a qualified teacher? What support and training will be required if a HLTA wants to take the Qualified Teacher route? Will there be training for student teachers to enable them to avoid the dilemmas that Jones describes in the Chapter 7 in her tale of the first encounters of an NQT and a nursery nurse?

There is currently a shift in government policy for continuing professional development towards school-based professional development for teachers. There is a recognition that teachers can learn from each other in inquiry-based learning, team teaching, focused discussion, joint planning and peer-coaching and mentoring situations (Campbell *et al.*, 2003). The opportunity to work and learn alongside each other is not just applicable to teachers. It can and should apply to a teaching assistant working with another teaching assistant and to teachers and teaching assistants working together. Good professional development should provide a balanced diet appropriate to the needs of the learners, and there are concerns that 'one size fits all' provision or lack of funding may result in poor-quality professional development (Campbell, 2003). Teachers and teaching assistants need to be vigilant and they need to articulate their needs. As Sachs (2003) advocated in her address to the British Educational Research Association in Edinburgh, educationalists need to become 'activists' in their profession, mobilizing for progress and development and asserting their rights.

There are many challenges and questions for the future, but there are also many opportunities. As this book goes to press the remodelling of the workforce is still a very contentious policy that is hotly debated. Let us hope that the challenges and opportunities can work collaboratively for a better future for children, teachers, support workers and schools.

●●● References

Anning, A. and Edwards, A. (1999) *Promoting Children's Learning from Birth to Five: Developing the New Early Years Professional.* Buckingham: Open University Press.

Bubb, S. and Earley, P. (2004) *Managing Teacher Workload: Work-Life Balance and Wellbeing,* London: Paul Chapman.

Campbell, A. (2003) 'Teachers' research and professional development in England: some questions, issues and concerns', *Journal of In-service Education.* 29 (3): 375–88.

Campbell, A., Hustler, D. and McNamara, O. (2003) 'Researching continuing professional development: the use of fictional pen portraits to illustrate and analyse teachers' perceptions and experiences'. *Professional Development Today.* 7, (2) Spring 2004, 13–19.

Campbell, A. and Kane, I. (1998) *School-based Teacher Education: Telling Tales from a Fictional Primary School.* London: David Fulton.

DfEE (2000) *Working with Teaching Assistants: A Good Practice Guide.* London: DfEE Publications.

Edwards, A. and Collison, J. (1996) *Mentoring and Developing Practice in Primary Schools: Supporting Student Learning in Schools.* Milton Keynes: Open University Press.

Fletcher, C. and Adelman, C. (1981) 'Collaboration as a research process', *Journal of Community Education,* 1 (1), 23–33.

Kerry, T. and Shelton-Mayes, A. (eds) (1993) *Issues in Mentoring.* London: Routledge.

McIntyre, D., Hagger, H. and Wilkin, M. (1993) *Mentoring: Perspectives on School-based Teacher Education.* London: Kogan Page.

Moyles, J. and Suschitzky, W. (1997) 'Jills of all trades?… Classroom assistants in KS1 classes', London: Association of Teachers and Lecturers Publications.

Randall, H. (2004) 'An investigation into some strategies for enhancing the role of teaching assistants in a Liverpool primary school.' Unpublished MEd dissertation, Liverpool Hope University.

Sachs, J. (2003) 'Teacher activism: mobilising the profession.' Plenary address, BERA conference, Edinburgh.

Summary

Of course, there are many other partnerships that could be explored. You have entered into a partnership with UWE alongside your school settings to gain the experience and qualification necessary to become a teacher. We, as a university have long-lasting partnerships with schools to support you in your goal. Most of all, of course, you, as a trainee teacher and then in your teaching career, must form a learning partnership with all the children you teach. Establishing this relationship with both individual children and the class as a whole is paramount if you are to be an effective and confident teacher.

Student activities
- List all the partnerships you have in your life
  - What makes them successful?
  - What makes them less successful?
- Which aspects of the partnerships you describe above are relevant to building partnerships within school?
- How will you build learning partnerships with the children in your class?
- What knowledge will you need to make this work?

Additional readings
Basford, J. and Hodson, E. (2008) 'Working with others to support children and families: the importance of multi-agency working' in *Teaching Early Years Foundation Stage*. Exeter: Learning Matters

Cox-Petersen, A. (2011) 'Schools and community: working together and respecting diversity' Chapter 6 in *Educational Partnerships-Connecting Schools, Families, and the Community*. London: Sage.

McDermott, D. (2008) 'Understanding parent involvement and engagement in schools today', Chapter 1 in *Developing Caring Relationships Among Parents, Children, Schools, and Communities*. London: Sage.

Nutbrown, C. and Clough, P. (2014) 'Including parents' in *Inclusion in the Early Years*, 2nd edn. London: Sage.

Roberts, S, M. and Pruitt, E, Z. (2009) 'The professional learning community: an overview, Chapter 1 in *Schools as Professional Learning Communities: Collaborative Activities and Strategies for Professional Development* 2nd edn. London: Sage.

Tutt, R. (2011) 'Schools working in partnership with other services' in *Partnership Working to Support Special Educational Needs and Disabilities*. London: Sage.

Whalley, M. (2007) 'Parents and staff as co-educators - 'parents' means fathers too', Chapter 5 in *Involving Parents in their Children's Learning*, 2nd edn. London: Sage.

Lightning Source UK Ltd.
Milton Keynes UK
UKOW06f1845220714

235581UK00001B/9/P